THE PLURALITY OF IMAGINARY WORLDS
The Evolution of French *Roman Scientifique*

THE PLURALITY OF
IMAGINARY WORLDS
The Evolution of French *Roman Scientifique*

by
Brian Stableford

cover by
Timothée Rouxel

A Black Coat Press Book

Acknowledgements:
    I could not have carried out this project without the support and assistance of Jean-Marc Lofficier of Black Coat Press, who published the translations I produced while doing the research and obtained reference copies of some of the texts I considered most vital, mostly with the invaluable assistance of Marc Madouraud. I am also very grateful to the many other people who kindly lent a hand in various ways to my searches for particular texts and to the facilitation of the overall project, including Jean-Luc Rivera, Jean-Luc Boutel, Guy Costes, Jean-Pierre Laigle, Xavier Legrand-Ferronière, Dominque Martel, Ellen Herzfeld, Sylvie Allouche, J. J. Pierce, Jean-Daniel Brèque, Henri Rossi, Denis Blaizot, Frédéric Jaccaud, Kevin J. Maroney, Sara Doke, Arthur B. Evans, Graham and Agnes Andrews and the late Robert Reginald.

Table of Contents

Introduction

1. The Nature of the Project

This book was planned as a companion project to a history of British "scientific fiction" entitled *New Atlantis: A Narrative History of British Scientific Romance*, which I had compiled three years earlier in order to compare and contrast the evolution of British speculative fiction based on scientific notions with American fiction of the same kinds. Previously all such fiction had been lumped together by historians under the label that eventually came to be applied to that kind of fiction: "science fiction," but I had come to consider that aggregation misleading.

The term "science fiction" was invented in 1929, after a brief period in which the more cumbersome "scientifiction" had been employed as a label applied to Hugo Gernsback's *Amazing Stories*, the first U.S. magazine specializing in fiction featuring hypothetical new inventions, scenarios set in hypothetical futures transformed by technological progress, scenarios in which the present world is disrupted by intrusions capable of rational rather than "supernatural" explanation, and "secret history" stories featuring past inventions and intrusions of the same sort. Those fundamental categories broadened over time to take in such marginal subgenres as "alternative history" stories and prehistoric fantasies based on scientific theories and discoveries.

All of those kinds of stories had existed prior to the invention of the label, so that generic label came with a "history" already built into it; indeed, in the introductory editorial to the first issue of *Amazing Stories* in 1926, Gernsback explained what the word "scientifiction" meant by referring back to previous works illustrative of the kind of fiction he wanted to gather together under the label, particularly works by Jules Verne and H. G. Wells. By so doing he defined "scientifiction," and thus "science fiction," as an essentially international enterprise, and in the first decade of their existence, Gernsback's magazines not only reprinted works by Verne and Wells but published a number of translations of contemporary works from French and German. Although the translations disappeared from generically labeled magazines after the mid-1930s, the American science fiction magazines continued to use material from a handful of British writers, the magazines having a limited circulation in Britain.

Following the end of World War II in 1945, the label "science fiction" was imported into Britain and France, where the kinds of fiction contained in the American science fiction magazines had previously only had casually-applied descriptive labels that were not applied with any great consistency. The result of the importation was that a good deal of material began to be written in those two countries with the intention of publication under the label, and some material not written with that intention began to be gathered under it, if not by publishers, then by commentators and by readers who had a particular fondness for the genre. Those specialist readers, while not numerous, tended to be avid; there was something about the genre conducive to attracting a "cult following" of fans, who formed a kind of community—a phenomenon noticed and encouraged by Hugo Gernsback in the 1920s, which undoubtedly helped to maintain the viability of science fiction magazines as a commercial product in times of fierce economic competition.

That tendency of commentators and fans to lay claim to works that had not been written with the intention of bearing the generic label caused some dissent and dispute. The early American magazines bearing the label were "pulp magazines": a term that referred to the cheap paper on which they were printed, but which also reflected a differentiation that had become very sharp in the U.S.A. during the 1920s when magazines supported by advertising revenue, which were printed on better quality paper and hence known as "slick" magazines, had increasingly focused on material calculated to appeal to better-off readers— particularly female readers, because market research had revealed that females had more influence on purchasing decisions—while those supported primarily by the purchasing price were those considered "lowbrow" and mostly read by males. Although science fiction was actually rather demanding of its readers, in terms of the elaborate terminology it employed and the intellectual efforts it required to follow its imaginative extrapolations, it was particularly favored by young male readers: the category in which advertisers were least interested.

Economically condemned to pulp magazines by virtue of the nature of its readership, American science fiction had taken on other general attributes of pulp fiction—primarily, an emphasis on melodramatic action-adventure fiction—as well as evolving to reflect the particular interests of its cult following. By 1945, when the label was exported to Britain and France, the American science fiction magazines were dominated by futuristic fiction routinely featuring space travel and adventures on other worlds, much of it colorfully melodramatic in its content, and positively garish in its illustrative packaging. Although there were writers in both France and Britain ready and eager to write that kind of fiction for that kind of packaging, there was a marked dissonance between that particular produce and much of the fiction previously produced in those two nations dealing with the same fundamental themes. That dissonance caused some dissent between writers eager to be packaged as science fiction writers and writers who wanted to avoid the stigmatization of the label—a dispute that continues, sometimes fiercely, in the present day.

The existence of that past and present dissonance inevitably creates problems for historians of the kinds of fiction that thrive under the science fiction label. Many simply take the view that the label can and should be extended to absorb anything susceptible of absorption—and, indeed, they often define "science fiction" operationally in a manner that makes that absorption compulsory. As interest developed in the compilation of some kind of definitive history of science fiction extending backwards as far as operational definition could take it, almost all such historians accepted the view adopted by Hugo Gernsback that it was a essentially international endeavor in which the relevant works of Jules Verne, H. G. Wells, and American pulp science fiction, were merely chapters in the same story.

That methodology has the side-effect of glossing over the fact that the British, French and American traditions of speculative fiction developed separately for more than a hundred years, with only slight overlaps of interest, prior to 1926, and continued to develop thereafter in accordance with quite different foci of interest and narrative methods, until the importation of the American label initiated a process of fusion that was still not complete even at the end of the twentieth century. My purpose in writing my two studies of British scientific romance—the preliminary *Scientific Romance in Britain 1890-1950* (1985) and the more definitive *New Atlantis: A Narrative History of Scientific Romance* (completed 2012 but not yet published at the time of writing)—was to identify and highlight those differences, and analyze the extent to which the evolution of speculative fiction, even within a common language, was not a common international endeavor but a process of parallel development of two separate traditions, with only a few bridges and entanglements.

While working on that project, I became acutely aware of the fact that if there was some historical insight to be gained by separating out the tradition of British scientific romance exemplified by H. G. Wells from the generalized "history of science fiction," a similar insight could be gained by separating out the French tradition of *roman scientifique* exemplified by Jules Verne, which had been isolated to a much greater degree by a language barrier. Even the cases where that barrier appeared to have been breached—the translation of all of Verne's relevant works into English being the key example—the crossover was far from perfect, because the original translations were, for the most part, corrupt and misleading.

To an even greater extent than British scientific romance, therefore, French *roman scientifique* seemed to me to warrant separate consideration as an independent tradition guided by its own particular interests and developing its own narrative strategies, rather than simply being subsumed, tacitly or explicitly, into a generalized "history of science fiction." That is what motivated me to undertake the present project, and that is what it attempts to achieve, at least in terms of a preliminary sketch.

Although the first significant study of the material that forms the subject matter of the present project, *La Littérature française d'imagination scientifique*

9

[The French Literature of the Scientific Imagination] (1950) by Jean-Jacques Bridenne did not adopt the "science fiction" label, most of those that came after it were content to do so, albeit with modifications and with a degree of separation. Most significantly, Pierre Versins' *Encyclopédie de l'utopie, des voyages extraordinaires et de la science-fiction* [Encyclopedia of Utopia, Extraordinary Voyages and Science Fiction] (1972) recruited it, along with two other generic labels, to the specification its field of concern. Although the book's format as an alphabetically-organized set of articles enables individual authors to be considered separately, the articles on the key themes of science fiction refer to French, English and American materials collectively.

Versins' prodigious effort was followed by Jacques Sadoul's *Histoire de la science fiction moderne* [The History of Modern Science Fiction] (1973; revised and augmented 1984 as *Histoire de la science-fiction moderne 1911-1984*), which separated its accounts of "le domaine anglo-saxon" and "le domaine français," the latter account beginning in 1905 rather than 1911, thus facilitating comment on contrasts between the twentieth-century development of two traditions as well as their common features. Sadoul's study does not have the same historical depth as Versins' endeavor, but the different direction of his approach—as a writer and publisher of contemporary science fiction rather than a collector and historian—differentiated his outlook sharply, and thus made his text a useful complement to its predecessor.

Those two books preceded most of the "histories of science fiction" written in English, although they drew on the preliminary work done by Sam Moskowitz in compiling the essay collections *Explorers of the Infinite: Shapers of Science Fiction* (1963) and *Seekers of Tomorrow: Masters of Modern Science Fiction* (1965). A significant model for generalized "histories of science fiction" was provided by Brian W. Aldiss' *Billion Year Spree: The True History of Science Fiction* (1973), which stirred up some controversy by its insistence on locating the "origin" of the retrospectively-constructed genre in Mary Shelley's *Frankenstein* (1815). Other historians and bibliographers hastened to identify other supposed points of origin, stimulating much debate about the essential nature of the genre and the manner in which it ought to be viewed, highlighting the fact that there is not just one "history of science fiction" but several, arranged in parallel like the alternative histories that genre had partially absorbed.

The most comprehensive account of retrospectively defined "science fiction" is Everett F. Bleiler's annotated bibliography of *Science Fiction, The Early Years* (1990), which lists and describes all the works published in English prior to 1926 that could, in Bleiler's syncretic view, be considered retrospectively to belong to the genre. His survey includes all the relevant works translated from French but none that had not been translated. That volume has become the definitive bibliographical guide to the "history of science fiction" prior to the invention of the label, although it is restricted to its manifestations in the English language. Investigation of the French tradition was, however, pursued by a number of critics and commentators in the last quarter of the twentieth century, most extensively by Jacques van Herp in his *Panorama de la science-fiction: les thèmes, les genres, les écoles, les problèmes* [A Panorama of Science Fiction: The Themes, Genres, Schools and Problems] (1975).

The most notable volume focusing on the entire history of French material that has been published since Versins' *Encyclopédie* is Jean-Marc Lofficier and Randy Lofficier's *French Science Fiction, Fantasy, Horror and Pulp Fiction: A Guide to Cinema, Television, Radio, Animation, Comic Books and Literature from the Middle Ages to the Present* (2000), which contains a useful synoptic history of various genres of French imaginative fiction and an extensive bibliography of relevant works. Another extensive study dedicated entirely to French material, although more limited in its scope, is Jean-Marc Gouanvic's *La Science-fiction française au XXe siècle (1900-1968)* [French Science Fiction of the Twentieth Century, 1900-1968] (1994), while other critics and historians who have significant contributions to the study of roman scientifique in the twentieth century include Jean-Pierre Fontana, Gérard Klein and Jean-Pierre Andrevon.

Although it is not exclusively devoted to French works, Daniel Fondanèche's *La Littérature d'imagination scientifique* [The Literature of the Scientific Imagination] (2012), which focuses mainly on the period from 1750 to 1910, places French materials in the foreground, and thus forms a useful complement to Sadoul's work, as do Irène Langlet's *La Science-Fiction: lecture et poétique d'un genre littéraire* (2006) and Simon Bréan's *La Science-Fiction en France* (2012). Natacha Vas-Deyres' account of *Ces Français qui ont écrit demain, utopie, anticipation et science-fiction au XXe siècle* [The French Authors who have written Tomorrow: Utopia, Anticipation and Science Fiction in the Twentieth Century] (2013) extends the account given by Sadoul to the end of the century, offering in-depth analyses of selected works; her bibliography refers to several recent academic theses on the subject that have not yet achieved book publication, reflecting an increasing interest in the subject.

The present project attempts to build on those endeavors and carry them a little further forward, within its own temporal range, from seventeenth-century foundation-stones to the 1930s.

The Versins *Encyclopédie* was the model for *The Encyclopedia of Science Fiction* edited by Peter Nicholls and John Clute, published in 1979 in England and America, which attempted to fix and clarify the notion of "science fiction's" range and history in the same fashion. The editors made an effort to include coverage of science fiction in other languages, and were careful to include entries on several notable French writers, although only a small minority of those covered by Versins. In order to help them cope with problems of definition, the editors commissioned an entry on "proto-science fiction," coining that term to describe works published before the genre label was invented, but which could be retrospectively gathered under its banner.

Coincidentally, that article in the 1979 *Encyclopedia* was assigned to me, and I patched it together without giving any serious thought to the propriety of the term. Indeed, I continued to use the phrase routinely for thirty years thereafter without giving it much thought. The article in question still exists, modified for the 1993 edition of the *Encyclopedia* and again for the current on-line version, which is enjoying a curious "pre-existence" by virtue of the fact that it is a work in progress that will never actually be finished, but can nevertheless be accessed in its incomplete and imperfect state. Nowadays, however, because of the insights developed during the research for the present project, I make a point of never using the term; I have recently preferred to subtitle the various anthologies of such material that I have compiled as translations of "French scientific romances." As well as asserting that the present project should not be considered as a "history of science fiction," I particularly want to emphasize the assertion that it should not be considered as a "history of proto-science fiction."

In wanting to do that, I am not attempting to deny the "science fiction" label because of any kind of imagined taint; my reason is that thinking of works produced before the genre label existed as "proto-science fiction" tacitly implies that they were somehow "leading to it," as if it were a kind of objective to attained. Science fiction fans in search of reading material inevitably look for works that resemble the objects of their affection most closely, and evaluate them according to the extent to which they do, but that kind of assessment ought not to be used to construct a historical narrative.

For example, futuristic fiction and interplanetary fiction are rightly regarded as the two most important elements of modern science fiction; indeed, if one looks at the narrow history of the American science fiction that evolved in the pulp magazines in the 1930s and 1940s, it is evident that those two subgenres became conflated into a whole that became the core, if not the essence of science fiction. Within that context, interplanetary fiction was almost exclusively futuristic, and although there was no logical necessity for the reverse to be the case, the futuristic fiction featured in the magazine almost invariably imagined space travel as a key aspect of future historical development. Although it is an admitted oversimplification, it is possible to characterize, if not actually to define, American science fiction as a genre based on that quasi-chemical combination of futuristic and interplanetary fiction, as one of the most influential editors in the genre, Donald A. Wollheim, did explicitly in his own survey of it, *The Universe Makers* (1971).

If one looks back at the history of those two kinds of fiction outside the narrow context of the American specialist magazines, however, there is little overlap between them; the majority of futuristic fictions make no mention of space travel, and those that do often regard it as a peripheral issue of no great significance, while the majority of interplanetary fantasies are set in the present or the past. Although both subgenres were, therefore "ancestral" to modern science fiction in some sense, it would be a mistake to look at them as if they were aspects of the *same* kind of fiction, and evaluate previous works in terms of the extent to which the two themes are combined therein.

Necessarily, the history outlined in these pages includes the evolution and development of French interplanetary fantasy and the evolution and development of French futuristic fantasy, and while doing that, I have had to bear in mind the eventual entanglement of the two kinds of fiction. What I have tried to set aside, however, is the notion that there was anything predestined about that eventual entanglement, and that authors working in those separate fields were somehow groping toward the connection.

It is, alas, tempting to look at interplanetary fantasy as if it were always somehow aiming toward the real space program of the 1960s and the actual moon landing that occurred in 1969—when science fiction writers were present at the launch of the spacecraft, exultant as having been "proved right"—and thus devaluing interplanetary fantasies that employed "*génies*" [genii, meaning spirits] or balloons as a literary device of imaginary spatial displacement as essentially lacking or inept. However, the writers who used those devices were not trying and failing to invent or anticipate *Apollo 11*; their aims and concerns were entirely different, and need to be weighed in their own terms if their contribution to literary history is to be accurately assessed.

That is one specific instance of a general problem. All history is to some extent distorted because, seen from the viewpoint of the present, the past inevitably seems to have been the process that produced that present, and what happened in the past thus tends to be seen in terms of the contribution the events in question made to the present state of affairs. In consequence, all history has a tendency to become not so much a mere record of past events as a narrative of the way in which those events combined to produce the present.

The problems involved in that kind of reasoning are unfortunately redoubled in a project that sets out to deal—not exclusively but to a considerable extent—with the history of images of the future. *Roman scientifique* is not a genre that consists entirely of futuristic fiction—one of the factors distinguishing it from modern science fiction is the reduced quantity of futuristic fiction it contains—but it does contain a good deal of it, and it would be difficult to rule many examples of futuristic fiction irrelevant to its development. It is, however, necessary to beware of considering those futuristic fictions purely and simply in relation to the actual future that developed in the interim between they writing and the time of their consideration.

It is perfectly natural for readers contemplating works of futuristic fiction produced in the past to measure the accuracy of their "predictions," tacitly awarding them credit for every detail of their images of the future and technological possibility that have actually been replicated in the interim between the writer's present and the reader's, and reckoning as a failure every detail that failed to achieve realization in that interim, but it would be a serious mistake for a historian to employ the same measuring-stick, as if all that past writers of futuristic fiction were attempting to do was anticipate the actual form that the future would take—a quest that is logically impossible.

In fact, writers of futuristic fiction frequently argue that they are not trying to predict the future, and are, in fact, far more interested in trying to *prevent* the hypothetical events they describe from actually coming to pass, but that does not prevent the readers of the present from picking through yesterday's images of the future with the interim in mind as a dimension of comparison. It should, however, serve as a dire warning to historians to be more sensitive in their evaluations, and to attempt to see the future-orientated fictions of the past as products of their own past rather than hit-or-miss contributions to the present from which they are being viewed, although it is also necessary to avoid going to the opposite extreme, and refusing to see anything in such works but reflections of their own present.

Alarmist writers attempting to prevent their futuristic visions coming true rather than to enhance their possibility are still attempting to be participants in the active process by which the future is made. It is necessary always to bear in mind that none of them had any idea what the actual shape of the future would be, and that their notions of what had previously counted and would subsequently count as "progress" were not the same as the notions that actually developed thereafter, but it is necessary to remember too that they would not have been writing futuristic fiction at all if they did not have a passionate interest in the nature and direction of progress. Such interests are, however, often much narrower than the future of the human race seen as a whole, and even when they are as broad as that, they are inevitably influenced by the standpoint of the observer. For that reason, British notions of progress have always tended to be different from American ones, and French ones have been even more different. In consequence, the history of *roman scientifique* is not something that can or ought to be simply gathered into a general "history of science fiction."

An argument can be made, and sometimes is, that it is a mistake and a distortion to gather texts together into genres at all, and to build narratives connecting them. In the present instance, that argument would assert that trying to establish a body of *roman scientifique* extending across two and a half centuries, and trying to make any kind of narrative out of the "evolution" of that work, is just as misleading and distortive as trying to assimilate that assembly of texts to a generalized "history of science fiction." Again, however, it would be silly to go to the opposite extreme and take the view that the generic similarities that the present text will attempt to identify and link together are purely accidental, entirely in the eye of the modern beholder.

Many of the texts that will be described and discussed in this volume are explicitly linked together by their own internal references, and many more by tacit connections resulting from their reaction to the same issues. Indeed, that is far truer in France than in Britain, let alone America, because of the concentration of French publishing, and the presence of a highly-developed French literary community, in the city of Paris. French writers, by and large, had more opportunity and inclination to read previously-written books relevant to their own projects, and to read one another's books, than writers in the English language. The *salon* culture that developed in seventeenth-century France, initially in association with Louis XIV's court, which spread and diversified throughout the eighteenth and nineteenth centuries, ensured that French writers, at least in Paris, were far more likely to get together and discuss what they were doing than writers anywhere else in the world.

That kind of opportunity is particularly relevant to imaginative and speculative fiction, which deals with ideas and possibilities rather than with the mimetic reproduction or elaboration of the familiar. As previously mentioned, one of the key features of the development of the labeled science fiction genre in America has been the evolution in association with the fiction of a community of writers and readers who went to considerable efforts to arrange regular meetings and discussions, partly for mutual support and encouragement, but also to "bounce ideas" back and forth. In France, it was not necessary to invent a labeled genre and make special provision for that kind of interaction to happen among speculative fiction's practitioners and enthusiasts; the social infrastructure was already in place.

By virtue of that circumstance, many of the authors whose works are discussed in the present text not only read many of the other works discussed, and responded and reacted to them, but were personally acquainted with at least some of their contemporaries, able to respond and react to them face-to-face. Not everyone, of course, could do that, but even those writers excluded from the meetings for one reason or another were aware of the culture of which they were a part; they sometimes made up the deficit with correspondence, or made what compensation they could by shadowy emulation or simple envy.

The result of that infrastructural support is that, even though no one before the 1870s could actually think in terms of "writing *roman scientifique*" and many people who can now be considered in retrospect as having done that actually thought of what they were doing in other terms, there was nevertheless always an awareness of some degree of common cause among writers interested in works of that kind, and an ongoing dialogue. The narrative of the evolution of French "scientific fiction" is blurred and complicated by all kinds of factors, but there is, nevertheless, a real narrative within it, and a real process of evolution. If it is to be understood properly, that evolution needs to be conceived as an evolution away from its actual past rather than an evolution toward what turned out to be its future, but it is a real and comprehensible process. (The same is, of course, true of biological evolution, although very few writers of speculative biological fantasies have understood that, and almost all of them tacitly or explicitly adopted the opposite point of view: that the progressive "purpose" of biological evolution had been, and still was, to "perfect" human being.)

15

In sum, therefore, the nature of this project is an attempt to produce a reasoned account of the evolution of scientifically-influenced fiction in France, paying heed to the differences between that evolution and the parallel processes going on in Britain and America. That cannot be responsibly done by looking primarily at the similarities between antique fiction of that sort and more modern fiction, as if the former were merely a prelude to the latter. It is, on the contrary, necessary to make the attempt, however difficult it might be, to look forward in the fashion that the authors of the past were looking forward, not toward our present but toward circumstances that never came about—and which, we now understand, never could have come about—but whose hypothetical construction can nevertheless be reckoned as a serious imaginative endeavor.

Tracking the evolution of a genre in order to cultivate the kind of understanding described above is a difficult process. The genre of *roman scientifique*, as I shall attempt to depict and characterize it, is a massive entity, with which it is no means easy for a single person to acquaint himself, even superficially. The bibliographical endeavor of accumulating a register of the relevant texts is Herculean in itself, and I could never have envisaged making the attempt without the enormously valuable groundwork laid by the bibliographers who have gradually put together the maps that I have employed in my attempted navigation.

The foundations of that endeavor were laid by Pierre Versins in his 1972 *Encyclopédie*. Although its coverage is limited to the number of texts that one person was capable of assembling and reading over a period of a few decades, it exhibits a remarkable breath and assiduity. Subsequent collectors have contrived to identify and locate numerous texts that Versins never happened across, so the body of work that can be identified as relevant to the present project has swelled steadily since 1972, thanks to the endeavors of such enthusiastic collectors and bibliographers as Joseph Altairac, Marc Madouraud, Guy Costes and Jean-Luc Boutel, assisting the bibliography contained in the Lofficiers' account of *French Science Fiction, Fantasy, Horror and Pulp Fiction* (2000) to extend the basic list of relevant titles considerably and usefully.

Although Pierre Versins bequeathed his collection to provide the basis of the library contained in the Maison d'Ailleurs at Yverdon, severe difficulties remained for subsequent scholars in obtaining access to the range of texts identified by him and subsequent bibliographers. Inevitably, those difficulties resulted in the vast majority of historical studies of generic materials produced before 2001 employing the standard academic strategy of simply ignoring the bulk of the material and focusing attention on a limited range of easily-available texts, tacitly suggesting that an understanding of the whole phenomenon can be gleaned from a handful of exemplary texts, without any need to consider the rest.

That situation has, however, changed drastically in the twenty-first century by virtue of the advent and extension of the world wide web. Consultation on line has made access to the bibliographical information much simpler; there are now several bibliographies of relevant material available on the web, the largest and most useful being those detailed at *noösfere.org* and the website of the BDFI (Base de Données Francophone de l'Imaginaire); the latter includes bibliographies of relevant works by some ten thousand authors, a useful forum in which authors can discuss possible candidates for the elaboration of the bibliography, and links to numerous other sites providing supplementary information.

Some of those other sites, most notably Jean-Luc Boutel's *Sur l'Autre Face du Monde*, and some more narrowly specialized sites such as *destination-armageddon.fr* and the section on *trussel.com* dedicated to prehistoric fiction, provide much more elaborate commentaries on relevant texts, and are increasingly providing direct access to previously-rare texts. The Bibliothèque Nationale's website *gallica* is gradually making the library's entire stock of out-of-copyright texts available for reading on line, and has already made a large quantity of texts that would otherwise be almost impossible to obtain available for downloading. It has therefore become feasible, as the twenty-first century has progressed, for anyone with sufficient determination not only to identify a wide range of texts relevant to the genre in which the present endeavor is interested, but to also read many of them; that is what I have tried to do, to the extent of which I was capable.

I cannot pretend that what I have contrived to produce in the present volume is anything more than a preliminary sketch, and it is arguable that its cut-off date for the considerations of texts, 1939, is at least a decade too early. Given another ten years of reading, during which time *gallica* would undoubtedly have made many more texts available, I could probably have done something a little more comprehensive, and should I live that long, I might well attempt a second edition of the present text, but it seemed worthwhile to produce something in the interim that was within my range of practicality, because I believe that there is some merit in trying to grasp the broad picture of the genre's early evolution, even while the jigsaw I am presently able to compile is necessarily missing many of its pieces.

In trying to identify and delineate the genre that I have chosen to call *roman scientifique* I thought it necessary not only to specify a starting-point—the beginning of the eighteenth century—but also to sketch a "prehistory" explaining how the seeds of the genre were able to begin germination in that century and proliferate greatly in the next. I have tracked the development of the genre through the nineteenth century and into the early twentieth as comprehensively as I could, but my coverage becomes increasingly patchy as the twentieth century progresses, partly because the volume of relevant material increases to unmanageable levels, and partly because I have focused my attention primarily on works in the public domain, because those were available for translation, and translating works automatically grants a more intimate insight into their narrative workings than merely reading them. It also creates a sense of investment invaluable to determined and protracted research.

The latter decision makes the text somewhat arbitrarily selective, especially with regard to its consideration of developments after the Great War of 1914-18, but one has to draw a line limiting such projects somehow, because it is not humanly possible to read and comment on everything. I hope that those I have been able to include offer a broader and more accurate representation than could ever have been achieved by the method of focusing on a mere handful of texts and trying to pretend that they are more representative than they are. I have tried to offer an image of the true extent and complexity of the genre, and if it lacks detail in places—as it surely does—I hope that disadvantage is somewhat compensated by its relative breadth.

In order to support the research for the book, and the book itself, I have translated more than a hundred and fifty volumes of material not previously available in English, the great majority of which have been published by Black Coat Press. The majority of the detailed references I shall have occasion to make are, therefore, to texts that interested readers will be able to find if they wish in English translation, most of them available in electronic formats as well as print-on-demand versions.

The volumes of translation provide a significant support function, in that the introductions and afterwords to the various volumes and sets of volumes generally provide more detailed information about particular authors and more detailed analyses of individuals texts than can be accommodated in the present general survey. The thematic manner in which the present text is organized requires coverage of the work of such important and versatile authors as Maurice Renard, J.-H. Rosny and André Couvreur to be distributed over several different subsections of the chapters relating to the periods of their activity, whereas the detailed introductions to the sets of translations of their works offer detailed biographies and overviews of their entire production. There is a sense, therefore, in which the present volume is simply the central element in a larger project, and is perhaps best regarded itself as a mere introduction. The set of translations will continue to grow, for as long as I am capable of producing them and Black Coat Press is able to publish them.

2. The Definition of the Genre

Like its closest English language analogue, "scientific romance," the phrase *roman scientifique* first made its appearance in the French language in the latter half of the eighteenth century, when it was initially used to refer to ideas in science that were thought to be, or had turned out be, chimerical scholarly fantasies. The earliest uses that show up in searching for the French term with the aid of internet search engines are dated between 1750 and 1754, but all the references from that period refer to a single observation by Élie-Catherine Fréron, referring to Isaac Newton's theory of gravity, which Fréron did not like. Other early uses include a footnote in a scientific encyclopedia of the period to the entry on phlogiston, and several sources citing Jean-Baptiste Delambre's scornful dismissal of a supposed calculation of the date of the Biblical Deluge by the astronomer William Whiston.

The term was subsequently employed by Honoré de Balzac in 1836 with reference to the New York *Sun* "Moon Hoax" of 1935, reporting supposed telescopic discoveries of lunar life, which became gradually more extravagant and absurd over the five days that the hoax extended, causing a sensation that was reproduced when the hoax was reprinted in French translation. Camille Flammarion employed the phrase in the same context in 1864. It was still being used in the 1860s to refer to scientific texts that the users considered fanciful, but it also began to be used increasingly in that decade to refer to works of fiction, including references to works by Edmond About, Léon Gozlan, and, of course, Jules Verne. Indeed, throughout the 1870s the term was used almost exclusively to refer to Verne's scientifically and technologically-enhanced adventure stories, considered by many of their commentators to be archetypal of a new kind of fiction, and it is in that decade that the term can be said to have acquired the meaning in French, at least tentatively, that I have adopted for the purposes of the present text.

That situation was, however, complicated in the 1880s when some critics, apparently provided with a lead by Édouard Rod, began to refer to the works of Émile Zola as "*romans scientifiques*"—a term which the author was happy to accept, on the grounds that his "Naturalist" fiction was typified by its employment of a scientific method of character analysis, based on the study of the influences of hereditary and environment in shaping individual behavior, although he actually preferred the term "*roman expérimental.*" The phrase was subsequently adopted in such studies of Zola's work as Henry Martineau's *Le Roman scientifique d'Émile Zola* (1907), although it was being used in the same era in the subtitles of Vernian novels such as Henri de Graffigny's *La Ville aérienne* [The Airborne City] (1911).

The conflict of reference that developed between the two usages of the term might have been one of the factors that prevented the generic label of *roman scientifique* from being more widely adopted than it was with reference to "Vernian fiction," although the fact that Verne's literary endeavors soon extended over a broader spectrum than the fraction that invited ready description as "scientific" inevitably generated problems of demarcation. From 1880 onwards, in fact, the terms "Vernian fiction" and "*roman scientifique*" began to diverge somewhat in their reference and implications.

The notion of Naturalist *roman scientifique* or *roman expérimental* was not very conducive to the development of speculative fiction, although there are elements of scientific and futuristic speculative fiction in some of Zola's later novels, most notably *Le Docteur Pascal* (1893; tr. as *Doctor Pascal*) and the quartet of novels begun with *Fécondité* (1899; tr. as *Fruitfulness*), which he did not live to complete. By the same token, only a minority of those of Verne's works that warrant consideration as "*romans scientifiques*" are speculative; although many of his adventure stories feature scientifically-inspired projects and methodical scientific thinking, they remain conscientiously naturalistic (with a small n). Neither characterization of *roman scientifique*, therefore, referred specifically to speculative fiction, and both covered a good deal of fiction that was naturalistic but nevertheless employed a method or subject matter that was in some sense, at least ostensibly, "scientific."

Numerous attempts had been made prior to the adaptation of *roman scientifique* to define literary genres that would subsequently be brought under that umbrella. Much fiction of that kind would previously have been categorized as "utopian," and the use of that term is distinctive in France because *utopie*, adapted from the title of Thomas More's classic *Utopia* (1516) acquired a broader meaning there than its English equivalent, routinely employed not simply to apply to imaginary locations of hypothetical societies to apply but more generally to fanciful and presumably-unrealizable ideas.

A more formal attempt to define a genre of imaginative fiction which has something in common with the such later nomenclatures as *roman scientifique* and Vernian fiction, also recognized in the complication of the title of the Versins *Encyclopédie*, was made in 1787 when the publisher Charles Garnier launched a series of *Voyages imaginaires, songes, visions, et romans cabalistiques* [Imaginary Voyages, Dreams, Visions and Cabalistic Fiction], which eventually extended to 36 volumes by 1789. The project was not only important in defining a particular set of concerns and bringing many of the relevant texts into juxtaposition, but also in providing future writers interested in similar endeavors with a kind of reference library, of which many took some advantage.

Another attempt to define a relevant genre was made by Félix Bodin in *Le Roman de l'avenir* (1834, tr. as *The Novel of the Future*), not, as in Garnier's case, by gathering previous texts together under a generic rubric, but by proposing the founding of a new genre that did not yet exist: *roman futuriste* [futuristic fiction]. As well as providing an exemplary sample of the genre in question, Bodin offered a analysis of its essential nature, differentiating it from former visions of the future and proposing that it might and ought to become an important aspect of the fiction to actually to be produced in the future. Time has proved him right in the latter connection, but his label never caught on.

One of the subsequent historians who made extensive use of the parts of Garnier's collection that were relevant to his own endeavor was Camille Flammarion, who tacitly delineated a genre of fiction in *Les Mondes imaginaires et les mondes réels* [Real and Imaginary Worlds] (1865), which set out to compare fictitious images of the worlds of the solar system with what astronomical evidence suggested to the author about their nature and possible inhabitants—a counter-narrative that turned out, inevitably but ironically, to be similarly fictitious. Flammarion's subcategory of "imaginary worlds" defined what would nowadays be called "interplanetary fiction" quite independently, and rightly so, of "futuristic fiction."

Because American science fiction became so heavily involved with interplanetary fiction, Flammarion's endeavor now looks like a treatment of French "proto-science fiction," and its method of evaluation anticipated one commonly practiced by some science fiction readers, of combing texts for inaccurate data and inept reasoning. Like futuristic fiction, however, interplanetary fiction is only a small fraction of what can now be defined retrospectively as *roman scientifique*—considerably smaller than utopian fiction, which was still the largest fraction prior to 1865, although that turned out to be the crucial year in which the balance tilted, and from then on, for nearly half a century, the largest fraction consisted of adventure stories inspired by the romance of exploratory geography, cardinally exemplified by the work of Jules Verne.

Flammarion added a supplementary section to later editions of his book commenting on numerous works published in the decade after the first edition's appearance, including Jules Verne's *De la terre à la lune* (1865) and its sequel *Autour de la lune* (1870), but the only elements of Verne's fiction that interested Flammarion were the interplanetary fantasies, which differed very markedly in narrative strategy from his own attempts to employ visionary fiction in the popularization of science and the dramatization of scientific discovery and possibility. That difference is so extreme, in fact, that within the context of the present endeavor it is useful to invent a vague category of "Flammarionesque fiction" in order to compare and contrast it with the "Vernian fiction" that became the most prolific category of fiction relevant to the development of *roman scientifique*.

The early fiction produced by both Verne and Flammarion was an aspect of a considerable boom in the popularization of science, which led a number of writers who had been involved in that kind of work for some time to experiment with fiction as a means of such popularization. The writer who had made a more significant contribution than any other to the use of fictional devices in the popularization of science prior to 1860 was S. Henry Berthoud, who had been publishing narrativized popular science articles in newspapers for many years, often using the pen-name "Dr. Sam." One effect of the new fashionability of the popularization of science was to allow Berthoud to compile of a four-volume set of his relevant work as *Fantaisies scientifiques de Sam* [Sam's Scientific Fantasies] (1861-2), thus making another bid to establish a category label.

Like *roman scientifique*, the phrase *fantaisie scientifique* had been used previously to refer to scientific ideas, but—perhaps oddly—not in the same pejorative fashion. Uses from earlier in the century referring to Galileo and Bernardin de Saint-Pierre seem to be at least neutral, if not actually complimentary. Berthoud's attempt to adopt the phrase as a generic label, which he first floated in an article bearing the title, which appeared in his regular column in *La Patrie* in 1859, did not catch on, but the range of works that he grouped under it is nevertheless interesting in the context of the history of French scientific fiction. Many of Berthoud's *fantaisies scientifiques* are really anecdotal essays rather than stories, and many of those more conscientiously formed as stories merely feature encounters between characters and odd phenomena of natural history, while others are items of historical fiction describing the endeavors of actual scientists, often distorting their real histories. Only a tiny minority include any speculative component.

If one adds Berthoud's characterization of *"fantaisie scientifique"* to the two different definitions of *"roman scientifique"* that became current in the latter half of the century, in fact, one of the most striking things about the putative genres thus described is how little speculative fiction they contained, especially by comparison with Camille Flammarion's category of the fiction of *mondes imaginaires*. Even Charles Garnier's category of *voyages imaginaires* had, in fact, started with naturalistic materials; the volumes of his enterprise being launched with a translation of Daniel Defoe's *Adventures of Robinson Crusoe*, which was a more important and influential exemplar in French thinking and French writing than it was in England.

In fact, the iconic character of Robinson Crusoe became a key reference-point for the French Romantic Movement in general, and Jules Verne's works in particular, to the extent that *"robinson"* became a familiar common noun in French parlance, in a far more robust fashion than "robinsonade" did in English. Like *roman scientifique* and *fantaisie scientifique*, therefore, *voyage imaginaire* was, during the period of its attempted popularization as a generic term, a description that included both naturalistic and fantastic works, and did not use a crucial distinction between those two kinds of fiction in laying down its boundaries.

Jules Verne's work attracted numerous imitators because of its enormous popularity, and eventually influenced the editorial policy of a specialist periodical, the popular geographical magazine *Journal des Voyages et des aventures de terre et de mer*, which acquired that title in 1877; the regular slot in the magazine dedicated to serial fiction concentrated thereafter on fiction in the Vernian vein. As conceived by many of Verne's imitators, including the editors of the *Journal des Voyages*, the essence of Vernian fiction was that it consisted of adventures set in remote parts of the globe; the fact that such missions often had a scientific purpose, and that exotic means of transport were sometimes used to facilitate the necessary voyages, were generally seen as peripheral issues.

The heroes of Vernian adventure stories were very often scientists, and those who were not were frequently assiduous in their application of the scientific method and the improvisation of technologies to solving the predicaments in which they found themselves, but the majority worked entirely within the confines of the known, without venturing beyond them in any but a geographical sense. Submarines and flying machines were often featured in Vernian fiction, and various kinds of exotic phenomena were routinely discovered in the course of adventures in *terra incognita*, but the core of the "Vernian genre," and hence of the Vernian version of *roman scientifique*, in the 1870s and 1880s, was displaced by a considerable distance from the speculative fiction that subsequently became the core of "Wellsian" British scientific romance and American pulp science fiction.

The first person to use the phrase *roman scientifique* not merely as a casual description but in a deliberate attempt to designate, delineate and exemplify a genre of fiction, was Louis Figuier, the editor of the weekly popular science magazine *La Science Illustrée*, who began running a regular *feuilleton* section in 1888 under that rubric. Figuier wrote no fiction of his own, save for using the occasional narrative device in his popularizations of science, but he was well aware of the fact that one of his early works of popularization had provided the basis for Verne's *Voyage au centre de la terre* (tr. as *Journey to the Centre of the Earth*), to such an extent of dependency that when he published a revised edition of the book in question, Verne felt obliged to revise his novel to take aboard a significant change of mind on Figuier's part. *Voyage au centre de la terre* would probably have been one of the first works of fiction that Figuier reprinted in *La Science Illustrée* had it not been too easily available—and he probably would not have been able to get permission to do so anyway—but he did reprint two shorter stories by Verne, in order to identify the author's centrality to the genre.

Over the next decade and a half, Figuier published dozens more works, which extracted a series of exemplars from the past, and mingled them with new works, in order to lay them out as a kind of tacit map of what he considered the genre of *roman scientifique* to constitute. It was, in essence, a Vernian genre, but Figuier seems to have urged the writers he recruited to be more adventurous in their endeavors than those who had previously appeared in the pages of the *Journal de Voyages* had been required to be therein. Although he published a number of naturalistic stories reminiscent of Berthoud's *fantaisies scientifiques*, he did edge his putative genre in the direction of bold speculative fiction, and began to do so even more wholeheartedly in 1898, when he discovered a new source of useful material in translations of the works of H. G. Wells, twelve of which he published over the next five years, alongside an even more extensive series of translations that appeared in the *Mercure de France*. Figuier's *feuilleton* slot did not last much longer, though, apparently having fallen out of favor with his audience, and the periodical was entirely devoted to non-fiction after 1905.

While Figuier was promoting the term it was taken up by a number of other critics who thought it useful, including Eugène Gilbert in *Le Roman en France pendant le XIXe siècle* [The Novel in France in the Twentieth Century]

(1900), who thought it more appropriate to consider Jules Verne as a pioneer of that genre than merely a member of the ranks of *"romanciers des voyages."* Another commentator, however, complained about the label's *"piperie"* [trickery] on the grounds that it was essentially self-contradictory.

One of the *Mercure de France*'s regular contributors, who made a substantial contribution to the genre himself, Alfred Jarry, adopted Figuier's generic term in an essay he wrote for *La Plume* in 1902 entitled "De quelques romans scientifiques." The difficulties involved in characterizing the new genre's relationship to previous forms of fiction, in terms of kinship and contrast, are very evident in the first two paragraphs of the essay. While the first states that *"roman scientifique* descends, in a direct line, from the *Mille et une Nuits*, many of the tales in which are alchemical, and the *Cabinet des fées"*, the second contends that *"roman scientifique*—which could be just as accurately described as hypothetical fiction—imagines what would happen *if* certain elements were brought together. That is why, in the same way that certain hypotheses will be realized one day, some of these novels will be found to be, at the time when they were written, futuristic novels." The tension between those two views is sustained through the remainder of the essay—and has been sustained throughout the entire history of critical writing about *roman scientifique*, scientific romance and science fiction.

Unlike Jarry, however, Alfred Vallette, the editor of the *Mercure de France*, refused to use Figuier's generic label to describe the Wells translations he published therein, perhaps because he feared confusion with the use of the term by Zola's followers. Instead, he encouraged the adoption of a substitute term. The *Mercure*'s first critical survey of Wells' work, by Marcel Reja, was entitled "H. G. Wells et le merveilleux scientifique" [H. G. Wells and the Scientific Marvelous] (1904). The designation of fantastic fictions in general as the genre of *le merveilleux* already had a long history; the term had been commonplace throughout the eighteenth century.

Like *roman scientifique* and *fantaisie scientifique*, the term *merveilleux scientifique* had previously been used with reference to scientific notions. Indeed, it had recently been used by the physiologist Joseph-Pierre Durand as the tile of his book *Le Merveilleux scientifique* (1894), which was a survey of research in mesmerism, hypnotism and suggestion, with a brief addendum on "Occultisme et Spiritisme." Raoul Gineste, an author who made a marginal contribution to *roman scientifique*, employed it in 1907 as a general description of recent scientific discoveries and technological developments, citing X-rays, radium, wireless telegraphy, etc.

In a literary context, *merveilleux scientifique* was employed by Pierre Larousse in the *Revue Universelle* in 1905 to refer to the relevant works of H. G. Wells and J.-H. Rosny, and it was adopted, at first eagerly, by Maurice Renard, one of the most important contributors to the genre, to describe his own work. Renard attempted to popularize it in an essay published in *Le Spectateur* in

1909, "Du Roman merveilleux-scientifique et de son action sur l'intelligence du progrès" (tr. as "On Scientific Marvel Fiction and its Effect on the Consciousness of Progress").

That label too failed to catch on more generally, although it was used significantly in Hubert Matthey's *Essai sur le merveilleux dans la littérature française depuis 1800* [An Essay on the Marvelous in French Literature Since 1800] (1915), which included a substantial chapter on "Le Merveilleux-scientifique," identifying the key French contributors to the genre as Verne, Villiers de l'Isle-Adam, Rosny, Renard, Jules Hoche and Gaston Danville. Maurice Renard abandoned the term after the Great War, however, and began to think instead in terms of "*roman parascientifique*" [Parascientific Fiction] (in 1923), and then "*roman d'hypothèse*" [Hypothetical Fiction] (in 1928)—but those suggestions had even less effect, and the very fact that he kept changing his mind implied that the problem of designation might be insoluble.

It is arguable that the advent and attempted popularization of *le merveilleux-scientifique* merely served to confuse the issue and help to prevent Figuier's preferred term becoming standardized. It also served, however, to place the focus on speculative fiction while exiling the naturalist fringe of Vernian fiction from the category, thus producing a concept more akin to the British notion of "scientific romance." For that reason, the term still has some resonance today, not only in some recent critical studies of the post-Wellsian period of French scientific fiction, but in such exercises as *Dimension merveilleux scientifique* (2015), introduced by Jean-Guillaume Lanuque, an anthology of pastiche materials, which also includes a substantial survey of the retrospectively-identified genre by Jean-Luc Boutel, conceived and contrived with considerable expertise.

In spite of the potential availability of more specific labels, however, most French scientific fiction of the first half of the twentieth century was simply lumped together in publishers' catalogues and advertisements with other *romans* or "*romans d'aventures*" without any distinguishing designation, and the absence of any widely accepted term left a void into which the American term "science fiction" began to creep not long after its coinage, becoming widespread and generally accepted, at least in the lower strata of the marketplace, after 1945. Whether or not that was a misfortune is a matter of opinion, but Figuier was probably not the only person to regret that the genre he attempted to define and promote in the pages of *La Science Illustrée* remained a shadowy notion after 1905. Presumably, he remained confirmed in the opinion that *roman scientifique* was a notion whose time had come in 1888, and which did not require further substitution, as I do.

In the same way that what can now be recognized as *roman scientifique* was mostly subsumed within broader descriptions in the nineteenth and early twentieth centuries, however, it had been similarly subsumed in the eighteenth century, in a fashion that would seem much more peculiar, looking back from today, if had not been largely forgotten. Because the present endeavor attempts to extend its evolutionary account back to the eighteenth century, and even to the seventeenth, it is also necessary to give some consideration to one of those broader categorizations here.

Many works of imaginative fiction produced in the late seventeenth century and throughout the eighteenth century, including most all those that might warrant consideration as early contributions to the evolution of *roman scientifique*, belonged to a genre that Voltaire called *contes philosophiques*. The literal translation of the phrase as "philosophical tales" does not embrace all the subtleties of the term *conte*, which will require further discussion in chapter I, but it also fails to grasp all the contemporary connotations of the word *philosophique*. Most importantly, in terms of the jargon of the literary marketplace in which Voltaire's works of fiction were issued, the word *philosophique* was conventionally used by booksellers as a euphemism for books that were legally proscribed.

Robert Darnton's meticulous study of *The Forbidden Best-Sellers of Pre-Revolutionary France* (1996) explains how books that were unlicensed by the censors were marketed and sold in Paris during the eighteenth century, clandestinely but in huge quantities, as "philosophical" works. His investigation attempts to determine which works were most in demand and sold most prolifically. At the very top of his list of prohibited best-sellers is one of the works now considered crucial to the evolution of futuristic fiction, Louis-Sébastien Mercier's *L'An deux mille quatre cent quarante, rêve s'il en fût jamais*, [The Year 2440; A Dream if Ever There Was One] first published anonymously in 1771 but considerably augmented in the course of twenty subsequent editions. Philosophical works by Voltaire, and the Baron d'Holbach's *Système de la nature* (1770, originally signed "Jean-Baptiste de Maribaud") also figure prominently on the list, but so do works that would nowadays by reckoned merely pornographic, like *Thérèse Philosophe* [Thérèse the Philosopher] (c1748; anonymous but probably by Jean-Baptiste de Boyer, Marquis d'Argens), and the scurrilously slanderous *Anecdotes sur Madame le Comtesse Du Barry* [Anecdotes featuring the Comtesse du Barry] (1775; anonymous but probably by Mathieu-François Pidansat de Mairobert).

Darnton observes that the concept of "pornography" did not exist when these works were published, and that when the equivalent French word was first coined by Restif de la Bretonne in *Le Pornographe or Le Prostitution réformée* [Writing About Sex; or, Prostitution Reformed] (1770) it was invented to describe an earnest tract calling for the legalization and organization of prostitution for the benefit of the public good and morality, and not what Jean-Jacques Rousseau had described as "books to be read with one hand." It only acquired its insulting connotations second hand, although it did so swiftly and irredeemably. Few eighteenth-century works that now invite consideration as *roman scientifique* have a significant erotic content, although some did take advantage of the freedom tacitly granted by their unlicensed status, but in the eyes of the law they were in the same category as books that were "indecent" in any other sense, whether because they were anti-religious, anti-royalist or simply scabrous.

Almost without exception, in consequence, the *romans scientifiques* of the eighteenth century were published in the same fashion as other texts considered to be dangerous. They were issued anonymously or pseudonymously, with title pages proclaiming, usually dishonestly, that they had been published in Amsterdam, Brussels, London, Geneva, or anywhere except Paris, although many of them were undoubtedly printed there. Some of the most interesting were published posthumously, because their authors dared not issue them while they were alive, even anonymously. One or two of them might have made money for their authors, but very little, and it is hard to believe that any of them was written with that purpose primarily in mind. They were mostly written as protests, sometimes mischievous and sometimes angry, not against the law *per se* but against the forces that were using the law to suppress free thought: the forces of dogma and tyranny.

The Revolution of 1789 was supposed to change all that, and did, so that authors of *roman scientifique* operating in the nineteenth century usually had much greater freedom to write what they thought, but the forces that had once had the law at their disposal had not vanished, and were not entirely stifled. The pseudonymous books of the pre-Revolutionary era that continued to be read mostly reclaimed their signatures—although Voltaire, who had originally become Voltaire in order to conceal his baptismal name, had become so thoroughly Voltaire that his former identity was completely forgotten—and few nineteenth century writers employed similar tactics.

In consequence, the euphemistic designation of "philosophical books" vanished, and the term was reclaimed for straightforward application to works of philosophy—but that strange episode of history was not without its legacy, and even when *roman scientifique* began to invite that straightforward description in the latter part of the century, in the staid and utterly respectable pages of *La Science Illustrée*, it still retained a fugitive consciousness of its own combativeness, a sense that it was still carrying the banner of valiant philosophical opposition against dogma, intolerance and ignorance, in a war not yet won.

For that reason, to a greater extent than contemporary British or American "philosophical fiction," French *roman scientifique* very often assumed a tacitly oppositional stance, defiant, pugnacious and unrepentantly radical, never completely domesticated even in its most comfortably tame versions. It would be impossible to define within the British or American traditions a significant subcategory of "anarchist fiction" but it would be very difficult to discuss *roman scientifique* seriously without doing that—and not simply in the political sense of the term. Alfred Jarry, one of the writers who immediately recognized the propriety of the term *roman scientifique*, and wanted to make contributions to the genre himself, was also inspired to step outside and beyond its implied boundaries in order to create a new genre of *roman pataphysique*, "pataphysics" going beyond physics in a more fundamental and more oppositional sense than metaphysics, proclaiming itself the science that dealt not with generalizations but with exceptions.

Although it is unnecessary, in the course of the present endeavor, to identify a strain of "Jarryesque" fiction in the same sense that it is profitable to talk about the "Vernian" and "Flammarionesque" elements of *roman scientifique*, there is a sense in which *roman pataphysique*, as a logical extrapolation of the Voltairean *conte philosophique*, does form an important terminus to its spectrum, and just as Jarry became one of the key precursors of Surrealism, so *roman scientifique* stands in special relationship to anarchism and surrealism, harboring and brooding a more significant element of the anarchic and the surreal than British scientific romance or American science fiction.

In conclusion, most of the early attempts to define fictional genres in France that can now be seen retrospectively as overlapping the genre of *roman scientifique* associated some naturalistic fictions with more fanciful ones, finding common bonds in terms of the involvement of scientific thinking and endeavor, the exploratory impulse, and interests in social reform or opposition to social strictures. Those overlaps add considerably to the terminological difficulties with which the present endeavor is forced to grapple, adding an unhelpful measure of confusion to the discussion.

It would undoubtedly be more convenient if it were possible to draw clearer boundaries and issue more specific operational definitions within this field of interest, but the simple fact is that it is not possible. Even such fundamental boundaries as the one between "naturalistic" and "imaginative fiction" become blurred and disappear if inspected carefully. The pioneering philosopher of esthetics Alexander Baumgarten proposed that the literary ideal was to produce textual mirrors to the world that would reflect it as accurately as possible, and that any kind of "heterocosmic" literary endeavor, featuring worlds within texts different from the experienced world, was *ipso facto* inferior. That is a prejudice that has always haunted literary criticism, to the detriment of any critic or historian specifically interested in heterocosmic fictions. Not only is it the case, however, that all fiction is heterocosmic to some degree, but it is also true that heterocosmic representations are sometimes far more informative about the experienced world than supposed slavish imitations of it—or, to put it proverbially, truth might well be stranger than fiction, but fiction is sometimes truer.

Most *roman scientifique* is heterocosmic, and its speculative components are heterocosmic by definition, but that observation is of no particular significance in itself. The whole point of attempting to define a genre of *roman scientifique* as something worth discriminating and worth discussing is to identify and elaborate the specific nature, direction and purpose of its differentiation from strict mimesis: to discuss the narrative strategies that it employs in order to accomplish the complex, but not paradoxical, mission of altering the experienced world in order to show that world in a different light, viewed from a different standpoint, from which it might potentially become clearer and more understandable, if not more changeable.

3. The Analysis of the Genre

The attempts made to define the various genres and subgenres cited in the previous section introduced a considerable number of terms that began the construction a vocabulary useful in the categorization and analysis of the works to be discussed in the history that follows. Before starting on the detailed survey of texts, however, it will be useful to make some further discriminations in order to broaden out the terminology.

There are two extra sets of terms that seem to me to be very useful in categorizing texts for the purpose of comparison and contrast, which also assist in making some further general points about the nature of the genre which might be useful to make in advance rather than being postponed to the substantive discussion of particular texts.

The first set of useful extra terms arose by degrees from the coinage of the terms "utopia" and *utopie*. Even setting aside the additional French meaning that allows *utopie* to be applied fanciful ideas in general, and sticking to the narrower sense of referring to hypothetical societies, the terms "utopia" and "*utopie*" soon acquired an awkward ambiguity in both languages because they were sometimes construed, as Thomas More had intended, as a derivative of the Greek *outopos* [no place], and sometimes as if they were derived from *eutopos* [better place]. Thus, the term could be used either as a label for any non-existent location imagined for literary purposes, or, more specifically, for attempts to design "ideal societies." For that reason, some critics and historians eventually began using "eutopian" as an adjective to refer specifically to the latter category of texts, while using "utopian" in a broader sense.

The complication did not stop there. The frequent use of "utopia" to mean, tacitly, "eutopia," encouraged the invention of an opposite term to refer to worse places: dystopia. The word appears to have been first used in English by John Stuart Mill in 1868, but it was not adopted into the critical jargon of historians of imaginative fiction as a necessary distinction until the 1960s. The equivalent French term, *dystopie*, took longer to catch on—it has no entry in the Versins *Encyclopédie*—but eventually crept into French usage in the late 1970s (slightly handicapped in its reference by competition from a pre-existent medical term defining a particular defect of eyesight). The English term seemed necessary to English literary historians to categorize a set of texts anticipating horrible futures, two of which had become highly significant texts that lent their titles to frequent use in common parlance: Aldous Huxley's *Brave New World* (1932) and George Orwell's *Nineteen Eighty-Four* (1949).

By the time "dystopia" became commonplace in critical parlance, however, other distinctions had become useful, and perhaps necessary. In his exemplary anthology *Utopias and Utopian Thought* (1966), Frank Manuel argued that the history of utopian thought had undergone two crucial transitions, the first in the late eighteenth century—primarily and crucially in France—when "eutopian" imagery and thinking had begun to be gradually and largely displaced by "euchronian" imagery and thinking, in which hypothetical ideal societies were located in a hypothetical historical future rather than in an imaginary space. The second shift, he argued, had begun in the twentieth century, when the emphasis of much imagery and thinking in that vein had gradually shifted into a "eupsychian" mode, which sought an existential ideal in a better state of mind instead of a better a better formula of government and social organization.

All of these terms do make useful discriminations for the discussion of the evolution of *roman scientifique*, and I shall therefore use them freely, routinely categorizing images of ideal societies as eutopian or euchronian, and occasionally as eupsychian, while retaining utopian as a more general description. including imaginary places that are merely different without necessarily being ideal. I shall frequently have occasion to combine those adjectives with the noun "satire" because, although there is not logical necessity for utopias to be satirical, the vast majority are. In so doing, they follow the precedent set by Thomas More, although it is not a matter of mere imitation.

The second set of terms that I consider to be useful in discussion of heterocosmic texts in general, and *roman scientifique* in particular, was first proposed by Farah Mendlesohn in "Toward a Taxonomy of Fantasy" (2002) and further elaborated in her book *Rhetorics of Fantasy* (2008). The core of the classification divides the majority of heterocosmic texts into three categories: intrusive fantasies, portal fantasies and immersive fantasies.

The literary framework of a voyage to a fictitious realm, which is fundamental to utopian fiction, falls into the category of portal fantasy. That narrative strategy involves transporting a viewpoint character from the familiar world into the constructed heterocosm of the story, where the character in question can provide the reader with a comfortable metaphorical pair of shoes in which to stand. Because they move from a familiar world into an unfamiliar one, such characters react and respond to the discoveries they make in the heterocosm in a manner with which the reader can readily identify and sympathize.

The narrative strategy of the intrusive fantasy effectively reverses the pattern of the portal fantasy, the heterocosmic element of the story being an intruder into a fictional world presumed to be similar to the experienced world of the present or the past known to history. Readers find it similarly easy to associate themselves with fantasies of that kind because the characters in the story react and respond to the intruder in readily comprehensible ways.

The narrative strategy of immersive fantasy, however, involves setting a story entirely within a heterocosm and employing a narrative viewpoint "native" to the heterocosm in question, whether it is associated with a character or functions as an impersonal narrative voice. That can be much more challenging for readers, who find themselves plunged into an alien environment, especially if the author elects to do without an "omniscient" narrative voice that can serve as an interpreter and commentator, explaining to the reader how the heterocosm differs from the familiar world. The stranger the heterocosm, the greater that burden of explanation becomes, and it poses very awkward technical problems for writers who want to tie their narrative viewpoint narrowly to a viewpoint character who will be just as alien to the reader as the world.

That problem is particularly acute because the central tendency of fiction, as the modern novel has evolved, has been the diminution and elimination of omniscient narrative voices, and the reduction of the narrative distance between readers and viewpoint characters, routinely taking the reader "inside the heads" of the characters to see things as they see them. That is far easier to contrive in naturalistic fiction, which can assume a fundamental similarity between reader and character, with parameters of difference comprehensible in terms of social or historical distance. In heterocosmic fictions featuring greater and more problematic distances in space, time and identity, that similarity is much reduced, and the burden of narrative labor that the author has to undertake in facilitating the association between the reader and the fictional world is increased proportionately.

Most antique heterocosmic texts did not run into that difficulty, partly because they automatically adopted the strategy of portal fantasy or intrusive fantasy, but also because they were more inclined to take advantage of omniscient narrative voices. The gradual evolution of narrative strategies permitting immersive fantasies to proliferate and flourish is, however, an important thread in the evolution of *roman scientifique*, to which I shall have occasion to call attention in the chapters that follow.

The category of portal fantasy is virtually synonymous with the subgenre of imaginary voyages, provided that one adds the observation that the most frequent portal employed to facilitate and abbreviate such voyages is the Homeric double gate of horn and ivory: the portals that led to true and false dreams respectively. The principal problem with employing dreams as portals to heterocosms, however, is that dreaming comes with a built-in assumption of unreality, and a suspicion of triviality that is difficult to dispel with the clam that some dreams are "visions" laden with special significance.

The use of an actual voyage, traditionally employing a ship—although other vehicles, especially balloons, were avidly embraced by writers of imaginary voyages as soon as their potential became available—supposedly avoids the taint of illusion, although that apparent evasion is somewhat illusory in itself. We can probably presume that travelers' tales go back to the remotest origins of travel, but we can probably also assume that they shared from the very beginning the invariable characteristic of suspected exaggeration: that every traveler's tale ever told was, in effect, a "tall tale" led to take on fantastic elements even when it was not designed specifically to entertain them. In literary works featuring voyages to exotic utopias, the ship or balloon is effectively a stand-in for a dream, and many of the more fanciful variants do indeed use a surprised awakening as a conclusion, which has the effect of "normalizing" the fantasy. Fantasies involving actual journeys typically have normalizing endings too, supplied by bringing the imaginary voyager home.

Intrusive fantasies usually have normalizing endings as well, although there is no logical necessity for them to do so. The great majority of intrusive fantasies end with the banishment or destruction of the intrusive element and an effective restoration of the situation prior to its introduction. That is an inherently convenient narrative trajectory or "story-arc," given that stories do have to end, and, in so doing, provide a sense of having ended appropriately. Indeed, the authors of stories involving dramatic intrusions often work hard not only to destroy the intrusive element but to destroy all lasting evidence of the intrusion, thus consigning the entire episode to a "secret history" that does not disturb the familiar pattern of acknowledged history.

In fact, normalization of the kinds typically featured in portal fantasies and intrusive fantasies is an important factor in the seemingly-natural capacity that stories have for providing a feeling of satisfaction on the part of the reader. It is a cliché that most readers love "happy endings"—"They lived happily ever after" is the archetypal concluding formula of the stories that people like best—and what is usually meant by a "happy ending" is a normalizing ending: the annihilation of the disturbance or the traveler's safe return home; the salvation of the *status quo*.

Not all stories end "happily," of course, but those that do not, in refusing to end "happily," tend to generate one of two particularly sentiments on the part of the reader: a sense of tragedy, or a sense of cruel irony. Both of those sentiments result from the awareness that that the story *could* have ended happily, and perhaps, in some sense, *should* have. The failure to save the status quo is regarded as inherently undesirable, an occasion for tears or sardonic laughter.

There are several corollaries of this state of affairs crucially relevant to the development of *roman scientifique*, which it is useful to point out before proceeding with an investigation of the texts contributing to that development. The most important is that because *roman scientifique*, by virtue of its scientific component, is intrinsically a literature of discovery and change, it is fundamentally incompatible with the formula of normalization that is the principal provider of a sense of satisfaction in other kinds of fiction. *Roman scientifique* is, quintessentially, less interested in saving the *status quo* than altering it, and there is, in consequence, an essential tension between the demands imposed by the conventional satisfactions of fiction and those suggested by the particular nature of the genre. *Roman scientifique* is, by definition, essentially awkward and problematic, and poses a challenge to writers and readers alike.

Normalizing endings remain possible in *roman scientifique*, and because of the satisfactions they offer, they remain very tempting, but there is a sense in which they never quite ring true. No matter how far a voyager travels in a portal fantasy, he can always come home, or wake up, and no matter how bizarre the intrusive element of an intrusive fantasy is, it can always be banished or destroyed, but if the heterocosms that have been visited or have intruded elements into the familiar world are to be taken seriously—if there is any component of real discovery involved, as there must be if they have any scientific relevance—then the return home or the banishment cannot be considered as entirely normalizing, because the knowledge of their existence is itself a change, and any implication that it is not can only be a pretence, or a lie. *Roman scientifique* is, by definition, a genre that not only recognizes the transience of normality but celebrates it; its primary purpose is the explorations of heterocosmic possibilities that are arguably potentially real, and at least meaningful.

To the extent that a story qualifies as a precursor of or participant in the genre of *roman scientifique*, therefore, it is necessarily at odds, to a greater or lesser extent, with the kind of satisfaction routinely supplied by other kinds of fiction, which many readers routinely seek. Writers of *roman scientifique* are often desirous of going against that particular grain, enthusiastic to engage in discovery, to violate expectations, and to celebrate change, and readers fond of the genre tend to be equally enthusiastic, but that does not alter the fact the genre is problematic from the viewpoint of marketing such work to a wide audience. It is intrinsic to the nature of *roman scientifique* that many readers, to a greater or lesser extent, find it discomfiting.

The majority of the texts described in detail in the next two chapters were published in frank defiance or determined opposition, most of them having to be published outside France—or, at last, pretending to be published elsewhere—because their publication and circulation within France was illegal. The fact that the agents of the establishment actively attempted to prevent them from being written, published and read is, however, merely a particularly striking instance of a broader problem, and if the evolution of *roman scientifique* is to be properly understood, it needs to be recognized that there is a fundamental conflict between the satisfactions that the majority of readers want and expect from fiction, and what *roman scientifique* is, or ought to be, intent on supplying. It is, as some of the critics of the term argued in claiming that it was oxymoronic, an enterprise that contains a crucial self-contradiction between its *roman* component and its *scientifique* component—a contradiction in which some readers and philosophers can take great delight, thus guaranteeing it a "cult following," but which many readers in search of conventional satisfactions find it easy to detest.

A second corollary of this observation arises with particular respect to immersive fantasies. Not only do the writers of such fantasies face problems at the start, because of the narrative difficulties of introducing their readers to the heterocosms they contain and enabling them to navigate their way through them, but they encounter problems at the end, because the convenient normalizing endings of the return home and the banishment of the intrusions are even more obviously artificial. Although the characters can return home, and inconvenient intrusions can be banished, the "status quo" that is saved by such narrative moves is not the reader's status quo, but an entirely arbitrary one.

There is one sense in which that "problem" is not a problem at all, but an advantage. If the reader's status quo were really worthy of invariable salvation, there would be no such thing as eutopian fiction. The sense of satisfaction that readers derive from normalizing endings is somewhat paradoxical itself, in that it tacitly credits the familiar with eutopian qualities that it clearly lacks. In heterocosmic fiction, however, a status quo can be established that really is worth saving: homes to which it is always worth returning, and milieux in which any possible intrusion really would be bad. *Roman scientifique* very rarely deals with such hypothetical worlds, but there is one genre of heterocosmic fiction that does: the only such genre that consists, necessarily, almost entirely of immersive fantasies, and, not by coincidence, a genre that is typically used for the entertainment of children.

In order to exist, however, that genre has to overcome the problem of the initial immersion in the heterocosm, but there again, within the genre in question, that "problem" becomes an advantage. Michel Butor points out in his essay "La Balance des fées" (1954; tr. as "On Fairy Tales") that it is easier for adults and children to communicate via the inventions of children's heterocosmic fantasy, of whose apparatus and conventions they have a similar knowledge and understanding, than it is for them to communicate through the medium of naturalistic fictions, because their experience and knowledge of the real world is so different.

The point is that it is easy for readers to orientate themselves in immersive fantasies if the heterocosms into which those fantasies take them are familiar, in terms of their fantastic equipment and possibilities. Everyone is sufficiently familiar with the milieu of *contes de fées* to read stories set there. Once that hurdle is overcome, the potential satisfaction offered by the conventional endings of the return home and the banishment of the intrusion can be increased rather than diminished, because the status quo can be defined as worthy of salvation, whereas the status quo to which naturalistic fiction is compelled to return its readers is inevitably flawed, if not thoroughly rotten. It might be a slightly shameful satisfaction, especially for adults, because they cannot help but be conscious of its unreality, but it is a satisfaction nevertheless—which arguably supports and sustains other genres than blatant fairy stories, perhaps embracing almost all fiction deploying normalizing endings, if one considers their illusions of naturalism to be intrinsically hypocritical.

In much the same way that *roman scientifique* has particular difficulties accommodating the initial artifice of immersive fantasy, however, it has particular difficulties accommodating the special kind of satisfaction that some such fantasies are capable of accommodating. "They lived happily ever after" can only be satisfying in a fairy tale if the reader is prepared to accept the heterocosm of the tale as one that genuinely permits that kind of outcome, and *roman scientifique*, by virtue of its *scientifique* component, tends to embody an intrinsic skepticism that rules out such acceptance *a priori*. In a sense, the whole point of immersive fantasies in the genre of *roman scientifique* is that they take the reader into unfamiliar milieux, where any kind of easy accommodation is necessarily out of the question.

The reality is, of course, not so straightforward, as can readily be appreciated by consideration of the overlap between readers of modern science fiction and readers of modern "fantasy," which strongly suggests that similar satisfactions are available from both genres. To some extent, of course, that simply signifies that a great deal of modern fantasy is skeptical and challenging in the same way that science fiction is, or ought to be—but it is also the case, to some extent, that some modern science fiction is more similar to fairy stories, in its narrative strategies and the satisfactions it provides, than its fans might be prepared to acknowledge.

American science fiction rapidly contrived, at least for its fans, a familiarity not unlike the familiarity that children are able to bring to the heterocosm of fairyland, thus allowing easy immersion; it did so by developing a kind of shared mythology of the future: a set of assumptions about the likely shape of the future that permitted readers to orientate themselves rapidly and easily within specific stories of that general type. The mythology in question was the mythology of "the Space Age," which fused futuristic fiction with interplanetary fiction in such a way as to make the kind of chemical compound previously mentioned.

Roman scientifique did not develop that kind of conventional "mythical future" of its own accord, and when it was imported along with the science fiction label after World War II, it never seemed as natural in French context as it did in the American context, largely because the myth in question was essentially an extrapolation into space of the preexisting American mythology of the Western, which made space into "the final frontier." While *roman scientifique* certainly connected many of its futuristic enterprises with the idea of colonization, it did so in the context of French ventures in colonization in North Africa and the Far East, which worked out very different from the U.S.A.'s conquest of the West.

35

One further result of that difference—which ought not to be reckoned a failure on the part of *roman scientifique*, although American historians of science fiction are sometimes tempted to see it as such—was that *roman scientifique*, like British scientific romance, retained an essential discomfort in the employment of immersive fantasy, and a consequent heavy reliance on portal fantasy and intrusive fantasy even in the decades of the twentieth century when American science fiction was developing its particular brand of immersive fantasy, thus remaining more disparate, and, as viewed through American eyes, more downbeat, by virtue of shunning the kinds of "happy endings" swiftly built into the science-fictional mythology of escape and conquest.

It is for those reasons that the distinctions identified by the Mendlesohn taxonomy of fantasy are as useful to an analysis of the development of *roman scientifique* as Frank Manuel's distinction between eutopian, euchronian and eupsychian images of hypothetical societies, and that is why I have elected to use them, when appropriate, in the following chapters.

In the text that follows I have used the convention of giving the titles of works published as independent volumes in italics, and those published in periodicals or collections in inverted commas. Where the same title appeared in both formats, I have used italics, except when referring specifically to the serial version. Where works have been translated into English I have employed the same formula, along with the indicator "tr. as"; where more than one translation exists I have given the title of the translation that seems to me to be preferable. Where works remain untranslated I have rendered a translation of the title in square brackets, except where the meaning seems obvious because the original version only employs words that have English equivalents.

Brian Stableford

CHAPTER ONE: THE PREHISTORY OF *ROMAN SCIENTIFIQUE*

1. The Legacy of the Merveilleux

Although it never caught on as a descriptive term, the attempt made in the early years of the twentieth century to define a genre of the *merveilleux-scientifique* did recognize and call attention to the fact that the more adventurous fraction of *roman scientifique* helped to carried forward the longest of all literary traditions: the heterocosmic fiction of the marvelous, which dealt with extraordinary events in order to inspire awe and wonder, with various subsidiary purposes, but primarily for the sake of the pleasure of imaginative stimulation; the fantastic element of folklore, legend and myth.

Modern readers and critics of science fiction often try to draw a fundamental distinction between science fiction and "fantasy," on the ostensible grounds that marvels based in scientific speculation have a particular plausibility that marvels drawing upon the vocabulary of myth and magic do not, although the present pattern of book marketing, in which books labeled as science fiction and fantasy tend to be shelved in adjacent locations in bookshops, advertised in the same spaces and aimed at overlapping audiences strongly suggests that the distinction is largely illusory.

The basis of the argument differentiating modern "science fiction" from "fantasy" is that the apparatus of the antique fiction of *le merveilleux* lost its currency in the Age of Enlightenment, being no longer capable of commanding belief, and needed replacement by something more responsible to the framework of modern philosophy. The briefest glance at the actual pattern of literary development, however, makes it clear that there is something seriously amiss with that argument. Far from seeing a decline in the fiction of the marvelous, the Age of Enlightenment witnessed a new boom in such fiction, not on the superstitious fringes of society but in the very core of the intellectual elite who prided themselves on the new wisdom. If the combination of enlightenment and the marvelous was paradoxical, then it was a paradox in which the imaginative writers of the era delighted, and strove to exploit. While writers working in genres of naturalistic prose fiction were striving to develop new narrative techniques of realistic representation, those exploring genres of fantastic fiction were simultaneously striving for new effects, sometimes within the canons of the same writers, and occasionally within the elaborate structures of the same works.

There is no better example of that kind of syncresis, in fact, than the renascent genre that was at the heart of the development of skeptical and philosophically enlightened prose fiction in eighteenth-century France: *contes philosophiques*, a label that deliberately fused philosophical ambition with the tradition of the *conte populaire* [folk tale] in order to emphasize its combination of previously-disparate elements. Nor was it the first such genre, having been preceded by the *contes de fées* [tales of enchantment] that had emerged from the *salons* of the late seventeenth century, deliberately reconfiguring folk tales with a modern spirit of irony and satire, and sometimes with sophisticated eroticism, as well as adapting them for the purpose of "civilizing" children.

The *contes de fées* intended for adult consumption and Voltairean *contes philosophiques* were eclectic in their plundering of sources; while they proudly advertised their willingness to draw on the humble folktale, they were also happy to draw, alternatively or simultaneously, on the more venerable resources of legend and myth, and in so doing suggested or recognized that the original literary sources from which they were extracting such materials might have more in common with their own endeavors than had previously been realized or admitted.

To some extent, French writers who took to the writing of imaginative fiction in the seventeenth and eighteenth centuries had the same remote sources to draw on as other European writers, sharing the same legacy of Classical Era and the same religious roots, but in terms of folklore and legend, a great deal more of it was local, and much of that local material had already been reprocessed by literary endeavors dating back several centuries. Even with respect to Greek and Latin sources, however, there was a distinction in the typical relationship between French writers and such materials, based in the particular emphasis placed on learning Latin and Greek by the French educational system, and the texts most prominent in the curriculum.

Although pupils in English schools were forced to learn Latin, and some Greek, just as pupils in French schools were, they did not have an equal advantage in the similarity of their native language to the Latin they were trying to learn, and did not become familiar with the same texts with the same intimacy, as is obvious by the typical range of Classical references made by English and French writers of the seventeenth and eighteenth centuries. To take one of the more obvious examples, French writers in general were likely to be familiar with the works of Virgil, and to assume such a familiarity on the part of their readers, in a manner only seen in England in advanced and specialized scholars, who were unable to make any such assumption.

By virtue of that fact, the French writers of the period were more readily able to observe a kinship between what they wanted to do and what Greek and Latin writers had occasionally done. Voltaire, for instance, would have found it far easier than the average enlightened Englishman to recognize Plato as the great pioneer of the *conte philosophique* and to appreciate, both intellectually and esthetically, the manner in which Plato employed fantastic and playful fictions to make philosophical points for didactic purposes in the *Republic*, which features the allegory of the cave, the story of the ring of Gyges, and the concluding story of Er. He would also have been better placed than English writers to appreciate the significance of the fact that in the *Symposium*, it is in the mouth of famous writer of comedies Aristophanes that Plato places a tale suggesting that human beings must once have been compound spherical entities, rolling along quite happily, until the gods split them up into misshapen fragments as a practical joke, condemning them all to spend their lives longing for reunion with their relevant "other halves" in the hope of recovering a more rounded character.

The most relevant of Plato's dialogues to the subsequent development of scientific enquiry is the *Timaeus*, which includes an elaborate version of his cosmology, as well as his comments on physics and biology, attempting to combine the mathematical ideas of the Pythagoreans with the Empedoclean theory of the elements. The same dialogue, however, also makes further innovative use of literary methodology, elaborating the ideal state sketched in the *Republic* by incarnating it on the fictional vanished island of Atlantis. Plato continued the description of Atlantis more elaborately in the *Critias*, but if that dialogue was ever completed, the full version did not survive. Atlantis, however, not only survived but thrived, becoming an archetypal focal point of scholarly fantasy, and retaining a far more significant role in French imaginative fiction, including *roman scientifique*, than it did in English fiction of the eighteenth, nineteenth and twentieth centuries, or English scientific romance.

Other Greek writers obviously influenced by Plato who dabbled in exemplary fiction included Plutarch, not only in his fanciful dialogue "On the Face in the Moon" but in some of his more straight-faced exercises, such as his biography of the legendary Spartan king Lycurgus in *Parallel Lives*, extensively adapted from such unreliable historians as Herodotus—an account that had a considerable influence on numerous French utopians. Such influences have been less obvious to scholars in considering the extravagances of the Greek satirists, most famously Lucian, but authors of *contes philosophiques* would have been more sensitive to it. Thus, not only was Lucian's *True History*—a ludicrously exaggerated account of a voyage to the moon—more familiar to French writers than English ones, but the French writers of the eighteenth century would have been more appreciative of its links to the Platonic tradition of calculated fabulation, and hence to the element of enlightenment contained within its blithe extravagance.

Because of the way the French educational system worked, French writers became familiar, without necessarily being consciously aware of it, with a wide range of mythological imagery that not only remained available to them as an imaginative recourse, but something within easy reach of consciousness. In studying Virgil, for instance, they would automatically come across his account of Orpheus' descent into the Underworld in the *Georgics*, and Aeneas' excursion to a rather more alarming Underworld in Book One of the *Aeneid*. Without studying descents into the Underworld as a topic in their own right, they would take aboard the motif, and there is, in consequence, nothing surprising in the fact that similar motifs, handled in a similar manner, are by no means infrequent in French imaginative fiction of the eighteenth century—far more so than in English fiction of the same period.

The distinction between the French and English heritage of the *merveilleux* is slightly confused by the fact that for a long period the history of the two nations was intricately entangled, and the period of the most complex entanglement produced a spectacular boom in literary endeavor, especially in respect of the literature of the marvelous. Important foundations were laid for both French and English literature by the same writers, in the context of what was almost a common culture—but the way in which that common legacy as carried forward in the two countries when they were split apart again was selective, and markedly different. The genre of the *merveilleux* in question is that of "Medieval Romance."

The word "romance" is ultimately derived from the Old French *romanz*, whose approximate meaning was "vernacular," and was initially used to refer to documents translated from Latin. By the twelfth century, however, the term and its evolving derivatives were more frequently and more particularly used with reference to a nascent genre of poetry and prose fiction that had moved on from translations of Latin epic poetry to prolific original composition. Just as the documents being translated had referred to what was by then a distant mythologized past, the imitations and pastiches also looked back nostalgically to a whole series of mythologized distant pasts.

The best-known of the verse romances of which twelfth-century copies survive, and the most important in terms of its familiarity to French readers and a key reference-point for writers in the Age of Enlightenment is *La Chanson de Roland*, which describes the ambush in the Pyrenees of a company of Charlemagne's knights returning from fighting Moors in Spain. Another cycle of poems referring back to the same era is the "Guillaume cycle" featuring Guillaume d'Orange, of which no twelfth century manuscripts survive, but which presumably dates from the same era and has slightly better connections with actual history.

Other early examples of the burgeoning genre included *Floire et Blancheflor*, about the love of a pagan prince for a Christian captive, and several versions of the story of Tristan's highly problematic love for Iseult, the intended bride of his liege-lord King Mark of Cornwall. The latter also became deeply embedded in French consciousness, as a key reference-point for the love stories of later periods, competing for that privilege with a much more recent legend deriving from the unfortunate fate suffered by the great twelfth-century logician

Peter Abelard as a result of his relationship with Héloïse, the niece of the violently-inclined Fulbert.

One version of the story of Tristan and Iseult that has not survived is known to have been written by Chrétien de Troyes, who became the most popular of the late twelfth-century writers of romance, and was also the most inventive. He was the great pioneer of romances featuring the court of the legendary English king Arthur, including *Le Chevalierde la Charrette*, also known as *Lancelot*, which tells the story of the conflict generated by the knight's deeply problematic love for Arthur's wife, Guenièvre. Chrétien's completed works in that subgenre were, however, eventually outshone, however—at least in terms of modern pseudoscholarship—by his unfinished allegory *Le Conte du Graal*, also known as *Perceval*, whose incompleteness left it with an intriguing aspect of mystery.

Although the particular popularity of Chrétien de Troyes was undoubtedly a major factor in establishing Arthuriana as a core topic of the evolving genre of prose Romance, contemporary politics also played a leading part, many of the key events of the period being the slowly-unfolding consequences of the event that subsequently made 1066 the best-known date in British history, when William I defeated his Saxon rival for the English throne, Harold, at the Battle of Hastings. The wealthiest and most powerful woman in Western Europe throughout the latter half of the twelfth century was Eleanor of Aquitaine, who first married Louis VI of France but almost immediately after the annulment of that marriage, in 1152, married Henry, Duke of Normandy; the latter became Henry II of England two years later, and the sons she bore him included the future kings Richard Coeur-de-Lion and John, both of whom became key figures in English legend.

Eleanor's court was undoubtedly an important source of patronage for writers and performers of romances, especially the epic-imitating *chansons de geste*, and her concerns undoubtedly help to shape the substance of the genre. Some subsequent historians credited her with the importation of an important element of southern "troubadour culture" into the chivalric romances of Northern France, hence generating the stories of problematic infatuation that played a central role in the genre, from Tristan and Iseult onwards. Although her personal role might have been exaggerated, the effective fusion of the Duchy of Aquitaine with Normandy undoubtedly formed the practical background to the amalgamation, as well as assisting its symbolization. The confusion of influences, however, extended much further than the central marriage of Eleanor and Henry.

The conquering Normans, who had originated as invaders from Scandinavia, were pillars of the feudal political system, glorified in romance by the retrospective extrapolation of the contemporary hierarchy of kings, barons and knights into imaginary pasts, where it could be more easily credited with imaginary virtues. Much of that mythology was borrowed from the Normans' neighbors in northern France, the Bretons, who were already taking a nostalgic delight in the twelfth century in looking back to lost glory days of heroic *preux cheva-liers* [gallant knights]. Meanwhile, the rulers of large parts of both France and England had long been descended from invaders—the Franks and the Saxons—who had partly displaced and partly absorbed previous cultures, loosely describable as Gauls and Celts, which had been previously conquered, at least briefly, by the Roman Empire. In consequence, the legendary pasts cooked up in France and England in the twelfth century were blessed with a rich complexity and confusion of inherited and improvised materials.

Literary romance was an inherently syncretic genre, tacitly celebrating the kind of blending obtained by conquest and reorganization that was inherent in the actual history of feudalism as well as the flattering ideological image that romancers tried to construct. Central to that syncretic process was the fundamental marriage of the Breton/Norman "chivalric romance" glorifying knightly prowess in combat with the Provençal/Aquitanian "courtly romance," which offered idealized depictions of intimate relationships. The writers were also willing, and often enthusiastic, to embrace other local folklores and superstitions, and to gather them into their generalized melting-pot—always, of course, with the proviso that threats originating from such dubious imaginative apparatus could not withstand the ideological forces of Christian faith and knightly heroism. It is against this background that the mythologies of Roland and Charlemagne's knights, on the one hand, and of King Arthur and his knights on the other, were invented.

Although the legendry of King Arthur was invented by Norman "historians" and developed in literary form by a French writer, it was not quintessentially French in the same way that the **Chanson de Roland** was, and it is therefore not surprising that the latter remained much more to the forefront of the French imagination in later centuries, along with related *chansons de geste* such as *Raoul de Cambrai* and, most importantly, *Renaut de Montauban*, also known as

Les Quatre Fils Aymon. The latter makes much of the hero's magical horse Bayard, later transferred to the ownership of Charlemagne. Like Roland, Renaud became an important character in imitative romances spun off from the Charlemagnian cycle in the Italian Renaissance, where he became Rinaldi or Rinaldo, as Roland became Orlando.

Many of the writers of twelfth- and thirteenth-century romance remained anonymous, or at least obscure, but another who achieved a measure of personal fame was Marie de France, who was probably a member of Henry II's court. She produced a number of *Lais* [Lays, or Lyrics] mostly featuring problematic love stories which end with the happy union of the long-frustrated lovers, many of them based, at least ostensibly, in Breton folklore, and which became standard sources for the subsequent literature of the *merveilleux*. Her celebrity was sufficient for numerous lays written by other hands to be attributed to her apocryphally, and she was also credited with a collection of *Ysopet* [Fables], which were represented—probably falsely—as translations from English. That genre too experienced something of a boom in the relevant period, reinforcing a tradition that remained unusually robust in France, and was carried forward with increasing assertiveness and style in subsequent centuries, reaching a striking climax in the seventeenth-century satirical fables of Jean de La Fontaine, which became a key foundation-stone of French literature and the object of exceedingly prolific references in the literature of the Age of Enlightenment.

Although the legendry of Arthur's court was somewhat de-emphasized in French memory and thought, by comparison with the parallel legendry of Charlemagne and Roland, it retained an international magnetism that spread further afield, especially the fantasy of the holy grail sketched in Chrétien de Troyes' posthumously-published *Conte du graal*, which was to prove one of the greatest imaginative inventions of all time, comparable to Plato's Atlantis in the quantity of scholarly fantasy that it engendered. Just as the Roland cycle inspired writers in Italy to adapt the material to their own purposes, so the story of the grail soon became an important literary export, most spectacularly in Wolfram von Eschenbach's Germanic *Parzifal* (c1210), which expanded the *Conte du graal* vastly, while claiming to be based on an entirely different source.

Another *chanson de geste* that became very popular, and whose substance became part of the standard apparatus of the international fiction of the *merveilleux*, was the early thirteenth-century romance Huon of Bordeaux, in which the eponymous knight, set a series of Herculean labors by Charlemagne after accidentally killing the emperor's son, is ultimately enabled to complete his penance with the aid of Auberon, a magically-talented dwarf. The latter was seemingly borrowed from the near-contemporary German epic *Niebelunglied*, where he is known as Alberich, and was subsequently retransfigured by numerous other writers, most famously by Shakespeare, who promoted him to king of the fairies as Oberon in *A Midsummer Night's Dream*.

The term *roman* became so ubiquitous in the thirteenth century that it acquired a flexibility carried forward into subsequent centuries, becoming virtually synonymous with fiction in general—as in the term *roman scientifique*—and eventually becoming the standard French term parallel to the English "novel." It is featured in a broad spectrum of works incorporating various kinds and degrees of fanciful material, including the **Roman de Renart**, a collection of beast-fables featuring a cunning fox, who made his way into English as Reynard but was little more there than a name. It is also featured in most famous allegory of the period, the *Roman de la Rose*, begun by Guillaume de Lorris and finished by Jean de Meun. The story is that of a dream in which the visionary enters the Garden of Delight in pursuit of ideal love, represented by the Rose, which he eventually gets to kiss, although the modestly defensive response is not the one for which he had hoped. Perhaps the most popular of all works of Medieval French literature, although probably always regarded as risible, its spirit and symbolism remained deeply, if somewhat ironically, entrenched in the French literary tradition.

Although further additions to the apparatus of Medieval Romance became sparser after the end of the thirteenth century, mention does need to be made of one particular tale that stuck in the collective memory and remained a source of continual citation by French writers, and several literary works produced elsewhere in Europe: the *Roman de Lusignan*, written down by Jean d'Arras circa 1390 in *L'Évangile des quenouilles* [The Gospel of Spinners], and there alleged to be the subject of a much longer work, the *Roman de Mélusine*, whose real existence is dubious. Mélusine is a hybrid snake-woman in magical disguise, whose true form is discovered by her husband, Raymond de Poitou, when he breaks a taboo she has imposed on him.

Some of the materials borrowed from French Medieval romance by writers in other countries fed back into the French tradition, including the substance of

Ludovico Ariosto's *Orlando Furioso* (full version 1532), which added a great deal more magic and marvel to the French account of the story of Roland, and also a leaven of humor; it introduced the hippogriff, on which the knight Astolfo journeys to Africa in search of a cure for the hero's madness before making an even more extravagant trip to the Moon, where everything lost and neglected on Earth can be found. That image of the Moon became a highly significant feature of subsequent literary lunar voyages, referenced in almost all of them.

One work of the reimported variety that became particularly familiar to French readers and writers, by virtue of its frequent use as an educational text in schools, was Torquato Tasso's *La Gerusalemma liberata* (1581; tr. as *Jerusalem Delivered*), known in French as *La Jérusalem délivrée*, which borrows heavily from Ariosto. French writers were particularly entranced by the witch Armida (Armide in French), who abducts Rinaldo to a magical garden, where she causes him to forget his knightly duties for a while. Based on Ariosto's Alcina—who enchants Ruggiero in the same fashion—and ultimately on Homer's Circe, Armide became an important archetype of the enchantress in French imaginative fiction.

The reinfusion of the French tradition by Italian sources was more noticeable and more significant because the French *chansons de geste* and other aspects of Medieval Romance went through a period of neglect in France, when, although still remembered, they came to be regarded as obsolete features of a dead past—to such an extent that when a new generation of writers began to advertise themselves proudly as a Romantic Movement in the early nineteenth century, one of their historians, Edgar Quinet, represented himself as the rediscoverer of a lost tradition of epic romance, and set out to reclaim Arthurian legend from the English by producing the great national epic that his forebears had shamefully neglected to produce, in *Merlin l'enchanteur* (1860; tr. as *The Enchanter Merlin*).

Although the neglect into which the old Romances had fallen was exaggerated by the new Romantics of the nineteenth century, it is true that the writers of the Age of Enlightenment who threw themselves wholeheartedly to the *merveilleux* generally derived their primary inspiration and their most prominent motifs from more recent sources, and that once the thirteenth century had ended there is something of a gap in the historical development of the French fiction of the *merveilleux*, which extended for nearly three hundred years until the next spectacular advent, which is of particular significance with regard to the situation of eighteenth century writers of "philosophical fiction" because it also marked the beginning of a long armed struggle between writers of a skeptical stripe and religious censors backed by the power of the law and the crown.

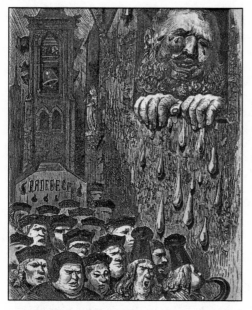

In the 1540s the faculty of the Sorbonne, reacting to the inexorable spread of literacy among the laity, based on the increasing availability of printed books, issued a list of books that were to be suppressed by all practical means. A licensing system by which legally-printed books required a royal warrant was already in existence, but was not yet protected with any great fervor, and the Sorbonne's list included, in any case, several works that had actually received a royal warrant. High on the list, and key targets for clerical ire and persecution on the grounds of their anti-religious inclinations, were two hectic ribald comedies featuring giants: **Pantagruel** (c 1532, anagrammatically signed "Alcofribas Nasier) and *Gargantua* (1534), by François Rabelais. The adventures of the giants in question were further elaborated in *Le Tiers livre des faits et dicts héroïques du bon Pantagruel* [The Third Book of the Adventures and Heroic Deeds of Pantagruel] (1546), which introduced the character of the knavish and licentious Panurge, and then by a *Quart livre* [Fourth Book] (1552) and a *Cinquième et dernier livre* [Fifth and Last Book] (1564) of dubious authenticity, all five of which volumes were subsequently combined into an omnibus usually known as *Gargantua et Pantagruel*.

Having taken holy orders himself and served terms as a monk with the Franciscans and Benedictines, Rabelais was in a unique position not merely to assault the tradition of monachism satirically, in his classic depiction of the Abbey of Thélème, a haven of gluttony and debauchery in which the presiding rule is "Do As Thou Wilt," and to lampoon the Sorbonne itself, but also to excite the particular resentment occasioned by perceived renegades. The fight to suppress Rabelais begun by the Church—which could not be won and ultimately produced the opposite effect—and the manner in which Rabelais had cloaked his serious humanist ideas in broad humor both became key exemplars for Voltaire and his contemporaries, even providing a veneer of justification for the writers of such scabrous works as *Thérèse philosophe*, in which libidinous Churchmen play an exceedingly prominent part.

Although Rabelais too went through a period of relative disrepute when his humor came to seem a little too coarse to delicate minds—which only enhanced his stature in the eyes of the *philosophes*—he was read very widely in the sixteenth and seventeenth centuries, throughout Europe, and his works became established as important landmarks and reference points in French literature.

Partly in order to obtain a royal warrant for its publication, Rabelais dedicated the *Tiers livre* to the king's sister, Marguerite de Navarre, who was also a writer, similarly committed to the ideals of humanism, and was thus also seen as an enemy by the Churchmen of the Sorbonne, albeit one who was by no means as easy to attack as Rabelais. Her major literary endeavor was a collection of stories inspired by Giovanni Boccaccio's *Decameron* (c1352), which was intended to number a hundred, although she only managed to complete seventy-two, with the result that the collection eventually became known as *L'Heptaméron* (published posthumously in 1558), notable not only for its frequent condemnation of corrupt clergy but also for its relatively robust defense of women, whose treatment in much contemporary literature was frankly misogynistic. The *merveilleux* plays a far less prominent role in the collection than it does in Boccaccio's assembly or other similar collages, and the enormous popularity of the work was more significant in its promotion of the *conte* as a literary form with moral purpose. Imitators were not slow, however, to replace the fantastic elements that Marguerite had largely purged.

Also largely purged of elements of the *merveilleux*, but similar influential in its form and content on works by other hands that were not so shy was Honoré d'Urfé's mammoth enterprise *L'Astrée* (1607-1619), to which further continuations by other hands were added following d'Urfé's death. The main narrative, a pastoral romance in which the central love-affair of the eponymous heroine and the ever-loyal Céladon, relentlessly troubled by the perfidies of other characters, is employed as a frame for a vast series of subplots and interpolated stories, which make the whole into a remarkable portmanteau text.

Like *L'Heptaméron, L'Astrée* provided a model for a kind of literary exercise that could contain many elements, as varied and disparate as the author cared to make them, and it became the model for a great many long novels—some of them incredibly long by today's standards—in which the mythology of amour subjected to languorous analysis and critical scrutiny by Marguerite de Navarre and Honoré d'Urfé could be subjected to further examination and celebration, while all kinds of other matters could be wedged in, to produce an eclectic and kaleidoscopic whole potentially accommodating the whole of human life and imagination.

Most such novels, inevitably, fell far short of that achievement, but Pierre Versins identifies one writer who made gestures in the direction of vast imaginative ambition as a significant precursor of *roman scientifique*: Charles Sorel, author of the exceedingly long *Histoire comique de Francion* (1623; expanded 1626). The second edition of the work features a character named Hortensius, a writer who describes projects he has in mind, which feature voyages to the moon, wars fought between lunar empires, attacks launched by lunarians on the Earth, submarine civilizations and the lives of microscopic beings.

Unfortunately, Versins also reports, the passage in question was dropped from subsequent abridged editions, although some compensation was provided by the similarly vast *Le Berger extravagant* (1627), a parody and response to *L'Astrée*, in which the Quixotic adventures of a shepherd intent on founding an ideal pastoral community include an excursion to a land populated by intelligent birds, humans with transparent flesh, and other wonders. Versins also describes highly fanciful descriptions of other imaginary realms by the author published in periodicals, which might have been intended to be gathered into a further portmanteau but never were, thus leaving Sorel's philosophical extravaganzas on the frustrating margins of existence, incomplete and effectively inaccessible: an allegory in miniature of what some modern commentators might consider to have been the fate of the entire genre, as the present project will inevitably illustrate.

Although eighteenth-century works employing the portmanteau procedure that have a slight element of *roman scientifique* are all shorter than *Astrée*, the longest of them do run to a quarter of a million words, and seem to the modern eye to be extraordinary jumbles of inconsequential fragments, but there are numerous shorter works that also reflect an awareness of the narrative utility of the method—a utility that was at last partly responsible for its fashionability. That utility is, in fact, twofold. Not only does the portmanteau method allow fantastic and philosophical materials to be introduced into a naturalistic frame narrative, but it also permits the reverse, whereby a fantastic frame can accommodate naturalistic intrusions, whose moralistic intent can be excused, and perhaps heightened, by that kind of framing. Some of the key works of eighteenth century philosophical fiction employed that inverted method, which now seems odd and eccentric, but is employed in its best examples with considerable artistry and vigor.

Although Marguerite de Navarre was not as generous as Boccaccio in the matter of including magical folk-tales in the stories that her hypothetical narrators relate to one another in *L'Heptaméron*, some of Boccaccio's other imitators went in the other direction, most particularly the Neapolitan writer Giambattista Basile, in a collection initially published in the mid-1630s that became known as the *Pentamerone*, which focused on such material, deliberately subjecting the fantastic materials of folk-tales to conscientious literary sophistication. That precedent was followed in numerous other countries, but nowhere more prolifically, eccentrically and effectively than in France, where it was taken up with particular fervor by the female writers who gathered in the literary salons associated with Louis XIV's court.

Perhaps inevitably, given the sexual politics of the day, it was a male writer, Charles Perrault, who eventually claimed center stage in popular attention, and was hailed as the archetypal exponent on the new genre, in a collection of six moralistic fantasies initially published as *Contes de ma mère l'Oye* (1697; tr. as *Tales of Mother Goose*) but the genre obtained its name from the near-simultaneous collection of works by the far more prolific and considerably more sophisticated Marie-Catherine Le Jumel de Barneville, Baroness d'Aulnoy, *Les Contes de fées* (1697). The nearest English equivalent to the French *féerie* is "enchantment," and *fées* are, strictly speaking, enchantresses, but the title of Madame d'Aulnoy's first collection was translated into English as "fairy tales," thus foisting that label on an entire genre, most of whose included stories do not, in fact, feature "fairies."

Because the genre was adapted, somewhat controversially, to a primary role in children's literature, which it still holds, and many of the particular tales continually reprocessed by Basile, d'Aulnoy, Perrault and others retain central roles in that usage, it is sometimes forgotten that the production of such tales in the French salons was intended for the amusement of adults, and that the versions circulated orally were probably a good deal more cynical, satirical and erotic than those eventually adapted for the *civilization* of children. It also tends to be forgotten that the literary battleground into which those stories were first rebelliously introduced was one tyrannically dominated by the theory of Classicism, which held that French literature ought to take its models—and hence, to a large extent, its themes and methods—from the masterworks of Greek and Roman literature. The playwright Jean Racine was explicitly attempting to reproduce the glories of Greek tragedy on the contemporary French stage, with ardent support from his friend, Nicolas Boileau-Despréaux, who became the most influential critic of the day. Their influence became so great that Classicism dominated the French stage for more than a hundred years, to such an extent that even Voltaire, the great rebel of the Enlightenment, fell into line with it in his theatrical productions, and blunted the criticism of his other endeavors considerably by the examples he set in carrying the tradition of pseudo-Classical tragedy robustly forward.

Classicism also dominated French epic poetry, but never had as much influence over prose fiction, mainly because Greek and Roman literature was conspicuously short of prose models—although Longus' proto-novel of *Daphnis and Chloe* [*Daphné et Chloé* in French] could be, and often was, held up as the ancestor of all pastoral fiction, including *L'Astrée*. In that context, therefore, the interest in the *conte* as a literary form could be represented as a challenge to Classicism, offering a rival proposal, to the effect that French writers might do better to seek inspirational sources in French materials: not merely local folklore but also the somewhat neglected fields of Romance.

Regarded contemptuously as a form fit for women, Perrault being granted an honorable exception, the salon *contes* of the latter half of the seventeenth century frequently failed to reach print, but they could nevertheless get their authors into trouble, as demonstrated by the fate of Henriette-Julie de Castelnau, Comtesse de Murat, one of whose tales was allegedly recognized as a satirical dig at one of the king's mistresses, and who was then renounced by her husband, exiled from the court and forced to spend the rest of her life under effective house arrest—which did not, of course, stop her writing. Charlotte-Rose de Caumont de La Force suffered a similar expulsion, being banished to a convent.

Murat's close friend Marie-Jeanne L'Héritier de Villadon dedicated her first collection of fairy tales to her, but got away unscathed, perhaps because she was Perrault's niece, and might well have played a role in prompting him to involve himself in the fad, as she published work in that vein before he did. Her own salon recruited a few writers who were not at court, including Catherine Bernard, who followed L'Héritier's example in refusing marriage in order to pursue a literary career, and was acknowledged by Voltaire as one of his influences. Her novel *Inès de Cordoue* (1696) features a competition between the heroine and her rival in which both invent fanciful tales.

Although some of the stories composed by the salon writers were based on pre-existing tales, most were original compositions. Many of them, however, fed back into oral tradition, becoming archetypal examples of "fakelore." Catherine Bernard's "Riquet à la Houpe" (tr. as "Ricky of the Tuft") was plagiarized by Perrault, and thus added to the standard repertoire of "traditional tales," along with material he adapted from Madame d'Aulnoy, while Mademoiselle de La Force's "Persinette" was later collected by the Brothers Grimm as an ostensible German folktale, under the title "Rapunzel." Perrault added one story to his collection that he made up himself, "Le Petit chaperon rouge" (known in English as "Little Red Riding Hood"), which subsequently became one of the most prolifically reprocessed tales ever written.

The writers of salon *contes* did not retain the credit for what they produced, but some of it proved remarkably enduring, and they helped to lay the groundwork for the extension of the tradition of literary *contes* not only through the eighteenth century but long thereafter. The element of the *merveilleux* expanded from *contes* into many longer works produced by aristocratic writers in the eighteenth century, much of which qualified as "philosophical fiction," the most famous being Claude-Prosper Jolyot de Crébillon's erotic fantasy *Le Sopha* (1742; tr. as *The Sofa*), which earned him a three month banishment, although that novel also shows the influence of a comedy in the same vein by a writer from outside the court circuits, *Le Diable boiteux* (1707; tr. as *The Devil on Two Sticks*) by Alain-René Le Sage, in which the hero is escorted by the demon Asmodeus on a tour of "Madrid"—a thinly disguised Paris—in order to see what is going on behind all the closed doors. That too became one of the key exemplars and reference-points for future fiction of the *merveilleux*.

The influence of the salon tale-mongers was further eclipsed by another male writer who came from outside their social circle—although he knew Charles Perrault—and stole their thunder spectacularly with a collection of *contes* taken not from European sources but from the Middle East, to which he added numerous items of fakelore presumably of his own composition: the diplomat Antoine Galland. To frame the stories, Galland invented one of the great narrative devices of all time: the story of Scheherazade, who must keep her husband avid to hear more by suspending the stories, in order to avoid having her head cut off. Twelve volumes of the stories appeared between 1704 and 1717, under the title *Les Mille et une nuits*, and although the portmanteau method had obvious precursors in *L'Astrée* and exercises in the vein of *L'Heptaméron*, it was henceforth dubbed "the Galland method" by many of its users, and the mythological apparatus of the tales became a more prolific source of fictional apparatus for Voltaire and other *philosophes* than native materials, their Orientalism adding a useful extra dimension of exoticism.

The sophistication of the elements of the *merveilleux* begun by the salon writers eventually laid the foundations for an important genre identified by twentieth-century French critics and literary historians, the *fantastique*: a genre recognized in France some time before American and British critics and historian began to delineate "fantasy." In much the same way that English-language commentators are sometimes torn between contrasting science fiction and fantasy, and making science fiction a subset of fantasy, so French commentators often seem uncertain as to whether to oppose science fiction to the *fantastique* or regard it as a subsidiary category—a dilemma clearly represented in the quotation of Alfred Jarry's observations on *roman scientifique* cited in the Introduction.

In much the same way that the material surveyed in this chapter can stand as a "prehistory" of *roman scientifique*, it can function equally well as a prehistory of the *fantastique*, if one were to take the operational decision to contrast the genres rather than conflate them. If one takes the view, however, that the works discussed in the next chapter represent something of a parting of the ways, when philosophical fiction drawing upon the scientific imagination gradually became distinct from the sequence of works providing the roots of the modern genre of the *fantastique*, then the key writer in the latter category was undoubtedly Jacques Cazotte, author of the fakeloristic tale "La Patte du chat" [The Cat's Paw] (1741), the absurdist comedy *Les Mille et une fadaises* (1742; tr. as *The Thousand-and one Follies*), the mock-Medieval romance Olivier (1762) and the irreverently inventive *Le Diable amoureux* (1772; tr. as *The Devil in Love*). It is worth observing, however, that although Cazotte wrote nothing himself that has any conspicuous relevance to the evolution of roman scientifique, he was a member in the late 1780s of the most important salon attended by two of the most significant writers who did, Louis-Sébastien Mercier and Nicolas-Edmé Restif de La Bretonne, with one odd consequence that will be mentioned in due course.

Thus were the foundations laid for the adaptation of the tradition of *merveilleux* to the particular purposes of writers who wanted to bring the burgeoning substance of natural philosophy into their tales of wonder, tentatively and peripherally at first but with increasing determination as the century went on, many of whom wanted to represent themselves as new Scheherazades deliberately substituting quintessentially modern marvels for the quaintly incredible substance of hers.

2. *Imaginary Voyages*

One of the oldest narrative frameworks for tales of the *merveilleux* is the imaginary voyage, for if wonders are to be encountered, they cannot plausibly be encountered at home, and the further from home a traveler has been, the less implausible it will seem to his hearers when he tells his story that he has found things different and strange.

The temptation to make a journey and its spectacles more dramatic in the retelling is undoubtedly forceful, and perhaps irresistible, further boosted by the occasional requirement to explain and excuse an absence, as Odysseus had to do when he made up the *Odyssey* to explain to poor Penelope why he was so late in returning from the Trojan War, thus providing an archetype for future tales of extraordinary adventure. The effect of such tales is heavily dependent on what Samuel Coleridge called the hearer's "willing suspension of disbelief," but that willingness is a problematic and perhaps paradoxical matter, which comes with a built-in suspicion and mistrust. It is possible both to love and resent illusions, with equal forcefulness, and that ambiguity has always haunted literary accounts of imaginary voyages, inevitably carried forward to the portal fantasies of *roman scientifique*, whose narrative bids for a special kind of plausibility were always deeply embarrassed by it, although it is the portal fantasies of *roman scientifique* that have the most to gain from going to imaginative extremes.

Inventors making up stories of imaginary travels are always inclined to go one step too far in their inventions; testing the limits of the willingness to suspend disbelief is intrinsic to the game. That extra step not only teases skepticism, but toys with the possibility of ridicule. Travelers in the imagination are often tempted to adapt the stories they invent to the interests of parody and satire, but in doing so, they have to bear in mind that real travelers who seem to be going over the top in their accounts of the dangers they have run and the prizes they just missed carrying off inevitably attract parody and satire regardless. There are, in consequence, imaginative travelers' tales whose extremism is encouraged by the intention of poking fun at other travelers' tales. That kind of sophistication is not recent; the cardinal example of that doubling of effect is a classic tale by the second-century Greek satirist Lucian, which is generally known, by virtue of an altogether-understandable sarcasm, as the *True History*.

The *True History* celebrates the innate tendency of travelers' tales to wild exaggeration by describing the most impossible of journeys to the most unreachable of places: a flight to the Moon. The journey also takes in a close passage of the Sun and numerous remote islands on Earth, following a splashdown in the sea, but it is the excursion to the Moon that established a key archetype and a fundamental reference-point for future inventors of traveler's tales. Lucian would undoubtedly have been delighted to discover that it eventually became a highly ironic reference-point, ultimately transformed in its significance by the subsequent evolution of scientific knowledge and mechanical technology, to the extent that the most conscientiously improbable of all barely-imaginable voyages not only became gradually more imaginable, but was actually accomplished, after a mere 1,800 years. The story thus became accidentally illustrative of an important feature of the human imagination, crucial to the notion and development of *roman scientifique*: that the limits of actuality sometimes lie beyond its reach.

Travelers' tales are not, however, mere lies, even when they have no manifest didactic purpose. The imaginary voyage, in its literary forms, including odysseys through the horn and ivory gates, is an authentic form of exploration. There is a sense in which the study of fictitious *terra incognita*, including lunar real estate, is just as illuminating, in providing us with insight into the human condition, as the actual exploration of the earthly lands that were still undiscovered at the beginning of the Age of Enlightenment eventually turned out to be.

The evolution of Lucianesque voyages to the moon, from deliberate nonsense and farcical satire to a recognition and understanding of the actual situation of the Moon within the solar system and its nature as a world, eventually gave them a significant role to play in propagandizing and popularizing the heliocentric theory of the solar system in the seventeenth and eighteenth centuries. The awareness of that role generated a certain sense of responsibility, although one that was admittedly more honored in the breach than the observance. The satirical tradition was still unsullied by philosophical considerations when Ariosto sent Astolfo to the moon in *Orlando Furioso*, to discovery a repository of everything wasted on Earth—misspent time, broken vows, unanswered prayers, and so on—but it was only twenty-seven years later that Copernicus' account of the heliocentric model of the solar system was published, in 1543, and paved the way for a significant imaginative reconfiguration.

Odysseus was by no means the only far traveler in Greek legend, although he was by far the most influential. Virgil's *Aeneid* is, in part, a deliberate recapitulation and extension of Homeric "history," and includes a new version of the excursion to the Underworld, which replaces the merely dismal Homeric afterlife with a place of punishments that bears a close resemblance to the Christian Hell. Christian writers, although more prolific in producing visionary fantasies, also produced the occasional traveler's tale, including the ninth-century legend of Saint Brendan's discovery of an island that might be the earthy paradise and his encounter with a monster, which appears to reprocess a pagan Irish legend written down two centuries earlier. The earlier legend describes the exploratory voyage of Bran maic Febail, which involves landings in the Land of Women and the Isle of Joy prior to a timeslipped return that brings him home centuries after his departure.

By far the most dramatic Christianization of Virgil's Underworld, in which Virgil is recruited to serve as a guide, was the account of the Inferno offered by Dante Alighieri as one element of his *Comedia*, completed in 1320, a year before his death. Described by his biographer, Giovanni Boccaccio as the "divina" *Comedia*, that descriptive adjective was subsequently added to its title. The imaginary voyages described therein, to Hell, Purgatory and Paradise, became a model and archetype as important in their distinctive fashion as the Odyssey, and added a further key reference-points to imaginary geography, although many later commentators seem to have overlooked the fact that it takes for granted the spherical shape of the Earth in placing Purgatory in the vast hemispherical ocean that was not yet known to be occupied by the Americas, preferring to perpetuate the fatuous myth that even educated people in the Renaissance believed the Earth to be flat.

Dante was, of course, writing long before Copernicus, and in the context of Christian theology, so it is not surprising that he placed his spherical Earth at the center of an Aristotelian solar system. In the *Paradiso*, he provides one of the very few accounts of space travel through such a solar system, although Dante finds that when he arrives with Beatrice at the Moon in a translucent cloud, he passes into it within no difficulty. The Moon turns out to be the abode of souls dominated in life by the virtue of virginity, and the other worlds that he visits similarly receive earthly souls in accordance with a categorization of their dominant virtues. The spheres containing the planets thus form a sequence approaching the divine presence, each world becoming more brilliant as it is more distant from the Earth's sink of iniquity, and populated by increasingly virtuous souls, with some of whom they converse. Eventually, Dante and Beatrice enter the sphere of the fixed stars, from which the poet can see Christ and chat to Adam, before going on to the ninth sphere, the *Primum Mobile*, and then the Empyrean.

By the time that Dante's account of travel to imaginary worlds was published, great steps were beginning to be made by real European travelers; although the era of the great navigations had yet to begin, because the technology of shipbuilding and rigging sails had not yet advanced sufficiently, Marco Polo had recorded an account of his overland travels in *Livre des merveilles du monde* [The Book of the World's Marvels] (c1300; tr. as *The Travels of Marco Polo*), a book that prompted advances in cartography, helped to inspire Christopher Columbus and was imitated—with suitable embellishments—by one of the most successful imaginary traveler's tales, known in English as *The Travels of Sir John Mandeville*, although it was probably first written in French and circulated in manuscripts in that language in the mid-fourteenth century. Although mostly pastiche, with added monsters, it includes a visit to the mythical Oriental Christian kingdom of Prester John, which had first became prominent in Christian legend in the twelfth century.

Another work produced outside France that became an important source of inspiration there was Thomas More's *Utopia*, originally published in Latin in 1516. In France, as in England, the title was adapted in to the language, but in the curiously different fashion noted in the Introduction. The list of landmark examples of literary utopias offered in Pierre Versins' *Encylopédie* includes two other works published in the sixteenth century—one of them being Rabelais's account of Thélème, a rather dubious inclusion—but he does not include the brief account of an imaginary island contained in Michael de Montaigne's *Essais* (1580; expanded in subsequent editions) in the list, although he refers to it elsewhere in the volume, noting that Montaigne takes care to distinguish it from Atlantis and another island mentioned in Classical texts before going on to describe an idealized primitive society ancestral to Jean-Jacques Rousseau's notion of virtuous social innocence.

Versins' list skips forward nearly a century, in fact, to a group of crucial examples produced in the early seventeenth century, none of them French, although two of them became well-known in French translation; J. V. Andreae's *Christianpolis* (1619), Tommaso Campanella's *Civitas Solis* [The City of the Sun] (first written in Italian in 1602 but known via the Latin version published in 1623), and Francis Bacon's incomplete and posthumously published *New Atlantis* (1627).

Those three works were of particular importance to the subsequent development of *roman scientifique* because all three of them, to some degree, incorporate the notion of scientific and technological progress into their notion of an ideal state, not as a means of producing it but as a natural consequence of its ideal quality. All of them consider the ongoing production of new knowledge to be an intrinsic feature of an improved society, and Campanella and Bacon take particular care to insist that one of the important effects of that new knowledge will be the development of new technologies; Bacon's catalogue of hypothetical new technologies is particularly impressive, as befitted one of the founders of the modern philosophy of science, and an acquaintance of James I's court inventor, Cornelis Drebbel—a man of considerable ingenuity, even if he never could get his submarine into working order.

Those three exemplars might, and perhaps should, have had more impact on the thinking of social reformers and other writers of utopian fictions, but they were regarded as *utopies* in the French sense as well as utopias in the English sense, and had no marked influence for some considerable time. Campanella and Bacon were read, however, by one French writer who took their ideas somewhat to heart, and who also read another English work by a contemporary of Bacon, the posthumously-published *The Man in the Moone* (1638) by Bishop Francis Godwin, published under the signature of its protagonist, Domingo Gonsales: the most significant lunar fantasy written since Lucian. Gonsales discovers a new species of birds, gansas, on the island of Saint Helena, capable of towing an aerial chariot, and eventually flies therein to the moon, where he discovers a Christian people living in a paradisal society, but eventually becomes too homesick to stay with them.

Prompted by those examples, Savinien Cyrano de Bergerac (c1619-1655) decided to write a fantasy of his own, *L'Autre monde* [The Other World], far more fanciful, satirical and far-ranging than Godwin's, in which a trip to the moon would merely be the first stage of a more adventurous odyssey that would take in the other planets of the solar system—taking the Copernican theory for granted—and perhaps go even further than that, although we have no way of knowing, because the second half of the middle part of the trilogy is missing, and so is the entirety of the third volume, presumed to have been stolen by agents of the Church and destroyed. Nor was the work published in the author's lifetime—a lifetime cut short by an "accident" that might well have been deliberate homicide—and the versions published after his death by his friend and executor Henri Le Bret were severely bowdlerized for diplomatic reasons. The full text was not restored from the surviving manuscript fragments until 1921, so no one in the Age of Enlightenment was fully aware of the adventurousness of the existing text, and nobody knows or ever will know the full extent of the adventurousness of the whole.

Our present image of Cyrano is inevitably colored and considerably distorted by Edmond Rostand's 1897 play, which makes altogether too much of the size of his nose—shown in contemporary portraits to be a trifle beaky, but by no means huge—his relatively brief career as a soldier, which actually interrupted much longer periods devoted to scholarship and writing, and his wholly imaginary pining after an inamorata he can never possess, the fictitious Roxane. In fact, Cyrano abandoned his military career after less than two years, having twice been wounded in action, and from 1641 onwards devoted himself to study, at the Collège de Lisieux, and to literary endeavor. He probably attended lectures given by the mathematician and astronomer Pierre Gassendi, a modified skeptic who attempted to reconcile the Epicurean philosophy popularized by Lucretius' *De Rerum Natura* with Christianity, and engaged in controversy with René Descartes. Cyrano was certainly aware of that dispute even if his actual acquaintance with Gassendi was slight; one of Descartes' fervent disciples, Jacques Rohault, was a close friend of Cyrano's, and he was also acquainted with another of Gassendi's one-time pupils, Molière, who borrowed elements from Cyrano's comedy *Le Pédant joué* for a scene in *Les Fourberies de Scapin*.

Cyrano apparently began work on *L'Autre monde* in 1649, shortly after reading Godwin's work, and finished it in 1650, circulating the manuscript to friends. He published two volumes of dramas in 1652 but did not attempt to publish *L'Autre monde*, and the performances of his tragedy *La Mort d'Agrippine* were soon interrupted when its anti-religious sentiments caused a reaction. It was at that time that a wooden beam fell—or was pushed—upon his head, causing him a crippling injury from which he never fully recovered, requiring nursing in the house of his aunt. He tried to work on the manuscripts of *L'Autre Monde* but they were removed, either stolen or taken away by friends who feared that they might be destroyed by the nuns helping to nurse him. Either way, by the time Le Bret published the copies he had, half of the work was missing, including the entire third volume, *L'Étincelle* [The Spark], one of the two great lost works of early *roman scientifique*. Le Bret published the first volume as **Histoire comique des États et Empires de la Lune** in 1657, not only abridged but with a preface apologizing profusely for the absurdity of the suggestion that the Moon might be a world. He issued the incomplete text of the second part as *L'Histoire comique des États et Empires du Soleil* [The Story of the States and Empires of the Sun] in 1662.

The first story, in the full version of the text, begins with the narrator being ridiculed for asserting that the moon is a world, citing Pythagoras, Epicurus, Democritus, Copernicus and Kepler to support his claim to no avail. He then finds a copy of a book by the mathematician Girolamo Cardano open on his desk at a page in which the writer describes a mysterious visit from two men claiming to be inhabitants of the moon. Taking this as a sign, the narrator attempts to reach the moon by filling bottles with dew, which lift him into the air under the effects of sunlight, but only contrives to get as far as Canada. After engaging in debates with the Viceroy of the province regarding Copernican theory and the infinity of the universe, he builds a machine powered by rockets in which he eventually completes his planned voyage, and finds himself in the earthy paradise, having landed in the branches of the Tree of Life.

There the narrator learns the "true" stories of Adam, Enoch and Noah's daughter Achab from Elijah, an earlier lunar voyager who explains his own magnetic method of arriving there. Unfortunately, the narrator cannot resist the temptation to make a joke, and is banished from paradise by Elijah for his irreverence. After eating an apple from the Tree of Knowledge he finds himself in a strange land to which all the now-mythical creatures of Earth have been banished, and where he is captured and enslaved. While he is in that ignominious situation, Socrates' "Daemon" tells him about his last visit on Earth, when he met Cardano, Faust, Campanella and various other scholars, and about his early life on the world of his birth, the Sun. The currency of the lunar country turns out to be one mentioned by Charles Sorel's Hortensius in the second edition of *Francion*, to which due credit is given.

Cyrano's narrator also meets Domingo Gonsales, with whom he engages in a long discussion of the theory of elements, but eventually, because of his claim that the Moon is a satellite and the Earth a planet, rather than vice versa, he is put on trial and forced to recant his heresy. Further philosophical discussions follow regarding the mores of the lunarians, atomic theory, the immortality of animal souls and other topics, before the narrator contrives, unwittingly, to return to Earth.

The Le Bret version of *Histoire comique des États et Empires de la lune* became a crucial model for later works in several significant ways. It is very rapidly paced by comparison with most of the proto-novels of its period, achieving that rapidity by keeping its philosophical discussions to brief exchanges of dialogue, and embedding them in sequences of farcical action, whose slapstick aspect helps take the edge off the more dangerous assertions of the dialogue by permitting readers so inclined to take the false inference that they need not be taken seriously and establishing what modern terminology would call "potential deniability" of the seriousness of the assertions contained therein. Although it has few kindred works to draw upon by citation, it is careful to do so, thus emphasizing that it belongs not merely to a continuing and evolving discussion of intellectual matters but to a continuing and evolving literary tradition employing similar narrative methods.

The second volume of *L'Autre monde* emphasizes the falsity of its normalizing ending by picking up the story exactly where the first part left off. The narrator hastens to write an account of his lunar journey, which promptly leads him to be denounced as a sorcerer. He is then involved in a series of discussions with his hosts—who address him as Monsieur Dyrcona—about enigmatic but seemingly revelatory dreams they have had, before he ends up in prison. After further earthly tribulations, of a farcically dire nature, he contrives to build another flying machine and set off on his extraterrestrial travels again, heading for the Sun and discovering the moons of Venus and Mercury *en route*. He makes numerous deductions in passing as to why he no longer needs food, why the Sun's heat does not burn him and why all planets have satellites.

After four months of travel Dyrcona lands on a sunspot, imagined as a small world, and finds a dwarfish inhabitant who can give him information on various matters, including a rapid account of cosmogony and the origins of planetary life. Then he sets off again, this time traveling so far that the Earth becomes lost to sight in the comic background. When he reaches the "firmament," he finds that it is not solid, although, when he passes through it, he and his vehicle become transparent. Having turned round, it takes him nearly two years to get back to the Sun, but he finally succeeds in landing thereon.

On the Sun, Dyrcona encounters sentient and articulate fruit and birds, and soon finds an informant able to give him an elaborate account of nature on that world of light, music and metamorphoses, where things work very different from earthly nature. The solar birds, far in advance of humans, initially regard Dyrcona as a mere ape, and subject him to a searching examination, which leads to a trial before the full Parliament of Birds to determine the extent and culpability of his humanity. The judgment does not go well, but he is enabled to escape to a forest of sentient trees, who tell him stories about various earthly humans—characters appropriated from Classical mythology—who ate their magical fruits, and other strange metamorphic and magnetic effects of those fruits.

Unfortunately, the trees are interrupted when the forest is threatened by the "plague" of conflagration, and Dyrcona has to leave, but he is able to do so in the company of Campanella, now a citizen of the solar Province of Philosophers, the Sun being the ultimate destination of all planetary souls. The two discuss Descartes' physics, but postpone judgment until they can consult the great man himself. A discourse on the physiology of the senses then links to an allegorical sequence featuring the rivers of Memory, Imagination and Judgment. Their long journey on foot eventually takes them to the Country of Lovers, whose sexual mores, as well as its vulnerability to flooding by tears, are briefly explained. Just as they catch up with Descartes, however, the narrative is abruptly cut off.

The second volume is not as rapidly paced as the first, and is less flagrantly farcical, though certainly no less extraordinary; it appears that it would have been more than twice as long; how long the third would have been, and where it might have taken Dyrcona, is anyone's guess. Various specific features of the image of the Sun were to crop up again in several eighteenth-century interplanetary fantasies, as well as the more general features of its narrative strategy, including the seamless inclusion of allegorical landscapes. The importance of its demonstrations were not, however, limited to the inventions of its content and method; the fact that it was incomplete, and had only been published in bowdlerized form after a the death of its author—to which foul play was suspected of having contributed—posted an important warning for future writers of philosophical fantasy. While providing a new cartography for didactic travelers' tales, it also marked its map, invisibly but ostentatiously, with the traditional warning of "Here be Tygers," advertising that future adventurers would need to be heroic as well as bold.

They were, even though most of them were conspicuously more modest in their inventions than Cyrano.

It was some time before further earthly utopian satires began to carry forward the inventiveness of Campanella and Bacon, most later seventeenth century accounts being more narrowly focused on political reforms. Versins identifies two French works that are more inventive than that, and hence of particular relevance to the present project. The first, oddly enough, was originally published in English in 1675 as *The History of the Sevarites or Sevarambi, a Nation inhabiting a Part of the Third Continent, commonly called Terrae Australes Incognita.* A somewhat different version of that text was published in two volumes in French in 1677 as *L'Histoire des Severambes*, and then supplemented by two further volumes in French in 1678 and 1679. Issued anonymously, although the preface was signed "D.V." the work was speculatively attributed to various authors before a supposedly-definitive attribution was made in the 1890s to Denis Verias or Vairasse d'Allais (c1630-1672), a Huguenot who spent part of his life in exile in England, anagrams of whose name can found in the work, akin to Cyrano's use of Dyrcona. If the attribution is correct, the whole publication history of the work was posthumous. A continuation of the original version was also published in English, but it is not the same as the French continuation and appears to be the work of a different author.

The narrative begins with the attempts by survivors of a shipwreck to establish and organize a society of their own, rather problematically, because their population includes far fewer women than men and the women in question were prostitutes who intended to practice their profession in Batavia. The temporary system of division devised to cope with that problem seems to be unnecessary, however, when scouts discover the city of Sporounde, whose exotic sexual mores seem attractive to the male castaways. Sporounde is, however, a vassal state of the empire of the Severambes, who do not practice the same sexual freedoms as the inhabitants of Sporounde, considered by them to be corrupt.

The Severambes trace their ancestry back to a second Eden created by God after the Flood, in which a new primordial couple became the ancestors of their alternative human race—although that mythical account is challenged by a less flattering alternative. They are sun-worshipers, who pride themselves on the rationality of their society, which maintains its purity by exiling deviants of all kinds. They are more advanced technologically than European societies, although the advancement is partially secured by espionage that allows them to appropriate and useful inventions made elsewhere in the world. They live in orderly cities whose vast buildings each contain a thousand inhabitants, and their economy has no need of money. Their food supply is guaranteed by agricultural methods that take advantage of ingenious soil technology and elaborate systems of land-irrigation. They can also cure diseases. They are, however, exceptional, all the other inhabitants of the austral continent remaining primitive.

In detailing the castaways' journey through the land of the Severambes, the narrative also plays attention to the unusual flora and fauna of the austral land, noting its difference from those of Europe in the same way that naturalists were sending back reports of the distinctive flora and fauna of the Americas. The location of the utopia clearly reflects a general interest in world exploration and the possibility of colonization, and also an increasing interest in the possibility of repeating Columbus' feat by discovering another new continent. Unlike America however, and however paradoxical it might seem, *Terra Australis Incognita* already figured, albeit speculatively, on some world maps.

Initially hypothesized in antiquity, the notion of Terra Australis had been repopularized in the sixteenth century by geographers who thought the world map unbalanced, and in need of a southern continent to "equilibrate" it, much as the Americas had provided a continent to fill a western hemisphere previously suspected to be oceanic. Those who believed in Terra Australis and placed it speculatively in their maps included Gerardus Mercator in 1538, and seventeenth century navigators who glimpsed new lands in the southern hemisphere, including Abel Tasman, assumed that they were parts of the land-mass in question.

The notion of the hypothetical "continent" was still sufficiently intriguing a century after Vairasse's work to prompt the British admiralty to instruct James Cook to search for it when he went to Tahiti to observe a transit of Venus. He looked hard, first in the *Endeavor* in 1769-70 and then in the *Resolution* in 1773-74, but failed to find it, although he did find Botany Bay, on what turned out to be the eastern coast of "New Holland," which paved the way for the substitution on more accurate world maps of the more modest island of Australia. For a hundred years after Vairasse, however, the undiscovered land remained wide open territory for writers of imaginative traveler's tales.

In between the volumes of Vairasse's work, another French Protestant, Gabriel de Foigny (c1630-1692)—a renegade Franciscan monk—published his own account of *La Terre australe connue* (1676; tr. of full text as *The Southern Land, Known*) in which a narrator named Jacques Sadeur—tacitly represented as the work's author—relates the story of his life and voyages. Banned on its first publication, not only in France but in Geneva, where that edition was printed, it was republished in 1693, a year after the author's death, in a severely bowdlerized edition; the latter was the version that was reprinted by Charles

Garnier in his collection of *Voyages Imaginaires* in late 1780s—the version of Vairasse's work that Garnier reprinted was also abridged—and the full text remained very difficult of access until it was restored in 1922.

After a preface offering an account of alleged sightings of the Austral continent, and presenting an elaborate argument for its existence, Sadeur explains how he overcame the stigma of being born a hermaphrodite to become an adventurer and explorer, initially in Africa, before being cast away in Terra Australis, where he is rescued from giant carnivorous birds by natives who turn out to be representatives of an entire race of hermaphrodites. By virtue of that condition, which permits a perfect equality impossible in a sexually differentiated society, the "Australiens" have been able to establish a truly egalitarian society with an economic organization that we would now call communist, although Foigny does not, the word not having yet been invented. Advanced agricultural techniques are allegedly supplemented by many other mechanical innovations, although few are described. The very perfection of their way of life, however, gives the Australiens an inclination to ennui, apathy and suicide, the latter facilitated by a powerful narcotic.

Much attention is paid in the text to the nature and organization of the Australiens' language, which is supposedly more rational than European languages. Like the Severambes, they have primitive neighbors, the Frondins, whom they treat very badly. It is Sadeur's sexually-motivated sympathy for a Frondin woman that eventually gets him into trouble with his hosts, exhausting the patience of the protector who had enjoyed debating with him on philosophical matters, and he is sentenced to death, although he manages to escape by exploiting one of the giant birds.

Foigny's utopia cannot be said to have been influential in the sense that it gave rise to very many further images of hermaphrodite societies, not even in the sense that the challenge it issued to utopian thinkers as to whether sexual differentiation permitted the development of a truly egalitarian society was seriously addressed by later thinkers. Indeed, this is one case in which the *philosophes* seemed to agree with the would-be suppressors of the work in considering it too dangerous to think about, and therefore simply refrained from doing so. Precisely for that reason, it is now entitled to be reckoned one of the most important works in the genre of imaginary voyages.

Imaginary voyages made further progress outside the context of utopian fantasies, most notably, with regard to the present survey, in *Voyage du monde de Descartes* (1690; tr. as *A Voyage to the World of Cartesius*) by Gabriel Daniel (1649-1728), in which the author—a member of the Society of Jesus—takes frank satirical issue with a contemporary philosophical system. He does so in an extravagant fashion, taking up where Cyrano's incomplete work was obliged to leave off, and introducing Descartes as a character for the purposes of debate.

The work begins with a prefatory section in which the narrator debates philosophical theory with "*un Vieillard Cartesien*" [an Old Cartesian], paying particular attention to Descartes' notion of the relationship between the body and the soul, and suggests that the philosopher had found the secret of separating the two. By utilizing that secret, rather than dying, as the world assumes, Descartes has actually set off into "*les espaces indéfinis*" [indefinite space] in order to build a world similar to ours. The Old Cartesian and the spirit of Marin Mersenne—a theologian, mathematician and musicologist who had died in 1648—invite the narrator to accompany them to see how the great man is progressing with that task.

After a brief digression, the author discorporates himself by means of Descartes' secret, and the trio set forth for the Moon, where they expect to find the philosopher. On the way, they investigate the nature of air and its particles, and the manner in which fluidity is contained by liquid bodies. Other spirits are encountered, including Socrates, Plato and Aristotle. The last-named disputes the conclusions of Descartes' *Discourse on Method* and *Meditations*, but some of his own ideas are ridiculed by Père Mersenne and the Old Cartesian.

The disembodied travelers arrive on the Moon, where they discover that Cyrano de Bergerac has been tricked and misled by Socrates's Daemon. They investigate the face permanently turned away from the Earth, and the author finds one of his former professors there, now teaching on the Moon. Gisbertus Voëtius, an old Calvinist enemy of Descartes from his days in Holland, recounts some anecdotes about his life there, and sends two peripatetic philosophers to accompany the author and Mersenne on the remainder of their journey. They also encounter Cardan, on the Peninsula of Dreams, and debate with a Chinese Mandarin, before finally arriving at the World of Cartesius.

Descartes welcomes the travelers and immediately engages them in discussions on various topics, including Blaise Pascal's supposed demonstration of a void, for which Descartes claims the credit, before offering various other unkind comments on Pascal. He is no more complimentary about the Jesuits, the Oratorians, including Nicolas Malebranche, or the Jansenists, including Antoine Arnauld. Descartes then constructs his new world in the presence of his visitors, explaining its principles as he goes along, and the narrator is convinced.

The story does not end with the author's return to his body, which proves slightly problematic, but continues with an account of his attempt to carry forward the Cartesian creed, to which he is now a convert; he is, however, hampered by objections raised by the peripatetics, and is eventually persuaded by their arguments that the Cartesian system is fundamentally flawed, leading to the conclusions that the Moon ought not to rotate around the Earth, that objects ought not to fall toward the center of the Earth but toward the Sun, etc. He implores Descartes to send him the solution to his difficulties; in the meantime the debates continue, and the peripatetics find themselves as embarrassed as the Cartesians in regard to matters concerning animals' souls, or lack of them. The ultimate result of the long string of arguments, unsurprisingly is that, the theory of vortices being judged to be fatally flawed, Descartes' entire system is thrown out by the author, along with much other philosophy.

Daniel clearly takes considerable influence from Cyrano, in order to try and turn the tables on that skeptic by using his own method, but he is unable to sustain that method for very long, and once he brings his narrator's soul back from the Moon the text becomes rather tedious in its accounts of the exchanges of ideas leading to his conclusion. In its early stages, however, it exhibits a considerable energy and some of the argumentative ingenuity for which the Jesuits were celebrated. In spite of its rapid translation into English, however, the book dropped out of sight almost completely until the text reappeared on *gallica*, and very few people appear to have read it, even though it is one of the few relevant texts of its period to have received a royal license and to have been printed legally; perhaps for that very reason, it is never referenced by the *philosophes*, although its omission from the Versins *Encyclopédie* presumably only signifies that Versins never found a copy.

Neither of the two significant seventeenth-century accounts of Austral utopias seem to have been widely read either—far less widely, at any rate, than Cyrano's comedy—and that reflects the general fate of utopian fantasies; although the name of Thomas More's book is well known, very few people actually bothered to read it, and Campanella's name often seems to have been bandied about by people who had no direct acquaintance with the *Civitas Solis*. There was, however, one very earnest and didactically-inclined account of an imaginary voyage published at the end of the seventeenth century that was widely read, and very strongly promoted as an educational text, to the extent that it became one of those books whole title and nature are familiar to every Frenchman, including many who would never dream of attempting to read it: *Suite du quatrième livre de l'Odysée d'Homère ou les aventures de Télémaque, fils d'Ulysse* [Sequel to the Fourth Book of Homer's Odyssey; or, The Adventures of Telemachus, son of Ulysses] (1699) by François de Salignac de la Mothe-Fénelon (1651-1715), generally known simply as "Fénelon's *Télémaque*" and translated into English as *The Adventures of Telemachus*.

Fénelon was a Catholic clergyman whose reputation as an orator resulted in his being commissioned, when Louis XIV revoked the Edict of Nantes—originally issued in 1598 by Henri IV to guarantee legal tolerance to French Protestants—to undertake missionary work to persuade the Protestants of France to convert to Catholicism, henceforth restored as the official State Religion.

Given that the alternatives to conversion were exile and, increasingly, "dragooning"—the forced confiscation of children from Protestant families, in order that they could be indoctrinated, by means of violence administered, often murderously, by soldiers—Fénelon's mission seemed simple enough, but did not prove so in practice, and he found it extremely distasteful to his conscience. Subsequently, however, he found an employment much more to his liking when he was appointed the tutor of the Dauphin's eldest son, Louis, Duc de Bourgogne, the second in line to the throne—although, like his father, he died before Louis XIV. His former friend and now rival, Jacques-Bénigne Bossuet, had served as the Dauphin's tutor, and had written a book in consequence fervently defending the divine right of kings; Fénelon decided to write a book of his own promoting his own reformist ideas about constitutional monarchy, but he decided to make it more child-friendly, for the sake of his pupil, by casting it as an adventure story, a sequel to the *Odyssey*.

The first version of the text, published in 1699, was censored because it was out of line with Louis XIV's views and therefore considered seditious, but in 1717, after the king's death, a full version was issued—posthumously, because Fénelon, like Louis XIV, had died in 1715. The book was an immense best-seller, and added a new concept to several European languages in the name of its hero, Mentor, who serves as the tutor who guides the young Télémaque around the various quasi-utopian realms of the Mediterranean, some borrowing the names of real places, such as Tyr and Egypt, some mythological realms like Arcadie and others frankly allegorical, such as Bétique, all serving as preludes to the description of the supposedly authentic ideal state of Salente.

Although considered tedious by its detractors, because of the minute care taken by its author, speaking through the mouthpiece of Mentor, in detailing the flaws of the various societies visited, thus justifying the amendments made to society in Salente, the book was praised by its admirers for precisely the same reason, and it remains the most carefully argued reformist tract of the period, although that definitely detracts from its appeal as an adventure story. We can only speculate as to the extent that the young Duc took Mentor's lessons aboard, and what might have happened if he had lived long enough to become Louis XV instead of his own son, who received a very different education under the tutelage of Philippe d'Orléans, the administrator of the notoriously Decadent Regency that held power while he was still a child.

Because it is so narrowly focused on political matters, and specifically with the rights and duties of monarchy, the content of *Télémaque* is less relevant to the subsequent development of philosophical fiction than that of many less earnest but more far-ranging works, and it seems less interesting to the modern eye than Cyrano's extravaganza. The *philosophes*, whose reformist ideas were much more sweeping, mostly regarded it with contempt. It was, however, important not merely because it was so widely read but also because of the model provided by its narrative method. Mentor was not the first "wise old man" to be featured in imaginative fiction or to function there as a mouthpiece pouring tutorial balm into the ear of a sorely confused hero, but he became the archetype of the species. Few later writers placed characters in exactly the same position, but many located mentors in slightly more convenient narrative situations, in order to deliver necessary lectures and homilies, and a few even granted some such role, at least temporarily, to their heroes. If *Télémaque* was not the most influential imaginary voyage employed as a reference-point by subsequent French writers in that vein, it was nevertheless the most immediate and the most readily-available, and it could only be avoided by an effort of neglect.

3. The Plurality of Worlds and the Evolution of Science

Looking back from the present, when it is taken for granted that the Copernican model of the solar system, in which the planets orbit the sun, is correct and the Ptolemaic or Aristotelian model, in which the sun and the planets all rotate around the Earth, mistaken, it is sometimes hard to appreciate that the contest between the two theses went on for such a long time. However, as the history and contents of Cyrano's *L'Autre monde* make clear, it was not only controversial in the mid-seventeenth century but so bitterly controversial that the battle between the two occasionally became violent, and perhaps murderous. Even the contention, which now seems ludicrous to us, that the Moon, the planets and the sun were not material bodies at all, but mere appearances, perhaps contained in a system of "crystal spheres" surrounding the one and only Earth, the center of the universe, was still an object of committed faith for many, and the contention that there might be more worlds than one was widely deemed heretical.

Even believers in the Aristotelian model, however, sometimes took the view that it was not only far from heretical to imagine that there were more worlds than one but blasphemous to think otherwise, because it was suggesting a crucial limitation of God's omnipotence. Some theologians considered it essential to believe that God could have created as many worlds as he wanted to, and might well have done so, whether they were visible or not. The Copernican theory thus appealed to some theologians in that it made some of those other worlds visible: not only the other planets within the solar system, but other suns—the stars—which doubtless had planets of their own, perhaps *ad infinitum* if there were more stars beyond the limit of visibility, as the invention of the telescope strongly suggested.

The case for the plurality of worlds was forcefully argued on theological grounds, based on the contention that the assumption of a single world was an insult to God's creative capability, in *De Docta Ignorantia* (1440) by Nicholas of Cusa, who proposed that the universe must be as infinite as God Himself, and filled with an infinite number of worlds of equal status. This became known as "the principle of plenitude," and was further developed in other works, including a didactic poem, *Zodiacus Vitae* (c1534) by "Marcellus Palingenius Stellatus" (Pier Angelo Manzoli), which suggested that the human race might be the only one to have experienced a Fall, while its multitudinous peer races remained perfect.

The notion of the plurality of worlds seemed, in theological terms, to be a relatively harmless speculation until the Church's Aristotelian orthodoxy was challenged and assaulted by Copernican theorists. Seventeenth-century writers in France were mostly aware of the fact that a version of the principle of plenitude had been strongly argued by the Italian Dominican Giordano Bruno in *La cena de le ceneri* and *De l'infinito universo e mondi* (both 1584) and that Bruno had been condemned to death by the Inquisition in 1600; although the two events were not necessarily connected, that became a cardinal legendary example, almost as important as the trial of Galileo, of the religious persecution of scientific ideas.

The theological dispute in France became much more intense when firm support was given to the argument for plurality, alongside the publication of Cyrano's satire, by Pierre Borel's *Discours nouveau prouvant la pluralité des Mondes, que les astres sont des terres habitées, & la terre une Estoile, quelle est hors du centre du monde dans le troisième Ciel, & se tourne devant le Soleil qui est fixe, & autres choses très curieuses* [A New Discourse Proving the Plurality of Worlds, that the Heavenly Bodies are inhabited earths and the Earth a star, that it is distanced from the center of the world in the third heaven and turns around the Sun, which is fixed, and other very curious things] (1657, published in Geneva). Although the arguments put forward by Borel, based on authority rather than empirical evidence, now seem futile and only interesting in filling out a history of the idea of the plurality of worlds and the principle of plenitude, the confidence with which the assertions contained in the title and subtitle were made was suitably defiant.

A crucial contribution to the debate in France was provided by **Entretiens sur la pluralité des mondes** (1686; tr. as *Conversations on the Plurality of Worlds*) by Bernard Le Bovier de Fontenelle (1667-1757), which was important not merely because its arguments were far more convincing than Borel's, but because their method of presentation was much more striking. Fontenelle was the nephew of Pierre and Thomas Corneille, the latter of whom was one of the editors of the *Mercure Galant*, one of the first Parisian newspapers. The paper's content was devoted primarily to literary matters, and Fontenelle became a regular contributor to it, thus becoming a pioneering journalist. He was also an enthusiastic contributor to salon culture, seemingly very popular with the hostesses because of his wit and

ENTRETIENS SUR LA PLURALITÉ DES MONDES

charm, and also because he increasingly began to orientate his journalism toward female readers, thus helping to broaden the *Mercure*'s appeal and sales.

Fontenelle's early literary endeavors were not very successful, but they included a comedy entitled *La Comète* (1681), a response to the great comet of 1680 and the alarm it provoked in those who regarded it as an omen of disaster—alarm that the play tried hard to calm, by argument cloaked in amusement. His first major success was *Nouveaux dialogues des morts* (1683; tr. as *Dialogues of the Dead*), which brought together mythological, legendary and historical individuals in unlikely couplings in order that they could debate their different ideas. The dialogues are unashamedly biased, routinely assaulting dogmatic ideas—especially those still current—in favor of a healthy skepticism and rational arguments based on empirical evidence.

In the same year as the *Entretiens*, when he was not yet thirty, Fontenelle published a protest against the revocation of the Edict of Nantes disguised as an apologue, *Relation curieuse de l'île de Bornéo* [A Curious Account of the Isle of Borneo] and a conscientiously skeptical comparative history of mythological and religious ideas, concealed beneath the relatively innocuous title of *Histoire des oracles* (tr. as *The History of Oracles*). The latter was undoubtedly intended as the more serious and ambitiously scholarly work but it was virtually eclipsed by the much lighter *Entretiens*, which immediately cemented the author's fame and became enormously popular.

In describing itself as a series of "conversations" rather than "dialogues" the *Entretiens* advertises its lightness, promising easy comprehensibility spiced with wit, but it goes beyond even that by introducing a distinct note of flirtatiousness into the relationship of the philosophical mentor and the Marquise to whom he sets out to prove the plurality of worlds. The conversations extend over five evenings, the first devoted to a comparison of the Copernican model with rivals, with careful arguments supporting the former, while the second and third focus on the status of the Moon as a world, including speculations about the possibility of traveling to it as an actual project not impossible of realization. The fourth evening moves into deeper philosophical waters in tackling the vortical theory of planetary motion advanced by René Descartes—a theory that the philosopher finds as difficult to accept as Gabriel Daniel had. The fifth is not as abstruse, but expands the perspective drastically, in arguing that the stars are suns, probably surrounded by habitable planets, and that the Milky Way is simply one star cluster among many, in a universe that might well be infinite. The philosopher also argues that stars change and eventually die, but admits that he would like to think that new suns also form and that there is a kind of continuous cycle in their manufacture and decay that will go on eternally.

Because of the casual, almost playful, context in which these ideas are presented, and the gradual escalation of the five phases of the argument, the *Entretiens* carries its readers along far more comfortably than earnest combative tracts like Borel's, or endeavors like Cyrano's, in which the serious is deliberately jumbled with the farcical to create striking discontinuities. Many of the novels of the period are, in effect, simply accounts of long series of conversations, set in a somewhat tokenistic matrix of occasionally-melodramatic happenings. By eliminating the events, Fontenelle removed one of the fictional elements of his narrative apparatus, but it is arguable that not only does the work not suffer from that omission but that it gains a fluency and continuity that Cyrano's narrative method could not possibly have contrived. Fontenelle continued to make amendments to his text in later editions, including the 1708 and 1742 editions, but most of the alterations simply updated measurements of the planets and their orbits derived from better astronomical observations.

Fontenelle's philosopher also challenges, in passing and discreetly, a notion taken for granted in the theological debate: that the inhabitants of other worlds, if there were any, must be human, because they too would be made in God's image. Nicholas Hill had, however, argued in *Philosophia Epicurea, Democritiana, Theophrastica* (1601) that the size of created individuals must vary in proportion to the size of their worlds and Johannes Kepler's posthumously-published *Somnium* (1634), which attempted to popularize the Copernican system by explaining the astronomical observations that could be made on the moon, had concluded with a remarkable section attempting to deduce the adaptations that lunar life would have had to make to its long cycle of day and night. Fontenelle did not add much to that line of argument in 1686—not as much as Cyrano, in fact—but a more significant addition was made a few years later in a text initially published in Latin but rapidly translated into French, the language in which the author had initially intended to write it, as well as English and several other languages: Christiaan Huygens' *Kosmotheoros* (1698). The decision to publish in Latin was probably precautionary, although the author did make every attempt to issue the book while he was alive, and the fact that it only appeared posthumously was, in this case, an accident.

Huygens' book begins with a defense of the Copernican theory, but effectively considers that case already proven, and moves swiftly on to the argument that the other planets in the solar system are highly likely to be inhabited, what the likely forms of animals there might be, and whether those animals might include rational species. He consider the possibility that there might be rational beings different in form from humans, but doubts that their rationality could be different, even if they were equipped with different senses. He argues that rational beings on other worlds are likely to be similar to humans, not because of any divine plan—although he does argue that the variety of life on all the worlds of existence is a reflection of the glory of God's creativity—but because of the kinds of physical adaptation that allow reason to develop and flourish.

In the second part of the text, Huygens goes on to consider the planets one by one, trying to estimate by means of astronomical observations and logic what conditions might pertain on their surfaces. He does not get very far with that, and is very tentative in the conclusions he draws, but the result is less significant than the method and style of argument that he employs, and the manner in which he attempts logical deductions in the same vein as Kepler's.

The book was widely read, and although its influence was slow to take full effect, it is noticeable that it reflects the beginning of a change of attitude. It remained the case almost throughout the eighteenth century that expeditions to the moon and other planets were undertaken in a satirical spirit, in order to parody earthly behavior, and the names of the planets were simply employed to signify displacements of society. Nevertheless, prompted by Fontenelle and aided by Huygens, some writers began to move toward a different way of thinking, not simply about the possible variety of life outside the Earth, but also the way in which to rationalize and make sense of that variety—thus moving the argument regarding the plurality of worlds, gradually, into a new phase that was ultimately to become one of the key characteristics of *roman scientifique*.

A year after Fontenelle's *Entretiens* and two years before Gabriel Daniel's *Voyage du monde de Descartes*, Isaac Newton published *Philosophiae Naturalis Principia Mathematica* [Mathematical Principles of Natural Philosophy] (1687), nowadays seen as *the* pivotal work in the history of science, entitling Newton to be considered as the central figure of a veritable scientific revolution, to which his own contribution was completed when he finally prepared his long-delayed definitive account of *Opticks* for publication in 1704. He augmented the latter text twice, in the Latin edition of 1706 and a second English edition of 1717-18, incorporating new material derived from his general physical theories and imported similar new material into a second edition of the *Principia* in 1713.

In England, even though Newton had had his enemies and rivals, most notably Robert Hooke, the *Principia* was immediately hailed as a work of genius, and literary celebrations of it in poetic form soon began to flow with some profusion, glorifying the new Age of scientific Enlightenment that it seemed to have ushered in. Science is supposed to be universal, and one might have expected similar reactions to occur elsewhere in Europe, in spite of Newton's feud with Gottfried Leibniz over who had invented what Newton called the method of "fluxions" and Leibniz called "calculus"—the mathematics that had permitted the explanation and perfection of Kepler's discovery that the planetary orbits are elliptical. In France, however, the reaction to Newton's work was quite different, provoking widespread skepticism—primarily, it seems, on nationalistic grounds. Newton was not French, and his ideas could not, therefore, be preferred to those of Descartes, even thought Descartes had been unwelcome in his own country for much of his life and had been obliged to do much of his work in exile.

The Newtonian theory had the tremendous advantage of being correct, in all its main features, and slowly gathered adherents on that basis, but throughout the eighteenth century the French scientific establishment was split between "attractionists" and "anti-attractionists," the latter stubbornly refusing to believe in the theory of gravity. It was the anti-attractionist Élie Fréron who coined the term *roman scientifique* in order to ridicule "attractionism." Newton did of course, have his champions in France, some of whom were very vocal in his support, but it did not work entirely to the advantage of his ideas that the most vocal of them all was Voltaire, who saw Newton as a welcome flood of common sense cleansing philosophy's Augean stables of undesirable detritus. Voltaire popularized Newtonian ideas in *Éléments de la philosophie de Newton* (1738), after his patroness at the time, Émilie Du Châtelet, had performed the Herculean task of translating the *Principia* into French. His defense was, of course, logically sound, but no one in France polarized opinion like Voltaire, and many of the people who loathed him, for whatever reason, automatically loathed Newton too—whose work, needless to say, they never read and could not have understood if they had.

For that reason, the most pivotal publication in the history of physics came to play a rather peculiar role in the history of the French Age of Enlightenment, held up as iconic by the *Encyclopédistes*, but persecuted by their enemies for that very reason, without any real concern for its actual merit as science. Numerous French writers set out to prove it wrong, having taken it as axiomatic that it must be, and rival theories of motion persisted there, with unusual and unwarranted strength, even into the nineteenth century. That ongoing battle is reflected in the backcloth of several eighteenth-century works of imaginative fiction, and perhaps conscientiously avoided by some others, whose authors did not want to get involved.

Litterateurs had, in any case, always been more interested in the dark shadow of science—the so-called "occult sciences"—than what we now consider, in retrospect, to be its most responsible fraction. Occult science inevitably tends to be more esthetically pleasing than real science, because the forces guiding its production and development are esthetic rather than rational.

It is significant that when Charles Garnier made the first attempt to formulate a new genre of imaginative fiction in 1787, he titled his enterprise *Voyages imaginaires, songes, visions et romans cabalistiques*, and although the collection put *voyages imaginaires* very much in the foreground, breaking them down into several subcategories, and only includes two volumes in the second class of portal fantasies, featuring dreams and visions, he tacked on four volumes of works in the third class of *romans cabalistiques* [cabalistic fiction]—and could, if he had revised his classification slightly, have moved some works from the other categories into that one. Some of the works Garnier collected in those four volumes are simply fantastic stories, but there is one volume that had a considerable influence on several imaginary voyages that also warrant attention in the present volume by virtue of their scientific inclusions, hybridizing them in a peculiar fashion: *Le Comte de Gabalis, ou entretiens sur les sciences secrètes* (tr. as *The Comte de Gabalis: Secrets of the Elementals*), first published anonymously in Paris in 1670, but thought to be the work of Nicolas de Montfaucon de Villars.

As the subtitle indicates, the book is essentially a series of conversations, although they are by no means as light in tone as those employed by Fontenelle, and it is definitely a work of fiction, almost certainly intended as a parodic satire, although it was widely misconstrued as an earnest handbook of initiation into the mysteries of the occult. It proved remarkable influential in European literature, influencing notable works in English and German as well as French, but its influence largely derives from its popularization of elements that its author borrowed from a more obscure occult text apocryphally credited to Paracelsus, although not written until some years after the latter's death, *Liber de Nymphis, Sylphis, Pygmaeis et Salamandris et de Caeteris Spiritibus* (1566). The system became known as the Paracelsian theory of elementals, linking each of the four classical elements to a particular kind of spirit: in the French versions, water to *ondins*, air to *sylphes*, earth to *gnomes* and fire to *salamandres*. The idea that there were special classes of spirits associated with the four elements had been previously broached by Cornelius Agrippa in his survey of *De Occulta Philosophia*, but it was the *Liber de Nymphis* that named them and *Le Comte de Gabalis* that popularized them.

As a literary device, the elemental spirits proved enormously attractive, even to popularizers of science like Erasmus Darwin, who blithely inserted them into his didactic poetry. In French *contes philosophiques* they vied for popularity with the *génies* popularized by Antoine Galland, which benefited enormously from the fact that the word *génie* meant "genius" (in both senses of the term) in French as well as being a serviceable translation of the Arabic *djinn*, usually translated in English as "genie." In many works of eighteenth-century fiction, in fact, elementals and *génies* are juxtaposed, or regarded as the same thing. Many such works carried forward other inventions from *Le Comte de Gabalis*, such as the notion that Rosicrucians could see elemental spirits by means of an ointment rubbed on the eyes, and frequently refrained from marriage with humans in order to enter into mystical unions with elementals—which come in two sexes in the book, a great convenience for writers of erotic fiction.

Although *Le Comte de Gabalis* is of no value intellectually and only of perverse value as a satirical literary hoax, its direct and indirect influence on the development of French imaginative fiction in the eighteenth century probably outweighed that of any other text except Galland's *Mille et une nuits*, and its relationship to the developing literature makes an interesting contrast with the lack of influence of such texts as Newton's *Principia*. Nobody loathed *Le Comte de Gabalis*, or even denounced it very ardently, in spite of its nakedly heretical content. Even if it was a farrago of nonsense, it was esthetically appealing—and French.

CHAPTER TWO: THE AGE OF ENLIGHTEN-MENT

1. The Nature of the French Enlightenment

In one of the utopian novels of the early nineteenth century, *Le Vallon aérien* (1810; tr. as "The Aerial Valley") by Jean-Baptiste Mosneron, Baron de Launay, a pioneering balloonist exploring the Pyrenees finds a valley, now inaccessible on foot, where Protestants fleeing persecution after the revocation of the Edict of Nantes formed a refugee community at the end of the seventeenth century, deliberately isolating themselves from a hostile society. They have therefore missed the entire eighteenth century and the Age of Enlightenment it supposedly represented. Asked to characterize that century and sum up its achievements concisely, the balloonist replies:

"The century of Louis XIV…has been followed not by the century of Louis XV but by the eighteenth century; for it is only great kings who give their name to their century, and that century will, in fact, be eternally celebrated by its litterateurs. Those who have principally honored it are four in number: Voltaire, Buffon, Montesquieu and J.-J. Rousseau."

Mosneron was not only person who saw the eighteenth century in that light. In *La Découverte australe par un homme volant* (1781; tr. as *The Discovery of the Austral Continent by a Flying Man*), Nicolas-Edmé Restif de la Bretonne, one of the writers to be prominently featured later in the present chapter, brought an agent of a refugee utopia established in the early part of the century on the far side of the world back to Europe in the 1770s, in search of things that the old world might be able to contribute to that burgeoning society; his shopping list includes a great philosopher, and he asks the author to name the one he ought to recruit. The author has no hesitation in naming the potential candidates as Voltaire, Buffon and Rousseau, and would surely have added Montesquieu to the list had the latter not been dead by the time the scene is set. Both during the era in question and afterwards, many people who regarded themselves as contributors to or products of the Age of Enlightenment characterized it as an era defined by its philosophical writers, of whom those four could be identified as the key pillars, not merely because of their personal genius but because of the collective range of their fields of operation.

"The first," Mosneron's balloonist says, "was a tragic and epic poet, a historian, a moralist and a writer of romances; in brief he exercised all the strings of the lyre, and all in an original and interesting manner." He could have added that

Voltaire (François-Marie Arouet, 1694-1778), of whom he was speaking, had also made a significant contribution to the physical sciences by virtue of his popularization and promotion of Newtonian physics, but he doubtless thought that a subsidiary issue.

To many of those who considered themselves enlightened, Voltaire was the most perfect incarnation of the Enlightenment, not just because he had the greatest virtues—among which his dramatic works and his *contes philosophiques* could be reckoned as important as his historical analyses and his moral and political crusading—but also because he had the very best of enemies, being loathed by the clergy, whose remaining authority over the minds of his contemporaries he was determined to destroy. He was also amazingly prolific in his writings, including his correspondence, tirelessly taking an interest in everything, and organizing and analyzing the results of his attention with his pen, consciously attempting to grasp the whole of the intellectual acquisitions of his time.

Not content with contributing extensively to the collaborative endeavor of the *Encyclopédie, ou dictionnaire raisonné des sciences, des arts et des métiers* planned by Denis Diderot and Jean Le Rond d'Alembert, and published between 1751 and 1772, Voltaire produced his own elaborate commentary on it—*Questions sur l'Encyclopédie* (1770) is one of the underground best-sellers identified by Robert Darnton—having previously issued his own extensive *Dictionnaire de philosophie* (1764), as well as many statements of his own opinions, commenced with *Lettres philosophiques sur les anglais* (1734; tr. as *Letters on the English*), which also made Darnton's list. By the beginning of the eighteenth century there were no more "Renaissance men" who could claim to know everything that humans could know, and a few other things besides, but Voltaire was *the* Enlightenment Man, who wanted to know as much as he could, and also to understand where the limits of that knowledge lay, and why.

"Another writer," Mosneron's balloonist continued in his summary, "has enriched with the most brilliant style the history he has made of all organic creatures. Humankind is the first link in the chain of those beings.... The genius of the great naturalist is deployed, above all, in the high station from which he contemplates nature. It is from there soaring above creation, that he unfurls the magnificent tableau before our eyes. Thus, the savant geographer, in raising his thought above the terrestrial globe, ceases to perceive the petty divisions of provinces and estates traced by the human hand, no longer seeing anything but the great masses of nature."

Georges-Louis Leclerc, Comte de Buffon (1707-1788) was, for his contemporaries, the great French scientist of his era. He was a mathematician as well as a naturalist, but it was his mammoth *Histoire naturelle, générale et particulière*, of which he lived long enough to publish thirty-six volumes beginning in 1749—although the last appeared posthumously and another was added by means of collating the notes he had not contrived to organize—that provided his monument, establishing him as the encyclopedist of nature. D'Alembert criticized him because he was not content merely to be a recorder of facts—Buffon's *Discours sur le style*, presented to the Académie française in 1753 insisted that writing well was the ultimate evidence of thinking well and that "*le style c'est l'homme même*" [the style is the very man]—but that was part and parcel of his thinking, and a significant component of his notion of Enlightenment.

Buffon's work was, of course, specialized, as all scientific work had to be by the eighteenth century, thirty-six volumes and a life's work only being able to contain a small part of it, but his endeavor was symbolic of the manner in which similar "magnificent tableaux" were being constructed in astronomy and the other science that Mosneron's narrator likens to Buffon's endeavor, geography. Nowadays, we take geography for granted, the map of the world being complete and detailed, but when the eighteenth century began, the navigational endeavors that were to make giant strides in the detailed mapping of the globe and provide the elements of an overall summary and understanding of its contents were only beginning. The information brought back by those voyages of discovery—including their mistakes and misapprehensions—were not only poured into Buffon's natural history, but provided the foundations of a more controversial ethnography, more sadly mistaken in many ways, but nevertheless groping conscientiously toward an eventual light.

Buffon's *Histoire naturelle* was primarily an endeavor of taxonomy, but it also had an important theoretical dimension; the stress it laid on the relationships between the different classes of living beings laid important foundations for evolutionary theory, although Buffon was naturally wary and tentative in suggesting that all life of Earth had evolved by differentiation from simpler forms, and diplomatically left humankind out of that account. He was more robustly challenging, however, in his speculations regarding the age of the earth, its geological evolution and cosmogonic origins, summarized in *Les Epoques de la nature* (1778; tr. as *The Epochs of Nature*), in which he integrated his studies of natural history with more general cosmological theories, carried forward from the speculations of René Descartes by such contemporaries as Pierre-Simon Laplace. Laplace subsequently began his own massive overall summary of physical and astronomical science in 1799 in *Mécanique céleste* [Celestial Mechanics], which ultimately ran to five volumes and completed the establishment, begun by Voltaire, of Newtonian physics and cosmology within the body of French science.

"What Buffon did for natural history," Mosneron's balloonist went on, "another author has carried out for civil history.... What sagacity, to penetrate through that rubble to discover the primitive disposition of the materials and the motive that directed them, to discern the parts of the edifice that were sagely ordered and those which sinned by some hidden vice, in order to render the faults of the fathers useful to the children, to draw the lessons of experience and instruct people in the science that touches them most intimately: that of living in society in the manner most appropriate for them to be happy!...

"History is filled with individuals born on a throne or in the ranks of the vulgar who have made great conquests, but where can one find elsewhere than among the Romans an entire people conquering by means of a political system, constantly followed for more than ten centuries? The event is almost prodigious, and for nearly two thousand years one has only been able to admire it. Montesquieu cast a glance over that phenomenon, unique on earth; immediately, the prestige vanished; but the admiration perhaps only increased, in relating the effects to the simple and natural causes that his book has revealed."

Charles-Louis de Secondat, Baron de la Brède et de Montesquieu (1689-1755) does not seem quite as important a thinker in distant retrospect as he did in 1810, but the hypothetical balloonist was right to signify that his particular combination of historical theory and political philosophy lay at the very heart of the Enlightenment. His *Considérations sur les causes de la grandeur des romains et de leur décadence* [Considerations of the Causes of the Grandeur and Decadence of the Romans] (1734) has since been superseded by far more detailed accounts of the rise, decline and fall of the Roman Empire, but it was extremely important at the time because it represented a new way of looking at history, not as the sum of the largely arbitrary actions of powerful men, but as a series of processes in which empires had natural life cycles, into which individual rulers merely slotted.

Whether or not that is true remains controversial, but it gave the *philosophes* eighteenth-century France a new perspective from which to consider the past and a new ideative framework in which to place their own present. Montesquieu is nowadays given more credit for popularizing the ideas of despotism, which came to be crucial in drawing analogies between the reign of Louis XIV to certain events in Roman history, but he also popularized the idea of decadence, which invited analogies between the aftermath of Louis XIV's reign—the Regency and reign of Louis XV—and the decadence of Rome. That second notion proved surprisingly versatile and persistent, resurfacing with a different slant in the nineteenth century, but in the eighteenth it made a crucial contribution to the routine representation of what eventually came to be known as the *ancien régime* as something rotting, and doomed by its corruption.

It was entirely natural, given the nature of that historical perspective, that Montesquieu should move on from his study of history to the production of his crucial work of political philosophy, *De l'Esprit des lois* [The Spirit of the Law], published anonymously and illicitly in 1748, ostensibly in Geneva, which caused more consternation in the French religious and political establishment than any other work published during the century—all the more so because it was so highly praised in other European countries, especially Britain (even though the British Establishment was equally relentless in is pursuit of its own home-grown troublemakers, especially Thomas Spence and Thomas Paine, the champions of human rights). Montesquieu's second great work was a comparative study of human societies and their institutions, which regarded laws as something essentially man-made, and, in comparing the different ways in which they had been and could be made, argued that the way in which they had been made and were administered in France could and ought to be reformed. The Church and State, whose leaders wanted laws to be considered divinely and despotically ordained, did not like that at all, but it was the very quintessence of active, evolutionary Enlightenment.

"Alongside those masters" Mosneron's balloonist concluded, "marches a man who combines the most profound knowledge of the human heart with the greatest talent for expressing the passions. No one has equaled him in the depiction of love, of its voluptuousness, its storms, and the succession of its pains and pleasures. Endowed simultaneously with an exquisite sensibility, a strong conception and a fortunate facility in embracing several different subjects, from the smallest details of domestic life he has risen to the highest questions of politics and morality."

Not everyone, at the time, would have recognized that characterization of Jean-Jacques Rousseau (1712-1778), the *enfant terrible* of the age. Reduced to destitution in childhood, Rousseau was rescued from poverty by the infatuation of an older woman, who debauched and educated him, but he subsequently sent the children to whom his own conspicuously uneducated mistress gave birth to the foundling home, where they all died. He was widely considered to be a lover of paradox for its own sake, having shot to fame when he won an essay competition held by the Académie de Dijon to address the question of whether the development of arts and sciences had been beneficial. Denis Diderot, who had befriended him, told him that he could not win it if he took the expectable line, and could only make an impression if he adopted and mounted a heroic defense of a controversial viewpoint; thus, Rousseau argued in *Discours sur les sciences et les arts* (1750), that the arts and sciences were, in fact, responsible for the degeneration of humankind, and that human beings must have been far more moral, and happier, when living in a state of cultural innocence—and was then forced to spend the rest of his life asserting that he believed it, although many people suspected that he did not. Whether or not that was the case, he certainly convinced many people, being possessed of a very considerable eloquence as well as a titanic intellect.

While not quite as versatile as Voltaire, with whom he maintained an uneasy and sometimes vitriolic rivalry, Rousseau was primarily remarkable for his versatility. Most of the articles he wrote for the *Encyclopédie* were about music, on which topic he considered himself a great expert—and in spite of his notoriety, Louis XV was so impressed by the music and libretto he wrote for the opera *Le Devin du village* [The Village Soothsayer] (1752) that he awarded him a lifelong pension—but he also contributed articles on political economy, having broadened out the considerations of his first essay in a *Discours sur l'origine et les fondements de l'inégalité parmi les hommes* [Essay of the Origins and Basis of Human Inequality] (1754), on the way to his magisterial summation of his political thought in *Du Contrat social* (1762; tr. as *The Social Contract*), which builds on Montesquieu's consideration of the spirit of law to a generalized notion of the essence of society as a contract between its members, amenable to and ready for renegotiation.

In the meantime, Rousseau wrote a novel—not just any novel, naturally, but a novel that helped to revolutionize the art of the novel, not so much in its epistolary form, which is a trifle clumsy, although it certainly permitted an intimacy of style, but in its sentimentality. *Julie, or la nouvelle Héloïse* (1761; tr. as *The New Heloise*) was not the first "sensibility novel"; the subject-matter had already been brought into narrow focus and extensively developed in the early work of the enormously popular Marie-Jeanne Riccoboni (1713-1792), but Rousseau was a man and a *philosophe,* and thus had an authority that his female predecessors and contemporaries did not; not only did *Julie* become a huge best-seller but it made its author the figurehead of a cult of *sensibilité* that expanded far beyond France, exemplifying a modern mythology of amour that still dominates fictional love stories today.

Rousseau followed up his classic tale of an ideal love bearing no resemblance whatsoever to his own amorous life with a treatise on the education of children, *Émile; ou de l'éducation* (1762), which conspicuously did not recommend sending them to the foundling home, but did argue, controversially, that children ought to be allowed to learn via play and experience, and that the only book from which they could learn anything useful was *Robinson Crusoe.* He did, however, ultimately set his own record straight—ostensibly, at least—in his warts-and-all autobiography, *Les Confessions,* written in 1770 but only published posthumously in 1782, along with its more recently-written supplement *Rêveries du promeneur solitaire* [Reveries of a Solitary Stroller].

By the time he wrote the latter book Rousseau was in poor health, apparently because of epilepsy resulting from a serious concussion—although his adversaries inevitably accused him of having lost his mind—and had to retire to a cottage lent to him by the Marquis de Girardin, where he spent his time in the company of his still-loyal mistress, studying botany, planning books he never wrote, and playing the piano, seemingly serene as well as perfectly sane between fits—one of which eventually caused a cerebral hemorrhage that killed him, although some of his friends spread rumors of suicide.

In a sense, Rousseau summed up the Enlightenment even better than Voltaire, Buffon and Montesquieu combined, not so much because his versatility, intelligence and style were match for theirs, and he was a talented musician as well, but precisely because, in his case, it was so very disorderly, always giving rise to suspicions of paradoxicality even though he denied it, and always inherently rebellious, instinctively opposed to dogma, perhaps to the point that he would far rather have been wrong than orthodox. In that regard, it might be considered that he was lucky to have lived in a time and place whose orthodoxy was not merely stubbornly wrong but backed up against the wall, manifestly teetering on the brink of collapse—but an analogue living in a different era would doubtless have been differently formed by his environment, so luck had nothing to do with it.

The only work of philosophical fiction that Rousseau published during his lifetime was his love story, although it might be worth noting in passing that in 1801 a short essay attributed to him—probably apocryphally, although allegedly taken from a manuscript of 1742—was published as *Le Nouveau Dédale* [The New Dedalus], which speculates fancifully on the practicality of artificial flight. Buffon's literary work, stylish as he considered it to be, was confined to his accounts of the natural world, and Montesquieu only ventured into fiction once, in a brief and modest moralistic utopian satire included in his *Lettres persanes* (1721), extracted and reprinted in Garnier's *Voyages imaginaires* as "Histoire des Troglodytes" [The Story of the Troglodytes], which attempts to exemplify and demonstrate the evil social consequences of extreme egotism. It is, therefore, to Voltaire that we look for the cardinal examples of the archetypal fiction of the Enlightenment: the *contes philosophiques*, including those relevant to the history of *roman scientifique*.

Although the publication of Voltaire's *contes* began in the late 1740s, with *Zadig, ou la destinée: histoire orientale* (1747; tr. as *Zadig; or Destiny*), "Memnon, ou la sagesse humaine" (published 1748 but written earlier; tr. as "Memnon; or, Human Wisdom) and "Le Monde comme il va, vision de Babouc" (published 1748 but written 1746; tr. as "The World As It Is: Babouc's Vision"), there is reason to believe that the first one he wrote, and which he sent to Frederick II of Prussia in 1739, during his extensive correspondence with that monarch, then titled "Le Voyage du baron de Gangan," was a first draft of the story that eventually appeared as a short volume under the title *Micromégas* (published 1752, but written 1750 in its final version).

In fact, the visitor from a world orbiting the star Sirius who visits the Earth in the last-named story, having collected and inhabitant of Saturn *en route*, is foreshadowed in "Memnon," whose protagonist, having decided to be wise and having came somewhat unstuck in that ambition, is visited in a dream by "*un spirite céleste*" [a celestial spirit] resplendent with light. The spirit tells the protagonist that his homeland is five hundred million leagues from the Sun, "in a little star near Sirius," and concludes his corrective lecture by telling Memnon that being perfectly wise is as impossible as bring perfectly skillful, strong, powerful or happy.

"There is one globe where all that is found," he observes, "but in the hundred thousand millions of worlds dispersed in the expanse, everything extends by degrees; there is less wisdom and pleasure in the second than in the first, less in the third than in the second, and so on until the last, where everyone is completely crazy." Memnon then opines that "our petty terraqueous globe" must be that very last one, and although the spirit tells him that it is not quite, although very nearly, he still judges that "Certain poets and philosophers are very wrong to say that all is well"—thus preparing the ground for *Candide*'s demolition of that attitude as well as *Micromégas*' expansion of the disdainful view that an alien giant equipped with far more senses than mere humans might take of the pretentions of Churchmen.

"Le Monde comme il va," which employs the fictional device of introducing Ituriel, a "génie" [genius, in the sense of a spirit, but sometimes translated as "genie"], in order to examine the question of whether "all is well" from the opposite perspective. Its hapless protagonist is delegated to decide whether "Persepolis" [Paris] is so utterly corrupt as to warrant destruction. Babouc judges, after due consideration, that its rich idol, at least, should be smashed, but Ituriel limits his own condemnation, on the grounds that "If all is not well, it is passable."

The brilliant *Zadig* offers a similar modified fatalism in its account of the luckless Babylonian philosopher whose skill in deduction, cultivated when he turns to science after being disappointed in amour, gets him into trouble and occasions a sequence of hectic and fantastic adventures. His exploits involve several abrupt changes in fortune before he is offered a conclusive enlightenment by a hermit, who turns out to be another celestial spirit, Jesrad. The latter's advice regarding the necessity of evil and the implacability of fate is somewhat belied by the happy ending attached to the tale, seemingly in accordance with

the conventional logic of fiction rather than the deliberately unorthodox logic of the story.

Micromégas is the text that is nowadays seen by many modern commentators as a crucial work of "proto-science fiction" because of its employment of a mathematically-talented Sirian and a Saturnian, who engage in discussions regarding the constitution of matter and light before setting off to visit Earth. Some modern commentators have been struck by the "prediction" contained in the story that Mars has two small moons, although the story makes it clear that the question was currently under discussion, on the basis of an argument suggesting that if Venus has no moon, the Earth one and Jupiter four, Mars ought, for reasons of arithmetical symmetry, have two. Seen from another angle, however, Micromégas can be seen as a modified "celestial spirit," admittedly one who can travel through interstellar space by virtue of his understanding of *"les lois de gravitation,"* sometimes with the aid of a ray of light and sometimes riding a comet.

Far from coming to Earth specifically to enlighten a chosen human individual, however, like his predecessors, Micromégas will not believe that such microscopic creatures can even exist until his Saturnian companion confronts him with the evidence. Numerous scientists and philosophers are cited in the story, sometimes—but not invariably—to treat their opinions and discoveries with amused disdain. Although the story concludes with the presentation of a blank book to a disciple of Thomas Aquinas, as a riposte to the *Summa Theologica*, the final paragraph begins with a much more sympathetic approval of the empiricist ideas of John Locke, whose own partisan has offered the view that "I affirm nothing; I am content to believe that more things are possible than one might think."

Further reflections on the modern scientific outlook are included in the brief "Songe de Platon" [Plato's Dream] (1756), in which the dreaming philosopher confronts "the great Demiurge, the eternal Geometer" who "having populated infinite space with innumerable globes, wanted to test the science of the genii who had been witness to his works" by giving each of them a ball of mud to work with, in a spirit of comparative experiment. Demogorgon, the genius given charge of the Earth, thinks he has created a masterpiece, but the Demiurge's commentary confirming that opinion is a trifle sarcastic, putting him on the defensive. The genii in charge of Mars and the other worlds of the solar system are, however, not spared criticism, and the Demiurge's final verdict is that, given a few more hundreds of millions of years, all of them might do better.

Having taken up that extremely distant narrative viewpoint, however, Voltaire's tales then returned to Earth, and began to concentrate on matters of fact and detail, first in "Histoire des voyages de Scarmentado" (1756; tr. as "The Travels of Scarmentado"), whose unlucky hero bears witness to a sequence of disasters, but has no philosophical lens through which to consider them. Because of that, he cannot find the experience as illuminating as the eponymous hero of Voltaire's greatest masterpiece, *Candide, ou l'optimisme* (1759), hopes to do, with the aid of his mentor, Doctor Pangloss. Poor Candide fails dismally to convince himself that all is for the best in the best of all possible worlds, although the author, while dutifully refraining from providing the kind of happy ending that he had earlier awarded to Zadig, does at least allow him to find a material refuge reflective of the philosophical refuge that Voltaire, having found it himself, felt free and obligated to offer to his readers.

The subsequent *contes philosophiques* are more playfully inclined. For the Oriental fantasy "Le Blanc et le noir" [The Black and the White] (1764), Voltaire invented a hypothetical narrator supposedly related to the recently-deceased songwriter Jean-Joseph Vadé, and then credited the moralistic tale of "Jeannot and Colin" (1764) to the same fictitious author. He did something similar with *L'Ingénu* (1767; tr. as "The Huron"), whose original subtitle represented it as being "taken from the manuscripts of Pierre Quesnel." That story proved to be one of his most successful, going through nine editions before the end of the year and many more thereafter—a success presumably not unconnected with the fact that it took Rousseau somewhat to task in its employment of a "Child of Nature" as a viewpoint for the examination of French society in the 1690s.

Voltaire returned to the satirization of scientific notions in *L'Homme aux quarante écus* [The Man with Forty Écus] (1768, published anonymously), whose principal target is the economic theories of the Physiocrats, but which includes a number of other documents, unconnected to the principal debate between the protagonist and a "Geometer." Those supplements include a critique of Benoît de Maillet's *Telliamed* (third edition 1755), objecting to its geological and evolutionary theory—a far less sympathetic reaction than that of Restif de la Bretonne, who built his own speculative cosmogonic and evolutionary theory on the basis of Maillet's, in combination with Buffon's, in the *Découverte australe*.

"La Princesse de Babylon" (1768; tr. as "The Princess of Babylon") and "Le Taureau blanc" (1773; tr. as "The White Bull") are more buoyant satirical fantasies, whose anti-religious arguments are relatively subtle, and whose appeal as fantastic stories was sufficient for Lin Carter to reprint both of them when he compiled a history of the "fantasy" genre that he had helped to define for the American paperback market in the 1970s. "Histoire de Jenni, ou l'athée et le sage par Mr. Sherloc" [The Story of Jenny; or, The Atheist and the Sage, by Mr. Sherlock" (1775), by contrast, is a more earnest dialogue and exemplary tale in which Voltaire defends his own version of deism—which attempted to strip the idea of God of all dogmatic paraphernalia while preserving its essence—against a more rigid atheism.

The last of the *contes philosophiques* to be written (although its publication was succeeded by that of one of the earliest, "Cosi-Sancta") again returns to metaphysical matters of some scientific relevance: "Les Oreilles du Comte de Chesterfield et le Chapelain Goudman" [The Earl of Chesterfield's Ears and Chaplain Goodman] (1775)—the individual to whom the title refers, Philip Stanhope, had died two years earlier—gives a leading role to Mr. Sidrac, a surgeon and anatomist who debates the existence of the soul with Dr. Goudman, in an attempt to convert him to materialism, their debate being confused by the introduction of the voyager Mr. Grou, recently returned from the South Seas, who adds an ethnographic dimension to the debate—without, of course, enabling it to reach a conclusion satisfactory to all parties.

The full set of Voltaire's philosophical fictions is by no means rich in precursors of *roman scientifique*, although *Micromégas* can certainly be reckoned one of the genre's most important foundation-stones, but it does serve to illustrate the breadth and complexity of the literary milieu in which such relevant works were produced, in which discussions of matters that would nowadays be considered "scientific" were then simply elements in a spectrum of philosophical issues that had not yet been subjected to the careful taxonomic sorting to which it would be subjected in the early nineteenth century by Auguste Comte, who defined physics, chemistry and biology as a positivist trinity of natural sciences, while mathematics and other disciplines, such as geography, geology and economics were carefully positioned at various distances therefrom.

The issues to be addressed in the eighteenth century seemed something of a jumble even then, but the kinds of treatment contained in Voltaire's *contes* and their analogues did not summon up the same kinds of discord in the minds of their contemporary readers that the modern eye picks up, and the invocation of celestial spirits and various items of Orientalia for use as plot levers and frameworks, although relatively new, seemed to be fair game in a way that many modern readers—especially readers of science fiction—would not license in contemporary fiction. Although the works discussed in the remaining sections of the chapter are selected for their relevance to the eventual emergence of *roman scientifique*, it ought not to be forgotten that they are elements in a broader spectrum, and that they share many interests and methods with other contemporary works of fiction, both heterocosmic and naturalistic.

2. Polar Landscapes

The first of the important eighteenth century precursors of *roman scientifique* whose work warrants elaborate discussion is Simon Tyssot de Patot (1655-1738), author of *Voyages et aventures de Jaques Massé* (tr. in 1743 as *The Travels and Adventures of James Massey* and more recently as "The Voyages and Adventures of Jacques Massé) and the book whose title is generally recorded as *La Vie, les aventures et le voyage de Groenland du Révérend Père Cordelier Pierre de Mésange* (tr. as "Discoveries in the Region of the North Pole by the Reverend Father Pierre de Mésange").

Voyages et aventures de Jaques Massé was first published anonymously, and four editions are known, all bearing the date 1710, some having title pages stating that it was issued in Bourdeaux or

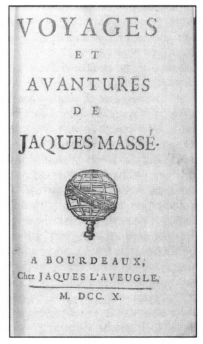

VOYAGES

E T

AVANTURES

D E

JAQUES MASSÉ·

A BOURDEAUX;
Chez JAQUES L'AVEUGLE,

M. DCC. X.

Bordeaux "Chez Jaques l'Aveugle" and one that it was published in Cologne "Chez Kaincus." The title-pages are fakes, and the likelihood is that the text was actually first printed in the Netherlands. Tyssot's biographer, Aubrey Rosenberg, concludes on the basis of indirect evidence that the actual first publication date of the text must have been between 1714 and 1717.

The attribution of the book's authorship to Simon Tyssot de Patot, first made in 1740 after his death, helps to explain the awkwardness of the publication strategy. Tyssot was a Huguenot whose family had been forced to leave France before he was born, and was subsequently forced to flee England as well, with the result that he spent most of his life moving around, living in various locations in the Netherlands, where he worked as a teacher of French and Mathematics, including a long spell at the Athenaeum in Deventer.

The preliminary title page of Tyssot's second novel, published in two volumes dated 1720, states that it was published in Amsterdam and does not cite an author, but the dedicatory epistle is signed "S. Tyssot de Patot." Page one of the second text, in both volumes, gives the title as *Voyage et découvertes autour du pole boreal du Révérend Père Cordelier Pierre de Mésange*, thus justifying the title of the translation; the term "Cordelier" indicates that the priest in question is a Franciscan—albeit a renegade, like Gabriel de Foigny.

Although the adventures of Pierre de Mésange are dated a year after the publication of Daniel Defoe's *The Life and Adventures of Robinson Crusoe* (1719) they were obviously written beforehand, with no knowledge of that work, or of the tidal wave of imaginary voyages that its example inspired, aided and abetted by Jonathan Swift's satirical account of the travels of Lemuel Gulliver, first published in 1726. It is not impossible, in fact, that Tyssot's fictitious account of the travels of Jacques Massé was known to Defoe, and helped to prompt his own colorful account of a mariner's trials and tribulations.

The seventeenth century had seen the publication of a number of accounts of actual voyages of exploration, but most such voyages had been extremely tentative by comparison with what was to follow in the eighteenth century. Dutch explorers had mapped much of the northern coast of what they called "New Holland," but had rarely attempted to land there, let alone explore it, although the privateer William Dampier did so briefly in 1688 and 1699; the island in question was still *terra incognita* for a further century until the English began the colonization that eventually transformed it into Australia. The island of Tahiti had also been sighted, but there was no record of anyone landing there, and it was not until the latter half of the eighteenth century that the great French explorer Louis de Bougainville, who landed there in 1768, would establish its native society as a key exemplar in the mythology of cultural evolution, in a context provided by Jean-Jacques Rousseau.

Tyssot was, therefore, writing in an era when the possibility of finding more vast islands, as yet unheeded as well as unexplored, was still entirely plausible. As Pierre de Mésange points out at one juncture, in a stirring speech, nobody yet cared about exploration for the sake of scientific investigation; the European invasions of the East Indies and Americas had been guided entirely by the quest for commercially valuable commodities and the lure of gold. The adventurous French navigators and explorers of the seventeenth century, without exception, followed the contemporary tide by heading for the Indies and Americas; only victims blown off course and shipwrecked, like Jacques Massé and Pierre de Mésange, ended up anywhere else, and they hardly ever lived to tell the tale.

Tyssot would undoubtedly have been aware of some examples of the utopian subgenre, and the imaginary societies visited by Jacques Massé and Pierre de Mésange are not without elements of comparison calculated to make European society seem a trifle sorry and more than a trifle sick, but neither the author nor his imaginary *alter egos* were social reformers. They were, however, pioneers and evangelists of Enlightenment, not merely in the sense that they have an insatiable appetite for discovering "curiosities," but also in the sense that they are ever avid to spread the knowledge they possess and to operate as fervent disciples for the training of minds by mathematical logic and the acquisition of new knowledge by means of the methods of science. Among the literary genres to which Tyssot's works feature a substantial foreshadowing contribution is that of "the popularization of science"—a project that both Massé and Mésange see as a kind of mission.

Jacques Massé introduces himself as the son of a family fallen on hard times when his father, the captain of a merchant ship, is accidentally killed in 1639. He initially tries to train himself for a career in medicine, apprenticed to a physician in Paris, where he makes contact with Jean-Baptiste Morin of the Collège Royal and Marin Mersenne, who involve him in debates regarding René Descartes' key works, then in progress. He subsequently finds another master in Dieppe—where he meets the Wandering Jew, who gives him an account of various curious resurrections following the crucifixion—before obtaining a post as ship's surgeon on a vessel bound for Martinique. A shipwreck strands him in Lisbon, however, where he makes curious discoveries in anatomy, engages in religious controversies with his new master and makes the brief acquaintance of a confidence trickster before joining a Portuguese vessel bound for the East Indies, setting sail in 1644.

Shipwrecked again in the South Atlantic, Massé and many of the crew are stranded on a landmass that is presumably part of Terra Australis, although its latitude and longitude place it somewhere near the Falklands. The castaways begin building themselves accommodation, but Massé soon tires of that, and sets off inland with two comrades. After a difficult journey, during which Massé educates his companions in Copernican theory and they find strange specimens of unknown flora and fauna, he and one of them, the other having been accidentally killed, reach an enclosed valley that is home to a peaceful and orderly society, technologically more primitive than those of Europe, but similarly civilized.

The castaways' advanced technical skills allow them to make a clock for the village where they initially find shelter, news of which attracts the attention of the ruler of the society, who asks them to make one for him too. They make the king various other devices, and Massé begins educating him in science, while becoming interested in the country's religious ideas and the mythology of its origins. The two foreigners run into trouble after manufacturing a watch, when one of the king's several wives, eager to acquire one like it, seduces Massé's companion with dangerous promises that she has no intention of fulfilling.

The ensuing complications result in Massé's companion persuading him to leave the valley, which they have to do clandestinely, and they are pursued along an underground river that eventually leads then back to the world outside. They find the other castaways again, now ensconced in an improvised fort, which they have to defend against marauding savages. Massé undertakes further educational enterprises with his new companions before they are eventually rescued; unfortunately, they are taken to Goa, where Massé falls into the hands of the Inquisition. While imprisoned he hears the story of a converted Chinaman, which occasions much debate about the foundations of Christian faith.

Condemned to the galleys by the Inquisition, Massé is captured by pirates and sold as a slave in North Africa—a career that goes through various phases, and involves him in further religious debates, one of them including an allegory of a beehive in which the clergy are represented as *frélons*—an ambiguous term that can mean both "drones" and "hornets," and retains that double meaning in the allegory. Eventually freed, he encounters the confidence trickster he once met in Lisbon, who gives him a long account of his mischievous life, including an ingenious career as a fake alchemist. Eventually, in 1694, he contrives to return to England, where he locates his long-lost brother, in the bosom of whose family he finally finds a haven of rest.

Pierre Mésange's story is set in a later period, 1639 being the year of his birth. Twenty-six years later, while living contentedly in a Franciscan monastery in Viviers, he falls victim to a deception on the part of one of his brethren, who wants to get rid of him. A friend who volunteers to help unmask the trickster is accidentally stabbed, and Mésange, fearing that he will be blamed, runs away to the Netherlands, where his initial attempts to work as a teacher are thwarted by religious prejudice. He fares better in Leyden, but again gets involved in a stabbing incident, which leads him to flee to Amsterdam, where he witnesses the early phases of the Anglo-Dutch War of 1672.

Mésange eventually signs on with a whaling expedition, which comes to grief in the Arctic ice. He and a small group of companions are cast away on a polar continent, where they find monstrous fauna and a curious society, living underground during the winter night but emerging to the surface in summer, whose extraordinarily elaborate history and legendry go back to pre-Christian times. Like Jacques Massé, Mésange befriends the ruler of the society, and enjoys a long sojourn as a privileged guest, reading the history of the colony, long anecdotal sections of which are inserted into the text. He undertakes to give lectures on the scientific knowledge accumulated by European science, two of which—one on the nature of weight and one on the question of whether a cannonball fired vertically into the air can ever come down again (he "proves," with the aid of his erroneous theory, that it cannot)—are reproduced in full.

The fictitious history of the polar continent involves a few fantastic episodes, although it also includes episodes of exotic imposture, and the most bizarre insertions—including an account of the discovery of a mysterious paradisal underworld—are represented as legends of dubious authenticity. Unfortunately, one of the pupils on his educational course, an ugly female relative of the king, becomes besotted with Mésange, and the only way that he can avoid being forced into marrying her is to claim that he is a eunuch. Exiled regardless to another city, he then becomes besotted himself with the beautiful wife of a neighbor, whom he sets out determinedly to seduce, but the affair ends disastrously.

Exiled yet again to a third city, he meets up with two of the other castaways, and makes plans with them to equip a boat for an attempt to escape through the ice-field—plans that have to be concealed by the strictest secrecy. Eventually, however, the refugees succeed in reaching Iceland, where Mésange hears the first of several interpolated stories as he makes his way back to Denmark, and then various other parts of Europe, before reaching Holland, where he meets his fellow runaway from the monastery, and his odyssey finally comes to an end.

Far more of a variegated portmanteau text than its predecessor, Mésange's own story being mingled with dozens of others, some of which seem ill-fitting—several of those inserted into the history of the polar continent seeming to be stories originally set in the world outside and wedged uncomfortably into an alien context—the second novel exhibits a greater imaginative range, and is not nearly as interested in religious disputes. Although the two scientific lectures it includes can now be seen to be completely false, and most of Mésange's other teachings are suspect too, there is no doubt that Tyssot intended them sincerely. His account of the paradisal Underworld, although it does not belong to its setting, still seems fascinating, precisely because it could not be superseded by actual discoveries, but his account of the northern polar continent, like his account of Terra Australis, is remarkable for its attempted naturalism, and his equipment of both societies with fanciful myths and legends can be seen as aspect of that naturalism.

The accounts of Terra Australis offered by Vairasse and Foigny had also been non-supernatural, but they are manifestly didactic tales of wonder, in which the reader is intended to marvel at the strange societies depicted and to make significant comparisons between their organization and beliefs and Europe's. In Tyssot's narratives, the attitude is markedly different. The societies depicted are interesting because they are different from ours—very different in the second case, because it has been forced to adapt to a hostile and unusual environment—but they are not presented as wonderful, nor is the reader invited to make any satirical comparisons with European society; they are far more akin to exercises in hypothetical ethnography, preserving the exoticism of travelers' tales, while trying to pretend that their extravagance is a matter of honest reporting rather than deliberate distortion. The story of Pierre Mésange is an extraordinary example of a portmanteau text juxtaposing narratives of markedly different kinds, perhaps endeavoring to use the plausibility of some to take the edge of the apparent implausibility of others. Rosenberg, who prefers Jacques Massé's story to Pierre Mésange's on the grounds that it is smoother and more coherent, argues that the second to be published was actually the first to be written, and that might well be true of some of its components, but the whole is probably a belatedly-assembled patchwork in which the author wanted to accommodate as much of his life's production as he could.

Written in the early years of the eighteenth century—whatever the actual publication dates of the two texts were, some elements of the portmanteau texts probably date back at least to 1700, and they were surely works in progress throughout the next two decades—the adventures of Massé and Mésange were produced at a crucial juncture of the "Age of Reason" and the "Age of Enlightenment," and help to illustrate a significant transition in ways of thinking, and the accumulation of knowledge in relation to what Massé or Mésange would call "the system of the world." Tyssot was contemporary with Isaac Newton, and Newton first published the *Principia* in 1687, but neither Massé nor Mésange, whose adventures mostly take place before that date, could have heard of the English philosopher, and it is possible that the author was unaware of his work, which was not popularized in France until after the publication of his own texts. The two voyagers are, in consequence, thinking and acting in advance of the influence that the Newtonian world-view and its associated scientific theories was to have in the history of ideas.

Analogies can easily be found between Tyssot and Daniel Defoe, and one or two other pioneers of the modern novel, but in many respects, his two imaginary voyages were unlike anything written before, and they illustrate the progress of the explorations and innovations that were paving the way for the rapid sophistication of prose narrative technique that was to follow in the next half-century. The second text, via the interest the narrator takes in the interpolated stories, exhibits a strong fascination with the nature of narrative, and the questions of reliability and import inherent in history and storytelling.

Both works, like many other foundation-stones of the modern novel, present themselves as "spiritual autobiographies," whose authors excuse themselves for the apparent narcissism of recording their lives with the suggestion that their humble experiences might provide a useful exemplar of the evolution of moral wisdom. Traditionally, that evolution had progressed in the direction of committed faith and trust in Providence, whose eventual consolidation provided a climax and denouement of sorts, but the whole point of Tyssot's works is that blind faith is a deceptive trap, and trust in Providence, although perhaps psychologically convenient, is essentially hollow. In narrative terms, the fundamental assumption of both texts is that life is ultimately anti-climatic and its only denouement is death; in the meantime, it is long and tortuous, and devoid of meaningful achievement, no matter how much movement and endeavor it involves. That developing awareness in the consciousness of both Jacques Massé and Pierre de Mésange gives the tone of their narratives a remarkable quality of laconism, which reaches an extreme in the manner in which the latter deals with the most horrific incident in his life, not only in the matter-of-fact description of the event itself, but in the way that little or no subsequent reference is made to its physiological or psychological effects.

The main difference between the two texts is the manner of the central characters' self-justifications. Massé is intensely interested in religion, and the puzzles that arise from his intensive reading of the Bible—such questions as whether *Genesis* ought to be construed literally or as a set of parables, and whether its chronology is trustworthy—and although he draws upon his knowledge of philosophy, mathematics and physics to help him work his way through those problems, they always remain his central focus of interest. When he is stranded in the imaginary civilization, although he is interested in all aspects of its culture, his primary focus is on the differences between the natives' religious beliefs and those current in Europe, especially their alternative version of the myth of Adam and Eve, and the influence of that variant myth on their social history and attitudes. He never makes up his own mind, and remains a passive listener to the various alternative views presented to him—although Tyssot obviously knew that the narrative strategy in question would not save his own text from accusations of heresy.

The spoiled Franciscan monk Pierre de Mésange, by contrast, is not primarily interested in religion. Religious bigotry is a perennial fact of life for him, and a perennial source of trouble, but his most intense interests are secular, inclined toward matters of mathematics, physics, cosmology and history. Most of the interpolated stories taken from the written history of the polar continent and the vast majority of the anecdotes related to him by the people he meets elsewhere are devoid of any theological or doctrinal implications. It seems, as Mésange's narrative proceeds, that he becomes gradually less interested in the actual substance of the stories that he hears and tells, and more interested in the psychological quirks that they reflect, as well as the reasons for their ability to seduce the interest of listeners.

Like its predecessor, and not by coincidence, Mésange's account of his life and listening acquires a particular fascination in its later phases with confidence tricks and impostures, perhaps not unconnected with the author's awareness that his texts are themselves impostures: accumulations of artifices embedded within artifices, sometimes stacked two or even three deep. Whether they are parables, fables, speculative fictions or mere tall stories, the tales are always told and carefully enfolded in the interests of prompting the quest for the truth via skepticism, ingenuity and intellectual ambition: the march of reason toward enlightenment. In that context, in the particular era of their publication, the two narratives are fascinating works, deserving of classic status in the evolution of imaginative fiction.

Tyssot published two more books after the adventures of Pierre de Mésange, to which he put his name, both in 1727: *Oeuvres Poétiques Tome I*, intended to be the first of three although it was the only one actually to appear, and *Lettres choisies*. The prefatory essays contained in the first book, framed as letters, and the more extensive letters contained in the second, revealed opinions that some critics thought indecent and atheistic, and Tyssot was apparently unable to continue teaching in Deventer thereafter, as well as being unable to publish any further works. The poems contained in the former volume are all long poetic adaptations of stories themes drawn from the Bible or the Apocrypha, but the full range of Tyssot's poetic endeavors was much broader.

Tyssot's use of the convention of fake title pages illustrates the problems inherent in the procedure. It allowed him to obtain a measure of posthumous celebrity, while permitting him to remain partly hidden during his lifetime, but had he been able to publish freely in his own homeland, he would undoubtedly have published a great deal more. On the other hand, the resentments and personal difficulties that led him to identify with his unfortunate heroes and sympathize strongly with the legendary Wandering Jew and the gypsy genius Beronice were presumably the sharpest spur urging him to write anything at all, and to triumph over all the obstacles making it difficult for him to reach an audience. Perhaps the adventures of Jacques Massé and Pierre de Mésange could not have been written by anyone but a rootless exile hopelessly in search of a viable haven of practical and spiritual rest—in which case, a perverse debt for their originality and inventiveness is owed the author's actual and potential persecutors as well as to his own idiosyncratic intellect.

It is difficult to determine how widely Tyssot's works were read, although the first of them seems to have been familiar to Voltaire and other writers of philosophical fiction, but there is one fantasy of Terra Australis that appears to show their influence very markedly: the anonymous *Relation d'un voyage du pole arctique au pole antarctique par le centre du monde avec la description de ce périlleux passage et des choses merveilleuses et étonnantes qu'on a découvertes sous le pole Antarctique* (tr. as "A Journey from the Arctic Pole to the Antarctic Pole via the Center of the Earth"), first published in Amsterdam in 1721. Its publication in Amsterdam was not the result of a refusal of approval by the royal censors in Paris; they issued certificates of license in 1722 used on three editions issued by different publishers in Paris in 1723, which were presumably pirated from the original. The story was reproduced from one of the latter editions in Garnier's *Voyages imaginaires*.

No one has been able to provide any information regarding the authorship of the text, and it is a much less considerable work in literary terms than Tyssot's novels, being primarily interesting for its eccentricity, in being written mostly in the first person plural and entirely devoid of dialogue. Like Tyssot's works, though, it is clearly a product of an era in which interest in the reports brought back by voyagers to remote and still-unknown lands was shifting from a context of purely economic interests to a context of scientific interest, in which exotic variations of natural history became a fascination in their own right.

To that fundamental shift of interest the author adds the remarkable narrative device of the journey from one pole of the Earth to the other via its center. Although all fantastic voyages are portal fantasies in which the narrative viewpoint is translocated from familiar to exotic surroundings, and many such fantasies introduce material portals in the interests of abridging the transition, very few imagine such an extravagant portal as the one employed in this text.

The work was produced not long after the English astronomer Edmond Halley had published an article, in 1692, arguing that the Earth might well be hollow—a serious speculation based on an error in Isaac Newton's *Principia*, which had miscalculated the relative densities of the Earth and the Moon. Halley was also attempting to account for variations in the Earth's magnetic field by means of a hypothetical internal body contained within the Earth's hollow interior, so his structure of cavities is much more complicated than the simple one imagined in *Relation d'un voyage du pole arctique au pole antarctique par le centre du monde*, but might nevertheless be considered an endorsement of sorts. At any rate, the idea cannot have appeared as absurd then as it does now, and does not disqualify the work from being considered as an early item of *roman scientifique*, albeit a minor one.

When the travelers who have been whaling off the coast of Greenland wake up after their unexpected plunge through the Earth they do not find themselves at the pole itself, but at a latitude of "seventy-one degrees eight minutes" south—ten degrees further south any anyone had actually attained as yet, not actually to be reached until 1774, by James Cook, so the story is explicitly set in unknown territory. Rather than trying to sail north, the crew take their ship closer to the pole, discovering several archipelagoes of islands and sometimes venturing ashore to discover exotic flora and fauna—including "white bears" that occasionally do battle with "sea-cows"—although they are also continually beset by strange meteorological phenomena far more complex than mere aurorae, and also geological upheavals akin to volcanoes. There are warm regions near the pole whose strange climate is explained by means of these meteorological and geological oddities, which are considerably stranger than anything found in other polar romances. The travelers find evidence of previous habitation and civilization in two places, but no living humans.

The narrator's story continues after the ship succeeds in reaching the Cape of Good Hope, adding a further incident of a different character, but it fails to inject any real life into the work, which remains remarkably devoid of conventional literary interest, and is little more than a catalogue of bizarre observations. As such, however, it is sufficiently inventive and peculiar to warrant attention in the context of the early development of fictitious natural history, as a topic of interest in its own right.

3. Cosmic Palingenesis

In terms of the chronology of publication, the next work of interest to the history of *roman scientifique* to appear after Tyssot's was the Chevalier de Mouhy's *Lamekis*, whose eight volumes appeared sporadically between 1735 and 1738 before the whole text was reprinted by Garnier in 1788. It was probably not the next one written however, as the Chevalier de Béthune's **Relation du monde de Mercure** (tr. as *The World of Mercury*), bears all the hallmarks of a posthumous publication, and the evidence of the text suggests that the bulk of it, at least, was composed not long after 1715,

The title page of *Relation du monde de Mercure* claims that it was published in Geneva in 1750. It was subsequently reprinted in Garnier's *Voyages imaginaires*, where it was slotted into the final category of "cabalistic romances" by virtue of its frequent references to alchemy and its deployment of Rosicrucianism and other varieties of allegorical mysticism, although all of them are obviously ironic. The Bibliothèque Nationale catalogue does not attribute any dates to the author, and no writer citing the work has been able to say anything at all about him. The resources of the world wide web provide considerable detail regarding the various branches of the prolific Béthune family, but none of the members cited in the various guides to the French aristocracy who used the title "Le Chevalier de Béthune" was alive in 1750. The most likely candidate to be the author of the text is Marie-Henri de Béthune, who died in Paris on 3 May 1744 at the age of 78.

It is possible that a family member who used a different title in everyday life—most of them had several, the majority being Comtes, Marquises or Ducs—employed a minor one for a signature, just as it is possible that someone who had no connection with the family simply borrowed their name as a pseudonym, but it seems more likely that the publication was simply posthumous, and might well consist of materials cobbled together by a relative, some of which might not belong to the portmanteau as originally envisaged by its author. There are numerous references in the text to individuals active in Louis XIV's court, and the latter's reputation as the Sun King is wryly reflected in the celebrations of the Court of Mercury's Solar Emperor, so it does not seem at all implausible that the text might have been the work of a man born in 1666 into a family prominent at the court of Versailles.

Relation du monde de Mercure does have some resemblance to the works of Tiphaigne de la Roche, which began to appear not long after its publication, in terms of its imaginative scope and, in particular, its eventual supplementation of a fanciful, satirical, Rabelaisian and quasi-allegorical narrative with an earnest exposition of a pseudoscientific thesis that was obviously dear to the author's heart, and it is possible that Tiphaigne took some influence from it, but in philosophical and literary terms, Béthune's text is evidently the product of an earlier era.

The text begins with a preface in which the narrator, while observing the planet Mercury shortly before dawn, is approached by a stranger who offers him the use of a "philosophical microscope" in order to see it more clearly—an instrument so powerful that it permits direct perception of "the stars and their inhabitants...the elementary peoples, the Atoms of Epicurus, and even the movements of the soul and human intentions." The stranger is a Rosicrucian who offers the narrator membership in the Order if he can pass the initiation test, and learn Arabic—for which purpose he hands him the manuscript account of life on Mercury that forms the main text.

The inhabitants of Mercury are introduced as winged humanoids of a stature less than that of a five-year-old child, although for much of the story, especially the many interpolated anecdotes included in Part Two, scant reference is made to their wings or their small size, and they might as well be human—and, indeed, as in the adventures of Pierre Mésange, one suspects that some of the interpolations were originally Earth-set stories that were belatedly wedged into the alien context. There is, however, not the slightest trace of Tyssot's attempted naturalism or laconism; Béthune's account is much more self-consciously fantastic, and several of the interpolations are allegories, some pretentiously earnest and other flamboyantly comical. Alongside the humanoid population of Mercury, the Emperor is a superpowered shapeshifting native of the Sun, who has a complex system of choosing his Empresses, and populations of "Paracelsian" elementals flourish—salamanders provide much of the society's technology—

while intelligent fauna, including fish as well as the more useful birds, provide much of the domestic service.

Part One of the story, consisting of seventeen short chapters, is a relatively coherent account of the various aspects of Mercurian life and society, following a pattern familiar in utopian fiction in a deliberately parodic and sometimes outrightly farcical fashion. Part Two is much more various and soon becomes disorganized; from chapter IX ("On Few Singularities of the Planet") onwards it begins to resemble a patchwork partially collated from different sources. The emphasis shifts markedly in the final chapters ostensibly dealing with "Medicine on Mercury," which include a diatribe against blood-letting treatments and offer an elaborate theory of disease that supposedly proves that such treatments do more harm than good. The chapters in question abandon any pretence of relevance to the world of Mercury before the rather abrupt conclusion of the text.

The author acknowledges in his text the influence of Fontenelle's *Entretiens*, and one of the narrative's many functions is to extend the long-running argument relating to the plurality of worlds on to a much vaster stage than Fontenelle's, or the one depicted by Huygens in *Kosmotheoros*. To the notion that God would not have made a universe full of stars and planets without populating all of them, Béthune adds an elaborate system of linkage involving a complex and highly ordered system of cosmic reincarnations—what would later be called palingenesis, although Béthune was writing some time before Charles Bonnet's *Palingénésie philosophique* [Philosophical Palingenesis] (1769) popularized that term in the context of the soul's survival after death.

Like Dante before him, Béthune imagines the progression of earthly souls to other worlds as a matter of organization on a moral scale, but he sees the other worlds in question in a much more modern fashion, and his moral scale is dynamic, in that souls are reincarnated indefinitely, in the interests of a gradual ascent of a scale of moral perfection, not only on the different worlds of the solar system but far beyond. Béthune's work was published more than a hundred years ahead of Camille Flammarion's repopularization of that notion in the classic *Lumen*, on which it probably had some influence; Flammarion included an extensive description of Béthune's work, which he had read in the Garnier edition, in his study of *Les Mondes imaginaires et les mondes réels*. Although Béthune's work cannot compete with Flammarion's for the sophistication of its thinking with regard to the relativity of space and time and the ecology of adaptation to alien environments, it does have an edge in terms of the inordinate complexity of its palingenetic schema.

Although it is innocent of any but the most rudimentary evolutionary thinking, and its notions of chemistry and physics are primitive and vague even by the standards of its time of publication, *Relation du monde de Mercure* is nevertheless possessed of an insistent sarcastic skepticism, which makes it one of the few "Creationist fantasies" entirely unhampered by any kind of religious dogma. In developing the elaborate secondary creation of his world of Mercury,

Béthune sets out to shape the kind of world that God might have built had he been somewhat more kindly inclined toward his creations than the existential situation of Earthly humans suggests. His description of that world is a tongue-in-cheek exercise, with many elements of pure comedy, and his account of life there is far closer in spirit to the land of Cockayne than to any kind of political eutopia, but that certainly does not rob the thinking behind it of any ingenuity or zest—quite the contrary, in fact. The elaborate metaphysics might well be intended as a joke, but it is impressive nevertheless in its cosmic scope

Seen as a whole, the work is certainly disorganized, but the fact that it seems to have been written in fits and bursts, probably over a long period of time, in response to a series of disparate whims, with sections ranging in kind from lewd anecdote to ponderous allegory, undoubtedly encouraged the author to let his fancy fly freer that it could ever have done if he had attempted a more focused narrative with something resembling a plot or a story-line.

Because we now know that the author's pet medical theory is pure nonsense (as were all medical theories in the eighteenth century) the concluding section of the text is bound to seem a trifle tedious to modern readers, although its negative component, attacking the then-conventional treatment of bleeding, is equally bound to attract sympathy—but that section at least has the merit of being left until last, and the lavish compensation provided in advance is more than adequate in terms of its originality, its adventurousness and, especially, its sheer bizarrerie. In particular, the description of the aerial conflict between the defenders of Mercury's Great Mountain and monstrous invaders from a sunspot—imagined as a fragment of "crust" expelled from the sun—is triumphantly eccentric, a match in its colorful extravagance for any space battle featured in the great tradition of twentieth-century space opera.

Whoever he was, if he was not, in fact, the late Marie-Henri de Béthune, the Chevalier de Béthune could not begin to compete with Voltaire as a literary stylist, and is inferior to Tiphaigne de la Roche in terms of his narrative coherency, but his text was a significant precursor of the new kind of *conte philosophique* that they developed, and he had a advantage on both of them in terms of the reach of his imagination; his scheme of cosmic palingenesis remains the ultimate model in terms of its organizational planning and sheer bravado. The book would be remarkable for that alone, although there are numerous other rewarding nuggets tucked away in the untidy folds of its sprawling patchwork. As "utopian novels" go, *Relation du monde de Mercure* is a long way from the serious end of the spectrum, and it would be difficult to find many works less earnest in their descriptions of a supposedly ideal society. If it really were the case, however, that immortal human souls could eventually live alongside Paracelsian elementals, not only on all the worlds of our Cartesian Vortex, but all the worlds of any other Vortex that they eventually decided to visit, it is difficult to believe that they could ever find a world where the living was easier and more fun than Béthune's Mercury.

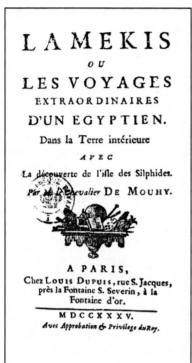

L A M E K I S

o u

LES VOYAGES

EXTRAORDINAIRES

D'UN EGYPTIEN.

Dans la Terre intérieure

A V E C

La découverte de l'isle des Silphides.

Par le Chevalier DE MOUHY.

A PARIS,

Chez LOUIS DUPUIS, rue S. Jacques,
près la Fontaine S. Severin, à la
Fontaine d'or.

M DCC XXXV.

Avec Approbation & Privilege duRoy.

The spirit of pure amusement found in the greater part of *Relation de monde de Mercure* is also found in ***Lamekis, Les Voyages extraordinaires d'un Égyptien dans la Terre Intérieure avec la Découverte de l'île des Sylphides*** [Lamekis: The Extraordinary Voyages of an Egyptian in the Interior World, with the Discovery of the Isle of the Sylphides] which comes nearer than other imaginative texts of the era to being a pure adventure story devoid of any philosophical pretentions at all. Its author, who styled himself Charles de Fieux, Chevalier de Mouhy (1701-1784), although it is extremely doubtful that he was really entitled to the *particule* or the knighthood, was a prolific writer who appears to have suddenly adopted that vocation in 1735, primarily to make money, and might be seen as one of the great pioneers of literary hackwork.

Several of Mouhy's multi-volume novels, including *Lamekis*, were effectively written as serials, each volume being issued separately with no decision made as to whether more would be added until they sold enough to warrant it, and individual volumes routinely being provided with teasing endings in a Scheherazadian spirit. His more conventional texts were often given titles similar to those of successful works, although *Lamekis* is a conspicuous exception, and its contents are so unconventional that one is tempted to think of it as a lapse into pure self-indulgence. It was, however, successful by his standards; the first volume, published in Paris in 1735, was followed by two more, from a different publisher, in 1737, and a further four in 1738, the last few bearing precautionary title-pages proclaiming publication in The Hague, although there is nothing in their content that seems likely to have attracted condemnation on religious or political grounds.

Fieux appears to have been perennially in need of money, and, having taken up the literary profession, he approached Voltaire touting for work, initially as an applauder during performances of his plays and increasingly as a secretary, literary agent and financial manager—functions he fulfilled between 1736 and 1740, until Voltaire suddenly took against him, apparently thinking him guilty of some treason, and sacked him. He claimed to have worked thereafter as an agent of Charles Fouquet, Duc de Belle-Isle and Maréchal de France, but all his claims have to be taken with a pinch of salt.

Mouhy might, however, have been responsible for one famous literary myth for which he is not routinely given credit: the man in the iron mask. Although the fictitious allegation that the mysterious prisoner in question wore a iron mask is routinely credited to Voltaire, the investigation of the origins of the story carried out in the nineteenth century by "P. L. Jacob the Bibliophile" (Paul Lacroix)—a close associate of Alexandre Dumas, one of the chief promoters of the myth—acknowledges that it might have been spawned by "a detestable novel by the Chevalier de Mouhy," issued anonymously in 1746, allegedly in The Hague, entitled *Le Masque de fer, ou les aventures admirables du père et du fils*. The novel in question is an early specimen of what later come to be known as a *roman de cape-et-d'épée*—a swashbuckling tale of derring-do. It remains uncertain as to whether Mouhy got the idea of the iron mask from Voltaire or whether Voltaire got it from him.

Because of its subtitle, *Lamekis* is often erroneously listed as a "hollow earth" story, Garnier having made that mistake when advertising the reprint in *Voyages imaginaires*, but in fact, most of the adventures of the eponymous priest of ancient Egypt take place above ground, in fictitious realms bordering the empire of the legendary Queen Semiramis. Most of those settings are far more mundane than the isle of the sylphs, which only features briefly as a setting, although it is the homeland of the philosopher Delahal, who pops up occasionally not only to pester Lamekis but also, in one eccentric section, to interact with the author. The most exotic episodes, however, do take place in subterranean caverns that are home to the loathsome worm-men, most of them in a convoluted story narrated to Lamekis by Motocoa, one of his various exotic informants. Giant birds sometimes provide a convenient means of travel between realms, and a super-powered dog also plays a crucial role in the embedded narratives, but the chaotic plot never looks like achieving any kind of coherency or any kind of serious philosophical implication.

The novel is perhaps best regarded as a remote ancestor of modern pulp fantasy, but if one sets aside literary disdain, that is not an unremarkable achievement. Its relevance to the developing tradition of *roman scientifique* is marginal, but, like Béthune's account of Mercury, it exhibits an imaginative exuberance and delight in exotic invention that was to prove stimulating and salubrious in works harboring more earnest intentions. Although clearly taking considerable inspiration from Galland, it does strive, however ineffectually, to cultivate a kind of plausibility derived from the supposed naturalization of at least some of its wonders.

4. The Secrets of Generation

Charles-François Tiphaigne de La Roche (1722-1774) was the writer of extended *contes philosophiques* who most obviously warrants representation as a proto-scientist. A physician by profession, he produced several entirely earnest treatises on natural philosophy and agricultural science, and he imported a considerable amount of material from that work into his satirical criticisms of contemporary French society, some of which are broadly comical while others are exploratory adventures in the realm of ideas.

Tiphaigne's first book, published in 1747, was *L'Amour dévoilé, ou le système des sympathistes* [Love Unveiled; or, The Theory of Sympathism], whose extended subtitle claims that it will explain the origin of "inclinations, sympathies, aversions, antipathies, etc." It belongs to the category of accidental scholarly fantasies, in that the author presumably intended his arguments seriously, although hindsight informs us that there is not an atom of truth in them. It was, however, a bold project for its time, even though it posed no challenge to political or religious authority. A text attempting a scientific explanation of sexual attraction, despite such august predecessors as Plato's *Symposium*—Tiphaigne was a great admirer of Plato—had the potential to be seen as suspect, even on the part of a devoutly religious author who went on to be loudly outspoken in his condemnation of the licentiousness of much contemporary literature.

Tiphaigne did not sign the book, publishing it under the pseudonym "l'A. de P***," the first item of the signature (an abbreviation of Abbé) suggesting that it was by a Churchman. The P might not stand for anything at all—Tiphaigne was a profligate inventor of unmeaningful names—but if it was imagined to stand for anything, the likeliest contender is Plato. As well as being one of the most important Greek thinkers, Plato was also one of the most playful—or at least, one of those whose playfulness shows through in his surviving works, albeit not always obviously in the eyes of his more humorless partisans and critics. Tiphaigne fully appreciated that element of playfulness in Plato's most adventurous dialogues, although he did not appreciate its presence nearly as much in the romances of Voltaire, whom he loathed righteously. There is a sense in which Tiphaigne's works can be seen as an attempt to reclaim the tradition of the *conte philosophique*, along with some of its modern apparatus, to serve what he considered be the right causes, as opposed to Voltaire's supposedly-mistaken ones.

Like Voltaire, however, Tiphaigne felt perfectly free to employ "celestial spirits" as literary devices, borrowing eclectically from Galland and *Le Comte de Gabalis*. He always strove to make it obvious that he was doing so playfully, with no prejudice to serious religious beliefs—an effort that gives a distinctive farcical flavor to his first *conte philosophique, Amilec, ou la graine d'hommes* (tr. as "Amilec or the Human Seed that Serves to Populate the Planets") first published in a single volume in 1753.

Like Tiphaigne's earlier book, *Amilec* was published under the pseudonym L'A. de P***, and its title page claimed that it had been published "à Luneville, aux dépens de Chr. Hugene, à l'enseigne de Fontenelle" [in Lunaville, at the expense of Chr(istiaan) Huygens, at the Sign of Fontenelle]. This device was a parody of the fake title pages standard in suspect works—the volume makes no secret of actually having been published in Paris by Michel Lambert—but there was probably a precautionary element to the parody, and Tiphaigne's later works in the same vein probably required their equally farcical disguises.

The story begins with the narrator in his study, becoming impatient with a treatise on "generation"—which is to say, the biology of reproduction—whose conjectural explanations he finds woefully inadequate. He then goes to sleep and is visited in a dream by the eponymous individual, who offers him an explanation of reproductive physiology in plants and animals in which hidden mechanisms are represented as "génies," here more reminiscent of Gallandesque djinn than the kind of spirits described in Latin as genii. Amilec is one of them, and he has a great deal to say about the collection and distribution of human "seed," not merely on Earth but all the other planets orbiting the suns of the Milky Way.

Having served previous tours of duty on Mercury and Venus, Amilec is about to move on from Earth to Mars, but before then he takes the narrator on a tour of his facility, explaining the problems that arise in sorting different species of human seed, and the advantages that can be derived from the interplanetary transplantation of seed, in the interests of moral progress. Between the comic and satirical episodes, he offers a speculative account of the biology of reproduction that is presumably meant seriously, the comic aspects of the story being intended as sugar-coating to help readers swallow it.

As with the earlier volume, this essay would now qualify as pure scholarly fantasy, although it does anticipate some aspects of cell theory. Tiphaigne was writing at a time when compound microscopes were still in their infancy, cursed by chromatic aberration, while the new era of analysis that would help to elucidate the problems he was addressing was still in the future. From the modern viewpoint, therefore, even the serious aspect of Tiphaigne's reproductive theory, let alone his satirical extrapolation of the manner in which "human seed" serves to populate other worlds, seems primitive and silly—but it is not unintelligent, give the paucity of the data with which Tiphaigne had to work, and its satirical frame has an admirable zest and some telling humorous observations.

Amilec proved sufficiently popular to be swiftly reprinted, and an augmented third edition was published in 1754, in three volumes. That form of publication was presumably a commercial ploy, because the augmenting text makes only the feeblest pretense to be a continuation of *Amilec*, and the second volume has a new title page, strongly implying that it was initially intended to be issued as a separate text. The sequel in question is *Zamar, député à la lune par Amilec,*

Grand-Maître de la Manufacture des Graines d'Hommes, augmentée de la Relation du Voyage d'un Sublunaire [Zamar, delegated to the Moon by Amilec, Supervisor of the Manufacture of Human Seed, augmented by an Account of the Voyage of a Sublunary] (tr. as "Zamar, Amilec's Delegate to the Moon"). The third volume also has a title-page of its own, but the only variation from the title-page of the second volume is its billing as *Suite de Zamar* [Zamar Continued], which is followed by the same supplementary material.

Unlike *Amilec*, which features a single essay with a relatively coherent fantastic frame, *Zamar* is a disorderly patchwork of texts, presumably written separately, which are stitched together by an exceedingly slight and wholly tokenistic frame narrative. Amilec does not appear in it at all, and Zamar only features as the author of a satirical letter about the accidental seeding of the moon and its comical social consequences, disappearing thereafter until he makes a brief personal appearance at the very end to close the narrative. In the meantime, the dreaming protagonist of *Amilec* undertakes a voyage to Venus, where he listens to a series of lectures on political and legal reform, and then goes to the Moon, where he gives a long lecture to his "son" about the iniquities of contemporary life in France. The most interesting part of *Zamar*, from a modern perspective, is an amusing utopian satire tacked on to the end of the text, where it is credited to a lunar writer and separately titled as "An Account of Nitramia and Nautopia."

Tiphaigne published two books in 1759: the essay-collection *Bigarrures philosophiques* [A Philosophical Medley], and a treatise on *Questions relative à l'agriculture et la nature des plantes* [Questions related to agriculture and the nature of plants]. The former features a brief visionary fantasy, "Voyage aux Limbes" [Journey to Limbo], which is in much the same vein as the earlier imaginary voyages, but the two-volume work with which he followed up those two books in 1760, *Giphantie*, is much more substantial.

Giphantie remains Tiphaigne's best-known book and is far more coherent than *Zamar*, or even *Amilec*, even though it is something of a patchwork that might have taken aboard some previously-written fragments; its narrative frame is, however, considerably more robust than that of *Zamar*. "Giphantie" is an anagram of Tiphaigne, and the imaginary landscape it presents is effectively a map of the author's ideas. The book was, however, unsigned even by a pseudonym, the only information on its bald title-page, save for the title itself, being a terse statement of a fictitious place of publication: "à Babylon." In the text, "Babylon" is clearly Paris, so the attribution to that place of publication has an element of double bluff about it.

The narrator of the story introduces himself in the preface as an inveterate traveler, and the story he is about to tell as the only adventure he has had worth recording for posterity. After getting lost in a sandstorm in Africa and falling unconscious, the narrator wakes up on the edge of a magical plain. A mysterious Voice explains that it is a land given to the elemental spirits before humans were created in Eden, and where the spirits that work hard on Earth, supervising the elements for the preservation of human life, take their vacations.

The Voice explains the nature of that virtuous labor to the narrator, and shows him a Globe whose map of the world consists of countless channels of communication, by means of which the elementals can overhear everything happening elsewhere on the planet's surface. One of the snatches of speech the narrator is enabled to overhear thereby is an unfavorable critique of Rousseau's *Julie*. The Voice then provides him with a magic mirror that enables him to see as well as hear, and thus obtain a broad overview of the whole human race—also unfavorable—before reverting to exemplary visions on a smaller scale.

It is while further sophisticating this process of eavesdropping that the text comes up with an original literary device that brings the text closer to the tradition of *roman scientifique* whose foundations it helped to lay. Requiring a synoptic view of human history, in order that the author can comment on its broad shape—in a vein closer to lamentation than satire—Tiphaigne hit on the idea of presenting a series of *tableaux* [pictures] "painted" by light itself, and offers a detailed description of a liquid substance that can be used to coat a mirror, so that if it is then placed in a dark room to dry out it will preserve the last image that formed on its surface: an "invention" that won him a place of honor in modern histories of photography.

After using that device to view a synoptic history of France, in a perspective markedly akin to Montesquieu's, the traveler's guided tour takes him to witness the vegetal productions of three pips salvaged by the elementals from the discarded fraction of Adam's fatal apple, and the compensations that they are enable to offer to fallen humankind via the elementals. The produce of the third pip, the Fantastic Tree, offers prophetic leaves, which provide the narrator with the substance of an "Epistle to the Europeans" and various fantastic technologies, including a "thermometer" and "lenses" whose functions are more metaphorical than literal, after which he returns by a subterranean route to the mundane world,

Tiphaigne evidently intended *Giphantie* to be a more serious work than the fantastic elements of *Amilec* and *Zamar*, more allegory than satire, although his irrepressible sarcasm and scathing wit come continually to the fore regardless of any attempts he might have made to hold them in check. It is nevertheless a relatively relaxed and earnest work by comparison with the volume with which he followed it up in 1761: *L'Empire des zaziris sur les humains, ou le zazirocratie* (tr. as "Zazirocracy; or, The Empire of the Zaziris over Humankind"), which seethes with barely-suppressed wrath. The volume has a page prior to the main title-page, which gives the title simply as *Zazirocratie*, and it seems likely, given the pattern of his previous titles, that that was Tiphaigne's original title, before he was persuaded to modify it. As with the previous volume, the main title page carries no indication of authorship and describes its place of publication and the name of its publisher as "*à Pekin, chez Dsmgtlfpqxz.*"

Although it is considerably briefer than the other volumes of Tiphaigne's work—which are not very long themselves by modern standards—*Zazirocratie* is also considerably denser, and covers a lot of ground, assisted by the fact that it does not attempt to simulate a *conte*, but simply consists of a kind of rant. It does not have the elegance or organizational complexity of *Giphantie*, but it makes up in sheer fervor what it lacks in gloss, and makes an interesting contrast with the earlier work in the way that it substitutes maliciously teasing Elementary Spirits for the gentle and benevolent ones featured in the earlier satires. It credits all human faults and disappointments to their malevolent practical jokes, tacitly arguing that such an explanation makes more sense than the supposition that we are solely responsible for our own sorry mess. In his *Encyclopédie* Pierre Versins describes *Zazirocratie* as "adorable," but that judgment has the advantage of historical distance; its contemporary readers must have found it an uncomfortable book to read, and it is still sharp enough for its splenetic thrust to be a trifle painful.

Tiphaigne's final utopian satire, *Histoire des Galligènes, or Mémoires de Duncan* [The History of the Galligenes; or, Duncan's Memoirs] (1765) is more reminiscent of the accounts of Nitramia and Nautopia appended to *Zamar* than to *Zazirocratie*, and seems to represent a mellowing on the author's part. He published his second book on agriculture in the same year, but then seems to have retired from literary activity, although he was still relatively young—his entire literary career, as presently mapped by subsequently bibliographers, only extended from his mid-twenties to his mid-thirties, although he did not survive his mid-forties, and might have done more had he not died so young.

Brief and restricted as it was by comparison with that of his multitalented *bête noire* Voltaire, however, Tiphaigne's career nevertheless deserves recognition for its breadth, its ambition and its wit. As a practicing scientist, he was not sufficiently far ahead of his time to make a very substantial contribution to the anticipation of future scientific developments, but the same is true of all the contributors to the prehistory of *roman scientifique*, and he was sufficiently of that time to make a significant contribution to the rebirth of the *conte philosophique*; for that reason, as well as for the particular artistry of *Giphantie* and *Zazirocratie*, he deserves to be remembered and applauded.

Tiphaigne de la Roche's interest in the problem of generation was confined to the mysteries of reproductive biology, but his accounts of fanciful reproductive mechanisms and his overviews of human history and endeavor do contain an awareness of patterns of change over time that might have drawn him into ideas that he would certainly have considered heretical had he not stubbornly refused to go there. He was probably not unaware that other people had already gone there, but he would have had very little opportunity to acquaint himself with what they had found. One such report did, however, appear alongside his utopian satires, cast, like *Giphantie*, as a traveler's tale whose narrator listens to a long account of the way of the world offered to him by an authoritative Voice, here cast as an Indian philosopher named Telliamed.

The work that eventually emerged was *Telliamed, ou Entretiens d'un philosophe indien avec un missionaire françois sur la diminution de la mer, la formation de la terre, l'origine de l'homme, etc.* (1748; tr. in 1750 as *Telliamed; or, Discourses Between and Indian Philosopher and a French Missionary on the Diminution of the Sea, the Formation of the Earth, the Origin of Men and Animals and Other Curious Subjects relating to Natural History and Philosophy*) had actually been written much earlier, the author's surviving notes having been produced between 1692 and 1718 and collated into manuscripts between 1722 and 1732. Their author, Benoît de Maillet (1656-1738), was a career diplomat who had been the French Consul General in Cairo between 1692 and 1708 before moving on to Leghorn and then, from 1715 until his retirement, the Levant. An amateur geologist, he had spent much of his spare time studying the local rocks, and had gradually drawn conclusions regarding their formation and antiquity that contrasted very sharply with Catholic dogma regarding the history of the Earth and its chronology, as derived from the early books of the Bible.

Maillet concluded from his observations that the rocks he was studying were sedimentary, having been laid down over long periods of time on the beds of seas that had long disappeared, and generalized that thesis to suggest that all of the Earth's continents consisted of sedimentary rocks that had been gradually exposed as waters that had once covered the entire surface of the Earth had diminished. One corollary of that theory was that the Earth's surface must have changed drastically over time at a pace estimable by calculation from rates of sedimentation (which suggested an approximate age for the Earth of two billion years, much greater than the six thousand preferred by Biblical chronologists, although that calculation was left out of the published versions).

A second corollary of Maillet's thesis was that life on land had initially emerged from the sea, life-forms colonizing the newly-emerged continents by gradual adaptation to the circumstance and the opportunities it provided. That process of transformism (the term "evolution" was still a long way from acquiring its modern meaning) had, in his view, gradually produced all extant animal species, including humans, from fishy ancestors. That idea, even more than the first, ran directly contrary to the orthodox version of the religious doctrine of creation.

Maillet left *Telliamed* unpublished when he died, but entrusted it to a priest, Abbé Jean-Baptiste Le Mascrier, with instructions to attempt to produce a version of it that might be acceptable to the Church. The task was plainly impossible, but Le Mascrier tried heroically—although his efforts, inevitably, only earned him the ire of modern commentators appalled by the extent of his bowdlerization—and did eventually publish the book, ten years after the author's death, in 1748, in Amsterdam. Two further editions followed, the second in 1749 bearing a title page claiming to have been printed in Basel, and the third in 1755 claiming to have been published in The Hague, although it was certainly printed in Paris by Nicolas Duchesne.

The later editions, especially the third, restored some of the text that Le Mascrier had removed from the author's manuscripts—probably with the Abbé's assistance—but not the whole of it; a full restoration of the most sensitive transformist material was not carried out until the 1960s. The third edition did, however, allow the outline of the transformist argument to be seen, and to cause offense, even to Voltaire, let alone the Church. That edition carries a fulsome dedication to Cyrano de Bergerac, probably added by Duchesne, as a further apologetic stratagem, tacitly representing the book as a fantasy.

The text represents the fictitious missionary's conversations with the Indian philosopher (whose name is, of course, an inversion of the author's) as having taken place in Cairo in 1715 and 1716 and written down by the former in 1724. The first volume of the third edition begins with an account of Maillet's life and a long apologetic preface by Le Mascrier defending his ideas against the suspicion of heresy. The first of the six days of conversation begins with Telliamed's account of investigations made by his grandfather of processes of sedimentation, with the aid of divers equipped with a specially-devised "Lanterne"—a kind of diving bell—which facilitates comparisons between the sea bed and nearby land, helping to explain the fact that seashells could be found embedded in the continental rocks all the way from the shore to mountain tops. The following days, including the fourth, which begins volume two, offer a detailed account of different varieties of sedimentary rocks and their various formations, including a commentary on recent discoveries of more advanced fossil animals—including human relics embedded in stone—augmented with theoretical arguments drawing conclusions from the data, considering various possible objections to them and dismissing them.

The conversation of the fifth day deals with cosmological matters, concluding with a long discussion of the plurality of worlds, and the probable habitability of the worlds of the solar system, drawing extensively on Huygens but also mentioning Cyrano, and discusses the possible extermination of the Earth's inhabitants by virtue of the further diminution and eventual exhaustion of its surface waters, although it also considers the possibility of the renewal of its waters by some cosmic means, and the possibility that the human race might endure until the sun dies, and even wonders whether the Earth might somehow find a new situation thereafter in another vortex.

The sixth day's conversation begins by addressing "The origin of humans and animals, and the propagation of species by *semences* [seminations]," with a preliminary insistence on the part of the philosopher that he is not attributing the origin of life on land to a process of "blind chance." After token references to ancient authorities, the argument moves on swiftly to logical arguments, including the anatomical resemblances between terrestrial animals—especially birds— and fish, and the facility of passing from water to air, making much of such air-breathing marine species as seals. That forms a prelude to a long account of reported sightings of "marine humans"—mermaids and the like.

The discussion then passes on to "savage humans," including "oran-outans," humans with tails, giants, etc., in order to support the argument that humans could have emerged from the sea by a process of transformation beginning with fish. Further support is added by the consideration of reproductive physiology and the similarities between processes of fecundation" in marine and terrestrial animals, and arguing that *semences* [seminations] widely distributed in sea water by marine species might also serve for the production of new species capable of terrestrial adaptation. The section concludes with an unconvincing assertion that this account of the origin of terrestrial life is not inconsistent with *Genesis*. The volume then concludes with various supplementary documents.

The new edition produced in the 1960s from Maillet's manuscripts demonstrates the vast extent to which the 1755 edition still differed from what Maillet actually wrote, and how much more detailed his transformist thesis and the arguments supporting it were, but all that the readers of the eighteenth century could read was the drastically simplified and censored version. It is not entirely surprising that Voltaire was not impressed by it, but nor is it surprising that some other readers accepted it as a startling revelation.

Telliamed is far more of a scholarly fantasy than a work of fiction; the dialogue framework is tokenistic and apart from the description of the invention and usage of the Lanterne there is no story component. The addition of the dedication placing it in the same genre as *L'Autre Monde* is a mere ploy. Nevertheless, the work is of more than marginal relevance to the development of *roman scientifique*, primarily because of its influence on Restif de la Bretonne and the encouragement it gave him to work out a much more elaborate version of the scholarly fantasy, making very extensive use of fiction as a means of that elaboration, but also because of references to is in several other significant works of the eighteenth and nineteenth centuries.

5. Lunar Follies

The third edition of *Amilec*, which added *Zamar* to the original, picked up the old notion of the Moon as a repository of Earthly follies so memorably exemplified by Ariosto. That example probably helped to restimulate the tradition of lunar satires, to which several significant works were added in the latter half of the century, each of them innovative in various ways and all of them unrepentantly eccentric.

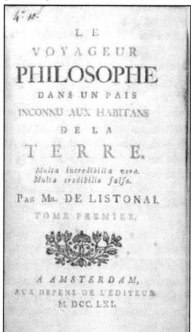

Le Voyageur philosophe dans un pais inconnu aux habitans de la terre (1761; tr. as *The Philosophical Voyager in a Land Unknown to the Inhabitants of the Earth*) signed "Monsieur de Listonai," was published in two volumes, ostensibly in Amsterdam, "at the expense of the editor," in 1761. It was placed on the Catholic Church's *Index Librorum Prohibitorum*, and "Monsieur de Listonai" presumably felt honored, given that his ostensible intention was to provoke thought in stagnant minds, and the ban placed him firmly in the august company of the *philosophes* and *Encyclopedistes*.

According to the Bibliothèque Nationale catalogue, "Monsieur de Listonai" was the pseudonym of one Daniel Jost de Villeneuve, who is credited with involvement in two other texts held by the library, one of them an essay on Italian opera, for which three authors are credited, and the other a printed version of an operetta, *Zephir and Fleurette* (1750, by Charles-François Panard, Pierre Laujon and Charles-Simon Favart), for whose first publication Jost paid, apparently because he had modified it slightly when he put on and starred in a production in Besançon in the south of France. The attribution is based on penciled notes added to manuscripts of two of the works in question.

In one sense, the extra information does not add a great deal to our knowledge of the works, as "Daniel Jost de Villeneuve" seems to have made no significant impression on history, and those penciled notes probably constitute everything known about him, as well as about "Monsieur de Listonai." The only potentially-significant item of information we have about the person who wrote *Le Voyageur philosophe*, therefore, is that he was an actor, although probably an amateur rather than a professional.

In fact, it would not have been too difficult to draw that inference from the text of the book, given the extent and the nature of the attention paid therein to the theater and the writing of plays. The author's footnotes demonstrate that he was an assiduous student of Horace's *Ars Poetica*, not merely as an enthusiastic Latinist but as someone who was intimately concerned with the problems and methods of dramatic construction. He agrees forcefully with Denis Diderot that a new theatrical genre of drama might and ought to break down the artificial barriers imposed by the rigorous division of tragedy and comedy and the regulatory impositions of Classicism. The text also reveals, however, that Listonai had a wide range of other interests and concerns, including an intense, if slightly eccentric, interest in Newtonian physics, an even more eccentric interest in natural history, and some highly idiosyncratic views on medicine and hygiene. Listonai demonstrates that the ambition to encyclopedic knowledge was not confined to scholars, and although he did not have the intelligence, let alone the wit and talent, of Voltaire, there is a sense in which that very weakness makes his attempt to venture into similar literary territory interesting.

Most of the writers who followed Voltaire's example in penning *contes philosophiques* did so with an agenda that imported a measure of narrow focus into their works, no matter how much they might digress as the Muse moved them. Listonai was, however, exceedingly curious, far more interested in asking questions than peddling theses, in spite of a couple of bees buzzing around his bonnet. As a result, *Le Voyageur philosophe* not only presents a broad spectrum of interests but does so, for the most part, in a spirit of open-minded enquiry that offers a useful insight into the kind of illumination to which an Enlightenment mind of relatively moderate scope might seek.

As with *Telliamed*, the straightforwardly fictional aspects of *Le Voyageur philosophe* are slight, but the text is by no means a scholarly fantasy. After a dedication addressed to himself and a long reflective preface, the narrator describes how, while visiting Niagara Falls, he came across a strange diaphanous spacecraft crowded with interplanetary tourists, somewhat reminiscent of the gossamer-rigged flying ships occasionally featured in *contes de fées*, and hitched a ride to the Moon. Unfortunately, he finds the civilization on the Earth-facing hemisphere of the satellite a mere reflection of ours, and regrets having bothered to make the trip, until he meets Arzame, a traveler from the far side, who tells him that things are very different there, and takes him via a tunnel through the center of the Moon to see for himself.

That is the whole of the action; the rest of the text details the narrator's observations of "Selenite" society, his conversations with Arzame on philosophical matters, and the books he reads on the Moon. Although he does pay attention to the utopian features of Selenite social organization, he is far more interested in their scientific knowledge, which he attempts to summarize as early as chapter III, while chapter IV moves on to metaphysics. Many of the opinions expressed in the text are defiantly unorthodox, although the author carefully attributes some of them to secondary sources, including a book he reads that mounts a sterling defense of despotism, on the grounds that it is more likely to generate and maintain human happiness than a libertarian society.

There is an interesting chapter in which the narrator visits a "cabinet of curiosities" in which everything lost on Earth is accumulated, after the fashion of Astolfo's discoveries, and another comprising an account of another Selenite treatise offering a theory of "intellectual attraction" ostensibly derived from the Newtonian theory of gravity, but the most starling of all the elements of the patchwork is a chapter on "Discoveries to be Made on Earth," which imagines a speech given in the Académie des Sciences in the twenty-fourth century, detailing the new technologies invented in the interim.

Although the list is somewhat short of predictive hits, the speech is certainly not lacking in ingenuity—its account of aerial travel is particularly bizarre—but the wonder is that it was done it all in an environment where there was no such thing as futuristic fiction, save for the peculiar affectation employed by Jacques Guttin in *Épigone, histoire du siècle futur* [Epigone, a Story of a Future Century] (1659), in which a conventional neo-Romantic adventure story is freed from any burden of historical responsibility by removing it into a hypothetical world called "the future" even though the known world does not feature in its imaginary history. Louis-Sébastien Mercier would not publish his dream of future Paris for another ten years, but he would derive his "future" simply by removing the things he hated from the Paris of the present day. Listonai, by contrast, firmly adopted the principle set out by Francis Bacon in *New Atlantis* and neglected for more than a century: that an improved society would be able to apply advanced scientific knowledge to the production of new technologies capable of transforming it drastically.

Presumably, writers prior to Listonai had been prepared to believe that, but none had ever grasped the nettle of actually trying to anticipate what those technological innovations might be, and what effects they might have on society. Listonai does not do it well, by modern standards, but those modern standards have been set by thousands of attempts made in the interim, while Listonai did not even have the advantage of inspiration by the robust philosophy of progress promoted in the latter half of the century by Jacques Turgot and the Marquis de Condorcet. Although it is technically possible for him to have heard the former lecture at the Sorbonne, where Turgot first exposed his "Tableau philosophique des progrès de l'esprit humain" [Philosophical Account of the Progress of the Human Mind] in 1850, the overwhelming probability is that he had never heard of either.

Although Listonai's futuristic chapter is not very long, and almost everything it contains has been rendered obsolete by the scientific and technological progress actually made on Earth since 1761, it offers a uniquely precious insight into the horizons of the eighteenth century speculative imagination, being far more extravagant, in its fashion, although less detailed, than the vision of twenty-fifth century Paris presented in Mercier's futuristic utopia. If Mercier read *Le Voyageur philosophe*, it is possible that the chapter in question might have played some part in prompting him to produce his own vision of the future, but Mercier exercised the restraint of earnest conviction, while Listonai felt free to be as extravagant as he could. The chapter is, in consequence, the most spectacular early attempt to put narrative flesh on the idea of technological progress, as it came to be understood in the Enlightenment, and it remained the boldest and most wide-reaching for at least half a century.

Unlike Tiphaigne de la Roche, Listonai found the serious aspects of Voltaire's philosophy very attractive, and the one point on which he differs strenuously from Voltaire is the one point on which Tiphaigne sympathized with him; Listonai claims to disapprove strongly of satire and might have disapproved of Voltaire's satires just as much as Tiphaigne's, in spite of their opposite targets. That did not mean that Listonai was not prepared to employ satire as a rhetorical instrument himself, but he did so in a more subdued manner than either of his august predecessors.

That is not the only evidence of flagrant inconsistency in Listonai's work; for instance, he includes a chapter on the unreliability of reasoning by analogy, but is not at all reluctant to reason by analogy himself when it suits him, and to put the icing on the cake, he also includes a sub-chapter on "inconsequentiality" in which he argues, somewhat inconsistently, that much of what passes for inconsistency is not as inconsistent as it seems. He is not in the least afraid of self-contradiction, being perfectly prepared to alternate the masks he wears, after the fashion he recommends in his prospectus for the actors of the future.

Subdued as Listonai's satirical impulse is, it remains effective enough to put the reader continually in doubt as to how seriously he means what he is saying. His fulsome dedication to himself is a parodic joke, but it is a pointed one, in juxtaposition with the preface, in which the author anticipates and defends himself against the charge that his work is a complete mess, devoid of any coherent order or "consequentiality." He mounts that defense not on the grounds that it is more orderly or consequential than it seems, but on the grounds that that is the kind of person he is, and so what? And, indeed, it obviously was the kind of person he was, and the disorderliness of his text, no matter how much it might offend lovers of coherence, does have certain virtuous consequences, not only in representing the vagaries of thought in something akin to their natural perversity, but in encouraging him to let rip, both argumentatively and imaginatively, in circumstances where more orderly authors would undoubtedly have exercised more discretion.

Voyages de Milord Céton dans les sept planettes, ou Le Nouveau Mentor (tr. as *The Voyages of Lord Seaton to the Seven Planets*), was first published in four volumes, ostensibly in The Hague, in 1765-66, with the by-line "*traduits par Madame de R.R.*" It was subsequently reprinted in Garnier's *Voyages*

Imaginaires. "Madame de R.R."—who was the author rather than the translator of the work—was Marie-Anne de Roumier-Robert (1705-1771). She was born into an aristocratic family that had already come down in the world by the time she was born; her paternal grandfather was a provincial procurator and her father was obliged to go into commerce to make a living; her mother was the daughter of an advocate. Her father was acquainted with Fontenelle, whom she met on more than one occasion when he came to dine in their home, and she retained a sufficiently elevated idea of his importance to grant him a place of honor on the world of the Cyranoesque Sun featured in her work, where all the great minds of Earth and other worlds go after death to live in the City of Philosophers, but if she ever read Fontenelle's masterpiece she does not seem to have taken its lessons aboard, as her own account of the solar system is extremely confused.

Marie-Anne's parents died while she was still young, and the debts her father left caused a posthumous bankruptcy that left her devoid of any inheritance; the relative who became her guardian put her into a convent, from which she only emerged to be married off to an advocate named Robert. The only biographical memoir written by someone who apparently knew her, Joseph de Laporte, contained in volume five of *Histoire littéraire des femmes françoises, ou Lettres historiques* (1769), does not make any mention of Monsieur Robert's death, but the preface of *Voyages de Milord Céton* finds her alone and "without support" in struggling with her tribulations, strongly suggesting that she was a widow by then.

Whether she was a widow or not, it was not until relatively late in life that Madame Robert decided to try her hand at writing. She was undoubtedly aware of some of the contemporaries featured alongside her in Laporte's volume, in which she takes second place behind the former actress Marie-Jeanne Riccoboni and ahead of Madeleine de Puisieux (1720-1798), an occasional collaborator with Denis Diderot. Madame Robert's works follow a pattern not dissimilar to theirs, including both naturalistic "sensibility novels" and fantastic "moral tales" borrowing motifs eclectically from Galland, *contes de fées* and Classical mythology.

Madame Robert published two sensibility novels prior to venturing into new literary territory in *Voyages de Milord Céton*, the first of which, *La Paysanne philosophe, ou Les Aventures de Madame la Comtesse de* *** [The Philosophical Peasant Woman] (1761-62), details the complex but relentlessly moral love life of an orphan peasant girl adopted and brought up by an aristocratic woman. That novel was reprinted three times, and thus appears to have been considerably more successful than *La Voix de la nature, ou Les Aventures de Madame la Marquise de* *** [The Voice of Nature] (1764), another tale of an orphan in quest of true love; the plaintive preface to *Voyages de Milord Céton*, as well as certain comments in the account of life on the Moon, suggests that the relative failure of the second novel might well have impelled her to attempt something more eye-catchingly unusual. The text of *Voyages de Milord Céton* contains some passages suggesting, somewhat disingenuously, a strong disapproval of the public's liking for fantastic fiction, but if Madame Robert felt some resentment at the fact that she was pandering to that appetite, it certainly did not prevent her doing so wholeheartedly, and at great length.

The first volume of *Voyages de Milord Céton*, published in advance of the others, belongs squarely to the tradition of lunar satires, containing echoes of Cyrano's *L'Autre Monde* and also of *Le Voyageur philosophe*, from which Madame Robert appropriated a passage, rather clumsily, to shore up a description of laboratory apparatus in which she was clearly out of her depth. It seems probable, too, that she was familiar with the Béthune's *Relation du monde de Mercure*; although her account of Mercury is very different from his, the patchwork narrative strategy she employs, including both allegorical and anecdotal inclusions, is very similar, as is the stratagem of an introductory encounter with a salamander. Her novel's subtitle, however, indicates that its principal literary model is not an interplanetary fantasy but Fénelon's *Télémaque*. Madame Robert's account of the more far-ranging educational tour to  which the *génie* Zachiel subjects his protégés Céton and Monime is to a large extent an homage, and echoes many of the criticisms that Fénelon made of the court culture of Louis XIV's reign, although it also rebukes the earlier Mentor for the implication of *lèse-majesté* contained in his more radical ideas about parliamentary government.

The story represents the "seven planets"—the Moon, Mercury, Venus, Mars, the Sun, Jupiter and Saturn, explored in that order—as Earth-clone worlds, in each of which a single human penchant is exaggerated to become an overriding theme of existence, thus exposing it to analysis, criticism and sometimes to ridicule. Most of the targets addressed are familiar: the follies of social affectation prominent on the Moon, the viciousness of avarice dominant on Mercury, and the relentless pursuit of social status on Jupiter are all conventional issues conventionally tackled; but there is an insistent quirkiness in the accounts of Venus, the planet ruled by Amour, the war-torn Mars, and the Apollonian Sun. The account of the supposedly-ideal society of Saturn is heavily influenced by the glorification of the pastoral so frequent in eighteenth-century French fiction, more reminiscent of Honoré d'Urfé than Rousseau.

The novel does not conclude with the visit to Saturn, but continues back on Earth, where the somewhat tormented relationship between Céton and Monime eventually reaches its conclusion in the context of a strange variant history, which employs several actual historical individuals—the novel is set in the mid-seventeenth century, although some of the visits to other planets involve drastic chronological inconsistencies—but soon moves into a spectacularly counterfactual account of the history of Georgia. Although it is not really an "alternative history" in the sense that the term was later attributed to a subgenre of fiction, its historical inventions are nevertheless interesting in that context.

It has to be admitted that Madame Robert does not go about her overarching mission with any great elegance; her seven-part narrative is not only prolix, repetitive and inconsistent, but in some respects remarkably lacking in seemingly-necessary intelligence, although certainly not in boldness; it requires a defiantly eccentric courage to set out to write an interplanetary novel if you are not only unsure as to whether the Ptolemaic model the solar system or the Copernican is the correct one, but not even sure as to why it makes a difference, and to offer an account of the population of the definitive City of Philosophers when you only have the slightest idea what any of the philosophers you feel obliged to name-check believed or opined, or why it was significant.

Like many writers of philosophical extravaganzas, Madame Robert appears to have been using the writing of her novel as a means of attempting to clarify her own ideas about various matters, and trying to fix her own moral compass by working on some difficult personal issues. That is undoubtedly the explanation of some of the story's inconsistencies, and also of its incessant repetition of the conclusions it attains. Not all the issues raised are resolved, and it is arguable that the remaining ambiguities and ambivalences are more revealing of the author's own state of mind and the confusions of her historical moment than the firm commitments she makes.

Her attitude to war offers one interesting instance, as her occasional polemics against it—many famous warriors receive exceedingly short shrift in her allegorical account of Céton and Monime's visit to the Temple Of Glory on Mars—are counterbalanced by her account of Céton's preparation for a military career in the same section, and even more so by the striking intervention of Monime in the battle fought in the climax of the plot. Throughout the text prior to that point, Monime had seemed distinctly timorous and squeamish, but once her true royal identity is revealed to her, she unhesitatingly takes command of her troops on the battlefield and far outdoes Céton in the business of enthusiastic slaughter; there, if nowhere else in the plot, a reckless feminism, albeit of a rather suspect variety, breaks traditional shackles in no uncertain terms.

The author's assurances that women are equal to men on both Venus and the Sun are not borne out by the events and subsidiary narratives set there, especially in the account of the amnesiac Monime's seduction by the handsome Prince Petulant, observed and occasionally impeded by the disapproving Céton in the guise of a fly. There is, however, a remarkable sequel to the account of Prince Petulant's infatuation with Monime in the episode set on Jupiter, in which the monarch of that world, echoing the tendencies of his planet's namesake, becomes determined to have his way with her, while his Junoesque wife sets her sights imperiously on Céton by way of reprisal—but the potentially-interesting carnal threats stand no real chance of consummation with the ever-watchful Zachiel standing guard, and that particular subplot fizzles out less melodramatically than the account of Prince Petulant's eventful wedding day.

As well as the interesting and partly-redeeming features of its faults, however, Madame Robert's narrative has some striking compensatory virtues. Not the least of those compensations is the sheer bizarrerie of certain parts of the narrative, both in terms of the intensely exotic imagery of its odder passages— the visit to a comet, during which Céton and Monime observe a necromancer at work in spectacular fashion, is a particularly striking example, although partly plagiarized from an obscure English text—and in the reckless mingling and confusion of the literal and the metaphorical, especially in the elaborate ventures into mythological allegory in the sections set on Venus and the Sun.

Most of the anecdotal inclusions Madame Robert inserts into her main narrative as supplementary asides are relatively straightforward, some of them being stereotyped exercises in sensibility fiction, but a few push that envelope quite considerably, including the most substantial ones related by secondary narrators on Venus, Mars, the Sun and Saturn. Although the Chevalier de Béthune was a far more accomplished writer than Madame Robert, if she was conscientiously trying to match the imaginative range, multiplicity and sheer eccentricity of his account of the solar system, she did not too badly.

After publishing *Voyages de Milord Céton*, Madame Robert went on to publish a third naturalistic novel, *Nicole de Beauvais, ou L'Amour vaincu par reconnaissance* [Love Vanquished by Gratitude] (1768) in the same year as the fantasy novella *Les Ondins, conte moral* (tr. as "The Water-Sprites") three years prior to her death. In spite of its subtitle, *Les Ondins* is a pure entertainment, far less ambitious than its predecessor, tackling no issues beyond the author's intellectual scope, but it does makes the most of her undoubted imaginative scope in its hectic and zestful eclecticism. It has closer affiliations with modern fantasy fiction than most contemporary works in a similar vein.

It might not be easy nowadays to sympathize with Madame Robert's intransigent monarchism and her absolutist views on sexual morality might also seem a trifle manic. Both attitudes were more than a trifle old-fashioned in her own day, but no one who read her works in the 1760s really wanted to be Mentored in that fashion, and undoubtedly found her two fantasies interesting for much the same reasons that modern readers might still be able to find some interest in them: their strangeness, their fervor and their occasional sarcastic wit.

Their contribution to the evolving tradition of *roman scientifique* was undermined by the author's almost-total ignorance of science, but her novel nevertheless set a significant precedent for subsequent planetary tours, including Duc Multipliandre's in Restif de La Bretonne's *Les Posthumes*.

La Nouvelle Lune, ou histoire de Poequilon par M. Le B*** (tr. as "The New Moon") was originally published, ostensibly in Amsterdam, in 1770. The author was subsequently identified by Antoine Alexandre Barbier's *Dictionnaire des ouvrages anonymes* as Alexis-Jean Le Bret (1603-1779). The Bibliothèque Nationale's data file relating to the author in question gives his place of birth as Beaune and his profession as Advocate and Royal Censor but two of those data are probably incorrect. Georges May, who wrote an excellent essay on the book, published in *Essays on the Age of Enlightenment in Honour of Ira O. Wade* (1977), edited by Jean Macary, sorted out the various confusions of identity that led to the false attributions, understandable given the profusion of Le Brets and Lebrets active at the relevant time. According to May, the birthplace of Beaune was that of the author's cousin Louis Lebret, whereas Alexis-Jean Le Bret was actually born in Dijon, and the Advocate of that name was Francois-Xavier Dardin Le Bret. On the other hand, May confirms, perhaps surprisingly, that the author of *La Nouvelle Lune* really was a royal censor, from 1759 onwards, who presumably spent a good idea of his time refusing official publication in Paris to licentious satirical works like *La Nouvelle Lune*.

Le Bret's work retains many of the sophistications taken on by lunar fantasies since Cyrano, but it also recovers in full measure the exuberance and—in the broadest possible sense—licentiousness of Cyrano's work. Unlike most of its predecessors, *La Nouvelle Lune* does not take the narrative form of a journey undertaken by a human from Earth to the Moon, describing instead the elaborate odyssey of a uniquely-favored lunar native, but that alteration only serves to emphasize that the Moon depicted here, like many of those featured in the earlier works, is not really the Earth's satellite at all but a distorted mirror image of the planet, displaced in order to put on a blatantly false pretence of not wanting to give offense to its various targets.

The hero of *La Nouvelle Lune*, Poequilon, is fortunate enough to be granted the privilege of an annual wish by the tutelary *génie* of the Moon, Selenos. Like many recipients of gratuitous wishes he uses them a trifle foolishly at first, but he retains enough in prospect gradually to learn wisdom. After finding and losing his one true love, Olympe, to whom he has difficulty remaining faithful, he has to undertake an odyssey through the various nations of the Moon to search for her, and then complete it in her company, before losing her for a second time and having to set forth on his penitential travels again, until his epic journey reaches its destined terminus in the island of Eutoquia, the fictional Moon's equivalent of the Earthly Utopia—without which, as Oscar Wilde once pointed out, no map of the world, or any world, can really be reckoned complete.

Although couched as a pure fantasy, in giving its protagonist an inexhaustible but carefully spaced-out series of wishes, the story nevertheless maintains the kind of rational skepticism typical of *contes philosophiques*, and its breezy hybridization of the attitudes and methods of Cyrano and Voltaire makes it one of the most lively satirical quests for Enlightenment produced in the pre-Revolutionary era. Eutoquia---loosely translatable as "good craziness"—is a particularly apt invention, and the story's sadly skeptical consideration of sexual mores is a significant anticipation of the examinations of that topic contained in several notable *romans scientifiques* of the last decade of the nineteenth century and the first decade of the twentieth.

Le Retour de mon pauvre oncle, ou Relation de son voyage dans la lune (tr. as "My Poor Uncle's Return: The Story of his Voyage to the Moon") was first published as an anonymous booklet in 1784. It was the first work of fiction by the architect and topographer Jacques-Antoine Dulaure (1755-1835), who had previously published *Pogonologie, ou histoire philosophique de la barbe* [Pogonology: A Philosophical History of Beards] (1780) and it remained the only one, although Dulaure went on to become a prolific writer of non-fiction, including many works on the city of Paris, its monuments and "curiosities," and a provocative work on *Des Divinités génératices, ou du culte du Phallus chez les ancients et les modernes* [Generative Divinities; or, The Cult of the Phallus among the Ancients and Moderns] (1808). He was also a prolific theater critic.

Dulaure was an enthusiastic supporter of the 1789 Revolution, a prominent Jacobin appointed to the Convention Nationale in 1792, although he abandoned politics for good following Bonaparte's coup, after shouting a farewell "Down with the dictator!" as he left the Chambre. He lost his entire fortune in the early 1800s owing to the bankruptcy of the notary with whom it was deposited, and obtained an administrative position in spite of his opposition to the Emperor, but lost it when the Restoration was affected, and had to live on the produce of his pen thereafter.

There is, of course, no hint of that colorful future to be found in his brief and amiable lunar romance, which is of minor interest in terms of its description of life on the Moon, because it treats the Moon as a straightforward Earth-clone in order to poke fun at contemporary Parisian society, but it is interesting and historically significant nevertheless, in offering a remarkably rapid reaction to the development of aerostatics in the wake of the Montgolfier brothers' pioneering public demonstration in June 1783.

Balloons were to become a key feature of fanciful French fiction for the next hundred years, but Dulaure was the first to seize upon their potential as an imaginative stretching device. He does not take the idea at all seriously— although the protagonist makes his return flight from the Moon in a balloon, he reaches it in the first place, ludicrously, by becoming a balloon himself, filling his own body with hydrogen—but Dulaure makes the central character of his amiable farce a "physicist," and his story pays continual homage to the manner in which aerostatics had suddenly made "physics"—which still meant science in general in his pre-Comtean era—an exceedingly fashionable topic of concern and discussion in Parisian society.

Dulaure acknowledges in the beginning of his story the utter absurdity of using hydrogen as a means of traveling to the Moon, but in its conclusion he similarly recognizes the convenience of the new narrative device, realizing that it really did not matter, for fictional purposes, whether people really could achieve interplanetary travel be means of balloons—the point was that they provided a potential iconic motif that could stand in for *"génies"* with an implication affiliated to physics rather than Gallandesque fantasy.

Dulaure's story therefore marked, with consummate neatness, a transition point in the development of *roman scientifique*. The day of the kind of narrative improvisations made by Madame Robert was over, and the kind of vessel glimpsed by Monsieur Listonai was about to lose its gossamer lightness and faeriesque connotations, becoming solid, and imaginatively connectable to visible technology in spite of being devoid of rational plausibility. *Le Retour de mon pauvre oncle* waved a fond *adieu* to the old era of lunar follies, which were retired to obsolescence, while issuing an enthusiastic welcome to the first light of a new era that had just begun to glitter on the imaginative horizon.

6. Glimpsing the Future

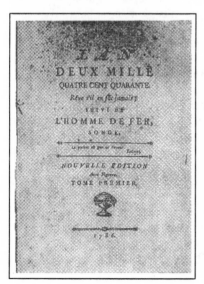

Louis-Sébastien Mercier (1740-1814) is seen from today's viewpoint primarily and essentially as a writer who made a crucial pioneering move in the development of futuristic fiction in *L'An deux mille quatre cent quarante, rêve s'il en fut jamais*, first published 1771 and subsequently revised and augmented several times. At the time however, he would have been seen as a prolific manufacturer of philosophical dream fantasies, whose initial sequence was aptly concluded by *L'An deux mille quatre cent quarante*. That dream was preceded into print by Mercier's *Songes philosophiques* (1768), which he signed, although the title-page claimed publication in London, and the anonymous *Songes d'un hermite* [A Hermit's Dreams] (1770), both of which contain material foreshadowing it, as well as other endeavors reflecting concerns and ideas familiar in *contes philosphiques* that can now be seen as ancestral to *roman scientifique*.

The former collection opens with "L'Optimisme," which begins with reflections on the iniquities of "this miserable Earth" that lead the narrator to abuse Providence, whereupon he is lifted up into the sky and confronted by a "*génie*" that he recognizes as an angel, who presents him with a sequence of exemplary visions in defense of God's mysterious ways. The same *génie* returns the following night in "L'Âme" [The Soul], this time taking the dreamer on an allegorical journey featuring more angels, nymphs and elementals, while the third dream offers him a more detailed image of the miseries caused by the incessant lust for gold, but also introduces a philosopher who tells him that collective human endeavor is capable of remedying those ills—after which his celestial guide offers him a vision of a happier world.

The fourth chapter, "Les Lunettes" [The Spectacles], opens with a diatribe against "ambulant rogues" who pretend to predict the future, after which the narrator goes to sleep and dreams that he finds himself in a vast library full of sealed books, in which he reads a story in the only open one. The story relates how Xuixoto "the God of the Indies and the Earth" deigns to look down on his work, and is surprised to hear the lamentations rising up from the world. Those complaining are sure that, in his place, they could have made a better world, and are particularly insistent that if they were able to foresee the future they would be much better off. Xuixoto, annoyed by the criticisms, has the news published that he will come down personally to listen to complaints and requests.

One plaint to which the god listens with particular care comes from the philosopher Zelon, who makes the case for allowing humans to know the future so eloquently that Xuixoto orders his minster to distribute spectacles with the double virtue of allowing people to perceive all the good fortune they might enjoy and all the misfortune of which they are at risk. The great beauty Aline is thus enabled to foresee the inevitable decline of her charms; the great captain Misnar sees that after his victories being glorified and celebrated, subsequent generations will judge him harshly and execrate him; and other users, ambitious for love, political authority or literary glory fare no better, all of them being horribly disillusioned by the fatal spectacles. Zelon suffers more than anyone, especially by comparison with the young Myope, who cannot see anything at all with the aid of the lenses. Eventually, humankind begins to curse Xuixoto even more than before—but, being a merciful god, he takes pity on them and removes the power to foresee the future.

Perhaps, in view of the fervor of that parable, it is surprising that Mercier wrote any futuristic fiction at all, but the temptation was perhaps a little too strong, and the search for a better world certainly continued to attract him; the sixth dream in the first collection, "D'un Monde heureux" [Of a Happy World] features a journey through space amid "a thousand blazing worlds" into "the frightful depths of the universe," and an eventual arrival on an Edenic planet where everything seems beautiful, peaceful and incorruptible, possessed of more colors than "the audacious prism of our Newton has been able to decompose." Its night-sky makes the order of the universe manifest, and sleep there gives the soul access to veritable enlightenment rather than confusing delusion. Pain is unknown and death brings manifest angels down from Heaven to collect the soul of the moribund. That series of contrasts causes the dreamer to regret all the more bitterly the extent of humankind's fall. His tears, however, only earn him a long lecture counseling him, in spite of everything, not to lose faith in the Providence that still presides over the Earth.

The third dream of the hermit in *Songes d'un Hermite* also features an interplanetary voyage, this time to the planet Mercury, where the excessive heat that makes the dreamer's blood boil only fills him with a greater vivacity. The planet's astronomers having anticipated his descent, a crowd gathers to meet him; the inhabitants of the world are simian, and perpetually agitated, but they speak French, and give him a fine welcome. Their chief is, however, entirely human and his immediately underlings half-human and half-ape; all of his subjects imitate him slavishly.

The next dream takes the hermit back to his garden, but presents him with a remarkable vision of biological metamorphoses, producing human beings from vegetables, which are explained by a theory of generation not far removed from the one that Telliamed employed to explain the metamorphoses that allegedly produced terrestrial human beings from marine ancestors. The dreamer's attempts to investigate the further possibilities of that remarkable thesis are, alas, interrupted when his informant is transformed into a nightingale.

The eighth of the hermit's dreams describes how the recluse, having lost his spectacles, finds an even better pair that allow him to see into the imagination of other people, which he naturally employs on various representative individuals—but without, this time, deriving any forceful moral from the expectable revelations of their ambitions.

Although brief and oddly inconclusive, that particular episode is worthy of note as an early investigation of the potential of an insightful "sixth sense" or "second sight" in the context of philosophy rather than superstition. It is not the first, but it makes an interesting comparison with an earlier venture by the Swiss writer Emerich de Vattel in "Voyages dans le Microcosme par un disciple moderne de Pythagore" (tr. as "Voyages in the Microcosm"), which appeared in his collection *Poliergie* (1757). The "microcosm" in question is that of occult science—i.e., human being—and the visionary journeys featured are expeditions into the human mind, in order to see its workings given visible form. The visions granted to Mercier's hermit by his dream-spectacles are not dissimilar, although they represent a primitive stage in the development of speculative depiction of what would ultimately come to be jargonized as "telepathy."

In his tenth dream, the hermit finds a tiny bell inside an oyster, which has the faculty of resuscitating the dead in miniature, permitting the juxtaposition of ancient priests, soldiers, etc., with more recent ones, to the detriment of the latter. In the eleventh he goes to sleep after reading a book of natural history which has shocked him by virtue of its materialism, and dreams about a sage who suggests to him that the wonders of nature, seen in their true breadth and complexity, can only invoke wonder at the genius of the Creator, and thus soothes away the burden of "the maledictions of modern philosophy." In a subsequent dream the hermit, having stumbled across the philosopher's stone by accident, takes it to the laboratory of a modern chemist prior to setting up in business as an alchemist, at first successfully, but eventually discovering the circumstances in which the stone loses its virtue.

Tacked on to the end of this sequence, *L'An deux mille quatre cent quarante* might seem a rather sober and pedestrian text, although it certainly caught the imagination of Mercier's peers in no uncertain terms, vastly outselling his previous volumes. In spite of Jacques Guttin's exotic literary ploy in labeling the secondary world of a conventional text "the future," Monsieur de Listonai's anticipation of a twenty-fourth century lecture reminiscing about five hundred years of technological progress, and the cautionary parable Mercier had offered in "Les Lunettes," there was still no such thing as "futuristic fiction" in 1770. On the other hand, the prophets of the past had routinely received news of the future in dreams, which they took to be divine revelations, although they rarely saw anything therein except the end of the world, threatened as a punishment for recalcitrant human wickedness by a God less generous than Xuixoto, and it must have been that imaginative context into which the vast majority of its contemporary readers automatically slotted the story

The anonymous *L'An deux mille quatre cent quarante*, ostensibly published in Amsterdam, is, at any rate, closer in its apparent nature to the tradition of prophetic visions than to the kind of progressive vision at which Listonai had hinted ten years earlier. Mercier, unlike Listonai, had probably heard mention of the new theory of progress promoted by Turgot and Condorcet, which proposed that moral progress is intimately linked to technological progress, and a natural effect of it, but he does not incorporate that thinking into his futuristic vision. Even so, the vision was spectacularly new in two ways that might now seem trivial, but at the time seemed a veritable "egg of Columbus." It inverted the normal direction of prophecy by revealing, not the end of the world by divine edict, but its improvement by human effort and endeavor, and it brought utopian design home from the remote islands and other planets to which it had previously been exiled, to the city of Paris.

The story begins with a dialogue between the narrator and an Englishman, in which the iniquities of contemporary life in Paris are discussed in angry terms, its horrors itemized and castigated. The narrator then goes to bed and dreams that he sleeps for hundreds of years and makes up in the year 2440. The first English translation altered that date to 2500 in the interests of roundness, claiming that the original has no significance, but in fact it does; when the narrator discovers the date at which he has "woken up" he realizes that he is seven hundred years old—exactly ten times the lifespan traditionally attributed to human beings. It also allows him to calculate that he has slept for 762 years, thus establishing the beginning of the narrative's composition in 1768.

The narrator is taken in hand by an obliging citizen, who volunteers to show him round the city as soon as he is decently clothed—fashions of dress have changed considerably, becoming much simpler and more comfortable. The tour proceeds rather randomly, and the substance of the dream is abundantly annotated by the dreamer who is reporting it, thus creating a kind of binocular vision in which the institutions of the future are compared with the rotten ones they have replaced. That structure, although cumbersome, greatly facilitated the further amplification of the narrative as it went through successive editions—of which there were a great many, as the book became the greatest underground best-seller of the century.

The innovations envisaged by the text are few and modest—for instance, the flow of traffic is organized, so that vehicles remain on the right-hand side of the road, but the vehicles themselves are even simpler than those of 1768, ornate and lavishly-decorated carriages having been replaced by plain, utilitarian vehicles. Its books are allegedly better, but there are far fewer of them, the bulk of the literary heritage having been obliterated as unnecessary or pernicious. The Temple is also drastically simplified, as an appropriate space for minimalist worship reflecting the awareness that nothing certain is or can be known about the Supreme Being. The horrors of the eighteenth century Parisian hospitals and prisons have vanished, health care now being largely provided by precautions of elementary hygiene, and punishments—including executions—being administered with tender regret.

In terms of its politics, the dream seems confused; the dreamer is informed that there is now much greater equality; the first edition actually states that in one chapter that monarchy no longer exists, although a later one credits the reform of the society to a wise king and modifies the judgment to the abolition of "absolute monarchy," later editions adapting the earlier moment to fit, although never removing the apparent contradiction between the allegations in one chapter that differences between rich and poor have been obliterated and in another that the rich are now benevolent and charitable toward the poor. That confusion was not ironed out in editions subsequent to the first, which expanded the 1771 edition's forty-four chapters to eighty-two by 1784, and also added further footnotes to the existing chapters.

Mercier was later to claim, falsely, that he had predicted the Revolution and helped to bring it about; although there is a general remark about the destruction of iniquitous systems often having to be effected violently, that is not what has happened in the future Paris he envisages—which has required nearly seven hundred years to have purged itself of its evil aspects, and the benevolence of a monarch to bring it about. Indeed, *L'An deux mille quatre cent quarante* includes a paean of praise addressed to Henri IV, offered as a model for hypothetical future kings in preference to the one reigning in 1768—the aging Louis XV—and his predecessor.

The absence of what would nowadays be reckoned futuristic anticipation is not surprising, given that Mercier was extremely skeptical about scientific progress, and in some of his writings seems not entirely convinced of Copernicanism, the plurality of worlds or the sphericity of the Earth. He did not consider himself to be a *philosophe,* and he was very fortunate to survive the Terror, being reckoned too conservative as a member of the Convention and thrown into prison after voting against the execution of Louis XVI; he was only released because Robespierre jumped the queue and went to the guillotine before him.

Dreams are, of course, entitled to be confused as well as rose-tinted, but that does somewhat undermine their entitlement to be considered serious anticipations. As with Listonai's futuristic essay, the wonder is that *L'An deux mille quatre cent quarante* was done at all, not that it was done particularly well, but it did not precipitate an immediate rush to do better, any more than previous landmark works such as *Utopia* and *New Atlantis* had done. Mercier never dabbled in futuristic fiction again, although he produced several more dream fantasies, including other dreams of some relevance to the development of *roman scientifique.*

"Les Lunettes" and most of the other *Songes philosophiques* of 1768 were reprinted in the later collection *Mon Bonnet de nuit* [My Night-Cap] (1786), mingled with essays, and were reprinted again in the collection of *Songes et visions philosophiques* included in Charles Garnier's *Voyages Imaginaires.* The latter included several pieces that had not appeared previously in book form, and one that Mercier had begun adding as an appendix to new editions of *L'An deux mille quatre cent quarante*, to which he was had begun adding his signature in 1784: "L'Homme de fer." The latter fantasy has slightly better credentials as a precursor of the Revolution. The dreamer goes into a cave where he is mysteriously transmuted into a man of iron—arguably the first human superhero—who then travels through France, responding to the evidences of injustice he sees by means of his iron fists, invulnerable to all reprisals, cataloguing at length the evils that he sweeps away with his metallic might.

The most interesting of the other new pieces contained in the Garnier version of the *Songes et visions* is "Nouvelles de la lune," in which a "luminous arrow" aimed from the moon inscribes a message on a series of wooden planks. The message reveals a vision of the afterlife somewhat reminiscent of, albeit more modest then, the schema of cosmic palingenesis mapped out by the Chevalier de Béthune. It is also reminiscent of the schema that Restif de la Bretonne began to map out in 1787 in the manuscript that eventually became *Les*

Posthumes, and might well have emerged from the same discussions in Fanny de Beauharnais' salon.

Nowadays, Mercier is only remembered for *L'An deux mille quatre cent quarante* and for his subsequent eye-witness accounts of life in contemporary Paris, accumulated in *Le Tableau de Paris* (1781-88), supplemented, after the eventful interim, by *Le Nouveau Paris* (1799). At the peak of his fame, however, at least while *L'An deux mille quatre cent quarante* was still cloaked with anonymity, and even thereafter in respectable circles, his greatest repute was a playwright, in which role he carried forward Diderot's thesis that the hidebound categories of tragedy and comedy ought to be broken down, to make way for a new and more generalized genre of drama. He wrote more than fifty of them, as well as several essays on dramatic art and other essays extolling the virtues of prose and denigrating the supposed obsolescence of poetry.

That battle was won, and so have many battles in the social crusade that Mercier fought in his dream fantasies, so he is fully entitled to be reckoned a man of progress, even though he did not believe in the kind of progress that his most fervent contemporaries came to believe in, and conspicuously left out of account in his fantasy of what kind of world he might see if he lived to be seven hundred.

7. The Romance of Phlogiston

Le Philosophe sans prétention, ou l'Homme rare. Ouvrage physique, chymique, politique et moral, Dédié aux savans (tr. as *The Unpretentious Philosopher; or The Rare Man: a Physical, Chemical, Political and Moral Work, Dedicated to Scientists*) was initially published under the by-line "M. D. L. F." in Paris in 1775, with the rare privilege of an official license, proudly reprinted in the text.

Someone has expanded the final two letters to "La Folie" in the Bibliothèque Nationale's copy of the book, reproduced on its *gallica* website (taking it for granted that the first two stand for "Monsieur de"), and that is how it is catalogued; it is unclear whether that is a mistake, or whether, if it is a mistake, it is deliberate. The book's author, Louis-Guillaume de La Follie (1739-1780), usually spelled his name with a double l, but spelling was rather haphazard in the eighteenth century, and the author might have used the double l in his more serious work to avoid the implication of "folly" contained in the single l—although he or someone else might have wanted to preserve that very implication, ironically, for the purposes of a satirical *conte philosophique* that embraces a calculated eccentricity for rhetorical purposes.

The translation of the final word of the title, *savans*, as "scientists" is inevitably dubious; in 1775, the word "scientist" did not exist in the English language—it was coined some fifty years later by William Whewell—and could not have been used in a contemporary translation, which would inevitably have preferred "scholars" if the translator did not want to retain "savants." In French, the word *savant*, equipped with a new orthodox spelling, continued in use with multiple meanings, used to refer to all kinds of scholars without any separation of those engaged in scientific endeavor, although it increasingly became to be seen as primarily synonymous with the English "scientist." The whole point of the argument contained in La Follie's book, however, and the core of his motivation for writing it, is to make the discrimination that the French language had not yet completed. He wanted to popularize a notion and an image that only existed, as yet, in embryo, in order to define himself, his protagonist, and a host of philosophers yet to come. His book is propaganda, not merely for scientific knowledge but for the scientific method, for the adoption of that method by all true philosophers, and for the recognition of a class of individuals who are routinely engaged in scientific enquiry by means of practical experimentation—i.e., *scientists*.

The purpose and innovative ambition of La Follie's book actually went one step beyond that, because it also attempted to embody, and ultimately to make explicit, a plea for a particular method of communicating scientific ideas and attempting to make them persuasive. That aspect of the text was, in essence, a plea for the popularization of science, and an argument to the effect that it is wholly appropriate to use entertaining fictitious devices in the service of that aim; in brief, it is a plea in favor of *roman scientifique* in the sense that the present text employs it. Given that purpose, the attainment of the royal license permitting its publication, and the instance on displaying it, is a significant feature of the work.

La Follie was sufficiently conscious of what might eventually be done in that regard to employ as the story's initial narrative hook the idea of an inhabitant of Mercury who has employed a spaceship powered by electricity to undertake a voyage of exploration to Earth, and has then become stranded after a crash, forcing him to embark on a long search for the exotic materials required to repair it. The individual who gives that account of himself—the eponymous Unpretentious Philosopher—explains his predicament to Nadir, an inhabitant of Chrysopolis (nowadays absorbed into the urban sprawl of Istanbul), who is in the process of refining his library by getting rid of all the superfluous texts. Although Nadir has several wives, he is only intimate with his favorite, Mirza, the others being wards under his protection. It is partly to obtain assistance in winnowing the science section of the library, and partly to assist him in Mirza's education, that Nadir welcomes the Philosopher into his home and begs him to explain all the enigmas of physical science, which the latter does at great length and in painstaking detail.

That didactic quest takes up about two thirds of the text, only slightly alleviated by Nadir's attempts to assist the Philosopher to find the materials he claims to require in order to repair his spaceship, although the plot eventually turns out to be more convoluted than it initially appeared, and the Philosopher not what he seems—but the supposed quest for materials intended for technological purposes also adds fuel to the propagandistic purposes of the text, representing scientific discovery as a means of facilitating a practical endeavor.

That particular combination of literary ambitions was new—so new, in fact, that it eventually turned out to be some way ahead of its time. Nothing else like *Le Philosophe sans prétention* was produced for a further fifty years, and by that time, La Follie's pioneering endeavor was forgotten. The novel was not included in Garnier's *Voyages imaginaires,* which became the chief reference-point for later writers with similar ambitions. Any writers of a later period who came across the book would probably have rejected it as an uninteresting text, because they would have paid far more heed to the theories it espouses than to its ambition and method—and the theories it espouses were soon proved to be completely wrong.

In terms of its scientific and fictional ambitions, therefore, *Le Philosophe sans pretention* unfortunately turned out to be a classic example of the manner in which elaborate and ambitious reasoning from a couple of mistaken premises can produce a vast web of ingenious absurdity. Indeed, it is such a perfect example of ratiocination from false premises that the text now has a rhetorical and esthetic charm quite different from the one intended by its author—but it is, admittedly, an esoteric charm that can only appeal to connoisseurs of the exotic. In its own day, however, it was a bold and innovative endeavor that represents a significant feat of the imagination.

La Follie's earnest writings consisted of papers published in the prototypical scientific journal, *Journal de Physique* [Journal of Physics], which were concerned with applications of recent discoveries in chemistry to the dyeing of textiles. His family, which belonged to the petty aristocracy, was heavily involved in the textile industry, and he became a researcher in chemistry with the specific aim of lending assistance to that concern. Whether his research contrived to increase the profits of the family firm is unclear, but he certainly had high hopes for it, and for the emergent class of professionals to which he belonged.

Not everyone was sympathetic toward the emergence of a new breed of experimental scientists primarily interested in possible industrial applications of their work; La Follie's endeavors seem to have been looked upon unkindly by the Académie des Sciences, which rejected the papers that ultimately ended up in the journal; he is, however, on record as one of the first people to deposit a sealed claim to a new invention with the Académie, in order that it might serve as proof of priority of discovery, in the days when patent law was still highly uncertain in its effects.

La Follie was ultimately a victim of his own enthusiasm—some might say hubris. As the text of *Le Philosophe sans pretension* makes clear, and his scientific papers confirm, he developed a particular interest in "oil of vitriol" [sulfuric acid] and was fascinated by reactions causing effervescence, conflagrations and explosions. Given the practical uses to which the hero of the novel puts oil of vitriol and "marine acid" [hydrochloric acid] when he is forced to call upon his scientific knowledge to enable him to survive in dire circumstances—enterprises that it would have been extremely unwise for readers to try at home, let alone if they were trapped underground—it is by no means surprising that La Follie eventually died in a laboratory accident in 1790, in his forty-first year; it is rather astonishing that he had not contrived to kill himself sooner. Had people of the era not been willing to carry out experiments that we can now see, in retrospect, to have been horrendously dangerous, however, the rapid progress that soon obliterated all of La Follie's theoretical convictions would not have been possible.

La Follie was, therefore, a true martyr of science—and, as a true philosopher in his own definition, surely could not have thought of any better way to die. It would have been a sadder fate had he fallen victim to the Terror, as he might well have done had he not made an earlier exit; *Le Philosophe sans pretention* also leaves no doubt that he was a supporter of the monarchy.

Although La Follie was, in effect, the first "professional scientist" ever to put quill to paper in order to write what would nowadays be thought of as a "science fiction novel," his endeavor was not entirely without precedent, and can be seen as a logical development of a tradition of work with which he would have been familiar. It is necessary to remember that the *Journal de Physique* in which he published his scientific papers was a radically new endeavor, and that science had been making progress for more than two thousand years (unsteadily, to be sure) without the aid of the system of publication that it now standardized and taken for granted.

As a petty aristocrat, La Follie was, inevitably, in Tiphaigne de La Roche's political camp rather than the other, and like Tiphaigne, he employed the devices of the Voltairean *conte philosophique* with a different political slant; although he took care to include a slightly-disguised tribute to Voltaire's efforts in his text, La Follie's principal influence, as well as his principal *bête noire*, was Rousseau. Rousseau's ideas regarding the corrupting effects of civilization and the iniquities of monarchy are specifically attacked at several points in *Le Philosophe sans prétention*, but on one issue, La Follie and Rousseau are in perfect agreement, and that agreement plays a major role in forming the narrative component of La Follie's novel. Unlike Voltaire and Tiphaigne, neither of whom had much time for Rousseauesque "*sensibilité*," La Follie was a whole-hearted subscriber to it, and was flatly opposed to the notion that there is any inherent opposition between science and sentiment, either in theory or in practice.

That ambivalent position, unusual in its day and still unorthodox today, introduces a further peculiarity into *Le Philosophe sans prétention*, which adds yet another dimension to its originality. In order to appreciate the work fully it is useful to be able to see it as both a logical continuation of the burgeoning tradition of the *conte philosophique*, and also a deliberate step outside it. As a result of that step, the narrative element of the novel becomes almost as distinctive and peculiar as the didactic element, which is never fully integrated with it. Unfortunately, because of the space it takes up within the text, and the drastic error into which it was unfortunate to fall, the didactic aspect became an anchor dragging the whole work down into obscurity.

In attempting to unify contemporary chemistry and provide it with a secure foundation in physics, La Follie had more data on which to draw than Tiphaigne had in supporting his theory of reproductive biology, including his own laboratory experiments, but he was also tackling a larger task, at what was arguably the worst possible moment. He was the first writer of *contes philosophiques* to put the "hard" sciences of physics and chemistry at the heart of his endeavor, and precisely because they are "hard" sciences, he was taking a much bigger risk than his rivals of not merely being disproved but made to look ridiculous.

1775 was a bad time for that kind of endeavor because it was only a few years in advance of some major discoveries and developments, which brought about to complete transformation of the entire world-view of the physical sciences. La Follie was aware of being on the brink of some such revolution, and his primary reason for writing his book, as he says in his preface, was corollary to his own attempts to think matters through, and to "instruct himself" as to the likely outcome of the impending transformation. In characterizing his eccentric hero, he was attempting to establish a hypothetical objective observer, from whose viewpoint it might be possible to unify physical and chemical science with the aid of a single omnipotent thesis: phlogiston. That was a laudable ambition, in spite of its impossibility, given the immaturity of scientific knowledge at the time. Unfortunately, as soon as the idea of phlogiston was abandoned, it became an archetypal "*roman scientifique*" in Élie Fréron's sense of the term; it has survived in all textbooks of chemistry as a horrible warning of how one might go astray in trying to understand the world.

By the time the nineteenth century dawned, no one was any longer likely to protest that phlogiston had seemed like a good idea at the time, but it *had* seemed like a good idea to its proponents, and even if reading *Le Philosophe sans prétention* serves no other purpose, it serves as a reminder of that fact, and an illustration of why phlogiston seemed like a viable notion, in a scientific community that was not yet quite ready to let go of the classical theory of the four elements beloved by Aristotle, in spite of all the accumulating evidence that the theory in question was unhelpful to a sensible understanding of chemistry.

The theory of the four elements, as promoted by Aristotle, was a tactful but paradoxical compromise. The whole idea of an element is that all material substance is ultimately reducible to one single principle, but Greek philosophers disagreed as to what that ultimate principle might be. Some plumped for "water," others "earth," others "air" and others "fire." The redefinition of common terms created a considerable legacy of confusion, especially with respect to "earth" (*terre* in French), which continued to be used to identify soil, land (as opposed to sea) and the planet as well as the element. Rather than trying to arbitrate in a debate that was intrinsically impossible to settle, Aristotle was not the only philosopher to admit all four. We can now see that three of the "elements" correspond to the three easily observable basic states of matter—solid, liquid and gaseous—while the fourth plays a key role in negotiating their transformations and transitions within and between those states.

By La Follie's time, the anomalousness of "fire"—which, with reference to the element, was closer to signifying "heat" than "flame"—was fully appreciated, and discussions of its essential nature had already begun to link it closely to other concepts, especially light, and the phenomena of static electricity. In order to explain such phenomena as combustion, however, some further elaboration of the concept was necessary, and because it seemed obvious, at first glance, that combustion was a process of emission, producing flame and smoke, it seemed only natural to add a further "principle" to the elementary system that would identify and characterize that emission, and facilitate the analysis of all the different phenomena associated with combustion.

Phlogiston theory was always controversial, and that controversy was thrown into sharper relief in 1772, along with the ailing theory of the classical elements, when the distinct properties of the residue of atmospheric air left after combustion were subjected to widespread study after its isolation by Daniel Rutherford. Rutherford initially referred to the separated component as "fixed air" or "noxious air," although others soon weighed in with "phlogisticated air" and "mephitic air" before Jean-Antoine Chaptal coined "nitrogen" in 1790, having determined that the gas in question was a major component of nitric acid. The negotiation between the terms was more than a mere competition of terminology, because the various concepts implied and embodied different theories— as a debate at the dinner table detailed in *Le Philosophe sans pretention* illustrates, although it would be overstating the case to say that it makes it clear.

Investigation of the supposed emission of phlogiston in different circumstances had already thrown up a host of anomalies, which had led some chemists to reject the theory, but it was not until the advent of "fixed air" that the accumulation and supplementation of those anomalies was ready to bring about a conclusive "paradigm shift," in which combustion came to be regarded as a process of absorption rather than emission. That now seems obvious, because we are familiar with the idea that the atmosphere is not a mixture of elementary air with "particles" of other elements, but a cocktail of gases, some of them elementary in the context of a much more elaborate scheme of "elements" and some compounded from other elements within that scheme, as well as the idea that one of those gases is oxygen, and that properly-defined combustion is really oxidation.

In 1775, however, the isolation of individual atmospheric gases had only just begun, and oxidation processes were still inextricably confused with other processes occasioned by heating. Oxygen had been isolated in 1773 by Carl Scheele, although the credit is usually given to Joseph Priestley, who was the first to publish the result he obtained independently the following year. The gas was not named, however, until 1777, when Antoine Lavoisier began the classic series of experiments that demonstrated the crucial role played by oxygen in combustion, and began hammering the final nails into phlogiston's coffin. Initially, the atmospheric component in question was labeled "dephlogisticated air," by contrast with "phlogisticated air." La Follie seems unaware of the isolation of "dephlogisticated air" and does not refer to it directly, but he is well aware that the amount of phlogiston supposedly contained in the atmosphere is very variable. In trying to defend phlogiston theory against the threat of the accumulating anomalies, albeit by revising it in an unorthodox manner, he is far more sensitive to arguments about "mephitic air," which derive from the then-unnoticed confusion of the nitrogen left behind by combustion and the gas we would now call carbon dioxide, familiar to La Follie primarily as a product of heating limestone.

In the article on La Follie in his *Encyclopédie* Pierre Versins points out the irony of the fact that, because La Follie designed his imaginary electrical spaceship before the Montgolfier brothers began the actual conquest of the air, his invention avoided the trap that almost all the imaginary space journeys undertaken in the next hundred years fell into by employing balloons as interplanetary vehicles. That sidestep was, of course, as accidental as the unfortunate error of trying to build a theory of everything on the basis of phlogiston, and was arguably spoiled by such follies as arguing that Mercury is habitable because the sun is not, in fact, hot (on the basis of a mistaken theory of light) but it is nevertheless true that La Follie deserves some credit for guessing the significance of the phenomena of electricity and anticipating an exciting future for electrical technology.

In sum, it is by no means surprising that the eponymous Philosopher not only gets everything wrong, but spectacularly wrong, in spite of his own smug self-confidence. Even though La Follie's endeavor would undoubtedly seem less crazy and more praiseworthy today if his Philosopher had got a few more things right, it is by no means deprived of all interest by its errors, which are intriguing and revealing in themselves, if only in reminding us what vast strides physical science has made in less than two and a half centuries, and how immensely difficult it was, at the beginning of that revolution, to shake off the burden of the old orthodoxies, even for a man utterly determined to do it.

8. Evolution and Cosmogony

La Découverte australe par un homme-volant, ou Le Dédale français (tr. as *The Discovery of the Austral Continent by a Flying Man; or, The French Daedalus*) was originally published in 1781, in a set of four volumes that also contained four shorter works, with a title-page falsely claiming to have been printed in Leipzig. A pre-title page announces it as the second in a series of the *Oeuvres posthumes de N****, with the shorter title of *La Découverte australe, ou Les Antipodes*, and the more elaborate title page does not indicate any author's name. The preface is signed by "T. Joly," who poses as an editor of a work attributed to his "friend Dulis," and the notes in the original version of the text are variously signed by Joly and Dulis. The book was actually the work of Nicolas-Edmé Restif de La Bretonne (1734-1806), who  made no secret of having written it, referring to it in several of his subsequent quasi-autobiographical writings and including his own name within the text twice, albeit written backwards.

The formula of representation linked the work to Restif's 1780 novel *La Malédiction paternelle, lettres sincères et véritables de N*** à ses parents, ses amis et ses maîtresses, avec les réponses; recueillies et publiées par Timothée Joly, son exécuteur testamentaire* [The Paternal Curse; Sincere and Veritable Letters by N*** to his parents, friends and mistresses, with the Responses, collected and published by Timothée Joly, the executor of his will], also allegedly published in Leipzig, but actually published by the widow Duchesne, the real publisher of *La Découverte australe*; its central character is Dulis, alias N*** [Nicolas].

The author of *La Découverte australe* was the son of Edmé Rétif, a peasant farmer, but a well-off peasant farmer, who also served the functions of a local magistrate; Nicolas was the eldest of the eight children of his father's second marriage, following a first that had been almost as prolific, two of the sons of which had taken holy orders. In 1742 the family had moved on to land that Edmé Rétif had recently bought, which included a field called La Bretonne; it was sold again later, but that did not prevent Nicolas from adding it to his signature, in a tongue-in-cheek fashion, in order to give it an aristocratic implication, further enhanced by changing Rétif to the more upmarket Restif, although he sometimes reverted to the earlier spelling. He might or might not have known that the "de Bergerac" that Savinien Cyrano had added to his name was a similar affectation.

His first schoolmaster detected signs of intellectual promise in Nicolas, which led his father to place him, in 1746, under the tutelage of his stepbrother, Abbé Thomas, in the hope that he might take holy orders too, but that expectation was dashed when Abbé Thomas sent him home, judging him an unsuitable pupil because of his insubordination and excessive interest in young women. Restif was to go on to cultivate a deep and abiding loathing for the clergy and to cultivate his exceeding interest in young women in an obsessive fashion. It was in that period that he began writing, beginning a diary of sorts from which he was later to draw details of his autobiography, writing various poems and a comedy in Latin imitative of his favorite classical author, Terence.

Nicolas found great pleasure in writing, and his exercises in poetry soon became voluminous. His first venture into autobiography—or, as he put it, his first account of his "adventures"—was in that form, begun in 1753 and concluded in 1755, by which time it ran to four thousand lines. That was preceded, however, by another substantial poem, tentatively entitled *Les Douze mois* or *Mes Douze travaux* [The Twelve Months, or My Twelve Labors], which was a long daydream fantasy in which the protagonist, having done a favor for the king, is rewarded with a plot of land enclosed by a high wall, containing a vast aviary and twelve beautiful young women, where he lives in an Earthly Paradise. That fantasy too was to recur resoundingly in his later work, vaguely echoed in the *Découverte australe*, but much more robustly recovered in a subsequent work.

Nicolas Rétif was apprenticed to a printer in Auxerre in July 1751, and went to Paris in 1754, working at the Imprimerie Royale du Louvre for a year before moving on to various other employers, with whom he rarely stayed for long. He returned to Auxerre for a while in 1760, and married Agnès Lebègue, with whom he eventually had four daughters. The couple returned to Paris in 1761, where Nicolas again worked for various printers until 1767, when he published his first novel, *La Famille vertueuse* [The Virtuous Family] and became

"Restif de La Bretonne." He became a full-time writer thereafter, pouring out a long series of prose works, eventually amassing a total that many of his contemporaries and subsequent historians thought prodigious: the final total, according to the most conscientiously detailed modern study, Pierre Testud's *Rétif de La Bretonne et la création littéraire* (1977), was 187 volumes, comprising 44 titles, and totaling some 57,000 pages—and Restif was presumably writing with goose-quills, as well as typesetting all his own works.

Restif's early works included *Le Pied de Fanchette, ou Le Soulier couleur de rose* [Fanchette's Foot, or the Rose-colored Shoe] (1769), which earned him the distinction, when psychologists began searching for technical terms to describe various sexual deviations, of encouraging some of them to name shoe-fetishism "retifism," as they had named sadism after the Marquis de Sade. He was not, in fact a fetishist in the psychiatric sense—which is to say, someone who substitutes the fetish object for the "real" desired object; while Restif appreciated a dainty foot and found high-heeled shoes sexy, there was never the slightest doubt that what he lusted after, incessantly and obsessively, was the real thing, and not any kind of substitute.

The other three books Restif published in 1769 included the previously-mentioned *Le Pornographe*, a eutopian tract offering practical proposals for the legalization and organization of prostitution in the interests of public order and morality. It was the first of several such tracts addressing various specific issues of concern, including *Le Mimographe* [Writing about the Theater] (1770), *Les Gynographes* [Writings about Women] (1777), addressing the social role and status of women, and the more generally political *L'Andrographe* [Writing about Men] (1782; also known, more accurately, as *L'Anthropographe* [Writing About Humans])

Restif's first considerable success was the quasi-autobiographical *Le Paysan perverti* [The Corrupted Peasant] (1775), which detailed the corrupting effects of life in Paris on an emigrant from a humble provincial background. The success of the earlier volume was, however, outstripped by *Les Contemporaines, ou Aventures des plus jolies femmes de l'Age présent* [Contemporaries; or, The Adventures of the Prettiest Women of the Present Era] (1780), a collection of short stories detailing the problematic lives of young women of various estates, to which the author continued to add further series under various other titles for the rest of his career. In the meantime, however, he was already working on his intended masterpiece: his multi-volume autobiography, to which he refers in the frame narrative of *La Découverte australe* as *Compère Nicolas* [Friend Nicolas], but which eventually appeared as *Monsieur Nicolas ou Le Coeur humain dévoilé* [Monsieur Nicolas; or, The Human Heart Laid Bare] (sixteen volumes, 1794-97).

The frame narrative of *La Découverte australe*, which provides a kind of self-portrait of the author circa 1780, also lays bare one of the existential cancers that was eating away at the author's soul during the period of his initial success: the distress caused by his wife's adultery, and his suspicion that at least one of his daughters was not actually his. From 1768 onwards, the couple were estranged, although still living together, and in 1778, when their youngest daughter found employment, Agnès went back to live with her father. Then Restif, temporarily left alone (two of his daughters eventually came back to live with him), took to prowling the streets of Paris by night, terming himself "le hibou" [the owl] and accumulating the observations that were to provide the raw material for another of his most famous works of quasi-autobiographical fiction, *Les Nuits de Paris ou le spectateur nocturne* [Parisian Nights; or, The Nocturnal Spectator] (four volumes 1788; augmented 1794).

La Découverte australe itself was, according to *Monsieur Nicolas*, begun in 1778 when Restif was confined to bed suffering one of his recurrent bouts of ill-health, before he began work on *Les Contemporaines*. It was a deliberately self-indulgent exercise, redeveloping one of his childhood daydreams, of what he might do if he were able to fly. That initial draft was probably restricted to the story of Victorin's adventures in the early years of the eighteenth century in devising a powerful set of artificial wings and using them to prepare carefully for the abduction and seduction of his beloved Christine, to whom he cannot pay court in any socially-sanctioned way, being too humble of status; he eventually establishes her on top of an Inaccessible Mountain as the queen of a utopian society in miniature.

Restif set the manuscript aside while he wrote the short stories making up *Les Contemporaines*, and it was probably when he took it up again thereafter that he added the frame narrative and the second half of the story, which describes Victorin's removal of his mini-utopia to the southern ocean and subsequent exploration of its archipelagoes. The island neighboring Île Christine is inhabited by "Patagons"—giants modeled on those described by Antonio Pigafetta, who reported on Ferdinand Magellan's circumnavigation of the globe, and which played a significant role in the arguments set out in *Telliamed* in support of the notion that the human species had originated by gradual metamorphosis as new species adapted to live on land newly emerged from the sea. Several other variant human species mentioned by *Telliamed* are also located in nearby islands, as well as many other kinds of "hommes-brutes" (beast-people) combining physical features of humans and various animals. The explanation for the existence of the beast-people is largely worked out by Victorin, his son and grandson, before a fuller explanation is obtained from superhuman Megapatagons, members of the most intellectually advanced culture on Earth.

The second part transformed the nature of the narrative very considerably, and made the book unique, not only within the pattern of the author's productivity, but within the context of French imaginative fiction to that date. By virtue of the deft combination of its technological element with the theoretical element derived principally from Maillet, *La Découverte australe* is undoubtedly the most significant work of science-based speculative fiction produced before the 1789 Revolution, and it remained so for some time thereafter. Although its cosmogony and evolutionary theory eventually turned out to be mistaken, and no one has yet found a means of devising artificial wings akin to those that allow Victorin to fly, that should not detract from the novel's imaginative achievement, seen as a work of art in its own right. The fact that it served as a springboard for further imaginative endeavors was a bonus, albeit a significant one.

The manner in which the attempt to rationalize the daydream fantasy that gave birth to *La Découverte australe* became a launching-pad for further thought was initially illustrated by the first edition of the book, which not only contains the novel but four other works, which take up part of the third volume and all of the fourth. The first of those supplements is a long essay on "Cosmogénies ou systèmes de la formation de l'univers suivant les anciens et les modernes" [Cosmogonies; or Systems of the Formation of the Universe According to Ancient and Modern Writers], which places Maillet's cosmogony in its broader historical context. The account progresses from a comprehensive survey of classical systems to those of Descartes and Isaac Newton before claiming that "Monsieur de Buffon has effaced all the other philosophers by the beauty, the clarity and the seductive light in which he presents his system." Restif then goes on to elaborate his own suggested elaboration and modification of his synthesis of Maillet and Buffon, as sketched out in *La Découverte australe* by the Metapatagon sage.

The second supplement is the satirical "Lettre d'un singe aux animaux de son espèce, avec des notes philosophiques," [A Monkey's Letter to the Animals of his Species, with Philosophical Notes] in which the letter-writer offers advice to his fellows on the tactics and necessity of self-improvement toward humanity and membership in a great confraternity of intelligent beings—which, according to the preface, "would have completed the revelation of the author's objective, if I had not made it perfectly graspable." The letter is supplemented by a very elaborate set of notes signed by the fictitious T. Joly.

The third and longest of the supplements is a "Dissertation sur les Hommes-brutes" [Dissertation on Brutal Humans], which is a massive survey of legendary and folkloristic accounts of exotic species of humans and beings hybridizing human and animal features, greatly expanding the brief survey contained in *Telliamed*. In essence, it tries to offer justifications for taking seriously the plausibility of *La Découverte australe*'s representation of various kinds of mythical humans, including some not featured in the main narrative but cited by Telliamed—tailed humans, monopods, albinos and "marine humans"—placing them all within the evolutionary theory sketched out in the main narrative.

The fourth and most eccentric addition to the collection is a set of six "diatribes" represented as speeches made by guests at a salon, entitled "La Séance chez une amatrice" [A Session in the Home of an Amatrice, the final word being a improvised feminine of "amateur," referring to a salon-hostess], which appear to have been stitched together arbitrarily, and attached to *La Découverte australe* because the author had nothing else to do with them

The research invested in "Cosmogénies" and "Dissertation sur les hommes-brutes" is both varied and intensive, and illustrates an aspect of Restif's tendency to obsession rather different from the one displayed in his relentless production of fiction, more akin to the earnest insistence of his plans for eutopian reform; both essays demonstrate that once he got a bee in his bonnet, he tended to pursue it assiduously, as far as it would go. That was certainly what he did with his own cosmogonic thesis; he eventually developed it even more extensively in non-fictional form in volumes supplementary to *Monsieur Nicolas*, which bore the separate title of *La Philosophie de Monsieur Nicolas* (1796), the first of which details his "physics," but before then he had extrapolated it very elaborately in graphic fictional form, in his account of the cosmic voyages and futuristic explorations of Duc Multipliandre in *Les Posthumes*, first penned in 1787-89, although not published until 1802, which is the strangest work of fiction ever penned by anyone, and half of the most far-reaching imaginative endeavor ever attempted—unfortunately, the only half that survived.

La Découverte australe was not a success, especially by comparison with *Les Contemporaines*, but N*** had not written it in order to make money. He followed it with another in his series of utopian tracts, which must have sold equally poorly, but he might well have redeemed himself in his publisher's eyes with the latest in the series of his quasi-autobiographical fictions, *La Dernière aventure d'un homme de quarante-cinq ans* [The Last Adventure of a Forty-five-year Old Man] (1783), which gave free rein to the erotic fantasies whose indulgence he thought of as a essential component of laying the human soul bare, but which some of his readers thought mere pornography, in the pejorative sense rather than the neutral one he had intended when he had coined the word—a mistake that did not hurt its sales at all.

La Paysanne pervertie [The Corrupted Peasant-Woman] (1784), a companion-piece to his earlier quasi-autobiographical novel, was in the same vein, and was similarly successful. He did publish one more of the intended "Posthumous works of N***," albeit without that designation and without the fictitious editorial interference of Timothée Joly, as *Les Veillées du Marais, or Histoire du grand prince Oribeau, roi de Momminie, au pays d'Evinland, et de la vertueuse* *primcese Oribelle, de Lagenie; tirée des anciennes annales irlandaises et récemment translatée en français par Nichols Donneraill, du comté de Korke, descendant de l'auteur* [Evenings in the Marsh; or, The Story of the great Prince Oribeau of Evinland and the virtuous Princess Oribelle of Lagenie; taken from old Irish sources and recently translated into French by Nicols Donneraill of the county of Cork, a descendant of the author] (1785), before publishing the next of his quasi-autobiographical novels, *La Femme infidèle* [The Unfaithful Wife] (1786) under the pseudonym Maribert Courtenay, although that probably did not enable his estranged wife to feel any better about it if she read it.

Restif focused thereafter, at least for a while, on his potentially infinite series of short stories about the women of contemporary Paris, for which he did intensive research in soliciting anecdotes from various acquaintances, and in literary salons. It was at this time, early in 1787, that he became a fixture at one particular fashionable salon, in which he appears to have received an unusually warm welcome (his reputation and appearance did not endear him to many people), not only attending the weekly "open house" but also the more intimate secondary gathering—equally conventional in institutions of that sort—organized by its hostess, Fanny de Beauharnais (1737-1813).

Running true to form, Restif fell in love with Fanny, although that passion, also true to form, remained hopeless. The regular attendees when Restif joined the more select group included Mercier, who probably introduced him to the salon, the feminist actress Olympe de Gouges, the mathematician Jean-Sylvain Bailly and the writer and self-styled Illuminist Jacques Cazotte. Fanny's nephew by marriage, Alexandre de Beauharnais, was married at the time to Joséphine Tascher de la Pagerie, who was later to marry Napoléon Bonaparte in 1796, after Alexandre had been guillotined during the Terror.

Restif collected anecdotes for use in his collections in Fanny's salon, whose members were as willing to supply them as any group of hardened and well-informed gossips. He undoubtedly made his own contributions to the conversation, where ideas for stories of all kinds were, inevitably, routinely circulated, most of which came to nothing. Restif, however, more obsessive then most, began developing one of the ideas he broached: that of a husband who knows he is going to die, and who writes a series of letters to be delivered to his wife one after another following his demise, in order to ease her mourning.

That idea was the seed of the text that ultimately became *Les Posthumes*, and its development can be tracked through its pre-Revolution version, then provisionally titled *Lettres du tombeau* [Letters from the Tomb], as it changed direction and focus several times while Restif was writing it, probably more for his own amusement and that of the members of the salon to begin with, although he must always have had the possibility of eventual publication in mind. He worked on it throughout 1787 and 1788, alongside two works that were intended for more immediate publication with clearly-defined professional intent: the third set of his exemplary short stories, *Les Parisiennes* (four volumes 1787),

135

and *Les Nuits de Paris*. Both of those projects "overflowed" into the slowly-growing text of the "letters from the tomb," somewhat incongruously at times, following an increasingly marked trend, greatly encouraged by, if not an inevitable result of, the manner in which Restif drew upon his life for source material even in his most extravagant and exotic endeavors.

It is evident from the first few letters that Restif's initial intention was to focus narrowly on the relationship between the letter-writer, Monsieur de Fontlhète ("font l'hète" is approximately equivalent to the English slang phrase "het up"—i.e., impassioned) and his beloved wife Hortense, analyzing its development by juxtaposing day-by-day accounts of the development of four years in their relationship, two past, one ostensibly present and one future, although the scheme is confused by the fact that the letters are "actually" being written some time ahead of their intended delivery date, thus confusing the "present" and the "future" in a manner that the author never did manage to sort out or clarify

At some point after his tentative beginning, however, the author apparently realized two things: firstly, that his initially-intended scheme was too complicated and confusing to be viable as a project; and secondly, that his format, vaguely planned in the image of the *Mille et une nuits*, might benefit from a much closer resemblance, in the sense that Fontlhète, instead of devoting himself to an over-complicated analytical remembrance of things past and present, could become a storyteller instead, not only possessed of a more interesting predicament that Scheherazade, but equipped with the same broad license to fantasize, in accordance with "the Galland method."

In consequence, Restif changed the direction of his self-indulgent whimsy, and began to develop the sequence of letters as a catalogue of fantasies, with the underlying subtext of trying to convince Hortense that death is not to be seen as a bad thing but rather an entrance into a wonderland of posthumous opportunity, echoing Mercier's "Nouvelles de la lune." Fontlhète does that by making contact with two discorporated souls who have remained closely united after death by virtue of the fact that they were accidentally slain on their wedding night at the moment of their first orgasm, Yfflasie and Clarendon.

The account of Yfflasie and Clarendon's adventures in the afterlife, as related mysteriously to Fontlhète, initially consists of meeting lots of famous dead people, discovering who they were in previous incarnations, and what has become of the recently-reincorporated in their new identities—a formula enabling a good deal of wry satire, which becomes increasingly self-indulgent as the author not only panders to his own political judgments and liking for salacious gossip but increasingly begins to give vent to his personal dislikes and hatreds, He does that in ever-more bizarre fashion, as he develops the notion of careers in the afterlife, which permits Yfflasie and Clarendon to progress from early days as pastors of desires ultimately to become the king and queen of the realm of the disembodied.

When that narrative sequence became too silly, Restif apparently had another change of heart, and abruptly, without bothering with any explanation, gave Fontlhète the wings that Victorin had invented in *La Découverte australe*, thus enabling him to become a more active nocturnal vigilante than the *alter ego* featured in *Les Nuits de Paris*. Unlike Victorin, who used his wings almost exclusively for selfish purposes, Fontlhète makes definite moves in what was ultimately to become the typical career path of comic book superheroes, using his power of flight to oppose evil, and fight crime—not on the local scale preferred in the comic books but on the world stage, taking on evil tyrants and warmongers. That particular narrative thread, however, was soon sidelined, as Restif appears to have been struck by another idea: that of giving scope to some of his other childhood fantasies and importing other superpowers into the plot: to begin with, the power of exchanging identities by taking over other people's bodies with one's own soul.

It is possible that Restif had already developed that idea in a separate story—and, indeed, that he had written several variants of that story while trying to figure out the best way to account for the origin and development of the power in question—and that he simply dumped that other story into his plot, as the "Galland formula" allowed him to do and as he had presumably already done with a few of the anecdotes associated with the careers of the discorporate souls. Indeed, he dumped several different versions of that other story into his framework, perhaps with some vague intention of deciding later which one to settle on, or perhaps realizing that the 366-day frame with which he had saddled himself was going to require a lot more filling than he had initially imagined. At any rate, the amazing Duc Multipliandre made his entrance into the scheme, in association with conflicting accounts of his birth and the back-story of his superpower, and began narrating his own adventures.

Multipliandre was a much more useful superhero than Fontlhète, for the simple reason that Fontlhète, being absolutely committed to Hortense, could not use any powers he acquired for the purpose that was, from Restif's viewpoint, the primary advantage of any superpower: the opportunity to lay women by the score, even while remaining deeply committed to the moral ideal of true love. Multipliandre's adventures thus involve not only the acquisition of several more superpowers, but the recounting of a vast series of varied erotic adventures, some second-hand but many of them personal. He too finds his one true love, but she is perfectly willing to share him, and not overly worried about what his soul might be doing when it is in other bodies than the handsome one she loves.

Restif was not, however, a man to waste the more extravagant opportunities now offered to him by his framework. Multipliandre, as a superhero, was naturally going to set the world to rights as well as having a lot of sex, but he was never going to stop there; having taken up where Fontlhète left off, he was always going to follow Victorin's example of boldly crossing the boundaries of the known world, in order to discover the hypothetical world of Restif's cosmogonic and evolutionary theories. That he did, and far more extravagantly than Victorin's descendants.

In so doing, Multipliandre not only transformed the languidly-evolving story of the letters from the tomb, but Restif's attitude to it. It ceased to be a dilatory self-indulgent spinoff from his salon conversations, and became a kind of mission: the ultimate development of his personal vision and philosophy, far grander than anything he had been able to imagine doing before, and something exceedingly dear to the heart he had not yet laid bare in his long-gestating masterpiece, which still remained to be completed.

That exploration takes Multipliandre to the other known worlds of the solar system, to examine their exceedingly peculiar inhabitants, and numerous worlds unknown to contemporary science, including trans-Uranian planets, a comet and three planets within the orbit of Mercury, the last of them, Io, being on the very brink of being dissolved in the Sun. After that, he sets off to visit several other solar systems, including those of Sirius and Vega, and several nebulae, before concluding his journey in the vicinity of the "astral center" into which the entire universe of stars will one day be dissolved, prior to being regenerated, phoenix-fashion, as an entirely new universe.

Multipliandre then returns to Earth, where, immortal by virtue of his superpowers, he settles down to witness the entire future of the Earth, initially coping with a new evolution of life consequent on a close encounter between the planet and a passing comet, which produces, among other plant and animal species, a new race of winged humans, whom Multipliandre naturally calls "angels." Some of that futuristic text was subsequently moved sideways into another overlapping project, and is missing from the published version of *Les Posthumes*, but the cosmogonic investigations almost certainly remained exactly where they had been in the summer of 1789, when the Revolution broke out, not only interrupting Restif's project but bringing an entire era to a spectacularly abrupt end.

9. The Protocosm

The last item of "philosophical fiction" published in French before the Revolution that is of considerable significance to the evolution of *roman scientifique* was *Icosameron, ou histoire Édouard et d'Élisabeth qui passèrent quatre vingt un ans chez les Mégamicres, habitans aborigènes du Protocosme dans l'intérieur de notre globe, traduit de l'anglois par Jacques Casanova, Chevalier de Seingalt, Vénétien* [Icosameron; or, The Story of Edward and Elisabeth, who spent eighty-one years in the land of the Megamicres, the aboriginal inhabitants of the Protocosm in the interior of our globe, translated from the English by Jacques Casanova, Chevalier de Seignalt, Venetian] (1788). It was not, of course, a translation, being an original work by the notorious Giacomo Casanova (1725-1798), ostensibly—and presumably in this case genuinely—

138

published in Prague. It is very long, consisting of five volumes, the first of them neatly printed by comparison with its clandestinely-produced predecessors.

In 1788 Casanova had not yet written the *Histoire de ma vie* [Story of my Life] that was eventually to secure his enduring fame. Restif de la Bretonne had not yet published *Monsieur Nicolas*, but Rousseau's posthumously-published *Confessions* had recently appeared, and probably played a considerable role in prompting Casanova to competition—Rousseau was an old acquaintance. Like those other ventures in laying bare the heart, Casanova's memoirs pretended an unprecedented honesty, but far less plausibly. He laid claim to a much more exciting life than either Rousseau or Restif, encompassing far more success in seduction, and easily out-competed them in scabrousness, thus becoming far more notorious.

According to his memoirs, Casanova first visited Paris in 1750, having called in at Lyon *en route*, where he had been inducted into Freemasonry, although it was only a substitute for the entry to the Rosicrucian Order that he really craved. He stayed in the capital for two years before moving on, eventually making his way back to Venice, where he wrote his first play, in Italian—the language in which most of his subsequent, fairly trivial, publications appeared. He was famously imprisoned for a while in the Piombi, the Republic's legendary prison, but following his release therefrom—a daring escape, according to his memoirs—he returned to Paris, arriving in 1757 in time, so he said, to witness the execution of Robert-François Damiens for his alleged attempt to assassinate Louis XV.

Casanova settled in Paris for some time, becoming a trustee of the state lottery—from which he creamed off a substantial income—and posing as a Rosicrucian, entering into rivalry with another occultist poseur, the Comte de Saint-Germain, whom the memoirs accuse, unsurprisingly, of being a fraud. He parasitized Jeanne Camus de Pontcarré, Marquise d'Urfé, a widow with a passion for the occult who was subsequently to entertain Cagliostro. He became acquainted with Rousseau and Voltaire during that sojourn. His expertise as a salesman obtained him a commission to sell state bonds during the Seven Years' War, which helped to increase his personal fortune considerably, but he claimed to have turned down an offer of French citizenship and a state pension.

Soon broke again, Casanova left France in 1760 after another spell in prison, adopting the *persona* of the Chevalier de Seingalt, although he sometimes promoted himself to Comte de Farussi. He went back to Paris briefly to attempt another exploitation of the Marquise d'Urfé, attempting to persuade her that he could rejuvenate her and change her sex by occult means, but settled for stealing her jewelry and fleeing to England.

He did not return to Paris for twenty years, but allegedly got back in time to watch an early balloon ascent with Benjamin Franklin before leaving for Vienna. There, in 1785, he made the acquaintance of the Graf von Waldstein, a would-be cabalist, who employed him as his librarian at his *schloss* in Bohemia, thus giving him the opportunity to settle down that his deteriorating health required; excruciating boredom, however, drove him to back to writing, not immediately to the memoirs that were to be his monument, but initially to philosophical romance—which he naturally set out to do in a fashion that had never been done before: hence the *Icosameron*.

The long dedicatory epistle of the book, addressed to Waldstein—who paid for the book to be printed—which is omitted from the drastically abridged English translation of the text published in 1986, cites *Robinson Crusoe* as a primary model, but suggests that Defoe's text, although assumed to be a novel, might really be an authentic account of actual experiences. It goes on to make the same claim for the *Icosameron*, representing it as a work bound to be assumed to be a fantasy, but perhaps a constituting a revelation that the interior of the Earth really is the terrestrial paradise, the actual Garden of Eden. The epistle goes on to provide highly dubious textual support for that supposition from *Genesis* and the Church fathers, and argues from the principle of plenitude that if God had taken the trouble to make such a capacious Earth he would surely have populated it internally to begin with, prior to using *"ses murailles, son écorce"* [its walls, its rind] as place of banishment for those unworthy of living within it, having *"tombé en suspicion"* [fallen under suspicion] after eating the fruit of the Tree of Life.

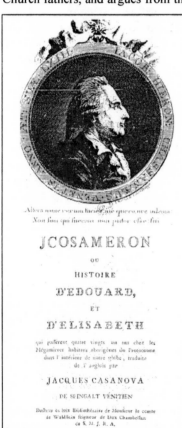

The epistle suggests, however, that God must have been very pleased with all the hard labor the exiles carried out on the surface, in spite of being subjected to all its inconveniences: pestilence, war, famine floods, earthquakes, stinking fogs, lightning, excessive heat and cold, ferocious beasts and biting, bloodsucking insects; in essence, a large-scale open-air version of the Piombi. (The first part of his memoirs, separately published immediately after the *Icosameron*, was Casanova's account of his imprisonment, which obviously rankled, and his escape, probably fantasized.) Those misfortunes, the epistle claims, do not exist in the world of the Megamicres, who still inhabit the Earth's Edenic interior.

Casanova admits that he cannot satisfy his patron "as a philosophical theologian" with an explanation of how his two protagonists, Edward and Elisabeth, contrive to get into Eden in spite of its armed angelic guards, but suggests that the sentence of exile was never intended to be irrevocable and that the Creator might have permitted it in order that witnesses could bring news back to the land of exile, thus shoring up faith in his bounty wherever it might be tottering. Indeed, the epistle contends that God might already be thinking of relenting in his wrath and allowing us to recover the immortality of which the other human race, the Megamicres of the interior, was never stripped—although they do, in fact, die, albeit delightfully.

The epistle calls its addressee's particular attention to the fact that the Megamicres "by virtue of being perfect and worthy of envy, have no need to be divided into two sexes, have no need of sleep to recover their strength, who nourish themselves on their own milk and have no need for nature to have furnished them, in order to eat, with teeth, bones devoid of a certain consistency and often unequal, which, on the globe's surface, quit two thirds of the living before they even reach the age of miserable decrepitude."

They live in a world of perpetual, mild light, provided by a motionless central sun, and their amour "cannot properly be called passion, for it is a sentiment that is not subject to alteration or diminution, which one could call the very substance of their life; for their entire life is one sole amour that always lasts with the same fire for forty-five of our years after having employed three to ignite. The two individuals that form an inseparable couple, born to love one another, die loving one another, giving one another the marks of the most ardent tenderness until the last moment of their existence. Their extinction cannot be called death, but a gentle passage of the same amour, which will become immortal in eternity."

The epistle also calls special attention to the language of the Megamicres— inventing, or at least envisaging, simplified languages had been a preoccupation of many writers of philosophical fiction, from Cyrano to Restif—which is "a true music in prose" and which does not merely enter by the ear but "takes a direct route to the soul by passing through a sixth sense that we do not have, and which God has elected to place all over their epidermis; it can only be produced by true poets, who are, as among us, very rare, and tells entire histories to the souls of the Megamicres that it is not possible to translate into words. Our heroes Edward and Elisabeth, his sister and wife, and their descendants, only experience in listening to it the sensations that the matter of their composition can excite: joy, dolor, astonishment, indignation, horror, pity and compassion, without their knowing why."

The epistle goes on to point out some of the advantages of the Megamicres' superior science, taking particular note of their domestication of a hundred species of horses, including those with wings, and the medical advantages of their chemistry, and promises the addressee that he will see in the story of Edward and Elisabeth a "true nobility...that can only be the child of nature," the triumph of truth over lies, modesty over nudity, and "science in the condemnation of indiscreet curiosity," but apologizes to his patron because the Megamicres might displease him by virtue of their small stature, being no taller than one of our legs (up to the knee)—although they will grow in his sight to such an extent that, in spite of their small material volume, they will end up seeming greater than us.

After several more pages of blatant flattery and philosophical posturing, the epistle finally gives way to the text, although, as with some modern cinematic "trailers," it has already summarized the entire schema, save for trivial supplementary details, arbitrary dramatic incidents and a great deal of prolix digression, and has provided a critique as well—a critique all the more revealing for its seasoning of bluff and nostalgia.

The epistle is followed by a second long commentary (also omitted from the English translation) addressed to readers in general, on the book of *Genesis*, arguing more intensively and exhaustively for the theological legitimacy of the account of the interior world and its consistency with the scriptures. As with the epistle, it is easy to suspect that the author did not mean a single word of it sincerely, and did not really expect anyone else to believe it, but as a lifelong confidence trickster, he knew that imposture is everything, and certainly works hard to put on an appearance of seriousness.

The scholarly tone of the analysis of the six days of Creation as recorded in *Genesis*, spiced with Latin and a little Hebrew, reflecting on the philosophical connotations of such concepts as existence, the void and the vault of Heaven before inserting the Megamicres and their realm into the account of the Earth's formation, is entirely earnest. The greater part of the commentary is not concerned with the Megamicres but with an intensive re-examination and reinterpretation of the myth of the Fall, although that provides the context for the subsequent reintroduction of the contrasted fictitious world, in which the history of paradise continues its own developmental course.

That scholarly fantasy takes up more than a hundred pages, following the dedicatory epistle's thirty, which is small by comparison with the length of the story itself—approximately 1,500 pages, totaling some 300,000 words, presented as a dialogue extended over twenty days in which Edward and Elisabeth tell their story to a group of interested listeners—but nevertheless gives the entire work a markedly different appearance from the abridged English translation that merely reproduces the bare bones of the story. The dialogues that introduce each of the twenty sections contain a great deal of material extraneous to the narrative of Edward and Elisabeth's long sojourn in the underworld, which is by no means free of digression itself, but they do serve to enliven an account of the mores of the Megamicres that is remarkably exhaustive by the standards of utopian fiction. As advertised in the dedicatory epistle, the Megamicres are not perfect, in spite of their unfallen status, but their vices are limited, unassociated with passion by virtue of the lack of sexual differentiation in their society—an argument that picks up where Gabriel de Foigny left off and extends a good deal further.

Only having had access to the drastically-abridged translation, and only aware of the existence of the prefatory commentary from secondary sources, Everett F. Bleiler's monumental bibliography of *Science Fiction: The Early Years* judges *Icosameron* to be "mostly a child of *Nils Klim*" and adds that "a touch of humor might have saved the work," but that is to assess it as a work of "proto-science fiction," which is an ill-fitting characterization. Casanova certainly knew of the existence of Ludwig Holberg's satirical account of the adventures of Nils Klim in a world inside the Earth, where numerous tiny planets orbit a central sun—first published in Latin in 1742 but translated into French not long thereafter—because he cites "Nicolas Klimius" in a list of four authors who gave him the desire to write his own novel offered in an introduction to volume two, the others being Francis Bacon, Thomas More and Campanella. However, his own account of a hollow earth only appropriates that framing device from Holberg. In terms of its overall narrative strategy it has far more in common with Restif's *Découverte australe*, save that its theological perspective owes its allegiance to the Bible rather than a coupling of Voltairean deism and Telliamedian evolutionary theory.

The forty-page introduction to the second volume also refers to Lucian and Don Quixote as "sublime," and contains some further reference to more recent writers, but mostly to denigrate them by comparison with Classical authors, although it compliments Voltaire. Casanova recognizes the achievements of modern science, but insists that Copernicus and Descartes could not have done what they did if Ptolemy had not done something similar centuries before, and, as a good occultist, suggests that if Ptolemy had only had the doctrine of Pythagoras to guide him, he would have come up with the Copernican system himself. Unsurprisingly, therefore, the account of the Megamicres "advanced" scientific knowledge is more an extrapolation of occult science than the kind of physical science that was beginning to take shape at the end of the eighteenth century—but that policy is shored up by the author's equipment of the Megamicres with a sixth sense akin to the one acquired by Mercier's hermit after discovering the dream-replacement for his lost spectacles.

Restif and Casanova make no mention of one another in their respective autobiographies, and presumably never met, but they share considerable similarities of outlook and inclinations, as well as a few conspicuous differences, and the elaborate account of Edward and Elisabeth's descendancy offered in the latter phases of their story mirrors the accounts of Victorin's and Multipliandre's descendancies in the *Découverte australe* and *Les Posthumes*, presumably included in the text for similar reasons of personal fantasization.

The juxtaposition of Restif's *Découverte australe* and the parts of *Les Posthumes* penned prior to the Revolution with *Icosameron* provides a useful collective image of the stage that philosophical fiction ancestral to *roman scientifique* had reached before the revolution, although hardly anyone now bothers to read *Les Posthumes* and the *Icosameron* is only read in drastically abridged form (the full text is available on *gallica* but is difficult to read in the later volumes because of the deterioration of the scanned pages). Their further juxtaposition with the adventures of Simon Tyssot de Patot's Jacques Massé and Pierre Mésange provides parentheses into which the relevant fictions of the century should be slotted, if they are to be properly understood and appreciated in their own terms rather than through the lens of the subsequent development of *roman scientifique* and its analogous genres, as they ought to be.

CHAPTER THREE: REVOLUTIONS: 1789-1851

1. The Four Revolutions and the Three Stages

The Revolution of 1789 was the most significant and traumatic event in French history, not only confused in its own hectic development but providing the prelude to an era of successive upheavals that extended over three generations. The National Assembly created in 1789 when the "Third Estate"—the equivalent of the English Commons—decided to verify its own political dominance without waiting for the other two Estates to agree to it, proceeded to abolish feudalism and all the symbolic paraphernalia of what was now called the *ancien* [i.e. former] *régime*, to pass the Declaration of the Rights of Man and the Citizen, and to effect a massive shift of power from the Church to the State, dissolving religious Orders and confiscating their property, making priests into State employees.

One of the side-effects of the demolition of aristocracy was to throw the French military establishment—whose ranks mirrored the ranks of the nobility—into chaos, leaving the nation vulnerable to invasion until an effective reorganization could be contrived—all the more so as émigré aristocrats were joining forces with the king's royal relatives elsewhere in Europe and actively trying to organize such invasions.

The new Constitution drawn up by the Assembly and signed, under duress, by the King, involved its own replacement by a Legislative Assembly, which first met in October 1791 but immediately fell prey to the fierce rivalries that had become manifest within the new political order, decisively separated into the radical Jacobin "left" and the conservative "right," with a center, mostly consisting of "Girondists," that was swiftly pulled apart as the edifice disintegrated. Its failure to govern led to a second Revolution by the Paris Commune in August 1792, when the city seemed to be under threat from advancing foreign troops.

The latter circumstance provided the pretext for a series of massacres of alleged "traitors," which started in the prisons but overflowed, soon spreading from Paris to the provinces, where priests and the privileged were more-or-less randomly slaughtered. The panic invaded the legislative Chamber, until the Convention Nationale elected to produce further revisions to the Constitution became the *de facto* government, abolished the monarchy, proclaimed a Republic and launched the series of purges that became known as the Terror.

Somehow, Paris did not fall to the invaders, and the new Republican army proved sufficiently well-organized and well-motivated to win a series of surprising military victories—but the tide swiftly turned, and France was to be at war for the next two decades against a shifting coalition of enemies, in which Britain always played a leading role. How France resisted swift defeat in 1793 it is difficult to comprehend, but it did, and the tables were soon turned again as the Republican army won more significant victories.

A new calendar was introduced in 1793 with ten-day periods instead of weeks, which effectively abolished the Sabbath, although still permitting one day's rest per "decad." The destruction of the Church's power paved the way for the institution of a new "cult of Reason" and Notre-Dame Cathedral, renamed the Temple of Reason, was the center of a city-wide celebration of a new Festival of Reason in November, the crowds singing the future national anthem, the Marseillaise, and cheering an actress symbolizing Liberty, clad in the red, white and blue of the tricolor flag and cockade. The Festival was not allowed to interrupt the Terror, although few observers can have thought that it rationalized it.

By the middle of 1794 the Terror had consumed most of its own instigators, Danton and Robespierre having followed Louis XVI and Marie-Antoinette to the guillotine, and the Girondists wrested control from the Jacobins before the Convention approved the new Constitution—the Constitution of Year III—in August 1795, issuing in the Directoire, which held power for the next four years, amid constant accusations of corruption, financial mismanagement—resulting in a dire famine—and treachery against its own democratic ideals, with the result that hardly anyone felt severe pangs of regret when Napoléon Bonaparte, the great hero of the Republican Army's continuing military victories, overthrew the Directoire on 18 Brumaire (9 November) 1799 and initially set up the Consulate, with himself as First Consul, before eventually declaring himself Emperor in 1804 and ushering in yet another new regime.

The new rule lasted for ten years, until military erosion caused Napoléon's expanding Empire to collapse again, although it experienced a famous hundred-day near-resurrection when the defeated Emperor returned from exile and attempted to reclaim power, only to meet his ultimate defeat at Waterloo in 1815. The precarious Restoration of the Bourbon monarchy, over which Louis XVI's brothers presided, was thus secured, for a while, but it never seemed convincing, although the July Revolution of 1830, which marked its end, was a very restrained affair by comparison with its predecessor, merely bringing in a different style of monarchy under Louis-Philippe, the son of the Duc d'Orléans, who had supported the Revolution but had not survived the Terror.

Louis-Philippe's reign lasted for eighteen years, often seeming to his subjects to be something less than entirely serious, until the vacillating order it had introduced broke down conclusively again, with a fourth revolution in 1848. After a brief interim under the caretaker presidency of the Romantic poet Alphonse de Lamartine, elections for the presidency of the new Republic brought back another Bonaparte as Head of State, until his *coup d'état* of 1851 issued in a Second Empire.

As might be imagined, the long series of political and economic upheavals of which the changes of regime were the tip of the iceberg was not conducive to the maintenance of a stable publishing industry, in spite of enormous demand and great determination to meet it. Parisian publishers were, however, long used to working in circumstances that were not merely difficult but actively hostile, and they continued the battle, no longer against the iniquities of the system of royal licenses—abolished along with all the other apparatus of the *ancien régime*—but against a combination of more-or-less continuous economic depression and shifting patterns of political censorship, imposed with varying degrees of ferocity.

Had circumstances been different, publication in Paris might have been more prolific, certainly in the early years of the period, and would not have been so completely dominated by political pamphleteering of various shades, but adventurous and innovative material, combative in broader and subtler fashions, began to reappear as new generations of writers emerged to do battle with the conservative esthetic ideals that were once again ensconced in the Académie Française, in spite of its temporary suppression by the external revolution, following its restoration by Bonaparte in 1803.

The Revolution and its aftermath were not good for French science either, some of its leading luminaries—most notably Antoine Lavoisier—having fallen prey to the Terror, which was probably as costly in its effects as the revocation of the Edict of Nantes had been a century before in driving Huguenot scientists abroad. Eighteenth century French science had labored under the oppressive authority of the Church, but nineteenth century French science did not get as much benefit from the removal of that yoke as it might have done had it not suffered such a crippling upheaval, followed by awkward economic difficulties.

Those circumstances made it rather difficult for the nation to follow the map hopefully drawn up before the Revolution by the philosophers of progress, who had expected progress in science and its technological spinoff to smooth the road for, and actively bring about, social and psychological progress toward the "perfectibility" of individual human beings and their society. Writers commenting on the phases of scientific and technological advancement would probably have been suspicious of that expectation anyway, but the context provided them with grounds for a deeper cynicism. The Industrial Revolution launched and powered by the steam engine and the host of new machines that it powered took in France as well as the rest of Europe, but its driving force was provided in England, and its effects were maximized there precisely because the English parliament, albeit with difficulty, kept the oppressive lid on its own rebellious masses.

If it was not good for practical science, however, the Revolution did provide an important stimulus to the philosophy of science, at least in the ideas of the most important French philosopher of science of the era, Auguste Comte. It was to counter what he saw as the malaise provoked by the 1789 Revolution and its aftermath that Comte developed his "positive philosophy" and such corollaries thereof as the taxonomic classification of the sciences previously cited, the famous law of the three stages, and his prospectus for a godless Religion of Humanity.

As secretary to Claude-Henri de Rouvroy, Comte de Saint-Simon (1760-1825), Comte worked in close association with the foremost eutopian philosopher of the era, whose ideas concerning the reorganization of the "working class" and the suppression of the "idling class" became the foundation of what became known as "utopian socialism," although his ideas regarding minimalist government also made a significant contribution to the development of Anarchist thought. Although Saint-Simon did not use fictional formats as a means of popularizing his ideas during his lifetime, he did make notes for such a popularizing text, intended as a possible "sequel" to his *Mémoires sur la science de l'homme* (1813), which were published posthumously, suggesting that the story in question would have described the sensations of the last human following the dessication of the planet and the extinction of the species, although it would somehow continue to provide a depiction of the race liberated from all superstition and "scientific charlatanism."

Comte did not employ fiction as a means of popularization either, but he did pick up where the *Mémoires sur la science de l'homme* had left off and did his best to usher in that era of liberation from superstition and scientific charlatanism. He saw himself primarily as an analytical scientist of society rather than a political reformer, and thus became the founder of sociology, initially summarizing his ideas in a series of texts collectively known as *Cours de philosophie positive* (1830-42) a summary of which was translated into English as *The Positive Philosophy of Auguste Comte.*

The first three volumes of the *Cours* contained the author's account of the physical sciences, and it was in strict relation to them that he mapped out his prospectus for social science. The latter included the assertion that social evolution progresses through three necessary stages, which he called the theological, the metaphysical and the positive; he applied that thesis to the history of France much as Montesquieu had applied the historical theories he had induced from his studies of ancient Rome to the condition of the French monarchy. In Comte's view, French society had been in the theological stage prior to the Enlightenment, when it had entered the metaphysical stage, prior to the 1789 Revolution, from which it was now emerging into the positive—i.e., the scientific—stage. He subsequently designed his Religion of Humanity as a form of reverence adapted to positive society, embodying the central dictum—of which such eutopian deists as Restif de La Bretonne would have approved wholeheartedly—of *vivre pour autrui* [live for others]: the source of the word "altruism."

Whether the law of three stages and Comte's assessment of the historical juncture that France had reached in the aftermath of the 1789 Revolution were true or not, Comtean philosophy became a major influence on the way intellectuals living in the latter part of that aftermath considered the nature and innate momentum of French society, and French thought. Many people, of course, disapproved strongly of the positive philosophy, not least religious believers, but those opposed to it had at least to arm themselves ideologically in opposition to it; they could not deny that it was an idea whose time seemed to have come.

The new utopian philosophers who appeared in the period between the revolutions of 1789 and 1848 were not only carrying forward and developing ideas whose foundations had been laid by Saint-Simon, but doing so in an intellectual and imaginative context largely defined by Comte. In the same way, Comte was the principal provider of the intellectual context in which serious writers of speculative *contes philosophiques* now had to work. Although he did not put the *scientifique* into *roman scientifique*, he was a major influence on the understanding of what the word could and ought to mean, and on the notion that the advent of some such genre was inevitable, as a matter of natural social evolution.

Immediate literary reactions to the Revolution were, for the most part, naturalistic, the reality of it seeming for too remarkable and urgent to require the distanced work of the imagination. Utopian pamphlets, and a few longer works, were not in short supply, but they were narrowly focused on political matters, and the specific questions of political reorganization facing the Assembly and the Convention. With regard to the development of *roman scientifique*, however, there was one immediate imaginative response that was as notable for its bizarrerie as for the irony revealed by hindsight relative to its optimism.

Le Miroir des événemens actuels ou la Belle au plus offrant (tr. as "The Mirror of Present Events; or, Beauty to the Highest Bidder") by François-Félix Nogaret (1740-1831), was first published, as the title page proudly proclaims, "*En l'an de notre salut 1790, et le deuxième de la Liberté*" [In the year of our salvation 1790, and the second of Liberty], paying homage to the Revolution that is "mirrored" therein with extraordinary eccentricity. The work acquired a certain belated celebrity in the early twenty-first century because of an essay and book by Julia V. Douthwaite, whose prize-winning article "The Frankenstein of the French Revolution: Nogaret's Automaton Tale of 1790" (2009, with Daniel Richter) made the claim, repeated in *The Frankenstein of 1790 and Other Lost Chapters from Revolutionary France* (2012) that it contains a character called Frankenstein. In fact, it does not—the character in Nogaret's story is called Frankestein—but the false allegation was widely repeated on the world wide web.

The work is remarkable in several ways, although it must have been a rather difficult text in 1790, as it is today, because of its stubborn esotericism, intricacy and perversity. It was emphatically not addressed to the masses granted democratic rights by the Assembly; although Nogaret was an enthusiastic supporter of the political ideals of the Revolutionaries and a great believer in the new philosophy of progress, his esthetic commitments remained exceedingly elitist.

In essence, the story is an irreverent political allegory, in which Paris is vaguely represented by the Syracusan beauty Aglaonice, who, following the unfortunate death of the inventor Archimedes in the siege of Syracuse by the Romans, offers her hand in marriage to the inventor who can produce the most effective innovative homage to the great man's mechanical genius. A series of suitors comes forward, each offering a mechanical device ostensibly more marvelous than the last. Thus, in the subtext of the story—made explicit in the final chapter—Lutèce [Paris] offers herself consecutively to a series of political ideologies before discovering an ideal of sorts. The allegory is partly modeled on Bernardin de St. Pierre's transfiguration of the early history of France, L'Arcadie [Arcadia] (1781; intended as the first part of a longer work that was never completed), and borrows several key images therefrom for an anti-clerical and anti-aristocratic tirade that would not have been recognizable to anyone unfamiliar with that text.

The story is set shortly after of the siege, one of its central characters being "Marcus Cornelius," the praetor installed by Rome to govern the island of Sicily, which had become a Roman province by virtue of the city's capture. The actual praetor in Sicily in 211 B.C., which is presumably the year in which the story is set, was Marcus Cornelius Dolabella, about whom very little is known, thus leaving space for Nogaret to improvise, in making his Marcus Cornelius a descendant of plebeians and a model of administrative intelligence. He takes a keen interest in the offer made by Aglaonice, and invites her to stay in his house in order to interview an assess the competitors, not least because he hopes that if no one can win the contest, he might be able to seduce her himself.

From the viewpoint of the present day, the principal interest of Nogaret's story is not so much its peculiar political allegorizing as its ingenuity in depicting the competing inventors and their new inventions. The first ones to come forward, all frankly disappointing, include the manufacturer of a mobile tripod that is ingenious but seems devoid of utility, an expert in miniaturization whose products, although equally ingenious, are similarly futile, and a confidence trickster armed with a fake telescope. In fact, the first really serious contender from the prize is a remarkable flying machine invented by one Aristos.

The machine in question is described as a light chariot made of a fine linen fabric, with large wings instead of wheels, activated by a hidden mechanism. Two large swans are also hitched to it, in order to provide extra lift and aid in steering. Naturally, Aristos does not intend to guide them himself—he has a man to do that for him. Unsurprisingly, given his name and symbolism, he ultimately comes to a sticky end while attempting to fly to the moon in order to recruit troops to invade his homeland and restore the power and authority that the Roman invasion took away. The author includes a tongue-in-cheek list of literary and supposedly actual precedents for the flying machine, although he does not mention the artificial wings invented by Victorin in *La Découverte australe* (1781).

Following Aristos' catastrophe, the way is open for the two exceedingly polite manufacturers of two equally charming and highly ingenious automata. The first automaton to be presented (by Frankestein, a descendant of the Franks) is a seductive flute-player, essentially an elaboration of one of the many devices constructed between 1737 and 1742 by the prolific maker of automata Jacques de Vaucanson. The second, however—the invention of Nictator, a descendant of the shepherds of Chaldea—proves to be even more engaging, in spite of its lack of musical ability, in wielding and pouring out a marvelous Horn of Plenty.

Although not particularly innovative, the two automata are marked improvements on their Vaucansonian models, and inevitably embody a great enthusiasm for technological progress and its potential social rewards. The second automaton, which eventually wins the prize—although Frankestein is rewarded too, by marriage to Aglaonice's sister Bazilide—is strikingly symbolic in that way, as well as in the symbolic political implication of its cornucopia.

Nogaret's novella is lavishly equipped with detailed footnotes, one of which reprinted the entirety of the article in Diderot's *Encyclopédie* on "Massacres," adapted by Voltaire from a calculation made in 1724 by John Trenchard adding up the number of deaths occasioned by the Christian Church in the course of its wars and schisms. The text ends, in association with that note, with a hopeful declaration that the events mirrored in the allegory might succeed in putting an end, not merely to religiously-inspired massacres, but to all massacres.

In spite of the brutal subversion of that hope by the Terror, Nogaret reprinted his story in 1800, in his collection *L'Antipode de Marmontel ou Nouvelles fictions, Ruses d'amour et Espiègleries de l'Aristénète français*, [The Opposite of Marmontel, or, New Fictions, Amorous Ruses and Mischiefs by the French Aristanaetus], under the title "Aglaonice, ou La Belle au concours" [Aglaonice; or The Beauty up for Competition] that subtitle having appeared as the title of the story in the actual text of the earlier volume, in contrast to the title page. It was typical of the author that he did not hesitate to reprint it, although he did remove both the footnote on "Massacres" and the original conclusion, leaving the story with a far more subdued and tentative ending, while retaining the implicit meaning of the role to be played by technology in a regeneration he still hoped to see.

As the title of the later volume observes, Nogaret had originally begun writing fiction under the by-line "l'Aristénète français," an appellation that demonstrated his extreme fondness for esoteric Classical references, Aristanaetus being the name apocryphally attached to two volumes of epistolatory mock-moralistic erotic tales published—long after the death of the actual Aristanaetus of Nicaea—in the fourth century A.D. The name was chosen because Nogaret's numerous *contes philosophiques* are in the same slightly salacious vein, although the satirical aspects of their mock-moralistic pose are inevitably as Voltairean as they are Rabelaisian even if their settings are usually Classical. They generated a certain amount of critical complaint in their day, and *L'Antipode de Marmontel* includes a few items cast in the form of letters from Nogaret in reply to his detractors; one of them objects strongly to comparison made between himself and "the author of *Justine*" (the Marquis de Sade) on the grounds that, whereas the author of *Justine* obviously hates women, he, Nogaret, adores them—a claim echoing the sentiments of Restif de la Bretonne, who praised Nogaret's poetic talents in *Les Posthumes*.

Nogaret's sympathy with Restif is further echoed in *La Terre est un animal, ou conversation d'une courtisane philosophe* [The Earth is an Animal: Conversation of a Philosophical Courtesan] (1795), which presents a cosmogony not dissimilar to Restif's in its fundamental assumption that all matter is living, but present a rather more violent image of worlds devouring one another and the Earth nourishing itself on everything lurking on its surface, including human beings. That work too was reprinted; the third edition of 1805 is supplemented by an epistle in verse addressed to Buffon, dating from 1771, and a preface addressed "Au Voleur" [To the Thief] in which Nogaret complains of the plagiarism of his ideas by one "Dessaudrais"—in *Clef des phénomènes de la nature ou la Terre vivante* (1805), signed Chevrel-Dessaudrais—in his usual flamboyant fashion.

Nogaret worked by day as a humble civil servant, under governments of very different complexion, probably aided in various transitions by his status as a high-ranking Freemason. He was awarded a pension by the National Assembly, which he initially kept during the early years of the Empire, but he was eventually rendered destitute in 1807 after getting on the wrong side of Joseph Fouché and, like Jacques Dulaure, was forced to make a living from his pen thereafter. Although he was never taken seriously by his contemporaries as a scholar because he was so witty, flippant and sarcastic, he was obviously an extraordinarily well-read and intelligent individual, and his refusal to make his philosophical fictions into *contes* in any but a strictly formal sense reflects a determination not to compromise those intellectual credentials.

The most prolific satirist to make use of imaginative materials of the kind later gathered into the fold of *roman scientifique* was "Le Cousin Jacques" (Louis-Abel Beffroy de Reigny, 1757-1811), who welcomed the Revolution with such theatrical pieces as *Nicodème dans la Lune ou La Révolution pacifique* [Nicodemus on the Moon; or, The Peaceful Revolution] (1790) and its sequel *Les Deux Nicodèmes ou Les Français dans la planète Jupiter* [The Two

Nicodemuses; or, The French on the Planet Jupiter] (produced 1791 but not printed).

Beffroy also published fictionalized says such as *La Constitution de la Lune, rêve politique et moral* [The Constitution of the Moon; a Political and Moral Dream] (1793) and a host of periodicals continuing the series he had begun before the Revolution with **Les Lunes de Cousin Jacques** [Cousin Jacques's Moons] (1785-87), including *Les Nouvelles Lunes de Cousin Jacques* (1791), many of which include the fanciful speculative snippets for which he was celebrated. His prolific production eased off after 1792, however, as economic circumstances grew harsher, and never recovered its former impetus or popularity. His multi-volume *Dictionnaire néologique* (1795-1800), which was intended to offer a definitive satirical commentary on the whole sequence of events,

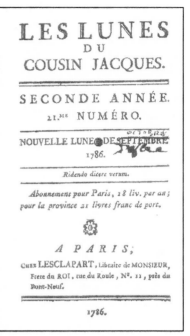

was suppressed and never completed, occasioning his retirement.

That was a kind of career trajectory that many other once-buoyant writers followed, and those who did not sink mostly avoided that fate by clinging precariously to fugitive planks in the 1790s.

The palm for the most imaginatively extreme of all the swift reactions to the Revolution undoubtedly goes to *Le Crocodile, ou La Guerre du bien et du mal, arrivée sous le règne de Louis XV: poème épiquo-magique en 102 chants* (tr. as *The Crocodile; or, The War Between Good and Evil* [omitting "which occurred in the reign of Louis XV, an Epico-Magical Poem in 102 Cantos"]), which was first published in Paris in *"an VII de la République Française"* [1798], advertised as an *"oeuvre posthume d'un amateur des choses cachées"* [posthumous work by a lover of hidden things]. It is not, in fact, a poem, although the story, almost entirely told in prose, does include numerous short bursts of flippant doggerel.

The original version of the work in question had actually been completed on 7 August 1792 by its author Louis-Claude de Saint-Martin (1742-1803), who was still very much alive in 1798. The precise date of completion is important because it was two days before the Paris Commune was established and three days before the suspension of the Legislative Assembly—which is to say, on the eve of the second Revolution in Paris. The published version is interrupted by a long essay, which, although not unconnected with the underlying themes of the story, makes no contribution to its plot. The essay was evidently written in 1797 in response to a competition for a prize offered by the Institut, so the "canto" containing it and the previous one excusing its insertion must have been added shortly before publication, so the original version of the work must have had a round hundred cantos. Saint-Martin subsequently published the essay separately, as if to admit that it did not belong where he had initially placed it. (It is removed from the English translation, on the grounds that the abrupt and arbitrary disruption of the story is a considerable disservice to the reader.)

LE CROCODILE,
ou *Phil 574*

LA GUERRE

DU BIEN ET DU MAL,

ARRIVÉE SOUS LE RÈGNE DE LOUIS XV;

POÈME ÉPIQUO-MAGIQUE
EN 102 CHANTS,

Dans lequel il y a de longs voyages, sans accidens qui soient mortels ; un peu d'amour sans aucune de ses fureurs; de grandes batailles, sans une goutte de sang répandu; quelques instructions sous le bonnet de docteur ; et qui , parce qu'il renferme de la prose et des vers, pourroit bien en effet, n'être ni en vers, ni en prose.

OEUVRE POSTHUME D'UN AMATEUR DES CHOSES CACHÉES.

A PARIS.

De l'Imprimerie - Librairie du CERCLE - SOCIAL,
Rue du Théâtre - Français, n°. 4.

AN VIIJ DE LA RÉPUBLIQUE FRANÇAISE.

Saint-Martin never signed any of his books with his own name, but the great majority were signed "*le philosophe inconnu*" [the unknown philosopher]. *Le Crocodile* was the only one to bear the pseudonym attached to it, and it was the author's only work of fiction. He is nowadays known almost entirely because of his connection with "Martinism," which—somewhat confusingly—was not named after him but after one of the unorthodox thinkers under whose influence he developed his own philosophy: a man generally known as "Martinez de Pasqually," although he sometimes decorated that appellation with various other ornamentations and his birth name remains uncertain, as does the year of his birth, although he died in 1774, seemingly in his fifties or sixties. Saint-Martin met Martinez in the 1760s, shortly after embarking reluctantly on a military career, which he swiftly abandoned when he fell under the older man's spell.

Martinez was the founder, in 1754, of the pompously-named *Ordre des Chevaliers Maçons Élus Coëns de l'Univers* [The Order of the Masonic Knights, the Priestly Elite of the World], an esoteric society modeled on the Freemasons and commonly known in English as the "Elect Cohens." Everything known about Martinez's theories is second-hand, mostly conveyed via his other celebrated disciple Jean-Baptiste Willermoz (1730-1824), the principal architect of "Martinism" as it became known when it briefly became one of the influential occult disciplines of its era, entangled with both Freemasonry and Rosicrucianism, with which Willermoz also involved himself. Martinism faded away after Willermoz's death before being revived and revamped by Gérard Encausse, alias "Papus," during the occult revival of the 1880s, which guaranteed a version of it a fugitive survival thereafter in the strange social fringe of occult lifestyle fantasy, where Saint-Martin's philosophical texts still serve as guide-books to a favored few.

Although Saint-Martin undoubtedly assisted Willermoz to formulate the original doctrine of "Martinism" he was not much involved in the esoteric societies in which Willermoz delighted, and although he had other associates and a handful of acolytes, he was essentially a writer, with little interest in ceremonial. His own esoteric philosophy was extensively reformulated in the 1780s under the influence of the German mystic Jakob Böhme (1575-1624), whose works he translated into French, and Böhme's ideas probably figure larger in the ideative background of *Le Crocodile* than Martinez de Pasqually's, although the story is so peculiar and, in parts, so deliberately enigmatic, that it would be difficult to trace all its individual elements back to their sources. Given that the story was evidently not intended to be read solely by initiates, it would, in any case, be wrong to regard it as if it were a kind of puzzle from which Martinist and Böhmian ideas are supposed to be deduced in detail, rather than simply dangled as teasing lures.

The story is, in fact, best read and appreciated not as a potential key to any kind of esoteric scholarly fantasy or lifestyle fantasy, but simply as a literary fantasy in its own right, akin to such calculatedly bizarre near-contemporary works as *Icosameron* and *Les Posthumes*. Like them, it employs fiction as a means of elaborating a highly unorthodox cosmogony, and like them—and Nogaret's *Le Miroir des événemens actuels* as well—it revels in a kind of teasing obscurantism that makes an extraordinarily elaborate use of symbolism in a challenging quasi-comedic fashion, thus acquiring a marked affinity with twentieth-century surrealism and the theater of the absurd.

The central theatrical absurdity in *Le Crocodile* is, unsurprisingly, the eponymous crocodile, an instrument of Evil whose spectacular manifestation in the Plaine des Sablons consists of surging forth from underground and swallowing two rival armies, one of Revolutionaries and the other of regular troops and volunteers attempting to suppress the revolution. The full title is deliberately misleading; the story cannot possibly have been set in the reign of Louis XV as it was known to history; it is, in essence, an apocalyptic fantasy of a kind that can only really be set in the future—or, given that it represents a Paris prey to Revolution and famine, a present day of immediate wish-fulfillment. In the interim between its writing and its belated publication, of course, things in Paris had gone from bad to worse, and the author, stripped of his modest patrimony (he was an aristocrat, but not rich) had been banished from Paris. His later non-fiction works are apocalyptic in a significantly different way, representing the Revolution as a day of divine judgment far more severe than the one depicted in the story—but that did not stop him publishing the work belatedly, any more than the stubborn continuation of massacres stopped Nogaret reprinting *Le Miroir des événemens actuels.*

After swallowing the armies, the crocodile, explaining that it has traveled to Paris without leaving Egypt, where its tail is bolted to the Great Pyramid, delivers a long "science lesson" to the crowd that has witnessed the disappearance of the armies, whose members are prevented magically from leaving. It claims to have created and shaped the material universe—although the author takes the trouble in one of his numerous personal intrusions to inform us that the monster's assertions are not entirely reliable—albeit within the context of a Divine Plan to which the it is opposed, as a dedicated saboteur, although it also functions as a container of a strange Hell, an account of which is eventually rendered by the volunteer Ourdeck, who manages to escape from the crocodile's entrails when it suffers an extreme internal commotion.

The story only offers oblique glimpses of the ultimate occult forces opposed to the crocodile, although Madame Jof [i.e. Jehovah], who supervises a Society of Independents, the members of which never meet but are always in session, pops up occasionally, and her husband—a jeweler by profession—eventually puts in an appearance of sorts (he is normally invisible) to explain to the Lieutenant de Police, Sedir, what has happened to the two armies after the crocodile is forced to vomit them up all the way to the realm of the heavens, where their attempts to continue fighting are thwarted by the elasticity of the heavenly bodies.

Long before that regurgitation, however, the crocodile and its associates have inflicted a plague on all books and paper, which reduces all human knowledge, especially science, to a soggy pulp. The pap in question is then fed to all the erstwhile users of books, including the members of a commission sent by the Académie to investigate the crocodile. The confusion imparted by the "broth of books" brings the story's deliberate surrealism to a peak in canto 41, which reproduces the address made by the spokesman for the Academy's commission while under its chaotic influence.

The passage is to some extent a parody of the calculatedly esotericism of academic discourse, but it is also deliberately paradoxical in its argumentative refrain, which is a remarkable admixture of contradictory positions, in which a crucial element of conviction is supposed to show through in spite of all the obfuscation. A compendium of images that includes numerous deliberately nonsensical juxtapositions is there employed as a matrix for sincere assertions, in a fashion that could not have been contrived in any context but that of a recklessly fantastic item of fiction. It is, after its own strange fashion, a *tour de force*.

Another report is rendered by Ourdeck following his escape from the crocodile's bowls and his return to Paris, initially orally, to a crowd assembled in a public square, but subsequently by way of the psychograph—a writer of thoughts—on one of the few supplies of paper spared from the plague. The portion transcribed by the psychograph explains that when the refugee first made his way out of the crocodile's body by means of a "capillary vessel" he found himself in the Euboean city of Atalante, here allegedly swallowed up during the great earthquake of 426 B.C. (In fact, Atalanti—now an island—was only damaged in the quake, although some land was inundated; Plato, born a year later, might have based his story of Atlantis on the incident).

In *Le Crocodile*, everything in Atalante is reported to have stopped dead at the moment of its submersion, although a vault of rock protected it from being inundated, and in the vacuum thus created, everything remains exactly as it was more than two thousand years before, uncorrupted and unaltered—except that the last words of its inhabitants, although they cannot be heard because there is no air, can still be read in something akin to cartoon speech-bubbles by Ourdeck, who is temporary freed from the need to breathe, as he had to be while in the crocodile's abdomen. The speeches he reads, as well as what he reads in annals and prophecies contained in an iron book, allow him to make numerous educative discoveries before he precipitates an upheaval that results in him being spat out into a drain in Paris.

Ourdeck arrives back just in time to witness the attack launched by a legion of evil genii on the most significant of their human adversaries: an aging Jew named Eleazar, who is armed with a little box containing a magic plant extract, and supported by his daughter Rachel as well as Sedir. For a moment, it seems that evil might win, as the boldest of the genii contrives to steal the box, but Eleazar has superheroic resources that allow him to come back from the brink of disaster, scatter the evil genii and go to confront the crocodile in the ultimate duel on the Plaine des Sablons. His victory there not only banishes the monster but enables the liberation of those inhabitants of its bowels who are worthy of clemency and convinces the two rival armies to lay down their weapons and swear eternal brotherhood.

More than that, Eleazar's victory also liberates the sciences, symbolically incarnated as beautiful maidens, from the long captivity in which the crocodile has held them, severing them from their divine origins and deflecting them into the allegedly-sterile intellectual wilderness of empiricism. They express their gratitude in song, and from then on, in the present day of the story, real progress is possible, both socially and scientifically—although Saint-Martin's notion of science is, of course, the very opposite of Auguste Comte's, and Saint-Martin's horror of Academic orthodoxy would have been mild by comparison with the anathema he would have uttered against positivism had he lived to hear it promulgated.

The difficulties faced by those writers who attempted to publish work after 1790 are illustrated very clearly by the travails of Restif de la Bretonne in trying to carry forward all the projects that were still incomplete in 1789—of which the one uppermost in his mind was necessarily his vast masterpiece, *Monsieur Nicolas*. Compared with that, the disorderly and misshapen *Lettres du tombeau* was a secondary issue. Nevertheless, he did take it up again when he had time, and he probably continued adding further letters sporadically, some of which detail a series of "dreams" in which Multipliandre describes the phases of the Revolution to Fontlhète as a futuristic prophecy.

In fact, Multipliandre had already given Fontlhète a different account of the future after 1787, in which he becomes Prime Minister of France by means of judicious body-swapping, unifies Europe under a Republican government and paves the way for the political unification of the entire globe, but Restif simply left that contradiction in place, along with numerous others. The dream sequence describing the Revolution is naturalistic, except for a brief episode when the dreaming Multipliandre uses one of his superpowers—invisibility—to escape arrest by Revolutionary Guards on suspicion of being a spy.

Restif never stopped writing during the years of the Revolution and the Terror, even when he was on the brink of starvation, as he eventually was, nor did he entirely stop publishing, although his productions necessarily slowed down. His principal publications, once the Terror was over and a measure of calm had returned, were *Le Drame de la vie, contenant un homme tout entier* [The Drama of Life, containing an entire man] (dated 1793, when it was presumably typeset, but it was not printed and distributed for some time thereafter) and the work from which it was spun off, *Monsieur Nicolas, ou Le Coeur human dévoilé* (1794). He also added new text to *Les Nuits de Paris* and continued his vast series of short stories detailing female lives with *Les Provinciales* (twelve volumes, 1795).

By 1795, having survived the Terror and famine, Restif was working with more fervor than ever before. He had already put together a non-fictional account of his "physics"—his cosmogony and evolutionary theory—in one of three supplementary volumes of his autobiography, collectively entitled *La Philosophie de Monsieur Nicolas* (1796), and in the early months of 1796 he set out on another dramatization of that science, taking up the plot of his early wish-fulfillment fantasy about a hero who acquires a private enclosure lavishly supplied with women in which to build his own private paradise, and developing it as a novel entitled *L'Enclos et les oiseaux* [The Enclosure and the Birds], which he wrote between January and May 1796.

There is no way to be sure, but Restif probably intended that project, to begin with, to be a replacement for the disorganized mess of the manuscript containing Fontlhète's inconsequential and incoherent *Lettres du tombeau*. He evidently translated many of the imaginative ideas from the Multipliandre sections of the manuscript into the new work, organizing them more coherently in an account of a new superhero, who indulges in the usual extensive gamut of sexual adventures before employing the secret of immortality to witness and participate in the entire future history of the Earth, from the end of the eighteenth century until the death of the planet, when it is swallowed by the Sun.

Even before finishing the manuscript of *L'Enclos et les oiseaux*, however, Restif was evidently inspired to wonder whether, in fact, the other manuscript might not be salvageable, and publishable as one of a pair with the new work, in spite of its incoherencies—which could, in principle, be partly written off as eccentricities and perhaps partly smoothed over. A note added to the final pages of *Les Posthumes* suggests that the future histories set out in the two texts were deliberately framed to complement one another rather than duplicating information, so the final phases of *L'Enclos et les oiseaux* were probably written with that intention, cannibalizing some futuristic material from Multipliandre's adventures.

Again, we cannot be sure, but it seems probable that *L'Enclos et les oiseaux* was a much more coherent and better-organized work than *Les Posthumes*, and that it contained a much more elaborate account of a long hypothetical future, informed by a scientific theory that (although we now know it to have been completely erroneous) had been worked out thoroughly and intensely. The indirect evidence we have suggests that it was the most important speculative novel produced in the eighteenth century, and the first great classic of *roman scientifique*, which would have been an enormously important reference-point for writers in the genre, had it only been published. Alas, it was not.

After completing *L'Enclos et les oiseaux*, Restif set out to prepare *Les Posthumes* for publication. His first move in so doing was presumably to supplement the existing text by bringing the sequence of Multipliandre's "prophecies" all the way to 1796, albeit briefly, before abruptly skipping back to 1787 in order to reorganize the denouement, before the Revolution can break out within the timeline of the narrative. Far more laboriously, however, Restif also decided to supplement the existing sequence of letters by adding a series of responses to them written by Hortense, interleaving those with the existing manuscript.

The immediate effect of that move was to add a further level of complication to a text that was already extremely muddled, especially in terms of its internal chronology, and the additions helped to transform an existing confusion into complete chaos. Nor is it immediately obvious why the new text makes any substantial contribution to the story, although it is obvious that the author wanted to pay some tribute to the story's origins in Fanny de Beauharnais' salon by adding her (lightly disguised) and some of her salon's guests into the weave of the narrative.

Hortense continually includes comments made by the other members of her "society," including Jacques Cazotte, which some of the individuals named might well have made while the series of letters as being drafted in 1787-89, and makes flattering remarks about them. The flattery might well have been fishing for financial aid to get the book published, because Restif had exhausted his own resources getting the last few volumes of Monsieur Nicolas and its supplement into print, and no publisher was any longer willing to take the financial risk of printing his more eccentric ventures. That fishing might have had some success, as the published version carries a note citing a subsidy from an unnamed "associate"—but *L'Enclos et les oiseaux* presumably contained no such incentive.

Apart from adding the last few letters, it is not easy to determine exactly what alterations Restif made to the existing manuscript in the 1796 version, but if appearances can be trusted, almost all of the other amendments consisted of dropping additional paragraphs into the text at various points, whose effect, once again, was to add a further layer of confusions and contradictions to a text that was already full of them. It might have been the case that Restif made a conscious decision at that point not to try to sort out any of those contradictions, but to leave them all in place, as essential features of a text whose peculiarity had already exceeded all known bounds. On the other hand, he might simply have realized that *L'Enclos et les oiseaux* was not going to get into print any time soon, that the whole joint project was a catastrophe from the viewpoint of publication, and abandoned the revisions half-done. On balance, the latter seems slightly more probable.

In the next five years, Restif only contrived to publish one new book: *L'Anti-Justine ou les délices de l'amour* [The Anti-Justine; or, The Delights of Amour] (1798), an ideological riposte to the Marquis de Sade, intended to demonstrate by example that pornography did not have to be disgusting and depraved, but could be delightful and virtuous. To its publisher and most of its readers, however, it was presumably just pornography, and the police certainly thought so when they seized the remaining copies in 1803 and banned it, as the sort of thing that was not going to be tolerated under the Empire. Inevitably, it remained, and still remains, one of his most popular works.

The economic and political corner was finally turned, for France, when Bonaparte overthrew the Directoire in 1799 and was appointed First Consul. An appearance of stability returned, and, far more importantly, a wave of optimism unfurled. Restif was still flat broke, but the son of the widow Duchesne, his old publisher, was eager to get the business running at full tilt again, and part of his business plan—probably in response to Restif's urgent persuasion—was a reissue of Restif's most successful works, supplemented by new volumes with ready-made reader appeal, such as *Les Nouvelles contemporaines* (1802). How Restif persuaded him to add *Les Posthumes* and *L'Enclos et les oiseaux* to his program is unknown, perhaps by begging, perhaps by promising to do more commercial work in exchange, but most likely simply by finding someone willing to put in a subsidy—the "associate" to whom the supplementary material of *Les Posthumes* refers.

At any rate, Restif set out to typeset *Les Posthumes* with a furious sense of urgency, which probably prevented him from making any of the changes that he might have made had completed his revisions in 1796 or had he been working in better circumstances. It was published as *Les Posthumes: Lettres reçues après la mort du mari par sa femme, qui le croit à Florence, par feu Cazotte* [The Posthumous: Letters received after the death of a husband by his wife, who believes him to be in Florence, by the late Cazotte] (tr. as *Posthumous Correspondence*) in 1802.

160

Restif knew, when he began to set the type, that the book would not make money, and that he was exploiting the good will of the widow Duchesne's son and his unnamed "associate," but he was desperate to get it into print at all costs, even in poor shape, for reasons that the text states explicitly. He knew that he was no longer capable of shaping it more elegantly and more coherently, and that if he did not publish it while he still had a little life left in him, nobody was going to do it for him after he was dead—so he did it, warts and all, laying bare its inner workings for anyone who cared to understand. He did not correct or alter anything in the confused mess that the manuscript still was, only dropping in a few extra notes in order to add flattering references to Bonaparte, as well as adding some supplementary material to the beginning and end of the text.

It was presumably in 1802, rather than in 1796, that he decided to credit the published work to "le feu Cazotte," Cazotte having been guillotined during the Terror. There is no trace within the text itself of any such imposture, save for one belatedly-added note, and although Fontlhète and Hortense inevitably refer to Restif in the third person when mentioning him or his works, no sensitive reader could possibly have been in doubt as to his complete involvement in the text. Even in the supplementary advertisements appended to the end of the text Restif refers to himself as "the editor," but only an exceedingly dim-witted reader would have failed to take the obvious inference from the fact that all the advertisements are for works by Restif, and that no mention at all is made of Cazotte's.

As to why Restif made that adjustment, we can only guess, but it is unlikely to have been a cynical attempt to increase the sales of the book. It might have been a simple tribute to a regretted friend whose comments in discussion might indeed have made a substantial contribution to the first draft while it was in slow progress, but it seems more probable that it relates to an anecdote circulating at the time that was due to a misinterpreted remark by Restif's arch-enemy Jean-François La Harpe, in which the latter commented wryly on how amazed the guests at one of Fanny de Beauharnais' dinners would have been if the Illuminist had told them, in 1788, where they would all be in five years' time. The comment was repeated as if it were a statement that Cazotte had indeed done that, and Restif might not have been able to resist the temptation to credit his late friend with such a "prophecy," made, like La Harpe's remark, after the fact.

Could Restif have done more to repair the work when he finally prepared it for publication? In theory, yes; in practice, probably not. After all, the one thing of which we can be certain is that it was the last thing he ever did by way of publication; he was not able to typeset *L'Enclos et les oiseaux*, either because he was physically incapable of doing it, or because Duchesne flatly refused to publish it, perhaps because the person who was going to pay for it backed out. Either way, that text was lost, forever—and whatever one might think of *Les Posthumes* as an undeniably crippled and clumsy literary work, that loss is undoubtedly a tragedy, in terms of the history of speculative and futuristic fiction, at least equal to the loss of the second half of Cyrano's *L'Autre Monde.*

Restif was sixty-seven in 1802, old by the standards of the day, and he had never enjoyed the best of health. When he typeset *Les Posthumes*, he believed that he was pressed for time and he probably identified his own predicament much more closely than he might have wished with Fontlhète's—with the crucial exception, of course, that he had no Hortense who would miss him, having never managed to find the deep and true mutual love for which he had yearned all his life, and which he never ceased to hold up as the great ideal of the human heart.

It was probably not at that point that Restif inserted Fontlhète's final cry of anguish into the text—"If ever death separates us, you will have things from me sufficiently extraordinary to reread them, and thus conserve my soul, rendered present by the particles of its intelligence that I am leaving you; for thoughts are the particles of the soul, and woe betide the man who does not leave behind those that are dear to him!"—but he must have felt its full force as he set it in type.

He was, by then, at the absolute end of his tether, even though he did not actually die until February 1806. By that time, he must, indeed, have been woebegone at the thought that *L'Enclos et les oiseaux* would never see the light of day, and probably could not take as much consolation as he would have liked from the knowledge that, direly imperfect as it was, bearing all the scars of its slow and uncertain genesis, *Les Posthumes* would at least conserve a few of the particles of his soul, which were even dearer to him than the heart he had never quite succeeded in laying entirely bare.

Les Posthumes seems to have been almost devoid of subsequent influence, with the possible and rather eccentric exception of a curious document published in 1834 in the form of a *Lettre d'un habitant de la lune*, which pretends to be a missive sent from the Moon by "feu Caron de Beaumarchais," reincarnated there among the "demigods" and assisted in the method of transmitting his memoir to Earth inside a projectile by the similarly-reincarnated Voltaire and Lavoisier. Restif included a particular tribute to Beaumarchais in *Les Posthumes*, which contained an element of apology, the content of which is much expanded in the substance of the letter from the Moon, addressed to the historian "M. Mary Lafont" (Jean-Bernard Mary-Lafon, 1810-1884), the presumable author of the work.

2. The End of the World

Catastrophic events tend to encourage apocalyptic fears, and although those fears remain tied to the catastrophe in hand while it is actually unfolding, they become easily negotiable once it seems to have ended into more distant and more generalized futuristic anxieties. It is not surprising, therefore, that the stuttering aftermath of the 1789 Revolution produced new apocalyptic fantasies; nor is it surprising, even though the Festivals of Reason had not lasted very long and the Church had soon reclaimed Notre-Dame and the other churches of Paris, that some of the new apocalyptic fantasies in question should take aboard a strong infusion of rationalistic thought and imagery. Most of the traceable poems and plays from the period employing the ever-popular title *Le Fin du monde* are straightforward Biblical fantasies, but there is no paradox in the fact that the longest and most spectacular apocalyptic romance of the period, *Le Dernier homme* (1805; tr. as *The Last Man; or Omegarus and Syderia, A Romance in Futurity*) by Jean-Baptiste Cousin de Grainville (1746-1805) should also offer a futuristic vision that owed far more to the new philosophy of progress than Mercier's *L'An deux mile quatre cent quarante* or Restif's *Les Posthumes*.

Cousin's novel was published posthumously, the author having died shortly beforehand; he had been a priest for more than twenty years but had had to abandon the priesthood during the Revolution. In his younger days he had won a prize for eloquence awarded by the Académie de Besançon, discoursing on the subject of the contribution made by philosophy to the eighteenth century. After quitting the priesthood he initially attempted to turn his eloquence to drama, his *Judgment de Paris* being staged at the Théâtre-Français; he apparently wrote two novels as well as a further play, and also produced numerous translations, without contriving to achieve anything further in the way of publication or performance.

When the situation of the Church eased sufficiently for Cousin to be able to contemplate returning to the priesthood he apparently made efforts to do so, but the new hierarchy did not want him. He seems to have become deeply depressed, and when he drowned in the Somme Canal, which ran past his house, on an exceedingly cold night, it was widely assumed—though not proven—that it was not an accident. His book was published at the behest of Bernardin de Saint-Pierre, a writer of imaginative fiction himself, who had supported Mercier when the latter had unsuccessfully recommended Restif for membership in the Académie Française before its abolition in 1793.

One of the modern critics to have examined Cousin's work thoroughly and perceptively, Paul Alkon, discusses it under the rubric of "The Secularization of Apocalypse," and the book does indeed offer a vision of the divinely-ordained end of the world that accommodates a great deal of secular imagery in its build-up to that moment, but the perspective can also be inverted, and it can be seen as a work that has a considerable contiguity with Casanova's *Icosameron* in attempting to place progressive utopian imagery firmly within a framework of religious faith. One suspects that Casanova was not entirely serious in doing that, but Cousin gives a much greater impression of sincerity—and also, perhaps, of a quest to resolve his own intellectual doubts.

Cousin initially projected *Le Dernier homme* as a epic poem, and the text, like that of *Le Crocodile*, is divided into "cantos" rather than chapters—and, indeed, two transfigurations of its substance into poetry were subsequently contrived, one by Auguste-François Creuzé de Lesser as *Le Dernier homme* in 1831, and the second, which elaborates its substance considerably, by Élise Gagne as *Omégar, ou le dernier homme*, in 1859. By then it was recognized as a classic of sorts, although it made little impact on first publication; in the second edition of 1811 Charles Nodier excused that relative failure by arguing that it had been "mistaken" for a novel and hence read as a mere story without a proper appreciation of its Miltonian poetic virtues. Nodier's championship kept the novel in the minds of other members of the Romantic Movement, to the extent that Jules Michelet devoted a chapter of his mammoth history of France to the tragedy of Cousin's life and death, holding his work up as an exemplification of the spirit of the early nineteenth century, when, in Michelet's view, the steam engine and the Emperor's Grande Armée had collaborated in unleashing the destructive forces of humankind in Europe.

Like the Apocalypse itself and Mercier's dream of future Paris, Cousin's depiction of the future is presented as a prophetic vision, granted by a celestial spirit to the narrator, by means of magic mirrors in a cave near Palmyra. Like the spectacles found by Mercier's hermit, the mirrors permit the narrator not merely to see and hear what Omégare, the man fated to be the last alive on Earth, says and does, but also to have access to his "most secret thoughts"—although, no sooner has his attention been absorbed by Omégare than the narrator regrets not having focused it on his female companion Syderie. He does have that opportunity, however, toward the end of the text, when Syderie, left alone, has her own apocalyptic vision. The story within the story begins some time in advance of the initial glimpse, however, before Omégare meets Syderie, with whom he might be able to become the parents of a new human race once the existing one has reached its terminus.

Indeed, the enclosed story opens not with the last man but with the first Adam, condemned to serve as Hell's doorkeeper in order to watch the passage of all the souls damned by his error. He is, however, offered the chance of release by Ituriel, God's messenger, if he can persuade Omégare not to perpetuate the human race with Syderie but to let it end. Adam, whose torment is increased by his ignorance of what happened to his own inamorata, Eve, has mixed feelings about that, but he accepts the mission. The situation is further complicated by the involvement of a "*génie*" as old as the Creation, who is determined to protect the human world, having been delegated by God to do that and who is now unready to accept the new orders from above. The *génie* has a laboratory inside the Earth, in which he toils away producing new devices for its salvation, and from which he reaches out in the attempt to ensure that Omégare and Syderie do get together and procreate, thus continuing the career of humankind.

The narrative voice seems to have mixed feelings too, and the reader—whose likely response to the situation outlined will presumably be to hope for Omégare and Syderie to defy God's dictatorial will and save humankind—could well experience a certain suspense in wondering what the eventual outcome will be. The possibility that God will not get his way this time is seemingly supported by the fact that the future world described seems to be devoid of Christianity, the Bible and any apocalyptic mythology of its own, although it is not entirely purged of superstition and pagan religion.

It is during Omégare's journey to his fateful meeting with Syderie in a "*globe aérien*"—a palatial airship—that the history of the world up to that point is summarized, with its various wars, but also its relentless scientific and technical progress, culminating in a Promethean remedy that enables the extension of the human lifespan. Carefully rationed in order to prevent the world from becoming overpopulated, that is a key element of an era of technological dominance over the entire world and its products, but natural forces remain more powerful; there is a drastic decline in human fertility, while the paling of the Sun and the disintegration of the Moon precipitate a new Ice Age, forcing the dwindling remnant of the human race to take refuge in Brazil. It is there that Omégare is united with Syderie, to create the only potentially-fertile couple left on Earth, but their union is opposed by various agents, on the grounds of visions suggesting that their progeny will be a deeply flawed race.

The couple flee to the ruins of Paris, initially intent on defying the prediction, but once they are there the situation becomes more complicated as "*la mort*" [a personalized Death] takes a hand in the game, haunting the *génie* and entering into negotiations with him, while Omégare and Syderie are plagued by further visions, in one of which Eve appears, in order to add her perspective to Adam's. In the end, God's will is done, and the narrative voice, as that of a stubborn man of God, has no alternative but to approve, outwardly at least—but the reader remains free to doubt, or at least to wonder, and to reflect on the apparent paradoxicalities of the plot and its import.

There is no other book like Cousin's *Le Dernier homme*, except for the two poetic adaptations of it, in spite of the fact that the early nineteenth century saw a positive rash of "last man" poems and stories spring up in England, several of which employ the equivalent title. They were far thinner on the ground in France, in spite of the attention paid to Cousin by the Romantics, under Nodier's encouragement. Mention perhaps ought to be made in this context, however, of the epic poem *L'Atlantiade ou La Théogonie newtonienne* [The Atlantiad; or, The Newtonian Theogony] (1812) by Népomucène-Louis Lemercier (1771-1840), which belongs to the subgenre of past-set apocalyptic fantasies featuring the doom of Atlantis, but is remarkable for the long preface in which the author explains the imaginary history on which the poem is based, and the supposed basis of the catastrophe—occasioned by a disruption of the Earth's axis—in Newtonian theory.

One notable example that places a modicum of futuristic speculation in a similar ideative framework is provided by *La Vision d'Hébal* (1834; tr. as "Hebal's Vision") written by the philosophical historian and Academician Pierre-Simon Ballanche (1776-1847), who had spent his entire life laboring on a comprehensive account of human history as an alleged reflection of cosmic history, embodying the principle of palingenesis. He never finished it, and barely made a start, because the task was simply too large, but he did eventually publish the summary vision in question in order to signify what its eventual reach might have been. The text is supposedly extracted from the incomplete third volume of the project, *La Ville des expiations* [The City of Expiation]. Like Cousin's *Dernier homme*, it remains a work of pure apocalyptic fiction in spite of its infection and invasion by scientific ideas and the author's attempts to adopt Catholic dogma to a philosophical frame that cannot logically accommodate it.

In its most general sense, "palingenesis" means regeneration, although it had come to have a more specific relevance during the eighteenth century, when it was adapted by some speculative philosophers to refer to notions of the reincarnation of the individual soul. The devout Ballanche would have been more familiar with its appropriation by theologians to dignify Christian baptism, and it was from that starting point that he developed his own eccentric notion of the history of the human race as a series of regenerative ordeals imposed by virtue of the Fall, in which the vicissitudes of individual life not only mirror the iterative emergence and collapse of civilizations and cultures but the entire story of Creation.

Hébal is a Scotsman—which might seem unlikely, but his name is derived from "clan Hébal," an anagram of the author's name—endowed with second sight, episodes of which are provoked by poor health that provoke fits of cataleptic hallucination. Although his visions do not present themselves sequentially, he is able to piece them together jigsaw-fashion, and eventually comes to see himself as "the universal man, living an infinite life, cosmogonically, mythically and historically"—to which three phases of human time he is able to add a fourth, the apocalyptic. He builds a vision of the entirety of human existence, from beginning to end, as a sequence of regenerations, which constitute steps in an ongoing redemption. Every component of his vision is divided into three—strophe, antistrophe and epode—in order to produce a "dithyrambic form…an endless concert, an eternal dance."

The series as set out in the story begins, therefore, with the Creation, and the formation of the Earth, followed by the appearance and pre-historic development of humankind, narrated in accordance with *Genesis*, but a *Genesis* revised in the hope of accommodating it to a post-Buffon period of thought, much as Casanova had done or pretended to do, in the preface to *Icosameron*. The histories of the Hebrews, the Greeks and the Romans get one swift chapter each, Christ is allocated a more substantial one, and the initial spread of his Church two, prior to the Reformation, but it only requires a dozen lines to pass from Luther via the Jesuits, Louis XIV, Oliver Cromwell and Peter the Great to the moment when "Descartes and Bacon give birth to the eighteenth century" and the French Revolution promptly brings it to an end. Napoléon, however, gets several paragraphs to himself, albeit short ones, and his aftermath—the present in which the story was written—an even more elaborate consideration.

The political future of the world only requires a string of terse statements, summarized by a transition to a new phase of existence when "at the remotest point of the future, at the limit of the final horizon of humankind, human beings complete the creation of the earth. By means of a new magism they spiritualize nature." But that is not the end in this vision, because it has to be followed by the real palingensis: the resurrection, which is itself only the antistrophe to the strophe of the fulfillment of human destiny, and still requires synthesis by the final epode: the ultimate enlightenment and the associated comprehension.

That kind of apocalyptic fervor was not easy to adapt to more down-to-earth accounts of the end of the world, which now seemed more likely to be a casual and humiliating accident than a road to glory, as is the case in one of the most extravagant fantasies provoked by the July Revolution of 1930, published in two parts as *La Fin du monde, histoire du temps présent et des choses à venir* [The End of the World; A Story of Present Times and Things to Come] (1830) and *Le Monde nouveau* [The New World] (1831) by the political journalist Antoine Rey-Dussueil (1798-1851).

The first part of the couplet is a political commentary in which the aftermath of the July Revolution is abruptly cut short when the Earth collides with a comet, precipitating a new Deluge that very few people escape. In the second volume, the hero, Brémond, who has escaped the Deluge in the company of four women, three of whom are aristocrats of different ranks, sets about founding a new society based on the radical Republican doctrines to which he is committed.

Brémond's attempt to shape his eutopia runs into problems, however, as one of his children recapitulates that story of Cain and Abel while others are gradually seduced by anti-egalitarian ideas, clandestinely encouraged by other escapees from the Deluge. The latter include "the 221"—the members of parliament who voted for new constitutional monarchy—including François Guizot, who became Louis-Philippe's first prime minister, and Pierre-Paul Royer-Collard, the leader of the "Doctrinaires" whose political philosophy guided the 221 through the evolution that prevented a complete obliteration of the monarchy and the return of a Republic. Brémond tries hard to resist the pressures of their skepticism, but cannot keep his children in line; in the end he can only escape from his own collapsing republic by awaking up from the bad dream.

France, however, did not have that option.

3. New Utopias

The longest, and perhaps the most interesting, of the numerous utopian tracts produced during the Revolution in order to give hopeful advice to its pilots was *Ma république* [My Republic] (1791) signed "Platon" [Plato], which was subsequently reprinted as *Eponine, ou De la République, ouvrage de Platon découvert et publié par l'auteur de La Philosophie de la Nature* [Eponine; or, On the Republic; a work by Plato discovered and published by the author of *The Philosophy of Nature*] (1793).

The author of *La Philosophie de la Nature* was Jean-Baptiste Delisle de Sales (1741-1816), although he sometimes signed himself simply as Jean de Sales, and was also known as Jean-Baptiste Isoard de Lisle, which was probably his original name. The earlier work was also vast, having first been issued in 1770 and then augmented in the course of numerous editions until it reached twelve volumes. Prior to the publication of Buffon's *Epochs de la Nature* Delisle de Sales had produced a cosmogonic theory of his own, which estimated the age of the Earth at 140,000 years. Although he rejected *Telliamed*'s much longer estimate of the Earth's age and Maillet's account of the evolution prompted by the diminution of the seas, Delisle de Sales was a more outspoken evolutionist than Buffon, arguing explicitly that orangutans were ancestral to human beings—which resulted in the aggressive condemnation of his book by the Church and his imprisonment, to be followed by banishment.

Delisle de Sales' friends launched a subscription to support his appeal, to which Voltaire famously made a substantial contribution, and although he did leave the country briefly when the appeal was successful, he soon returned to continue the elaboration of his text and supplement it with numerous others, mostly historical. Versins lists *Ma république* as an alternative history rather than a euchronia, and the many appendices of *Eponine* include a more explicit alternative history, "D'un nouvelle séance Royale," which explained how the revolution might have gone if Louis XVI had proved more robust in his response to it. Unfortunately for the author, *Ma République/Eponine* fared no better than *La Philosophie de la Nature*; some members of the Convention did not like the advice it offered at all, and Delisle de Sales was imprisoned again, although he was released in 1795, and became a founding member of the Institut National des Science et des Arts established to replace the abolished Académie (which provided a framework for Napoléon's reformulation of the latter in 1803).

Delisle de Sales' writings were almost universally declared to be mediocre because of their prolixity and lack of organization, but he is fully entitled to recognition for his combative contribution to the development of evolutionist thought, and his ponderous contributions to philosophical fiction continued with the four-volume *Le Vieux de la montagne, histoire orientale* [The Old Man of the Mountain, An Oriental Tale] (1799) and a sequel to Voltaire's masterpiece, *Mémoires de Candide sur la liberté de la presse, la paix générale, les fondements de l'ordre social et autres bagatelles* [Candide's Comments on Press Freedom, World Peace, the Foundations of Social Order and Other Trivia] (1802).

The latter exercise was rapidly followed, or countered, by Louis Bellin de La Liborlière's *Voyage de M. Candide fils au pays de Eldorado vers la fin du XVIIIe siècle, pour servir de suite aux aventures de M. son père* [Voyage of Candide junior to the land of Eldorado, to serve as a sequel to his father's adventures] (1803), which offers a scathing transfiguration of the Revolution from the viewpoint of an émigré ex-priest, who had fought against the Revolutionary Army before turning to the production of *romans noirs*—the French equivalent of the English Gothic novels made fashionable by Ann Radcliffe.

Another utopia of the period deserving of brief mention here, which remained unpublished until the days of the Empire, although it had surely been written earlier was *Voyage d'un habitant de la lune à Paris à la fin du XVIIIe siècle*, signed P. Gallet. The Bibliothèque Nationale unpacks that signature as "Pierre Gallet," although the author had signed himself "Citizen Gallet" ten years previously when he published *La Véritable évangile* [The True Gospel] (1793), representing Christ as being fully in tune with the ideals of the Revolution. Like Félix Nogaret, however, he had failed to anticipate the Terror, and he subsequently signed himself. M. [for Monsieur] A. Gallet. Those shifts encourage the suspicion that the P. might have stood for "Père" but that, like Cousin de Grainville, Gallet had changed his status when the Revolution arrived.

The story of the lunar visitation is, in fact, little more than a glorified sermon, but the story is notable as an early example of the "reversed utopian" strategy in which an observer comes from a supposedly eutopian milieu to the writer's imperfect society in order to evaluate and castigate its faults by making a series of comparisons with his own. Gallet's example is also exceptional among lunar fantasies for the means of interplanetary transport employed: a giant winged elephant that subsequently causes some inconvenience while having to be stabled, fed and cared for in Paris.

What can, perhaps, be seen in retrospect as one of the most interesting utopias of the period was written in 1800 by the political economist Jean-Baptiste Say (1767-1832), *Olbie, ou Essai sur le moyens de réformer les moeurs d'une nation* [Olbia; or, An Essay on the Means of Reforming the Mores of a Nation], but it remained unpublished until 2014, when the Institut Coppet made a pdf version available gratuitously on line.

Although primarily concerned with economic issues, the text does digress to describe the consequences of economic reform on such matters as the sexual mores of the Olbiens; women, liberated from the necessity to work, have become utterly dependent, personifying "douceur" [tenderness] and resolutely chaste. The amount of space given to the issue suggests that it is one about which Say felt very strongly, in a fashion that distances his work enormously from such fellow utopians as Restif and Nogaret, thus enriching the spectrum with an opposite extreme.

Although the philosophy of progress did have a very considerable development on utopian thinking after the 1789 Revolution, especially in ideas and works inspired by Saint-Simon, the aftermath of the upheaval also produced a kind of backlash, in the form of "retreatist utopias" that took the view that the supposed progress the world had already made had actually taken it in the wrong direction, and that the acquisition of a happy society could only be achieved by a step backwards, in a direction variously indicated by the Patriarchal Era described in the Bible, the mythology of Arcadian Pastoralism or Rousseauesque images of primal social innocence.

Perhaps the most eloquent utopian novel of that kind produced in the aftermath of the 1789 Revolution was the previously-mentioned *Le Vallon aérien ou Relation du voyage d'un aéronaute dans un pays inconnu jusqu'à présent; suivie de l'histoire de ses habitans et de la description de leurs moeurs* (1810) signed "J. Mosneron, ex-Législateur." The author, whose full name was Jean-Baptiste Mosneron, Baron de Launay (1738-1830) was the son of a Nantes shipowner who had made his money in the slave trade. After studying law in Paris he returned to his home town to practice, and did a good deal of work for the family firm, while pursuing his literary interests as a sideline, albeit with a considerable degree of interest and intensity. His early work was mostly done for the theater, but he also published a translation of *Paradise Lost*, a biography of John Milton and several other items of non-fiction, plus two novels.

Following the Revolution, Mosneron was appointed as a delegate to the Legislative Assembly in 1791 and was sent to Paris with a specific mandate to defend the slave trade against possible prohibition by a government ostensibly committed to the rights of man. The artful speech that he made in that cause became his most notorious work; it was published in a number of places and can now be read on-line. He sat on the right of the Chambre and opposed the execution of Louis XVI, in spite of the fact that his Protestant family had absolutely nothing for which to thank the Bourbons. Consequently, he was arrested and imprisoned during the Terror, but he escaped execution and was released, like Louis-Sébastien Mercier, when Robespierre fell. He came back to the legislative assembly after Bonaparte's coup overturned the Directoire, but did not remain there for long.

Mosneron's combative tendencies are displayed in both of his novels, the first of which, *Memnon, ou le Jeune Israélite* (1806), was the earliest of several French novels that provided accounts of the life of Jesus—although Citizen Gallet's *Véritable Évangile* had made a move in that direction. Mosneron's version is carefully stripped of any miracle-working and naturalized—a project calculated to cause offense to devout believers, but carried out with care and craft; other writers who repeated the project subsequently included Alexandre Dumas and Félicien Champsaur.

Le Vallon aérien might be reckoned uncombative by comparison, and also somewhat disjointed—its numerous chronological inconsistencies might well stem from an attempt to stitch together several different fragments into a more-or-less unified whole—but it is nevertheless notable within the rich history of French utopian fiction as one of the more readable, as well as one of the most conscientiously self-doubting works of that kind.

Although it follows a relatively orthodox line of argument in suggesting that a utopian society can only maintain stability if it is limited in size and isolated from outside influences—Restif had made the same case in *La Découverte australe*—Mosneron added the stern insistence that it must at all costs resist the disruptive effects, not only of technological progress but also of the very idea of progress. The text examines that proposition with an even-handed approach that scrupulously gives consideration both sides of its principal arguments—as a lawyer accustomed to considering both sides of a case might be expected to do.

The patchwork account of the "aerial valley" and its inhabitants is awkwardly-structured, mostly derived from the "annals" constructed by various hands over the course of a century, a copy of which is obtained by the balloonist who rediscovers the fugitive society and is treated well until he is politely asked to go away, never return, and never to reveal its location. The extracts from the annals are also annotated by a hypothetical "editor," who adds his own quibbling footnotes to those supplied by the aeronaut. The eccentric product is nevertheless successful in building up a mosaic account of the circumstances that led the founders of the fugitive society to flee from France, the evolution of the society and its politics, and the reasons for its commitment to continued isolation.

The multi-sided consideration is sufficiently dutiful to introduce an interesting thought-experiment into the story, in the form of the importation into the rigidly stable and naïve society of a well-meaning but subtly dangerous outsider, whose endeavors serve to test both the resilience and the justice of the story's fundamental assumptions. That inclusion also helps to make the plot of the story more enterprising and more robust than is commonly the case in utopian fiction.

As a modest anti-progressive utopia *Le Vallon aérien* cannot be reckoned, with the aid of hindsight, to be in the mainstream of the development of French utopian thought, but it is interesting as a presentation of the "anti-euchronian" case, and its challenge to the philosophy of progress as an instrument of perfectibility.

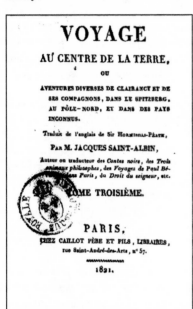

Mosneron's utopia shares several interesting features with *Voyage au centre de la terre, ou Aventures diverses de Clairancy et de ses companions, in Spitzberg, au Pôle-Nord, et dans des pays inconnus, traduit de l'anglais de Hormidas Peath par M. Jacques Saint-Albin* [Journey to the Center of the Earth; or, Various Adventures of Clairancy and His Companions in Spitzbergen, at the North Pole and in Unknown Lands, translated from the English of Hormidas Peath by Jacques Saint-Albin] (1821; tr. as *Voyage to the Center of the Earth*).

The signature "Jacques Saint-Albin" had previously appeared on two flippant satires, *Les Trois animaux philosophes, ou Les Voyages de l'ours de Saint-Corbinia, suivis des Aventures du chat de Gabrielle et de L'Histoire philosophique du pou voyageur* [The Three Philosophical Animals; or, The Travels of Saint Corbinian's Bear, followed by The Adventures of Gabrielle's Cat and the Philosophical History of a Traveling Louse] (1819) and *Voyages de Paul Béranger dans Paris après 45 ans d'absence* [Paul Béranger's Travels in Paris after an Absence of 45 Years] (1819), among other works, but the author had already signed the version of his own name that he adopted permanently, J. A. S. Collin de Plancy, to a parallel series of publications; his name was actually Jacques-Albin-Simon Collin (1793-1881), but he added the suffix as an affectation, in the manner of Cyrano de Bergerac and Restif de La Bretonne.

That works to which Collin added his preferred signature included the oft-reprinted *Dictionnaire infernal, ou Répertoire universel des êtres, des personnages, des livres, des faits et des choses qui tiennent aux apparitions, à la magie, au commerce de l'enfer, aux démons, aux sorciers, aux sciences occultes* [The Infernal Dictionary; or Universal Directory of Beings, Individuals, Books, Facts and Matters Pertaining to Apparitions, Magic, Commerce with Hell, Demons, Sorcerers and the Occult Sciences] (1818; augmented in subsequent editions; tr. under various titles, including *The Encyclopedia of Demons and Demonology*) and its companion volume *Le Diable peint par lui-même, ou Galerie de petits romans, de contes bizarres, d'anecdotes prodigieuses sur les aventures des démons, les traits qui les caractérisent, leurs bonnes qualités et leurs infortunes; les bon mots et les réponses singulières qu'on leur attribue; leurs amours, et les services qu'ils ont pu rendre aux mortels, etc.* [The Devil Depicted by Himself; or, A Collection of short stories, bizarre tales and prodigious anecdotes concerning the adventures of demons, the features that characterize them, their good qualities and misfortunes, the witticisms and singular responses attributed to them, their amours, and the services they can render to human beings, etc.] (1819).

At the time he wrote the abovementioned texts Collin was a thoroughgoing skeptic and ardent Voltairean, who recorded demonological legends in a spirit of ridicule, and allegations of his eventual conversion to devout faith probably need to be taken with a pinch of salt, given that some statement of that kind seems to have been required of him before he was allowed to return to France after seven years in exile in Belgium and the Netherlands from 1830-37. In addition to "Jacques Saint-Albin" he occasionally put other pseudonyms on his various works, including the pamphlet, *Le Marquis de Condorcet, épisode de la grande Révolution, par le neveu de mon oncle* [The Marquis de Condorcet: A Episode of the Great Revolution, by My Uncle's Nephew] (1847), a signature that might offer some assistance in understanding how Collin not only elected to become an encyclopedist of the Devil's works but also to be prepared to look at such matters from the satanic point of view.

The uncle to whom Collin refers in that signature was his mother's brother, the Revolutionary leader Georges Danton. It could not have been easy for Collin's mother to be known as Danton's sister even under the Directoire, let alone the Empire, and much less the Restoration; Collin probably had to face a certain amount of hostility and prejudice himself on account of his relationship with the notorious Montagnard, which doubtless served to hone the scathing quality of his Voltairean mockery to an exceptional keenness.

Voyage au centre de la terre is most evidently Voltairean in its contemptuous attitude to priestcraft and its espousal of a kind of minimalist deism that many Voltaireans adopted—including Restif de La Bretonne, whose utopian writings might well have had some influence on the design of the society of the Alburians depicted in the novel. Nowadays, the work is viewed as an element of a fairly extensive library of "hollow earth" fantasies, and it appeared the year after the first significant work of that kind written in English, *Symzonia* (1820) by "Captain Adam Seaborn."

Collin had obviously heard of John Cleve Symmes, jr. and his proposal that an expedition be mounted to discover one of the hypothetical openings at the Earth's poles and perhaps pass through into a world within our globe, but he probably had not had an opportunity to read the propagandizing novel popularizing Symmes' ideas, although he was presumably aware that his characters were following in the footsteps of Ludwig Holberg's Nils Klim and the protagonists of *Icosameron* (1788). Casanova's population of the inner world with diminutive "Megamicres" is echoed in Collin's depiction of miniature humans, but if Collin had *Icosameron* in mind while writing his own novel it was probably in order to oppose himself sternly to the argument that the inner world is the Garden of Eden featured in *Genesis*, which Collin wryly inverts in the beliefs of the Felinois featured in his novel, whose religion places a paradise of delights on the Earth's surface.

Voyage au centre de la terre is at least as much of an adventure story as it is a utopian fantasy, and its eutopian element is haunted by a skeptical consciousness that no matter how excellent an ideal society might be in theory, and even in practice, it would be a difficult milieu for ordinary human beings to tolerate for long, by virtue of its tedium if not its awkward restrictions. In that, it sometimes seems a rather modern work, although its closest literary analogues are Tyssot de Passot's accounts of the adventures de Jacques Massé and Pierre de Mésange, which take a similarly distant and quasi-clinical view of the strange societies they represent.

Although it places its alien world inside the Earth rather than in the distant reaches of space, and is content to represent it as an Earth-clone populated by humans who only differ from those living on the surface in their size, *Voyage au centre de la terre* stands at the beginning of a new phase in interplanetary fiction, marking a significant step forward in attempted verisimilitude from the interplanetary fantasies of the eighteenth century. The means by which Collin's visitors to the inner world reach it without being injured, and return therefrom, are devoid of any rational plausibility—or, indeed, any real attempt at explanation—but that is inevitable, given the nature of the exercise; the real point is the way in which the "small globe" is designed and depicted.

Although there are satirical elements in the distorted reflection of our world that it provides, the world within the Earth is treated, in the main, simply as another planet, with its own geography and history, a mildly exotic fauna and flora, and nations with different politics and religion. The account of it provided by the self-effacing Hormisdas Peath (his name is misspelled in the subtitle) aims for a level of narrative realism that adds an extra measure of laconism to Gulliverian mock-sincerity. Although it pretends to be earnest in order to tell an exceedingly tall tale, the manner of its pretence links the novel firmly to the tradition of exotic adventure fiction that was to become important in the latter part of the century, when its title had been usurped by a work that became far more famous.

Approximately half of the narrative set on the small globe is dedicated to the depiction of the society of the diminutive Alburians, which is similar in many ways to that of the inhabitants of the Aerial Valley, in terms of its devout but dogma-free religion and its relatively limited technology; the latter is not a matter of lack of technical advancement—the nations of the small globe have had printing technology for fifteen hundred years and invented gunpowder so many millennia ago that they can no longer remember its origin—but a matter of conscious selection in the matter of adopting technologies and the purposes to which they are applied. Thus, printing is carefully controlled and channeled, and gunpowder is not used in firearms. The society is not strictly egalitarian, but its education ensures equality of opportunity for all, and all administrative authority is awarded strictly on the basis of merit.

The novel is interesting not merely for its careful depiction of a eutopian society that has preserved happiness largely by rejecting progress, but because Peath and his companions, while recognizing it as a eutopia—especially by comparison with the first of the other nations that they visit, Sanor, which initially seems more pleasant but turns out to have a dark underside—feel that they cannot live there, partly because it is a rigidly vegetarian society and they yearn to eat meat, but mainly because it is simply too tedious. It does not help that the inhabitants are only two feet tall, but the extra erotic benefits the visitors obtain from living among the four-feet-tall Sanorlians do not, in the end, solve the particular problems of adaptation posed by that society.

Insofar as it is a utopian fantasy, therefore, Collin's *Voyage au centre de la terre* is representative of a deep-seated disenchantment, not so much with the practicality of euchronian social reorganization, but with the very idea of eutopia—the notion that an ideal social organization, in terms of its politics, religion and morality, could actually provide happiness and contentment, except to those born into it and completely adapted to it psychologically. The utopian fantasy is probably hybridized with an adventure story partly for marketing reasons, but it also reflects the fact that the six protagonists are, in essence, adventurers, restlessly in search of new horizons, unable to settle for an ideal way of life, not so much because of the flaws it retains as because it is, in too many ways, *too* perfect.

L'An deux mil huit cent, ou Le Rêve d'un solitaire, (tr. as "The Year 2800") first published as a pamphlet in Tours in 1829, is a euchronian work set firmly in the tradition of Mercier's *L'An deux mille quatre cent quarante*, which serves, like its immediate predecessors, to illustrate the fact that the nascent genre of euchronian fiction remained skeptical for some time about the notion that technological progress would be an essential component of social progress; like Mercier, its author bases his anticipations of future improvement almost entirely on social reforms.

The booklet is listed by the Bibliothèque Nationale as an anonymous work, although it bears the signature "Turrault de Rochecorbon" at the end of the text. That signature also appears on one other text of the period, similarly published in Tours, the three-act comedy *L'Épreuve de l'amour* [The Proof of Love]

(1827), and Turrault appears to be a moderately common name in the département of the Indre-et-Loire, in which the commune of Rochecorbon is located. The work's utopian scheme is unremarkable, but it is interesting for its resurrection and extrapolation of the ideas of Charles Castel de Saint-Pierre (1658-1743), a social theorist now most famous for having proposed the establishment of an international organization responsible for maintaining peace between nations. Although he was briefly at Louis XIV's court when he was chaplain to the king's sister-in-law, the Princess Palatine (whose husband, Philip II d'Orléans subsequently served as regent during Louis XV's minority), Castel's reformist ideas got him expelled from the court and kicked out of the Académie.

Turrault's futuristic vision attempts to repopularize all Castel's ideas by showing them in action. The plot takes the simple form of a dream-tour guided by a helpful cicerone, in exactly same fashion as Mercier's model, focusing primarily on political reform and the reorganization of the legal system to minimize corruption. Like its immediate predecessors however, its representation of religious practice favors a minimalist deism relatively free of cumbersome dogma and the encouragement of early marriage coupled with simple arrangements for divorce. Technological development is simply not an issue, although agricultural methods are tacitly assumed to have been improved as well as rationalized.

The most important utopian philosopher of the period, who had by far the most influence on subsequent utopian fiction, although he did not use fiction as a medium of propaganda himself, was Charles Fourier (1772-1837), whose ideas were so radical, influential and futurological that Everett Bleiler appointed him as an important writer of "proto-science fiction" by including a volume of his translated selected writings in the non-fictional appendix to his *Science Fiction: The Early Years*, alongside Fontenelle.

Initially ambitious to be an engineer, Fourier was thwarted by the prejudices of rank inherent in the pre-Revolutionary regime, not being of noble descent; he became a travelling salesman instead, doing business all over France before, during and after the Revolution, but always retaining a base in the south, initially in Besançon and then in Lyon, and gradually becoming deeply disillusioned by the "knavery" of merchants and the deceits that his occupation forced upon him, for which his writing provided a distraction and a medium of increasingly fierce reaction. He was inspired by the writings of Saint-Simon to take up the utopian torch himself, and extrapolated Saint-Simonian schemes for reform in a thoroughly Comtean context.

Fourier first set out his reformist ideas, in the rather disjointed manner that was typical of his writing, in *Théorie des quatre mouvements et des destinées générales* [Theory of the Four Movements and General Destiny], published anonymously in Lyon in 1808, further elaborating it in *Théorie de l'unité universelle* [The Theory of Universal Unity] (1822); *Le Nouveau monde industriel et sociétaire, ou invention du procédé d'industrie attrayante et naturelle distribuée en série passionelle* [The New Industrial and Social World; or, The Invention of an Attractive and Natural Industrial Method, Distributed in a Loving Manner] (1829); and *La Fausse industrie, morcellée, répugnante, mensongère, et l'antidote, l'industrie naturelle, combinée, attrayante, véridique, donnant quadruple produit* [False Industry, fragmented, repulsive and deceptive, and its Antidote, Natural Industry, integrated, attractive and veridical, producing four times as much] (1835-36). Those three texts were supplemented posthumously by *Le Nouveau monde amoureux* [The New Amorous World] (1845) and various reorganizations of his writings, made in the attempt to make them more orderly and coherent.

In spite of the Comtean elements of his thought, Fourier was religious, conceiving his reformist schemes as a literal redemption, and he also embraced a kind of mysticism not unlike Restif's notion that "everything in nature is model and image," oddly akin to the proposition sketched by Listonai in one of the books his protagonist reads on the Moon, in which Newton's theory of gravity provides the model for a theory of psychological attraction. He also seems to borrow from Restif, or perhaps more generally from the interplanetary fantasies of the previous century, in setting out his own divinely-ordained schema of life on the other planets of the solar system, and might be reckoned a significant, if somewhat deviant, disciple of *La Philosophie de Monsieur Nicolas*.

In terms of social theory, Fourier agreed with Mosneron that technological progress had taken a wrong turn and that industrialism, as exhibited by contemporary societies, was producing horrible results; unlike Mosneron, however, he believed that the appropriate alternative was not a freeze on technological development but a redirection of progress into "natural industry" that would employ technology responsibly, founded on a program of agricultural reform that that would collectivize agricultural endeavor, encouraging fraternal sentiments rather than the rampant egotism fostered by the existing system of ownership. Following Rousseauesque precedent, Fourier always used "civilization" as a term of abuse, and considered himself so much an outsider in the intellectual realm that he also used "philosopher" routinely as if it were an insult.

The key unit of Fourier's model of collectivization is the establishment of coherent social units called *phalanges* or *phalanstères* [phalansteries]: communities working together on the exploitation of an area of land by means of agriculture, animal husbandry and, where geographically appropriate, fisheries, as well as devoting artisans to various métiers and manufacturing projects. In the first phase of development the income of the phalanstery would be shared by all the members, but not equally, rewards being commensurate with the amount and quality of the contributions of labor made by each individual, but he believed that in the fullness of time, the harmony induced by that way of life would result in a complete communism of property, including the "sexual property" of marriage.

The hypothetical organization of Fourier's phalansteries was based on his thesis that there are twelve fundamental passions, whose various combinations produce 810 kinds of character, the duplication of which could produce an ideal society in miniature of 1,620 people; eventually, he proposed, the number of phalansteries would extend to six million, collectively organized and controlled, initially by an omniarch but eventually by a democratic world congress. He considered that once it was "naturally" ordered, labor would cease to be burdensome and become pleasurable, in a quasi-sexual sense, while actual sexual relations would be "industrialized" by matchmakers armed with card-indexes of appropriate personality types.

The detailed sophistications were mostly ignored, or even treated as jokes, by Fourier's followers and by writers of futuristic fiction who drew on his ideas, but the basic model was sufficiently attractive to prompt numerous experimental attempts to construct actual phalansteries, and the term entered the common parlance of futuristic thought, featuring in numerous literary images of hypothetical societies.

The third influential utopian theorist of the period, who did use fiction as a means of promoting his ideas, was Étienne Cabet (1788-1856), who moderated Saint-Simonian and Fourieresque ideas considerably, while retaining the fundamental notion of the collectivization of labor, which he envisaged not in terms of intricately-organized phalansteries but more loosely aggregated workers' cooperatives. He became the great popularizer of "communisme" and is sometimes credited with having coined the term, although assiduous researchers have found an earlier reference in a review of works by Restif de La Bretonne—who clearly advocated and detailed a communist economic organization in his eutopian writings and in *La Découverte australe* but always described it as "communauté" [community] rather than improvising a new term.

Cabet received the education that was denied to Fourier, training as a lawyer, and went to work in that capacity. He was an active propagandist for reform during the Restoration, producing numerous political tracts, and was rewarded with a government post after the July Revolution, but he was swiftly dismissed because, like Rey-Dussueil's Brémond, he was far too radical for the Doctrinaires—although he was a devout Christian, and was thus considered not radical enough by many subsequent communists; taking up where Citizen Gallet had left off, Cabet was an enthusiastic pioneer of the notion that Christ was the first communist and that his teachings, properly construed, were orientated toward social reorganization on communist lines.

As a député in the new parliament, Cabet positioned himself in the Chambre on the far left. He founded the radical newspaper *Le Populaire* in 1833. Accused of treason because of the paper's agitations, he sought political asylum in England, and probably wrote his utopian romance there, although he returned to France in 1839, the year of its first publication as *Voyages et aventures de Lord William Carisdall en Icarie, ouvrage traduit de l'anglais de Francis Adams par Th. Dufruit, maître de langues* [Voyages and Adventures of Lord William Carisdall in Icaria, a work translated from the English of Francis Adams by Th(éodore) Dufruit, language teacher]. Subsequent editions, signed with his own name, issued frequently from 1840 onwards, shortened the title to *Voyage en Icarie* (tr. as *Travels in Icaria*).

In the story, Lord Carisdall sets off from the port of Tyranna, and travels to Icara, the capital of Icarie, a meticulously ordered and perfumed city, although each district has a different style of architecture, in order to avoid uniformity, with edges smoothed in order to reduce the damage inflicted by accidental collisions. All labor is collectivized, within State ownership, and all meals are prepared and eaten communally. That state of affairs is relatively recent, a fifty-year plan put in place after the Icarian Revolution of 1782 having been completed in thirty, due to public enthusiasm. Although travel and transport are still largely dependent on horses, they are lent significant assistance by railways and airships, and also by submarines.

Disillusioned by the lack of political progress made in France during the reign of Louis-Philippe, Cabet left France before the Revolution of 1848. Under the influence of the English practical utopian Robert Owen, he set sail for America in order to found an Icarian community there; his first attempt, in Texas, failed dismally, but he fared better in Illinois. His administration became increasingly dictatorial, however, and he was eventually thrown out in 1855, dying in St. Louis the following year. A number of Icarian communities staggered on for a while, but none survived into the twentieth century.

The fundamental idea extrapolated by Fourier, that contemporary industrialization had taken a wrong turn and was heading away from perfectibility rather than toward it, took root widely in the first half of the nineteenth century, and is dramatized in some of the most striking works of imaginative fiction produced in the period. One particularly far-reaching image is found in a short work that set out to parody the scientific reports sent back in profusion by voyagers who set out to conduct disciplined geographical investigations in the wake of Louis-Antoine de Bougainville and James Cook, and which were becoming an item of popular reading matter. The parody in question is *Voyage pittoresque et industriel dans le Paraguay-Roux et la Palingénesie australe, par Trédace-Nafé Théobrôme de Kaout't'tchouk, gentilhomme Breton, sous-aide à l'établissement des elyso-pompes, etc. etc. etc.* (tr. as "A Voyage to Paraguay-Roux") by the humorist Henri Delmotte, first published in 1835, ostensibly in Meschacébé [Mons, in Belgium] by Yreled-Sioyoh [Hoyois-Delery],

The text in question was reprinted in 1841 in an omnibus of *Les Oeuvres facétieuses de Henri Delmotte* [The Facetious Works of Henri Delmotte], by which time it had acquired a wider, if slightly paradoxical, celebrity by virtue of a substantial review-article published in the *Revue de Paris* under the pseudonym Docteur Néophobus and subsequently reprinted under the name of its prestigious author, Charles Nodier. The celebrity won for the story by that article was "paradoxical" because Nodier somehow forgot to mention the author's name, with the result that many subsequent writers interested in the text referred to his paraphrase of the text rather than to the original.

In consequence of that omission, Nodier effectively usurped much of the credit awarded by subsequent commentators to the quasi-futuristic sections of the text describing the technological innovations encountered in Polynesia on "l'île de Civilization," where the vehicles that run on its railways are glass-sided capsules fired by a "Voltaic pistol," which fly along an electrified metal wire. The island's monarch is a wooden automaton, while chemistry has allowed the supersession of conventional gas lighting in favor of "phosphoriculine," derived from flammable components of bodily excreta.

Although Delmotte's account is more obviously a parody of scientific reportage than of utopian fantasy, the description of "Civilization Island" remained by far the most interesting section for its readers. As in other satirical works poking fun at euchronian dreams, the exaggeration inherent in the narrative method required a greater imaginative reach than the objects of parody—which eventually had the ironic effect of bringing them much closer to the extravagance of actual subsequent technological achievement.

The broad humor of Delmotte's parody of scientific reportage soon found a much subtler counterpart in *Publication complète des Nouvelles découvertes de Sir John Herschel dans le ciel austral et dans la Lune* (1836; tr. as "The Complete News from the Moon") by Victor Considerant (1808-1893), which is a sequel to the text of the New York *Sun*'s "Moon Hoax," presenting a detailed continuation of the study of the Moon's intelligent species and the social relationships between them, in the form of a series of extracts ostensibly taken from Herschel's complete report, of which the pages of the hoax are assumed to be a journalistic popularization of the initial observations.

The text begins with preliminary materials that include a seemingly earnest account of astronomical observations of the moon and a discussion of the evidence for its possession of an atmosphere. The bulk of the main text then offers an elaborate description of the civilization of the angelically-winged "Séléniens" and their interactions with the bat-winged "Vespertilios," many of whom have been domesticated and now provide Sélénien civilization with one of its servant classes, although the "savage" Vespertilios living on the part of the Moon's surface invisible from the Earth still mount occasional nocturnal raids on the Séléniens, stealing and eating their children, having long since obliged the Séléniens to place their heavily fortified homes on mountain-tops and to maintain a constant vigilance. The domesticated Vespertilios only fill the median position in the lunar social hierarchy, the heaviest and dirtiest manual labor being carried out by the wingless "Castors" [Beavers], thus completing a parallel of sorts to the Earthly social hierarchy of the aristocracy, the bourgeoisie and the proletariat.

Viewing from a long distance with a limited field of vision, there is only so much that the Earthly astronomers can see, and the early sections of the text show them very scrupulously recording and collating their observations, gradually building up an image of the hypothetical "anthropology" of the three alien races, including the effects on their culture of the long cycle of their days and nights. Up to that point, the work is doubly interesting, both as the most elaborate description yet provided of a fictitious alien culture in terms of its adaptation to its environment, and as the most elaborate fictional account yet provided of scientific observations made and reported in a careful and disciplined fashion. It is, however, a parody, which comes not to praise its hypothetical observers but to undermine them—or, at least, to cast a skeptical eye on one faulty aspect of their attitude. The later sections, which deal with the astronomers' attempts to study the lunar religion and to draw inferences from their observations, take the rhetoric in a different direction, mounting a subtle but devastating attack on a tendency among contemporary scientists to what was known in England as "natural theology": the idea that by studying nature one could obtain an insight into the mind and methods of the Creator that would support and confirm religious faith rather than threatening it.

While continuing hypocritically to assert their objectivity, the astronomers describe a religious ceremony in which an unbiased reader might well see nothing but a ruthless and sadistic expression of the Séléniens' dominance over the domesticated Vespertilios, but which the reporters insist on construing as evidence that the God they worship has revealed His existence and the mystery of the Trinity to the people of the Moon. In case any reader might be tempted to take that seriously, the text concludes with a ludicrous essay arguing that the condition of society on the Moon provides just as good an example as conditions on Earth of the essential benevolence of the Lord and the Harmony of Nature—a mockery that might well have Bernardin de Saint-Pierre's lyrical account of *Harmonies de la nature* (1815) in mind. Even that chapter is slightly risky, as any text is that uses a narrator to assert an argument with which the reader is expected to disagree, without any explicit hint to that effect. That potential uncertainty as to exactly what the text intends to imply might well have been one of the factors involved in the work's relegation to almost-complete oblivion, although it is one of the most sophisticated, ingenious and striking precursors of *roman scientifique.*

Victor Considerant went on to become one of the staunchest disciples of Charles Fourier before and after the latter's death, and wrote a good deal of nonfiction in that cause, but no further fiction. He eventually followed the example of Étienne Cabet in attempting to found a utopian community in America, in 1852, but it did not survive the Civil War.

Henri Delmotte's brief sketch of the bizarre Island of Civilization was soon superseded by a far more wide-ranging satirical account extrapolating the wrong direction that "progress" had allegedly taken: *Le Monde tel qu'il sera* (1846; tr. as *The World As It Shall Be*) by Émile Souvestre (1806-1854), in which a young couple speculating optimistically about the future are invited by the obliging John Progrès to accompany him on an a excursion to the year 3000 aboard his flying steam locomotive—arguably the first fictional time machine.

The couple find themselves in a hectic world equipped with all manner of rapid transit systems, including hollow containers fired by cannons, submarines and subterranean railways, and instant telephonic communications. Everything is built and manufactured from synthetic materials, fruits and vegetables having been transformed by new technologies, and similar methods, in association with educational techniques, are applied to human beings in order to adapt them to particular tasks and careers. Europe-based corporations run the world, having destroyed competition from abroad by means of opium wars and engineered economic collapses, national governments merely being their instruments, and the medical industry maintains demand for its products by keeping everyone in a state of ill-health.

The description of the future society is offered with a degree of artistry not often seen in utopian fictio, but it is notoriously easier to be clever and elegant while indulging in aggressive criticism and depicting horrors than it is while representing life running smoothly in an approving fashion—although the author's subsequent account of *Un Philosophe sous les toits: journal d'un homme heureux* [A Philosopher in a Garret: The Journal of a Happy Man] (1851) was awarded a prize by the Académie. The caricaturish imagery of *Le Monde tel qu'il sera* was all the more effective because it was supported by suitably lurid illustrations.

Regarded at the time of its publication as a sharply satirical but wildly implausible comedy, the reputation of *Le Monde tel qu'il sera* has shifted over time as its resemblance to actual developments in the modern world have become increasingly striking, and it was eventually singled out by historians as the first great "dystopian novel," although, as previously noted, the term "dystopia" was not coined until some time after its appearance.

That eventual coinage was, however, inevitable, as Fourieresque skepticism regarding the horrors of "unnatural" industrialism grew apace with the inexorable spread of steam engines and all the devices that they powered. Euchronian fiction did not die out—and, indeed, it became increasingly robust and ambitious as technological advances lent optimists more encouragement and a broader basis for speculation—but it was increasingly forced after the middle of the nineteenth century to operate in an environment of skeptical suspicion, often extending to mockery and denial.

4. The Romantic Movement

The birth, or rebirth, of Romanticism in the first half of the nineteenth century was an international phenomenon, in which several strands overlapped and intertwined. It was a broad cultural phenomenon, which affected philosophy, literature, music, painting and even politics and natural science. It was represented by its adherents are a reaction against the esthetic philosophy that looked to the Classics for its models—the last remnant, as it were, of a Renaissance that had long ago reached and passed maturity and now seemed decrepit. Eighteenth-century esthetics seemed to its detractors to be excessively rule-bound and also rather austere, over-intellectualized to the point of freezing out sentimentality and a certain spirit of individualism.

Although the Movement, as such, did not begin in France, the example of the French Revolution seemed important to all its adherents, as an example not merely of the fact that old systems could be overthrown and smashed to smithereens, but also that a new voice was breaking through old networks of common beliefs and assumptions, from an implicitly anti-authoritarian standpoint that held everything to be challengeable, and challenge as a good thing in itself.

The adherents of Romanticism were not against Reason and Enlightenment—far from it—but they were prepared to wonder whether Enlightenment itself was becoming overly strict in its edicts, excessively focused on the intellect, logic and materialism, and losing sight to some extent of the less disciplined and less rational elements of mental life, which were not only seen by the champions of the new Romanticism as precious in themselves, but also to harbor explanatory resources that dutifully Enlightened minds had skimmed over or rejected. The manner in which the Enlightenment, in the aspect exemplified in France by Buffon, seemed to have subjected Nature to a disciplined classification and rationalization, seemed to some nature-lovers to be robbing her of a valuable mystical element. The parallel advancement of physics and chemistry, in gradually squeezing the mystery and magic out of phenomena, seemed to have costs as well as benefits, in terms of what the esthetic theorist Edmund Burke had called the sense of the "sublime." Some artists felt that a squeeze was being put on their imagination and creative spontaneity by new theories of all kinds, including scientific theories as well as esthetic theories.

The first Movement that can now be seen in retrospect to have been "Romantic" took form in Germany, embracing a number of idealist philosophers—including Johann Fichte and Friedrich Schelling—and writers, whose literary adherents termed their reaction to the perceived situation as *sturm und drang*: storm and stress. Its first archetypal work of prose fiction was J. W. Goethe's *Die Leiden des jungen Werthers* (1774; tr. as *The Sorrows of Young Werther*), although Goethe, not atypically for a writer of the Romantic stripe, later denied that he belonged to any Movement, on the grounds that it was an insult to his individuality to try to subsume him to some such phenomenon.

One of the interesting side-effects of the German movement was the popularization of the idea that there was a distinctive collective German soul—the *volksgeist*—whose roots could be detected in and unearthed from the regional folklore, as collected by the brothers Grimm, and celebrated by the production of sophisticated fakelore, as practiced by Ludwig Tieck and Friedrich de La Motte Fouqué and further recomplicated by the hallucinatory fantasies of E. T. A. Hoffmann. The French, of course, had already done something similar at the end of the seventeenth century for purely literary reasons, although no one had taken it seriously at the time and its products had been considered mere play, primarily fit for women and children. The salon culture that had given rise to it, however, now played a significant role in giving rise to the new Movement in France.

The term "Romantique" was repopularized in France by Germaine de Staël, the daughter of the Swiss banker and statesman Jacques Necker. She had sat in as a child on her mother's salon, attended by the Comte de Buffon and such *Encyclopédistes* as Marmontel and Baron von Grimm, as well as many other luminaries. Educated partly in accordance with Rousseau's theories, she became a great admirer of his works, and the first book she published in 1788 consisted of laudatory reflections on his work. Indeed, Rousseau became a key point of reference for French Romanticism and a strong influence thereon, which helped to differentiate it from the parallel German and English Movements.

Having been vociferously opposed to Louis XVI, Madame de Staël felt safe in Paris when the Revolution broke out, in spite of her father's close association with the *ancien régime*, which forced him to leave the country, but on the eve of the Terror she felt it politic to leave, and later gave lurid accounts of her "escape." She took up residence at Coppet on Lake Geneva, and there founded the salon that was to become the most famous of its era, although she moved back and forth between Coppet and Paris for a while, until she became she became an equally strident opponent of Napoléon. She eventually befriended the Duke of Wellington, and also Lord Byron, who became the most important English model of French Romantic writing, and found it politic once again to stay away from Paris. It was during that second period of what she termed her "exile" that she published *De l'Allemagne* [On Germany] (1810-13), which publicized the German Romantic Movement in France and gave potential French adherents their label.

Like virtually every female French writer of the eighteenth century, Madame de Staël wrote some "sensibility fiction," and must have been very well aware that sensibility fiction was so thoroughly Romantic that it would have been regarded as the fountainhead of the French Movement had it not been for the fact that it was mostly written by women. The cult of *sensibilité* chimed harmoniously with the Romantic emphasis on emotional spontaneity at the expense of calm intellectualism, and many of the Movement's novels were, in es-

184

sence, more feverish and more pretentious versions of stories that Madame Riccoboni and her counterparts had been telling for years.

Other salons that became cauldrons of the Movement included those hosted by Juliette Récamier (1777-1849), which played host to René de Chateaubriand, unanimously elected as the figurehead of French literary Romanticism, and Sophie Gay (1776-1852), who made a major contribution to the Movement with her own novels and plays. Those establishments were, however, overtaken and overshadowed, in the eye of history, by the masculine salons founded in competition, which became known as *cénacles*. The first of them was founded by Charles Nodier (1780-1844); its regular participants included Alphonse de Lamartine, Alfred de Vigny, Victor Hugo and Alexandre Dumas, and it quickly spun off others, most significantly the one hosted by Hugo, which spun off in its turn the *petit cénacle* of even younger writers, spearheaded by Théophile Gautier.

Nodier, a prolific essayist, expressed his opinions abundantly during the early 1820s, and became the Movement's first literary theorist and principal propagandist, but he was overtaken in that regard by Victor Hugo, who published what is nowadays regarded as the manifesto of French Romanticism in the Preface to the published version of his unperformed play *Cromwell* (1827). Nodier subscribed wholeheartedly to the idea that fakeloristic fantasy could and ought to be an important literary vehicle, although he was unconvinced that there was a French equivalent of the German *volksgeist*, and sought a more general esthetic essence by that route.

Not everyone followed Nodier's example; Stendhal adopted the general idea of Romanticism ardently, but felt that it ought to engage directly with contemporary reality in a newly frank naturalistic fashion, while Victor Hugo and "P. L. Jacob the Bibliophile" became intensely interested in reinterpreting the past. Both schools of thought helped to pave the way for the dramatic breakthrough of Romanticism into popular fiction in the mid-1840s boom in feuilleton fiction, when Eugène Sue's contemporary fictions ran in head-to-head competition with Dumas' historical novels in rival daily newspapers. Feuilleton fiction had initially been popularized by the journalist Émile de Girardin, the illegitimate son of the aristocrat who had given a home to Rousseau at the end of his life, and the husband of Sophie Gay's famously brilliant and beautiful daughter Delphine (named after a novel by Madame de Staël).

Delphine de Girardin's salon also became an important focus of the Movement, not least because her husband used it to recruit editors for the new periodicals he founded in quantity, and they, in turn, found many of their leading contributors there. Girardin hired Honoré de Balzac's friends S. Henry Berthoud and Jules Janin as editors, and they provided useful new opportunities for other writers, supplementing the *Revue de Paris* and the *Revue des Deux Mondes*, both cradles of the Movement in the 1830s, although the latter went on to become a very different periodical once the Movement had passed its heyday and had begun to seem obsolete itself.

The fraction of fiction produced in association with the Romantic Movement that has any relevance to the evolution of *roman scientifique* is tiny even by comparison with the quantity of fakeloristic fiction celebrating the *merveilleux* in a frankly nostalgic fashion, and melodramatic "Gothic" fantasy ancestral to modern horror fiction, but that tiny fraction was by no means insignificant, in terms of pioneering new developments and providing significant exemplars for later writers.

During the 1820s, when the Movement was still getting under way, attention was focused on poetry at the expense of prose, and the traditional *merveilleux* at the expense of imaginative fiction inspired by more modern notions. One of the more important benchmarks laid down in that decade for future development by writers of *roman scientifique* was by an Academician firmly associated with the Classicist old guard who doubtless intended it as a parody not only of Romanticism but of pseudoscientific travel literature, albeit of a more relaxed variety than that subsequently travestied by Henri Delmotte. The fact that it is a parody has not, however, been evident to all modern readers, and the fact that later stories in a similar vein were written in earnest has allowed it to be slotted into the origins of a curious subgenre as a pioneering work.

The story in question—which would be a mere short story if its elaborate footnotes and large print had not blown it up in order to make it into a volume, is *Jocko, episode détaché des lettres inédites sur l'instinct des animaux* [Jocko: An Episode Extracted from Unpublished Letters on Animal Instinct] (1824; tr. as "Jocko") by Charles Pougens (1755-1833). It appears to have been successful—the copy reproduced on *gallica* is from the third edition of 1827. The English translation omits the "preliminary narration" in which the narrator claims to have spent his youth "laboriously examining the mechanisms that move us and debating contrary axioms…especially to discovering differences between similar things; all philosophy begins thus." Having reached old age however, he finds his perspective inverted, now devoted to discovering identities between seemingly different things—which, he contends, is "where all philosophy ends."

In particular, the narrator explains that he has produced a treatise on instinct in animals, emphasizing the unity of life on Earth and the great chain of their being, and is planning a new work extending those ideas, which will be a work of theology as well as science. In the meantime, he offers a second-hand anecdote allegedly taken from a Portuguese manuscript, although he suspects that it might be a translation made from English, or even French. At any rate, he has annotated it very extensively by referring its details to everything known about orangutans, whether reported by naturalists such as the Comte de Buffon—quoted very extensively—or travelers in the East Indies.

"Jocko" is a term used by Buffon to refer to smaller members of the ape family, by contrast with larger "pongos"—in which category he initially confused orangutans and gorillas, although he subsequently corrected his mistake. We now recognize that his "jockos" are chimpanzees, but the term seemed looser in its application in 1824, so it is not implausible that a European functionary in the East Indies might have decided to nickname a relatively small female orangutan "Jocko."

The story offers an account of the relationship formed between the isolated functionary and the orangutan in question, which becomes closer when he nurses her through injuries sustained during a fall. She builds a hut for him in the forest, where they set up a household of sorts, and fall in love. Although the author of the manuscript represents the attraction as a one-sided infatuation on Jocko's part, and the footnotes profusely citing reports of the observed behavior of great apes support that view, there is sufficient reason in the text for the reader to suspect that it is more mutual than the writer or the annotator care to admit. At any rate, Jocko's eventual death, after a highly implausible battle with a giant snake, is represented in the lachrymose fashion of sensibility fiction as a tragedy, even though it saves the writer from what would otherwise have been a painful decision when summoned to return home.

Although the footnotes are included by way of a joke, they are, in fact, a useful compendium of what was known and believed at the time regarding orangutans, and must have been a useful source for other writers over the next hundred years who penned tales of great apes possessed of near-human intelligence and emotion—tales that include more than one account of tragically or comically doomed love. Two of the most significant were written by prominent members of the Romantic Movement, but not until the Movement's Golden Age was passed and a new phase of its evolution had begun under the Second Empire. Interestingly, however, the most striking immediate extension of the theme of *Jocko* was written in 1837 by a writer who, like Goethe in Germany, could never be persuaded that he was a Romantic at heart and in method, although nobody else was in doubt about it: Gustave Flaubert (1821-1880).

In 1837, at the age of sixteen, Flaubert wrote "Quidquid volueris" [Whatever one wishes], a short story that did not see print until many years later in 1910, but offers a striking anticipation of several other works that will warrant mention in subsequent chapters. It describes how an experimental scientist, Monsieur Paul, allows a girl to be raped by an orangutan and then takes possession of the daughter to whom she gives birth, Djalioh, in order to track the progress of her semi-human intellect. The project, not unexpectedly, ends in tragedy.

Another early story of the Romantic era that is some note because it similarly stands at the head of a sequence of stories on the same theme is "Mademoiselle de La Choupillière," which was published in a collection of *Nouvelles* (1832) by an archeologist and paleontologist who signed his works Jacques Boucher de Perthes, although his baptismal name was Jacques Boucher de Crèvecoeur (1788-1868). It is one of a number of fanciful stories extrapolating ideas inspired by the activities of Jacques de Vaucanson, the famous builder of automata, whose machines were long gone by the time the story was written but had left behind a legacy of rumor whose marvels were exaggerated by the passage of time.

Félix Nogaret had made two automata the star turns in his tale of a Syracusan technology competition, but they were obvious automata that could not be mistaken for anything else. One of the hallucinatory tales by E. T. A. Hoffmann that were among the favorite reading of the French Romantics, however, was "Der Sandmann (1816; tr. as "The Sandman"), in which the deluded protagonist mistakes a mechanical doll for a real woman and falls in love with it at a distance, before his delusion is cruelly shattered. Boucher, in importing that idea into his own tale, deploys it not as a horrific motif but as a satirical one, employing the lovely female automaton as a counterfoil to highlight the automatic features of the behavior of the foppish protagonist and all her rivals for his affections.

Although it was not followed swiftly by other tales in the same vein, "Mademoiselle de La Choupillière" became the stereotype for many other stories in which humans become erotically involved with automata, with consequences just as disappointing as those awaiting characters who became erotically involved with great apes. The remainder of Boucher's collection is thoroughly Romantic, including several Oriental fantasies, two of which include brief hallucinatory visions of life on other worlds. He was, however, to have far more influence on the development of *roman scientifique* indirectly, by way of his paleontological endeavors, largely devoted to finding evidence of prehistoric human habitation in France, initially publicized and popularized by his book on *Antiquités celtiques et antédiluviennes* (1847).

One of the most significant exemplars provided by the Movement was produced by Charles Nodier himself, while his conversations with one of the attendees at his salon, Félix Bodin, helped to encourage the latter to produce his previously-mentioned manifesto for a new fictional genre, *roman futuriste* [futuristic fiction].

Nodier was the son of an active Jacobin, and thus, in effect, a child of the Revolution. Although he was living in Besançon during the Revolution rather than Paris, he was deeply affected by it, particularly the nightmare of the Terror—which led to an extreme disenchantment, not merely with the Revolution itself but other ideologies that he considered partly to blame for it. He was no more charitably inclined towards the Empire that followed in its train, which he considered to be a natural extrapolation of the same ideologies; when a satirical poem he wrote about Napoléon bought down the wrath of the authorities on his head, his animosity was further intensified. The ideology that he considered most culpable of all, however, was not specifically political but more abstractly theoretical: the idea of progress and its eutopian corollary, the ideal of social perfectibility.

Nodier made several unsuccessful attempts to find a congenial means of earning a living before turning to professional writing, and struggled to make ends meet during the early part of his literary career. His first novel, *Le Peintre de Salzbourg, journal des émotions d'un Coeur souffrant* [The Painter of Salzburg: A Journal of the emotions of a Suffering Heart] (1803) was a chronicle of anguish strongly reminiscent of Goethe's *Die Leiden des jungen Werther*. While Goethe initially refused to recognize himself as a member of the German Romantic Movement, however, and had to be persuaded against his will that he was its cardinal exemplar, Nodier was a wholehearted Romantic from the outset, ambitious to take up a position at the heart of such a Movement. He continued to lead by example with *Jean Sbogar* (1818), a novel about a noble Illyrian bandit, and the lachrymose love story *Thérèse Aubert* (1819), but it was his fantastic stories—examples of what the Germans called *kunstmärchen* [art-folktales], most notably *Smarra, ou les démons de la nuit* (1821; tr. as "Smarra; or the Demons of the Night"), *Trilby, ou le lutin d'Argyll* (1822; tr. as *Trilby, the Goblin of Argyll*) and *La Fée aux miettes* (1832; tr. as "The Crumb Fairy") that set more memorable and enduring examples.

It was also in a fantastic vein that Nodier worked in collaboration with Jean-Toussaint Merle, the director of the Porte-Saint-Martin theatre in the early 1820s, working in collaboration with other writers on stage melodramas loosely adapted from John Polidori's "The Vampyre" and Mary Shelley's *Frankenstein*. In an anecdote recorded in his autobiography, Alexandre Dumas recalled that he went to the first night of *Le Vampyre* when he had not been in Paris very long, and found himself seated next to an irascible gentleman who expressed his continual displeasure with the script so loudly as to be ejected at the intermission; he subsequently discovered that the man in question was Nodier, taking violent offence at the way in which his contributions to the script had been mangled by Merle.

Nodier's health deteriorated significantly in the 1830s, by which time his *cénacle* had been overtaken in its influence by others, but he continued to write stubbornly, if not prolifically, and it was in that context that he produced a two-part futuristic narrative reacting with typical irascibility against the idea of progress, consisting of "Hurlubleu grand Manifafa d'Hurlubière ou la perfectibilité" and "Léviathan le long Archikan des Patagons de l'île savante ou la perfectibilité" (tr. collectively as "Perfectibility"), both published in the *Revue de Paris* in 1833.

The protagonist of Nodier's story is Berniquet, a present-day philosopher of progress, who is introduced as he seeks to entertain Hurlubleu, a tyrant ruling an Ottoman-style empire ten thousand years in the future, with the tale of how he set off on a quest with others of his ilk to discover the perfect man, who would be able, willing and delighted to live in the perfect world that technological and social progress seemed destined to forge. Berniquet relates that the journey proved to be a terrible one, which cost the lives of all his companions; some fell by the wayside when their first vehicle, a high-powered steamboat, ran out of control and blew up, and others died when their second, a vast and heavily-armed airship, was caught up in atmospheric turbulence and crashed. (Both vehicles are symbolic, the former of the 1789 Revolution and the second of the Empire.)

After surviving the fall from the airship, poor Berniquet explains, he ended up buried neck-deep in a rut in the middle of the road—symbolic of the *juste milieu*, whose quest became the watchword of Louis-Philippe's government—from which the well-meaning philosophers of the utopian Île des Patagons were unable to extract him, although the local children easily improvised a means of so doing.

Hailed as a hero by the Patagons, whose lives have been completely freed from the inconvenient demands of nature by science—they are fed and maintained in good health by advanced biotechnologies—Berniquet relates that he unfortunately fell victim to a medical error that put him to sleep for ten thousand years. After waking up again, he conceived a nostalgic desire to return to Paris, and his obliging hosts dispatched him to Europe by means of an electrically-powered flying-machine even more powerful and even more dangerous than his earlier means of travel.

That machine crash-landed in the court of the despotic Grand Manifafa of the empire whose capital had long replaced Paris. There he has been recruited to the *collège des mataquins* [Mataquin is an imaginary realm featured in several *contes de fées*] to serve as Hurlubleu's *grand loustic* [court jester] because his new master finds his story quaintly amusing, and requests its repeated recitation as a reliable means of lulling himself to sleep. The attraction of that amusement only endures, however, until the philosopher incurs the potentate's wrath by being caught *in flagrante delicto* with a favorite concubine.

In consequence of that heinous crime, Berniquet is exiled to the depths of a vast excavation, in order that he might continue his quest for the perfect man in the center of the Earth—where, it is rumored, a secret formula by means of which the great sage Zérétochthro-Schah (Zoroaster) once made such a perfect man was lost in the wake of a cataclysmic earthquake. Nodier did publish is another brief story featuring Berniquet's pursuit of that quest, "Zérothoctro-Schah, Proto-Mystagogue de Bactriane" but it is not really a continuation of the two parts of "Perfectibilité," being far more stylized and devoid of any real evidence of being set in the future.

Félix Bodin (1795-1837) was the son of a noted local historian who had done military service in the Armée de l'Ouest, and had then served a term in parliament during the Restoration, as a député for Maine et Loire. A sickly child, he was rarely in good health as an adult, and his premature death did not come as a surprise. He developed a passion for history while collaborating in his father's historical research and he published a number of "résumés"—single-volume synoptic histories—but in the early 1820s he established a career as a journalist, writing for various Republican newspapers.

Bodin published a substantial collection of his journalistic essays, *Diatribe contre l'art oratoire, suivi de mélanges philosophiques ou littéraires* [Diatribe Against the Art of Oratory, followed by Philosophical and Literary Pieces] (1824), but his greatest popular successes appear to have been a series of "*complaintes*" [mock-ballads in a satirical vein] and his one completed novel, *Eveline* (1824). The precedent set by his father obviously influenced his decision to stand for parliament after the July Revolution of 1830 but he was also heavily influenced by his friendship with Adolphe Thiers (1797-1877), whom he had assisted to complete and publish a ten-volume *Histoire de la révolution française* [History of the French Revolution] (1823-27). Thiers went on to enjoy a much longer and more successful political career than Bodin, eventually becoming the first president of the Third Republic in 1871.

Bodin's political career was troubled even before it was cut short; he was regarded as a radical by other Republicans, by virtue of his opposition to the prevailing governmental philosophy of *juste-milieu*, which sought to strike a balance between opposing parties by negotiating a balanced compromise on every practical question, but he played a role in the establishment of *caisses d'épargne* [savings banks] and *salles d'asile*: a new kind of foundling home, which aspired to provide effective quasi-maternal care. Previously, foundling homes had been virtual death-traps, as Rousseau had discovered and illustrated.

His work in the Chambre cannot have been helped by his continuing poor health, nor did it help to ameliorate his condition; it is a wonder that he managed to continue writing at all, but not at all surprising that he found it difficult to finish what he started, or that he ended up cobbling together the fragments of his project to write a novel of the future, together with a manifesto for that kind of fiction, while they were still far short of a satisfactory state, simply to place his inspiration on the record, much as Restif de La Bretonne had done with *Les Posthumes*.

In the "Préface" to **Le Roman de l'avenir** (1834)—which is derived from an article first published in the *Gazette Littéraire* in 1831—Bodin begins his prospectus for *roman futuriste* by distinguishing between two fundamental patterns of anticipation: the *péjoriste* thesis and the *mélioriste* thesis. In the former case, anticipators "place the Golden Age in the cradle of humankind and the Iron Age on its deathbed"; in the latter, "the future is offered to the imagination resplendent with light." Anticipators of the first sort, Bodin argues, tend to produce *apocalypses* when they adopt literary methods; anticipators of the second kind generate *utopias*.

What Bodin proposes for the *roman futuriste* is that it should avoid both of those tendencies, and should instead aim to present an image of the future as if it were a novel written in the future. Effectively, what he proposes is a genre of immersive fantasies that ought to replace the portal fantasies traditionally used for apocalyptic and utopian visions, although he felt obliged nevertheless to equip his own fantasy of that kind with a frame narrative explaining how the text contrived to reach the present day.

Bodin admits that he has raced his book into print in the hope of claiming the honor of being the originator of the idea of writing a *roman futuriste*—and in one of several appendices to the text of his own fragmentary sample he lists previous attempts to envisage the future in literary terms, but dismisses all the examples he cites as apocalypses or utopias: expressions of hope and/or fear rather than sober attempts to imagine the future as it might actually be and to describe the lives of people living in the future in the fashion of a novel, establishing them as interacting characters with various personal ambitions and problems.

Bodin was being a trifle disingenuous in his summary of precedents. He gives his friend Nodier credit for mentioning to him the existence of one of those earlier works—Cousin de Grainville's *Le Dernier homme*—and adds a fulsome note to the effect that "if the novel of the future had been due to be written by anyone but me he [Nodier] would certainly have been the one to do it." He does not, however, mention the fact that Nodier had already published a two-part futuristic narrative of his own, which had been formulated as a genuine im-

192

mersive fantasy without the kind of apologetic frame-narrative that Bodin had used himself; although he must have become aware of that publication before his book went to press, he evidently could not be bothered to update the existing text when he hurriedly put the book together.

Nodier's two-part story does not fit neatly into either of the categories to which Bodin had attempted to relegate previous futuristic fictions; it is, in fact, a parodic anti-utopia, which mocks the *mélioriste* pattern of anticipation mercilessly, while refusing to endorse the *péjoriste* position or even adopt a neutral one. It might thus be regarded as the first significant example of dystopian satire. In that respect, it is also bears an interesting relationship to Bodin's sample of a *roman futuriste*, which tries hard to adopt an enthusiastically *mélioriste* outlook but cannot quite manage the feat, although it sternly refuses to retreat to a *péjoriste* position, or even a neutral one.

The lack of neutrality in both narratives is conscious rather than merely accidental; Nodier and Bodin both take the trouble, in somewhat different ways, to pillory the procedural philosophy of the quest for the *juste milieu*. Although they were in complete disagreement as to the direction in which the world ought to be going, Nodier and Bodin were equally convinced—as Antoine Rey-Dussueil and Étienne Cabet also were—that the *juste milieu* was a road to nowhere, to be avoided if at all possible.

The futuristic speculations of Nodier and Bodin were similarly driven by a conviction that the path of progress—the idea of progress being the foundation-stone of *mélioriste* faith—had gone badly awry in France, but they adopted very different attitudes in consequence of that awareness. Nodier took it as proof that the idea of progress had always been silly, and that the late-eighteenth-century philosophers of progress had been starry-eyed fools. Bodin took it as proof of the unfortunate strength of the various ideologies opposed to a noble and sacred cause.

The central character of Bodin's fragmentary *roman futuriste*, Philirène, is also a philosopher of progress, but one who is in the much more fortunate position of having been elected president of the world-governing *congrès universel* in the late twentieth century. While he is addressing a meeting of that congress held in Centropolis, the capital of the Central American republic of Benthamia, however (Bodin had been a house-guest of the utilitarian philosopher Jeremy Bentham while visiting England), Philirene's fiancée Mirzala is kidnapped from her home in the rebuilt city of Carthage by agents of his great rival, Philomaque. Philomaque is about to make a bid for world conquest under the pseudonym of Aëtos, exploiting the great prestige he enjoys as a military leader among the barbaric tribes of the Far East, and wants Mirzala for his queen, although he has already married and deserted her adoptive sister Politée.

Philirène has to raise an army to combat Philomaque's planned invasion, aided by Politée, who is the heir to a heroic dynasty of technologists and capitalists—a crucial alliance that has secured the tremendous social and technological progress made in the previous century and a half. Unfortunately, the external threat posed to the *congrès universel* by Aëtos is supplemented by an internal threat posed by its dark counterpart: the subversive *association anti-prosaïque universelle* [Universal Anti-Prosaic Association] or *association poétique*, which holds its own assemblies in subterranean caves. That loose alliance of dispossessed aristocrats, unreformed Churchmen and redundant military men is a parody of the opposition that Bodin faced on a daily basis in the chamber, in his capacity as a radical *député*, sitting alongside Cabet and not far from Rey-Dusseuil. Bodin's narrative voice regretfully admits, however, that the association also includes a great many artists and writers of a Romantic stripe, and the same voice observes more than once that his potential readers—especially his female readers—might well have more sympathy for that opposition than for the defenders of progress, and will probably find Philomaque more attractive, as a fictitious hero, than Philirène.

Bodin's fragment comes to an end long before the climactic confrontation between Philirène and Philomaque can take place, although it does take the trouble to sharpen their contest by revealing that they are half-brothers, and drops enough hints for the reader to deduce that the battlefield on which they will meet will embrace the geographical location of Armageddon. The narrative voice offers no clear indication as to who will win that contest, but has established while introducing the story that the magnetically-induced visions permitting the story to be reconstituted in 1834 cannot recover any information at all about the twenty-first century—a suggestion that does not bode well for any readers hoping that Philirène and his *mélioriste* cause might triumph and that his victory will ensure that the long march towards *perfectibilité* can continue unchecked.

Because he had been born in 1795, Félix Bodin had not actually lived through the 1789 Revolution and the consequent Terror, as Charles Nodier had in his youth. Nor had Bodin been persecuted on account of his political satires, as Nodier had for penning his satirical verses about Napoléon in 1803. Such differences in experience cannot account for the differences in their attitude to the possibility of future progress, but do help in some measure to explain the contrast between Nodier's stubbornly cantankerous certainty that progress was a myth and Bodin's querulously reluctant suspicion that, even if progress really is possible, its cause might well be betrayed, not merely by the lurking forces of Reaction but the capricious seductions of Romance.

Like the pre-Revolutionary literary popularizers of the new philosophy of progress, Bodin had convinced himself that the principal means of social improvement lay in the elaboration of technology, carefully fostered by economic reform. He had great hopes for the steam engine and even greater ones for the future of aerial transport, once a method of steering airships could be devised. More rapid communications and more effective means of production, in his

opinion, were bound to bring people closer together and ameliorate the economic causes of conflict between them—but he could not suppress a lurking suspicion that economic causes were not the only, or even the most important,
sources of human conflict. While economic wellbeing might be a necessary
condition of social improvement, Bodin doubted that it was a sufficient one.

Nodier, by contrast, regarded both steam engines and airships as hazardous
contraptions more likely to prove destructive than constructive. That suspicion
can hardly be dismissed as ridiculous. When Richard Trevithick first developed
the "Cornish Engine" that worked at much higher pressures than James Watt's
original contraption—during the 1790s, while Nodier was in his teens—early
models, including Trevithick's first steam locomotive, did indeed have a tendency to explode. The conquest of the air pioneered by the Montgolfier brothers in
1783 also demonstrated its hazards quickly enough, especially when highly
flammable hydrogen was used as an agent of buoyancy. In Nodier's view,
moreover, rapid communications and effective means of production were just as
likely to reduce the quality of human life as to improve it, even if they did succeed in reducing conflict, because of the danger that they would gradually remake humans in the image of the machines on which they depended. Although
he did not suppose that the whole world would ever be remade in the image of
the Île des Patagons, he did assume that the cost of avoiding that fate would be
the persistence of crass dictatorships and all their attendant injustices.

Bodin's depiction of giant bird-like flying-machines in *Le Roman de
l'avenir* is extravagantly enthusiastic, but his airships, like Nodier's, are heavily
armed and the aerial battle he describes between Philirène's ship and a pirate
vessel—by far the most dramatic incident in his sample text—costs several
lives. Again, Bodin's narrative voice is uncommonly honest in admitting that it
is the *romance* of flight that is attractive, not only to would-be readers and writers of *romans futuristes* but to the characters within them, and there is an obvious incongruity between that addiction to romance and the hypothetical Platonic
ataraxia of a perfected world. Although Bodin did make the effort to imagine a
world of routine commercial air travel, which does not contrast completely with
the matter-of-fact world of contemporary air tourism, his own stubborn anti-
prosaic tendencies would not allow him to leave it untroubled by pirates, or even
to regret the fact. As a would-be *mélioriste*, he was perhaps his own worst enemy—considerably worse, at any rate, than Nodier, whose *loustic* tendencies
blunted the force of his own attempts to shoot down the buoyant airship of progress. Nodier's successor as the doyen of French Romanticism, Victor Hugo,
was prepared to take a very different view in "Plein ciel" [Open Skies] (1859),
the element of his epic *Légende des siècles* that celebrates the future conquest of
the air as the ultimate achievement of the Romantic imagination.

Interestingly, the most striking differences between Nodier's anticipations
of technology and Bodin's are not in their anticipations of the future development of steam-powered industry and transport but in their starkly contrasted de-

pictions of the artificiality of everyday life. When Philirène spends a brief sojourn in the Loire valley, after his skirmish with the pirates, he describes a rural idyll that might almost be Rousseauesque were it not for the fact that the valley now has a railway line and much of the river traffic consists of steamboats. The fact that Mesmeric "magnetism" has become the chief form of domestic medicine further enhances the general atmosphere of rustic simplicity.

Evidently, Bodin would have been just as antipathetic as Nodier to the latter's depiction of the life of the everyday life of the Patagons, whose island utopia has been cleansed of all other living organisms and whose food is manufactured—albeit with consummate culinary artistry—in chemical factories from raw materials. It is not entirely obvious, however, why Nodier finds this prospect so intrinsically appalling, given that the resultant nourishment reproduces the same gustatory and nutritional effects as animal flesh without the need for callous butchery. On the other hand, it is all too obvious that Bodin's affection for conventional rural productivity stems from the same romantic wellspring as his infatuation with flying machines, providing further tacit support for his anxiety that readers and voters alike will never be able to forsake their anti-prosaic tendencies sufficiently to embrace reason and progress wholeheartedly.

There is a sense in which Bodin, like Berniquet, set off in search of the perfect man when he sat down to write his *roman futuriste*, and there is a sense in which, like poor Berniquet, he got lost *en route*. It is not only Bodin's narrative voice but Philirène himself who wonders whether he really can pass for perfect, even in a dim light. Is his calm, reasonable and reliable love for Mirzala really superior to the violent, irrational and unreliable passion of a Philomaque? He cannot, in all honesty say so—and neither can his loyal friend Politée, when he consults her on the matter. If perfection really does involve drying up the well of the passions—as Plato assumed when he suggested, tongue-in-cheek, that Romantics might have to be expelled from his ideal Republic—is the prize really worth the cost? Bodin and Philirène, although by no means as certain in their own minds as Nodier and Hurlubleu, are desperately anxious that it might not be—and that desperation might, in itself, be enough to demonstrate the hopelessness of their quest.

The explicit and tacit arguments raised by Nodier and Bodin continued to run through all the *romans futuristes* produced after 1834, and continue to do so today. It is hardly surprising, given the compromises to which Bodin was forced, that very few of the minority of subsequent literary images of the future that have pledged allegiance to the *mélioriste* perspective have ever lent any but modest and hesitant support to the cause of *perfectibilité*, while very many of them have accepted the Romantic opinion that passion is indispensable to human wellbeing. Although *mélioristes* have continued to disagree with *péjoristes* on the question of whether the advancement of technology, and economic reforms that foster it, are inimical to that wellbeing, their apologetic cases are routinely haunted by anxiety. As Bodinesque *romans futuristes* gradually displaced

Mercieresque euchronias, they brought all the weighty baggage of Bodin's uncomfortable fragment with them.

There was no immediate rush of writers after 1833 to follow in Nodier's footsteps, but there were plenty in later periods equally avid to scoff and satirize, and to proclaim that only fools believe in progress. Nor was there any eventual shortage of writers enthusiastic to adopt Bodin's perspective, ready to suggest that progress has much to be said for it, but conspicuously hesitant by virtue of recognizing their own ideological frailties and weak-kneed Romantic proclivities, although his work struck no immediate chord and was virtually forgotten. Perhaps that is not unconnected with the fact that both writers were evidently correct in suggesting that no attempt to apply the philosophy of the *juste milieu* was ever likely to unstick the situation from that morass of confusion.

Two years after Bodin's attempted invention of *roman futuriste*, another writer with obvious affiliations to the Romantic Movement pioneered another new kind of fiction, which set out to extrapolate an alternative—and somewhat futuristic—version of the present by constructing a variant history departing from one of its crucial junctions. As with futuristic fiction, the subgenre of alternative history fiction was eventually to thrive and become extraordinarily rich, but as with *Le Roman de l'avenir*, its first exemplar did not serve as a prolific inspiration in its own day. The text in question was initially published anonymously in 1836 as *Napoléon et la conquête du monde, 1812-1832: Histoire de la Monarchie universelle* [Napoleon and the Conquest of the World, 1812-1832: A History of the Universal Monarchy]; it was reissued in 1841 as *Napoléon apocryphe* (tr. as *The Apocryphal Napoléon*), with the addition of the by-line Louis Geoffroy.

"Louis Geoffroy" was an abbreviation of the name of Louis-Napoléon Geoffroy-Château (1803-1858), a magistrate in the civil tribunal of Paris. He was the son of Marc-Antoine Geoffroy-Château (1774-1806), an officer in the engineering corps who had attracted the attention of General Bonaparte while fighting in the Egyptian campaign, but had subsequently died in battle in Europe in 1806. Like all the children of officers killed in action, Louis was then formal-

ly adopted by the Emperor, but it is doubtful that he ever met his adoptive father. A more active role in his upbringing was doubtless played by his uncle,
Étienne Geoffroy Saint-Hilaire (1772-1844)—all four sons of the advocate Jean-
Jacques-Gérard Geoffroy added arbitrary suffixes to their surname. Geoffroy
Saint-Hilaire was a colleague of the Chevalier de Lamarck, who carried forward
the latter's theory of evolution, with a heavier emphasis on the unity of life and a
quasi-transcendental notion of adaptive evolution that has numerous echoes in
his nephew's novel. He too had accompanied Bonaparte to Egypt, as part of the
scientific mission attached to the military one.

In the alternative account of Napoléon's life featured in the novel, the Emperor does not retreat from Moscow in 1912 but heads for Saint Petersburg immediately after reaching the burned city, and defeats Czar Alexander' army convincingly. The Grande Armée then returns to France in time to repair the reverses suffered in the Peninsular War and smash the English forces there, eliminating the Duke of Wellington from history. Having invaded and conquered England, and put down an attempted revolt by Russia, Sweden and Prussia, thus securing Europe, the Grande Armée sets out to conquer Asia. That requires four
years, but proves relatively facile once the crucial Battle of Jerusalem has obliterated the forces of Islam, and establishes the Emperor's reputation so magnificently that all the rulers in Africa capitulate without a shot being fired, and the
precarious leaders of the Americas, both halves of the continent having been
torn apart by revolutions, beg Napoléon to accept their homage and integrate
them into his Universal Monarchy.

The somewhat tongue-in-cheek narration reaches a climax of straight-faced
absurdity during Napoléon's coronation as Sovereign of the World, when God
obligingly extinguishes two stars in order to reconfigure the constellation of
Orion so that it can be renamed in his honor. Alongside his conquests, Napoléon
has taken care to obliterate the religion of Islam utterly and absolutely, never
hesitating to use massacre as an instrument, and, having installed his uncle as
Pope, reclaimed the Orthodox Church from the ex-Czar and whipped all the
Protestant sects into line, he welcomes the Jews into the Catholic fold when they
vote unanimously to convert (except for one dissenting rabbi whom God
promptly strikes dead). He has also taken time out to excavate the ruins of Babylon, including the tower of Babel, and to discover the central seas in the heart of
Australia and Africa, a buried antediluvian city in Mexico and lost civilizations
preserving pristine relics of the Egypt of the first pharaohs and the survivors of
the Deluge. In the meantime, the sciences and arts make phenomenal progress
under his reign, solving the problem of steering airships, developing a worldwide network of electrical telegraphy, inventing new means of enhancing senso-
ry perception and clarifying the fundamental nature of life, with abundant medical spinoff.

Unlike the real Napoléon, Geoffroy's swiftly makes the effort to reconcile
himself with Madame de Staël, not only seducing her with sudden goodwill but

ordering the Académie Française to admit her as a member, immediately. The Emperor credits his conversion to his reading of the books that gave the French Romantic Movement one of its key exemplars and its name. When Geoffroy lists the important publications of his alternative 1820s he includes masterpieces (all unknown in our history) by Alphonse de Lamartine, Victor Hugo, Alfred de Musset, Charles Nodier, Honoré de Balzac, Stendhal and Jules Michelet, as well as adding works by the English Romantics Lord Byron and Walter Scott, written in French following the addition of England to the French Empire, and the "final and most eccentric" work by J. W. Goethe. As to whether Geoffroy attended meetings of Nodier's *cénacle* himself, we can only speculate, but a biographical note on his father in a book co-authored by Nodier mentions that Marc-Antoine Geoffroy-Château left behind several unpublished manuscripts, and Nodier might well have got that information from Geoffroy. Prior to becoming the first classic novel of alternative history, therefore, Geoffroy's work is primarily, essentially and spectacularly an embodiment of the spirit of Romanticism, and its utopian dreams and excessive glorification of its hero need to be seen in that light if they are to be fully understood.

The novel has mostly been viewed as an earnest glorification of Napoléon, and if its author ever took his theoretical status as the Emperor's adoptive son seriously, perhaps he had reason for hero-worship, but the text's most conspicuous feature is its sharp wit; it is a manifestly sarcastic work, and deliberately shocking in places. Although it is difficult, in consequence, to measure the exact depth of its satire, it remains the case that the publication of the book in 1836 and again—with the author's signature—in 1841, was not without bravery. Louis-Philippe was not unready to exile people who offended him, and Bonapartist sympathies, even if not entirely sincere, were definitely liable to offend him.

Louis-Napoléon Bonaparte was one of those thus exiled, but he published his *Rêveries politiques* [Political dreams] in 1833, expressing the belief that he was one of the elect "Volunteers of Providence" in whose hands the destiny of their countries lay. In 1836, almost simultaneously with the publication of Geoffroy's book, he attempted to stimulate an uprising in Strasbourg, but failed and had to flee the country again, henceforth regarded as more dangerous than before—as, indeed, he proved to be. He attempted a second coup in 1840, which failed as catastrophically as the first, and was imprisoned thereafter for six years, until he contrived an escape that made him seem once again to be an active threat to the regime.

Against that background, it is perhaps surprising that Geoffroy's text was reissued in 1841, although the second reissue in 1851, by which time Louis-Napoléon had been elected president of the Second Republic (but had not yet carried out the *coup-d'état* in December of that year, which made him Emperor) no longer seemed in the least undiplomatic. The Revolution of 1848 had prompted Émile Girardin to run Théophile Gautier's feuilleton "Les Deux étoiles" [The Two Stars] in *La Presse* in September and October, a secret history

story featuring a heroic attempt made by a group of conspirators to rescue Napoléon from Saint Helena, which was also reprinted in 1851 as *Partie carrée* (tr. as *The Quartette*), but in the twelve-year interval separating Geoffroy's book from Gautier's serial there was a definite risk in expressing Bonapartist sympathies, even in the fanciful guise of secret history, let alone the more combative form of alternative history. The option was available of producing alternative histories referring to other historical turning-points, but no one, at the time, was prepared to grasp that nettle as firmly as Geoffroy had grasped his.

Another writer associated with the Romantic Movement who was to make highly significant contributions to the evolution of *roman scientifique*, although many of those contributions were not made until the days of the Second Empire, was **Samuel-Henri Berthoud** (1804-1891), who anglicized the spelling of his familiar name as an affectation when he elected to sign his literary works "S. Henry Berthoud." Born in Cambrai, in the region of Flanders in north-western France, he was the son of a printer and bookseller who also had the first name of Samuel, which is probably why he preferred his second forename in his usual signature.

Berthoud obtained his first publication in 1822, when his father published his *Premiers essais poétiques* for him, and his talent was endorsed in 1823, when he won a competition organized by the Societé d'Émulation de Cambrai, the literary society of his home town. By 1829 he was the permanent secretary of the Societé d'Émulation de Cambrai, and was also editing a periodical founded the previous year by his father, the *Gazette de Cambrai*. He had probably been working for his father since leaving school, in the family business, but whenever his formal education had been suspended, his lack of advanced qualifications did not prevent him from thinking of himself as a scholar. His first passion was natural history, but he was also interested in literature, music, history and local folklore. He was an enthusiastic adherent of Romanticism from the very beginning, taking in German and English influences as well as French ones. Ernst Hoffmann is featured as a character in some of his historical romances and he was an admirer of Lord Byron, to the extent of adopting some affectations of dandyism—but not the Byronic "satanism" that made such a deep impression on many French Romantics; Berthoud never compromised his devout Catholicism.

Berthoud moved to Paris in 1830, when his story "Prestige" was published in the *Revue des Deux Mondes*. He met Balzac in that year, and became part of the curious community of would-be writers graphically described by the latter writer in *Illusions perdues* (1837-43; tr. as *Lost Illusions*). Exactly where Berthoud fitted into the spectrum of types identified by Balzac's novel is unclear, except for the fact that he was one of those who "sold out" by falling prey to the temptations of journalism, perhaps compromising his original ideals and ambitions in the process. Before then, however, he must have written the bulk of the items in his first collection, *Contes misanthropiques* [Misanthropic Tales] (1831), whose contents leave no doubt about the fact that, whatever illusions he might have bought to Paris regarding literary life and the prospects of finding success therein, he had none at all about life in general and the roles played therein by love, marriage, fickleness and recklessness.

Berthoud's *Contes misanthropiques* have strong thematic, methodical and philosophical links with the short stories that Jules Janin began collecting in 1832 and those that Petrus Borel collected in *Champavert: contes immoraux* (1833; tr. as *Champavert: Immoral Tales*). Although Berthoud's work lacks the fire and ferocity of Borel's and the slick dexterity of Janin's best work, there is no doubt that it is Berthoud who was the true originator of the rich tradition of cynical short fiction that eventually came to be known as *contes cruels*. Had it not been virtually impossible to find for such a long time, *Contes misanthropiques* would have been recognized as a crucial contribution to the *conte cruel* tradition. Its fall into oblivion was doubtless aided by the fact that Berthoud never produced another volume like it, although the studied disillusionment that fueled those early stories continued to influence all of his works. In particular, it was to color his scientific journalism and his "scientific fantasies" in a distinctive fashion, which distanced his work in that vein considerably from that of such fellow pioneers of the popularization of science as Camille Flammarion and Henri de Parville.

Berthoud's first real literary success was obtained by the three volumes of *Chroniques et traditions surnaturelles de la Flandre* [*sic*, Chronicles and Supernatural Traditions of Flanders] (1831-34). The collection does include some genuine items of folklore, only slightly modified in giving them literary form, but it also contains a considerable number of works that do not even bother to mimic the form of folktales, simply being items of modern supernatural fiction based on the kinds of materials found in folktales. Such mixtures are not unusual in collections of that sort, but Berthoud is further removed from being an authentic folklorist than most prominent Romantic contributors to the field, including the brothers Grimm in Germany, Robert Hunt in England and Anatole Le Braz in France; the French successor with whom he had most in common was probably Julie Lavergne, whose own mock-folkloristic tales include a marginal item of *roman scientifique* featuring artificial wings, "L'Horloger de Nuremberg" (1882).

In a single-volume reprint of his collection published as *Légendes et traditions surnaturelles des Flandres* (1862), Berthoud added the novella *Asrael et Neptha*, originally published separately in 1832, to the reprinted short stories—a move re-emphasizing the fact that its contents are more readily considered as literary works that draw some inspiration from Flanders folklore than attempts to record the folklore in question in anything resembling its "original" anecdotal form.

As with the *Contes misanthropiques*, Berthoud never made any concerted attempt to write more supernatural fiction in the same vein as the *Chroniques et traditions surnaturelle de la Flandre*, but as with the former volume, its legacy left an indelible legacy on his future work, where folklore and fakelore continue to occupy a situation "in the wings," always available for recruitment, at least for the purposes of comparison and subsidiary reference. His literary production slowed after 1834, because he found employment as an editor under the auspices of Émile de Girardin, whose periodicals always put a particular emphasis on popular education. Girardin's first periodical, *La Mode*, was supposedly a women's magazine with an emphasis on fashion, but more typical of his projects were the enormously successful *Journal des connaissances utiles* [Newspaper of Useful Knowledge] (founded 1831), published under the banner of La Societé Nationale pour l'Émancipation Intellectuelle [National Society for Intellectual Emancipation] and his launching of the popular daily press with *La Presse* (founded 1836), which helped to found the tradition of popular feuilleton fiction that brought about a revolution in French popular fiction in the 1840s. Berthoud contributed to all those projects, and his commitment to the cause of mass education played a major role in shaping the remainder of his literary and journalistic output. It was, however, for the illustrated *Musée des Familles*, founded in 1833, that Berthoud was hired as editor in 1834.

In 1834 children's literature, in the sense of books and magazines designed for children to read by themselves, hardly existed; it was still assumed that children would provide an audience for adult readers, and even the *Journal des Enfants*, founded in that year with Jules Janin as editor, was aimed at parents rather than the supposed "end consumers." The *Musée de Familles* was by no means designed with child listeners exclusively, or even primarily, in mind, but the whole point of it was to construct an all-inclusive audience, addressing content to children and women as well as to the adult males who had previously constituted the core of the audience for periodicals, thus adding significant impetus to the crusade for universal literacy—which was proceeding more rapidly in France in the 1830s than any other nation.

It was in connection with the crusade for universal literacy, and in trying to cater to it with his editorial policy, that Berthoud apparently first became intensely interested in the popularization of science, and it was in the *Musée des*

Familles that his career found the fundamental orientation that it would maintain for the rest of his life. His own contributions mostly appeared under the rubrics "Études Historiques", "Études Morales" or "Études Artistiques," and all of them consisted of robust melodramatic narratives set against a historical backcloth, including one or more famous people, writers and artists more frequently as kings and soldiers.

There is no doubt that Berthoud urged his other contributors to dress up their own didactic enterprises in robust fictional form, and those who responded to his urging included one of his leading writers on scientific topics, Pierre Boitard (1789-1859), who was led by that urging to produce two of the most eccentric, but also most ground-breaking, early-nineteenth-century exercises in *roman scientifique*: "Paris avant les hommes" (tr. as "Paris Before Humankind"), which appeared in two parts in the June 1837 and November 1837 issues, and "Voyage au soleil" (tr. as "Journey to the Sun") published in four parts in the issues for December 1838, February and November 1839, and February 1840. The second item was never reprinted, and although the author began work on a revised version of the former before his death, its subject-matter had made such vast advances in the previous twenty years that only small fragments of the original survived in a far more elaborate text, which was posthumously published as *L'Univers avant homme* [The World Before Humankind], in 1861.

Boitard's early publications were in the field of botany, his first book being *Traité de la composition et de l'ornement des jardins* [Treatise on the Design and Ornamentation of Gardens] (1925), and most of his later ones were concerned with the relevance of botanical knowledge to the planning and maintenance of gardens and agricultural endeavor. Because of his interest in botany he also became fascinated by the nascent field that would nowadays be called paleobotany: the study of extinct plants and the sequence of their development over time, by means of the fossil record. That led to a more general interest in paleontology, including the development of animal fossils over geological time, and hence to an interest in cosmogony, the history of the Earth as revealed by the geological record, and what that might imply regarding the nature and development of the entire solar system in the course of cosmic time.

Partly because of that direction of approach, Boitard had no difficulty at all in becoming a believer in "transformism"; it seemed obvious to him that plants had originated with simple forms that had, over long periods of time, developed into more complicated ones. That pattern was very obviously set out in the fossil record and relatively easy to comprehend. It was, therefore, natural enough for him to transfer the same kind of thinking to his contemplation of the record of fossil animals, where it was much more controversial.

The development of geological studies since the days of Benoît de Maillet had long made nonsense of the chronology inferred from *Genesis*, which suggested that the world was only six thousand years old and had been created in six days; the realization that the Earth contained a large number of rock strata laid down by successive processes of sedimentation made that account utterly incredible. Some people therefore considered geology—and science in general—to be a dire threat to religious faith, and one to be opposed at all costs. Others took the view that it made no difference to the real foundations of religious faith, but merely required the six days of creation to be construed metaphorically. Some geologists even took the trouble to divide geological time up into six periods that conserved the same number—an adjustment with which Boitard was quite happy to go along.

There was, however, an additional and particular problem with regard to the sixth day of *Genesis*, which included the creation of humankind. By 1837, paleontological discoveries had begun to suggest, although the crucial evidence was still thin, that humans had appeared on Earth a long time before six thousand years ago, which cast the rest of the chronology of *Genesis* into the same rubbish bin as the six days of creation, without there being any readily available metaphorical shift to save its essence. Worse than that; if it were generally accepted that animals as well as plants had developed over an exceedingly long period of time by virtue of a complex pattern of transformations, then the possibility that human beings were a product of that process too, and not a special and unique creation, became increasingly hard to deny. That, for many devout believers, was a line that could not and must not be crossed.

Some scientists saw no particular problem there either. For them, transformism simply became God's painstaking method of creation, and the truth of transformism—even if it included the origin of human beings, supplying them with relatively recent ancestors that they had in common with the great apes—need not challenge belief in God as the creator of the world. Boitard apparently belonged to that camp too. There was, however, a considerable difference in 1837 between being prepared to believe that and being prepared to say so publicly. Most geologists and biologists were extremely diplomatic in writing, if only in the interests of avoiding persecution, of which there was still a real danger.

Even in esoteric publications directed at an academic audience, it was still advisable, in France in 1837, to be very careful of what one said, and how, about transformism, especially where its relevance to humankind was concerned. That diplomatic risk was, however, magnified very considerably when it was a matter of addressing a popular audience in a "family magazine." It seems probable, in retrospect, that it was not Boitard's idea to do it; he certainly never did it again while he was alive, although he did prepare the revised and expanded version of "Paris avant les hommes," for posthumous publication. Even if the idea of publishing "Paris avant les hommes" and then following it up with the even more ambitious and equally provocative "Voyage au soleil" did originate with Boitard, the notion must have been very wholehearted endorsed by Berthoud, and Berthoud surely had something to do with the narrative strategy they adopted, which was something else that Boitard never attempted again—and nor did anyone else for the next two decades, although subsequent writers have certainly made up for the delay.

In being asked to adapt his exercises in the popularization of science to narrative form, Boitard was facing a far more difficult task that Berthoud took on himself in packing his own narratives with information about history. The simplest way to do it was simply to embed scientific ideas in conversations, after the fashion of Fontenelle, and that is what one of Berthoud's other scientific contributors, Auguste Bertsch, did in his series on "Le Monde invisible" (1839), which presented early discoveries in miscroscopy is the context of a series of dialogues between the narrator and his doctor. Boitard did that as well, but in the context of far-reaching journeys that displayed, on the one hand, recent discoveries in the science that would become known as paleontology, and on the other hand, a speculative cosmogony based on recent discoveries in astronomy and physics.

Paleontology and cosmogony are inherently narrativized sciences, which set out fundamentally to tell stories, but the stories in question necessarily extend over very long periods of time and treat large-scale events with no immediate human involvement. It is, therefore, not easy to blend their inherent narrativization with the kinds of story that fit so readily into the context of historical depiction. Indeed, in order to for a human viewpoint to be introduced into them, the narrative strategy requires at a minimum, the invention of some kind of time travel, and, in the latter case, space travel as well. In 1837, there was only one previous literary work that had done both: *Les Posthumes*. Without going to Restifian extremes, however, there was one narrative device readily available to fulfill both of those functions, and that was dreaming.

Dreaming can supply interlocutors as easily as it can supply visions of elsewhen and elsewhere, but a far-reaching scientific dream of the kind envisaged by Boitard requires an interlocutor of a special kind, not only in terms of what he knows, and can therefore discuss, but also in terms of what he can do within the dream to guide it and steer a course through it. Given the provocative nature of Boitard's enterprise, and the attitude that those hostile to it were bound to strike, there was one very appealing contender available in French literary tradition, and that was the one that Boitard selected: Lesage's lame devil, Asmodeus.

In the first part of "Paris avant les hommes," Asmodeus takes the narrator back to the earliest days revealed by the record of the geological strata, before the addition of any sedimentary strata or any fossils, and then walks him through the entire sequence of geological history, pointing out salient details of plant and animal evolution, as excavations had thus far revealed it. The scientific basis of the account is provided by the work of Georges Cuvier (1769-1832), the first person to develop the idea that fossils were the remains of plant and animal species that had long become extinct, but which could nevertheless be accurately depicted, even from incomplete skeletal remains, by means of analogical reasoning—although Boitard took leave to disagree with Cuvier with the regard to some of the logical consequences of that theory.

In the second part, Asmodeus becomes more active in offering his own speculative accounts of such contemporary puzzles as the nature of the skull labeled *Dinotherium*—which he gets completely wrong—but more importantly, he completes the journey that he had cut timorously short in part one, showing the origins of humankind as a natural consequence of the sequence of primates. That theme is picked up in "Voyage au soleil," in which Asmodeus takes the narrator on a tour of the solar system, beginning with the Sun itself, here made habitable, like all the other solid bodies in the solar system, by an ingenious extrapolation of the theory of "caloric" introduced by Antoine Lavoisier to substitute for phlogiston theory when the defects of the latter became too obvious.

Before the tour begins Asmodeus gives the narrator a lecture while they take a rest on a lump of rock orbiting the Earth: a miniature moon. It is possible that Boitard had taken the inspiration, for that scene in particular and perhaps for the whole exercise, from *Voyages et aventures du docteur Festus* (1833) by Rodolphe Töpffer, written around an album of illustrations published three years earlier, in which the protagonist is hurled no space by the rapidly-rotating sail of a windmill and goes into orbit himself as an artificial satellite, before being carried away by an "aérolith." Asmodeus' guest gets a close-up view of a similar object and the demon explains the nature of meteorites at some length.

In subsequent phases of the journey Asmodeus provides his explanation of comets, introduces the narrator to the four minor planets so far discovered and explains the logic of the then-novel thesis that they must be fragments of an exploded planet. He also explains what the inability to measure the distance of stars by means of the parallax of the Earth's orbit implies about the awesome size of the universe. The real point of the tour, however, is to present the narrator with a series of images of life on other worlds that not only confirm and emphasize the thesis that humans evolved by a natural process from ape-like ancestors, but also presents an image of what future evolution will probably make of human beings, and how humans will be replaced when their evolutionary development has led to the decadence and extinction of the species.

The logic that Boitard applied to both of the latter notions produced images that were eventually to be reproduced, and even to become clichéd, although it is virtually certain that their reproducers had no knowledge of Boitard's anticipations. His Solarian, with his huge head and tiny body, is the prototype of one of the standard images of far-future humankind, and his Mercurian, an intelligent ape reminiscent of an orangutan, whose species has replaced humankind following that species' decline and extinction, also recurred several times in twentieth-century imaginative fiction. Although Boitard uses the conventional argument that evolution is bound to follow the same course on all worlds because it is working with the same materials, he does allow adaptive modifications of human form, which produce the rabbit-like troglodytic humans of Saturn, and he also allows himself one remarkable leap into the extraordinary in populating Pallas with seeming humans composed of an exceedingly refined matter, which requires some exceedingly exotic amendments to their physiology.

Hindsight informs us that all Boitard's speculations about the solar system were incorrect, partly because the theory of "caloric" is mistaken, but partly too because his understanding of physics was faulty even for 1837. His account of the evolution of Earthly life is also severely flawed, although that was almost entirely due to the inadequacy of his data—but in the fundamental matter of the origins of humankind his brave decision was correct. "Paris avant les hommes" and "Voyage au soleil" were both far superseded, by future prehistoric fantasies and future interplanetary fantasies that had far better data on which to build their speculations, but that did not happen for nearly thirty years, and Boitard's works remain among the ranks of deeply-flawed but heroically bold precursors. "Voyage au soleil" was not entirely without competition in its era from other voyages into space, but its most immediate predecessor, a brief account of a journey to the moon by balloon included as a digression in a long account of the *Aventures de Robert-Robert* (1836) by Louis Desnoyers, is exceedingly pale by comparison.

S. Henry Berthoud's most successful book, after the *Chroniques et traditions surnaturelles de la Flandre*, was his account of the life of *Pierre-Paul Rubens* (1840), based on work published in the *Musée des Familles*, and issued as a supplement to the magazine, but the publication had already changed hands twice by then, after losing money consistently, and he was replaced as its editor in 1840, forced back to freelance journalism. It was then, however, that he picked up the thread of what he had encouraged Boitard to do, and began using fiction as a vehicle for the popularization of science himself, making significant strides in developing narrative strategies and motifs that were to become standard features of *roman scientifique*. His work in that vein was only a tiny fraction of his output, most of which consisted of domestic melodramas, but it was obviously precious to him.

Berthoud's first notable work of *roman scientifique* was "Voyage au ciel" (tr. as "A Heavenward Voyage") originally published in Girardin's *La Presse* in 1841. It tells the story of Ludwig Klopstock—a nephew of the German epic poet—whose tendency to imaginative meditation and fascination with science leads in youth to social isolation, only temporarily ameliorated when he marries a poor orphan, whose attentions adapt him a little better to social life. Unfortunately, his wife goes mad when their first child dies, and his refusal to put her away in an asylum increases his ostracism by his neighbors. He plunges deeply into his scientific research, and makes two significant discoveries, only to find that he had been anticipated in both of them. Having become interested in aerostatics, he becomes obsessed with building a flying machine that can take him to altitudes that balloons cannot reach, and thus beyond the divine limit apparently set on human ambition.

The flying machine itself, similar to those envisaged by Félix Nogaret and Félix Bodin, is of relatively slight interest by comparison with the intensive study the story makes of the particular character of scientific obsession: a psychological analysis of "the scientific mind." That project fascinated Berthoud, both as a journalist seeking information from actual scientists and as a writer of fiction constructing imaginative archetypes. It became the dominant feature of his *fantaisies scientifiques*.

The concern is particularly evident, almost to the point of obsession itself, in the contributions Berthoud made to the devoutly Romantic *Revue Pittoresque*. In "Le Maître du temps" (1844; tr. as "The Master of the Weather"), a scientist who discovers references to a method of controlling the weather in pages of a manuscript used to seal jam-pots sets off on a desperate quest to locate the rest of the document, or its writer, and thus acquire the secret. Even more typical of his subsequent work is "Le Fou" (1844; tr. as "The Madman"), which offers an account of the final days of the exiled English scientist Sir William Congreve (1772-1828), adapted and tailored to present Congreve as an archetypal scientific genius driven insane by the crass and ingrate incomprehension of his fellows.

In one sense, Berthoud's stories are forebears of countless subsequent literary depiction of "mad scientists," but Berthoud is insistent from the very outset that his scientists are, to begin with, possessed of a distinctive, and perhaps superior, kind of sanity, which is only warped by frustration and a lack of sympathy and understanding on the part of their fellows. He recognizes that the special sanity of the scientists makes social relationships—particularly marital relationships—awkward and difficult, but he does not see that awkwardness as an incapacity for love, simply as a deflection of affection inherent in a greater love of solving problems. The eventual and seemingly inevitable annihilation of his protagonists by their overwhelming compulsive obsession is presented as stark tragedy, akin, in a more than merely metaphorical sense, to martyrdom. Two of the three stories cited above were, in fact, eventually reprinted in Berthoud's *Fantaisies scientifiques de Sam* in a section entitled "Martyrs."

That section contains another story that has close thematic links with them and was probably first published in the same period, "Le Second soleil" (tr. as "The Second Sun"). Another of the stories that Berthoud contributed to the *Revue Pittoresque*, "Le Chaudron de Bicêtre" (1845; tr. as "The Cauldron of Bicêtre") belongs to the same sequence, but adds further layers of complication to the basic pattern. It offers a highly fanciful account of the career of Salomon de Caus (1576-1626), who had been hailed by the nineteenth-century scientist and statesman François Arago as the true inventor of the steam engine. "Le Chaudron de Bicêtre" can easily be imagined as a pivotal work in Berthoud's career—a kind of summation of his more exotic endeavors so far—being an extended *conte cruel* in a form that was later to become one of the standard templates of that genre, a tale of diabolism, the force of which is only slightly diminished by a frame narrative placing it in the mouth of an inmate of the lunatic asylum at Bicêtre, and an account of fatal compulsive obsession and frustrated scientific discovery, in exactly the same fashion as its three (or perhaps four) recent predecessors.

It might conceivably have been pangs of conscience, or complaints from others, about the cavalier distortions of historical fact in "Le Fou" and "Le Chaudron de Bicêtre" that persuaded Berthoud to be more discreet in future; while few of his other stories featuring real individuals can be commended for their accuracy and authenticity, most are more conscientious in treating their heroes—but his fascination with the psychology of the scientific mind remained, developed in numerous other accounts of scientific eccentricity, many of which blur the distinction between reportage and fiction.

The four stories produced in the early 1840s—five if "Le Second Soleil" was also first written then—were Berthoud's earliest attempts to invent a form of "scientific fiction," and they remain distinctive; there is nothing else in the historical record of precursors of modern science fiction quite like them. They are not only interesting because of the detail in the account they offer of the scientific mind, and the similarity of that account to some modern analyses— "Voyage au ciel," in particular, contains what is nowadays recognizable as a textbook description of Asperger's syndrome—but because of their parallel study of the hostile manner in which people possessed of a different psychology react to the eccentricities typical of dedicated scientists.

Because all his accounts of hypothetical scientific discoveries are set in the past, Berthoud had to find narrative means of obliterating them all from the historical record: a strategy that prevented him from extrapolating their possible social and intellectual consequences, and thus prevented him from inventing a kind of fiction more akin to modern science fiction. What it did enable him to do, however, by way of partial compensation, was to add a particular dimension of tragedy to his accounts of the frustrations of genius occasioned by incomprehension, which is markedly different from the more clinically ironic tone of his *Contes misanthropiques.*

That achievement would not be without interest even if it were an isolated example without consequence, but in fact, whether Berthoud's influence had anything to do with it or not, that fascination with the psychology of science, its tendency to lead to a kind of martyrdom, and its frequent culmination in tragedy, was to become one of the abiding preoccupations of *roman scientifique*, echoed in some of its most affectively-powerful works—works in which, very often, the speculative element is similarly marginal.

Berthoud's popularity and perceived importance in that first phase of his career is reflected in the fact that he was appointed a *Chevalier de la Légion d'honneur* in 1844, but his endeavors on behalf of the education of the masses presumably had more responsibility for that award than his reputation among his literary peers; at the very best, he would have been ranked alongside some of the other "foot-soldiers" of Romanticism who contributed extensively to both the *Musée des Familles* and the *Revue pittoresque*, such as Joseph Méry, Jules Janin and Léon Gozlan, and he might well have been ranked some way beneath them because of the increasing banality of his didactic novels. In that context, the short stories he did for the *Revue Pittoresque* can probably be considered his most ambitious work, and might also be reckoned as a peak of aspiration that he did not attempt to scale again after the abrupt interruption of his career by the 1848 Revolution.

The other contributions made by writers associated with the Romantic Movement to the evolution of *roman scientifique* prior to the overthrow of the Second Republic now seem even more anemic than the handful of stories contrived by Henry Berthoud, although it is worth mentioning a group of minor works by Honoré de Balzac (1799-1850), who was one of Berthoud's closest friends when they were in the early phases of their careers.

In the Gothic potboiler *Le Centenaire ou les deux Behringeld* (1822 as by Horace St. Aubin; tr. as *The Centenarian; or, The Two Behringelds*) the eponymous predator who distils vital fluid from victims in order to prolong his own life uses technological methods of extraction and possesses a laboratory that seems more chemical than alchemical. *La Recherche de l'absolu* (1834; tr. as *The Quest for the Absolute*) is more interesting, not so much because of the elements of scientific method in the protagonist's quest for the philosopher's stone as for the minute analysis of his obsession and its effects on his family: an evident precursor of Berthoud's psychological studies of more orthodox scientists. Equally interesting is the short novel serialized in 1843 as "Ève et David" and subsequently incorporated into the later versions of *Illusions perdues* as "Les Souffrances de l'inventeur" [The Inventor's Sufferings], which details the difficulties faced by the inventor of a new technology of paper manufacture in developing his technology, which is stolen by an insidious competitor.

Perhaps surprisingly, many of the younger participants in the movement only made extensive contributions to the foundations of *roman scientifique* after the establishment of the Second Empire, when the Movement seemed, even to its stalwarts, to have gone into something of a decline—a decline encouraged by the challenge to the Movement's ideals by new literary fads but also reflected the oppression of Napoléon III's censors, who were fierce in their suppression of anything suggestive of political criticism in the first few years of his reign. Some of those younger writers, however, did produce a few items of note before the 1848 Revolution. One of the most significant was Joseph Méry (1798-1866)—who might, in fact, have produced more than is now evident, as the original dates of his shorter pieces are difficult to establish because their periodical publications have not yet been determined by bibliographers of the genre.

Four items by Méry—who did not use his forename in his signature—subsequently gathered together for book publication as "Les Lunariens" (tr. as "The Lunarians") must have been written in the mid-1830s, because they are all explicitly inspired by the recapitulation in French newspapers of the New York *Sun*'s "Moon Hoax" of 1935, and one of them is explicitly dated 1836. All of them are, however, mere jokes, which represent a brief topical renewal of the tradition of lunar satire rather than a step forward in the tradition of interplanetary fiction.

Rather more significant, in terms of its subsequent influences, is what was presumably the first of Méry's futuristic fictions, "Les Ruines de Paris" (tr. as "The Ruins of Paris"), which, if the internal evidence of the story can be trusted, must have been originally published in 1844. Like the pieces making up "Les Lunariens," it is a joke, in which archaeologists of the future return from the Atlasian Phalanstery in New France—the heart of civilization having now shifted to North Africa—to the site of ancient Paris, where they examine the ruins of various buildings, some of which were uncompleted projects when the story was written, including the Madeleine and the Panthéon. The result of those inclusions is to make the story seem slightly surreal to modern readers because many of the details discovered were not actually incorporated into the buildings in question, which do not resemble the representations in the story.

Not unnaturally, perhaps, the archeologists from Méry's New France draw various false inferences from the relics of ancient Paris that remain, concluding that Catholicism was unknown in France in the early nineteenth century and that nymphs were still worshiped there. The experience is, however, edifying, as the inspection of the ruins serves to remind the people of 3844 how far they have advanced in two millennia, and how different the present earthly paradise is from the primitive beginnings of civilization. The story appears to have been reprinted at least once before the 1848 Revolution, and was reprinted again after the advent of the Second Empire, thus achieving a familiarity that helped it to inspire an entire series of imitative exercises, which became increasingly elaborate and sophisticated. Méry added his own supplements to it, which will be discussed in the next chapter, although it is possible that at least one of them was initially published before 1850.

The fact that the Romantic Movement took in art and music as well as literature and philosophy is reflected in one of the most curious utopian fantasies of the period, penned by the exceedingly Romantic composer Hector Berlioz in 1844 and describing the small town of "Euphonia" (tr. as "Euphonia") in the year 2344, in which the sole purpose of the community and its inhabitants is the making of music. Life is organized and disciplined in accordance with signals given by a steam-powered organ situated at the top of its central tower, in an aural telegraphic language understood by all the inhabitants—who communicate between themselves by means of a system of visual telegraphy that avoids the prosaicism of speech. The story features a concert played by an entire mechanical orchestra commanded by its conductor.

One of the most bizarre works relevant to the development of *roman philosophique* published the period is *L'Uraniade, ou Ésop juge à la cour d'Uranie, scènes dialoguées au sujet des hypothèses Newtoniennes: songe scientifique* [The Uraniad, or Aesop judges in Urania's Court; dialogue scenes on the subject of the Newtonian hypothesis: A Scientific Dream] (tr. as "The Uraniad") signed Père Brémond and first published by the author in Avignon in 1844. It harks back to the original coinage of the phrase *roman scientifique* by Élie Fréron, as Brémond is also a diehard opponent of Isaac Newton's theory of gravity. In 1844 the term had not yet been adapted for application to new kinds of literary work, so Brémond's work was an example of literary protest against *roman scientifique* in what he would have considered to be the meaning of the phrase, although it can now be seen in retrospect as a uniquely pure exercise in *roman scientifique* in the modern sense, akin—like Guillaume La Follie's championship of the phlogiston theory and Pierre Boitard's extrapolation of caloric theory—to what is nowadays called "hard science fiction," in spite of its flagrantly fantastic allegorical trappings.

Those allegorical trappings consist of a trial held outside the gates of the palace of Urania (the muse of astronomy), in which the followers of Newton—including Voltaire, although the prosecution is undertaken by less celebrated scientists, led by Willem s'Gravesande—attempt to have a book by an unnamed author (Père Brémond) banned for attacking the great man. Urania refuses to head the tribunal herself and nominates the fabulist Aesop to judge the case, as a man of common sense beginning from a position of neutral ignorance. The defense is undertaken by the pioneering popularizer of science Noël-Antoine Pluche, author of *La Spectacle de la Nature* (1732) and Bernardin de Saint-Pierre, whose unorthodox account of *Harmonies de la Nature*, including attempted descriptions of life on the other planets of the solar system, had been published posthumously in 1815.

We now know that the criticisms leveled against Newtonian theory by the unorthodox theorists featured in *L'Uraniade* are utterly mistaken, and any modern schoolboy could probably poke the holes in them that Newton's defenders conspicuously fail to bring up when invited by the *ad hoc* judge to argue their case. The real individuals on whom those characters are based could undoubtedly have put up a far more robust and devastating show, but their failure to do so adds a perverse interest to a debate that is intriguing not so much in regard to the problems it addresses, but in respect of the issues in the philosophy and sociology of science that it raises in the process. In particular, it contains severe criticisms of the manner in which the scientific community operates to maintain an orthodoxy against criticism, whether the criticism is justified or not, and in that

212

respect it anticipated a theme that was to become very important in *roman scientifique*, which is replete with brilliant scientists whose unorthodox ideas lead to all difficulties and frustrations because they cannot make their voices heard and only attract hostility and persecution by trying.

Little seems to be known about Brémond except that his first name was Pierre and that he was a Jesuit; his supposed *magnum opus*—or *pièce de resistance*—criticizing Newton's theses, which *L'Uraniade* was written and published to advertise, was never published, in spite of Aesop's favorable verdict. Whether or not the manuscript that he left on deposit in his local library in Avignon still exists, it is highly unlikely ever to see print, and equally unlikely that the earnest work in question could have had the saving graces that allow *L'Uraniade* to retain some interest above and beyond its status as a literary and philosophical curiosity. In spite of that, however, the work is notable for its enterprise, its liveliness and its sheer bizarrerie.

In all of subsections of this chapter, reference has been repeatedly made to ground-breaking works that set significant precedents for future endeavors in roman scientifique. Viewing them collectively, however, the most striking thing about them is that they were not followed up rapidly; the works that eventually took up their themes productively were occasionally produced by authors aware of their existence, but in many cases, the reiteration seems to have been an accidental result of independent inspiration. The entire history of speculative fiction between 1789 and 1851 thus seems, in retrospect, to have been a matter of occasional spectacular feats of the imagination that were not subsequently followed up, for one reason or another, until after 1851.

Perhaps that was only to be expected of a period of such continual instability, when everything seemed temporary and contingent, or perhaps it simply reflects the fact that imaginative breakthroughs, in the epoch in question, appeared in the eyes of their contemporary readers to be objects of potential admiration rather than stimuli to further imaginative endeavor. At any rate, the entire period can seem, on looking back from a distance, to have been one of frustrated efforts rather than triumphs. The social and literary environment was not yet ready for the establishment of a coherent genre of fiction taking its inspiration from the progress of science and technology, but the pioneering exercises carried out then, and the thinking that promoted them, nevertheless added an important supportive layer to the foundations laid down in the eighteenth century, and they give the impression in retrospect of ideative seed-cases whose kernels were capable of robust germination, in the right intellectual soil.

It is perhaps arguable that the metaphorical germination in question might have happened earlier had it not been for the political disruptions of the period, but comparison of the precursors of French *roman scientifique* with the parallel precursors of British scientific romance and American scientific lend no support at all to that thesis. Indeed, the opposite is the case; the French precursors are far more prolific and considerably richer in imagination than those laid down in Britain and America in the same interval, and the impression suggested is, therefore, that it might well have been the turbulence and uncertainty of the period that promoted the production of those intellectual seeds, and thus helped to ensure their eventual fertility and the quality of their heritage.

CHAPTER FOUR: THE SECOND EMPIRE: 1851-1870

1. Future Paris

The *coup d'état* staged by Louis-Napoléon Bonaparte, the elected president of the Republic, on 2 December 1851 initially consisted of a dissolution of the National Assembly, which left him in sole charge of government, but nevertheless still as President, and the new Constitution enacted in January 1852 merely confirmed his presidency for ten years. He did not let much time elapse thereafter, however, before restoring the Empire, ostensibly by popular demand, and confirmed his new status on the anniversary of the coup. Authoritarian at first, backed by forceful censorship and the intensive surveillance of opponents, that pressure gradually eased, and by 1860, which turned out to be its half-way point, the Empire had become considerably more liberal.

Many of the writers affiliated to the Romantic Movement had been ardent supporters of the 1848 Revolution and several had accepted posts in the Republican government; Alphonse de Lamartine had been its interim president, and Victor Hugo, Alexandre Dumas, Edgar Quinet and Eugène Sue were all prominent therein. All of them were exiled, although some took advantage of an amnesty that allowed them to return after a few years. Hugo and Quinet refused to do that, and remained stubbornly and ostentatiously in exile until the Empire ended, a permanent if rather minor embarrassment to the regime.

Things were difficult for many writers for some years, but the Empire did eventually bring a measure of economic stability that France had not enjoyed for a long time, and also military successes that had not been seen since the days of Napoléon I, initially in the Crimean War and subsequently, more spectacularly, the war against Austria in 1859. In the meantime, Paris underwent a spectacular growth, prompting an even more spectacular metamorphosis. Already the largest city in continental Europe in 1851, over the next two decades its population doubled, from one million to two. Eleven surrounding Communes were annexed, creating eight new arrondissements, while Napoléon III and the Prefect of the Seine, Baron Haussmann, set out in 1853 to reshape the center of the expanded city completely, effectively tearing the old Paris down and building a new one around its key monuments—a project credited to Napoléon I in the alternative history constructed by Louis Geoffroy.

The project was still unfinished when the Second Empire fell, smashed by the catastrophic Prussian invasion of 1870, but while it was in progress it was an important stimulus to both regret for the old and enthusiasm for the new. Napoléon III saw himself as a euchronian in the mold of the wise king of Mercier's *L'An quatre cent quarante quatre*, and he was fond of quoting Fourier, even though he had no intention of building phalansteries. He wanted the streets widened to facilitate the flow of traffic and he was determined to bring air, light and water into the center of a city that had long come to seem stifling, dingy and unclean. He wanted spaces for recreation—parks, theaters and museums—and new railway stations to connect the city effectively to the rest of the nation, and he commissioned Haussmann to make his desire a reality.

Nothing similar had ever been attempted in any other city, and although others were eventually to clear away their slums and open themselves up, nowhere else was that done in such a swift and disciplined fashion as in Paris. For much of the Second Empire, Paris was one vast building site, and the question of what it was becoming—and what it might and ought to become—was ever-present in the minds of Parisians. In such an environment, the euchronian speculation whose seeds had been planted by Saint-Simon, Comte, Fourier and Cabet was perhaps bound to bear further fruit, and to thrive in a relatively coherent fashion, as an active debate rather than in isolated flurries of individual activity, albeit one impeded by the scrupulous vigilance of the Emperor's censors.

In the second of Charles Nodier's stories featuring Berniquet's misadventures in the far future, when the philosopher expresses his intention "to go to that capital of science, that metropolis of art, that headquarters of civilization, that inexhaustible arsenal of perfectibility, Paris," his interlocutor laughs and tells him that Paris was destroyed ten thousand years ago by a rain of aeroliths, and that the place where Paris stood is now occupied by "the superb city of Hurlu." It is not improbable that when Nodier wrote that, he had Louis-Sébastien Mercier's vision of Paris in the year 2440 in mind, and thought that his own travesty of the idea of progress would not be complete without the destruction and replacement of the French capital. Napoléon III agreed, and those of Nodier's followers who dabbled in futuristic speculation also followed in Mercier's footsteps in developing a particular fascination with the future of the city, albeit in a decidedly ambivalent fashion that counterbalanced images of its improvement with images of its destruction.

Joseph Méry had pointed the way to one end of the spectrum of debate in his brief account of "Les Ruines de Paris," but Baron Haussmann pointed the way to another, and there was little about the *milieu* that any longer seemed *juste* to anyone: the visions that were produced frequently tended to an extreme of some sort. Discussions between Méry and his friend Théophile Gautier, partly fed by Méry's ironic depiction of a Paris obliterated by time and catastrophe, prompted both of them to address the issue further, and more adventurously, in a number of brief works that became the wellsprings of a significant series of endeavors by other hands.

By 1851 **Théophile Gautier** (1811-1872) was solidly established as one of the central and most famous members of the Romantic Movement, and the temporary exile of his most notable rivals for the position made him even more prominent, even though the Movement now seemed to many observers to be a thing of the past, effectively finished. His own *Histoire du romantisme* (1872; tr. as *The History of Romanticism*), the last work he completed before his death, was a nostalgic personal memoir rather than a history, looking back on times long gone, celebrating the legendary status of the opening night of Victor Hugo's *Hernani* in 1830 as  the pivotal moment of the history of the Movement; it made much of his own allegedly-heroic role, in turning up in a bright red waistcoat that was to serve as the standard of the claque led by Petrus Borel, whose members were ready to use their fists, if necessary, against any decriers. Gautier spent his entire life in Paris, although his fiction ranged far and wide in its settings, and it is not at all surprising that he took a keen interest in its potential future when the Second Empire began, or that his pivotal account of that potential future should display all of his customary flamboyance.

Gautier's account of "Paris futur" was initially published in *Le Pays* in December 1851, almost exactly contemporary with the *coup d'état*, and reprinted several times elsewhere, including his collection *Caprices et zigzags* (1872). "Paris," it begins, "is infinitely self-obsessed; it regards itself, with the greatest naivety, as the center, the eye and the navel of the universe." the narrative voice goes on to complain, in no uncertain terms, about what a mess the city is presently in, and how poorly it compares with the author's dreams of ancient Babylon and Nineveh, which he describes with great enthusiasm in exceedingly fanciful terms, in order to heighten the question of whether a new Paris can be built to outshine them, once the old one has been steam-rollered and the Seine broadened out in order to bring the Ocean to the threshold of the city: a dream that became known as "Paris Seaport," which was to figure continually in euchronian projects and imaginative fictions, until the end of the century and beyond.

Gautier's vision switches into the future tense in order to describe the munificent Paris to come. It will only have one temple, on the site of the Panthéon, but it will be the finest temple ever. The present site of Notre-Dame will become that of the new leader's palace, built with the aid of the rubble produced by the razing of the Butte of Montmartre. It will be the finest of its kind, as befits its tenant, who will be the finest specimen of humanity, maintained perpetually young and healthy by "a rational diet and transcendent hygiene." His processions will be fabulous in their ostentation. There will be double railway lines in every street and fountains in every immense and florid square. Even the sewers will be magnificent. Canvas awnings over the streets will protect pedestrians from the summer sun, and glass ceilings will shield them from the winter cold. Every house will have thermostatically-controlled central heating, although "thanks to studies in climate management" Paris will have a climate like Naples and a vast girdle of forests will block winds and hold fog at bay. There will be no night, electric lighthouses substituting for the sun—and the people will rarely sleep, because "their existence will be so well-organized that they will never experience fatigue; the resistance of matter will be vanquished, and alimentation detached from all its grossness."

Joseph Méry responded to that vision twice, in his own speculative essay on "Paris futur" (1854; tr. as "Future Paris") and more substantially in a longer narrative account of "Ce qu'on verra" (tr. as "What We Shall See"), the date of whose periodical publication is unknown, assuming that it did appear in a periodical before being reprinted in *Le Château des trois-tours* [The Château with Three Towers] in 1860. Méry's sarcastically comical account of "Paris futur" opens with a diatribe against the Parisian rain—which, as a southerner, he always thought excessive—and his first concern, in his prospectus for the twentieth century, is to equip the city with effective technologies of weather-control, which involve firing enormous cannons. The sun's light is also augmented, in its absence, with a huge central artificial beacon and twelve subsidiary ones. Aqueducts have secured the city's water supply, feeding its fountains with spring water and multitudinous overpasses allow pedestrians to cross every street and boulevard in safety.

"The future, which always comes too late for the living," Méry proclaims, "will see these things, and many others too, for the world is born, nowadays, of the union of steam and the railways. Everything that existed the day before yesterday no longer has any reason for being; the new order is already the antipodes of the old; the impossible will regenerate the world; interests are never disunited, they combine; Nelson fraternizes with d'Estaing, there is no longer any distance; wheels are wings, mountains corridors, ships bridges, oceans streams."

That imagery of metamorphosis was very much a product of its time and place, and it was echoed prolifically in the second half of the century.

The fact that "Ce qu'on verra" is set in the year 3845 might imply that it first appeared, or was at least written, as early as 1845, not long after the 3844-set "Les Ruines de Paris" but it reads more like an expansion of the final sentiment expressed in "Paris futur." It is a breezy comedy in which "France" now extends all the way to the Cape of Good Hope, although Paris is by no means in ruins, and the story opens with its hero embarking on a railway journey from the southern tip of that vast France to the great capital in search of a wife, celibacy now being "an impossible vice" (Méry never married).

The electric train, which travels at eight hundred kils per hour—future language has been streamlined—has all the facilities deemed indispensable, including a theater, a library, a dormitory, an restaurant and a "steam orchestra." In fact, the hero falls in love before the train has even reached the African super-city of Lupata, and is married there in a simple ceremony: "Michel declared his love to his wife in calm and rational terms, which solidifies belief in progress."

After a stopover in Marseille, the couple are able to marvel at a Paris that still puts all other cities in the shade, although not quite as ostentatiously as Gautier's "Paris futur." They enjoy a sumptuous meal and see all the sights, but are repeatedly drawn back to theatrical performances, which encapsulate the spirit of the age, although spoken plays are out of fashion because "the vices, farces, petty passions and all the gossip of the old world are of no interest today. The tiny breath of human beings is lost in the intelligent noise of the creation taking place around us. The world is staging a drama, not in five acts but in five continents; a thousand electric links are recounting a thousand scenes, forming an eternal dialogue at every instant between the two worlds."

The couple are, however, also eager to see the port of Paris, with its symbolic statue of Prometheus, holding the sacred flame of electricity, having chained the vulture sent to torment him to the rock in its turn, and the monument of the Arc du Soleil, celebrating the glorious achievements of the world's scientists and engineers, with brief accounts of their feats of imagination. The story foregrounds some of the key ideas that lurk in the background of much of Méry's work, including the conviction that the euchronian prospects of human progress are dependent on a drastic southward shift of endeavor, but it also allows Paris to continue its own evolution, under the guidance of science. Its imagery is no less striking and its sociological speculations are no less intriguing for being narrated in a comical tongue-in-cheek fashion that serves to disguise the author's earnest hopes and expectations.

Gautier's piece was also the direct inspiration of Arsène Houssaye's "Paris futur" (1856; revised 1889 as "En 3789"; tr. as "Future Paris"), which appeared in a collection of essays to which Gautier was also a contributor, and probably of Victor Fournel's "Paris futur" (1865; tr. as "Future Paris"), although the latter is a far more direct reaction to Baron Haussmann's ambitions and procedural policies.

Houssaye's vision is very similar to Gautier's although described as an "apocalypse" glimpsed by a "miracle seeker—a modern Cazotte-Swedenborg" in the form of "a newspaper printed on Indian silk, *textilis aër*; it was the *Moniteur de l'Empire universel* for the first of May 3855." Again, Paris is a sea-port, and is now thirty leagues around. The Institut is vast and when the Emperor returns to his capital after vacationing in Australia he passes through fifty trium-phal arches as his fifty-horsepower carriage transports him to the Louvre. Again the sky is permanently radiant, and that reflects the condition of the populace: "Now that the energy of the living has obliged the dead to frequent the eternal fatherland of intelligence and surrender their secrets, too long buried; now that for Paris, capital of the universe, all is serenity, light and joy, who will dare to say 'No!' to progress?" Only a few "amorous oldsters," we are assured, "the buffoons of Paris metamorphosed"—but the author's jocular skepticism regard-ing the desirability of that kind of progress, unlike Méry's, is obviously real.

Fournel's vision is even more sarcastic, and set much closer to home, only a hundred years in the future, in 1965, although, even then, his future Paris is a hundred kilometers around, filling the entire département of the Seine, and has completed "half its journey to the Ocean." The city is now remarkable for its geometric order and its amazing uniformity, all the old monuments having been made to look "presentable" and mechanically transported to occupy more sym-metrically-arranged positions. Artificial light does not turn night into day, but steam-driven machines labor all night long cleaning and polishing the streets.

The discipline is not excessive, though: "By way of compensation for the Romantic soul, however, the authorities of the year 1965 had put flower-beds in the Place Saint-Sulpice, around the Obelisk and the Arc de Triomphe at the Étoile, thus according nature its right to sunlight, but without permitting it to in-fringe that of the boutiques." The city's most ornate celebratory statue is its trib-ute to Baron Haussmann.

Although Méry's account of "Les Ruines de Paris" is less substantial than "Ce qu'on verra," it turned out to be by far the more significant work of the pair, in terms of its influence, because it has the distinction of having prompted a whole series of further stories on the same theme, beginning with Alfred Bonnardot's "Archéopolis" (1857; tr. as "Archeopolis"), a visionary account set in 9957, initially rendered in a lyrical tone, which becomes gradually more mat-ter-of-fact and finally sarcastic.

A visionary wandering in the ruins of Paris and recognizing the relics of his own time encounters a party of tourists from the eponymous African city that is now the heart of civilization, and follows them around, attempting to correct the false interpretations offered by the tour guide, but is only dismissed as a madman. In order to correct his supposed misapprehensions, the tourists take him back to Archéopolis with them. There he eventually hears the reports rendered on discoveries made in the ruins of Paris, which include the ludicrous errors that were to become the standard feature of such stories.

While wandering beforehand in the corridors of the Academy, the narrator is able to eavesdrop on history lessons that provide scattered items of information regarding the evolution of the world in the interim. They include interplanetary travels and the perfection of phrenological medicine, but are most interesting in their account of the decadence that followed the twentieth century, in which the vast multiplication of machinery had freed humans from all labor. Although the vast network of telegraph wires disrupted the natural electricity of the atmosphere and unleashed a series of natural disasters, it was internally that the rot had set in:

"Dispossessed of the benefit of manual labor, entire populations lived inactively from day to day, ennui and the cold sentiment of realism in their souls. Everywhere, idleness, having become chronic, had engendered a disgust for life that was translated into thousands of suicides.... Never had a more ardent thirst for the superfluous, the marvelous and unrealizable projects changed the human imagination for the worse. The study of arts, letters and the sciences was no longer the exception but the banal objective of everyone. Everyone thought himself called to a great intellectual role; everyone wanted to be an enchanter, but there was no more enchantment. Printing presses, multiplying everywhere, relentlessly vomited out millions of books at rock-bottom prices. All the evil passions spread their contingent of redoubtable poisons through those vast arteries of social life known as literature.

"Great moral convulsions followed close on the heels of this mortal virus. Reason deserted brains as religion had retired from consciences. Rivalries of love, wealth, commerce, celebrity and political influence degenerated into desperate battles, basely hypocritical, egotistical and perfidious. About 2050, an epidemic madness propagated from individual to individual. The civilized nations were then ruled by governments impotent to master the passions in the absence of religious restraint, and composed of strangely complicated mechanisms.... An accusing voice went up, from no one knew where, to signal the hatred of the masses for the chief engineers who represented financial power, and the aristocratic class. Thousands of newspapers made themselves the echo of that fatal voice.... By virtue of the weakness of a fictitious authority and the rapidity of the means of communication, all the peoples rushed toward the same abyss at the same time. A conspiracy was organized that burst forth simultaneously at all points. Everywhere, the engineers were stripped of their wealth or massacred and the machines annihilated, save for those designed for destruction—the only ones that were to survive, to the misfortune of humankind."

This diatribe in delivered in the context of a comedy, but in itself, it manifests the urgency of apocalyptic prophecy, albeit inverted by narrative strategy and offered as ancient history from the hypothetical perspective of a world in which a much saner eutopian equilibrium has been achieved in the relationship between humans and machines, and the Paris that gave birth to the hypermechanical Age of Iron has been replaced, not by a portentously ludicrous Hurlu built on the same site but by a proud Archéopolis displaced sunwards. The contest between pessimism and optimism has been resolved, not by finding a *juste milieu* but by a Ballanchian palingenesis: disaster followed by regeneration.

Increasingly, that was the way the future came to be conceived by a considerable number of speculative visionaries, its fundamental pattern being neither an endless upward curve nor a sequence of merely repetitive cycles, but as a process in which the smashing of eggs might, in the end, achieve the cooking of a eutopian omelet.

That pattern was reproduced in particularly spectacular fashion in one of the most elaborate futuristic fictions of the period, which continued the sequence of stories centered on the future ruins of Paris, but set it in a far more complex context: *L'An 5865, ou Paris dans quatre mille ans* (1865; tr. as *The Year 5865*) by "le Docteur H. Mettais." It is a remarkable novel in several ways, the bulk of it consisting of a first-person narrative related by a character living four thousand years hence, after various disasters have obliterated almost all the documents relating to the world with which the readers of 1865 were familiar. The narrator's knowledge of the reader's world is severely limited and densely clouded by myth; in his world, archeological investigation is in its infancy, and has only just begun to provide corrective evidence allowing some slight penetration of that fog of myth.

That situation reflects an assumed similarity between the world of 5865 featured in the book and the world of 1865, in which archaeological endeavors— particularly those in Egypt sparked by the legacy of Napoleon's Egyptian campaign—were beginning to cut through the fog of myth clouding the past of several millennia before, creating a heady combination of intellectual excitement and threats to entrenched belief. The project of writing such a novel must have seemed exciting and challenging, but it posed awkward technical problems, for whose potential solution there was no literary precedent in 1865. The establishment of a

L'AN

5865

ou

PARIS DANS QUATRE MILLE ANS

par

LE DOCTEUR H. METTAIS

Auteur des Souvenirs d'un Médecin de Paris

PARIS
LIBRAIRIE CENTRALE
24, BOULEVARD DES ITALIENS, 24
1865
Tous droits réservés

first-person narrative viewpoint that is both radically different from that view-point of the reader and ignorant of huge amounts of information known to the reader creates obvious problems for a writer, because of the considerable disso-nance between what the narrator knows—especially the things he takes for granted—and what the reader knows and takes for granted.

Most previous works providing elaborate descriptions of the future, from *L'An deux mille quatre cent quarante* to "Archéopolis," had been portal fanta-sies employing protagonists from our own time who were able to observe the future in visions, and were thus able to transport the reader's awareness into the future with them. The handful of much shorter works that had attempted to do away with such artifice and offer straightforward accounts of future reality, in-cluding the fragment of Bodin's *roman futuriste* and Méry's "Ce qu'on verra," had used omniscient narrators able to serve, at least to some extent, as interpret-er ready and able to explain to readers what is happening in the future being de-scribed, in terms of their own experience.

Mettais scorned the use of both of those explanatory crutches; even when he interpolates fragments of texts supposedly originating from the nineteenth or twentieth centuries into his immersive fantasy, as he occasionally does, they on-ly make information available to the reader elliptically, and even though he equips the principal first-person narrative with a documentary frame, that too is strictly limited in its assumed vision. Given that the unreliability of remembered history and the vagueness of transtemporal understanding are important themes of the novel's didactic endeavor, the essentially fractured viewpoint is uniquely appropriate to the project, but that does not make it any less difficult for the writer or for the reader.

Hippolyte Mettais was, as his by-line indicates, a physician who practiced in Paris from 1834, when he left his native town of Blois, until the 1870s. His birth date is given in the first edition of Pierre Larousse's *Grand Dictionnaire* as 1812, and that datum is reproduced in the catalogue of the Bibliothèque Nationale, but he was not considered important enough to warrant inclusion in subsequent editions of Larousse and the date of his death is unrecorded in any of the standard sources.

Although he had previously published a medical treatise, Mettais' first manifest literary endeavor was in the early 1840s, when he published two novels of his own, *Rupert* (1841) and *Le Portefaix, roman de moeurs* [The Street-Porter; a novel of (contemporary) mores] (1842) and one in collaboration with the prolific but now-forgotten writer of popular fiction Georges Touchard-Lafosse (1780-1847), *Un Lion aux bains de Vichy* [A Lion (in the social sense) at the Vichy Spa] (1842). Touchard-Lafosse also contributed an introduction to *Le Portefaix*, and the fact that he published nothing more after his collaboration with Mettais suggests that he probably recruited the latter to help him complete a project imperiled by ill-health. Mettais might well have been his doctor.

That first foray into literary publication was presumably unsuccessful, because there was a long gap before Mettais resumed that aspect of his career, publishing another naturalistic novel, *Le Père Thuillier* [Old Thuillier], in 1857. His next publication was a reformist pamphlet, *Des Associations et des corporations en France* [Associations and Corporations in France] (1859), whose propagandist argument in favor of the elaborate development of trade-union-based insurance and pension schemes is summarized in one of the more arbitrary chapters of *L'An 5865*. He then published *Souvenirs d'une médecin de Paris* [Memoirs of a Parisian Doctor] (1863), which is a novel rather than an autobiography, but claims in its introduction to be factually based. The literary ambitions of the young doctor who is its protagonist, and the similar ambitions of his friends in Paris in the late 1830s and 1840s, are peripheral to the plot, but the story gives walk-on parts to Alexandre Dumas, Alfred de Vigny and Émile de Girardin, and places the young protagonist very firmly in the Romantic camp.

In Mettais' 5865 the center of world civilization is based in the Caucasus, from which the hero, Daghestan, sets out on his travels. What used to be France is now New Cosaquia, and the site of Paris is occupied by the glorified shanty town of Figuig, still dominated by the descendants of the Moroccan invaders who conquered France in the remote past, although their fading hegemony is under threat from other populations, including Cosaque refugees and the ancient French, much of whose culture has long been driven literally underground.

Daghestan, an interested historian, locates the ruins of Paris after being put on the trail of an ancient book, which he has to go to the "semi-savage village" of Copenhagen to acquire. There he has the first of several encounters with a mysterious woman, who saves him from sticky situations in the course of his travels more than once, with the aid of a combination of apparent magic and an airship—which proves far more effective as a means of long-distance travel than Daghestan's mechanical "horse."

Before he reaches Figuig, however, he visits other parts of the world, including the Sudan and the island of the mysterious Androgenes—which appear to have resulted recently from an evolutionary process similar to the one outlined in *Telliamed*—and his first dangerous landing in Figuig is brief; he is only able to make his way back there after an excursion to Borneo. When he returns, still in a very precarious situation, he is able to explore the relics of ruined Paris more elaborately, and to take a hand in the three-sided conflict to determine the city's new future—a conflict that is not resolved, and leaves him with wounds likely to prove fatal once he has finished telling his story to his fellow Caucasians, via the medium of a newspaper *feuilleton*.

As a vision of the future, *L'An 5865* is a trifle murky, and is perhaps more interesting as a pioneering exercise in exotic storytelling, heroic in its attempt to deal with unprecedented problems of narrative strategy, but it does provide a striking endorsement of the pattern of futuristic anticipation laid down by Bonnardot—whom Mettais probably knew, just as Méry certainly did. Mettais followed it up with another novel in which Paris is the central focus, *Paris avant le Déluge* (1866), which provides a fictitious account of the founding of a colony by stranded explorers from Atlantis, "the Atlantis of the Pah-ri-ziz," on the site of modern Paris, and tracks the history of that colony all the way to its destruction by a deluge caused by the Earth's close encounter with a comet, after the fashion of the planetary deluges featured in *Les Posthumes*.

The last phase of *Paris avant le Déluge* is to some extent a transfiguration of the pre-Revolutionary history of the present-day Paris, but the story is by no means a simple political parable. The author's preface, like his preface to *L'An 5865*, includes a forceful argument to the effect that Biblical chronology cannot be taken seriously, which reflects the fact that it was still a controversial issue—more controversial than before, in fact, because of the direct challenge posed by Boucher de Perthes' recent discoveries of relics of ancient human cultures in France—but that is only one part of the overall argument of the two texts that if history is to be properly understood and its underlying mechanisms appreciated, it must be considered in the broadest possible frame.

Following the publication of *Paris avant le Déluge*, Mettais wrote a further fantasy, *Simon le magicien* [Simon Magus] (1867), but reverted thereafter to more conventional literary fare with *Docteur Marat* [Dr. Marat] (1874), *Les Amours d'un tribun* [The Love-Life of a Tribune (i.e. a popular spokesman)] (1876), two further novels and a one-act play, but following his unremarked death, his works appear to have been completely forgotten—although *L'An 5865* is mentioned in passing in a essay on futuristic fiction, "Dans 100 Years" [In a Hundred Years] (1891-2), by the physiologist Charles Richet, who wrote *roman scientifique* of his own under the pseudonym Charles Epheyre.

The fascination with the city of Paris and its possible future is further reflected in the work of the popular humorist **Pierre Véron** (1833-1900). When he first began to carve out a successful career as a journalist in the early 1860s, Véron became a frequent contributor to two of the most popular Parisian humorous papers, both founded by Charles Philipon, *Le Charivari*—the satirical magazine which served as the model for the English magazine *Punch*—and the more broadly humorous *Journal Amusant*. Most of his contributions to the periodicals were made during the editorial reign of Charles' son and heir Eugène Philipon, which began in

1862, and Véron succeeded Eugène in his turn as editor-in-chief of both periodicals in 1874, retaining that position until his retirement, only a few months before his death.

Once he had taken over the editorial chairs, Véron's own contributions to the magazines became considerably less prolific and less mordant, and he did his best satirical work in the early 1860s, most of it in the form of vignettes. Almost all of his prose pieces, whether fictional or non-fictional, were ironic reflections on Parisian life, and several strayed into realms of speculation, including his account of "Le Déluge en Paris" (1859; tr. as "The Paris Deluge"), the episodic novellas *Les Marchands de Santé* (1862; tr. as "The Merchants of Health") and *Monsieur Personne* (1864; tr. as "Monsieur Nobody"; reprinted as *En 1900*—misleadingly, since it is deliberately set in 1901, that being the first year of the twentieth century), and "L'Omnibus aérien" (1867 tr. as "The Aerial Omnibus").

Les Marchands de Santé is an interplanetary romance set on the Planet Fantasia, but Fantasia is simply Paris writ large—even larger than the immense future Paris featured in *Monsieur Personne*. The former is a satire on contemporary developments in medicine, especially its commercialization, but its incidental exaggerated representations of Parisian life are not without a quirky charm. *Monsieur Personne* is, however, of much more direct interest, as well as being more advanced in narrative terms, employing an immersive fantasy strategy not dissimilar to the one employed by Mettais in *L'An 5865*, although the story is told in the third person; it is able to make use of far more contemporary reference-points, even though its gigantic future Paris has been transformed far more extensively than the one featured by Victor Fournel after a similar lapse of time.

The strangely anonymous protagonist arrives in the city rich, but finds the cost of living so high that he will soon run out of cash, and desperately needs to find work and affordable long-term accommodation. The quest proves enormously difficult, as his innocent moral sensibilities—he is something of a Rousseauesque child of nature—make him woefully unsuitable to the career in journalism that he attempts, or the toils of the Bourse, in which he refuses to involve himself when he discovers how corrupt it is. Even his attempt to pay court to a young woman runs on to the reefs of future commercialism when he is referred to a marriage bureau that operates with stern materialistic efficiency.

The context in which these works were produced is worthy of some note; *Le Charivari* had run into serious trouble with Napoléon III's censors in the first decade of the Second Empire, and had been forced to adapt in order to survive; by the time Véron began publishing in its pages it had become an exceedingly diplomatic and somewhat chastened periodical. Although the censors were easing up by then in the pressure they put on the more general themes tackled by novelists, they were still sensitive to anything resembling direct political criticism of the Empire or the Emperor in satirical periodicals; that helps to explain the near-total absence in Véron's work of any political argument, or any reference to the political order of the Planet Fantasia and the Paris of the year 1901 featured in *Monsieur Personne*.

While that absence might seem regrettable now, it still left plenty of scope for Véron to turn his satirical lens on features of contemporary life whose consideration was not likely to get him or the periodical into hot water. His satire is undoubtedly weak-kneed by today's savage standards, but if it had attempted more it might well have ended up achieving nothing at all. Unlike Fournel's *Paris futur*, *Monsieur Personne* makes no mention of Baron Haussmann, but of the two accounts of Paris in the not-too-distant future, it is Véron's that offers the more telling indictment of the physical transformations that Haussmann was endeavoring to effect, and the economic ideology associated with them.

Political satire returned in some quantity when censorship was eased in the 1860s, but most of it retained the careful diplomacy exercised by Véron. Not all such satire was Republican, and one of the most interesting examples, from the viewpoint of the evolution of *roman scientifique*, came from a very different direction, hinting ironically that Napoléon III's Bonapartism might not be Bonapartist enough. *L'Homme à l'oreille cassée* (1861; tr. as *The Man with the Broken Ear*) by the Romantic humorist Edmond About (1828-1885) transplanted Colonel Fougas, an officer from Napoléon I's Grande Armée, into the Second Empire, by means of the novel device of imagining that he had been frozen stiff after capture by the Russians during the retreat

from Moscow and preserved by a German scientist whose studies in the revivification of desiccated infusoria have suggested a means of prolonging his suspended animation indefinitely.

Brought back to France as a "mummy," Fougas is reanimated, but immediately becomes a troublesome presence. Determined to track down the descendants he might have via his former lover, he attempts to approach the new emperor to demand his help, on the basis of his past loyalty, but does not get very far, his brand of Napoleonic fervor now being considered out of touch with the contemporary political reality. His advanced age is used as an excuse to "retire" him from the army and render him harmless. His personal affairs are granted a happy ending, blunting the already-mild satire into an amiable comedy, but the novella left a considerable legacy in helping to popularize suspended animation as a means of time travel. Although dreaming still retained the advantage of an easy return to the present, the long sleep did have the advantage of a certain scientific plausibility, thanks to the arguments About set out in support of it, and the popularity of the novel in English translation spread the example far and wide.

Alongside Véron's mild satires and Mettais' boldly extravagant extrapolations, other writers took advantage of the relaxation of censorship after 1860 to produce more orthodox euchronian accounts of future Paris. *Paris en songe: essai sur les logements à bon marché, et le bien-être des masses, la protection due aux femmes, les splendeurs de Paris et divers progrès moraux tels que chambres de transactions, justice à trois degrés, tribunaux d'indulgence et pardon, honorariat du commerce, parlement de paix* [Paris in Dream: An essay on cheap housing, the wellbeing of the masses, the protection due to women, the splendors of Paris and various items of moral progress, such as transaction courts, a three-stage legal process, tribunals of indulgence and pardon, a commercial system of honors and a parliament of peace] (1863; tr. as "Paris in Dream") by "Jacques Fabien" is solidly set in the tradition of Mercier, and the author probably thought of it as a similarly daring work, given the political climate if the day. The signature is obviously a pseudonym, but there does not seem to be any published indication as to who the person behind it might have been.

Like Véron, Fabien employs a conspicuously soft pedal in avoiding any direct consideration of the governmental system ruling his future Paris, but maneuvers around that issue in a fashion that leaves no doubt as to his radical affiliations. As his subtitle indicates, his story is primarily focused on economic and legal reforms, which have made the Parisian proletariat comfortable, if not rich, and well-provided with accommodation and recreation facilities, as well as assuring them of just and efficient treatment by the law.

The narrator of the story, returning to Paris after an absence of ten years on a train from Lyon, is told by the companion who meets him there that he will no longer recognize the city—as anyone would have done in 1863 because of the changes already wrought by Haussmann. Having fallen asleep on the train, however, the narrator arrives to find much more sweeping changes, seemingly resulting from a further hundred years of progress.

Interestingly, the two chapters of the novella dealing with the effects of the two most visible technological advances of the period—electric lighting and telegraphy—suggest that no good has come of either of them, the former having unleashed an epidemic of blindness due to eyestrain and the latter an epidemic of nervous breakdowns due to the informational overloading of the brain. Thus, as in Mercier's vision, technological progress has played no significant role in the utopian reorganization, which is entirely due to the removal of manifest social evils and their substitution by sanitized alternatives.

By 1863, however, that was a minority view, and Fabien's reluctant to embrace technological progress offers a stark contrast with a succinct account of "L'Avenir" (tr. as "The Future") by Victor Hugo, which formed the first chapter of the great man's introduction to a guide-book produced for visitors to the Exposition Universelle of 1867, although most surviving copies of the text date from 1869, when the text of the guide was reprinted as a book for sale to the general public. The article was published while the author was still living in exile in the Channel Islands, having refused to return to Paris while Napoléon III was still in power. The invitation to the exile to write the preface to a guide book to one of the principal showpieces of the emperor's reign might be reckoned a trifle unusual, but Hugo was universally recognized as the greatest writer in France, and thus by far the most appropriate individual to sing the praises of an Exposition Universelle staged in Paris.

In any case, the futuristic vision offered in the essay—written in the future tense, following Gautier's precedent—is not unduly revolutionary in its political suggestions, which are mostly restricted to an insistent pacifism, and the political censors obviously saw no occasion to interfere with it, especially in view of its nationalistic fervor, which anticipates Paris being elevated in the twentieth century to the capital of a unified Europe, where massive irrigation systems have increased the fertility of the land and provided cities with abundant clean water, while aerial transport has ensured convenient travel and the shipment of goods.

Napoléon III's censors were, on the whole, far more effective than the *ancien régime*'s; they did not manage to suppress the publication and circulation of material attacking the State completely, but, by narrowing their focus, they were able to avoid the absurd situation of a hundred years before, when Paris was bursting at the seams with illicit publications. Among the political activists they fought hard to suppress was Louis Ulbach, whose journalism, much of it produced under the pseudonym "Ferragus," was incendiary but whose fiction was mostly historical and frankly nostalgic; throughout the period of the Second Empire he only produced one item of speculative fiction with an element of political satire, which is carefully set in a fictitious city dealing with a fictitious leader, "Le Prince Bonifacio" (1864; tr. as "Prince Bonifacio").

The political satire in the story has little interest now and probably had little enough then as a critique of Napoleonic Empire, but the novella is far more remarkable in the narrative device it employs to poke fun at the State's hapless ministers, which involves an exotic method of brain surgery—a cross between lobotomy and brain-transplantation—which inevitably goes awry. The scientist Marforio, who pioneers the method, and has many other ideas regarding the progressive transformations he could bring to the realm if only he were only given a free rein by the intellectually-challenged monarch, is a significant stereotype of the highly intelligent scientist who is neither mad nor bad, in a strict sense, but whose narrowly focused psychology makes him direly dangerous to know: the kind of man who might wreak utter havoc with the very best of intentions, simply because his innovations are so far-reaching.

Ulbach might not have intended Marforio to be an archetype of science in general—the satire in the story is definitely aimed at bad politics rather than the pursuit of technical progress—but he can easily be construed in that way, just as many ambitious fictitious scientists can. Whether their authors intended them as horrible examples of hubris or not, the logic of fiction often nudges them in that direction, and Marforio is an interesting example of the exaggeration of Berthoudian analysis of the scientific mind, precisely because he is a likeable comic figure rather than a pitiable tragic one.

It is necessary to remember that Napoléon III had his ardent supporters as well as his opponents, and that they too could produce visions of future Paris in the interests of their cause. Fernand Giraudeau's *La Cité nouvelle* (1868; tr. as "The New City") even takes care to include a joke about censorship in his introductory preface, deleting several lines and adding a note to the effect that they contained unkind references to opponents of the regime that it seemed diplomatic to efface. In the story, the narrator is arbitrarily translocated a hundred and thirty years into the future by a character identified as Graymalkin, with no further comment, and he finds Paris full of vast, ugly, dirty buildings, which he is assured are *"utilitaire."* The same utilitarian principle determines that people, and everything else, now have numbers rather than names.

The streets are dangerous, horse-drawn vehicles having been replaced by rapid automatic vehicles named "smashalls," uncontrolled by any regulation. Indeed, there is no regulation of any kind anywhere, because the sacred principle of *liberté* cannot be infringed—except for women, who are not allowed to work, and employers, who are not allowed to dismiss their workers, and must pay them exorbitant wages (inflation is rampant and the cost of living very high)—although the "workers," being free, do not actually do any work, the high-powered machinery that ensures production is manned by children.

Religion is free too—save for certain prohibitions—but the old orthodox religion has virtually disappeared, largely replaced by the philosophy of "lanism," based on the theory of "nousthymique" fluid, which notionally puts everyone in touch with venerable ancestors via the fabric of their garments and the dirt thereon. Science, the arts and all intellectuality are in steep decline—the advanced technologies in use are left over from an intermediate period of history—but theaters are thriving, thanks to obscene tableaux, and books are still being published, although the narrator can only bring himself to report a few of the less offensive titles.

Half way through, however, the story gives way to a long account by a historian, who assesses Napoléon III's reign as the greatest in the history of European society. The nature of the exercise compels that account to extend beyond the date of the book's publication, which we can now see, with the aid of hindsight, to have been a trifle unfortunate, being only two years ahead of the Franco-Prussian War that brought the reign in question to a catastrophic end. In the "future history" mapped out by Giraudeau—which the passage of time rapidly turned into a an "alternative history," that does not happen, of course; in a brief military campaign that hardly qualifies as a war, the Emperor puts the Prussians in their place and secures Alsace and Lorraine for France permanently, and goes from strength to strength until he is succeeded by his son, who is compelled to engage in the first genuinely worldwide conflict, when France, England and Germany are allied against Russia and the U.S.A., and from which that alliance emerges triumphant.

The imaginary history is then obliged to progress, however, to account for the bizarre society described in the opening chapters, which, although it contains numerous comical episodes, is by far the angriest and most detailed account of a comprehensively wrecked society produced in the nineteenth century, and a much closer analogue of many twentieth-century anti-socialist dystopias than Souvestre's *La Monde tel qu'il sera*. The sequence concludes when the population rises up against the tyranny of the trade unions and proclaims Napoléon VII emperor. The remainder of the book is filled out by reprinted documents from the Second Empire, some arguing in support of Napoléon III's more controversial decisions, and others condemning the alleged inconsistency of such opponents as Émile de Girardin.

The most striking thing about Giraudeau's text is its peculiar narrative strategy. No other work of the period demonstrates so very clearly the policy of imagining the future as a dire warning, not of an apocalypse visited by God, but as a catastrophe contrived by a political philosophy in action. It is uncommonly bold as well as unusually detailed in presenting a speculative history of the future, and the fact that the history mapped out was rendered impossible only two years after its production does not detract from the bravery of the project. The story is also unusual in its juxtaposition of the euchronian optimism of the first phase of its future history with the extreme dystopian imagery of its depiction of Paris in the year 1998, which runs counter to everything that Baron Haussmann was attempting to achieve in remodeling the city.

In the meantime, however, euchronian ideas were still being more abundantly developed in fictional form than dyschronian warnings, and in euchronian visions of future Paris, the socialist ideals the Giraudeau loathed were still the most powerful driving force of the imagination.

It was difficult in Paris, under the Second Empire, to be more radical than Louis Ulbach and speak one's mind any more freely. The most fervent criticisms of it were thus written by exiles, including the physician Ernest Courderoy (1825-1862), whose *Hurrah!!! ou the Révolution par les Cosaques* [Hurrah!; or The Cossack Revolution] (1854; ostensibly published in London) includes two chapters of visionary futurism, of a kind with which his autobiographical account of his *Jours d'exil* [Days of Exile] (2 vols., 1854-55) is also liberally spiced.

The most extreme writer in the French language, however, was Joseph Déjacque (1821-1864), a poet who was imprisoned for socialist agitation even before the *coup d'état* of 1851 and seems to have escaped from prison during that upheaval, initially fleeing to England; he was in Jersey when he published an article that is now regarded as one of the foundation-stones of French Anarchism, although he preferred to refer to himself as a "*libertaire*" [libertarian].

It was in the U.S.A. that Déjacque eventually founded a periodical, *Le Libertaire*, which published twenty-seven issues between 1858 and 1861; he serialized therein a series of related texts, samples of which were subsequently reprinted in a summary form as *L'Humanisphère, utopie anarchique* [The Humanisphere: An Anarchist Utopia], which set out the author's design for a society even more radical than Étienne Cabet's communist utopia, concluding with a vision of the future in which the author sees his egalitarian dreams fulfilled (separately translated as "The Future World (of the Humanisphere)"). The copy of *L'Humanisphère* reproduced on *gallica* is dated 1899 and was published in Brussels, but its ideas were certainly known to French anarchists long before that, and it is almost certain that the book had initially appeared much earlier in a clandestine printing; the edition reproduced by *gallica* is advertised as a reprint, but gives no indication of the date and place of its prior publication.

Whereas most later writers attempting to design an "anarchist" eutopia compromise to some extent with the principle of total liberty, Déjacque does not; although he is aware that skeptics might consider his account of the probable consequences of a complete absence of any regulation or restriction in education, labor and matters of amour a trifle over-optimistic, he defends his position robustly. From a purely literary viewpoint, the narrative of the futuristic vision is relatively uninteresting, containing no characters, no dialogue and little concrete description of the anarchist way of life, but it does contain some plangent rhetoric, and a concise summary of the anarchist ideal that is particularly interesting in the context of the present project, and with reference to subsequent accounts of the role of science and technology in hypothetical eutopian societies.

Déjacque's ideal anarchist society, organized around huge edifices of a kind that would be dubbed "urban monads" in the late twentieth century, is only feasible because of dramatic improvements in technology, intrinsic to which are abundant power supplied in the form of electricity, elaborate agricultural and industrial machinery, and sophisticated means of transport, including aerial transport. It is a highly mechanized and largely automated world, which inevitably places Science at the very heart of its educational system and makes it central to its Comtean reverence. In Déjacque's vision, Anarchism and advanced technology are intimately interlinked, and his thesis is, in a sense, the ultimate extrapolation of the eighteenth-century philosophy that saw technological and social progress as different aspects of the same process.

Other political philosophies, of course, could equally well envisage the future development of science and technology, and would have been foolish not to do so in the years of the Second Empire, but at the very least, Déjacque's vision of a high-tech society, more elaborately advanced than the vast majority of such visions produced previously, and his forging of a firm link between the image of an electrically-powered, mechanically elaborate society and the philosophy of anarchism, was not likely to incline diehard opponents of anarchism in favor of such imagery. Nor could the ban on his ideas discriminate between his politics and his technological anticipations, and anyone who contrived to become acquainted with his work in spite of the censors was bound to associate the thrill of the forbidden with all the aspects of the text.

Although Déjacque's writings undoubtedly achieved some covert circulation in Paris, very little material of a similar kind was actually produced there; the censors were simply too effective, and the threatened punishments too heavy. One political radical, however, was willing to grasp the speculative nettle that Louis Ulbach let carefully alone, which "Jacques Fabien" and even Victor Hugo handled with scrupulous care. Even while remaining in the heart of Paris, he produced the most remarkable euchronian novel of the era, focused with exactitude and clarity on a Hausmannian transformation of the city more radical than anything the Baron had been prepared to contemplate himself.

Paris en l'an 2000 (tr. as *Paris in the Year 2000*), by-lined **Docteur Tony Moilin**—his forenames were Julius-Antoine—was published in Paris by the author "in association with the Librairie de la Renaissance," in 1869. Moilin (1832-1871), a practicing physician, had previously published three medical treatises and three political pamphlets, *Programme de discussion pour les sociétés populaires* [A Discussion Program for Popular Societies] (1868), *La Liquidation sociale* [Social liquidation] (1869) and *Le Suffrage universel* [Universal Suffrage] (1869), but *Paris en l'an 2000* was his first venture into fiction. It was also his last.

Chapters II-VI of the text, which deal with the reorganization of labor and society, involving a State monopoly on all commerce—but not manufacture—and a determined minimum and maximum level of earnings, all income over the maximum being taxed at 100%, the institution of a new system of education, and new system of socialist republican government, and various minor matters, follow a line that was relatively orthodox for the socialists of the era, although rather extreme. What was not ortho-dox, and makes the work uniquely striking, is the first chapter, on "The Trans-formation of Paris," which depicts the transformation of the outer first-floor rooms of all the buildings of the city into a continuous network of covered corri-dors—effectively a system of pedestrian streets one level above the network of vehicular streets, itself greatly refined, much of the mechanized transport and distribution system consisting of subterranean railways.

The architectural practicality of the envisaged transformation is certainly dubious—although new building technologies are invoked to compensate for the sacrifice of load-bearing walls as the work of transformation progresses—but its scope and daring is impressive, and very much a product of the era. Although Moilin's political ideals were not much more radical than Jacques Fabien's, and exhibit many of the same detailed concerns, he has a very different attitude to the utility of technology and the practicality of large-scale engineering projects, and his narrative method stands in stark contrast to the dream fantasies in which so much previous euchronian writing had been packaged, either overtly, as by Mercier and Fabien, or covertly, as by Gautier and Méry. Its mere existence would make the work remarkable in the context of the Second Empire, but its contents, especially that of the first chapter, make it considerably more so.

2. The Popularization of Science

It was in the 1850s that S. Henry Berthoud, for want of other publishing opportunities, settled down to work primarily as a popularizer of science and commentator on scientific progress. Émile de Girardin was still active as a pub-lisher, but had switched his major effort to his political career, and was no long-er the pillar of support for the members of the Romantic Movement that he had once been. He was one of Louis-Napoléon's most outspoken supporters before the coup, and although he subsequently became a diehard opponent of the Em-pire, he kept his opposition within diplomatic bounds. After 1849, Berthoud seems to have worked as a columnist for *Le Pays* for a while, although he sub-sequently transferred his primary allegiance to *La Patrie*, where the bulk of the non-fictional materials subsequently reprinted in his four-volume collection *Fantaisies scientifiques* made their original appearance, under the avuncular pseudonym of "Dr. Sam." He did other work as well, including fiction for chil-dren, and might well have been active as an editor in that field. The Romantic Movement, as such, seemed to him and most observers to be a thing of the past, and those leading contributors who were still in Paris had moved on, although those who remained famous all maintained its ideals in one form or another.

Where Berthoud stood politically is not entirely clear—his works exhibit an almost total disregard for contemporary politics—but his eventual association with the conservative and imperialist *La Patrie* suggested that he accommodated himself comfortably within that camp. If so, that might help to explain why the devoutly Republican Pierre-Jules Hetzel, when he accepted amnesty and returned from the exile to which he was condemned after the coup, does not seem to have had any dealings with Berthoud, who would otherwise have seemed an ideal contributor to, if not a collaborator with, the "family magazines" that Hetzel founded and promoted so enthusiastically in the 1860s, in imitation of the old *Musée des Familles*—a periodical that had by then become far more staid and conservative.

When there was a new boom in periodical production, book production and the popularization of science in the early 1860s, however, Berthoud was more than ready to capitalize on it, and his publications in volume form became prolific again throughout the decade. With specific regard to the popularization of science, he became the editor of and leading contributor to the annual *Les Petites chroniques de la science* [The Pocket Annals of Science] (1861-72) and in addition to the four volumes of *Fantaisies scientifiques* he published several other volumes of popularizing fiction, most notably *Contes du Dr. Sam* [Tales of Dr. Sam] (1862), *L'Homme depuis cinq mille ans* [Humankind over Five Thousand Years] (1865), *Les Féeries de la science* [The Enchantments of Science] (1866) and *Les Soirées du Dr. Sam* [Dr. Sam's Evening Entertainments] (1871), all of them slanted toward juvenile readers. *La Cassette des sept amis* [The Seven Friends' Casket] (1869) is similar in structure, although its inclusions are mostly unconcerned with scientific themes. He also published a series of orthodox non-fictional popularizations, including *Causeries sur les insectes* [Conversations about Insects] (1862), *Le Monde des insectes* [The World of Insects] (1864), *L'Esprit des oiseaux* [The Intelligence of Birds] (1867) and *Les Os d'un géant, histoire familière du globe terrestre avant les hommes* [A Giant's Bones: An Informal History of the Terrestrial Globe Before Humankind] (1868).

Much of Berthoud's work in the latter category recalls the endeavors of Pierre Boitard, who had died in 1859, but whose *L'Univers avant les hommes* was published posthumously in 1861, and might well have lent some encouragement of Berthoud's endeavors, particularly the "Le Château de Heidenloch" (tr. as "Heidenloch Castle"), published in the June 1962 issue of the *Journal des Demoiselles*—a long-running magazine aimed primarily at teenage girls—without a by-line, before being reprinted in *Contes du Dr. Sam*. The story features a "prehistoric tour" akin to Boitard's.

Berthoud's *fantaisies scientifiques* are mostly anecdotal accounts, whether first- or second-hand, of encounters with curious natural phenomena, often featuring insects, in a fashion subsequently developed to best-selling effect by J.-H. Fabre, or birds. The most remarkable, are, however, the accounts of past, present and fictitious scientists at work, and their trials and tribulations. Those that pretend to be based on fact—"drama-documentaries" in modern parlance—are more extensively fantasized than most of the items in that genre nowadays pro-

235

duced for the television medium, but it is arguable that it makes them all the more interesting, and certainly makes them more extensively "personalized."

It is often difficult in reading the stories to determine where the factual material ends and the fiction begins. In "Les Cruautés d'un savant" (tr. as "A Scientist's Cruelties"), for instance, an account of an experiment involving the blinding of bats in order to investigate their system of navigation, rendered as an autobiographical anecdote, is almost certainly invented in order to provide a graphic illustration of the mind-set of a vivisectionist and to support a more generalized commentary on the activities of named scientists—but there is nothing impossible about it, and the specific dating of the phases of the experimental series creates an impression of plausibility. The unreliability of those dealing with named individuals, which are open to checking against other sources, however, suggests that factual accuracy was always low down on Berthoud's list of priorities, as might be expected from the title of the four-volume set.

The collections of children's stories Berthoud assembled after the *Fantaisies scientifiques* frequently recycle stories therefrom—especially the longer stories that predate the articles reprinted from *La Patrie*, some of which were reprinted from the *Musée des Familles*—but usually added new items intended to round out their themes. The latter are presented in a supposedly child-friendly manner, but that does not always serve to conceal the author's cynicism, and certainly does not suppress the periodic surges of his imagination.

In those more extravagant endeavors, Berthoud was inevitably working under the handicap of the imperfect knowledge of his era and the limitations of his own particular idols of thought, as Pierre Boitard had done before him. The limitations of the fossil record as a basis for fictional reconstruction are painfully obvious to the modern eye in "Le Château de Heidenloch." However, Berthoud's pioneering account of Stone Age humankind, "Les Premiers habitants de Paris" (1865 in *L'Homme depuis cinq mille ans*; tr. as "The First Inhabitants of Paris") remains something of a *tour de force* for its time, having been produced a full decade ahead of the next significant attempt to do something similar in *Le Monde inconnu* [The Unknown World] (1876, tr. in 1879 as *The Pre-Historic World*) by his fellow veteran of the Romantic Movement Élie Berthet, who presumably took his cue from Berthoud.

"Les Premiers habitants de Paris" is all the more interesting for being bracketed in *L'Homme depuis cinq mille ans* with "L'An deux mille huit cent soixante-cinq" (tr. as "The Year 2865"), which appears to be his only item of futuristic fiction: an account of a hallucination caused by a chemical spill, in which the mysterious Azrael takes the author on a tour of a future Paris that has a good deal in common with the images offered by Gautier and Méry—with both of whom Berthoud had long been acquainted—featuring a rapid-transit "atmospheric highway," the electrical regeneration of tissues during and after surgery, an Artillery Museum to which all weapons of war have been permanent retired—including the electric thunderbolt machines whose irresistible slaughter

236

finally made war unthinkable—powerful microscopes that enable all pathogens and the particles producing odor to be seen, pocket cameras producing colored images, weather control, round-the-clock illumination, a Paris Seaport with an elaborate associated pisciculture, and electrical news displays updated every hour.

One of the most remarkable of Berthoud's later *fantaisies scientifiques* is a long chapter in *Les Hôtes du logis* [The House-Guests] (1867) entitled "Les Mystères de la lune" [The Mysteries of the Moon], in which he describes a dialogue taking place "twenty-five years ago," whose participants include Pierre Boitard and Boitard's adopted daughter Marguerite, in which Boitard and his friends respond to Marguerite's question as to whether the Moon might be inhabited, firstly with a summation of recent astronomical discoveries tending to imply that it cannot be, and then with equally elaborate narrative summaries of Cyrano de Bergerac's supposed voyage to the moon, Edgar Poe's account of Hans Pfaall's observations, and the supposed discoveries of John Herschel, as set out in the New York *Sun* Moon Hoax. The framework of the educative conversation not only allows Berthoud to juxtapose fictional images with astronomical data in a fashion that is more lyrical than critical, but also to pay homage to his late friend and one-time collaborator.

Berthoud's renewed popularity in the 1860s obtained him a second dose of brief celebrity, and a promotion to the rank of *officier* in the Légion d'honneur in 1867. The brief description of his lifestyle contained in "L'An deux mille huit cent soixante-cinq" is confirmed by one of the few journalistic sketches available, contained in Jules Brisson and Félix Ribeyre's account of *Les Grands Journaux de France* (1862); he really did live in a house cluttered with books and his various collections of specimens, in company with a dog named Master Flock and a pet lemur he called Mademoiselle Mine. That success and renewed popularity did not, however, prevent him from being almost completely forgotten after his death, and his works from falling into near-total neglect.

The modest fame won for Berthoud by his popularizing endeavors did not last, but between 1851 and 1870 he was one of the leaders in that field, and one of the first to make an impact, partly because of his ingenuity in using fiction as an instrument of popularization. He was, however, overtaken toward the end of the period by two other writers, both of whom outshone him in terms of reputation, partly because they only dabbled tentatively in fictionalization, and devoted the core of their effort to much more earnest and detailed non-fictional endeavors: Henri de Parville and Camille Flammarion.

Henri de Parville (1838-1909) had been baptized François-Henri Peudefer, but never used that name in adulthood. After completing his education at L'École des Mines—which specialized in the education of would-be mining engineers, although its courses had perforce to take in more theoretical issues in geological science—he joined a scientific expedition to the Americas, spending time in Central America and the southern U.S.A. before returning to France in 1860. He immediately embarked on a career as a science journalist, eventually writing articles for many of the leading periodicals of the day, but his principal position was at *Le Pays*, for which Henry Berthoud had earlier worked. He was still building his career when he produced his one and only work of fiction, initially intended as a single hoax article, but so successful that he was required to spin it out for nearly a fortnight; it was subsequently reprinted in book form as *Un habitant de la planète Mars* (1865; tr. as *An Inhabitant of the Planet Mars*).

The genesis of the work was an article in the form of a letter that appeared in *Le Pays* on 17 June 1864, signed "A. Lomon"—that being the name of the paper's American correspondent, responsible for reporting on the progress of the Civil War. The article asserted that an "aerolith" excavated from an ancient geological stratum in Colorado by an oil prospector had turned out to contain a mummified humanoid, believed to originate from the planet Mars.

The immediate inspiration of Parville's hoax was a combination of circumstances deriving from the fall of a stony meteorite—a "carbonaceous chondrite" unlike the more familiar metallic "siderites"—near the French town of Orgueil on 14 May 1864. Various fragments of it were distributed to many scientific institutions, where they were examined by numerous scientists. In France, they took on a particular significance in the context of a controversy that had been bubbling away for five years, in which one of the contenders, Louis Pasteur, had delivered what he believed to be a lethal blow a few weeks earlier, on 7 April. On that day, Pasteur had delivered an address to a regular "scientific soirée" at the Sorbonne in which he reported the results of a series of experiments that he had carried out in order to demolish supposed experimental evidence for the theory of spontaneous generation previously reported by his rival, Félix-Archimède Pouchet. Parville, as an ambitious scientific journalist, would have been present at the soirée, on the bench set aside for the press, and would have seen Pouchet walk out, complaining that the audience was prejudiced against him.

Pouchet, who preferred to call his thesis *"hétérogénie"* [heterogenesis] had carried out a series of experiments in which he concocted mixtures of the various materials he thought necessary to the spontaneous generation of life and left

238

them alone for a while; in every case, living creatures eventually appeared. Organic chemistry was then in its infancy, and microbiology was still working under the severe handicap of microscopes whose acuity was limited by chromatic aberration; bacteria were not yet included on the official roster of living organisms, although the suspicion that organisms too tiny to be visible—as yet—was widespread. Pasteur was convinced that Pouchet's experiments had been contaminated by such invisible "germs" and he repeated them, sterilizing all the mixtures with heat, and then sealing half the containing vessels to avoid the possibility of external contamination. The unsealed vessels "generated" life while the sealed ones did not—this was what Pasteur reported to the soirée, with the claim that he had proved thereby that spontaneous generation did not occur.

Pasteur's address became famous; it was widely cited as a classic application of the experimental method, although the impossibility of proving a negative meant that he had really only provided evidence that Pouchet's experiments could have been subject to external contamination. Pouchet continued to fight his corner until he died, and was not entirely without sympathy in the French scientific community; although largely forgotten today, he had a considerable reputation at the time as a popularizer of science, and one element of his retaliation to Pasteur's address was the publication in 1865 of *L'Univers*, a lavishly-illustrated summarization of contemporary ideas regarding the cosmos, its origin and development, which was reprinted several times. Perhaps more significantly, he was also one of the leading French supporters of Charles Darwin, who had published *The Origin of Species* in 1859, the year that the Pouchet-Pasteur feud had kicked off.

Although Pasteur's victory was, and still is, regarded as a heroic triumph of science over pseudoscience, his convictions owed as much to his Catholic faith and his antipathy to Darwinism as to his scientific principles. He was opposed to both heterogenesis and natural selection on the grounds that they were essentially "materialistic", threatening the elimination of God's creative role in the history of the universe. His diehard belief in invisible "germs"—which also won him the credit for revolutionizing the theory of disease and thus laying the foundations of modern medicine that was really due to François Raspail—was, in essence, a means of saving God's creativity from the menace of a materialistic model of life's emergence. Pasteur would have been disappointed had he been able to anticipate that his own theories would one day be considered to be pillars of materialism, sidelining God just as rudely as he considered Pouchet to have done.

The relevance of that to the Orgueil meteorite—and thus to Parville's hoax—was that the scientists examining the fragments of the chondrite soon began to report the existence within it of organic materials. The finding was rapidly confirmed by Pasteur and Marcellin Berthelot, and seemed to many observers and commentators to have a significant bearing on the issue of spontaneous generation, especially if—as some analysts suggested—the organic materials were fossils.

The extraterrestrial origin of meteorites had been a hot topic of controversy itself earlier in the nineteenth century, figuring along with fossils in Pierre Boitard's propagandizing popularizations in the late 1830s, and although the matter was largely settled by 1864, there was no universally-agreed theory as to where meteorites originated, or why they differed in composition. It seemed to some interested parties that if there really was, or ever had been, life inside "bolides," then spontaneous generation offered a more plausible explanation than what later came to be known as the "panspermia hypothesis": the notion that life that had originated elsewhere in the universe had reached Earth—and many other planets—by means of a migration.

At any rate, the potential significance of the Orgueil meteorite's organic contents briefly became a significant source of speculation in the burgeoning world of French scientific journalism. The publicity given to the analyses of the fragments and the presence within them of organic material not only prompted Parville's hoax but provided it with a media environment that guaranteed it a measure of superficial plausibility.

When the decision was made to extend the original articles into a series, it was entirely natural that Parville should elect to construct an imaginary "scientific commission" not unlike the one that had sat in judgment over Pasteur's experiments at the Sorbonne, which would not only settle the question as to whether the aerolith containing a mummified human really had come from Mars, but examine what that conclusion might imply for contemporary science's model of the universe and the evolutionary process, with particular reference to the role therein of spontaneous generation. It is possible that Parville had not made up his own mind about the issue when he started out on the extrapolation, and that he used the imaginary debate to clarify his own thoughts and to decide where he stood—for the time being, at least.

Parville evidently began to struggle with the task of extrapolating his original article. Although the notion of describing the proceedings of a scientific conference summoned to study and discuss the discovery must have seemed both obvious and attractive to him, he found considerable practical difficulty in formulating that project. The first chapter of the extrapolation clearly intends to develop the description of the conference as a satire on the conduct of contemporary scientists; it mostly consists of a series of more-or-less brief descriptions of eccentric stereotypes. He decided, however—or was advised by his publisher—that he was on the wrong track, and abruptly changed direction. His subsequent attempts at satirical humor were tokenistic, and he settled down to the more earnest business of constructing a summary account of the universe.

Parville never wrote anything else as expansive as the cosmic vision featured in *Un habitant de la planète Mars*. The fact that he was writing fiction, putting his ideas into the mouths of hypothetical individuals, gave him a freedom to speculate and associate disparate ideas that he did not allow himself in his customary reportage. The struggle he experienced in fictionalizing the material, however, illustrated one of the key difficulties under which the genre of *roman scientifique* always labored: the fact that conventional "mimetic" fictional representation is not easily adapted to the discussion of scientific issues, especially those involving the development of Grand Theory. In general, storytelling techniques make a much better metaphorical microscope than telescope, while non-fictional formats are far more amenable to the opposite tendency.

Inevitably, everything that Parville thought about the nature of the universe was eventually falsified by the progress of scientific knowledge. The whole ideative edifice is, in retrospect, nothing but a work of fantastic fiction. That does not mean, however, that it was unintelligent; nor does it mean that it became uninteresting the moment the falsity of its core assumptions was revealed by the further theoretical progress of geology, physics and organic chemistry. Parville's cosmic vision is a distinctively French one, different in significant ways from the kindred visions built in Britain by Robert Hunt, in *The Poetry of Science* (1848), and in America by Edgar Poe, in *Eureka* (1848). The fact that those distinctive features also show up in the work of his rival popularizer, Camille Flammarion, and were preserved in a considerable fraction of subsequent *roman scientifique* is due to a common intellectual background rather than any direct influence.

Nicolas Camille Flammarion (1842-1925) formed an interest in astronomy at an early age, later relating that he had been fascinated by his observation of solar eclipses in 1847 and 1851. He began to record his astronomical and meteorological observations at the age of eleven, and began to write voluminously in his teens. He was apprenticed to an engraver when his family moved to Paris in 1856 but continued his studies in amateur astronomy alongside assiduous attempts to increase his education. By the time he was sixteen had produced a "Voyage extatique aux régions lunaires, correspondence d'un philosophe adolescent"
[A Visionary Journey to the Regions of the Moon, related by an adolescent philosopher] and a 500-page manuscript immodestly entitled "Cosmologie Universelle" [Universal Cosmology]. The latter was noticed by a physician called to treat him, who was sufficiently impressed to recommend the young man to Urbain Le Verrier, then in charge of the Paris Observatoire.

Le Verrier accepted Flammarion as an assistant, putting him to work in the Bureau des Calculs. Flammarion did not find that routine work to his taste, and was frustrated by the lack of opportunity to make his own observations, so when the successful publication of his study of *La Pluralité des mondes habités* [The Plurality of Habitable Worlds] in 1862 gave him hope that he might be able to make a living as a writer, he left. Advertised by its subtitle as a study of the conditions of habitability of the planets in the solar system from the viewpoints of astronomy, physiology and natural philosophy, *La Pluralité des mondes habités* went through thirteen further editions in the next thirty years, and Flammarion swiftly became a frequent contributor to several periodicals, but he could not support himself adequately on his writing income and he obtained a position in the Bureau des Longitudes.

Flammarion did not allow his duties at the Bureau to impede his literary production. He might have seen his next book, *Les Habitants de l'autre monde: révélations d'outre-tombe* [The Inhabitants of the Other World: Revelations of the Afterlife] (2 volumes, 1862-3) as a companion-piece to its predecessor—he had met Allan Kardec, the French founder of "psychic research" while researching *La Pluralité des mondes habités*—but he must soon have been apprised of the fact that reporting alleged revelations from beyond the grave channeled by a spiritualist medium would not do his scientific career any good. His next book of the same kind, *Des Forces naturelles inconnues* [Unknown Natural Forces] (1865) was initially issued under the pseudonym Hermès, but he abandoned such subterfuges thereafter. He was always careful, however, to make it clear

that his interest in psychic research was that of an open-minded scientific researcher; he was not a follower of the Spiritualist faith and refused to consider the texts he produced during his experiments in automatic writing as anything other than the product of his own imagination.

He followed up his first work of speculative science with **Les Mondes imaginaires et les mondes réels** [Real and Imaginary Worlds] (1865). The first part of the book was a revisitation of the various worlds in the solar system, supplemented with a speculative note about planets illuminated by double stars, but the second was a thoroughgoing historical and critical survey of mythological, philosophical and literary speculations about the inhabitants of the planets and stars. As previously noted, it includes the first general survey of interplanetary fiction, tracking the progress of the ideas developed therein.

Flammarion constructed a telescope of his own in 1866, and returned to the Observatoire in 1867 to take part in a project observing and mapping double stars. He also continued his meteorological observations, undertaking many balloon flights in order to observe atmospheric phenomena at closer range. He continued to produce popular articles and books with increasing rapidity, taking in vulcanology and climatology as well as astronomy. He was a frequent contributor to such periodicals as *Le Cosmos*, and the newspapers *L'Intransigeant* and *Le Siècle*.

Much of Flammarion's work for periodicals was hastily-composed, and many of his books give the impression of being unchecked first drafts, but he worked harder than any other man of his day to make the revelations of science accessible to ordinary readers, experimenting with every narrative device he could imagine in order to make his communications more effective. Although his reputation within the scientific community suffered, partly because of his success as a popularizer, partly because of his fondness for flights of wild fancy, and partly because of his unceasing attempts to apply the scientific method to studies in what would now be called the "paranormal," he did more to prepare the way for public acceptance of the cosmic perspectives of modern science than any other nineteenth century writer. The scope of his imagination was inevitably restricted by the limitations of the scientific knowledge on which he drew (especially in biology), but no one else matched his imaginative avidity or audacity.

Flammarion first began to publish didactic fiction in popular magazines in the mid-1860s, most notably in a series of dialogues that eventually made up a work entitled *Lumen*, which set out to dramatize the content of *La Pluralité des mondes habités* and *Dieu dans la nature* [God in Nature] (1867) but changed direction in mid-stream to take aboard a third influence: the translation he made in 1869 of Humphry Davy's *Consolations in Travel* (1830). *Lumen* is a manifestly shaky start to the business of constructing didactic fictions, the various dialogues comprising it having been composed in three separate batches between 1866 and 1869, but once the text finally hit its stride it enabled Flammarion to produce a new and truly spectacular vision of the universe, which laid the groundwork for an entire tradition of modern visionary fantasy.

Lumen's first book publication was in the collection *Récits de l'infini* (1872; translated as *Stories of Infinity*, 1873), where it was supplemented by his next endeavor of the same kind, "Histoire d'une comète" (1869; tr. as "The History of a Comet"), which views episodes in the history of the Earth from the viewpoint of Halley's Comet. He revised and expanded *Lumen* for separate publication in 1887, and made further amendments in later editions, but it remained, in essence, a product of the imagination of the 1860s. As in Fontenelle's *Entretiens*, the narrative voices that Flammarion employs in the dialogues constituting *Lumen* are not disputants but a willing teacher and an eager pupil. Although the teacher, Lumen, gives an elaborate account of his life on Earth, his name declares that he is also light itself: the light of the stars, as observed and analyzed by astronomers. His interrogator, Quaerens, is partly Flammarion and partly his imagined reader, but his name signifies "Seeker (of Knowledge)."

The first dialogue, which labors long and hard to establish its elementary ideas, is stodgy and repetitive; Flammarion—or perhaps his editor—seems to have been exceedingly doubtful as to the readiness and ability of his readers to take aboard the simplest corollaries of the limited velocity of light. The most interesting idea that the first dialogue raises—the principle that time and space are not absolute, but only exist relative to one another—is left stranded, and never properly developed. The second dialogue, whose central idea is that a viewpoint moving faster than light would be able to see events in reverse order, suffers from the same faults, partly because Flammarion did not take the trouble to remove from the collected version material that had originally served to recap the basic thesis for the benefit of new readers.

It is only at the end of the second dialogue that the author picks up the pace and begins to broaden his imaginative horizons to take in wider vistas in both time and space, but, once having done that, he fails to carry the extrapolations of the third dialogue very far forward. He might have cut it short when it had hardly got going because he simply ran out of steam, but it seems more probable that the editor of the periodical in which the serial version appeared aborted it—in which case, Flammarion's decision to keep the first dialogue simple and to labor every point it made might have been wiser than it now seems.

Although the gap between the first and second dialogues made no evident difference to Flammarion's outlook, he seems to have emerged as a changed man from the two-year interval between the third and fourth. Perhaps the marked change of attitude and tone merely reflects the fact that he now felt free to express himself more freely and say what he really thought about such matters as the human tendency to war and French prevarication over the principles of Republicanism, but he might well have undergone a change of heart. The crucial point in Lumen's discourse arrives when he explains that the form of the human body results from its adaptation to a specific set of physical circumstances rather than divine design, and that sentient beings elsewhere in the universe are likely to be very different, by virtue of being adapted to a wide variety of environments. Lumen also insists that physical forms are the products of slow and never-ending processes of evolution.

Flammarion's evolutionary theory is thoroughly Lamarckian, and its extrapolation from an earthly to a cosmic scale easily assimilates the notion that evolution is moral as well as physical, souls being subject to their own evolutionary process as they move through successive incarnations. Flammarion was not the first writer to apply such a theory of evolution to the wholesale construction of authentically alien beings, having been preceded by Restif de la Bretonne, but his evolutionary theory and his cosmogony were far more advanced than Restif's, and he was able to produced a more convincing set of exemplars in the fourth and fifth dialogues. Although he continued to take an interest in hypothetical aliens, however, especially Martians, he never again exercised that kind of invention on the scale that he did in *Lumen*, and the text remains a uniquely interesting and astonishing product of its era.

It is not easy to judge the effect that this boom in the attempted popularization of science had on the audience at which it was aimed, although the success of some of the works it produced, most notably those by Camille Flammarion, and, less directly, those of Jules Verne, certainly demonstrate a demand that was being fed. The marked increase in the production and consumption of *romans scientifiques* in the decades that followed the 1860s can probably be taken as evidence of an increased understanding among the laity of science that scientific ideas were becoming more familiar and more welcome.

That welcome was, of course, far from universal. The collection of S. Henry Berthoud's studies of the particular psychology of the scientific mind in 1861-2 were swiftly followed by a sharp reaction against the traits that Berthoud was pointing out in René de Pont-Jest's Faustian parable "La Tête de Mimer" (1863; tr. as Mimer's Head"), whose protagonist is tempted—seemingly deliberately, by the Devil himself, albeit in disguise—by the acquisition of the eponymous legendary head, which is a fount of all knowledge and can answer any question: a symbol of science. There is, however, another life ready and waiting for him if he only cares to seize the opportunity: the love of a good woman, marriage, children, and the conviviality of society. The author is very strict in dictating that he can only have one; he can become an obsessive recluse, shut away in his library with his magical head, in pursuit of abstract ideas and theoretical understanding, or he can be a normal member of society, contributing to the well-being and enjoyment of others and reaping the same returns, but there is no possible compromise.

Pont-Jest is unusually extreme in offering that contention, but he was by no means the only writer to make that point in their characterization of scientists, and even the most ardent supporters of science, including Berthoud and Verne, took it for granted that the obsessive dedication required of the true scientists would create difficulties in social relationships in general, and marital relationships in particular. Many scientists featured in the fiction of the 1860s and afterwards are either unmarried, or in marital relationships fraught with difficulty. It is not that they are incapable of love, but that the love of women always takes second place to science in their affections, and always loses out if any conflict arises, great or small. A noticeable pattern soon began to emerge, first exhibited in stories like Berthoud's "Le Fou," but soon to become a cliché, in which fictitious scientists love their daughters far more passionately than their wives, that being a kind of love intrinsically less demanding in terms of practical involvement.

245

The conviction expressed so fervently by Pont-Jest was exceptional, however, and it is worth taking note of an interesting counter-example, produced by a writer who was a close friend of Camille Flammarion, by virtue of being an ardent participant in his psychic experiments: Victorien Sardou. Sardou went on to become one of the most successful playwrights of his era, but before he began to specialize in that kind of work he wrote some prose fiction, including a story initially known as "Le Médaillon" [The Medallion] when it was published in 1861, but subsequently known as "La Perle noire" after the author adapted it for the stage under that title, and its English translations are titled "The Black Pearl." The story is intriguing not only because it is one of the few stories in which a young scientist in love is assisted to pursue his suit by his science, but as an early instance of the "scientific detective story."

The young scientist is introduced to the reader as a typical eccentric, flying a kite in a storm after the fashion of Benjamin Franklin because he wants to attract and observe lightning, having become particularly intrigued by the phenomenon now known as "ball lightning." His esoteric knowledge comes into its own, however, when the young woman he loves, intensely but secretly, is accused of robbery and murder by a policeman applying the method of deduction later to be summed up by Sherlock Holmes as "when you have eliminated the impossible, whatever remains, however improbable, must be true." The ingenious detective proves, beyond any apparent shadow of doubt, that no one but the young woman could possibly have committed the crime—but in this case, he has mistaken the limits of the possible; the scientist proves, by an even more dramatic process of deduction, leading to incontrovertible proof, that both the "robbery" and the "murder" were the accidental effects of a lightning-strike.

As in the case of Pont-Jest's story, the plausibility of the particular sequence of events depicted by Sardou is less significant than the implication that it is calculated to support: the superiority of logic enhanced by scientific understanding over logic that, by virtue of ignorance, is working from faulty premises. The point is hammered home dramatically by virtue of the fact that the hero is motivated by love for a damsel in distress and he is, in the inevitably climax of the story, rewarded by the consummation of his desire.

Seen in isolation, one case evidently counterbalances the other—but historically speaking, placing both items in context, it has to be admitted that it was Pont-Jest's story that posted the more accurate signpost to the shape of things to come. Although few of those who came after him represented science as an explicit diabolical temptation inevitably leading those who make a pact with it into the hell of lovelessness, the general opinion did tend in that direction, rather than regarding it as the kind of vocation likely to lead a young man into the arms of the girl of his dreams and guarantee that he would live happily ever after, at least in the conventional understanding of the phrase.

Had Victorien Sardou not found success in another medium, he might have become a significant pioneer of *roman scientifique*; in his incomplete novel *Car-*

lin (written 1857; published 1932) the eponymous androgyne invents several new gadgets, but the existing text stops short of the voyage sketched out in the author's notes, which would have taken him to an island populated by bipedal animals possessed of a language, an island constituted by a "progressive city" whose human inhabitants have alienated themselves completely from nature, an island when the female of the human species has been eliminated and men have found a new means of reproduction, and a submarine society. Had the rest ever been written, *Carlin* might have been the most important utopian novel of its era, but its surviving text is, alas, merely one more item in a long list of incomplete works indicative of a frustratingly hypothetical genre.

3. The Romance of Geography

Perhaps the most surprising of Joseph Méry's exercises in speculative fiction is the longest, comprising the second significant contribution to the alternative history subgenre pioneered by Louis Geoffroy. "Histoire de ce qui n'est pas arrivé" (book publication 1854; tr. as "The Tower of Destiny: A Story of Events that Did Not Happen"). Whereas Geoffroy had imagined a history that deviated from ours during Napoléon's Russian campaign in 1812, avoiding the terrible losses of the retreat from Moscow, Méry, reverting to the hero-myth created in his early epic poem written in collaboration with Auguste Barthélemy, *Napoléon en Egypte* (1828), imagined an earlier deviation taking place in May 1799, while the protagonist was still General Bonaparte.

In the story, Bonaparte succeeds in something he could not actually accomplish during his Egyptian campaign, taking the port of Acre by capturing the tower defending it. Having taken it, he decides that, rather than return to France, as he did in our history, he will take his army eastwards, join forces with the Indian rebel Tippoo Sahib, and expel the English from the subcontinent, in order to build a French empire there. In fact, the story is anachronistic, Tippoo Sahib having been killed while Bonaparte was still attacking the tower, but Méry ignores that detail and offers an account of a triumphant overland journey that concludes with a series of battles, the first of them fought in Afghanistan. All of them are won, by virtue of Bonaparte's tactical genius and the bravery of the Republic's soldiers, culminating in a triumphant alliance with Tippoo Sahib and the obliteration of England's influence in the jewel of its own imperial crown. The story is interrupted by a whimsical *entr'acte*, in which the members of a Parisian opera troupe, sick of life under the Directoire, decide to sail for the east in expectation of the campaign's success and the opportunity to lend their artistic support to the nascent empire.

There is an inevitable temptation to regard "Histoire de ce qui n'est pas arrivé" as a celebration of the advent of the Second Empire, although it might conceivably have been written beforehand, at much the same time as Gautier's

"Les Deux étoiles" and perhaps for the same editor. Whenever it was written, however, the argument of the story is a little more subtle than it might seem at first glance, and, like Geoffroy's alternative pattern of events, it has as much do to with geography as history; it is as much a reaction to the expanding horizons opened up by the colonial quest as a perpetuation of the Bonapartist mythology. Its conclusion is not simply a celebration of an amazing military victory but an anticipation of things to come:

"It is the awakening of a whole world; it is the renaissance of the primal world; it is the creation of the globe, after God's creation; it is the second endeavor of Shem, Ham and Japhet after the deluge of barbarism; an immense and noble endeavor confided to France, which Bonaparte alone had understood."

In his numerous adventure stories set in the Far East and Africa, Méry was already a pioneering participant in a new wave of fiction set in exotic regions of the globe. His fiction in that vein, like the vast majority of works of a similar stripe tended to glory in exoticism in a supposedly naturalistic fashion, leavened by vague mysticism, but the general endeavor was increasingly supplemented by work that drew more extensively and more elaborately on the reports brought back by the scientific expeditions sent out to map the world.

The purpose of those reports was to describe the various aspects of faraway places with a meticulous exactitude as far away as possible from exaggerated and deceptive traveler's tales. Most of the fiction that began to draw upon them, and to use them as a basis for exotic adventure stories, did so not in the jadedly mocking fashion of Charles Pougens and Henri Delmotte, but in enthusiastic earnest. When geographical fiction of the new era took on a dimension of the marvelous, it often did not come from the traditional resources of myth and magic, which seemed somewhat ill-fitting in a positivistic era, but from scientific and technological speculations, not different in kind from those employed by Pougens and Delmotte, but deployed with a markedly different narrative attitude.

Méry was not the only survivor of the Romantic Movement to assist in the beginning of that transition, and two of the novels that took off, in a sense, where *Jocko* had left off were produced by the Romantics whose Rousseauesque ideas he had been parodying: Méry's fellow Marseillais and close friend Léon Gozlan (1803-1866), and Élie Berthet (1815-1891).

Léon Gozlan's *Les Emotions de Polydore Marasquin* (1856; tr. as *The Emotions of Polydore Marasquin*) was his most successful novel, and probably helped to prompt several later exercises in a similar vein. It is a satire, but a subtle one, which can be read as an unusually melodramatic Robinsonade, and its initiating incident derives from an unfortunate personal experience. Gozlan's father was an arms dealer who was ruined by the depredations of English privateers during the Napoleonic wars. Hoping to restore the family fortunes, Léon chartered a ship, filled it with bottles of champagne and set off to make his fortune in Africa; unfortunately—but perhaps predictably—all the bottles broke *en route* and he was stranded in Senegal, penniless, for some years before making his way back to France in the 1830s, and becoming a journalist and feuilletonist. *Les Emotions de Polydore Marasquin* is, to some extent, a satirical transfiguration of his experiences in Senegal, with the natives replaced by various species of apes.

While managing a menagerie-cum-bazaar he has inherited from his father, Polydore Marasquin learns to see many animals as representatives of human types and many humans—especially criminals—as superficially-civilized animals: a blurring of categories and boundaries that sets the tone for the novel. Polydore becomes increasing alienated from the "society" of his captives after his father is killed by a tiger, forming a particularly antipathetic relationship with two huge baboons. When he splits up the pair by selling one of them, the one left behind takes his revenge in a distinctively human manner, by a premeditated act of arson, forcing him to go in search of new stock to restore his fortunes. Unfortunately, he is shipwrecked and cast away on a remote island.

Unlike most such fictional islands, the one on which Polydore is cast away has been recently colonized by civilized Europeans, but they have been forced to flee by pirates, leaving behind most of their possessions. Those trappings of civilized life have been taken over by the legions of monkeys which inhabit the island, whose leaders—members of the larger species—mimic the habits of the departed colonial masters in an odd anticipation of South Sea "cargo cults." The monkeys had been no match for the colonists—their former "king," a giant mandrill, had been summarily shot and skinned, and his skeleton displayed as a warning—but the lone Polydore provides a ready target for their vengeful spite, until he finds the skin of the ape-king and puts it on, thus becoming the acknowledged emperor of the island, at least for a while.

Polydore dreams about his role as King of Kouparou eventually being consecrated by an archbishop, but his reign is inevitably uneasy, perpetually threatened by exposure. His imposture eventually ends, absurdly, because his all-too-human backside eventually bursts through the seams of his costume, whose real owner had been designed for climbing rather than sitting. His consequent rescue by the returning colonists is fortunate, but he can only return to civilization as a pauper, doomed to dream forever after, nostalgically, of the glorious time when he was a king among apes.

Seen from one point of view, *The Emotions of Polydore Marasquin* can be construed as a racist parable, but it is not as simple as that; the fact that some humans are transmuted by the sarcastic plot into baboons and mandrills is partially compensated by the early observation that Marasquin has also learned to find human qualities in animals, and the hierarchy of contempt is not divided simply on racial lines; the noblest creatures in the entire plot are the chimpanzees Mococo and Saîmira. Gozlan's critique of savagery is scathing, but its most significant element is the sardonic account of savagery mimicking the trappings of civilization, which spills over into skepticism regarding civilization itself. What had given the colonists temporary mastery over the apes of Kouparou was not intelligence but fire-power, and the clear implication of the situation Polydore leaves behind on the island when he leaves, the cunning and enterprising Karabouffi having succeeding him as King, is that the apes will soon domesticate fire on their own account, and will begin to erode the technological advantages of the colonial adventurers significantly.

Élie Berthet's feuilleton "L'Homme des bois" (1861; tr. as *The Wild Man of the Woods*), is a much more earnest and focused account of an encounter with apes. The story is set in Sumatra, introduced as a paradoxical mixture of fertile ground and deadly menaces, both natural and human. The female members of a family of colonists imperiled by a man-eating tiger are saved by a "large hairy man" armed only with a club, identified by the local Malays as an "orangoutang," more to be feared than tigers. The family has secrets that eventually catch up with them, and the real threat to them comes from their fellow humans, but the orangutan is pursued nevertheless, not merely by hunters intent in killing him, but by a scientist desperate to measure his facial angle and evaluate the precise relationship between great apes and humans.

An uneasy alliance grows up between the son of the family and the persecuted orangutan, which culminates in the boy and the ape disappearing together into the forest, where the child becomes, for a while, an adopted orangutan, forming a close relationship with one of his new peers while his father tries in vain to recover him. The boy is eventually returned to his own species, but the situation ends tragically. The complex human problems unwind in suitably melodramatic fashion, as befits a feuilleton, but the conclusion of the story focuses on the scientific enigma as to whether the orangutans are "the first of apes or the last of humans," which is left scrupulously hanging in the balance, the implications of the story as tantalizingly unclear as those of the frustrated scientific investigation.

That kind of narrative balancing of melodrama and scientific curiosity was to become a major feature of the geographical fiction of the 1860s, and a key feature of the work of one of its most successful popular writers: Jules Verne (1828-1905). It was Verne who mixed melodramatic and scientific raw materials most cleverly, and took the compound swiftly to unprecedented and productive extremes.

Jules Verne, the son of a lawyer in Nantes, began to write in his teens, heavily influenced by Victor Hugo. He was first sent to Paris in 1847 to study law, but returned to his home town for some time; he was distracted from his studies by a frustrated love affair, after which his inamorata was married off to someone else by her parents, in search of a safer match—the second time that had happened to him. The experience fueled his writing and embittered him somewhat against the prejudices of bourgeois society. He returned to Paris to continue his studies just as the Revolution of 1848 broke out, throwing everything into confusion.

While continuing his studies, Verne began to attend literary salons, which led him to write even more, still under the influence of Victor Hugo, and now ambitious to be a playwright. He met Alexandre Dumas, and became friends with his similarly-named son, with whom he wrote a play that Dumas *père*'s influence helped reach the stage. His health was frequently poor—which spared him from military service—but he continued to maintain both his studies and his writing.

Verne obtained his qualification to practice law in 1851, but in the same year he made contact with another writer from Nantes, Pierre Chevalier, known by the nickname of Pitre-Chevalier, who had taken over as editor of the *Musée des Familles* when S. Henry Berthoud was sacked, and was carrying it forward with the same stress on popular education, but in a more conventional manner. Verne began supplying him with material, including "Un drame dans les airs" (1851; tr. as "A Drama in the Air"), which offers a more melodramatic version of a crucial episode in Berthoud's "Voyage au ciel," presumably by coincidence.

Dumas *fils* obtained a position for Verne as secretary of the newly rebranded Théâtre Lyrique, which greatly encouraged his writing for the stage. He was subjected to pressure from his family to return to Nantes and take up a law practice there, but he resisted and committed himself to Paris and literature. He befriended the veteran geographer and explorer Jacques Arago, who had sailed around the world with Louis de Freycinet and had written a light-hearted account of the voyage; Arago was now blind, but still loquacious, and Verne found his anecdotes inspiring.

Verne published a number of increasingly long stories in the *Musée des familles*, of various kinds, including the polar romance "Un hivernage dans les glaces" (1855; tr. as "A Winter amid the Ice"), but he eventually quarreled with Pitre-Chevalier and refused to supply more. Verne later claimed that it was during the period when he was writing for the *Musée des Familles* that he first thought of developing a new kind of fiction, *roman de la science* [science fiction], and that he discussed the possibility seriously with Alexandre Dumas. Most of his efforts were, however, directed toward drama, in connection with his work for the theater, although his position there did not enable him to get much of his work into production.

When he returned briefly to Nantes in 1856, Verne fell in love once again, this time with a young widow with two children. Her brother was a stockbroker, and Verne took a job with him in order to have a secure income with which to marry and support his instant family. When he returned to Paris, it was to go to work at the Bourse, but he continued to write in his spare time and consort with his literary friends. He was also able to do a little traveling, visiting England and Scotland in 1858 and Scandinavia in 1861.

In 1862 Verne met Pierre-Jules Hetzel, a publisher who had returned to Paris some years before, following a period of exile after the 1851 coup. Hetzel was an ardent promoter of educational fiction for children, and wanted to convert his series of books, *La Bibliothèque Illustrée des Familles*, into a magazine that would rival, and hopefully overtake, the long-running *Musée des Familles*. The periodical in question eventually materialized as *Le Magasin d'Éducation et de Récréation*. Verne showed Hetzel a work in progress, which enthused the publisher considerably, as exactly the kind of thing his new magazine needed, but he demanded extensive revisions, which Verne hastily made.

The resultant novel, *Cinq semaines en ballon* (1863; tr. as *Five Weeks in a Balloon*), was a narrative describing the employment of a new kind of hydrogen balloon, capable of long voyages, for an exploration of the heart of Africa and a search for the sources of the Nile—an intense focus of geographical interest at the time. The three protagonists, a scholar, his manservant and a hunter, run into various kinds of difficulty, including the rescue of a missionary from a hostile tribe and an attack by large birds, but their melodramatic adventures are punctuated by technical descriptions and scientific discourses in a manner that was to become Verne's dominant narrative strategy, at least for a while.

Although similar hybridizations had been tentatively attempted before, as in *L'Homme des bois*, there had been nothing to compare with the intensity and expertise with which Verne went about the task, with the active encouragement of Hetzel, and a measure of editorial instruction. If Hetzel played a part in formulating "Vernian fiction," however, Vernian fiction also played a major role in shaping Hetzel's new magazine, and giving it an edge over the *Musée des familles* that carried it almost immediately to predominance.

In anticipation of that success, Hetzel offered Verne an almost-unprecedented long term contract, by which Verne would deliver a specified amount of wordage every year in return for a guaranteed payment—an arrangement that lasted until the end of his life, although the precise terms had to be re-negotiated along the way. Verne's second novel, the polar romance *Voyages et aventures de Capitaine Hatteras* (serial 1864-65; book 1866; tr. as *The Adventures of Captain Hatteras*), was further adapted after its serialization for publication as the first item in a lavishly illustrated series of books collectively entitled *Voyages Extraordinaires*, although it was advertised as the second, anticipating the placement in chronological sequence of *Cinq semaines en ballon*. The series became a major feature of Parisian publication for decades, a multiple best-seller.

An adventure story spiced with technical and scientific punctuations, like its predecessor, the new novel was also a study in obsession. Captain Hatteras, an Englishman modeled on the ill-fated explorer John Franklin, is determined to reach the pole and to overcome all obstacles, driving his associates relentlessly, surviving mutiny, shipwreck, attacks by polar bears and the rigors of the Arctic winter. He eventually reaches the open sea that was then widely thought to exist beyond the Arctic ice, and discovers a volcanic island directly over the pole. Verne wanted to conclude Hatteras' obsession with a fatal leap into the crater, but Hetzel, not for the first and certainly not for the last time, demanded that he rewrite it, so that the Captain survives—although he never speaks again and is committed to an asylum, where the residue of his obsession persists.

It is not known to what extent that ending is a compromise between Verne and his editor, but the impression it gives is that of an *injuste milieu* resulting from a contest in which neither party wanted to yield completely. In fact, unbreakable as it proved to be, Verne's relationship with Hetzel seems to have been one of continuous tension, in which, although both were pulling in the same general direction, they had different notions of exactly where they were heading and how to get there. Notoriously, Hetzel not only rejected one of Verne's early productions but strongly advised him—or even demanded—that he not attempt to publish it elsewhere, because it would damage his burgeoning reputation.

The novel in question, probably written in 1863, remained unpublished until 1994, when it was said to have been rediscovered unexpectedly in an old safe, and was issued as *Paris au XXe siècle* (tr. as *Paris in the Twentieth century*). In complete contrast to the *Voyages extraordinaires*, it begins as satire reminiscent in many ways of Émile Souvestre's *Le Monde tel qu'il sera*, depicting a 1960 Paris ruled by the commercialism of the Bourse, in which rampant technology has transformed all aspects of life, but it ends in morbid tragedy. The protagonist, a poetry-writing misfit, manages to find a precarious position in a bank, working with a fellow misfit to maintain the accounts contained in the quasi-sacred Ledger, until an accident results in their dismissal. He is in love, but evil circumstance spoils that too, and he goes mad, beset by the paranoid certainty that he is being pursued and persecuted by the demon of Electricity, eventually dying in despair.

Although it clearly reflects many of Verne's personal travails and anxieties, the novel is a startling addition to the long sequence of descriptions of future Paris, and the most downbeat of them all. It is perhaps understandable, however regrettable it might be from a purely literary viewpoint, that Hetzel not only refused to publish it but told Verne to bury it—and perhaps understandable too that Verne's resentment of that circumstance, even though he doubtless understood the logic of it, can occasionally be glimpsed, in a fugitive fashion, in such later amendments as Captain Hatteras' eventual fate, which Hetzel would surely have preferred to be more upbeat.

The extent of Hetzel's influence over Verne's future career is impossible to measure precisely, but the likelihood is that, left to his own devices, Verne would have let his speculative imagination roam much more freely and much further than Hetzel was prepared to license, and that the trajectory of the first phase of his career was a compromise between Hetzel's desire to publish earthbound and stubbornly naturalistic adventures stories wrapped around nuggets of didactic discourse, and Verne's ambition to produce much bolder and fanciful work. Without Hetzel, Verne might not have become as rich as he eventually did, and might have been less famous, but his imagination might not have spent four decades shackled to a ball and chain.

Before that ball and chain began to weigh too heavily, however, Verne did have the opportunity to stretch himself, and he did so triumphantly. His third-published novel, *Voyage au centre de la terre* (1864) took a party of adventurers even further into unknown territory than Captain Hatteras had been able to go. Again, the story employed a foreign protagonist, using as its viewpoint character Axel, the nephew of the obsessive scholar Otto Lidenbrock—a carbon copy of one of S. Henry Berthoud's case-studies in the strange psychology of the scientific mind. Lidenbrock's discovery of an old manuscript to which a cryptogram has been added, and the subsequent decoding of the cryptogram, lead him to follow in the footsteps of an occult scientist, Arne Saknussemm, descending into the crater of an extinct volcano in Iceland in search of a realm within the Earth, and dragging the reluctant Axel along.

Having recruited a hunter as their guide, to complete what would become a standard Vernian trio, Lidenbrock and Axel descend through the strata of the Earth's crust, aided by new technological devices and guided intellectually by the geological analyses set out in Louis Figuier's recent account of *La Terre avant le deluge* (1863). They recapitulate the contrived descent featured in Berthoud's "Le Château de Heidenloch," and discover similar specimens of prehistoric life, not as artificially-generated images but in the flesh, having survived the ages in their isolated enclave.

All the translations of the novel are taken from a revised edition published in 1867, in which Verne made a few changes in the story to take aboard amendments that Figuier had made to his own book in a new edition published the same year. Initially committed to preserving the Biblical account of the history of the human race, Figuier had decided in the interim that the evidence collected by Boucher de Perthes and others had become overwhelming, and that he had to integrate the prehistory of the human species into his account of the evolution of the world's surface over an extent of hundreds of thousands of years rather than six thousand. Verne was a little more hesitant about doing that explicitly—his family was devout, although he was not—and although he accommodated human fossils within his account of the underworld featured in the novel, he left Axel's sighting of a living human giant in a highly ambiguous section that licensed the reader to interpret it as a hallucination.

The first translation of *Journey to the Center of the Earth* published in Britain was utterly careless of such niceties, and the "translator" rewrote the story extensively, introducing other melodramatic incidents, changing the characters' names, and contriving a complete travesty—which unfortunately remained the standard English-language translation long after a more accurate one had become available. Although nothing quite as extreme happened to English language editions of Verne's other novels, it became commonplace for the translators to minimize the scientific and technological intrusions that were an intrinsic element of their *raison d'être*, thus transforming the novels into more straightforward adventure stories, adapted to what was considered by English publishers to be "the boy's book market."

The view of Verne's work in the English-speaking world has always been distorted by that process of adaptation, and it was not until the 1970s that full and accurate translations of his most famous novels began to appear in the U.S.A. Those translations still remained largely excluded from the English market by the priority obtained by an extensive set of adaptations commenced in 1958 under the editorship of I. O. Evans, which, although better than the worst of the nineteenth-century translations, were still frequently cut and shaped to fit a particular format, often being split into two parts and deliberately simplified. Although intended to be complete, the series was not quite finished.

The bibliographical mess resulting from all these misshapen endeavors left English speaking scholars interested in Verne's work with an enormous amount of reconstruction to do. Even the task of tracking the atrocities perpetrated by translators required a Herculean labor on the part of Arthur B. Evans, and the job of producing a complete set of accurate translations is probably too daunting ever to be tackled.

In spite of the restraint imposed upon him by his publisher, Verne continued to write speculative fiction bringing an unprecedented verisimilitude to the description of the bolder exploratory ventures he constructed. In *De la terre à la lune, trajet direct en 97 heures 20 minutes* (1865; tr. as *From the Earth to the Moon*), the members of the Baltimore Gun Club, an association of armaments manufacturers and merchants formed in association with the Civil War, find themselves at something of a loose end once hostilities are concluded, and the club's president, Impey Barbicane, comes up with the project of building an unprecedentedly huge cannon, the Columbiad, capable of firing a projectile at the Moon, in order that the satellite's inhabitants, if there are any, will be able to marvel at the prowess of American technology.

The initial project is transformed by a proposal from a Frenchman, Michel Ardan, that the projectile should be equipped to carry a passenger—for which role he volunteers. Ardan arrives in America in time to smooth things over in a fierce dispute between Barbicane and his chief opponent within the gun club, Captain Nicholl, and the result of his arbitration is that the projectile will be adapted to carry all three of them, together with all the requisite life-support apparatus and provisions for a year. The narrative, although by no means uneventful, is less of an adventure story than its predecessors, being primarily concerned with the practical planning required to adapt the gun to the theoretical requirements of launching a projectile out of the Earth's field of gravity and of equipping the projectile with an adequate life-support system. Such questions had never been addressed before in any work of fiction with the seriousness and intelligence that Verne brought to the task, and the work was a significant watershed in the evolution of interplanetary romance.

Largely because of the publicity given to it by Verne's novel, people rapidly became aware of the fact that the project as planned therein was inviable, because the passengers inside the projectile could not possibly withstand the acceleration of the shot. Verne did not want to address that problem, or the problem of how his would-be lunar travelers might return from the Moon if they contrived to reach it, and thus left the consequences of the cannon-blast to be observed from Earth. The wind from the blast uproots trees for twenty miles around, destroys a hundred buildings and sinks numerous ships, causing storm-winds that blow all the way across the Atlantic. The resultant bad weather prevents terrestrial observatories from catching a glimpse of the projectile for some time, but it is finally spotted a week later (impossibly) from Long's Peak, still 23,000 miles from the Moon—but there the story ends, the fate of the travelers left unknown.

That was clearly not an ending satisfactory to readers, most of whom construed it as a cliffhanger rather than drawing the logical conclusion that the ridiculously ambitious voyagers have, in fact, committed suicide. Whether moved by Hetzel or his own regret, Verne was eventually forced to add a sequel in *Autour de la lune* (serial 1869; book 1870; tr. as *Around the Moon*). Before then, however, he penned a long adventure story of a far more orthodox kind, *Les enfants du Capitaine Grant* (serial 1865-67; book version in two volumes 1867-68; tr. in various formats under various titles, including *In Search of the Castaways*).

The story begins with the discovery of a bottle in the sea, which is found to contain an enigmatically-incomplete document written by the shipwrecked Captain Grant. When the bottle comes into the custody of Lord Glenarvan, he informs the Captain's children. The government refuses to send a vessel to search for the castaways, so Glenarvon and his wife decide to do it themselves, joined accidentally by a French geographer, Jacques Paganel. Their search takes them to South America and then to Australasia, facilitating detailed descriptions of the geography of various locations and the naïve flora and fauna, enlivened by the occasional natural hazard and the staple menaces of pirates and savages. Eventually, by luck rather than judgment, they attain their goal. Hetzel probably liked the novel more than Verne, who might well have considered it pedestrian by comparison with its predecessor and its successor.

Autour de la lune, however, picks up the story of the moon shot from the viewpoint of the three heroes; having survived the launch, they experience the long journey through space, experiencing a few problems *en route*—notably when they overdose on oxygen and become intoxicated—and carry out a detailed close-range study of the lunar surface, eventually looping around the moon under the effect of the satellite's gravity before their momentum carries them back toward the Earth. They land safely, by courtesy of another extreme but dramatically necessary improbability, landing in the sea in a cushioned impact. The rather remote view of the Moon that they obtain, somewhat spoiled by the fact that the hemisphere permanently hidden from the Earth is in darkness when they pass over it, strongly suggests that it is lifeless, but dutifully leaves open the possibility that it was once inhabited, and that some vestiges of that life might still persist there.

As with the earlier novel, the narrative of *Autour de la lune* only includes a few incidents to spice up an exhaustive account of astronomical discoveries and an elaborate description of the satellite carefully and dutifully derived from recent astronomical observations. Although that pattern is a relatively straightforward inversion of the basic schema of *Cinq semaines en ballon* and *Voyage au centre de la terre*, the drastic alteration of the balance made a big difference to the reader experience, and that might not have been to Hetzel's liking. It was certainly not to the liking of the novel's early English translators, who made extensive cuts and alterations to the first edition, which combined the two parts together in a single volume. At any rate, Verne never again tilted the balance of his work quite as far in the direction of scientific discourse, at the expense of dramatic action.

The precedent set by the compound work, however, really did institute a new kind of *roman de la science*, and that status permitted it, at length, to serve as a powerful inspiration, not merely to future novelists—several of whom set out as assiduously as they could to correct the "error" of the lethal gun and find ways for their travelers to land on the Moon and take off again—but also to the twentieth-century generation of rocket pioneers, all of whom had the ultimate ambition of paving the way for a moon shot, in explicit celebration of Verne's vision. That was a kind of ambition to which no previous literary work could have aspired, but it added a new potential purpose to the repertoire of *roman scientifique*, which several subsequent writers of speculative fiction attempted to exploit.

Immediately after supplying the belated sequel to *De la terre à la lune*, Verne produced the most famous of all his *romans scientifiques*, the classic **Vingt mille lieues sous les mers** (serial 1869-70; book 1870: tr. as *Twenty Thousand Leagues Under the Sea*), which attempts to add an element of suspense and mystery to the adventure format. The story begins with reports of strange disruptions of merchant shipping by a "monster," which prompt the U.S. Navy to send a warship to find and destroy it. The crew of the warship is supplemented, as an afterthought, by the marine biologist Pierre Aronnax, a Berthoudian eccentric of a slightly milder stripe than Professor Lidenbrock.

When the ship locates the strangely luminous monster and fires at it, the result is a reprisal that casts Aronnax into the sea, with his manservant Conseil. In company with a harpooner named Ned Land—who makes up the typical Vernian trio, providing abundant scope for educational conversations—Aronnax and Conseil end up on the monster's "back," where they discover that it is made of metal; the reluctant passengers hasten to attract attention to their plight, and are taken aboard the huge submarine. Some time passes, however, before they are finally allowed to meet its master, the enigmatic and misanthropic Captain Nemo, who employs his ultra-sophisticated *Nautilus* as a refuge from the terrestrial world, which he dislikes in general, and as a weapon against the naval power of the English, whom he hates more particularly.

Nemo gives Aronnax a tour of the ship, and then takes him on long excursion through the undersea world, the incidents of which include an underwater hunt with the aid of electric rifles, a siege by savages, and visits to the ruins of Atlantis, the Sargasso Sea and the island imagined in the text to occupy the center of an open sea at the south pole, mirroring the one found by Captain Hatteras at the north pole. The sequence of adventures concludes with an encounter with giant "*poulpes*"—now identifiable with giant squid, although the incomplete knowledge of the day always represented such monsters as giant octopodes, and litterateurs generally did likewise. Such creatures are far more common in fiction than is warranted by rumors of their actuality, but Victor Hugo had recently employed one in *Les Travailleurs de la mer* (1866; tr. as *Toilers of the Sea*), and if the device was good enough for Victor Hugo, still the doyen of Romanticism, it was surely good enough for Verne's brand of scientifically-sophisticated neo-Romanticism. The three castaways eventually manage to escape from the *Nautilus* in a small boat, and the last glimpse they catch of it sees it on the brink of being swallowed by the Maëlstrom.

It is possible that Verne initially made Nemo an enigmatic and fugitive individual simply in order to be better able to hide his plot away as an episode of secret history, rather than bringing it into too brutal a confrontation with known recent history, as he had arguably done with the conclusion of *De la terre à la lune*, but it is also probable that he invested the character fervently with some of his own buried frustrations and dreams of escape. At any rate, the character created a precedent at least as important as that of his charismatic vessel, and became an iconic figure in the burgeoning mythology of popular fiction, with the *Nautilus* the pedestal on which he stood.

Although he is so full of hatred and contempt that he is much less appealing as a human being than Ned Land or Professor Aronnax, that does not make Nemo any less enviable in his splendid quasi-Byronic isolation. Most contemporary readers were probably unwilling to share his misanthropy wholeheartedly, although there could be a certain guilty pleasure in its appreciation, but it fitted him all the better for his role as a bold pioneer of science. As George Bernard Shaw observes, the fact that reasonable people make every effort to fit in with their surroundings leaves the responsibilities and rewards of progress to unreasonable men, and the defiantly unreasonable Nemo is a fine symbol of progress and enterprise, at the extremity of the Berthoudian spectrum of scientific psychology. It is not surprising that he far outshone Aronnax in that regard, the latter being too reasonable for his own good in a contest of charisma.

Although it is rightly regarded as one of the central classics of *roman scientifique*, the technology featured in *Vingt mille lieues sous les mers* is less inventive that some of its admirers thought and proclaimed. Verne had had several opportunities to observe submarines being tested in the Seine, and had certainly seen the model of Charles-Marie Brun's *Le Plongeur* displayed at the Exposition of 1867. His most significant fictitious inventions were the powering of the ship by electricity extracted from sea-water—a technology that continues to prove elusive—and the diving-suits used by Nemo and his crew, which would be fatal to users because of their lack of pressurization. As with the story of the lunar voyage, however, *Vingt mille lieues sous les mers* prompted real technological endeavors; it encouraged inventors to begin manufacturing better diving suits, and it was the desire to make a better cinematic version of *Twenty Thousand Leagues Under the Sea* that provided the principal inspiration for the development of the first underwater camera by the Williamson brothers in 1916.

On the other hand, it is difficult for modern readers to appreciate how mysterious the undersea world was in Verne's day, and what a boldly innovative endeavor his attempt to describe it was. Thanks to underwater photography and television, we now have a clear window into that world, but Verne had none. The surface of the moon, which the heroes of *Autour de la lune* observed at close quarters, had been thoroughly mapped on the side facing the Earth by careful telescopic observation, but the world under the sea was almost entirely hidden, known only indirectly, by virtue of what was cast ashore or hauled out by fishermen's nets. Verne's fictitious travelers were venturing into an unknown world, almost for the first time, affecting to lay some of its wonders bare to an audience whose members had none of the preconceptions that modern readers cannot help but bring to the text. His research was as conscientious as it could be, given the limitations of the available information, and he did a superb job of weaving a memorable picture around that research. Pedants can complain that he makes seawater far more transparent than it actually is, but he did so with the best of motives.

There was something of a hiatus in the production of Verne's fiction after *Vingt mille lieues sous les mers*, partly occasioned by the intervention of the Franco-Prussian War, although he did publish a novel while the invasion in full swing, and did not stop writing during the conflict and its aftermath. The novel in question was not serialized by Hetzel but in the newspaper the *Journal des Débats*, during August and September 1970 (the war had started in July). Entitled *Une Ville Flottante* (book 1871; tr. as *A Floating City*) the novel is primarily a documentary account of the enormous transatlantic liner *Great Eastern*, a routine crossing of which is only slightly troubled by the insanity of a passenger. Although Hetzel did reissue it in the *Voyages Extraordinaires* series, it does not really belong there. As a punctuation mark, however, it signaled the end of a distinct phase in Verne's career, which never again reached the imaginative heights attained before the war, even when he made conscious and deliberate attempts to do so.

Verne's impact in France was immediate; he was already recognized as a writer of great importance by the time the war broke out, and became a Chevalier de la Légion d'honneur in 1870. It was obvious right away that his *roman de la science* was something new, and perhaps something important, although journalists and critics, searching for a term by which to describe it, thought *roman scientifique* more economical, and that was the description that caught on in critical parlance. There was a brief moment, too, when Jules Hetzel thought that there might be some potential in the new genre. Not only did he reprint Henri de Parville's newspaper hoax in book form but he also reprinted another work that had appeared in a recent periodical, although it was not "Vernian fiction" at all, being cast in a very different satirical mode.

"Prodigieuse découverte" (tr. as "A Prodigious Discovery") was originally published in the monthly *Revue Moderne* in the December 1865 and January 1866 issues under the signature of "X. Nagrien"—the pseudonym employed by the story's central character. Hetzel reprinted it under that by-line in 1867 as *Prodigieuse découverte et ses incalculables consequences sur les destinées du monde entier* [A Prodigious Discovery and its Incalculable Consequences for the Destiny of the Entire World]. In the novella, mysterious notices appear overnight all over Paris, many of them posted in seemingly impossible locations, inviting the populace to come and witness "the first manifestation of the greatest of revolutions past and future" in the Place de la Concorde the following Sunday. Those who accept the invitation see a spectacular demonstration by a flying man, who then—while maintaining the strictest secrecy regarding his identity and methods—builds a larger flying machine, in which he invites numerous passengers to accompany him, first on a tour of France and subsequently of the world, communicating with his eager audience via the pages of a newspaper.

The story is partly a satire aimed at politics and publicity, using the hypothetical invention of a technology of antigravity as a means of highlighting the problems that an inventor might experience in the profitable exploitation of an epoch-making discovery, and partly an exercise in wry logic, pointing out the economic and social upheavals that a truly prodigious discovery might provoke, even while furthering the cause of progress. That nexus of issues was to become a popular theme of *roman scientifique*, seeming particularly thorny in France because French scientists routinely saw their work overtaken by entrepreneurial American inventors like Samuel Morse and Thomas Edison, who reaped the glory and well as all the profits of discoveries that they succeeded in patenting, but had not necessarily made.

Unfortunately, Hetzel did not like the ending of the *Revue Moderne* story and insisted that the author alter it. The alteration did not work to its advantage, although that probably had nothing to do with the fact that the book version of

Prodigieuse découverte sold very poorly. That poor performance, probably matched by Parville's *Un habitant de la planète Mars*, might well have helped to put Hetzel off *roman scientifique* and enhanced his inclination to steer Verne away from its excesses toward more orthodox adventure fiction.

However, the fact that the manifestly-pseudonymous work had been issued by Hetzel prompted some eager translators of Verne's work to appropriate it, and the versions published in Spanish, Italian and Portuguese were misrepresented as Verne's work. That misattribution remained commonplace in bibliographies for many years, although the novella was actually the work of the lawyer and Republican civil servant François-Armand Audoy (1825-1891), who wrote a number of non-fiction books under his own name and subsequently published a second book under the Nagrien pseudonym, *Un Cauchemar. Manoeuvres, intelligences, délits fantastiques* [A Nightmare. Fantastic Maneuvers, Intelligences and Misdemeanors] (1869). The catalogue of the Bibliothèque Nationale does not as yet attribute the Nagrien pseudonym to Audoy, but there is no doubt about it, a search of Hetzel's archives made in 1966 and publicized by Simone Vierne having revealed the truth.

It is difficult to know exactly what to make of the failure of Hetzel's other experiments in *roman scientifique*, and his apparent subsequent distaste for the genre. It is certainly plausible that what readers liked most about Verne's works was their adventure story component, and that they found the didactic components difficult to swallow without that kind of sugar-coating, but *De la terre à la lune* and its sequel, the Verne works that bore least resemblance to orthodox adventure fiction, do not seem to have been any less successful commercially, and were certainly far more successful, in terms of their subsequent reputation and influence, than *Les Enfants du Capitaine Grant*.

Seen as a work of coherent fiction rather than a hastily-improvised series of newspaper articles, Parville's book is frankly inept, and Audoy's, although much more fluent, is frustratingly anti-climactic even in the version of the ending that Hetzel forced upon it, so it might simply be the case that the publisher made an unfortunate choice of supplementary materials and might have fared much better had he contrived to find better books to exemplify the new genre. The result of his experiment, however, is not in doubt: he left it alone thereafter, except for occasional experiments by Verne, which he seemed merely to tolerate. It is hard to blame him; it would be difficult to find an example of any publisher, anywhere in the world, who ever lost money by indulging a distaste for speculative fiction.

Verne's early exercises in the speculative fiction of geographical exploration soon began to give rise to similar exercises, although the genre of "Vernian fiction" did not begin to blossom extensively until the aftermath of the Franco-Prussian War. One of the earliest examples was *Voyage sous les flots, rédigé d'après le journal de bord de* L'Éclair (tr. as *Voyage Beneath the Waves*), whose first book edition also bears the heading *Aventures extraordinaires de Trinitus* and the signature "Aristide Roger ." It was first published in that form by a similarly-pseudonymous publisher "P. Brunet" (Paul Bory) in 1868, but it was also serialized in *Le Petit Journal*, beginning in October 1867. The book version was issued in Brunet's Bibliothèque de la Science Pittoresque, and advertised as "a fantastic voyage in which the author describes, in an exceedingly curious and interesting fashion, the innumerable marvels of the submarine world."

Jules Verne, who came across the serial version of **Voyage sous les flots** while the serial version of his own *Vingt mille lieues sous les mers* was in preparation, wrote a letter to *Le Petit Journal* in order to make it clear that he had come up with the notion independently of "Aristide Roger"—or, more accurately, of Pierre-Jules Rengade (1841-1915), the author behind that pseudonym—his own story of an underwater voyage having been advertised as forthcoming in Hetzel's *Magasin d'Éducation et de Récréation* in September 1867, but evidently having been delayed in production.

Verne probably did that because his sensitivity to such issues had been considerably sharpened by an attempt made to sue him for plagiarism by René de Pont-Jest, on account of similarities between the initiating incident of *Voyage au centre de la terre* and the one featured in "La Tête de Mimer," which had appeared in the September 1863 issue of the *Revue Contemporaine*. Pont-Jest had abandoned his suit, presumably persuaded that he could not win it—although he was probably right to assume that Verne had "stolen" his idea of prompting a voyage of exotic discovery to Scandinavia by means of a runic cryptogram—but the incident had been unfortunate. George Sand was later to allege that it was she who had fed the suggestion of writing a novel about an underwater voyage to Hetzel, who had then passed it on to Verne, so Verne was probably correct to feel that people might get the wrong idea if he did not make his position clear.

There was, of course, nothing new about the notion of a submarine, *Le Plongeur* having been on public exhibition, and previous literary use having been made of one by Théophile Gautier in *Les Deux étoiles*, but the point at issue was not so much that Verne's *Nautilus* might seem to have been inspired by Rengade's *Éclair*, but that the wonders of the undersea world that the vessels in question revealed might seem excessively similar.

There is, in fact, no obvious similarity between the magnificent *Nautilus* and the rather petty *Éclair*, but it is not surprising that the imagery of the under-sea worlds glimpsed by their passengers had a good deal in common, because the authors were drawing on exactly the same meager resources, not only in terms of the scant knowledge provided by divers and fishermen but in terms of traditional melodramatic potential. In 1867, even the most advanced diving-bells could not go down very far and had not brought back very much in the way of eye-witness accounts of undersea life, and although the catches of fishermen and other dredgers of the sea-bed had brought back large numbers of samples of un-derwater organisms, it was by no means easy to perform the imaginative gym-nastics required to envision those specimens in their natural state.

Modern readers know full well that the sea-bed is not brightly illuminated by vast hosts of phosphorescent organisms, that the notion of the weed-choked Sargasso Sea popular in the nineteenth century was more myth than reality, that narwhals do not engage in titanic battles with other whales, and that the notion of dangling a trapeze underneath a fast-moving submarine to serve as a viewing platform for men in canvas suits breathing air from the interior of the submarine through long rubber tubes is monumentally silly. The fact that such narrative devices did not seem entirely ridiculous to Rengade and his contemporary read-ers, however, serves to remind us that the reason that no one prior to 1867 had dared to write a novel about an underwater voyage is that no one had any but the slightest idea of what such a voyage might reveal.

Although *Voyage sous les flots* and *Vingt mille lieues sous les mers* do not seem very similar to the modern eye, the narrative differences that distinguish them result from Verne's far greater sophistication as a thinker and writer. In terms of their "scientific content," as well as their didactic purpose they have a good deal in common. In the latter respect there was, of course, some direct in-spiration involved in the coincidence between the two works, but it was not to do with the machines that provided their central motifs, and the flow of that in-spiration was not so much from Verne to Rengade as from P.-J. Hetzel to P. Brunet.

As *Voyage sous les flots* illustrates very obviously, the strategy approved by Hetzel and appropriated by Brunet, of interweaving an exciting adventure story with brief lectures on geography, natural history and physical science was risky in the absence of the craftsmanship required to put it into practice with due elegance. Rengade also demonstrated that a writer can easily be carried away by the more exciting passages of his endeavor to the extent that the popularization of science tends to fade away as the story progresses, so that the climactic phas-es of such endeavors can easily become pure and unalloyed melodrama. If Verne did not reproduce all of Rengade's errors in chronicling the exploits of Captain Nemo, that was partly because he had already made many of them be-fore, in *Les Enfants du capitaine Grant*, from which Rengade seems to have bor-rowed considerable inspiration in shaping his plot, which is, in essence, a brutal abridgement of Verne's story of a long-distance rescue, in which the submarine functions as a means of curtailment as well as a vehicle of revelation.

In spite of its faults, *Voyage sous les flots* was by no means a commercial failure. The Brunet edition went through half a dozen printings, and the story was given a further lease of life in 1889 when Louis Figuier reprinted a slightly-revised serial version in *La Science Illustrée*. That led in turn to a new book edition, with a preface by the author in which he proudly reprinted Verne's letter, in order to demonstrate his ideative kinship with the great man.

The other book of a similar kind that "Aristide Roger " contributed to the series in which *Voyages sous les flots* appeared—*Les Monstres invisibles* [Invisible Monsters] (1868), a non-fictional study of life in the microcosm revealed by microscopy enlivened by a few stylistic affectations—also went through half a dozen editions, but Rengade made no further attempt to repeat the trick. Brunet advertised a third Aristide Roger title in the series, *La Machine humaine* [The Human Machine], but it did not appear, although Rengade subsequently used the title on a series of articles featuring different organs of the body, and it might well be the case that the projected book would simply have been a collection of those articles.

Rengade was a qualified physician—he always signed the plays that he regarded as his most important contributions to literature "Dr. J. Rengade"—but does not seem ever to have practiced medicine after finishing his stints as an intern in two Parisian hospitals. Instead, he preferred to follow Henri de Parville's example in following a career as one of the first generation of full-time scientific journalists; he launched a popular periodical of his own in 1867, *La Santé, journal de vulgarisation médicale et scientifique* [Health, a Magazine of Medical and Scientific Popularization], although it ceased publication a year later. Given that he was a professional writer, and that his two exercises in fictional popularization sold so well, it is perhaps surprising that he did not do more in that vein, but it is possible that he simply realized that he could not compete with Verne, and conceded defeat in that particular arena. If the idea of writing *Voyage sous les flots* and *Les Monstres invisibles* had, in fact, been Brunet's rather than Rengade's, it is also possible that Rengade regarded them as mere hackwork.

Verne and Rengade both deserve credit for taking on the task that they did; it really was a bold attempt to explore the unknown by means of the imagination. The lack of success they enjoyed in terms of accurate prediction of what future underwater exploration would actually reveal is somewhat beside the point; no one can know today what will only be discovered tomorrow. The real issue at stake is whether such journeys are worth undertaking, regardless of the scant chance of predictive success. Verne surely demonstrated that they are, and that entitled him to become the figurehead of an entire genre, which not only collated such attempts but also enabled them to achieve a measure of collective progress.

Contrary to what René de Pont-Jest thought, it is actually healthy for writers to take inspiration from one another, borrowing one another's ideas in order to extract further mileage from them and exhibit the true breadth of their potential. Mere copying is fruitless, but development is anything but, and although much of the material contained in the melodramatic component of *Voyage sous les flots* is inept imitation, the narrative does have developmental ambitions in its depictions of underwater life, and Brunet and Rengade were correct in their belief that there really was additional mileage to be obtained from jumping on to the Hetzel-Vernian bandwagon, in terms of seeing how far it could go, and in what directions.

4. Travels in Space and Time

Camille Flammarion's survey of previous interplanetary fantasies in *Les Mondes imaginaires et les mondes réels* finds several examples of non-fictional treatments of the theme in the previous decade, but only one significant work of fiction, of whose central supposition he observes, wryly, that it is "not uningenious, although it is far from revealing the hand of an astronomer."

The work in question is *Star ou Ψ de Cassiopée* (1854; tr. as *Star: Psi Cassiopeia*) by Charles Defontenay (1819-1856) and the oddity that provoked Flammarion's remark is that it envisages a distant solar system that has three suns, one of which orbits the central sun within the orbit of the planet Star and its retinue of five satellites, and another externally to the planet—thus making the cycle of its differently colored daylights very complicated, and night almost unknown.

The peculiarity of that arrangement is further enhanced, at least for English readers, by the author's decision to call the planet "Star"—which, of course, does not mean "star" in French, the equivalent term in that language being *étoile*. The uniqueness of the work is not limited to that central eccentricity; it is undoubtedly one of the strangest works of fiction every produced, in terms of its form as well as its subject-matter. Its first section is in blank verse, its second a sequence of brief chapters each only a few lines long—and they are merely parts of a prefatory frame describing how the "Starian books" that form the main body of the text came into the hands of the narrator, having apparently been transported to Earth aboard a meteorite, after spending an exceedingly long time drifting through interstellar space.

The relics are even more various, interleaving a history of Star, its sentient inhabitants and their migrations to its various satellites with poetry and fragments of plays illustrating the mentality of the people in question, and concluding with a "historical poem in prose" and three epilogues in verse. The reading of these documents prompts the narrator to undertake his own visionary journey there, in order to offer a visual description of the system to the reader, as well as an account of the exotic fauna of Star, including its two human species, before reproducing the documents themselves.

The history of the Starians commences with an account of the primitive religion of the Savelces, the fanatical adherents of which provoke wars, in stark contrast to placidity of their irreligious neighbors the Ponarbates, the more flexible "mythologists" the Tréliors, the domesticators of the second human race, and the sexless but extremely long-lived Nemsèdes, three of whom avoid falling victim to the "slow plague" that almost obliterates the three principal peoples, and thus assist in the development of the technologies that permit migration to the Starian satellites, where a sequence of separate but interrelated histories unfolds, mostly focused on Tassul, the nearest satellite of Star and the initial refuge of the fleeing Starians.

There had been previous literary ventures outside Earth's solar system, by Voltaire and more notably by Restif de La Bretonne, but nothing remotely similar to *Star*, which attempts to give a synoptic patchwork account of the entire history of an alternative human race inhabiting an alien system that does not appear to have been produced by the same simple cosmogonic process that had previously been assumed—generalizing from the single known example—to be universal. The account is necessarily a summary, but the inclusion of a few more intimate glimpses of Starian and Tassulian ways of life, filtered through works of art, supplies a kind of binocular vision that enables a greater understanding as well as a greater sympathy.

Although Théophile Gautier appears to have reviewed the book when it first came out, *Star* was virtually forgotten after Flammarion's brief mention until it was rediscovered by Raymond Queneau, whose complimentary remarks about it, made in 1949, brought it to the attention of Pierre Versins, and, via his *Encyclopédie*, to other historians of science fiction. Versins' subsequent research discovered that Defontenay was a physician who also published a treatise on tuberculosis, an early essay in "*calloplastie*" (cosmetic surgery) signed "Dr. Cid," and a collection of four plays, before dying prematurely of stomach cancer. Clearly, the work had no literary influence on anyone, but that does not alter the fact that it is a work of enormous imagination, now recognizable as a classic of its genre.

Aventures d'un aéronaute parisien dans les mondes inconnu, à travers les soleils, les étoiles, les planètes, leur satellites et les comètes (1856; tr. as *The Aventures of a Parisian Aeronaut in Unknown Worlds*) by Alfred Driou (1810-1880) was originally published in Limoges by Barbou Frères; it was reprinted by the same publisher in 1880, and again under the title *En Ballon, voyage fantastique dans les mondes inconnus* [In a Balloon; a Fantastic Voyage in Unknown Worlds] in 1888. The story does not, alas, live up to its subtitle; the Parisian aeronaut gets no further than the Moon—a paradisal world described in lyrical terms—before returning to Earth in the company with a party of lunarians

AVENTURES

D'UN

AÉRONAUTE PARISIEN

DANS LES MONDES INCONNUS

PAR A. DRIOU.

LIMOGES
ANCIENNE MAISON BARBOU FRÈRES
CHARLES BARBOU, IMPRIMEUR-LIBRAIRE
Avenue du Cruciﬁx.
—

to undertake a rapid tour of Earth, with extensive discussions of what they see there.

Driou was a very prolific author from the 1850s until his death, credited with well over a hundred titles under his own name and various pseudonyms. He was the nephew of Jean-Baptiste Driou (1761-1830), the curé of Montier-en-Der in the Haute-Marne, to whom *Aventures d'un aéronaute parisien* is dedicated. A history of *Les Moines de Der* [The Monks of Der] (1843) by R. A. Boullevaux states that a monument to Jean-Baptiste Driou was erected by his nephew "M. l'Abbé Alfred Driou," which implies that the delay in the commencement of the latter's literary career was occasioned by his being in holy orders beforehand. Although he apparently decided, a trifle belatedly, that he had no priestly vocation, he evidently remained devout, at least until *Aventures* was published.

Driou's first substantial literary work was *Études littéraires, ou Introduction à la littérature* [Literary Studies; or, An Introduction to Literature] (1843), a textbook designed for use in girls' schools, and many of his subsequent works, including *Aventures d'un aéronaute parisien*, were written with young readers in mind. He seems to have begun *Aventures d'un aéronaute parisien* intending to write a didactic interplanetary tour, but changed his mind. The book has an Earthbound companion volume, *L'Album merveilleux, épreuves d'un daguerreotype aérien, ou Scènes historiques, monuments, moeurs, coutumes et costumes de tous les temps et tous les âges* [The Marvelous Album, Prints of an Aerial Daguerrotype; or, Historical Scenes, Monuments, Mores, Customs and Costumes of All Times and All Ages], similarly issued by Barbou Frères in 1856, which was probably written first, and the decision might have been belatedly made to wind *Aventures* around it as a kind of advertisement. *L'Album merveilleux* was, however, the less successful of the two, being one of the few works by Driou that appears never to have been reprinted.

The *Aventures* marked something of a watershed in Driou's career; there was a distinct hiatus in his original publications between 1857 and 1860, when he might well have spent a good deal of time traveling; the pattern of his publications changed noticeably in 1861, when he began to churn out travel books in some quantity. In the midst of his hectic but mostly pedestrian production, *Aventures d'un aéronaute parisien* stands out as a markedly anomalous item, not merely for its imaginative extravagance but also for its keen interest in techno-logical progress. An interest in ongoing scientific discoveries was reflected in a handful of his later works, but for the most part, Driou set such matters aside—oddly, given that he might otherwise have become a significant pioneer in the 1860s boom in the popularization of science.

The novel is just as anomalous in the history of imaginative fiction as it is in the context of Driou's literary career, because of its awkward hybrid status, uneasily suspended between religious fantasy and travelogue—an effect of the author's manifest uncertainty as to what he was trying to do. Like many works of imaginative fiction, *Aventures* may have become an endeavor in pure explora-tion in the course of being written; although it poses as an exploration of the ma-terial world, it is actually nothing of the sort; what it really explores is its au-thor's subjective notion of the world, with far more emphasis on judgment than description.

An unusually large proportion of early English writers of speculative fic-tion were the sons of Protestant clergymen who had lapsed from the stern and narrow faith of their fathers and used their fiction to explore alternative world-views, in which the God of the scriptures was either absent or greatly transfig-ured. That pattern is not reproduced in the parallel history of the French *roman scientifique*, because lapsing Catholics tend to follow a different psychological trajectory, but if Driou's literary career was the sequel to a forsaken religious vocation, that would help greatly, not merely to explain how he came to write *Adventures d'un aéronaute parisien* but why it is such a deeply peculiar book. Although it refuses to give up on a restrictive form of devout Catholicism, the protagonist's adventures, which supposedly confirm that faith, actually subject it to enormous stress, often giving the text the appearance of protesting too much, and somewhat hypocritically. The author often seems to be aware—although he never permits his protagonist to realize the fact—that his quasi-Miltonic attempt to "justify the ways of God to men" does no credit at all to God or to stubborn belief.

The fact that the protagonist's partly-extraterrestrial balloon flight turns out to be a dream is no surprise—it could hardly have been otherwise, given the lit-erary conventions of the day—but it is more important to the story than a mere matter of supplying it with a bathetic pretext; it is the story's free indulgence in "dream logic" that both permits and encourages it to be so revealing about the author's interests, opinions and doubts.

Had *Aventures* not been a dream-story, not only could the protagonist not have set out to explore the Moon, but the author could not have confronted him-self with the practical problem of trying to imagine a material Paradise—a chal-lenge that no author has ever been able to meet successfully, but whose dimen-sions of failure are frequently interesting. The images of transport in Paradise by balloon and railways, which are central to Driou's description, might seem quaint to modern readers, but they are revealing. The telling point is not that

Driou was able to imagine a Paradise inhabited by enthusiastic aeronauts, but that he found himself no longer capable of imagining one that was not.

The Limoges publisher Barbou was also the publisher of all the works of Edmé Rousseau, including two small volumes *Le Songe, ou voyage aérien* [The Dream; or, Aerial Journey] (1864; but written 1859) and *Le Rêve, ou Promenades dans les espaces imaginaires* [The Dream; or, Excursions in Imaginary Spaces] (1876; but written 1860), which constitute an interplanetary fantasy considerable more peculiar than Driou's, although not quite as odd as *Star*; they are run together in translation as "The Aerial Journey." The Bibliothèque Nationale refuses to identify their author with the artist Edmé Rousseau (1815-1868), who was best known as a miniaturist, presumably because the publication dates of the editions it possesses of the works credited in its catalogue to "Edmé Rousseau, *romancier*" are mostly later than that of the artist's death, but their publication pattern is strongly suggestive of some posthumous publication, and the two individuals might well be one; if not, nothing at all is known about the writer—and, indeed, very little is known about the artist, except that he worked for a while in America, although his paintings are nowadays very collectible.

The episodic story told in the two texts fully justifies the original titles describing them as dreams; the visits to the various major and minor planets, especially the exceedingly strange "imaginary" planets featured in the latter half of the narrative, do indeed have something of the texture of dreams, and Freudians would have no difficulty finding material there for interpretation in accordance with Freud's theory of dreams as wish-fulfillments laden with sexual symbolism. Although the final section of the narrative clearly reflects the modifications to the city of Paris being carried out under the aegis of Baron Haussmann, the translation of a similar project to an exotic other world and its concentration on the erection of a colossal symbolic column make it far stranger than any of the other utopian fantasies prompted by that endeavor.

Rousseau's story is deliberately old-fashioned in using "*génies*" as a method of interplanetary travel, after the fashion of Madame Robert a hundred years earlier, in addition to the second layer of apology provided by dreaming, but that does help to license a certain flamboyance that is interesting, and perhaps admirable in itself. The narrative presents an image of the solar system far more bizarre and complex than any other work of interplanetary fiction, refusing to be fettered by the inconvenient details of astronomical observation.

The first part of the story begins conventionally, with a visit to an Earth-clone Moon that the dreamer find tedious, quickly asking the obliging genius Zadir to take him to Venus instead. There he soon becomes close to Queen Venusté, but that excites the jealousy of her courtiers, who immediately start plotting to get rid of him, and contrive to have him tried on a trumped-up charge of treason. Zadir gets him out of trouble easily, but he thinks it diplomatic to go on; finding Mercury too hot he passes swiftly on to Iris (one of the recently discovered minor planets, whose location within the solar system the author misconceives). There he becomes intimate with Queen Irisa, whom he begins to instruct in Earthly science and Christian religion. He saves her from drowning but cannot save her life a second time when she breaks her leg and contracts gangrene.

Passing on to the planet Flora, he begins to give its Queen lessons in drawing and painting, but all her ladies-in-waiting demand a similar education and the excessive pressure causes him to go on to Parthenope, where Queen Partha is equally welcoming, but whose subjects once again exhibit disturbing signs of jealousy. From there he goes to the Sun, but finds it even less comfortable than Mercury, and soon asks to goes home.

No sooner has the dreamer landed on Earth than he asks to make a second journey "beyond the fixed stars" to "imaginary space," but Zadir tells him that it is impractical, and suggests that he visits the imaginary spaces that are much nearer, within the solar system: island worlds shaped like demi-spheres that keep their flat surfaces permanently turned to the sun and oscillate pendulum-fashion instead of orbiting it. He agrees, and visits the Island of Reveries before going on to the Island of Tricks, where he finds a duplicate of Paris in which his dead relatives are still alive. He stays for longer on the Isle of Prodigies, where he is entertained by a lady he names Belladonna, and does indeed witness prodigies before her attentions become too inconvenient (he is a married man) and he asks to be transported to the isle of Marvels. He spends the rest of his vision there, in and around the city of Mirabilis, whose buildings float in mid-air and are thus subject to drastic displacement by storms—until he brings his engineering genius to bear and anchors them, after first rearranging them neatly and redesigning the entire city in a rational and elegant fashion, adding the *pièce-de-résistance* of a massive central column topped by his own sculpture of the king.

Compared with Edmé Rousseau's bizarre visionary fantasies, *Voyage à Vénus*, (1865; tr. as *Voyage to Venus*) is exceedingly moderate in its imagination, although the author is careful to leave the reader the option of interpreting the voyage in question as a dream. The novel is reckoned to have some historical significance in the ancestry of modern science fiction because it was the first to use a rocket to propel a hypothetical space-

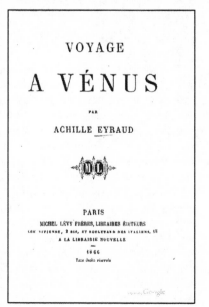

VOYAGE

A VÉNUS

PAR

ACHILLE EYRAUD

PARIS
MICHEL LÉVY FRÈRES, LIBRAIRES ÉDITEURS
RUE VIVIENNE, 2 BIS, ET BOULEVARD DES ITALIENS, 15
A LA LIBRAIRIE NOUVELLE

1866
Tous droits réservés

ship—unless one counts Cyrano's calculatedly absurd suggestion—and to include an argument explaining why that would be the only practicable means of doing so. Its author, Achille Eyraud (1821-1882) studied law in Paris before returning to his home town of Puy for a while to practice, and then returned to the capital, where he obtained a post in the Ministère de Justice, in which he spent the remainder of his career. He had a strong interest in literature and, if the evidence of *Voyage à Venus* can be trusted, he would far rather have made a success of his literary career than his profession, although his services to the government in the latter capacity did eventually win him the title of Chevalier de la Légion d'honneur.

Eyraud's first publication, in 1840, was a monograph, *Les Deux tombeaux du grand homme* [The Great Man's Two Graves] (the titular reference is to Napoleon), which was followed in 1842 by an account of the early life of Louis-Philippe, written for children. In 1843 he published a *complainte*, but his real love appears to have been the theater, especially the musical theater, and the bulk of his subsequent output consisted of comedies and operettas, several of which were initially signed Achille Lafont. He made a contribution to the libretto for Florimonde Hervé's opera *Scaramouche* (1854) and collaborated with Gustave Labottière on *Francastor* (1855), with music by Frédéric Barbier, but went on to more conspicuous success with the librettos for Joseph-Auguste Ancessy's operetta *Jean et Jeanne* (1855) and Louis Heffer's comic opera *Brin d'amour* [Love-Child] (1857). His dramatic career languished thereafter, however, and his record must have seemed painfully thin to him when he penned *Voyage à Venus*, at which point he appears to have regarded himself as a near-complete failure in his literary endeavors; he devotes an entire chapter of the novel to railing against the difficulties that hopeful authors experience in getting plays produced in Paris.

Although the account of the protagonist's construction of his spaceship and the description of his journey through space—sound while repeating the observations of balloonists, but increasingly bizarre once the ship leaves Earth's atmosphere—now seem to be its most interesting features, *Voyage à Venus* is essentially a utopian satire. Its primary purpose in describing the Earth-clone society of Venus is to allow the author to vent his spleen against all the aspects of contemporary Parisian life of which he disapproves—of which there are a great many. Indeed, it is difficult, on reading through his extensive catalogue of complaints, to judge Eyraud as anything but a deeply unhappy man, accomplished in finding fault with absolutely everything, although the preface to his posthumously collected comedies and operettas claims that he was a very likeable person with a great many friends.

The novel demonstrates that he was not without wit, occasionally deploying his talent for sarcasm to good effect within its pages, but for the most part, he seems therein to be rather morose, prey to bitterness whenever he contemplates the world in which he is condemned to live. There is a Voltairean element to his misanthropy, but it frequently seems merely curmudgeonly. Even so, there is something to admire in the wholeheartedness of his disenchantment, and although disappointments in literature and love must surely have been major factors in shaping his hostilities, his obvious intelligence and curiosity help to counterbalance his pessimism in the novel, as they presumably did in life.

The political standpoint of the utopia is oddly confused. In some ways, including his literary tastes, Eyraud is an arch-conservative, but in others he is distinctly radical. He disapproves strongly of both revolutions and monarchs—although he is careful never to mention Napoléon III—and is a relentless champion of social equality, but his notion of equality is peculiar, in that it assumes little change in the structure of society, but merely in its attitudes. He extends his championship of equality to a strident argumentative support for feminism, but his image of life on Venus provides no instances at all of women in influential positions, or of women behaving in a manner significantly different from their Earthly counterparts. He claims to be wholly in favor of plain speaking in matters of law, religion and education, and against the use of rhetoric in any context, but he does not speak plainly himself, according to his own stated criteria, and his method and style are saturated with rhetorical manipulation.

The principal model for *Voyage à Venus* was presumably Cyrano de Bergerac's interplanetary fantasies, which are cited in the text, but Eyraud also mentions Edgar Poe's account of the misadventure of Hans Pfaall, which he had presumably read in a version carrying the prefatory note appealing for more verisimilitude in accounts of interplanetary travel; that might be why he forsook the traditional means of literary space travel—which ranged from the frankly magical and blithely absurd to the highly improbable use of balloons—by not only designing a new kind of spaceship but supporting his design with an elaborate argument and describing its voyage in a fashion that made continual appeal to logic and science.

How seriously Eyraud took his own invention we cannot know; although we can now see several glaring flaws in his account, it is possible that he was unaware of them—but it is equally possible that he was only intent on papering over the fatal cracks in order to cultivate a purely superficial plausibility. The most obvious defect of his rocket is that he includes a secondary system for collecting and recycling the reaction mass once it has been expelled from the rocket, thus converting the vessel into a kind of perpetual motion machine. The machine is also vulnerable to the chief criticism that was made of the space gun featured in *De la terre à la lune*, which appeared in the same year; in order to cover the distance from Earth to Venus rapidly enough, Eyraud imagines an acceleration far too extreme to permit his space-traveler to survive.

There is no doubt that Eyraud's interest in science was genuine, although his opinion of contemporary scientists appears to have been low and he seems to have thought himself well-qualified to demolish their favored theories on the basis of his own common sense and argumentative flair. He is not in the least

273

intimidated in tackling some of the major scientific controversies of his day, including the argument about spontaneous generation that had been recently heated up by the Pasteur/Pouchet debate (the book version of Parville's *Un inhabitant de la planète Mars* appeared in the same year as *Voyage à Vénus*), and the ongoing controversy about the existence of the luminous ether; he seems to have had every confidence in his judgment on those matters, in spite of the fact that his citation of evidence is remarkably superficial.

Eyraud did enjoy some further success after the publication of *Voyage à Vénus* in his true literary vocation, but he was in his late fifties by the time that his one-act comedy *L'Éternelle comédie* [The Eternal Comedy] (1877) was produced at the Théâtre Français, swiftly followed by the two-act comedy *Mademoiselle Pivert* (1878). The last of his operettas to be performed before his death was *Le Rat de ville et le rat des champs* [The Town Rat and the Country Rat] (1881), with music by Germain Laurens. Although the relevant chapter of *Voyage à Venus* strongly recommends dying as the best career move a playwright can make, it does not appear to be the case that Eyraud achieved any more success as a result of his demise, although a commemorative collection of his comedies, librettos and monologues was issued in 1883, featuring twelve items, five of which had never been produced. He never published another novel, having had no way of knowing that *Voyage à Venus* would one day constitute his sole claim to a retrospective celebrity.

The same year that produced Eyraud's novel, alongside *De la terre à la lune*, also saw the publication of another novel, in addition to Rengade's, to take its direct inspiration from Jules Verne. One of the numerous writers associated with the Romantic Movement that P.-J. Hetzel had badgered into writing children's fiction for him was George Sand, and he showed Sand a copy of *Voyage au centre du monde*. As previously noted, she later claimed that it was her suggestion, made to Hetzel during that meeting, that prompted him to encourage Verne to write a novel exploring the world under the sea. Whether that was the case or not, she was certainly prompted to write her own account of an imaginary "journey to the center of the Earth," albeit in a manner far stranger and more quintessentially Romantic than Verne.

Laura: Voyage dans le cristal (1865; tr. as *Laura: A Journey into the Crystal*), begins with the protagonist being shown a geode—a rock incrusted with crystals—the interior of which he examines with a magnifying glass, seeing it as a kind of landscape. He then reads a manuscript whose writer relates that, when afflicted by visions as a child, he was taken under the wing of his Uncle Tungstenius, who hoped to cure him by guiding him into scientific studies of mineralogy.

When the author of the manuscript falls in love with his cousin Laura, however he has a hallucination in which he walks with her in a fantastic landscape like those glimpsed within geodes. After a two-year separation he meets her again, but finds that a marriage has been arranged for her. That precipitates a far longer and more detailed hallucination, in which the mysterious Nasias, who claims to be Laura's father, offers to break the arrangement and allow the narrator to marry Laura if he will accompany him to the Arctic in order to descend into the volcanic crater at the pole into the world of gems that occupies the heart of the planetary geode.

The journey is phantasmagorical—part of the descent is accomplished by riding on the backs of giant scarab beetles—but every time the narrator begins to doubt its reality, Nasias makes him look into a mesmeric gem that renews the lure of the crystalline landscapes inside the Earth: a world more alien, in its fashion, than anything yet imagined by Restif de La Bretonne, Charles Defontenay or Camille Flammarion in their excursions beyond the solar system.

Romantic writers always made elaborate use of environmental symbolism, extrapolating the "pathetic fallacy" by which the phenomena of nature are interpreted as if representative of emotions, and it could be argued that all fantastic landscapes are in some sense representations of the "inner space" of the mind as well as, or instead of, mere hypothetical geographies, but *Laura* is an unusual and highly exceptional attempt to do that consciously and extensively. Sand's deliberate and distinctive use of imagery borrowed from a slightly esoteric science in that quest added a new facet to the expanding pattern of *roman scientifique*.

Camille Flammarion's salon, which became increasingly popular in the latter half of the 1860s as his celebrity increased, must have been one of the strangest in Paris, not only playing host to his psychic experiments but also hosting lectures on scientific topics and, in one instance that as to prove highly significant for the future of *roman scientifique*, speculative technology. One of the salons with which Flammarion's had an overlapping membership was hosted by a fashionable physician, Antoine Cros, who had strong literary interests, and who numbered Paul Verlaine and François Coppée among his friends.

Antoine Cros had a younger brother, Charles, who was both a poet and a would-be inventor, interested in the attempt to develop color photography, and when Antoine brought him along to Flammarion's salon, the astronomer took the younger man under his wing. It was through the friends he made in Flammarion's salon that Charles Cros was introduced to the far more lavish *avant garde* salon hosted by Nina de Villard—described by the Goncourt brothers as "l'atelier de détraquage cérébral" [the mental breakdown factory]—where he met and befriended Villiers de l'Isle-Adam, and soon became Nina's "official lover."

In the meantime, however, Flammarion invited Cros to talk to his guests in May 1869 about one of his hypothetical inventions: a possible means of establishing interplanetary communication using light signals potentially visible from Mars. Cros submitted the text to the Académie des Science in July, and it was published in *Cosmos*, a periodical then edited by the popularizer of science and radical socialist Victor Meunier, in August, before being reissued as pamphlet, *Étude sur les moyens de communication avec les planètes* [A Study of Means of Communication with the Planets].

Charles Cros began publishing poetry the same year, and his involvement with Nina de Villard increasingly deflected him in that direction—as well as the absinthe drinking that eventually led to the breakdown of his health—but his proposal for interplanetary communication made a far greater impact on the imagination of his contemporaries than any of his literary endeavors, and it became a standard feature of French futuristic and interplanetary fantasies. The essay helped to focus the attention of those writers on Mars as a possible abode for life, also promoted enthusiastically by Flammarion, who produced numerous hypothetical images of the planet's surface featuring possible inhabitants and civilizations.

Cros dramatized the notion himself in a brief account of an interplanetary love-affair conducted by means of light signals, "Un drame interastral" (tr. as "An Interastral Drama"), but did not manage to publish it until 1872, after the upheavals of the war and the Commune, which caused Nina de Villard to flee Paris, and Antoine and Charles Cros to be denounced as Communards because they had given medical assistance to the wounded during the battle for control of the capital.

Fortunately, Antoine Cros' clientele was sufficiently influential to get him out of trouble, but the salon culture that had been so intriguingly interwoven before the war was shattered, and although its parts eventually re-formed, they did not connect up again in the same way; the flow of ideas in Parisian society, decisively interrupted by the siege of 1870 and its aftermath, never fully recovered the moment of communication they briefly contrived in 1869, which might, in kinder circumstances, have been more productive of hybrid imaginative endeavors.

In an alternative history—perhaps the one mapped out by Fernand Giraudeau in his account of the extended reign of Napoléon III and his succession by Napoléon IV—the literary seeds of the scientific imagination that had begun to germinate in the 1860s, some of them spectacularly, might have sustained their momentum more smoothly, but the devastating Prussian invasion appears to have applied an icy brake. It certainly did not kill the burgeoning genre—far from it—but it did have a marked effect on the form and coloration of its subsequent efflorescence.

CHAPTER FIVE: BETWEEN THE WARS, 1871-1914

1. The Commune, Anarchism and Euchronia

The Second Empire fell on 1 September 1870, when 120,000 French troops, accompanied by Napoléon III, engaged the invading Prussian army commanded by Helmut von Moltke, accompanied by Wilhelm I and Otto von Bismarck, at Sedan, and suffered a catastrophic defeat. Napoléon III surrendered the next day, leaving the French government headless. The Germans marched on Paris and besieged the city on 19 September. The siege lasted until 28 January 1871, after Bismarck, taking control of operations from Moltke, had ordered the bombardment of the city with large-caliber siege guns, which inflicted tremendous damage and prompted the surrender within three days.

In the turmoil that followed, radical socialists, with the support of the National Guard, wrested control of the city's administration from the Third Republic hastily proclaimed in the wake of the Emperor's capture, and established the Paris Commune on 18 March. The Third Republic and the Commune were thrust into a small-scale Civil War, which concluded, after *"la semaine sanglante"* [the Bloody Week], on 28 May with the crushing of the Commune and the National Guard by the regular Army. Fierce reprisals followed on the part of the re-established Third Republic, headed by Adolphe Thiers, which created political martyrs by the score, and cast an exceedingly long shadow over political debate and euchronian speculation in France for a generation and more.

The brutal suppression of the Commune, followed by the execution of its leaders and the mass deportation of a large number of its participants to the prison colony of New Caledonia, further radicalized the socialist opposition to the Third Republic, which gained a newly sturdy far-left wing, adopting a political philosophy of Anarchism further refined from the manifesto set out by Joseph Déjacque. Ironically, that fracturing of the opposition took some pressure off the ruling party; for the remainder of the century the radicals marching behind the red flag of Socialism expended as much effort disputing with those marching behind the black flag of Anarchism as they did with the Republic, which was deemed by both to be simply a new form of monarchism in disguise. Indeed, the Thiers government came very close to inviting the Comte de Paris, one of the pretenders to the French throne, to resume it; legend asserted that the negotiation only broke down because the would-be king refused to consent to the tricolor remaining the national flag.

Futuristic political speculation after 1871 was thus dominated by the idea of Anarchism, either as the ultimate ideal at which to aim, or as the ultimate bugbear to be avoided at all costs. In spite of its ultimate commitment to pacifism, as expressed in Déjacque's vision of the "Humanisphere," the creed was soon mythologized by its association with bombs, represented by its own extremists as "propaganda by action," on the grounds that it would be impossible to establish a new society without first destroying the existing one.

As a footnote to that sketch of the key events of 1870-71, it is worth calling attention, within the context of the evolution of *roman scientifique*, to the marginal role played in the siege by the Compagnie d'Aérostiers [Company of Balloon-Pilots], founded in order to help besieged Paris maintain communication with the world beyond the encamped Prussian troops by the flamboyant "Félix Nadar" (Gaspard Félix Tournachon, 1820-1910), and who was usually known simply as "Nadar."

Nadar had earlier founded a *Société d'encouragement de la navigation aérienne au moyen du plus lourd que l'air* [Society for the Encouragement of Aerial Navigation by Heavier-than-Air Means] in 1863, not long after his fascination with ballooning had assisted his friend Jules Verne to make a crucial literary breakthrough with the publication of *Cinq semaines en ballon*. Verne was the first secretary of the society, although the two men appear to have quarreled thereafter, and his association with it was brief. Nadar's active promotion was soon compromised when he commenced experiments with his own balloon, the aptly-named *Le Géant*, which crashed on its second flight in October 1863 and left him crippled, but that did not prevent him from helping to found the periodical *L'Aéronaute* in 1867.

Although the efforts made by the Compagnie d'Aérostiers' balloonists to assist in alleviating the siege of Paris had only limited success, they did provide useful data about enemy positions and carried a great many dispatches. One of the balloons, the *Armand-Barbès*—named after one of the revolutionaries of 1848 who had gone into exile after the *coup-d'état* that founded the Second Empire—carried the Minister of the Interior, Léon Gambetta, from the besieged city to Tours in order that he might help to organize resistance to the invading Prussians.

Like Barbès before him, Gambetta was a far-left Republican, and one of the other two balloons forming Nadar's initial fleet (which eventually expended to sixty-six) was named the *Louis-Blanc* after another similarly-exiled hero of the 1848 Revolution, leaving little doubt that the aeronauts had set out to defend the Paris of the embryonic Commune, not Napoléon III's corrupt and collapsing empire. The third member of the initial trio was the *George-Sand*, named after one of the key figures of the French Romantic Movement, whose Verne-inspired fantasy *Laura* was described in the previous chapter.

A second footnote worth inclusion here is the fate of Tony Moilin, the author of *Paris en l'an 2000*, published by the author shortly before the fall of the Empire, in defiance of the censors. In August 1870, as the Prussians invaded, Moilin was charged—without any foundation in fact—with involvement in a plot to assassinate Napoléon III, and sentenced to prison for five years. He was, however, released during the Prussians' siege of Paris, and enlisted in the National Guard as a surgeon-major, presumably under compulsion.

When the Commune subsequently took control of Paris, Moilin refused to join it, but he did agree to accept the position of Maire of the 6th arrondissement when the Communards attempted to organize an Administration for the city. He was taken prisoner by the army of the Third Republic in May 1871 when the Commune fell, rapidly court-martialed, ostensibly for having accepted the administrative post, condemned as "a socialist of the most dangerous kind," and summarily executed by firing-squad, thus securing the unsuccessful would-be censors of his work the vengeance that they doubtless desired.

The first eutopian works to appear when the publishing industry got back into gear again following the re-establishment of the Republic had presumably been written before the war but had not been able to find a publisher then. *Voyage de Théodose à l'île d'Utopie* (1872; tr. as "A Voyage to the Isle of Utopia") and *Le Monde renversé* (1872; tr. as "The World Turned Upside Down") by Léonie Rouzade (1839-1916), were the third and fourth of five items issued by their publisher in rapid succession, following *Connais-toi toi-même?* [Do you Know Yourself?] (1871) and *Le Roi Johanne* [King Johanne] (1872), and being followed in their turn by *Ci et çà, çà et là* [This and That; Here and There] (1872).

The first and last of those items were non-fictional pamphlets, more akin to meditations than essays, whereas the second, which had a considerably lower page-count than the two novellas that succeeded it, was a visionary fantasy reflecting the same socialist and feminist concerns as its successors, in a similarly oblique fashion. *Voyage de Théodose à l'île d'Utopie* is dated September 1872 at the end, but the last chapter of the novel is radically different from the remainder, and the chapter in question was probably added at that date to a story that had been written some time before. The epilogue of *Le Monde renversé* suggests strongly that the author had experimented with more earnest utopian fictions before developing the more adventurous rhetorical strategies applied tentatively in *Voyage de Théodose à l'île d'Utopie* and far more wholeheartedly in the second novella—in which the author's scathing sarcasm and righteous wrath are given much freer rein—but that her earlier efforts had been unappreciated.

The author was born Louise-Léonie Camusat, the daughter of a Parisian watch-maker; she liked to boast that she was the grand-daughter of a delegate to the 1789 Estates-General. She apparently worked as an embroideress before marrying Auguste Rouzade, the municipal accountant of the wealthy suburb of Meudon, at the age of twenty-one. Léonie Rouzade's activism increased markedly after her attendance at the International Congress on Women's Rights held in Paris in 1878. In 1880 she was a co-founder, with Eugénie Pierre (later Potonié-Pierre) and the ex-Communard Marcelle Tinayre, of the *Union des femmes* [Women's Union], a group designed to obtain representation for women in the *Parti ouvrier* [Workers' Party] and she was one of the authors of its manifesto. In 1881 she stood as a socialist candidate for the Municipal Council in Paris—the first woman to do so. Contemporary reportage of her political activism suggests that she was an outspoken and controversial figure who annoyed many of her fellow feminists almost as much as the male socialists she continually castigated for their lack of concern regarding the oppression of women. She was one of the most radical of the Parisian feminists of the day, notably in her advocacy of the collectivization of motherhood.

Voyage de Théodose à l'île d'Utopie is a depiction of a relatively orthodox socialist utopia in much the same spirit as Cabet's *Voyage en Icarie*, but it is considerably enlivened by employing a bourgeois Parisian snob as its viewpoint character, following his shipwreck on the island in question, leading to much ironic misunderstanding—which persists stubbornly as the narrative follows him home, where he gradually realizes that his ideas are obsolete. *Le Monde renversé*, on the other hand, is highly exceptional, and remains outstanding within the canon of feminist fiction; it is not only the earliest lengthy fantasy of sex-role reversal ever penned, but is more striking than almost all of those that came after it, in terms of its flamboyant imagination of the operation of that reversal and its description of its possible consequences. It is a grandiose Voltairean *conte philosophique*, but it takes its satire to a comic extreme that is on the edge of absurdism, and can now be seen as a work that was far ahead of its time in its method as well as its angry intent.

The novella presents the history of the divine Célestine Chopin, the ultimate *femme fatale*, the most beautiful daughter of a family of Montmartrean whores, who learns all the arts of the only power that women retain in a masculinist society—the power of sex-appeal—and contrives to cajole and bribe her way to a temporary sultanate. Once in power, she tells her subjects that, as they have never sought to change their laws, they are obviously very content with them, so that she will retain them all integrally—except that she will invert the terms "woman" and "man," so that women will henceforth have all the powers over men than men previously had over women.

The resultant upside-down society cannot endure, of course, if only because Célestine's only reason for doing anything is to stave off the deadly effects of ennui, and nothing amuses her for long, but while it lasts, its effects are spectacular and hilarious. The story must have seemed utterly bizarre to anyone who read it in 1872, and not at all the sort of book that a respectable married woman ought to write, but it became publishable at that particular moment in time, and it does shine a ray of light into the dark realm of the works that had found it impossible to achieve publication under the Second Empire.

1873 can only be presumed as the original publication date of "L'Amour en mille ans d'ici" (tr. as Love a Thousand Years Hence") by "A. Vémar" (Gustave Marx) by means of its internal references, although that fits in with the relative short career of its author, the version presently accessible being derived from a reprint periodical of 1889. The misleadingly-titled story is a satire of the glut of utopian accounts of future Paris, perhaps penned with both "Jacques Fabien" and Victor Hugo in mind, as well as such earlier contributors to the sub-genre as Gautier and Méry.

As is normal with satires, the exaggeration of Vémar's goes beyond the standard routine of possibilities featured in the earnest utopias of the period, although the longest section of the future history filled in by the dreaming protagonist's guide to future Paris, dealing with the invention of artificial wings in a fashion similar to Restif's Victorin is relatively sober. That chapter contrasts sharply with the charmingly absurd consequent account of the exploration of the solar system by winged travelers unreeling long metal cables behind them, in order that all the planets—except, for some unstated reason, Mars—can enter into communication with one another by telegraphy.

A similar ebullience and calculated absurdism can be found in *La Commune en l'an 2073: au bout du fossé!* (1874 tr. as "All the Way: The Commune in 2073"), signed "R. de Maricourt," one of the most striking direct responses to the experiences of 1871. The signature was one of the versions of his name employed by Comte René du Mesnil de Maricourt (1829-1893), who had established a reputation before the war with the historical novels *Lucie, épisode de l'histoire* [Lucie, an Episode of History] (1860) and *Marcien, ou le magicien d'Antioche* [Marcien; or, The Magician of Antioch] (1866) and had resumed publication thereafter with *Une femme à bord* [A Woman on Board] (1873), a contemporary romance set in Brittany and dedicated to Flaubert. In later life Maricourt acquired a certain reputation as a scholar of the occult, although *Souvenirs d'un magnétiseur* [Memoirs of a Mesmerist] (1884) was a theoretical essay rather than a memoir, and he was actually more interested in archeology, publishing a good deal of serious non-fiction in that field.

The story begins with the protagonist, disgusted with present society, deciding to put himself to sleep for two hundred years in the hope of finding a better world, ordering his children to wall up the room in which he is confined. Instead, when he wakes, he finds a grotesquely overpopulated Paris somewhat reminiscent of Giraudeau's *La Cité nouvelle*, in which the streets have been reduced to mere gutters because the houses are so densely packed, and respirable air has to be pumped in—at a price. All travel is necessarily by aerostat.

There is perfect equality between citizens, who now have numbers instead of surnames, but liberty in love has been abolished because it led to chaos, and the duties of "repopulation" are now strictly regulated, couplings being organized by lottery and individuals possessed of beauty being artificially handicapped to level the field of attractiveness. All social behavior is monitored by censors who can impose fines for misdemeanor and organize disappearances for more serious offenses. War has become impractical because of the awesome destructive force of electrical weaponry, and the European Pact regulates relations between the half-dozen "duchies" of the former France and similar mini-states in most of the other former nations. Domestic politics are, however, a chaos of rival industrial factions, and the fact that the President is an automaton does not save him from assassination—or prevent his maker submitting a bill for damages.

Although the author scrupulously acknowledges the fact that he borrowed one of the story's key images from a skit in the English *Cornhill Magazine*, his elaborate development of what was simply a passing mention in the *Cornhill* piece, of the extremes to which a society devoted to the principle of equality might have to go, is amusingly scathing, and more polished than Giraudeau's similar assault. Maricourt's novella is similarly more extreme in its "dystopianism" than Souvestre's *Le Monde tel qu'il sera*, and some of its imagery anticipates that of such earnest twentieth-century dystopias as George Orwell's *Nineteen Eighty-Four*, testifying eloquently to the strength of feeling that the aftermath of a war can leave behind.

Le Monde dans deux mille ans (1878; tr. as *The World in Two Thousand Years*), signed "Georges Pellerin" is an orthodox euchronian tract, although its use of hypnotism as a means of prompting access to the future places a heavy emphasis on the "double vision" of its mesmerized protagonist, and the fictional frame allows the resultant comparisons of past and future to be further developed in dialogue and interrogation.

Although *Le Monde dans deux mille ans* is a work of "scientific fiction" in the purest sense, the science in which its speculations are developed is economics, rarely used as a basis for fiction published under that label, in spite of the Voltairean precedent provided by *L'Homme aux quarante écus*, partly because its reputation as "the dismal science" is not entirely unjustified, at least in terms of its potential as a source of action, adventure and melodrama.

Economics is, however, not merely a descriptive science but a prescriptive one, not in the sense that it provides vulgar prophesies, but in the sense that it attempts to map out strategies of individual and political action by means of which certain particular goals might be efficiently attained. It is a frustrating science because, as we know from the bitter experience of hundreds of years of economic history, such plans usually go awry, sometimes because the actions in question have unintended consequences that were unanticipated, but mostly because individual economic interests are inevitably in conflict, and whatever plans are made, one can be certain that active attempts will be made to exploit, pervert and subvert them. As its analyses become more sophisticated, economic theory gives further scope to such perversion and subversion, thus continually undermining itself.

The economic theory on which *Le Monde dans deux mille ans* is based is now obsolete, but its obsolescence pertains not so much to its notions of cause and effect as its specification of fundamental objectives. Economics as currently taught and practiced is basically the science of making a profit; but in the future described in *Le Monde dans deux mille ans*, the primary objective of economic policy is the prevention of the accumulation of money in the hands of relatively few individuals or institutions. While making money remains an objective, it is subsidiary to the determination to redistribute it in such a way as give every member of society the opportunity to earn a living free of hardship and strife.

Unlike many euchronian writers, the author of *Le Monde dans deux mille ans* is not primarily concerned with designing an "ideal society"—a notion that he considers to be essentially relative—and is not foolish enough to believe that, if ever such a plan were agreed, such a society could simply be legislated into existence at a stroke. His concern is not so much with the goal as the possible route, the mapping out of a process of economically-guided social evolution. Whether the policy that the author maps out would fulfill that purpose remains a matter of opinion, as the Third Republic never tried it, and nor has anyone else, but in terms of its narrative strategy the novel deserves some credit for innovation and originality.

The developing tension between eutopian and dystopian images of hypothetical societies, and its association with variant uses of similar technologies was subjected to an interesting literary thought-experiment in a manuscript entitled *L'Héritage de Langevol* submitted to Jules Hetzel on behalf of a former Communard who had escaped from New Caledonia and only recently returned to France, named Paschal Grousset. Grousset had published two brief political tracts in 1869, *Le 26 octobre* [The Twenty-Sixth of October] and *La Rêve d'un irreconcilable* [The Dream of an Irreconcilable], the second of which included a hypothetical description of the establishment of a Paris Commune, albeit with a membership very different from the one that actually came into being. The new manuscript, however, reflected his ambition to take up a career as a professional writer.

Hetzel asked Jules Verne to redevelop the novel—perhaps oddly, given that Verne had been horrified by what he had seen of the Commune's rule when he visited Paris in 1871—and he subsequently published it under Verne's name, although it is not at all the kind of novel that he had previously encouraged Verne to write. By way of compensation, he did go on to publish numerous books by Grousset, under the pseudonym of André Laurie, and two further novels rewritten by Verne under Verne's name. It is arguable, however, that Grousset never published anything else as interesting as *Les Cinq cents millions de la Bégum* (1879; tr. as *The Begum's Millions*) and the novels he wrote as André Laurie in the Vernian mold, alongside other materials, which will be discussed in a subsequent section, seem a trifle uncomfortable in their careful avoidance of political issues.

The published version of the story describes what happens when two very different men each inherit a half-share in a vast fortune accumulated by a French adventurer in India. The French physician Sarrasin elects to build the new city of Franceville to his own eutopian model, while the German scientist Schultze, convinced of the superiority of his own race over his rivals decides to incarnate his own ideals of technological progress in the city of Stahlstadt, effectively an immense armaments factory, both of the cities being located in the American north-west. The plot takes up the story five years later, when a friend of Sarrasin's son obtains work in Stahlstadt under a pseudonym and discovers that Schultze is building a huge cannon with the specific intention of destroying Franceville. He is caught spying and sentenced to death, but contrives to escape to carry the warning to Franceville.

The story is, to some extent, an allegory of the Franco-Prussian conflict and its climax is a reaction to Bismarck's bombardment of Paris, but it is also a study of the manner in which technology can be used either for life-enhancing or life-despoiling purposes, depending on the economic and political motivations of its users, and tacitly poses the question of whether the present world is heading in the direction of a society akin to Franceville, or one more akin to Stahlstadt. The textual description of life in the "City of Steel" pays particular attention to the extreme regulation of time and effort within the vast factory-complex and its associated mines, and also to the dire effects of environmental pollution: two issues that were to become increasingly important in dystopian imagery.

In Stahlstadt, advanced technology enables its owners to enjoy the leisure denied to the workers and its pollution is held at bay for their benefit; the centre of the city is a privileged enclave centered on a beautiful tropical park, populated with plants and animals transplanted from distant parts of the globe. Perhaps the most obvious impact of late-nineteenth-century reality on literary imagery of this sort was the lesson of social division: the notion that bad places would be for the abandonment of the poor, while the rich and privileged would build exclusive eutopian microcosms for themselves. In late-nineteenth-century naturalistic and speculative fiction alike, therefore, eutopia and dystopia can sit side by side, as two sides of the same coin, the eutopia of the few being built at the expense of the dystopia of the many.

The immiseration that takes place in such conventional dystopian locations as Stahlstadt is, to a large extent, a straightforward representation of the actuality of nineteenth-century slum life; it is a matter of living in squalid conditions in a spoiled environment with barely enough to eat, to which the excessive regulation of the workers' tasks and shift-patterns, in consequence of which they become mechanized themselves, adds an extra turn of the screw. *Les Cinq cents millions de la Bégum* provides a striking depiction of that kind of immiseration, which was somewhat ahead of its time; it must have seemed an anomaly to Verne's readers, although it doubtless sold far better with Verne's name on it than it could ever have done with Grousset's signature.

Anxieties about the darker side of rapid technological progress, represented by fears of excessive mechanization, were fed by news from America, where Thomas Edison was in the process of becoming a national hero after such loudly-publicized feats of innovation as patenting the phonograph in 1877—causing some heartache in France, where Charles Cros had invented a similar device, but had not been able to develop it rapidly enough to claim the credit. The celebration of Edison is parodied in "Josuah Electricmann" (1882; tr. as "Josuah Electricmann") by Ernest d'Hervilly, in which the inventor of photoplumographer, the colorofix, the vultograph and many other useful devices is so busy working on his household galvanomaster—designed to "replace the father of a family"—that he hardly has time to get married, even with the aid of the scribograph in identifying and locating an ideal mate and the telegraphic operation of the ceremony; a meeting between the spouses is, alas, out of the question because he has not yet completed his aeroveloce, and international travel still requires days rather than hours, but he hopes to compensate by inventing an amouradistanceophone as soon as he has a minute to spare.

Similar ideas regarding the accelerating pace of invention and the consequent transformations of the pattern of social life that it would enable or compel generated one of the most striking images found in the fiction of the period, in the second part of **Ignis** (tr. as *Ignis: the Central Fire*), a novel first published anonymously, in 1883. Three more editions followed, the third and fourth, issued in 1884, bearing the signature "Le Cte Didier de Chousy" and boasting that the book was an "ouvrage couronné par l'Académie française," although there is no independent evidence of any such accolade.

The identity of the "Comte de Chousy" remains something of a mystery, the only surviving evidence of the existence of such an individual being two letters bearing that signature, one sent to Charles Cros and the other to Villiers de l'Isle-Adam thanking him for *L'Ève future* (1887), of which Villiers had presumably sent him a complimentary copy; if so, it presumably signifies that Villiers had read *Ignis* and was aware of its relationship to his own novel—both texts feature humanoid machines. The one thing that seems certain regarding the author of *Ignis* was that he was an applied scientist whose literary activity was a sideline, intent on using satirical narrative as an instrument for the dramatization and discussion of scientific ideas. *Ignis'* publisher, Berger-Levrault et Cie, was a specialist in scientific and military texts, and *Ignis* was something of a departure from its normal policy, although its success seems to have inspired them to one further venture of a kindred sort, which will be discussed in another section.

The first target to receive a whiff of satirical grapeshot in *Ignis* is not science *per se* but the capitalistic financing of large-scale technological projects. The novel begins with the launch of the Central Fire Company, dedicated to digging a deep shaft to tap the energy of the Earth's hot core, and is an evident echo of the hullabaloo occasioned by the Suez Canal Company in the 1860s. The target for which the author reserved his heavy ammunition, however, was the controversy raised by mid-nineteenth-century advances in geology and paleontology, which had already prompted major rows between devout men and freethinkers as to the age of the Earth and the duration of its human occupancy. The author of *Ignis* throws himself into the controversy with a fine fervor, and the fact that he lined up on what was subsequently established as the wrong side should not be allowed to detract from the significance of his work as a precursor of modern speculative fiction.

Although the second of those issues is clearly a matter dear to the author's heart, which he settles in startling fashion by having the diggers of his great pit excavate the remains of the garden of Eden—to the delight of Cain, who is still alive and laboring under his curse—it is the final phase of the novel that seemed the most stirring at the time and still seems so now. The energy derived from the Central Fire is used to build the city of Industria, a huge eutopian complex replete with all the splendor that metal and glass can provide: an ultimate vision of the futuristic city, where all work is done and all human needs are supplied by a vast population of "atmophytes"—functionally-designed automata of every shape and size—with the aid of devices that might have come straight out of Josuah Electricmann's workshop, including the "*téléchromophotophonotétroscope*." The government of the city, in which every citizen is at least a millionaire, is as liberal as can possibly be contrived, characterized as "*pantopantarchique*": the role of everyone over everything.

Although the exaggeration of the city of Industria is every bit as grotesque as the world of Josuah Electricmann, and its narrative function is similarly satirical, there is an intensity about it that goes far beyond the casual flippancy of Hervilly's story. The description of the various atmophytes is detailed and graphic—and so is the melodramatic conclusion, in which the mechanical slaves demand their own share in the pantopantarchy, and the independence to serve themselves rather than humans; the rebel machines eventually corner the novel's main characters in the most pretentious of all their palaces, which the giant steam hammers among them set about assaulting with a steely determination.

There is a certain beguiling symmetry in the fact that *Ignis* was published almost simultaneously with a work that adapted some of the ideas associated with the city of Industria, albeit much more modestly, to an image of the future produced very carefully by the caricaturist who was to become one of the leading French writers of *roman scientifique*, **Albert Robida** (1848-1926). He had moved on from the extravagant Vernian pastiches that will be described in some detail in the next section to produce the first of his masterpieces, in an extraordinarily extended but conspicuously mild satirical account of *Le Vingtième siècle* (1883; tr. as *The Twentieth Century*).

The protagonist of the novel is Hélène Colobry, the niece of a rich man trying to find a vocation by sampling the various professions open to her in the world of 1952, which is dominated by ubiquitous electrical power and machinery, and new means of transport, including private rapid aerostats and trains dispatched at high speed through flexible tubes by compressed air. Much is made, in particular, of the téléphonoscope, imagined primarily as an extrapolation of the telephone rather than as an anticipation of broadcast television, but which has inevitably taken on some of the functions of the latter, as well as some of the extra features spelled out in the name of Chousy's téléchromophotophonotétroscope, becoming an important news medium, facilitating the live transmission of significant events, and also an important medium of commerce, permitting people to shop from the comfort of their own apartments.

The heroine tries her hand at legal practice, journalism, politics and finance, following much the same agenda as Pierre Véron's Monsieur Personne, with a similar lack of luck, sometimes for the same reasons—like Monsieur Personne, she finds that journalism is an exceedingly dangerous career because of the number of duels one has to fight, but she is more fortunate than he was in finding the world of finance not quite as utterly corrupt, and when she goes in search of love she does not run into the same insurmountable barriers that doomed his quest. Her exploration of the society of 1952 is further enhanced for the reader by the changes induced by greater sexual equality, some of which are exploited for conventional sexist comedy, but which nevertheless display, taken as a whole, a significant shift in attitude of which many euchronian writers seemed to be quite incapable, much to the annoyance of progressive feminists like Léonie Rouzade.

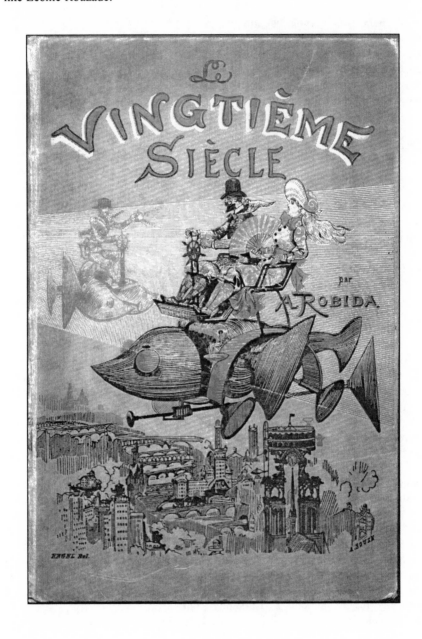

The satirical tone of *Le Vingtième siècle* is thoroughly amicable; the novel might not qualify as a euchronia, but it is certainly not a dystopia. Indeed, it comes as close as any futuristic fantasy written prior to 1883 to qualifying as a *roman futuriste* in Félix Bodin's sense; it is neither *amélioriste* nor *péjoriste*, but simply interested in how the fabric of everyday existence in the twentieth century might be woven by courtesy of its new machinery. On the other hand, it is not a straightforward satirical transfiguration of the world of 1882, when it was presumably begun and mostly written (the gap between that date and 1952 being equivalent to the standard calculation of a human lifespan), but a genuinely extrapolative study, injecting a good deal of thought into its humor.

Robida's tone is humorous but his attempts to anticipate the kind of social changes that might be provoked by certain kinds of new technologies are earnest. He assumes the continuation and expansion of the existing capitalist system—which permits the occasional contrived revolution by way of a safety-valve to let off a little resentful steam—rather than putting forward any scheme for euchronian reform, but also takes an interest in manner in which that expansion might be evolutionary. It is humorous primarily because Robida was a professional humorist, and that was the vein in which he worked, but he takes full advantage of the fact that humor provides a narrative energy that reduces the need to try to maintain reader interest with melodramatic incident. Many future writers of *roman scientifique* were to exploit the same facility, using ironic humor to spice speculative visions that might otherwise have seemed too uneventful to keep readers hooked.

Despite what Anatole France was subsequently to say about H. G Wells being the only writer who had ever approached the future as an explorer, without making up his mind in advance what he was going to find there and how he ought to judge it, Robida gives every appearance of having done that in *Le Vingtième siècle*—all the more so as what he did find there gradually altered his own perception and formulated the judgments he had largely withheld in this pioneering exercise. He was not a dystopian pessimist when he wrote the book, but he certainly moved closer to that outlook as he followed his train of thought further, partly because of what he found with the aid of his own fertile imagination, and partly because the pressure of external events seemed to him to have left him no choice.

A more conventional euchronia is *Dans mille ans* (tr. as *In a Thousand Years*), which was published in a handsome illustrated edition signed E. Calvet in 1884, having been serialized the previous year in the now-venerable *Musée des Familles*, where the author's name was given in full as Émile Calvet. That seems to be the sum of what is known of the author, who is highly unlikely, on chronological grounds, to have been responsible for any of the handful of other works signed "E. Calvet" or "Émile Calvet" listed in the catalogue of the Bibliothèque Nationale. Anything deduced about the author from the contents of the novel remains conjectural, but the evidence suggests that he was a Parisian schoolmaster specializing in the teaching of the physical sciences.

The story begins with the physicist J. B. Terrier being summoned by his friend Dr. Antius, who wants to make him party to a discovery he has just made. The eccentric in question also summons his frivolous nephew Gédéon, who completes a trio not unlike the one favored by Jules Verne as participants in exploratory adventures, albeit one unbalanced by the presence of two scientists at the expense of a commonsensical practical man. The discovery consists of a plant-derived drug that permits the user to enjoy the privilege of "ubiquity": being in two places at once; and, as it turns out, two times at once. When they experiment with the drug, they project their "alternative selves" a thousand years into the future, and set forth to explore a future Paris set firmly in the tradition established by Gautier and carried forward by Méry and Berthoud.

The time travelers of **Dans mille ans** soon make the useful acquaintance of Monsieur Herber, the director of a school, who becomes their guide and Mentor. Conveniently, as it eventually turns out, his school not only has its own museum but is located within easy walking distance of a larger one, and also of the Necrological Palace where the genealogical records of the city are kept. Herber introduces them to all the domestic marvels of the new world's kitchens as well as the external developments of communication and transport systems, including the "atmospheric railway." Almost nothing survives of the Paris of their own day except the towers of Notre-Dame, and their acquaintance with the ancient city becomes intensely interesting to antiquarians; ironically, it is Gédéon's familiarity with the mores of fashionable society rather than the scientists' specialized knowledge that proves especially fascinating to the denizens of Paris a thousand years hence.

In general, Calvet seems to agree wholeheartedly with the late-eighteenth-century philosophers of progress that social and technological progress go hand in hand and he assumes that if the technological problems restricting the adequate supply of human needs can be solved, then political problems of distribution and social order will simply sort themselves out, through the medium of efficient universal education. That view probably seemed a trifle naïve in 1883, but the entirely-justified skepticism casting suspicion on it cannot detract from the interest that Calvet's work retains, because it provides an unusually clear and definite example of that particular train of thought, developed with as much conscience as determination. Seen from the viewpoint of the early twenty-first century, Calvet's text is a remarkable combination of innocence and ingenuity, unparalleled at the time and perhaps since.

290

It is important to remember, in evaluating such texts as Robida's *Le Vingtième siècle* and Calvet's *Dans mille ans* from today's standpoint, how closely they followed on the heels of the key inventions that they extrapolate. The telephone had been patented in 1876, the phonograph in 1877 and Joseph Swan's electric incandescent lamp—the first genuinely practical one—in 1880. The first electric power network, producing 110 volts of direct current, had been developed in 1882 to supply a mere 59 clients. The steam-turbine that would provide the basis for efficient electric power generation had not yet been invented. The problem of steering aerostats was still painfully unsolved, in spite of long effort, as was the problem of heavier-than-air flight. Heinrich Hertz had not yet demonstrated the existence of the electromagnetic waves that would eventually give birth to wireless telegraphy, and it would have been astonishing had any such notion been on Robida's or Calvet's intellectual radar.

Given that timetable, Calvet's notion of a world transformed by prolifically-distributed electric power and aerial transportation is as remarkable as Robida's. His tongue-in-cheek representation of the widespread uses of gold and platinum have little technological basis, but his notion of the potential utility of aluminum—which was still more expensive than gold and platinum when a bar was exhibited as "the new precious metal" at the Paris Exposition of 1855—proved much more prescient, although he could not have anticipated that significant new methods of production would make it available for widespread industrial use in the late 1880s. Although his slightly awestruck descriptions of an electric kettle and an electric grill with a rear reflector might seem quaint to readers perfectly familiar with such devices, whose actual design eventually followed exactly the same logic as his extrapolations, envisioning them really was a daring imaginative venture on his part, and exhibits an attention to utilitarian detail rare among constructors of eutopias—and not, alas, reflected in other aspects of Calvet's somewhat tunnel-visioned description of life in the future.

The fact that Calvet avoids any direct discussion of politically controversial issues, and makes no mention whatsoever of organized religion—although his characters occasionally take the Lord's name in vain—is presumably the result of rigorous self-censorship, required to obtain serialization in a self-declared "family magazine." In the early 1880s the *Musée des Familles* had a long-running regular feature entitled *Science en famille* [Science in the Home] and frequently published articles glorifying the exploits of explorers in Africa—a part of the world to which Calvet' story pays particular attention—so his story seems to be very closely adapted to the magazine's editorial policies. That selective pattern of omission undoubtedly weakens the novel as an all-encompassing euchronian schema, but it nevertheless provides, especially in juxtaposition with *Le Vingtième siècle*, a useful insight into the horizons of the futuristic imagination at the moment of their production.

Because Robida's image of *Le Vingtième siècle* is presented as a lengthy novel, it is relatively staid, and its humor leisurely in its development. A complete stylistic contrast is found in the collection *Fantasmagories: Histoires rapides* [Phantasmagorias: Fast-paced stories] (1887), which includes half a dozen futuristic items carrying forward the tradition of humorous speculative fiction begun by Pierre Véron. The collection appeared under the by-line Jean Rameau, the pseudonym of Laurent Labaigt (1858-1942), which had previously appeared on a volume of *Poèmes fantastiques* (1883) and was subsequently to appear on many other novels, poems and short stories.

The relevant stories adopt a breezily irreverent attitude to future possibilities, featuring such standard motifs as electric guns and automata substituting for real individuals as well as novelties like energy-capturing mechanisms that permit no human action to go entirely to waste. One particularly striking image offers a vision of a future Paris in which people have become so accustomed to environmental pollution that they have become dependent on it, and most of the population has been forced to take up residence in the sewers. The works are primarily remarkable, however, because of their frenetic minimalistic style, which aspires to a certain futurism in itself, although it was never likely to catch on in a world where writers get paid by the word.

A tantalizingly brief glimpse of an Anarchist eutopia is supplied in *Le Nouveau monde* (1888) by **Louise Michel** (1830-1905), who had become by then the most notorious of all the surviving Communards who had returned from exile in New Caledonia when they were granted amnesty. The glimpse is all the more tantalizing because *Le Nouveau monde* itself is a patchwork of incomplete stories hastily stitched together, even messier in its unsatisfactory improvisation than *Les Posthumes*, and because the novel had been previously envisaged as part of a much larger project that would have given a much more elaborate representation of the Anarchist dream.

Louise Michel had spent her childhood in the Château de Vroncourt in the Haut-Marne, where her mother was a servant, having been fathered either by the châtelain or his scion. She was brought up there by the châtelain's family, to whom she was invited to refer as her "grandparents," and given a liberal education, in the course of which she took considerable delight in the works of Jean-Jacques Rousseau and Voltaire; as a bastard and, in terms of social class, a "half-breed," she was well-primed for hostility to the prevailing social order, and even for a certain resentful truculence.

In 1852 she obtained a certificate that qualified her to work as a schoolteacher, but she was unable to obtain employment in state-approved schools because she refused to recognize Napoléon III as head of state following his *coup d'état* in the previous year. In 1856 she went to Paris, where she worked in a private boarding-school. She wrote a good deal, including poetry, short stories and legendary tales; she corresponded with the exiled Victor Hugo, and was considerably influenced by his ideas. She contributed to radical periodicals, but her active political involvements in the 1860s were moderate, and she would surely have remained an obscure schoolteacher and unsuccessful writer indefinitely had not circumstances in Paris changed dramatically in 1870.

Her initial involvement in the upheaval was patriotic rather than revolutionary; she did what she could to support the cause of National Defense during the siege, running a canteen and working in field hospitals as well as taking an active role in the local citizens' "vigilance committee." As president of that committee she met various people who were later to become important political figures, including Georges Clemenceau, then Maire of Montmartre, and Théophile Ferré, a member of the National Guard who became one of the prime movers of the Commune. Ferré was sixteen years her junior, but Louise became infatuated with him, and her subsequent actions were partly guided by that infatuation.

It is now impossible to separate fact from fiction in trying to determine exactly what part Louise Michel played in the Commune; her memoirs are coy and self-serving, and the accusations leveled against her in her subsequent trial were obviously trumped-up. The most sensational allegations made against her—that she volunteered to assassinate Adolphe Thiers and that she personally set fire to the Hôtel de Ville while wearing a National Guard uniform—were fantasies invented by the newspapers when she became a celebrity of sorts.

Her legend began to take form when, having escaped after the military suppression of the Commune, she was blackmailed into surrendering by threats made against her mother. Detained with thousands of others in a camp at Satory, she witnessed the summary execution there of numerous friends and associates, including Ferré. Like Ferré, she refused to defend herself at her trial, on the accurate grounds that it was a hollow travesty of justice, and one anecdote more likely to be true than the rest is that she demanded loudly that her judges sentence her to death. Perhaps, if she had not done that, they would have, but in the event they sentenced her to deportation to New Caledonia. By the time of her embarkation she had already become famous, assisted by Victor Hugo's campaigning on her behalf and by extensive press coverage, which stuck her with such nicknames as La Louve rouge [the Red She-wolf].

It was in the course of the four-month voyage to New Caledonia, in company with the other Communards who had escaped the firing-squad, that Michel's political views became refined into the Anarchism, initially under the influence of the polemicist Henri Rochefort. If the government of the Third Republic had hoped to export her burgeoning legend along with her, however, they failed. She remained a person of interest to the Parisian press, and there was no longer anything standing in the way of her promotion as a heroine, initially for the assiduity with which she attempted to arrange for the education of the children of the exiles and those of the native islanders, and then for allegedly being the only anarchist among the former Communards to side with the native Kanaks in their rebellion of 1878. She remained in communication with Hugo, Clemenceau and other supporters, who campaigned for her release.

When the transported Communards were given amnesty in 1880, Michel was welcomed by cheering crowds in Dieppe and Paris. She became a popular public speaker and seemed set for a successful career as a political agitator, but in March 1883 she took part in a demonstration on behalf of the unemployed, inevitably placed at the head of the march, which ended with a confrontation with the police, during which three bakers' shops were pillaged. For that participation she was tried in June and was sentenced to six years' imprisonment for "incitement to riot"—with the provision that she was to be kept in solitary confinement and not allowed any communication with the world outside, apparently in an attempt to shut her up for good.

In the event, her silence proved more eloquent than her speechifying had been, and further campaigns on her behalf eventually forced her release. While she was in jail, however, she staved off the effects of solitary confinement by writing: letters of protest to the government, her memoirs (focusing on the rank injustice of her trials) and several works of fiction, apparently for light relief. Although there is no doubt that no one else would have been able to publish those works of fiction in the dire state they were in, the simple fact that she was famous made her an exception.

The first of the two volumes of fiction derived from her prison writings, *Les Microbes humains* (tr. as *The Human Microbes)* was published by Dentu in 1886, not long after her release from jail, half way through her sentence. Although it was clearly written with publication half in mind, the primary motive guiding its composition can only have been to provide a distraction and an internal refuge from her awful circumstances. *Les Microbes humains* is the work of an author who was poorly-nourished, in poor health, under very considerable mental stress and seething with furious resentment. It was written in dribs and drabs with poor implements, on odd scraps of paper, without any access to reference books. There are several places where text is obviously missing from the published version, including one entire chapter, and the incoherency is further compounded by the fact that the fragments of several other stories are wedged arbitrarily into the main story.

The main story is modeled on the classic feuilleton serials of the 1840s, especially Eugène Sue's *Les Mystères de Paris*, and Michel might originally have intended to string it out through the full term of her imprisonment. By the time of its publication, however, or shortly thereafter, she had formed a very different plan. *Les Microbes humains*, as published, was to be the first volume of a six-novel series. Several periodicals reported in 1887 that the titles of the other five would be *Le Monde nouveau*, *La Débâcle, ou le Cauchemar de la vie* [The Debacle; or, The Nightmare of Life], *Première Étape* [The First Stage], *L'Épopée, ou la légende nouvelle* [The Epic; or, The New Legend] and *D'Astre en astre* [From One Planet to Another]. The schema seems, on the suggestion of those titles and further hints dropped into *La Nouveau monde*, to have embraced not merely a worldwide transformation of the Earth but an expansion of humankind to other worlds, which would have made it an unparalleled epic of Anarchist *roman scientifique*.

Exactly why the project was aborted is unclear, but Michel was jailed again late in 1886, for four months, and an attempt was made to assassinate her in 1888, when she was shot in the head. She was subsequently imprisoned yet again, and then fled France in order to live in London from 1890-1895. She did continue writing through all of that, but, as always, had other priorities to juggle. The second and third volumes of her *Mémoires* also remained unpublished while she was alive, although she had produced a rough draft of the entire text while in prison, either because she was never able to get around to preparing it or because it ran into problems with its prospective publisher.

Les Microbes humains is a deeply problematic text; the *Revue Britannique*'s reviewer called it "le roman le plus incoherent, the plus fou, le plus drôle qui ait jamais paru" [the most incoherent, craziest and oddest novel that has ever been published]—but the reviewer had not yet seen *Le Nouveau monde*. The prose and the plot have a pulp-fiction crudity, deliberately calculated to make the jaw drop. The first chapter has a sleeping tramp being eaten alive by rats, followed by the laconic observation that there are far worse things to come in the story—and there were. One might perhaps be able to imagine some other follower of Eugène Sue writing a human vivisection scene in 1886, and perhaps even getting it into print, but not a scene in which the victim is hypnotized in order to be able to report on her agony, let alone one in which she gives birth mid-vivisection.

Similarly, one can imagine a successor of Sue or an admirer of Zola writing and publishing a scene of brutal child rape in 1886, but not a scene of necrophiliac child-molestation, set against a background in which it is taken for granted that avid violent pederasty is rampant in the upper strata of society, and that the invariable practice of the law in those and all other circumstances is to let the guilty go free while mercilessly imprisoning or executing the innocent. Given the nature of her legend and her past, however, what else could be expected of a melodrama by Louise Michel? All standardized nineteenth-century melodramas were virtually compelled to conclude with a nick-of-time rescue, a joyous family reunion, a loving marriage and an abundant inheritance, those being the essential elements of a "happy ending" back then, but Michel, having carefully provided the narrative raw material for all of them, refused every single one. Her narrative is one long blast of unmitigated wrath against the corrupt society that had treated her, and all her unfortunate peers, so very badly.

Les Microbes humains is, admittedly, a very bad book by purely literary standards, but it is a remarkable one nevertheless, and unique, at least within its own era. *Le Nouveau monde* is even worse, by the same pure literary standards, but still remarkable for the hysterical pitch of indignation it achieves in depicting and castigating a society in which women, and little girls in particular, are cruelly and relentlessly debauched, tortured and murdered, while the law invariably sides with the torturers—unsurprisingly, given that its representatives are among the most ruthless perpetrators. There are, however, glimpses of relief within the horrific imagery: heroic anarchists who, having as yet no realistic chance of overthrowing the existing order, establish a utopian enclave of their own in the Arctic, to which they recruit escapees from New Caledonia and other places of exile. It is very successful, until the villain contrives to blow it up, by means of a new kind of explosive invented there and stored a trifle carelessly.

The details of the eutopia given within the text are slight, but there is an inevitable insistence on the fact that women there are safe from the terrible oppressions that they suffer in the outside world, and able to take a full and equal role in the maintenance and progress of the society. The most interesting aspect of the text, however, is the hints it offers as to the intended, or hoped for, contents of the four unwritten volumes, which were to tell the story of a massive geological upheaval that would bring down the existing social order, followed by a process of reconstruction that would eventually see the triumph of Anarchism, and then a further phase of human evolution, involving travel between the different worlds of the solar system, and perhaps the integration of human society with a much broader society of intelligent beings. One of the fragments appended to the story told in *Le Nouveau monde* offers some significant clues as to what the new phase of evolution and the expansion into the solar system would have involved, and the role to be played therein by science.

Science is symbolized in both extant texts by the enigmatic Dr. Gael, initially introduced in *Les Microbes humains* as a vivisectionist, seemingly as a stock villain. In one of the extraneous fragments dropped into the story we find him in Africa, operating on the brains of a human child and a number of chimpanzees, hoping to make discoveries regarding the relationship between brain and mind. He is also the doctor who carries out the bloodcurdling experiment mentioned above, in which a pregnant woman undergoing vivisection while hypnotized gives birth in his laboratory. In *Le Nouveau monde*, however, Gael is no longer a villain, but has joined the anarchists in order to lend the support of his scientific genius to their utopian enterprise. In another extraneous fragment he has built a device that allows him to communicate with the inhabitants of Mars, with whom he is busy trading information, and he has developed a means of replacing the cells of his body with more resilient ones, which effectively make him superhuman, and perhaps immortal. Presumably, both of these elements were scheduled to play a significant role in the future volumes of the series, facilitating the recovery of society after the great catastrophe and the eventual expansion of that society beyond the Earth.

Could Louise Michel actually have written those books if she had not been shot and imprisoned, and harassed until the day she died? If she had, would they have been any good? Even if they had been any good, would they have been published? One suspects that the answers to the first question was "no," rendering the others redundant, but there was certainly a moment in time when she had the ambition to write the great Anarchist epic, mapping out the future course of human society's evolution from the utter corruption and degradation described so luridly in *Les Microbes humains* to a condition of true liberty, equality and sorority: a world fit not merely for heroes but also for wives and little girls.

The image of a technologically-advanced future civilization shifted forward seventy years by Robida and a thousand by Calvet was kicked ahead by a further order of magnitude in *Dix mille ans dans un bloc de glace* (1889; tr. as "Ten Thousand Years in a Block of Ice") by Louis Boussenard, in which the scientific genius featured in the author's Vernian novel *Les Secrets de Monsieur Synthèse* (1887; tr. in *Monsieur Synthesis*) is woken up in the distant future, after being held in suspended animation in the Arctic ice.

The tour of the world undertaken by Synthèse takes in the usual museum, with the standard contemplation of mislabeled fragments of antique hardware, and includes an elaborate version of Charles Cros' method of interplanetary communication—Boussenard and his older brother used to drop in, between voyages, on Nina de Villard's salon, where Boussenard had met Cros, and he might well have been present at Camille Flammarion's salon when Cros read his paper—but its principal focus is upon the people of the future, who are very different from their nineteenth-century ancestors.

Climatic changes have limited the habitable parts of the globe to the tropics, and the humans who live there are hybrids descended from Oriental and Negro stock, who have evolved physically, their bodies being reduced in size while their heads have grown, after the fashion of the Solarians in Pierre Boitard's "Voyage au soleil." The huge brains associated with this change have developed new mental powers of a kind that would later be called "telekinetic," which have alleviated the need for many of the technical devices featured by Robida and Calvet; the ability to levitate renders all of Robida's beloved personal aircraft redundant, and electrical power has been largely displaced as a motive force by mental energy.

That shift in perspective not only changes the apparatus of the technologically advanced future drastically, but also adds a new dimension to the evolving distinction between eutopian and dystopian applications of technology. The entire mythology of progress is confused by the new ideas developed in the story. The resultant shift is not exactly what Frank Manuel meant when he suggested that utopian fiction, having moved into a euchronian phase after Mercier, subsequently moved into a "eupsychian" phase, but it is nevertheless a particularly stark illustration of that kind of evolution.

When Turgot and Condorcet had imagined technological progress and social progress proceeding hand in hand, they had presumed that human beings would retain something closely akin to their present form and mentality, and even though Restif de La Bretonne and Charles Nodier had both pointed out that the assumption was not necessarily sound, the potential modifications they had presented had either been modest alterations of size or, in the case of Restif's inhabitants of Io, bizarre transfigurations removed by hundreds of millions of years (although we do not know what he did in the more detailed description of the future evolution of humankind in *L'Enclos et les oiseaux*). Boussenard, therefore, helped to introduce a new kind of progress into the pattern of possibility, which might have transformed the ongoing debate had anyone else taken it up robustly.

In fact, Boussenard did not know how to continue the argument himself, and brought his serial novel to an abrupt conclusion while it was still some way short of normal book length, and much shorter than its slow-paced predecessor, exactly as Pierre Boitard had done half a century earlier. The ideas broached therein did crop up again in a handful of works of *roman scientifique*, but they were left largely unexplored and undeveloped until they were taken up more affirmatively by American science fiction writers in the 1930s.

The manner of the abrupt closure of Boussenard's narrative is also relevant, in that Synthèse realizes that there is no place for him in the future society except as a museum piece himself, an exhibit for study: in essence, that the kind of "perfectibility" attained by the humans of the future is one from which he is definitively excluded, even though he had been an unparalleled genius in his own time. The world into which he has survived might well qualify as a eutopia from the viewpoint of its participants, but for him it is utterly alien, beyond mere questions of pleasantness and unpleasantness, and intolerable.

La Cité future (1890; tr. as *The Future City*), signed "Alain le Drimeur," reverts to much more familiar and much safer narrative ground. The text reveals that the author wrote it in 1888, probably inspired by the publication in America of Edward Bellamy's best-selling *Looking Backward, 2000-1887*, which caused something of a sensation and rapidly became the best-selling book of its era in the U.S.A. *La Cité future* is one of numerous texts that were produced in the wake of Bellamy's, offering an alternative account of life in a socialist republic in the early years of the twenty-first century. Although it was nowhere near as successful commercially as Bellamy's book, or some of the other utopias inspired by *Looking Backward*—most notably William Morris' *News from Nowhere* (1890)—*La Cité future* is a carefully-wrought text, and its attention to detail makes it one of the most significant contributions to the French futuristic fiction of its era.

Like Bellamy and Morris, the author of *La Cité future* uses a viewpoint tacitly transported from his own milieu as a lens through which the hypothetical future can be viewed; the imaginative device he employs might be no more probable than suspended animation or visionary dreaming but is considerably more ingenious and intriguing in its corollaries. "Le Drimeur" carefully sets up a historical thought-experiment, in which the principal reactionary forces in late nineteenth-century France, disturbed by the centenary celebrations of the 1789 Revolution, emigrate *en masse* in 1891 to the island of La Réunion, where they establish a Roman Catholic kingdom that deliberately cuts itself off from the homeland for a century. Not until the early years of the twenty-first century is a mail service established between Marseille and La Réunion's capital, Saint-Denis, of which two young men take advantage in order to discover what has been happening in France since it was abandoned to the mercy of secularist Republicans.

The thought-experiment involves the use of two protagonists, one of whom remains immovably committed to the religious and political ideals of his insular home, while the other is evidently ripe for conversion to the socialist ideals put into practice in the new France—and, indeed, the new Europe. The author also insists, early in his text, that he is not writing a "purely sociological work" but a novel—"which is to say, a love story," as he puts it—and he therefore provides each of his male protagonists with a potential female lover in the new France, so that the two women can function as rival temptresses as well as propagandizing informants.

The romantic aspect of the experiment provides a useful distraction from the fact that the book otherwise consists of a long series of conversations in which the politics, economics and educational system of the socialist state are explained to the protagonists by various pontificating interlocutors. The author would probably have liked to make the story even more reader-friendly, but he was obviously not an experienced novelist, and was not able to take full advantage of the ingenuity of his plan. None of the standard sources offer any clue as to who "Alain le Drimeur" might have been, and the pseudonym was never used on any other text.

Although accounts of hypothetical socialist organization were becoming abundant by 1890, and *La Cité future* is standardized in its representations of political organization, the narrative has some elements that are unusual for a work of its time, especially its slightly peculiar but unusually strident feminism and its taken-for-granted atheism—which makes the religiosity of one of the protagonists stick out like a sore thumb. The tentative nature of the technological extrapolations featured in the story makes *La Cité future* less interesting as a work of *roman scientifique* than such explorations as Calvet's, but the lack of specific description of the mechanics of the bird-like aerostats featured in the text is compensated by the detailed description of the abundant advertisements displayed within their cheaper cabins—an opportunity for the author to deploy his sarcastic wit, also displayed when the characters visit a sculpture park commemorating the "lustrum" (demi-decade) of the late 1880s; the spectrum of his antipathies then displayed placed the author's sympathies on the radical left of the French Republican movement, although not so far along the spectrum to qualify as an Anarchist.

An interesting utopia following the theme of Léonie Rouzade's vision of the world turned upside-down, viewing a similar situation from the male side of the fence, is Henri Desmarest's *La Femme future* (1890), in which the narrator travels in time to the year 1999 when women are in dictatorial control of the government and the "femmes-hommes" of the future dress in suits, carry briefcases and smoke cigars. He is forcibly married to Néolia Cortive before meeting an "unevolved" woman who is much more to his taste, but only women can initiate divorce proceedings.

As in other novels of the same type produced by men, such as Walter Besant's *The Revolt of Man* (1882), Desmarest's superficial misogyny is only apparent, the real rhetoric of the satirical argument being a criticism of the familiar tyrannies of patriarchy. Eventually, the narrator runs for political office on a reformist platform, but timeslips back to 1890 before he can suffer the expectable heavy defeat in order to carry the lessons he has learned into his everyday life.

The serialization of *Dix mille ans dans un bloc de glace* in the pages of *La Science Illustrée* was followed not long after by the boldest imaginative work ever featured in the pages of that periodical, *La Vie électrique* (serialized 1891-92; book 1892; tr. as *Electric Life*) by Albert Robida, a sequel to *Le Vingtième siècle*, which extrapolates the technological imagery of that novel considerably, taking full account of the technological discoveries made in the real world in the interim.

The story of *La Vie électrique* opens on 12 December 1953, when a violent electrical "tornado" causes massive disruption to communication and transport throughout western Europe. The authorities responsible for weather control react immediately, ordering emergency measures to ameliorate the disaster, and providing a hook for which the author to hang an account of the domestication of the "Great Slave" of Electricity and its multiple applications in the world of 1953: an enormous success that has its downside when things go wrong, as they occasionally do; the tornado is the result of an accident at a power station.

When the tornado bursts, the great Parisian scientist Philoxène Lorris is in the middle of berating his son Georges over the Tele (as the telephonoscope is now familiarly called) for his supposed idleness and lack of application. Although not far distant from the Berthoudian image of the obsessive and eccentric scientific mind, Lorris is by no means unworldly, having been the first person to issue shares in his genius to stockholders in order to finance the research projects—all directed toward practical ends—that have made him fabulously rich. Georges, by contrast, is "a mere lieutenant in the Chemical Artillery," seemingly lacking the drive and determination to dedicate himself obsessively to science or to make millions. Philoxène attributes that to an effect of atavism, having discovered an artist lurking in his wife's ancestry, and hopes to prevent further genetic disaster in the next generation by arranging a "rational marriage" between Georges and a female scientist of perfect intellectual pedigree.

When the tornado cuts off communication with his father, and a crossed line connects him to a young woman names Estelle Lacombe, the lovely daughter of an engineer employed as an inspector of the Alpine Beacons, Georges naturally falls in love. He pursues his passion in spite of his father's marriage plans, causing much further dispute and disruption. The story also introduces Philoxène's assistant, Sulfatin, rumored to be the product of a biological experiment to manufacture an artificial human, and his associate Adrien La Héronnière, who is introduced as a typical product of the modern era:

"He is the man of the present day: the sad and fragile human animal, whom the truly electric excess of our breathless and feverish existence wears away so rapidly when he does not have the will-power or the opportunity periodically to rest his mind, tormented by an excessive and continual torsion; to go and steep his body every day in the bath of reparative nature, in complete relaxation, far away from Paris, that pitiless twister of minds; far away from centers of business, factories, offices, shops; far away from politics, and, above all, from those tyrannical social agents that make life so harsh and enervating, the Teles—all those phones, those pitiless engines, pistons and motors of absorbent electric life in the midst of which we live, run, fly and pant, carried away in a formidable and fulgurant whirlwind!"

That is the central theme of Robida's updated image of the future, reflected in the fact that the narrative of *La Vie électrique* moves at a much faster pace than that of *Le Vingtième siècle*. The technology that has made life so much "easier" has also accelerated its pace dramatically; in its freneticism, it has become vulnerable to catastrophic stumbles, but even when nothing goes wrong, its general effects are gradually deleterious. The mortal threats posed by the technology are dramatized by the electrical tornado, one of Philoxène's projects in progress and Georges' participation in training maneuvers in his capacity as an officer in the Chemical Artillery, practicing the defense of his nation against a mock invasion, but such exceptional events as those are temporary, and capable of avoidance or repair; the everyday effects of the pace and pressure of "electric life" are far harder to oppose or compensate.

Georges eventually succeeds in marrying Estelle and setting up house with her, in the distinctively modern fashion, but their honeymoon, in a vacation resort in which the primitivism of the old way of life is artificially retained, as the "reparative nature" in which overtaxed citizens like Adrien la Héronnière occasionally need to steep themselves, brings into sharper focus the question of what they are going to do with the rest of their lives, in the flawed euchronian society in which they find themselves stranded.

"La Vie électrique" is far more critical of the way the world appeared to the author to be going than its predecessor; even when it settles contentedly into blatant farce for a while, it retains a trenchant edge. Other nineteenth-century writers had anticipated the expansive future development of technology, in association with big business, and envisaged changes to the pace of everyday life in consequence, but no one else envisaged a state of affairs in which almost everyone might be in a perpetual state of fatigue and nervous stimulation, even the masters of the society being *surmenagé* [overstressed] to the point of debility and illness. Robida was not alone in suggesting that improved technologies of communication might increase friction between nations rather than diminishing it, thus increasing the likelihood of armed conflict—and the commercial opportunities thus created for arms dealers—especially in combination with dramatic increases in population facilitated by technology, but he was unusual in depicting such matters as routine aspects of everyday life, simply taken for granted.

There are, inevitably, aspects of *La Vie électrique* that now look like gross errors, if the novel were to be mistakenly construed as a series of "predictions." The most significant specific element of non-resemblance to the actual future is the fact that virtually all traffic in Robida's twentieth century is air traffic, and most of that consists of dirigible airships. That assumption leads to corollary architectural fancies with regard to the construction of the houses of the future and technologies of traffic control. Even that nexus of anticipations, however, has a basic intelligence that was ahead of its time.

If the specific focus on airships is set aside, what is being suggested—radically, at the time—is that in the twentieth century, large numbers of people would have their own private vehicles, and that houses, public buildings and the environment in general would have to undergo sweeping changes in order to accommodate those vehicles. Seen in that light, the novel does indeed have a prophetic dimension that displayed a considerable foresight and extrapolative intelligence, only partially masked by its jocular tone and farcical intrusions. It deserves to be reckoned the classic work of the *fin-de-siècle*, so far as the evolution of *roman scientifique* is concerned.

Politics was subject to patterns of change itself, as it continued to play a leading role on speculative fiction of the period. Pacifism, increasingly becoming isolated as an independent political creed, came more prominently to the fore in several futuristic visions. It is brought into specific focus, in a heartfelt fashion, in *Le Conte futur* (1893; tr. as "A Tale of the Future") by Paul Adam (1862-1920), framed as a tale of martyrdom akin to many of the traditional Christian folktales of the Golden Legend. A much sharper parable taking an opposite view was, however, swiftly provided by *L'An 330 de la République* (1894; tr. as "Year 330 of the Republic") by the conservative journalist Maurice Spronck (1861-1921), which is one of the most graphically violent literary reactions against socialism, with particular reference to its pacifist tendencies.

The story opens on 16 Messidor 330 (2105 in terms of our calendar) when the city of Orléans is about to celebrate the centenary of its liberation, and also the end of a long wrangle over an equestrian statue of Jeanne d'Arc, which the Progressivist party has long wanted to remove as an obsolete symbol of the ignorance and primitivism of past eras, and which has finally been replaced by a statue of an illustrious chemist, responsible for great advances in the manufacture of artificial foodstuffs—by now an iconic fascination of *roman scientifique*, partly due to the widely-publicized assertions of the chemist Marcellin Berthelot regarding the possibilities of synthetic food, although the notion had previously been featured in Charles Nodier's futuristic fantasy.

In Spronck's year 330, weather control guarantees a fine day for the celebration, to which all of the delegates turn up in electric wheelchairs, universally employed by a population whose younger members are so unaccustomed to physical exercise that they are morbidly obese and can only walk short distances, while older ones are preserved by sophisticated medical technologies. They watch a dramatic enactment of gruesome scenes from the bad old days, which serves as the introduction to a summary of French history, from the pivotal moment of the Franco-Prussian War and the suppression of the Commune to the eventual triumph of the ideals credited to the Commune's martyrs.

The establishment of peace in Europe and general disarmament has led to widespread socialist reforms and a surge in technological invention associated with the exploitation of electricity and a sophisticated organic chemistry that has rendered agriculture superfluous. The French have been completely freed from the necessity of labor, the remaining requirements being fulfilled by imported Chinese laborers, supervised and disciplined by similarly-imported Muslim mercenaries.

One side-effect of that universal leisure, however, has been universal ennui, occasioning "psychological lesions" in the brain and incurable degenerations of the nervous system. The population is also in decline, because so many women have ovariotomies in order to avoid the inconveniences of childbirth, although medical science has compensated, not by keeping everyone healthy but by keeping all of the unhealthy alive, in spite of the widespread recreational use of toxic compounds.

This remarkable vision of a twisted technological euchronia, populated not by "perfected" people but by the most imperfect people imaginable, is the prelude to a depiction of its inevitable collapse, overrun by Muslim "barbarians" led by a charismatic leader intent on conquering the entire world, against whom no effective resistance can be mounted, in spite of the enormous technological sophistication of Europe, because no one can effectively use such weapons as can be hurriedly manufactured and distributed. After describing the swift and ignominious defeat, the novella ends with the laconic observation that: "The barbarians have reconquered the world. Civilization is dead."

Spronck went on to be one of the founders of the right-wing pressure group Action Française and he joined forces with other conservative writers—including Maurice Barrès and Jules Lemaître—in the Ligue de la Patrie Française, under the aegis of which he was elected as a député in 1902 and served as a member of parliament until 1919, although he gradually moved away from the far right to a more liberal stance.

The possibilities opened up by futuristic fiction for philosophical speculation of a broader kind than the simple modeling of a hypothetical society were explored by Gabriel Tarde (1843-1904), the professor of Modern Philosophy at the Collège de France, in one of the first such fantasies to be published in an academic journal, *Fragment d'histoire future* (1896 in the *Revue internationale de sociologie*; tr. as *Underground Man*). The narrator reflects from the viewpoint of the thirty-first century on the social developments of the previous millennium, primarily those forced by a global catastrophe similar to the one anticipated in Louise Michel's aborted schema.

In advance of the catastrophe in question, the world makes spectacular scientific progress under the stimulus of a series of wars, which force the development of increasingly advanced weaponry of the varieties described in Albert Robida's specialist supplement to *Le Vingtième siècle* (to be described in detail in the chapter on "Future Wars"), from which they might have been borrowed. The wars in question succeed in establishing a world state possessed of many euchronian features, although still beset by periodic economic crises, but erratic diminutions in solar radiation culminate in a sudden drastic decline that fatally freezes much of the world's surface. The survivors of the catastrophe take refuge in the southern reaches of the Arabian desert, in a region rich in coal deposits capable of meeting their fuel requirements, at least for a while.

Under the influence of a messianic preacher, the survivors then decide that, in order to survive in the long term, they must seek to exploit the Earth's inner heat, and move their entire society underground. In the evolving Underworld of tunnels and chambers thus created, a new culture evolves, adapting to its confinement esthetically as well as materially, which thrives as it gradually expands, learning to take comfort in an existential situation that, by courtesy of technology, is by no means as dark as might have been feared.

Socialist eutopians were, of course, largely undeterred by the alarmist criticism from the right launched by the likes of Maurice Spronck, although the wry quality of Gabriel Tarde's conditional optimism was perhaps more in line with the humor of the times than the innocent enthusiasm of Émile Calvet and the meticulous social design of "Alain le Drimeur."

A particular deft example of a similarly wry humor, albeit still in combination with fervent euchronian optimism, can be found in "Un Roman historique" (1896; tr. as "A Historical Romance") by Henri Ner, who was later to change the form of his name, presumably without altering its pronunciation, to Han Ryner. The story is a striking parable, whose narrator, a determined rebel against the peaceful socialist euchronia of the year 2347, wants to reinspire the passion and excitement of Romance by setting a striking example. He is seen by his serenely contented contemporaries as a lunatic, worthy of pity rather than punishment—which, of course, only makes him angrier—and he does, indeed, come across as utterly insane in his ranting, even before his antics lead to a tragic conclusion.

A far more ominous irony can be found in the elaborate utopian exercise with which Paul Adam followed *Le Conte futur*, *Lettres de Malaisie* (1898; tr. as "Letters from Malaisie"). The story starts from the premise that a disciple of Étienne Cabet disillusioned by the fate of Cabet's Icarian colonies in the U.S.A, set out to carry out a similar experiment in the isles of the Indian Ocean, under the collective influence of Saint-Simon, Fourier and Cabet, and that the experiment, after overcoming initial difficulties, was spectacularly successful; the author is carefully to emphasize in advance, however, that the society depicted by the letters is *not* an ideal, and puts that statement in capital letters to make sure that the reader gets the message. In fact no other work more clearly justifies the utility of differentiating between utopias and eutopias.

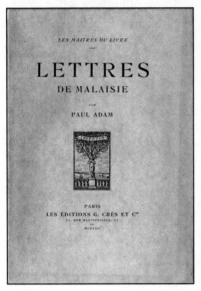

The preface to **Lettres de Malaisie** refers to all the utopian writers of the early nineteenth century, in whose ideas the thought experiment is firmly rooted, and also likens the exercise explicitly to Thomas More's pioneering exemplar, but the story is also equipped with an extensive series of footnotes consisting of long quotes from *Télémaque*, drawing explicit links between Mentor's advice on how to construct a wisely-governed society and the society described by the letters, although the contrasts are far more striking than the similarities, and Fénelon would doubtless have been appalled by the frank horror and even franker obscenity of many of the descriptions in the text. Clearly bearing in mind what actually happened to the communities that Cabet, Victor Considerant and others of their ilk tried to establish in various parts of the world, Adam describes a society that has been forced to become extremely authoritarian in order to maintain a philosophy of liberty that really does not extend much beyond the orgiastic application of complete amorous license.

The eponymous letters are sent by a diplomat sent to investigate reports of French "aerial pirates" based on a high plateau on the island of Borneo, who are lending support to indigenous insurgents against colonel rule in the Philippines. The ship in which he is traveling does not take long to encounter one of the flying machines in question, which hovers overhead, suspending "torpedoes" like the sword of Damocles, but an unprecedented exception is made to allow the diplomat to make his representations. Since its establishment in 1843 the colony has expanded to occupy an area in the interior of Borneo a third the size of France, and in fifty years its technological progress has far outstripped that of Europe.

Joseph Déjacque would have disagreed strongly with Paul Adam's account of the likely consequences of amorous anarchy, but he would have found much that was familiar to him in the advanced electrification and mechanization of the cities of the new society, although the complete community of property and the corollary absence of money are reinforced by law rather than merely voluntary. Tobacco and alcohol are also banned, and backed by powerful sanctions, any possession thereof being considered as attempted murder and punished accordingly

Unlike Déjacque's standardized "humanispheres," the cities of Adam's new society are carefully specialized. The diplomat's journey, in the company of two female guides, Théa and Pythie—who quickly introduce him to the joys and (for him) sentimental stresses of free love—begins in the city of Minerve, which is the center of education and bureaucracy, although it is in his conversations there that he learns about the elaborate rituals surrounding reproduction, involving the cities of Diane and Venus, which he never gets to visit. It is also in Minerve that he witnesses the extraordinary elaboration of Christian dogma wrought by the founder of the colony, the new catechism adopted there, and the elaborate philosophical allegory contained in the new credo.

From Minerve the diplomat goes to the city of Jupiter, where Authority resides, and makes unpromising initial contact with the Oligarchies that make up its Dictatorship. Although no final decision is made, he sees that his diplomatic mission has little chance of bearing fruit, all the more so when he is handed a document outlining the political reforms that the Dictatorship intends to impose on the nations of Europe as soon as its airfleets have bombed them into surrender—which they expect to do as soon as the factories of Vulcan have produced enough of them.

The diplomat next visits Mars, which lodges the army and the abattoirs, on the grounds that all slaughter ought to be aggregated in the same hands, but which is also the entirety of the society's penal system, conscription into the army being the only penalty for any and all crimes, in order that antisocial tendencies can be productively channeled. It is also where all culinary activity is carried out and where the dead are cremated. The orgies occurring there horrify and sicken the diplomat more than the ones he has so far seen, seeming to him to be direly perverted—but, perhaps surprisingly, not as perverted or as nauseating as the one he is privileged to witness in Mercure, the city of science, where a remarkable initial rhapsody on the wonders of science and the glory of the intellect is brutally juxtaposed with an account of a discovery that has made of a means of channeling erotically-generated "psychic force" and making it available for the purposes of scientific inspiration.

The diplomat's journey concludes in the industrial city of Vulcan, whose automated machinery and multitidinous fitters are busy churning out the flying machines that will be used for the conquest of Europe and—allegedly—the greatest leap forward in social progress that the world has ever made. Naturally, he sets out try to discover the secret of the flying machines, in the hope of enabling Europe to mount a defense, even though his beloved Pythie warns him that he is being deliberately tempted and set up, in order to facilitate a charge of espionage that will permit the Dictatorship to send him to Mars...

Lettres de Malaisie is one of the most interesting nineteenth-century utopian satires, in the way it gathers so many threads of eutopian thought together, in order to expose their supposed paradoxicality and potential perversion, while simultaneously allowing the voices of the imagined society to argue, forcefully and cogently, that the societies of Europe are far worse and more absurd than theirs. It is certainly the most sophisticated and ingenious of the century's ambivalent dystopias, and really does provide a significant series of dispatches from the psychological realm of Unease. No other work is as conscientiously nightmarish in amalgamating eutopian ideals with their dark underside.

Adam scrupulously includes in his survey all the imagery of technological advancement that *roman scientifique* had enabled to become conventional by the end of the century, combining the relevant wonders, hopes and anxieties in a more insidious but no less effective fashion than Robida's account of *La Vie électrique*. *Lettres de Malaisie* illustrates, more graphically than any work had previously done, the clash of euchronian determination with an insidious disenchantment that was part and parcel of the shift toward eupsychian thought; it has a distinctly *fin-de-siècle* feel about it, but it also provides a kind of foundation-stone for the uneasiness that was to haunt twentieth-century euchronian thought even before the Great War seemingly abolished the optimism of such thought permanently.

Paul Adam was one of the writers who was most conspicuous in spanning the supposedly rival schools of Naturalism and Symbolism, and was therefore ideally placed to combine their influences and methods in works like *Lettres de Malaisie*, which not only benefited from that alloy but required it. The difficulties of dealing with the potential for social progress and its seemingly-inevitably complicity with technological progress, while working entirely within a Naturalistic framework, are amply illustrated by Émile Zola's final project, originally intended as a trilogy but which he replanned while it was in progress as a quartet—*Les Quatre Évangiles* [The Four Gospels]—but then failed to finish because death intervened, leaving the volume that was originally planned to complete the trilogy, *Justice*, unwritten.

Because the group of novels features the children of the couple featured in Zola's previous trilogy, its action was committed from the start to begin in the present day, but because it tells the story of their entire lives, it was also committed to extending seventy years into the future. In the first of the novels, *Fécondité* (1899; tr. as *Fecundity*), that has the rather peculiar effect of detailing the aging of the central character over the course of the greater part of the twentieth century, while the world in which he lives hardly changes at all—an absence of transformation that is not particularly noticeable or relevant because the plot of the story is, as its title suggests, very narrowly focused in the issue of fecundity: that of the characters and that of the barren land that Mathieu Froment takes over in order to make it productive. Vague references are made to advances in agricultural techniques and machinery, but the tunnel vision of the story allows it simply to ignore what else might be going on in the world while an elaborate pattern of marriages and childbirths, quarrels and estrangements, gradually unfolds.

That is not the case, however, with the second novel, *Travail* (1901; tr. as *Work*), whose focus is on labor, especially the social reform of labor, and hence on industry, and the technological development of industry. Luc Froment, the hero, and his many neighbors, form a similar network of relationships, marriages and conflicts, and ultimately produce a posterity that is only slightly less fecund than his brother's, but that can only be part of a story in which Luc must not only found a worker's co-operative that will grow into a city, withstand or absorb all economic competition, and show the characters modeling anarchism, socialist collectivism and diehard capitalism the error of their various ways, but must also improve the technological apparatus of his factory and its environment. In order to help with that, Zola has to introduce an innovative scientist, Jordan—an obsessive recluse, of

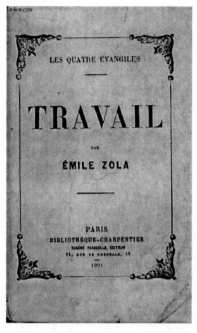

course—who will strive to be the motor of that facet of improvement. Not only that, but he has to give some consideration to patterns of demand and the kind of goods to be manufactured, and because Luc manufactures steel, the question of armaments cannot be left out of account. Thus, *Travail*—unlike *Fécondité*, although it is notionally happening in the same world—includes mention of war: a world war, fought with advanced weaponry.

Remarkably, Zola contrives to leave that war entirely off-stage, and most of the other technological developments that his plot has to include are only given tokenistic mention. Jordan gives the occasional rhapsodic speech about glorious possibilities but achieves very little in manifest practical terms, and as marginal items of *roman scientifique* go, *Travail* sets the record for being the most reluctant, the most hesitant and the one whose progress proceeds at the slowest possible pace—not because Zola believed that future technological progress would actually be glacially slow, but because it would have severely compromised the conscientious Naturalism of his narrative if he had not operated in that fashion. Perhaps the result is absurd, and it is certainly peculiar, but that only serves to make it a more interesting specimen.

It would have been interesting, too, to see what *Justice* would have made of the further reaches of the twentieth century, especially as the last of the

Froment brothers, Jean, was to be a soldier, and would have been obliged to involve himself in the mysterious world war mentioned but not detailed in *Travail*. Like Luc, Jean too was to be working toward a broad social goal—nothing less than the Universal Republic—although there is no way to know whether he would actually have achieved it, and one suspects that he might only have achieved a distant hopeful glimpse of its possibility. *Vérité* (1903; tr. as *Truth*), however, is as narrowly focused as *Fécondité*, the battle for truth reproducing in its general aspect the Dreyfus Affair but transfiguring its substance into a war between Church dogma and lay skepticism; it has no need to stray into speculative areas, and its insertion into the series as a belated adjustment condemned *Justice* to the same realm of the imagination as several other texts mentioned in the present survey whose non-existence we can only regret.

By the end of the century, the imagery of euchronian and dystopian fiction, in their technological and political dimensions, was becoming far more widespread in popular melodrama, where it was inevitably coupled with the sense of dire threat featured in Paul Adam's carefully-interrupted series of fictitious letters. A particularly extravagant version is to be found in the four volumes of *La Conspiration des milliardaires* (1899-1900; tr. as *The Dominion of the World*) by the debutant novelists Gustave Le Rouge and Gustave Guitton, whose incidental features involve a city akin to Stahlstadt constructed in the American wilderness by an Edisonian inventor in order to build an army of automata and a fleet of submarines for use by the consortium of billionaires planning the conquest of the Old World.

The plan is thwarted by a loose association of heroes, including an American engineer, a French inventor, a brilliant chef (Le Rouge was a renowned gourmet) and the irrepressible Parisian *gamin* without whom no feuilletonesque adventure story could really be deemed complete. The pattern of the long novel, in which virtuous inventors must strive to counter the machinations of evil inventors, quickly became standard in downmarket *roman scientifique*, with the commonsensical ingenuity and intrinsically anarchic irreverence of the gamin frequently tipping the balance of forces in favor of the righteous. Guitton was later to write a much more straightforward didactic vision of a future city more reminiscent of Franceville than Stahlstadt, in *Ce que seront les hommes de l'an*

3000 [How the Humans of the year 3000 will live] (1907), but Le Rouge stuck thereafter to fanciful action-adventure fiction devoid of any interest in social evolution, although some are interesting in their relevance to other aspects of the evolution of *roman scientifique*.

Particularly intriguing in the same context was a seemingly-unlikely literary partnership formed between two former childhood friends whose paths had diverged significantly, François Goron having become the head of the Parisian Sûreté and Émile Gautier a prominent Anarchist who spent time in prison. On his release, however, Gautier had abandoned political agitation for scientific journalism, and had been the editor for some years of the popular science magazine *La Science Française*. In the meantime, Goron, having retired from the Sûreté, had successfully serialized his memoirs of fighting crime, and was keen to continue his literary career by branching out into *feuilleton* fiction.

Wanting to write a novel about a supervillain far more accomplished than those he had boasted about bringing down in his old job, Goron recruited Gautier to help equip the evil genius in question with advanced technological means and an organization of anarchists to exploit cynically, including an idealistic but unworldly scientist who has perfected a scientific means of manufacturing gold. *Fleur de Bagne* (1901; tr. as *Spawn of the Penitentiary*) ran for several months in one of the leading daily newspapers of the day, *Le Journal*, and was reprinted the following year in three separately-titled volumes.

Like many feuilletons of the day, and similar exercises like *La Conspiration des milliardaires*, *Fleur de Bagne* is a rambling exercise in crude pulp fiction, but is unusual for its sympathetic treatment of Anarchism as well as its introduction into the plot of a heavier-than-air flying machine, the weaponization of radioactivity, and other devices borrowed from the image of the emergent future that was now becoming familiar, thanks to the endeavors of euchronians like Robida and Calvet, with staunch support from the more adventurous writers of Vernian fiction. It illustrates the extent to which that kind of imagery was becoming "domesticated" in a literary sense, readily available for recruitment to spice up routine thrillers and pander to their need for melodramatic inflation.

The lead provided by Gabriel Tarde in taking a clinical historically-distanced view of future possibilities was echoed by the historian Daniel Halévy

(1872-1962) in his *Histoire de quatre ans, 1997-2001* (1903), which necessarily affects to take for granted the intervening century separating the publication date from the four years ostensibly in focus. The story behind the surface is that of the consequences stemming from the laboratory synthesis in 1925 of an alimentary substance called albumine, which can be produced so cheaply as to be potentially capable of liberating humankind—or Europe, at least—from the threat of hunger.

The massive reduction of effort involved in agricultural production and the processing of food leads to a dramatic reduction in labor time and a consequent expansion in leisure time—which, the author assumes, following a similar line of thought to Maurice Spronck, will lead to a dramatic increase in vice, drugtaking and other symptoms of moral decay, in turn leading to epidemic mental disturbance. In order to counter the plague, governments attempt to suppress psychotropic substances, but fail to solve the problem, although it seems that it might contain the seeds of its own solution—or at least obliteration—when new stimulants, extreme in the pleasurable sensations they provide but also fatal, begin to cut through the ranks of the decadent masses: a Darwinian culling regarded with complacency by social scientists and politicians alike. Further distraction is eventually provided by new Moorish incursions into Europe and the threat of a war between a unified Western Europe and Russia—a war whose perceived imminence closes the four year period actually specified by the title.

In much the same way that the real substance of the story is lightly masked by the ostensible subject-matter implied by the title, the author's real political sympathies—affiliated to a somewhat unorthodox variant of socialism—are somewhat concealed by a superficial rhetoric that is ironically orientated in a different direction. The complexity and subtlety of the work have the effect of making it difficult to see exactly where the sarcasm ends and the sincerity begins, but that might well reflect some uncertainty on the part of the author, as well as an understandable pessimism regarding the likelihood of the lower orders of society reacting with sufficient gratitude and enthusiasm to the prospects of socialist reorganization offered to them by the left-wing intelligentsia.

Hindsight might now give the impression that *Histoire de quatre ans, 1997-2001* was somewhat ahead of its time, both in terms of its narrative strategy and its philosophical sophistication, but there is also an argument to be made that it was very much of its time, reflecting an awareness, even while the early years of the twentieth century gave the impression of a new beginning, that euchronian optimism might well be obsolete, its aerostatic dreams punctured, and that the notion of future progress, whatever relationship was supposed to exist between social and technological progress, would henceforth have to be regarded as something essentially problematic, and perhaps essentially paradoxical.

Louise Michel and Émile Gautier made only tentative beginnings to literary careers that they did not carry very far, but some other anarchists and ex-anarchists adopted the strategy much more wholeheartedly, after the fashion of Paschal Grousset. The most successful of them all was Michel Zevaco (1860-1918), who continued his political agitations while writing *cape-et-épée* novels on the side from 1900 onwards, swiftly achieving huge success as a *feuilletoniste* in the mold of Alexandre Dumas. Most of Zevaco's works were formularistic action-adventure stories, zestfully designed for maximum reader appeal, and in adopting that strategy he was clearly following an example set by a veteran anarchist who had been involved with the cause before he was even born, Jules Lermina (1839-1915).

Lermina was still a child when the revolution of 1848 was followed by Louis Napoléon's *coup d'état*, but he grew up as a dedicated opponent of the Second Empire, embracing a radical socialist viewpoint. Having married at eighteen, with a baby daughter to support, he tried his hand at various clerical jobs, but could not hold on to them because of his political opinions, and turned his hand to freelance journalism instead. He attracted the attention of the censors when he eventually founded a political periodical of his own, *Le Corsaire*, in 1867, which led to his being imprisoned. He was released in response to protest—from the ever-reliable Victor Hugo, among others—but promptly repeated his crime, founding a new journal called *Satan*, and was imprisoned again.

Lermina was still in prison when the Siege of Paris began, but he was released when the new Government of National Defense took office and he was enlisted, presumably by compulsion, in the National Guard and sent away from Paris to fight the Prussians. He was only in uniform for a matter of months, but must have had a terrible time; he was short, thin, pale, puny and of a somewhat nervous disposition even when not fresh out of prison—and his regiment, which engaged the enemy on at least two occasions, had no chance whatsoever of stemming the Prussian tide. Military discipline did not shut him up; he prepared campaign literature with which to stand for elections to the new National Assembly, before the promised elections were cancelled, and he wrote an angry open letter of protest to the government when the chief protagonists of Communist agitation were imprisoned. Had he not been posted outside Paris, he would certainly have taken an active part in the Commune, and might well have been shot or transported when it was overthrown, but the experience seems to have been traumatic nevertheless, and he took a new direction in life thereafter. He launched a new phase of his journalistic career, concentrating on the writing of popular fiction, in which he had only dabbled before the war.

Jules Claretie, who wrote an introduction to Lermina's first collection of fantastic tales, *Histoires incroyables* [Incredible Stories] (1885), records that he and his friend had both been strongly influenced in their early days by E. T. A. Hoffmann and Edgar Poe, and that they had both attempted work of that sort when they launched their careers in 1859. Almost all the work that Lermina published in the first phase of his journalistic career and his first decade as a *feuilletoniste* was, however, naturalistic, in accordance with the prevailing priorities of the marketplaces in which he worked. He only published a handful of Poesque tales before the war, most significantly "Les fous" (*Le Gaulois*, 1869 as "Edgar Poe"; tr. as "The Lunatics"), one of several "case study" stories. After the war, he published several more, including items of Poesque *roman scientifique* but he was more active in the 1880s as a writer of occult fiction.

Shortly after 1880, when she was in her early twenties, Lermina's daughter Marie-Pauline met, fell in love with and married one of the *bouquinistes* who kept stalls on the banks of the Seine, Henri Chacornac, who specialized in books on the occult. Lermina presumably provided the financial backing for Chacornac to open a shop on the Quai Saint-Michel in 1884, Librairie Générale des Sciences Occultes. The shop and its associated publishing enterprises were able to cash in on a remarkable explosion of interest in the occult, and became very successful. Lermina jumped on to the bandwagon, publishing *La Comtesse Mercadet* (1884), the first of several stories about "animal magnetism", before assembling and filling out his two collections of *histoires incroyables*. He also wrote fiction and non-fiction in collaboration with one of Chacornac's most avid customers, the Martinist Gérard Encausse (1864-1916) who used the signature "Papus."

After 1890, however, Lermina's fiction began to take on more of the attributes of popular scientific romance, in stories that will be discussed in other sections of the present chapter, and he also stepped up his political writing, initially in the pages of *Le Radical* and in the preparatory work he did for his most significant political work, the anarchist reference book *L'ABC du Libertaire* [The ABC of Libertarianism] (1906). It was perhaps only natural that the two lines of interest should intersect, in one of the most remarkable utopian satires of the era, published in the unlikely venue of the Vernian *Journal des Voyages*: **"Mystère-ville"** (1904; tr. as *Mysteryville*). It is not unlikely that it took some inspiration from *Lettres de Malaisie*, which he surely read in the course of his research for the reference book, but his own novella develops the ideas on which Adam's story was based in a far more garish fashion, adapted for downmarket publication.

The narrator of the story, an inveterate world traveler, gets caught up in the Boxer rebellion in China and is forced to flee into the Gobi desert. There, on the brink of death, he find a way into an almost-inaccessible hidden valley, where a

314

party of Huguenots fleeing the persecution that followed the revocation of the Edict of Nantes had been cast away two centuries before. Starting with virtually no resources, except that their number included Denis Papin—the scientist and inventor whose papers on the possible adaptation of steam engines, presented to the Royal Society when he first fled France, probably assisted England to take the lead in the Industrial Revolution—the refugees have built their own technologically-advanced and determinedly egalitarian society, taking advantage of the externally-unknown power sources of light and sound to supplement steam power.

Like Albert Robida, who also seems to have provided a significant fraction of the inspiration for "Mystère-Ville," Lermina employs broad humor to lighten the tone of his story and to compensate for a relative dearth of action while the unwelcome visitor is being shown the wonders of the hidden world, but as with Robida's work, the story's farcical quality overlays a serious argumentative pattern. The arrival of the outsider in the long-isolated enclave reignites debate as to whether the "New Paris" produced by the heirs to Denis Papin's inventive genius should attempt to renew contact and commerce with the old one. His news allows the inhabitants to obtain information as to what that might involve, but his account of what the original Paris has become, technologically, culturally and politically, does not make the decision any easier.

As things turn out, the debate is overtaken when the latest developments in the ongoing rivalry between the enclave's two contemporary scientific geniuses, who are striving to outdo one another, one in the development of "phonism" (sound power) and the other in the development of "aromatism" (odor power), precipitates a catastrophe, but that merely leaves the challenging question to the reader's judgment. The anarchist political system that organizes the society of New Paris is presented as if it were mere comedy, posing no serious challenge to any firmly-held political convictions that the reader might have, but the comparison is nevertheless set out for contemplation, and the underlying rhetoric of the adventure story is more subversive than it seems—something that was to become a routine feature of the *roman scientifique* adapted for the purposes of entertainment in popular magazines as the twentieth century progressed.

Although Lermina's thoroughly professional fiction, unlike Michel Zevaco's, did not exclude his political sympathies entirely, their fellow anarchist Jean Grave (1854-1939), a prolific author of propagandistic pamphlets, casually went to an opposite extreme, embedding his philosophy straightforwardly in books designed to be read for children, initially in *Les Aventures de Nono* (1901), whose nine-year-old protagonist visits the land of Autonomie, and subsequently in the more elaborate *Terre libre: Les Pionniers* [Free Land: The Pioneers] (1908), aimed at older children, which follows a group of political deportees cast away on a desert island, where they build a society enshrining their ideals.

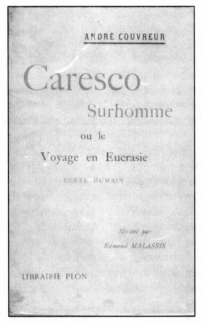

Befitting the advent of a new century, euchronian fiction obtained a significant updating in its imagery and philosophy with the publication of *Caresco surhomme, ou le voyage en Eucrasie* (1904; tr. as *Caresco, Superman; or, A Voyage to Eucrasia*) by André Couvreur (1863-1944). Couvreur, a practicing physician had began his literary career as a Naturalist with a trilogy of novels *Le Mal nécessaire* (1899; tr. as *The Necessary Evil*), *Les Mancenilles* [a noun improvised from the specific name of *Hippomane mancenilla*, a highly toxic shrub] (1900) and *La Source fatale* [The Fatal Source] (1901), collectively entitled *Les Dangers sociaux* [Social Dangers]. He had then begun a second trilogy of the same kind, collectively entitled *La Famille* [The Family] but interrupted it after two volumes in order to take up the story of the unscrupulous surgeon featured in his first novel, Armand Caresco, by extrapolating his philosophy to its limit. Significantly, the novel is fulsomely dedicated to Paul Adam, and it deliberately takes up several of the themes broached in *Lettres de Malaisie*.

In the sequel to his mundane exploits, Caresco has become fabulously rich and has bought an island newly-thrust out of the sea by volcanic eruption, where he constructs the closed and heavily-defended utopian society of Eucrasia [good health]: a society in which everyone is beautiful, thanks to the assistance of his advanced surgical techniques, and easy sexual fulfillment is permanently available to everyone, although only a select few males and a larger but still limited population of fertile females are allowed to breed, in the interests of eugenics, most of the population being contentedly sterilized.

Various sexual inclinations are abundantly supplied in Eucrasia, thanks to the provisions of entire classes of highly-trained and versatile female "courtesans" and male "gitons"—catamites—who supplement the wide-open marriages between sterile males and fertile females. Pedophilia is routine and even necrophilia is given appropriately sensitive technological support. Anyone in need of artificial assistance—as the few breeding males routinely are, being required to fertilize a much larger population of females—has access to sophisticated aphrodisiac technologies. Possible political resentments due to the stratification of the society, which extends as far as institutionalized slavery, are soothed by a carefully-designed religion that offers compensation for present status-deficiency with the promise of reincarnation: a religion of which Caresco is the prophet, and—in the eyes of the subjects to whom he has delivered perfect health and happiness—the incarnation of god.

The plot of the novel describes the arrival in the eutopia of two new recruits, the exceedingly handsome and romantically inclined, but deeply disillusioned Marcel Girard and his mentor, the neo-Stoic philosopher Zéphirin Choumaque. They arrive in the company of a visitor, the political activist Mary Hardisson, who has come to implore the assistance of Caresco's awesome military technology in order to save her African homeland from annexation by imperialist colonial powers. Inevitably, Marcel falls in love with Mary before the bizarre flying-machine ferrying them to the mysterious island even touches down, but she is completely immune to sexual arousal—a situation that becomes extremely dangerous for both her and Marcel when the Superman, Caresco, also becomes obsessed with her. Caresco is forced to refine his aphrodisiac technologies even further in the quest to break down her resistance, and also has to go to considerable trouble to ascertain that her resultant gradual arousal does not get deflected in the direction of the amorous Marcel.

In the meantime, Choumaque provides a skeptical eye that tries hard to pass scathing judgment on the supposed falsity of the eutopia, although he is by no means immune to its seductions, especially when he discovers that his own long-lost first love, an ex-child prostitute, is now applying her hard-won expertise to training Eucrasia's courtesans. Marcel, selected as a male breeder, is even more distracted, although his determination to escape with Mary, if her resistance can ever be broken down, is dramatically increased when Choumaque discovers that Caresco's particular sexual fetish—in which he naturally intends to indulge with Mary—is surgical in nature, and drastic. Caresco remains aloof from his eutopia, still obsessively continuing his own progressive scientific endeavors, which include attempts to perfect transsexual surgery, to create human hermaphrodites, and also to perfect "the human Monad": the surgical reduction of human being to the minimum of flesh, coupled with a complementary enhancement of the power of the mind.

Given that the island of Eucrasia is scrupulously designed in the form of a human body, with Caresco's secret lair situated in its loins, inside the cone of the volcano that gave birth to the island, few readers familiar with Symbolism would have been surprised, in 1904, by the nature of the climactic eruption that brings the entire thought-experiment to a close. Not all of them, however, would have been convinced by the subsequent post-apocalyptic discussion, in which Choumaque offers a conspicuously weak-kneed championship of his pseudo-Stoical doctrine and his principle of philosophical equilibrium. The latter insists that the satisfactions provided by a eutopia, even one as physically satisfying as Eucrasia, can only be temporary, because "happiness" becomes meaningless once there is no unhappiness to sharpen it by comparison, and that a desire completely fulfilled is bound to disappear, but even Choumaque is unconvinced that he is really doing Marcel and Mary a favor by returning them to the awful pressures and frustrations of a mid-twentieth century society that is suffering the symptoms of Robidaesque *surmenagement*.

The question of sexual relations in an ideal society had been somewhat sidelined in the nineteenth century, and a hundred year gap separated Couvreur's pornotopia from the enthusiastic libertinism of *Les Posthumes*, several eutopians having gone to an opposite extreme in assuming that in a perfect society, passion would naturally fall into line with a moderate "normality." Couvreur, as a Parisian doctor, had abundant evidence available to him of the actual range of contemporary sexual behavior and the wayward fervor of sexual desire, the unfortunate consequences of which he had mapped extensively in his first trilogy of novels. Caresco's eutopia is designed to accommodate and facilitate all manner of eccentric desires—including his own fetish, which surely qualifies as pathological, no matter what one might think of the rest—in order to guarantee the kind of happiness that people characteristically seek via that route, as well as the simpler ones provided by the supply of more elementary bodily needs.

Most eutopias produced since Plato have been vulnerable to the objection raised explicitly early in the nineteenth century by Collin de Plancy's depiction of the society of the Alburs: "Yes, it's perfect, but would you really want to live there?" Employing Choumaque as his hypothetical assessor, Couvreur inverts the thrust of that question: having once experienced the pleasures of Eucrasia, can he really bear the idea of living anywhere else, and can he sincerely recommend that to this young pupil, once Caresco's dangerous insanity has been taken out of the equation? Readers are scrupulously left to form their own judgment—but it is worth observing that Couvreur abandoned naturalistic fiction after completing his trilogy in progress; almost all of his subsequent fiction, as future sections of the present text will detail, consisted of scrupulously skeptical speculative extrapolations of individual topics raised in the course of *Caresco surhomme*.

In 1905, the writer who, in the opinion of many critics, had become the greatest living writer in France when Victor Hugo died, **Anatole France**, who had become a convert to communism after involving himself ardently in the Dreyfus affair, produced his own vision of a communist eutopia in the final section of *Sur la pierre blanche* (1905; tr. as *The White Stone*), a philosophical novel in which a dialogue regarding the difficulties of anticipating the future serves as a frame for debates about various more specific topics, including the possibility of world peace, and the respective roles of political reform and technological advancement in securing that goal, in the face of hazards generated by colonialism and racial conflict.

France had written a good deal of imaginative fiction prior to *Sur la pierre blanche*, including numerous extravagant *contes philosophiques*, but he had usually drawn his motifs from Classical mythology, save for an elaborate Voltairean comedy poking fun at occultism, *La Rôtisserie de la Reine Pedauque* (1893; tr. as *At the Sign of the Reine Pedauque*), which had drawn the greater part of its imagery from *Le Comte de Gabalis*. *Sur la Pierre blanche* was not a pivotal work in his production in the sense that it changed his fundamental *modus operandi*, but the satires he produced thereafter, especially the classic *L'Île des pingouins* (1908; tr. as *Penguin Island*) do have a forward-looking dimension, which is extremely skeptical of euchronian ambitions, while nevertheless recognizing their force and relevance.

The discussion in which the characters in the novel engage is punctuated by two long exemplary narratives. In the first, a group of Roman intellectuals in exile encounter Saint Paul in the course of his missionary travels, and confidently conclude in consequence that Christianity has no future, whereas the Roman Empire will undoubtedly recover all of its glory under the governance of its new and artistically-sophisticated emperor, Nero. The second, "Par la porte de corne ou par la porte d'ivoire" (tr. as "Through the Horn or the Ivory Gate") is a Mercieresque dream-fantasy which begins which the narrator contemplating the night sky on the eve of his thirty-ninth birthday (23 September 1903—probably the date on which the passage was written) and wondering whether all the stars, like our sun, illuminate worlds that are host to the same "innumerable sufferings" as ours.

The narrator believes that he can predict exactly how his birthday will go, and is not at all delighted by the prospect. When he wakes up, however, he finds himself in a Robidaesque future of universal aerostatics, in which the workers have obtained political hegemony, while reducing the burden of labor considerably thanks to advanced technologies of production; a handful of men can now bake enough bread to feed an entire Parisian district merely by monitoring the efforts of an automated bakery. The language is no longer entirely recognizable, but he is able to understand references he sees to 28 June in the year 220 of the "Federation of Peoples," which he is soon able to translate as 2270 A.D.

The narrator's immediate thought on realizing that he is in the future is to compare his situation with those of Colonel Fougas in *L'Homme à l'oreille cassée*, H. G. Wells' time traveler and the dreamer in William Morris' *News from Nowhere* (1890)—thus illustrating the fact that the accumulation of literary accounts of the future had by now produced a vocabulary of ideas that would provide a ready intellectual resource not merely for future writers but future time

319

travelers, even if the latter were to remain confined to visionary methods of transport.

The vision of the future is typical of those assuming that social problems will simply vanish if society is organized properly in an egalitarian fashion; there are no more courts of law because there is hardly any crime; marriage no longer exists but people tends to live monogamously by choice; money has been replaced by coupons registering work done, but assistance is available to those unable to work, and work is easily obtainable for those who can; the dreamer has no difficulty in being taken on at the marvelous bakery. There, one of his fellow workers turns out, conveniently, to be a spare-time historian able to fill him in on the evolution of the society, which has come about by means of a classical Marxist proletarian revolution—surprisingly rare in futuristic fiction, considering the political force of the notion—and to make comparisons with the evil olden days. Happiness, however, still proves elusive, and the worker wonders whether humans are really psychologically equipped for it, even in a world from which the traditional evils have been largely banished

Considering that one of the spokesmen in the framing dialogue has complained that H. G. Wells was unfortunately alone in endeavoring to set forth into the literary future as a curious explorer rather than simply using the relevant fictional space to paint hopes or fears, "Par la porte de corne ou par la porte d'ivoire" might be judged something of a weak-kneed venture, in that it is a perfectly straightforward depiction of euchronian hopes, with very little in the way of exploratory extrapolation. It does summarize, however, with unusual neatness and literary elegance, a euchronian viewpoint typical of the imaginary horizons of the time, purified of humor and melodrama alike. The deliberate avoidance of those narrative crutches does not necessarily add to the story's reader-appeal, but it does give the account an honest frankness that one might expect to be more common in euchronian fiction than it actually is. It is noticeable, however, that Anatole France did not repeat that strategy of plain-speaking frankness in his subsequent social commentaries, a much more flamboyant sarcasm coming to the fore in *L'Île des pingouins* and in the magisterial *La Révolte des anges* (1914; tr. as *The Revolt of the Angels*).

A far more radical eutopian transformation is imagined in *L'Amour dans Cinq mille ans* (1908; tr. as *Love in Five Thousand Years*) by "Fernand Kolney" (Fernand Pochon de Colnet, 1868-1930), which could be construed as a reply of sorts to *Caresco surhomme*, going to an opposite extreme in its imagination of a society from which the sexual urge has been banished by scientific contrivance, thus removing a fundamental source of tension and inequality. Pierre Versins' *Encyclopédie* gives the date of the undated first edition as 1905, implying that it followed directly on the heels of Couvreur's novel, but a footnote in the 1928 edition gives the date of the original publication as 1908, and there does not seem to be any reason to doubt the author's word.

The novel is set in a utopian enclave originally established in the wake of a global catastrophe, in which the problems corollary to amorous desire were sternly canceled out by a system of technological castration, enabling everyone to devote themselves to quests for purely intellectual satisfaction—allegedly less implicitly frustrating in their outcomes than quests for erotic fulfillment—resulting in the rapid and extensive scientific progress required to hold the after-effects of the global upheaval at bay.

That premise of *L'Amour dans Cinq mille ans* has the inevitable corollary of posing problems for the reproduction of society, but the author constructs and institutionalizes an elaborate technology of what J. B. S. Haldane would later call "ectogenesis": the creation and development of embryos *in vitro*, in artificial wombs subjected to much more sophisticated and delicate control than those provided by nature. The novel opens in the "Artificial Fertilization Laboratory" in question, with the hero, Sagax, hard at work pursuing his sacred task as a "Creator of Humans," carefully providing the next generation of Superhumans with the prenatal potential necessary to produce not only appropriate numbers of males and females, but adequate quotas of mathematicians, physiologists, pedagogues, etc.

The process of artificial fertilization has not quite eliminated all human involvement, but what remains has been religiously ritualized in a public ceremony in which Sagax employs a golden syringe to inseminate the selected Reproductress who is to supply the next batch of artificial wombs with the fruits of her own. In the particular instance described in the novel, however, the ritual described in the second chapter is disturbed by the unexpected phenomenon of the Reproductress Formosa's apparent sexual arousal by the ceremony—something that ought to be impossible. Although subdued, all the potentials of the sexual act still remain, and they gradually begin to make an unwelcome turbulent reappearance in the supposedly tranquilized society.

Kolney's plot maps the unfolding of the apocalyptic breakdown of his eutopia as it is invaded, slowly at first and then uncontrollably, by the force of erotic desire, returned to it by virtue of an irreparable breakdown of the technology of technical castration to a society that has no social and psychological apparatus for coping with such an urgent disruptive force. Sagax watches as others are gradually overtaken by lust, and observes himself with equal horror as libidinous urges invade and take possession of his own flesh, until the general unleashing of fervor rips the society apart. In a sense, what happens to the characters in Kolney's story is no different from what happens to Mary Hardisson in *Caresco, surhomme* as a result of Caresco's insidious aphrodisiacs, but the altered context makes all the difference in the world to the chances of adaptation, and hence to the nature of the reaction.

Kolney's novel is unusually melodramatic within the context of the euchronian subgenre, the symbolic eruption being much longer drawn out and far more graphically detailed than the climactic volcanic blast that puts paid to Caresco's obsession. It accommodates temporary distractions, such as a visit to the ruins of Paris, supplied with the usual humorous archeological misinterpretations, and the opening of communication with Mars, but those embellishments only supplement an excess that is deliberate and uncompromising in all its narrative aspects. Few other authors have ever made such reckless use of exotic words, many of them improvised, nested in conscientiously overblown descriptions, assertions and speeches. Although the riot of verbiage does make the novel a trifle challenging for the reader, it is a strategy appropriate to the task the author set himself, which necessitated an extremely ambitious imaginative reach and a baroque narrative style.

Kolney's previous endeavors in literature and social crusading—he was a militant atheist, a fervent anarchist, and loathed all politicians, especially the ones currently in power—demonstrate an extreme annoyance at the fact that no one took any conspicuous notice of his strident attempts to persuade the French people and government to institute a policy of national birth control on Malthusian grounds. He was already an angry man even before he published his first novel, *Le Salon de Madame Truphot* (1904), and *L'Amour dans Cinq mille ans* is to a large extent an expression of that anger, in its violence as well as its pugnacious desire to shock.

The reception of his first novel must have fed Kolney's anger, although he cannot have been entirely surprised by the reaction it produced. *Le Salon de Madame Truphot* is a satirical *roman à clef* in which the various members of the salon in question are easily recognizable. The poet Jehan Rictus, parodied in the novel as "Modeste Glaviot," brought a prosecution for libel and demanded twenty-five thousand francs in damages. Madame Truphot is based on Henriette Maillat, a would-be occultist and literary muse who is nowadays most famous as the principal model for Hyacinthe Chantelouve in Joris-Karl Huysmans' *Là-Bas* (1891); she had previously been the mistress of the pseudo-Rosicrucian occultist and prolific novelist Joséphin Péladan and the outspoken Catholic polemicist and writer of *contes cruels* Léon Bloy, both of whom are pseudonymously featured among Madame Truphot's associates, along with the flamboyant dandy Comte Robert de Montesquiou, the Symbolist writer Frédéric Boutet, then best-known for his Poesque horror stories, and the Socialist journalist and politician Jean Jaurès.

Kolney's contemporaries took the view that he must have had source of "inside information" on which to draw, if, in fact, he had written the book at all, and pointed the finger of suspicion at his brother-in-law, the Symbolist poet Laurent Tailhade (1854-1919). The two had been friends for some years before the marriage, both being ardent polemicists with strong anarchist sympathies. Even if Tailhade did make an informational contribution to *The Salon de Madame Truphot*, however, Kolney's subsequent work strongly suggests that he really did write the book himself. The author's *alter ego* in the novel, Eliphas de Béothus, crops up in three of Kolney's later novels, including *Les Aubes mauvaises* [Evil Dawns] (1905) as well as *L'Amour dans cinq mille ans*, but other books listed in the latter volume as forthcoming—including *L'Androphobe* [The Man-Hater] and *La Bacchante des noires ivresses* [The Bacchante of Black Intoxication] failed to materialize at the time, and any ambition that Kolney might have entertained then to build a literary career seems to have been derailed at that point.

L'Amour dans cinq mille ans might have been circulated to commercial publishers and rejected, but it seems more likely that the author knew before he set pen to paper that no commercial publisher would touch it at the time of writing, and always planned to issue it himself. It was not his first venture into self-publishing, being preceded by *La Grève des ventres* [The Womb-Strike] (1907), a more straightforward exercise in Malthusian propaganda. Kolney founded the monthly periodical *Le Malthusien* in 1908, although it did not last long, and *L'Amour dans cinq mille ans* was probably printed on the periodical's press; the latter is credited as the publisher of the pamphlet *Le Crime d'engendrer* [The Crime of Breeding] (1909), which mostly consists of quotes from *Le Salon de Madame Truphot* and *La Grève des ventres*.

Because the idea of artificial fertilization, as applied to human reproduction, is now perfectly familiar to us, it is a trifle difficult to imagine how shocking it might have seemed in 1908. It had been treated in French literature prior to that date, but very tentatively, notably in *Le Faiseur d'hommes* (1884), signed "Yveling Ram Baud and Dubut de Laforest" but probably written by the signatory of its preface, Georges Barral. The novel is a sentimental melodrama in which a husband who initially believes that his pregnant wife must have committed adultery eventually has difficulty deciding whether that explanation might have been preferable to the truth of her technologically-determined conception. The gap between that tentative approach to the notion and Kolney's depiction of a society whose sole mode of reproduction is based on artificial fertilization is, however, an exceedingly wide one, further widened by the supportive logic of the hypothetical institution.

In fact, the ambition explicitly expressed in the preface to *L'Amour dans cinq mille ans* to be forerunner of a new post-Romantic school of fiction proved more justified than might have been expected; in retrospect, the narrative can be regarded as a significant precursor of Symbolism's own descendent school of Surrealism; the images it deploys are manifestly better regarded as the raw substance of nightmarish dreams than the products of rational extrapolation, disciplined speculation and considered opinion. Many of the inconsistencies in the text are explicable in terms of the fact that the author obviously made up the story as he went along, changing his mind in regard to some points and being unable to make it up in regard to some others, but there is also a manifest and insistent dream-illogic about some of his narrative shifts, which has deeper psychological implications.

As well as expressing a qualified residual allegiance to Romanticism, Kolney's preface represents his novel explicitly as a Nihilist text, and although French Anarchists such as Louise Michel regarded Russian Nihilism merely as an alternative term for the same political philosophy, Kolney attempts to map out a further philosophical dimension. His insistence in *L'Amour and cinq mille ans* that an Anarchist eutopia would be doomed to collapse just like every other supposedly-ideal society might have been regarded as intellectual treason by some of his associates, but, although there is undoubtedly a tongue-in-cheek element to Kolney's assertion that Nihilism is the only viable philosophy, and that the development of the novel's narrative is an alleged exemplar of that philosophy, a serious point is nevertheless being made in lurid jest.

Another leap into a technologically advanced future is detailed in *La Cité du sommeil* (1909), signed "Maurice Barrère," in which a number of Parisians volunteer to use a suspended animation serum that will put them to sleep for three hundred years in order that they can see what will become of the great city in the meantime. They find a placid Robidaesque milieu in which everything works by courtesy of electricity, roads have become redundant, and thoughts can be read at a distance. The socialist député included in the party of temporal explorers, however, cannot resist the urge to stir up trouble, with the aid of a disaffected scientist, and their antics conclude in disaster—which some of the still-hopeful characters escape by returning to suspended animation.

The observation made by one of the participants in Anatole France's dialogue that too few writers ventured into hypothetical futures with an open-minded spirit of enquiry rather than simply using it as a medium to paint their hopes and fears, thus preventing the full emergence of a *roman futuriste* of the kind that Félix Bodin had hoped to find, probably prompted more than one writer to try the experiment, assisted by the exemplary exercises provided by H. G. Wells in the final years of the nineteenth century and rapidly translated into French. One who took the notion quite literally was the playwright and dramatic theorist Jean Jullien (1854-1919), who pretended to do exactly what France had requested, in *Enquête sur le monde futur* (1909; tr. as "An Investigation of the

World of the Future") in which the narrator represents himself as a reporter for the *Universal Informer* dispatched to America to interview the people whose projects and discoveries are in the process of laying the foundations for the future development and transformation of human society.

If Anatole France read Jullien's book he would probably have dismissed it as a relatively insignificant text because it does not appear to take its quest very seriously, offering a series of sarcastic fantasies, which eventually takes care to obliterate its own dubious authority, but if one looks at it in the context of previous attempts to explore the future with attitudes that have something in common with Bodin's proposal, it is evident that it reproduces and extrapolates features typical of many, if not all of them, and is more significant than a casual glance at its frothy surface might suggest.

The first person the reporter interviews is a would-be prophet who, while retaining many aspects of the typically American version of the tub-thumping prophet, is a mathematician whose statistical methods allegedly constitute a genuine "prescience." The possible paradoxes that might arise from accurate anticipation of future possibilities are, however, immediately thrown into sharp relief when the reporter, intent on seducing the scientist's seemingly-complaisant wife, has to wonder every step of the way whether he has been anticipated, and whether, if so, his quest will be thwarted as a result.

The reporter is subsequently uninspired by the religiously-inspired eugenic plans of the New Life Club, and is rendered slightly queasy by the physiological experiments of Professor Fuss, who is attempting, under the inspiration of *Telliamed*, to develop artificial superhumans directly from the marine womb, by means of an accelerated evolution that will surpass the stage currently reached by the natural one. More evident results seem to have been achieved by a system of intense technologically-assisted education applied in an ultra-modern school, and even more so by the engineer John Eddy, whose studies of "radiant matter" have led him to develop means of storing and redeploying mental energy.

The reporter gets personally involved with his research again more than once, notably when investigations of a "rational marriage bureau" more advanced than the one featured in *Monsieur Personne*, which has every feature of modern computer dating except the computer, all the sorting and analysis having to be done by hand. Disappointments set in again thereafter, however, and his ingenious efforts to win admission to the secret establishment of Immortality Co. Ltd. endanger his life when he finally succeeds—after which he decides, perhaps wisely, to give up.

When he is put on the spot by his editor, the reporter finally has to confess that he has not actually done the legwork of trailing all over America, and has simply made up his account of the makers of the future—as, indeed, the author really has—but that does not affect the fact that they provide an interestingly laconic survey of early-twentieth-century euchronian ideas, all treated with a similar combination of curiosity and cynicism.

The narrative strategy of attempting to weigh the euchronian or dystopian potential of new technologies while showing them "in embryo," as Jullien does, became increasingly common as the twentieth century progressed; in more sophisticated fiction dealing with hypothetical technologies, that kind of evaluation gradually became an intrinsic part of the exercise, if not the whole point of it. A particularly graphic early example is provided by **Edmond Haraucourt**'s "La Découverte du docteur Auguérande" (1910; tr. as "Doctor Auguérande's Discovery"), which subjects an old idea—in this case, an "immortality serum"—to that kind of scrupulous re-examination, wondering how society might and ought to react to the news, not only of the existence of the new technology, but also to the proposed manner of its distribution.

In this particular instance, the new serum is discovered by a humanitarian scientist who is not concerned to exploit it commercially. Indeed, he wants to give it away, free of charge, to everyone, and so, after having announced his discovery, he invites the population of Paris simply to form a queue: a naïve move that complicates the various problems that immediately emerge as the world reacts to the news of his triumph far less enthusiastically that he had anticipated. Indeed, the press-stimulated public reaction is so hysterically alarmed and reflexively negative that Auguérande's clinic and his defenders have no chance of surviving the violent backlash, and the remote possibility left at the end of the story that he has not been killed suggests that the circumstances and cost of his survival might lead to consequences even worse than his death.

Haraucourt's biological inventor is explicitly likened to Christ, recapitulating his messianic role by bringing humans the gift of new life, and crucified for his pains. Whereas conventional technophobic thrillers routinely present accounts of "mad scientists" making dangerous discoveries that threaten to upset worlds whose sanity is taken for granted, Haraucourt sarcastically overturns the formula, representing Auguérande as a quintessentially sane individual caught up in a whirlwind of violence that exposes the inherent insanity lurking beneath the surface of civilization. The euchronian potential of the invention, potentially capable of creating a society largely liberated from the threat of death, if only its adaptation can be sanely organized, is obliterated by the swift reaction of those alarmed by the immediately-evident costs of disrupting the status quo.

The particular satirical irony of Haraucourt's narrative remained relatively rare for some time, but the simpler notion that euchronian dreams were, after all, mere "*utopies*" in the sense that they were inherently unrealizable, even in possession of the technological means and engineering skills necessary to build them, remained convincing as well as convenient as a means of concluding parables offering accounts of eutopia-builders. One particularly striking example almost exactly contemporary with Haraucourt's, serialized in a more downmarket periodical, was "Un Monde sur le monde" (1910-11; tr. as "A World Above the World") by Jules Perrin and the illustrator Henri Lanos, in which a billionaire's attempt to construct a technologically advanced eutopian supercity elevated literally as well as metaphorically above the existing society, by virtue of its placement on top of a huge pedestal, eventually comes to grief, as it is inexorably eroded in its social as well as its technological foundations.

En plein vol [In Full Flight] (1913), the only novel by the innovative printer and publisher Albert Quantin (1850-1933), opens on 1 January 2001, with the President of the French Nation finishing a speech delivered in the Palais National to an audience of thirty thousand people, his voice relayed to the remotest corners by a novel sound system. He has devoted his speech to the glorification of the socialist society that has been functioning smoothly for 69 years, after the initial difficulties of its establishment. The last debts owed by the State to the former holders of private capital have now been paid off.

The protagonist, Elie Montorier, meets Claire Landin and the disabled Marie Denvol while marveling at the edifice and they take a stroll together through the new city of Paris. They agree to meet again to watch a meeting of the national assembly, and that becomes the prelude to a series of meetings in which they witness and discuss the various aspects of the socialist society. The text is interrupted by long expository sections, some complete with statistical tables, adding further detail to Elie's educational discourses.

Elie and Claire marry—in Church—and take a rapid honeymoon tour of France before returning to the capital to provide opportunities for the reader to see its museums and its education system, and to continue the economic description. They also have the opportunity to try out its medical facilities after an accident, but the time of forced rest enables Elie to make a useful invention that will speed up the manufacture of shoes; that stroke of luck involves him with the new society's encouraging management of science and discovery.

Like Alain le Drimeur, however, Quantin is determined to make his text a novel as well as a tract, and his plot eventually gets into gear when Elie is seduced away from Claire and their children by an actress, creating the kind of emotional turmoil that was commonplace in the old imperfect world of the early twentieth century, thus testing the marital laws and mores of the new society.

Victim in her turn to the attempted seductions of a poet, Claire is counseled by the saintly Marie, who becomes the story's supposed voice of reason—reason that Elie conspicuously lacks when tested, folly leading him to violence and hence to trial, judgment and imprisonment. When his sentence ends, however, hope still remains, and the final lesson delivered by Marie is that although Socialism cannot eliminate sin, as some previous eutopians had hoped, it can still fulfill the task of humanity by making reparation possible.

In Quantin's view, therefore—and he was by no means alone—although criticisms of social design and cynicism regarding human nature admittedly had to be taken into account, euchronian dreams were still in full flight in 1913, without having yet been conclusively shot down by the hunters' blasts. Perhaps, at that moment in time, he was right—but the guns were nevertheless thick on the ground, fully-loaded and ready to fire again.

Les Pacifiques (1914; tr. as "The Pacifists") by **Han Ryner**, redeploys the narrative strategy of employing an unsympathetic narrator, which the author had earlier employed effectively in "Un Roman historique" while he was still spelling his name Henri Ner, this time to react against an explicitly Anarchist utopia situated in a fugitive remnant of Atlantis, the author's politics having become more extreme in the interim.

Like Théodose in the first of Léonie Rouzade's utopian novellas, the narrator of the story—who refuses to provide his name on the grounds that he intends running for political office and does not want his campaign to be vulnerable to accusations of fantasization—find refuge after being shipwrecked on an island whose society is very different from the bourgeois French society of which he is an allegedly-typical product. Of all the castaways, however, he is the last to be welcomed into the hospitality of the natives, finally being taken into the home of an old man named Makima.

Makima guides the stranger to his land very patiently through its customs, explaining its vegetarianism, based on biologically-enhanced fruits and vegetables, the operation of the "belts" that give every individual the power of flight, and the elements of its egalitarian and leaderless social organization. The narrator runs into difficulties, however, when Makima invites him to address an informal class of children eager to know about the society of the wider world, whose members raise naïve objections to his account of its religion and politics, initially refusing to believe in them and eventually concluding that the "Cruels" must be insane. He runs into further trouble when he attempts to service his sexual needs in a society where prostitution does not exist and the rituals of courtship associated with free love requires polite formalities to which he cannot accommodate himself.

Although he is impressed by the technology of the pantoscope, which allows him glimpses of the world he has left behind, and the advanced mechanical technologies of Syndynamics, the castaway deems the uses made of them in anarchist society far too modest, and thinks that capitalist society could make far more of their exploitation. With that in mind, he joins a conspiracy headed by the Captain of the ship whose foundering stranded the castaways, to take over the island by armed force—they know that the Atlanteans, being confirmed pacifists, will not put up any resistance—in order to establish themselves as its rulers and open it up to a commerce that is bound to be extremely profitable. Some of their fellow castaways, having "gone native," refuse to join the conspiracy, but enough of them do pledge support to provide an appearance of certain success. The plan goes badly awry, of course, but the Atlanteans are finally obliged to agree that there is no place in their society for the likes of the Captain and the narrator, who are sent back to the Cruel world that they love so stubbornly.

By virtue of its ironic narrative method, *Les Pacifiques* is the most violently melodramatic of all pacifist utopias, adopting that strategy as a means of loading the dice in favor of non-violence. It does not, however, shirk the central problem of describing a pacifist anarchist society in some detail, and it takes care to offer robust arguments in its favor as well as leveling scathing criticism at its opposite—a bullet that only a handful of anarchist polemicists were willing and able to bite.

Although it was probably written some years earlier—the evidence of the text suggests 1905—*Les Pacifiques* was published on the eve of the Great War, a matter of weeks before that conflict exploded; the only review currently accessible via *gallica* appears in the 5 July 1914 issue of *Les Annales*. That was undoubtedly not the best timing for the publication of a pacifist utopia, although the dearth of other reviews probably reflects prejudice against its anarchism rather than awareness of the untimeliness of its pacifism. At any rate the novel dropped out of sight somewhat in consequence, although it is one of the most striking and effectively challenging of all Ryner's works.

Les Pacifiques was by no means the last eutopia to be published, but its appearance weeks before the Great War broke out did mark the end of a historical phase that was uniquely rich in the production of speculative fiction fascinated by euchronian ideals, anxious either to promote or decry them, and in which the importance of the potential roles that technological progress might play in the amelioration or spoliation of future society made euchronian and dystopian fantasies an important branch of *roman scientifique*, or *roman scientifique* an important branch of utopian fiction, depending on the viewpoint adopted.

The importance of that association did not change, of course, but the fundamental attitude underlying any and all approaches to the question did, to such

an extent that there is no need for the next chapter of the present project to devote a special section to eutopian fantasies, that being a sector of thought in
which all dreams, even if they had not turned to nightmares, had become deeply
steeped in the kinds of anxiety that had invaded such *fin-de-siècle* exercises as
Lettres de Malaisie. After 1914, all utopian dispatches had to be sent from a land
of Unease, even if they were conscientiously stamped with other postmarks.

2. Verne and the Vernians

Jules Verne was one of the few writers in France whose career did not
seem to observers to have suffered any significant interruption by the war of
1870-71—and, indeed, mostly staying in Amiens, although he had not yet established a permanent residence there, he continued working through the time of
the upheaval, although he did visit Paris during the brief rule of the Commune
and was deeply shocked by what he saw. The impression of seamlessness in his
production was encouraged by the publication in 1872 of *Aventures de trois
Russes et de trois Anglais dans l'Afrique australe* (tr. as *The Adventures of
Three Russians and Three Englishmen in South Africa*).

That account of a scientific expedition in the 1850s to make measurements
permitting an accurate deduction of the Earth's shape, which is disrupted when
news of the Crimean war causes conflict between its participants, was one of
two novels that Verne wrote when the troubles were at their worst; the other,
originally titled *Les Naufragés du Chancelor*, inspired by the story immortalized
by Géricault's famous painting *Le Radeau de la Méduse* [The Raft of the Medu-
sa], was deemed too horrific by Hetzel, and was not published until it had been
completely rewritten, as *Le Chancelor* (tr. as *The Survivors of the Chancellor*) in
1875.

Verne had apparently not been paid the money that Hetzel owed him during the war. He was also beginning to find the obligation to deliver three volumes a year taxing, but post-war inflation threatened to render the contractual
payments even for three volumes inadequate to meet his needs. Fortunately, he
was able to renegotiate his contract, increasing the payment while reducing his
obligation to the provision of two volumes a year—but Verne then disagreed
with Hetzel again over the best means of extending the length of his next novel
in progress, the Canada-set *Le Pays des fourrures* (1873; tr. as *The Fur Country*).

The scientific element in *Le Pays des fourrures* is more marginal than in
Aventures de trois Russes et de trois Anglais dans l'Afrique australe, where the
scientific expedition provides the backcloth to the plot and the primary motivation of all its characters. In *Le Pays de fourrures*, an astronomer's mission to observe an eclipse is merely tacked on to the main narrative, the long climax of
which concerns the slow and suspenseful diminution of a fragment of the Arctic

ice-sheet on which a trading post has been unwisely built, as it drifts south-wards; the novel is very much an adventure story with a minor component of scientific observation, perhaps too slight to give the novel any real interest in the context of the development of *roman scientifique*. In the meantime, Verne had published one item of pure *roman scientifique* in the novella "Une fantaisie du Docteur Ox" (1872; tr. as "Dr Ox's Experiment"), a light-hearted story in which a project to bring improved gas lighting to a small town has unexpected side-effects when an escape of oxygen causes general inebriation, but the scientific component of the majority of his longer works continued to shrink like the ice-berg in *Le Pays des fourrures*.

The latter novel was followed by the work that brought Verne to the peak of his celebrity and remains his most famous, *Le Tour du monde en quatre-vingts jours* (1872 as a *feuilleton* in *Le Temps*; book 1873; tr. as *Around the World in Eighty Days*). It sold well from the start, but its popularity was further boosted a few years later by an extraordinarily lavish adaptation for the stage, which gained enormous publicity. Verne was once again trying to make an im-pact in the medium that had been the focus his initial ambition, but he found the path far from smooth, in spite of his acquired fame. His next major project in prose was the languorous completion of a Robinsonade of which he had pro-duced a first draft in the 1860s but had not taken up again in the interim because Hetzel, when it was first shown to him, did not like it. The new version became *L'île mystérieuse* (1874-75; tr. as *The Mysterious Island*).

In the story, five assorted castaways—the usual trio of participants in dis-cussion, plus a negro servant and a child—eventually contrive to make life on a desert island comfortable, due to the incessant ingenuity of the scientist of the party, Cyrus Smith, with subtle assistance from an unknown benefactor—who eventually turns out to be Captain Nemo, perhaps making a return appearance by popular demand, but more likely because Verne had a particular soft spot for the character. Nemo's death provides the novel with an unusual climax, strange-ly heartfelt in its sense of tragedy, almost as if Verne were bidding adieu to a fraction of his soul—and his next few works gave the impression that, along with Nemo, he had put away his fascination with progressive science. The raw material was not entirely banished from his work, but the forthright attitude of such early works as *Voyage au centre de la terre* and *De la terre à la lune* did not survive with it.

Verne's next novel, serialized as *Le Courrier du Tzar* in 1875 and reprint-ed in 1876 as *Michel Strogoff* was a straightforward adventure story, with no scientific component at all, although it features an imaginary invasion of Russia by Tartars. Like *Le Tour du monde en quatre-vingts jours*, it was a big hit when adapted for the stage, and that success might have played some part in restrain-ing the fantastic elements in Verne's subsequent works, although the trend al-ready seemed firmly set before then.

In contrast to that trend, however, Verne did set off into space again in *Hector Servadac* (1877), in which a fragment of the Earth's surface is dislodged by a cometary impact and carried away on a journey through the solar system. An assorted group of castaways establishes a tolerable *modus vivendi*, with the exception of an English contingent, whose stubborn isolationism is rewarded in kind when the comet eventually splits into two. The obligatory scientist, Palmyrin Rosette, is considerably more eccentric than Verne's previous studies of the scientific mind, but the text as a whole shares that peculiarity; the ending is nonsensical, and presumably bears the hallmark of Hetzel's meddling, although it could hardly have made sense however it was handled.

After publishing his rewritten version of Paschal Grousset's utopian fantasy in 1879, Verne inserted an elephantine automaton into *La Maison à vapeur* (1880; tr. as *The Steam House*), but the novel is otherwise a straightforward adventure story; so were the next half-dozen novels he published, although a few technological devices play a marginal role in *Mathias Sandorf* (1885). He reverted deliberately thereafter, however, at least to the pattern of his early works, if not their attitude, when he reproduced the basic formula of *Vingt mille lieues sous les mers* in *Robur le conquérant* (1886; tr. as *The Clipper of the Clouds*), substituting an airship for the submarine.

As the ex-secretary of Nadar's society for encouraging the development of aerial navigation, Verne had long been interested in the possibility that heavier-than-air flying machines would one day take over from aerostats in a new phase in the human conquest of the air. The Nemoesque Robur is of the same opinion, but his *Albatros* bears very little resemblance to the actual aircraft that were to make their tentative debut in actuality some fifteen years in the future, having a hull like a sailing ship and masts decked with numerous helical propellers to provide lift. The members of the trio of aerostatic enthusiasts kidnapped aboard the vessel in order that they might learn the error of their ways nevertheless persist in their own line of research when they escape, and nearly pay the price when their own buoyant craft is engaged in an aerial duel with the *Albatros*. Unfortunately, Robur has only a fraction of Nemo's charisma, and as an eccentric obsessive scientist, he considerably less likeable than Palmyrin Rosette.

Verne followed up *Robur le conquérant* with an explicit sequel to *De la terre a la lune* in **Sans dessus dessous** (1889; tr. as *The Purchase of the North Pole*), but it is only a sequel insofar as it features the bickering luminaries of the Baltimore Gun Club, Barbicane and Nicholl, whose scheme to alter the world's axis, in order to exploits the mineral deposits of a polar island the Club has bought, fortunately comes to nothing, because the scientist they have commissioned to make the necessary calculations, stunned by a fortuitous lightning-strike, makes a fatal artithmetical error. To an even greater extent than *Robur le conquérant*, whose partly-repentant anti-hero had suggested that technological progress might be better if made slowly, *Sans dessus dessous* seems to indicate a very considerable waning of Verne's enthusiasm for scientific interference with nature—and, indeed, a growing hostility to the idea of change, such as many people experience as they grow older, but which enthusiastic fans of Verne's ebullient early works would not have expected of him.

The belatedly-issued *Le Château des Carpathes* (1892; tr. as *Carpathian Castle*) is also a *roman scientifique* after a fashion, but in the limited sense that it uses hidden scientific contrivances to explain seemingly-supernatural occurrences. Verne was by no means finished with the substance of *roman scientifique*, however. A marked return of innovative energy is visible in *L'île à hélice* (1895; tr. as *Propellor Island*), in which the world's richest men construct a movable island as a tax-avoidance measure, in an unspecified era of the future that has numerous similarities to Albert Robida's image of the 1950s. The subsequent adventures of the peripatetic island are partly satirical and partly farcical, in a spirit akin to Robida's, although the story eventually turns into melodrama as the explosion of conflict within the city results in it being literally torn apart, thus licensing dire warnings against technological hubris dutifully issued by the narrative voice.

Face au drapeau (1896; tr. as *For the Flag*) is similarly enterprising, tracking events following the invention by a French scientist, Thomas Roch, of a kind of ultimate weapon, the fulgurator: a flying torpedo carrying an enormously powerful explosive charge. Having tried unsuccessfully to sell his invention to several nations unwilling to meet his price, Roch suffers a mental breakdown and is hospitalized, precipitating a contest to winkle his secret out of him by hook or by crook. Eventually persuaded to sell the device to pirates, Roch continues to be parsimonious with the ultimate details long enough for an appeal to be made to his patriotic sentiments at a crucial moment. The success of that appeal, however, only gets him blown up, along with his invention. That kind of normalizing denouement was always popular with writers of thrillers with a component of *roman scientifique* because it supplied such a neat story-arc and such spectacular climaxes, but it also has an inherent negativity more considerable than the normalizing moves made at the end of Verne's earlier enterprises in *roman scientifique*.

The endless repetition of that particular narrative formula has a cumulative effect giving the impression that all technological innovation is inherently evil, and that all innovators are best destroyed along with their inventions—a syndrome that one of the twentieth century's most prolific popularizers of science, Isaac Asimov, eventually dubbed "the Frankenstein complex"—but *Face au drapeau* was written in an era when it had not yet become conventional, and Verne cannot be blamed for its formularization, although his version was definitely one of his more ominous anticipations of things to come. The evolution of the image of the scientist within his work, from Professors Lidenbrock and Aronnax through Nemo and Palmyrin Rosette to Robur and Roch, shows distinct symptoms of an increasing psychological pathology.

S. Henry Berthoud had been aware of the pathological possibilities of his descriptions of the scientific mind from the very beginning, but had felt them more than adequately balanced, not so much by the equally pathological potentialities of the non-scientific mind, as by the tremendous technological rewards that their obsessive inventiveness might produce. The explorations of Jules Verne and his many followers increasingly suggested, however, as the nineteenth century drew toward its close, that there were fewer crumbs of comfort to be gleaned from that apparent compensation than had once been hoped.

There are elements of speculative fiction in *Le Sphinx des glaces* (1897; tr. as *An Antarctic Mystery*), Verne's sequel to Edgar Poe's *Narrative of Arthur Gordon Pym* but the story uses its simple imaginative devices in the same deflating and anti-climactic fashion as those in *Le Château des Carpathes*, which robs them of any real interest. The most interesting of Verne's later ventures in *roman scientifique* is the one contained in the climactic chapters of *Le village aérien* (1901; tr. as *The Village in the Treetops*), which offers a thoughtful account of the discovery of a new primate species by two explorers who flee into dense forest in order to escape an attack by elephants. There they discover evidence of the passage of the primatologist Professor Johausen, and eventually Johausen himself. Having been captured by the Wagddis [changed to Waggdis in the English translation], members of a species intermediate between great apes and humans, who can speak, use fire and have a fairly elaborate culture, including a religion, although they are hunter-gatherers who do not plant crops, Johausen has contrived to make himself their king. The novel clearly endorses evolutionism in a tacit fashion, although the narrative voice treats the issue rather diplomatically, perhaps for fear of giving offense to the devout members of Verne's family.

The last significant speculative work that Verne completed himself was *Maître du monde* (1904; tr. as *Master of the World*), a lackluster sequel to *Robur le conquérant*, in which Robur, now armed with a submarine called the *Terrible*, which is also capable of traveling on land at high velocity and of sprouting wings, adopts the eponymous title in vainglorious fashion, but is soon severely punished for his arrogance, without having made any real progress toward the mastery in question. Verne's career continued beyond his death, however, by courtesy of his son Michel (1861-1925), who published a number of works under his father's name that he had edited or rewritten— sometimes extensively—from existing drafts, several of which are of interest in the context of *roman scientifique*.

L'invasion de la mer (1905; tr. as *The Invasion of the Sea*), describes a project to flood the Sahara desert, for which a surveying expedition is mounted. In spite of harassment by Touaregs, who would rather the desert remains unameliorated, work on a canal connecting the parts of the desert below sea level to the Gulf of Gabès begin—but an earthquake renders the effort redundant by establishing the connection without the need of human endeavor.

La chasse au météore (1908; tr. as *The Chase of the Golden Meteor*; restored text 1986; tr. as *The Meteor Hunt*) describes the conflict between two amateur astronomers, both of whom claim the priority of the discovery of an anomalous "météore" that turns out to be a bolide—a meteorite, in modern terminology—and whose consequent bitter quarrel threatens to wreck the marriage of the hero and heroine, which requires the consent of one of them. Michel's version introduced the character of Zéphyrin Xirdal, an exceedingly eccentric scientist whose genius enables him to invent a machine to deflect the bolide's course, in order to cause it to fall on land hastily acquired by a billionaire intent on exploiting the gold that has been detected within it by spectroscopy—but the plan goes awry, and when Xirdal realizes the upheavals that the mass of gold is likely to precipitate, he uses his machine to get rid of it, at the cost of some minor physical disturbances.

Les Naufragés du Jonathan (1909; tr. as *The Survivors of the Jonathan*; re-stored text 1987 as *En Magellanie*; tr. as *Magellania*) is a novel extensively re-written by Michel, based on a manuscript that Verne had written in 1897-8 and set aside, perhaps because, on reflection, he thought to too embittered. It employs the archipelago containing Tierra de Fuego as a background for a charac-ter-study representing Verne's reaction against anarchism: a philosophy that he had not only encountered in Paschal Grousset, but with which Michel had toyed for a while before settling for a more moderate form of socialism. The latter was still somewhat at odds with his father's views, so Michel's version removed some of the critical elements of the original story as well as complicating the plot in the interests of melodrama. The anarchist anti-hero of the novel is known as Kaw-Djer, a name bestowed upon him by the indigenes of Magellania, where he has sought eremitic refuge from the society he abhors, and which allegedly means "benefactor." The arrival on one of the islands of survivors of the wreck of the *Jonathan*, a ship carrying assorted emigrants who decide to found a colo-ny there instead of going on to their original destination, ends his isolation and poses a challenge to his ideals.

Le Secret de Wilhelm Storitz (1910, but based on a first draft written in 1904; tr. as *The Secret of Wilhelm Storitz*) is more interesting in the present con-text, by virtue of inviting a direct comparison with the work of H. G. Wells, which Verne read and of which he affected to disapprove when journalists sug-gested to him that his glory as a pioneer of *roman scientifique* was being eclipsed. It is one of several French responses to Wells' *The Invisible Man*, simi-larly couched as a thriller, although its initial mystery, which results in the even-tual discovery and ultimate destruction of the Prussian scientist Wilhelm Storitz and his elixir of invisibility is rendered rather petty by the fact that Storitz em-ploys it in attempts to disrupt the marriage plans of a young woman who reject-ed him as a suitor. The novel was shelved in 1904 because Michel, who was by then his father's first reader and principal confidant, confirmed—accurately—that that it was not as good as Wells' novel and would suffer by comparison. The amendments that Michel made to the text before publishing it did not help—as, alas, his amendments rarely did.

The posthumous novels were supplemented by an elegiac novella pub-lished in the collection *Hier et demain* (1910; tr. as *Yesterday and Tomorrow*), developed by Michel from a fragmentary text abandoned by his father, "L'Eternel Adam" (tr. as "The Eternal Adam"), in which a historian of the far future discovers a manuscript account of a 20th-century world catastrophe. The setting of the story, a hundred and seventy thousand years hence, is unusual in imagining that the Earth's surface only has a single remaining land mass, where the Atlantic Ocean was in our time, and where a new evolution has taken place, *Telliamed*-style, the only surviving species of ancient terrestrial life being hu-mankind. The historian who finds the aluminum capsule containing the key to the mystery is distressed to discover that the philosophy of progress is not a reliable guide for future hopes, and that a cyclical palingenesis seems to be the best hope that nature has to offer.

The last of the "posthumous publications," almost entirely the work of Michel although based on his father's last incomplete manuscript, *Voyage d'étude* [Educational Journey], was *L'Étonnante aventure de la mission Barsac* (serial 1914; book 1919; tr. in two volumes as *Into the Niger Bend* and *The City in the Sahara*), essentially an African adventure story, although it does feature a secret Saharan city, Blackland, tyrannically ruled by the brutal Harry Killer and possessed of advanced technologies by courtesy of the obsessive scientific genus Michel Camaret. The most interesting of the devices in question, although they did not require a great stretch of the imagination by 1914, are pilotless aircraft with adaptable wings, and televisual surveillance systems. The geographical romance of the first part of the story derives from Verne *père*'s manuscript; the account of Blackland and its eventual orgiastic destruction is all Michel's—but it is not so very different in its working out from the climax of *L'Île à hélice*, nor different in spirit from the regretful aspects of Robur's dreams of mastery.

Although many of the later works are rightly reckoned minor, and Verne never recovered the verve of his first few endeavors in *roman scientifique* once the Franco-Prussian War and its aftermath has shaken his once-optimistic faith in the fundamental, if slightly problematic, virtue of scientific progress, the sum total of Verne's contributions to the evolving genre is impressive in its quantity, and it might reckoned a tragedy of sorts that it eventually became so narrow in its range, not so much in terms of its inventions—although others did better in that regard—but in terms of its attitude to scientific possibility, which varied from anxious trepidation to reluctant but resigned hostility. Even when he deliberately returned to his own themes, probably with the intention of recapturing something of his early zest, Verne did so only to subvert them, incapable any longer of summoning up, or at least of maintaining, the kind of enthusiasm that had infused his early works. He had changed markedly as the nineteenth century moved toward its close. He was, however, by no means the only person to be afflicted in that fashion by a sense of the creeping decadence of society and a suspicion of the impotence of technological progress to stop the rot.

The great popularity of Verne's early work spawned abundant imitations, and drew numerous other writers into a subgenre of "Vernian fiction," which thrived throughout the period between the Franco-Prussian War and the Great War of 1914-18, and even survived the trenches, albeit in a somewhat traumatized fashion. Only a handful of the works produced within that subgenre, however, did any better than Verne himself in trying to recover the intensity and energy of his early *romans scientifiques*, no matter how committed they were to making the attempt. The Vernians who followed in the great man's footsteps were partly handicapped by the fact that they were lesser writers, unequipped with his artistry, but there were also more fundamental factors. Verne had changed, in part, because the world had changed, and because everyone else had changed with it, the imaginative trajectory followed by Vernian fiction was broadly similar to that followed by Verne's own work.

One crucial aspect of that change was that the romance of geography was an intrinsically wasting asset. Almost as soon as it had reached its peak, inspired by the rapidity of new discoveries and the principal projects of colonialism, the discoveries in question became familiar aspects of the world map, and European colonial projects began to run into all kinds of trouble—economic, climatic and political—which bogged them down and threatened them with inevitable doom. Adventure stories set in the distant parts of the world could still be exciting, even as their locations passed from the unexplored category to the merely exotic, but the quality of the excitement changed drastically; while not necessarily inferior, it was cheapened and standardized as it was subjected to mass-production.

Vernian fiction was, in essence, a subgenre born in decline, whose funeral oration had been declaimed in advance, by the example of *Le Tour du monde en quatre-vingts jours*, the hypothetical record of which was beaten in actuality in matter of months; the fiction had not necessarily become tired, but it could no longer keep far enough ahead of prosaic reality. That decline was particularly fatal for the aspect of Vernian fiction that related it to the evolutionary development of *roman scientifique*. Vernian writers were careful to retain some of the key motifs of mid-century *roman scientifique*, especially the submarine and the flying machine, but those devices were cheapened and standardized along with everything else, always available for evocation in response to temporary narrative necessity, but very rarely deserving of being objects of intense and enthusiastic focus.

The chief exception to that generalization was the space shot featured in *De la terre à la lune*, which was, in general, considered a little too far out to be standardized, and which, by definition, removed characters from the map containing the slowly-diminishing romance of geography into territories that were not merely unknown but perhaps essentially unknowable. The Vernian romances that retained their innovative drive and their bespoke distinctiveness were, therefore, the interplanetary romances that deliberately picked up where Verne, even in his glory days, had felt obliged to leave off: with the missile fired by the Columbiad turning back as it swung around the Moon and coming back to Earth with a splash. The most ardent of the Vernians were those who understood that the romance of geography had reached its limit, and that if original imaginative inspiration were to be sought, it had to be sought by solving the problems inherent in the attempted realism of *Autour de la lune*: by finding imaginative means of not only landing on the Moon, but of going further.

The one central motif of Vernian fiction that was not securely rooted in Verne's early work was the flying machine. Balloons could be found there in abundance, but in spite of his initial enthusiasm for Nadar's society for the championship of machines that could not only raise humans up to the realms of the birds but give them freedom to maneuver there, Verne let that idea alone until he was himself merely one of a host of imitative Vernians. In spite of such primitive precedents as Restif de La Bretonne's *La Découverte australe*, the Vernian epic of the true conquest of the air had remained unwritten in the 1860s and early 1870s.

The most significant early attempt to fill that gap was made by the most conspicuous Vernian writer to emerge after Jules Rengade's brief incarnation as "Aristide Roger": Alphonse Brown, whose *La Conquête de l'air: 40 jours de navigation aérienne* (tr. as *The Conquest of the Air*) was first published in 1875. The preliminary page devoted to listing other works by the same author clearly spelled out his Vernian ambitions; it lists one title as *"sous presse"*—*La Retraite des quarante-cinq* [The Retreat of the Forty-Five]—and four *"en preparation"*: *Avant le deluge* [Before the Deluge], *Le Fleuve mystérieux* [The Mysterious River], *Aventures extraordinaires du capitaine Bob Kincardy* [The Extraordinary Adventures of Captain Bob

Kincardy] and *L'Ère nouvelle* [The New Era], a prospectus less bold than the one subsequently set out by Louise Michel—who had obviously begun a Vernian romance of her own, some chapters of which are inserted awkwardly into *Les Microbes humains*—but similarly far-reaching.

In the event, only one of those titles appears to have been published, *Aventure de capitaine Bob Kincardy* being the subtitle attached to Brown's second published book, *Voyage à dos de baleine* [A Journey on a Whale's Back] (1876). There is no way of knowing whether the others were completed or not, although the first-named must surely have existed in a finished state, and would presumably have appeared had the publisher survived, but Brown was not able to publish anything more for some while, and when he did continue his career, the great majority of his published works stuck closely to the groove hollowed out by the burgeoning subgenre, leaving *La Conquête de l'air* somewhat isolated in its greater ambition, until a new opportunity opened up.

Alphonse Brown was actually Joseph-Maximilien-André Brown (1841-1902), a resident of Bordeaux and member of the Societé de Géographie Commerciale de Bordeaux. The *Bulletin* of the society designated "A. Brown" in 1877 as a *publiciste*, which would normally mean "journalist" but might, in this instance, simply mean "writer." *La Conquête de l'air* was by no means the first literary work to address the question of aviation, but it was a landmark nevertheless in its determination to tackle the question earnestly and to provide propaganda for its importance. Brown's description of a hypothetical heavier-than-air flying machine was by far the most detailed so far produced, and it set a standard that several subsequent writers attempted heroically, and undoubtedly consciously, to follow.

We now know that Brown's model of heavier-than-air flight is flawed, but it seemed plausible at the time that technologists might well find the secret of such flight by imitating birds. Brown is given credit by some historians for an early use of the term "aéroplane" in the novel (the term had actually been coined by Joseph Pline in 1855) but he does not intend that word to mean what it subsequently came to mean. In common with all his contemporaries, Brown had no inkling of the principle of physics by virtue of which a fixed wing can generate lift, and therefore had no idea that flight might one day be possible using rigid and immobile wings. He takes it for granted that if humans are to emulate birds, their technological wings will have to flap.

We also know now that Brown's solution to the problem of powering his hypothetical machine is similarly impractical—but again, it was by no means implausible at the time. He was right to conclude that the best motors then available—steam engines—were unlikely ever to be adaptable to aviation, because they were simply too heavy in proportion to their power output, and his attempt to get around that problem shows commendable ingenuity for its time. The design of the aircraft featured in *La Conquête de l'air* is, however, a secondary matter, even though the novel goes to such great pains to offer details of its construction and functioning. The real issue at stake is what it can do, and what it will mean for the future of human society.

It is implausible that anyone inventing such a machine would try to go around the world in it without any preliminary trials, but the journey in question, in spite of the wealth of detail carefully added to it, is purely symbolic. The trip around the world is ostentatiously made in forty days, that being exactly half the duration given tremendous emblematic significance by *Le Tour du monde en quatre-vingt jours*, effectively constituting a flag hoisted to signify the novel's affiliation.

As in Verne's novel, the question of whether the circumnavigation can be made within the time-limit becomes the subject of a wager, in this case between the builder of the flying machine, Marcel Valdy, and the Russian and American who chip in to make up the stake he initially puts up against the boastful Englishman Sir Walter Donderry—although the betting frenzy eventually bursts the original bounds spectacularly. Again, as in Verne's novel, the journey is plagued by all kinds of problems, mechanical and political, as the *Céleste* comes down in various locations around the world, not always within easy reach of the fuel-dumps that Marcel has wisely distributed along his planned route. Naturally, the race against time goes all the way to the wire.

Voyage à dos de baleine is also definitively Vernian, but is a trifle implausible as well, featuring an excursion of essentially limited scope. It is effectively an inflated tall tale, which only made a marginal contribution to the tributary subgenre that it was helping to found. That subgenre took its first great leap forward in 1877 with the founding of the *Journal des Voyages*, whose regular *feuilleton* slot became and remained the central venue of Vernian fiction throughout its lifespan. The magazine published more than a thousand issues in its initial series, from 1877 to 1896 and more than nine hundred in a second series from 1896 to 1914. The title was revived again in 1925, died again in 1928 and then rose from the dead once more, very briefly, in 1946, but only the first two series were of any real consequence.

The first feuilleton that ran in the *Journal* was "Un drame au fond de la mer" [A Drama on the Sea-Bed] (1877) by Richard Cortambert, the second "Les Robinson des mers" [The Robinson Crusoe of the Seas] (1877-78) by Pierre Ferragut and the third—considerably shorter than its predecessors—"La Mer libre" [The Open Sea] (1878) by Jules Claretie. None of the three writers went on to make any significant contribution to the Vernian subgenre, although Claretie became famous for other reasons, and made a significant contribution to a different subgenre of *roman scientifique* in a much later phrase of his glittering career. "La Mer libre" is interesting, not so much as a polar romance—the sea, once reached, is an essentially tedious expanse of water—but because of its study of the rivalry between its two protagonists, ex-soldiers who become scientific explorers under the spur of different obsessions, but arrive at the same fatal psychological juncture.

Three of the subgenre's leading contributors made their debuts in the periodical in 1878-80, the first being Jules Gros (1829-1891), with *Le Volcan dans les glaces, aventures d'un mission scientifique au Pôle nord* [The Volcano in the Ice: The Adventures of a Scientific Mission to the North Pole] (1878-79). The second was Armand Dubarry, whose several serials for the periodical are pure adventure stories of no relevance to *roman scientifique*. The third was Louis Boussenard, whose first novel, *Le Tour de monde d'un gamin de Paris* [A Parisian Street-Urchin's World Tour (serial 1779-80; book 1880) spawned a long series of sequels. Boussenard initially worked in the same vein as Dubarry, adapting his work more specifically for teenage readers, and thus hollowing out a niche that enabled him to become the most successful writer in the subgenre for the next two decades. As previously mentioned, he eventually did more imaginatively innovative work, but not until he was specifically requested to do so by the editor of a periodical of a more ambitious kind.

Le Volcan dans les glaces was reprinted in book form in 1879 and again in 1895, in the Nouvelle Bibliothèque Illustrée de Vulgarisation [New Illustrated Library of Popularization]. It describes with minute realism the equipping of an international scientific expedition in 1875 by the American explorer John Wilson, after announcing his intention at a scientific congress. After various conventional adventures on the ice-sheet, where the explorers spent the winter, the discovery of the Arctic volcano is followed by a descent into the crater by the young French scientist Henri Ledru and Alexis Polowskine, where they become trapped following an earthquake. While trying to find a way out, Henri discovers that "Alexis" is actually Mirrine de Kolikef, the daughter of a Russian aristocrat who has adopted a disguise in order to join the expedition, thus providing the plot with a love interest and a conventional denouement.

The novel is unexceptional, but it established Jules Gros as the most solidly Vernian of the three early contributors to the *Journal des Voyages* in terms of erecting frameworks of scientific investigation for his works, just as Boussenard's novel established him as the liveliest and most readable writer of imaginary travelogues. It was Gros who produced the works most closely related to the evolution of *roman scientifique* that appeared in the periodical until Alphonse Brown was recruited to its pages in 1884 with "L'Oasis" (1884-85; reprinted in book form as *Perdu dans les sables* [Lost in the Sands] in 1895), a year before "Pierre Maël" and Louis Jacolliot made their first contributions, and two years before Gaston de Wailly first appeared in its pages.

Because of the effects of its editorial policy on the content and ideological thrust of its *feuilletons*—Pierre Versins describes them collectively as "racist, sadistic, chauvinistic, credulous to the point of imbecility, flattering the worst instincts of the Beast," somewhat unfairly but not wholly inaccurately—the *Journal des Voyages* contributed forcefully to the standardization of Vernian fiction, and to its stereotypy as a form of adventure fiction in which speculative elements played a very marginal role. Its pages cramped the imagination of Louis Boussenard and Alphonse Brown, and later recruits like Jules Lermina, although the latter's anarchism, as previously mentioned, eventually intruded mischievously even into the implicitly hostile environment provided by the periodical. For that reason, therefore, the significant contributions made to the development of *roman scientifique* by some of its regular writers were mostly postponed or displaced, and from the viewpoint of the present history, the most interesting items of Vernian fiction were published elsewhere, on the fringes of the subgenre rather than at its ostensible heart.

Vernian fiction was not, of course, the only kind of fiction that made use of the uncertainties and romance of geography; a rich tradition of "Gulliveriana" had extended from the early eighteenth century, in France as well as England, and it was still producing occasional works in the late nineteenth century of a kind markedly different from Verne's. Thus, *Voyages de Lord Humour; le pays des retrogrades: île de Servat-Abus* [The Voyages of Lord Humor: The Land of the Retrogades, the Island of Servat-Abus] (1876) by Edmond Thiaudière (1837-1930) features a narrator who is declared to be a direct descendent via his mother of the great voyager Gulliver, and offers a marked contrast to the general run of contemporary traveler's tales.

Lord Humour describes his rescue, following a shipwreck, by a crew of cynocephali—dog-headed humans—manning a strange sailing ship, *El Kokass*. They take him to the port of Oua-Oua in their homeland of Servat-Abus, where he is removed from the ship covertly and taken to the home of the teferp, to which he is admitted in the capacity of a domestic servant. The cynocephali are not the only quasi-human species in Servat-Abus; they are mingled with the fox-headed vulpiminois, who seem to be common in the clergy. Lord Humour also sees depictions of dog-headed soldiers—whose maneuvers look odd because of their habit, commonplace among the people of Servat-Abus, of marching backwards—fighting enemy soldiers with the heads of ostriches, whose maneuvers also seem eccentric because they are mounted on gnus that can only walk and run sideways.

Having been granted a status more akin to that of a guest than a servant, Humour is able to see something of Servat-Abusan society and study its mores, witnessing an election and attending a ball in honor of one Effutrat. He is also able to visit the great capital city of Hak-Hak, where he is introduced to the court, familiarizing himself with the royal family, and is assisted to learn the language. He is present during a *coup-d'état* carried out by Prince Nobruob against the reigning King Snaëlro, but continues to enjoy a privileged status that enables him to carry forward his observation of local customs and to learn more about the relationship between the church and the state, the censorship of the news, the operation of bureaucracy and other matters of marginal interest to him. He becomes the subject of a sermon preached in the Temple, somewhat to his discomfort, but is not surprised to find the local lunatic asylum filled with sane and honest individuals.

The political upheavals in Hak-Hak continue with a further coup, this time carried out by Prince Etrapanob, whose eagle takes against the narrator's peculiar head, forcing him to wring the bird's neck in self-defense—which naturally gets him thrown in prison, until he is rescued by a helpful vulpinoise, in whose complex family affairs he has also become entangled, and is enabled to flee aboard the *Zarre-bi* to the isles of Foederia. A further report was promised of his adventures there, but does not seem to have materialized.

In addition to the future war story to which reference will be made in a later section, Thiaudière produced several other works of marginal relevance to the present project, most notably the novella "Le Docteur Melanski," in *Trois amours singulières* (1886), which references Allen Kardec and animal magnetism in its account of a exceedingly peculiar relationship between the eponymous protagonist, a skeleton and a miniature portrait. The others are the moral tale *Le Chien du Bon Dieu, conte céleste* [God's Dog, a Celestial Tale] (1894) and *Contes d'un éleveur de chimères* [Tales of a Chimera-Breeder] (1902). The author had studied medicine and was the founder and editor in the late 1870s of the *Revue des idées nouvelles: Bulletin du progrès dans la philosophie, les sciences, les lettres, les arts, l'industrie, le commerce et l'agriculture.*

Although Lord Humour's relationship with the development of *roman scientifique* is marginal, the satirical tradition represented by Thiaudière and other contemporary humorists became entangled with the history of Vernian fiction, perhaps inevitably, in a long quasi-Gulliverian part-work that was part-parody and part tribute in respect of its Vernian inclusions, which are specific to the extent of probably being legally actionable—although Verne, who was apparently amused by it, was in no mood to sue—while remaining broadly comical in a fashion reminiscent of the exploits of Lord Humour. The work in question was ***Voyages très extraordinaires de Saturnin Farandoul dans les 5 ou 6 parties du monde et dans tous les pays connus et même inconnus de M. Jules Verne*** [The Very Extraordinary Voyages of Saturnin Farandoul in the World's five or six Continents, and in all the Countries known—and even unknown—to Monsieur Jules Verne] (1879; tr. as *The Adventures of Saturnin Farandoul*) by Albert Robida.

Each installment of the part-work consisted of an eight-page pamphlet, of which there were a hundred in all. The pamphlets were rebound and reissued in 1880 as an eight-hundred-page paperbound book, with the modification that the full-page color illustrations that had served as covers in the part-work, which were blank on the rear, were stripped of text repeating the title and mostly relocated within the text. A contents section was also added as a supplement. The novel was never reprinted again thereafter, although a silent movie version of part of the text was made in Italy in 1914 by Marcel Perez.

Robida had already built up a considerable reputation as an illustrator and caricaturist before embarking on the serial, but it was his first novel, and it represented a very ambitious undertaking. Its format and magnitude must have been planned in advance, and Robida must therefore have blithely undertaken to produce a 200,000-word text, organized into five equal sections, each of which would be further divided into ten chapters, without any significant experience of writing long fiction. He probably intended each chapter to consist of two pamphlets, but some actually ran to three, thus requiring others to be restricted to one. Each pamphlet had to fill up the available space more-or-less exactly, meaning that its text had to be tailored to fit the space available once the illustrations had been set in place—a task that inevitably provided a stern challenge to the writer's organizational skills, and probably required a good deal of editing.

In each of the five parts of his own worldwide adventures, Saturnin Farandoul meets one of Jules Verne's characters. Captain Nemo appears in Part One, initially to save Farandoul and the crew of his ship when they are under attack from a legion of pirates, and then to serve the same function again, following the hero's conquest of Australia at the head of an army of apes, recruited via the orangutans who raised him when he was cast away as a baby. His subsequent reign as monarch is treacherously undone by English cunning and apish vulnerability to flattery and alcohol, and Nemo's rescue arrives once again in the nick of time.

In Part Two it is Farandoul who first fills the role of rescuer, by getting Phileas Fogg and a host of damsels that Fogg has saved from distress out of a sticky situation in North America, but when the two meet up again in a more southerly region of the same continent they become rivals, taking different sides in a Civil war fought with weapons far more advanced than any yet seen in Europe, in which the seeds were sown of an important strand in Robida's future work.

Part Three begins as an African adventure, in which Farandoul employs all his ingenuity and superhuman strength to liberate the captive European "queens" of a primitive tribe, but he and they are then carried off into space by the comet that abducted Hector Servadac and are transported by it all the way to Saturn, where they are stranded among exotic aliens and imprisoned as exhibits in a zoo, until they can contrive an escape—after which they manage to hitch a ride on the comet again, now on its way sunwards.

In Part Four, set in the Far East, Farandoul and his much-harassed companions have great difficulties fitting in with the exotic culture, and excite the enmity of an evil Oriental mastermind of a kind that was later to become a cliché of popular fiction. Following a siege in a harem, they are obliged set out in pursuit of an escaped white elephant, whose long flight eventually brings them into contact with Michel Strogoff in the wastes of Siberia.

In Part Five, an adventure set mostly at sea, Farandoul runs into Captain Hatteras, who has turned pirate, before visiting European Russia and finally concluding his far-flung adventures with a hectic ride on a gradually-diminishing but solidly-packed shoal of herring, inherently less stable but more conveniently nourishing than a whale or an iceberg.

Even though Verne raised no objection, he surely cannot have approved of the manner in which Robida developed and altered some of the characters he borrowed. Captain Nemo is the only one whose manifestation in *Saturnin Farandoul* is approximately faithful to Verne's model; he plays the same supportive role with respect to Farandoul as he does to the castaways of *L'Île mystérieuse*, albeit in a more violent manner. All four of the other characters, who play broadly heroic roles in Verne's originals, become Farandoul's enemies, routinely undermining his projects and threatening him, actively or by neglect, with death. In spite of the inherent absurdity of the situations in which they become involved, that transfiguration of Verne's characters is more than mere parodic or caricaturish exaggeration, amounting to a sinister kind of role-reversal.

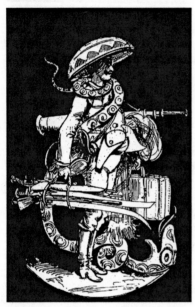

The use that Robida makes of Verne's characters is all the more surprising because Robida was a sincere admirer of Verne's work, who loved his books. After publishing **Saturnin Farandoul**, he persuaded Verne to contribute to one of the humorous periodicals he founded, and wrote a glowing tribute to Verne's work to accompany the contribution. There is certainly a celebratory aspect to *Saturnin Farandoul* as well as a satirical one, but that serves to throw its contrasts and darker aspects into even sharper relief. Had Robida not recognized that Verne was a great writer, whose work had begun a significant new era in adventure fiction, changing that *genre* irredeemably, he would surely never have bothered to write *Saturnin Farandoul*—but nor, in all probability, would he have bothered if he had not had a simultaneous sense of the cost involved in that irredeemable transformation, and some regret for the imaginative restriction that conscientious Vernian verisimilitude entailed.

Robida clearly loved the satirical tradition of traveler's tales that went back to Lucian, for its humor and its extravagance—new editions of its classics provided some of his best opportunities as a illustrator—and his love of that tradition clearly put him in two minds when he encountered the further transfiguration of *voyages extraordinaires* achieved by Verne. Verne's sophistication of the traveler's tale was clearly an advancement of sorts, reflective of the technological progress it celebrated, but it also delivered a potentially mortal blow to the unfettered imaginary extravagance of previous traveler's tales. The principal reason why Saturnin Farandoul continually meets Vernian characters in the remotest regions of the world is that Robida was all-too-conscious of the fact that, from 1878 onwards, nobody would be able to write a story of the hypothetical exploration of any earthly setting without being uncomfortably aware of the fact that Jules Verne had not only got there ahead of him, but had de-mystified the territory in question.

The Vernian characters borrowed by Robida become Saturnin Farandoul's enemies because there is a sense in which they are the implicit enemies of all future adventurers who desire to find something unprecedentedly rich and strange in the places they visit, and a sense in which they will give the lie to all future tellers of munificently absurd tall tales. Saturnin Farandoul is not of their ilk; he belongs wholeheartedly to an earlier and incipiently-obsolete tradition. He is the kind of traveler who routinely falls into grotesque adventures and routinely extricates himself from them by equally grotesque means. He is more a Sindbad than a Robinson Crusoe, and far more of a Baron Munchausen than a Phileas Fogg, a Hector Servadac or a Captain Hatteras—all of whom pose a threat not only to his person but to his whole *raison d'être*.

One of the principal means by which Verne cultivates verisimilitude in his *voyages extraordinaires* is the use of an unusually measured and modest third person narrative. Of all his major works, only one—*Voyage au centre de la terre*—uses a first person narrator, and the objective narrative voices he employs in his other novels make every effort to cultivate the rhetoric of reliability. Robida likewise tells the tale of Saturnin Farandoul's adventures in the third person, but his narrative voice is considerably more intrusive than Verne's; that is because it serves a commentary function, continually making observations about the kind of modern world that Farandoul is now cursed to inhabit and to which he is, crucially and essentially, ill-fitted. Farandoul's world is not entirely Vernian yet, but it is in the process of becoming Vernian, inexorably and irredeemably, and when it has completed its transition, it will be even more hostile to the likes of Saturnin Farandoul and his trusty crew of comic mariners. The narrative voice is polite enough not to labor this point too much, allowing it to emerge naturally from the narrative by demonstration, but its eventual conclusion is quite explicit and leaves no room for doubt.

Robida's use of some of Verne's characters as villains seems particularly striking, not simply because Verne cast those same characters as heroes, but because Verne was initially reluctant to use villains at all. One of Verne's most admirable qualities as a writer, in fact, was his reluctance to employ the cheap melodramatic currency that can be derived from giving heroes explicitly evil enemies to fight. Unlike the majority of writers of his era, including the majority of writers of "Vernian fiction," Jules Verne was not a jingoist prepared to trade on popular xenophobia by using foreigners as villains; indeed, he was remarkably cosmopolitan in his choice of heroes, and was always willing to entertain apologetic arguments for seemingly-heinous behavior.

The challenges of bad weather and incipiently hostile terrain, together with the well-known tendency of even the best-laid plans to go awry, provide most of the challenges for the bold pioneers in Verne's romances of exploration, and it is fairly rare for him to equip one of his heroes with a vicious adversary whose eventual thwarting will provide a suitable sense of climax; Michel Strogoff's treacherous rival, Ivan Ogareff, is exceptional in that regard. Robida's transformation of Verne's own characters is, in part, a wry observation of this fact—a suggestion that the Vernian world-view is a trifle rose-tinted, and that the kinds of people who do the kinds of things that Verne's characters do are very often less noble, and carry more social and psychological baggage, than Verne's characters, with the crucial exception of Captain Nemo, tend to do. The narrative voice slyly suggests, on more than one occasion, that Verne has been a little too trusting in accepting the tales that his heroes told him, accepting their self-serving distortions at face value.

On the other hand, Robida does seem to have approved of Verne's ambitions in that general regard, and his approval seems to have increased considerably during the writing of *Saturnin Farandoul*. Although he was by no means unwilling, at any stage of the novel, to evoke human villains to serve the purposes of his plotting, he became more careful in its later stages to give narrative space to their apologies and excuses. Even the evil Siamese mastermind Nao-Ching is allowed to plead, albeit somewhat hypocritically, that he is only trying to support his family, and he is left conscientiously unpunished for his treacheries. After the violent suicides of Valentin Croknuff in Part One and Phileas Fogg in Part Two, none of Farandoul's principal adversaries suffers a narrative death-penalty in consequence of opposing the hero.

In view of the trajectory of Robida's subsequent career, it is worth pointing out that neither Farandoul nor his author display any conspicuous pacifist tendencies in Part One of the novel, when Farandoul briefly entertains Napoleonic ambitions of world-conquest; after the brutal war that forms the climax to Part Two, however, Farandoul undergoes a gradual but decisive transformation, forsaking his early bellicosity entirely after a brief battle early in Part Three and becoming completely uninterested in revenge. In Part One he is willing to subject captured pirates to summary justice, and in Part Two he is still reluctant to let any affront go unpunished, but by Part Four he is quite content to let Nao-Ching go about his treacherous business indefinitely, and in Part Five it does not even cross his mind to make any attempt to hunt down the pirates who have subjected him to so much injury by stranding him at the North Pole with no apparent means of escape. That is a significant progressive change of attitude, in seeming response to the darker episodes described in the text.

Jules Verne was, of course, well aware of the fact that the world in which he lived had a dark underside, whose primary expressions were the ugly politics of colonialism and warfare, and his later works include several narratives set against the background of actual or threatened wars, but before 1879 the only story he had written in which warfare formed a significant background element was *Michel Strogoff*—the Crimean War is a long way from the theater of operations in *Aventures de trois Russes et de trois Anglais dans l'Afrique australe*. Robida was evidently more anxious about warfare, and the potential of technology to sophisticate warfare, than his model; the second of his savagely satirical accounts of *La Guerre au vingtième siècle* (1883 & 1887; both tr. as *War in the Twentieth Century*) became his most famous work. The groundwork for that exercise and its predecessor were, however, laid in *Saturnin Farandoul*, in the climactic "duel" in part two between Farandoul and Phileas Fogg.

Although that civil war is conducted in a blatantly farcical spirit, the comedy has a distinct black edge; not one violent death is explicitly described, but the accounts offered of the devastation of cities leave no doubt as to the horrific casualties that must be incurred, purely as an unconsidered side-effect of the main protagonists' slightly-injured pride. That is not only point in the story at which Farandoul seems every bit as bad as his adversaries, in terms of his blithe disregard for the fate of bystanders, innocent and otherwise, but it is a turning-point, and he becomes noticeably more scrupulous thereafter. So does his author, who similarly becomes increasingly reluctant to kill or maim anyone and spends most of Part Three engineering escapes from ingeniously horrible condemnations to death.

Part Two is the phase of the narrative in which Robida's misanthropy shows through most frankly in its fullest black depth, and although a certain laconic cynicism continues to underlie the entire narrative, perennially poking sharp reminders through the narrative surface, there are also increasing signs of moderation and repentance from then on. Robida's criticisms of colonialism are not as carefully muted as those in Verne's early works, and are by no means entirely restricted to the explicit war against English imperialism depicted in Part One, but they change in tone, becoming more plaintive and more resigned as the story progresses.

Jules Verne was not the only direct influence on Saturnin Farandoul, and the opening phase of the narrative, in spite of its corollary evocation of Captain Nemo, owes considerably more to Leon Gozlan's *Émotions de Polydore Marasquin*. Although Robida borrows the plot device by which Gozlan's hero becomes unstuck in Part Two of *Saturnin Farandoul*, the more important influence of Gozlan's novel is seen in its similar employment of apes as quasi-human characters possessed of a particular kind of primal innocence. It is the fact that Saturnin Farandoul has been raised as a feral child by a population of inoffensive monkeys that fits him for his heroic role when he re-enters human society, but also ensures that he can never properly fit into that society.

Whereas Polydore Marasquin was a fake while dressed in his monkey-skin, Saturnin Farandoul really is a quintessential Rousseauesque innocent, born into such natural freedom and goodness that civilization can never be anything to him but a set of shackles, which perpetually threaten to turn him into the same kind of morally-defective, money-grubbing, luxury-loving, war-mongering boor that civilization has made of almost all its native victims. Farandoul does not try very hard to resist that fate—indeed, he tries actively to embrace it at first—but he proves, by slow degrees, not only to be immune to it himself but also to have

349

alienated his immediate companions, to such an extent that they, too, can no longer be content with such hideously vulgar ambitions. In this respect, he not only anticipates Edgar Rice Burroughs' Tarzan but eventually outstrips him in sharing the wealth of his fortunate heritage.

Jules Gros was not confined to the pages of the *Journal de Voyages*, but the project that would surely have been the most adventurous of his works, far too extravagant for the *Journal*'s tentative pages, *Voyages extraordinaires du docteur Boldus* (1881), suffered the rather strange fate of only being published in woefully incomplete form, as a kind of teaser. Its sixty-four pages were published and bound by the press associated with the newspaper *La Lanterne*, as if it were a section of a reprinted feuilleton, but no such feuilleton was ever published in the newspaper, and no further sections appeared.

Boldus is introduced as a raconteur whose accounts of his travels includes scientific marvels that are stated as making the inventions of Hoffmann and Poe pale into insignificance; he immediately shows off a new kind of flying machine, and follows up with demonstrations of the alchemical secrets of making gold and the panacea. A former professor of physiology at the Imperial University of Prague, he explains that his meditations and studies there had led him to conclude that the Earth is a living being; he set off on his travels in order to visit all the world's volcanoes in order to "interrogate the entrails of the planet," and spent thirteen years at the north pole.

Boldus' next demonstration is the revival of "living mummy" nearly five hundred years old, by means of artificial blood of his own invention. The operation is described at length in a long letter from a witness, Dr. Jéhul, on which the narrator reflects before receiving another letter inviting him to accompany Boldus, Jéhul and others on a new expedition—but he cannot do so because the Franco-Prussian War breaks out and he is obliged to take up arms.

Following that introduction, the main narrative begins, in which the narrator receives a package containing Jéhul's journal of a Vernian tour of the world, with Boldus standing in for Captain Nemo as the mysterious sage supervising the educational voyage. The story then abruptly breaks off in mid-sentence, apparently only a quarter or a fifth of the way through an envisaged novel that, if completed, might have been the second most extravagant work of Vernian romance, after *The Adventures of Saturnin Farandoul*, but far more earnest. No explanation was given for the abrupt cessation, and perhaps the whole exercise was imagined as a parody, but it would certainly have been interesting to read the rest of the story, if the author had ever cared or contrived to complete it.

The most interesting of Gros' serials in the *Journal des Voyages* is "L'Age de pierre et l'homme fossile, aventures d'une expedition scientifique dans les mers australes" [The Stone Age and the Fossil Man: The Adventures of a Scientific Expedition in the Austral Seas], which ran there between 17 September 1882 and 25 February 1883. It was reprinted in book form as *L'Homme fossile, aventures d'une expedition scientifique dans les mers australes* (tr. as *The Fossil Man*) in 1892 and reprinted under the imprint of the Librairie d'éducation de la jeunesse in 1898; the latter edition was reprinted at least twice. The story is a mildly satirical comedy describing the progress of an international scientific expedition to a fictitious island south-west of New Zealand, which sets off in 1876 to observe a transit of Mercury. In fact, there was no such transit, although there was one in May 1878, which was observable from the northern hemisphere and was, in consequence, tracked by several American astronomers. No sightings of the planet had been recorded in the previous sixteen years.

One of the principal sources on which Gros' story draws, and presumably the most significant inspiration for its composition, was Henri Filhol's *Rapports géologiques et zoologiques de l'Île Campbell avec les terres australes avoisinantes* [Geological and Zoological Reports on Campbell Island, and the Neighboring Austral Lands], published in February 1882, which was a report of one of six French expeditions sent to observe the transit of Venus in 1874. That particular expedition was unsuccessful in astronomical terms—bad weather ensured that very little was visible—and it was a far more limited operation than the one described by Gros, but the fictitious island described in *L'Homme fossile* is a clone of Campbell Island, situated at the same latitude a little way to the east, and many of the details of its geology and natural history are appropriated from Filhol, whose explorations were the only substantial result of the 1874 expedition.

The modeling of the story on an actual expedition places *L'Homme fossile* at the documentary end of the spectrum of fiction routinely offered by the *Journal des Voyages* and it reads for much of its narrative span as if it were an exercise in the popularization of geographical science rather than a novel, although a "love interest" is carefully added. The scientist at its core, Arthème Charmillon is a declared enemy of marriage, and has sworn that he will never allow his beloved daughter Angèle suffer such a fate; she is, however, in love with his assistant and secretary Émile Colin. The plot is contrived in order to construct an acute problem of a kind that could only arise in the context of an organized scientific endeavor, and although the solution provided by the narrative—whose discovery by Émile gives him the opportunity to overcome Charmillon's opposition to Angèle marrying him—is artificial, the problem is sufficiently real to prompt the reader to wonder how much effect its analogues might have had on the development of the body of scientific knowledge. The novel is, in consequence, one of the purest examples of "scientific fiction."

In 1882, when religious opposition to the idea of the great antiquity of the human species, was still ardent and forceful, the idea that the human species had undergone a long process of gradual evolution was still anathematized, and the discovery of a fossil human skeleton by a scientific expedition like the one described in the story would still have been a matter of import and controversy,

351

even though half a century had elapsed since Pierre Boitard had first dramatized the import of fossil finds in "Paris avant homme."

By the time Gros wrote *L'Homme fossile* the scientific notion of paleolithic culture had crystallized into a reasonably clear picture, and the finds of bone fragments made in the first half of the century had been augmented by the discovery of entire human skeletons, but there still was no way to date such remains with any degree of certainty, so the antiquity of such remains still remained open to challenge, in spite of their association with the remains of extinct animals. Nor was there any way to determine, at that point in time, how widespread paleolithic culture had been in geographical terms, and how its chronology related to the changes that had taken place in the physical surface of the earth, which were equally impossible to date accurately. That too is an important issue at stake in Gros' novel, and the discovery of quasi-Magdalenian remains in the southern seas would, indeed, have seemed as exciting and significant to real scientists in 1876 as it does to the fictitious ones in his story.

Whereas the much younger Louis Boussenard was able to settle down once he became a popular writer via the periodical's pages, in order to devote himself to a substantial productive career as a fiction writer, Jules Gros was nearing the end of his life when he began writing for the magazine, and the novels serialized there enjoyed their greatest popularity after his death. Most of his books were non-fictional, including historical accounts of the exploration of Africa, the polar regions, and, perhaps most significantly, South America, in *Les Français en Guyane* [The French in Guyana] (1887). Gros involved himself intimately in Guyanese politics, under the influence of an old friend, the explorer Henri Coudreau, to the extent of accepting the presidency of an enclave on the country's disputed border with Brazil, where Coudreau had founded the supposedly-independent but universally-unrecognized République de Counani.

Gros moved his family from Paris to Counani in 1888, and although he returned to France before his death in 1891, he probably still considered himself to be the President of the Republic in question at that time, and was doubtless deeply disappointed by the fact that France had refused to recognize its existence. The episode was considered rather comical by many observers, but its consequences proved extensive, as other adventurers attempted to take up the slack once Coudreau and Gros had abandoned the cause, and diplomatic conflicts between France and Brazil continued for some years thereafter, eventually being settled after their referral to arbitration by the Swiss government.

In spite of his brief career as an unacknowledged head of state and the posthumous popularity of his novels and histories of exploration, Jules Gros faded almost completely from public view after the Great War, soon eclipsed by his namesake, the Breton writer Jules Gros (1890-1992). Even during his lifetime he had a lower profile than another namesake, the politician Jules Gros (1838-1919), a long-serving député and the founder of the newspaper *Le Petit comtois*. He does, however, retain a significant niche as a writer of Vernian fiction, especially with respect to the work occupying one of the extremes of the subgenre's spectrum.

Jules Verne appears as a character in *Histoire de la fin du monde, ou La Comète de 1904* [A Story of the End of the World; or, The Comet of 1904] (1882), signed "Verniculus," when he is asked, in spite of his advanced age, to serve as general secretary of a scientific Commission meeting to discuss the threat of a comet scheduled for a close encounter with the Earth. It has been discovered that the comet's atmosphere is composed almost entirely of methane, which will break down eventually if it mingles with the Earth's air—unless someone strikes a match during the interval when the mixture is still explosive. The Commission issues the relevant precautionary warning, but has not reckoned with the determination of the Russian nihilists to take their philosophy to the limit.

It is perhaps not surprising that one author who moved to the end of the Vernian spectrum opposite to the one where Jules Gros stationed himself was Paschal Grousset, whose manuscripts supplied the basis for two other novels signed by Verne, while he gradually emerged completely from Verne's shadow, as "André Laurie," initially with the first of a long series of fictionalized documentaries of school life in various times and places, which proved highly successful, and then with an adventure story for young readers, *L'Héritier de Robinson* [Robinson Crusoe's Heir] (1884), in which the mummified body of Defoe's hero is discovered by a subsequent castaway. He also published the naval

romance *Le Capitaine Trafalgar* (1886) before venturing with unusual boldness into the realm of *roman scientifique* with **Les Exilés de la terre. Selene-Company Limited** (1887; tr. as *The Conquest of the Moon*).

Les Exilés de la terre begins with three crooks planning a scam of a kind widely featured in French fiction of the period, selling shares in a company for mining the Moon. Their sales pitch is interrupted when a young astronomer attached to the Paris Observatoire, Norbert Mauny, demands to know how they intend to reach the Moon; when they cannot provide a satisfactory answer he hijacks the pitch and tells the prospective shareholders that the fundamental mechanism of planetary motion is magnetism, and that, given a big enough electromagnet, he could sidestep the problem of traveling to the Moon by bringing the Moon down to earth.

In spite of the improbability of the suggestion, Mauny gets the backing of those eager to purchase shares, and sets off—with the three con men serving as finance directors of the company—to turn an iron-rich Sudanese mountain into a gigantic magnet. The plan runs into political difficulties because of the Sudanese war of independence led by the Mahdi, and Mauny encounters personal complications when he falls in love with a young Englishwoman, who is also coveted by a sinister dwarf. All these problems intersect when the Mahdi's forces attack the station and Mauny switches on his electromagnet. The Moon does indeed, descend, until one of those present panics and reverses the current—but the near miss enables the Moon to skim the surface and carry the mountain away into space.

The castaways have what they need to manufacture oxygen, and are thus enabled to survive on the moon and explore it, discovering relics of an extinct civilization of giants. While the various parties transported to the Moon follow their conflicting agendas, the satellite's disturbed orbit then carries it toward the Earth again, sufficiently far into the atmosphere to allow Mauny and his companions to parachute down to the surface.

Most critics, then and now, considered *Les Exilés de la terre* to be mind-boggling implausible, to a degree that Verne would never have tolerated for a moment, and the judgment is undoubtedly sound. Indeed, the novel became a kind of horrible example held up to all would-be Vernians tempted to let their imagination run away, and Grousset seemed to take the lesson to heart himself, albeit a trifle reluctantly. André Laurie's next Vernian novel, *De New York à Brest en sept heures* (1888; tr. as *New York to Brest in Seven Hours*), although definitely on the melodramatic side as Vernian romances go, was considerably more modest, limiting the grand project at its heart to a transatlantic oil pipeline, although the inevitable love story that pulls the levers of the plot eventually compels the hero to attempt a journey through the pipeline in a sealed capsule; he runs into trouble, but it only proves fatal for the tunnel, while he gets the girl and the fortune, as the hero of a melodrama has to do.

Le Secret du mage (1890; tr. as *The Secret of the Magian*), in which an archeologist discovers evidence of an advanced technological civilization in the remote past, retains a Vernian affiliation, as did some of Laurie's subsequent work, although he seemed to suffer a loss of impetus parallel to Verne's in some of his subsequent fiction. *Le Rubis du Grand Lama* [The High Lama's Ruby] (1892), *Le Géant de l'azur* [The Giant of the Skies] (1904) and *Le Maître de l'abîme* [The Master of the Abyss] (1905) give the impression of being weak exercises in pastiche. Some of his work, however, retained considerably more imaginative verve, although the fact that some of it only achieved periodical publication suggests that the pastiches were more easily marketable.

The more adventurous works in question include the interplanetary eutopian novella "Un Roman dans la planète Mars" [A Romance on the Planet Mars] (*La Revue Illustrée*, 1895). The protagonist of the story gets around the problem of interplanetary travel in much the same fashion as Restif's Duc Multipliandre, having discovered the secret of separating his "astral body" from its corporeal shell. Mars has a society more advanced than those of Earth, mechanical technology providing the needs of its members while they devote themselves to intellectual pursuits. The equality of the sexes has been achieved, and the visitor is guided there by a beautiful woman with angelic wings. Animals have also been liberated, because food technology has evolved to the point at which biologically-engineered vegetables can mimic meat for culinary purposes.

Much of André Laurie's subsequent work was done for the *Journal des Voyages*' rival periodical *Le Globe-Trotter*, to which he contributed *Le Secret du volcan* [The Secret of the Volcano] (1902-03), *Le Toit du monde, aventure sur l'Himalaya* [The Roof of the World: An Adventure in the Himalayas] (1903-04), *L'Obus invisible* [The Invisible Shell] (1905) and the most interesting of his late works, *Spiridon le muet* (1906-07; book version 1908; tr. as *Spiridon*).

In the last-named novel a traveler stumbles across a fugitive remnant of a species of ants, which once included an entire caste of intelligent giants, although only the eponymous individual now remains, conducting scientific studies in isolation, which involve the capture and dissection of any humans who stray into his territory. The protagonist of the story, amazed by Spiridon's surgical skills, enters into an uneasy compact with him after narrowly avoiding dissection himself, and takes him back to Paris, heavily disguised, in order that he can continue his studies there, while parsimoniously releasing his secrets in exchange.

The imposture soon goes awry, and the protagonist's attempts to keep his associate's murderous inclinations in check are soon canceled out when his fellow humans exhibit their own ruthlessness in dealing with the new phenomenon, even before realizing that he is, in fact, an insect. The story is a rather slapdash melodrama, but is redeemed by the adventurousness of its theme, which helps to demonstrate the imaginative potential that Vernian fiction always had, but allowed far too frequently to remain in embryo, developed only tentatively if at all.

In 1887 Louis Figuier created the popular science magazine *La Science Illustrée*, into which he soon introduced the previously-mentioned feuilleton slot bearing the rubric of *roman scientifique*, under which heading he eventually collected enough texts to define and delimit a genre considerably broader than the stereotyped sequence of adventure stories that had so far appeared in the *Journal de Voyages*, and eventually broader than the entire subgenre of Vernian fiction. He might well have invited the more adventurous writers who appeared regularly in the *Journal de Voyages* to contribute to his own slot, and, if so, doubtless requested them to spread their imaginative wings more broadly, but it is possible that writers keen to do that immediately leapt at the new publishing opportunity as soon as they became aware of it, without having to be asked. At any rate, the two who responded most rapidly to the opening were Louis Boussenard and Alphonse Brown.

Boussenard's first contribution to *La Science Illustrée*, **Les Secrets de Monsieur Synthèse** (tr. as "The Secrets of Monsieur Synthesis") was published in book form in 1888 while it was still running as a serial, from 10 March 1888 to 9 February 1889. The story's internal dating suggests that the author had probably started writing the text some years earlier, but had abandoned it at least once, having changed direction markedly in the course of its construction. Given the marked difference between the main plot and a more conventional subplot in which the scientist's daughter and the mariner who loves her are shipwrecked and must cross the Malaysian peninsula on foot, he might even have run two previously-separate manuscripts together in order to form a new whole, to which the extremely hasty conclusion was added belatedly. More text might also have been interleaved with the existing material, reinforcing its scientific content with the didactic supplements that are rather awkwardly intruded into the story, in order to adapt it more closely to Figuier's priorities. The result is confused and uneven, but the parts dealing with Monsieur Synthèse's "Great Work" remain fascinating nevertheless.

"Monsieur Synthèse" is not the real name of the scientist at the center of the story but a symbolic pseudonym, reflecting his ambition to personify science in its synthetic rather than its analytical aspect, as his motto, *Et ego creator* [I too am a Creator] boastfully proclaims. The account provided of him is initially filtered through the eyes of a French policeman sent to investigate him as a potentially-suspicious alien, and the novel shapes up for a while as a mystery story, but it soon reverts to the kind of adventure fiction set in remote parts of the globe that was Boussenard's usual stock-in-trade, hybridized in this case—a trifle awkwardly—with the account of the central character's scientific quest to recapitulate the entire pattern of earthly evolution from primordial slime to human being.

In order to accomplish that re-creation, within the bosom of a new coral island especially created by a similar process of accelerated evolution, Synthèse

356

proposes to engineer something similar to the kind of metamorphoses imagined by Restif de La Bretonne on the basis of his reading of *Telliamed*. Significant further dimensions had been added to evolutionary theory since Restif had written *La Découverte australe*, however, not merely by the Chevalier de Lamarck and Charles Darwin but by the German biologist Ernst Haeckel. Haeckel was not only one of Darwin's most enthusiastic supporters and promoters, but had greatly elaborated ideas put forward by Lamarck's colleague and successor Étienne Geoffroy Saint-Hilaire, with respect to parallels between the sequence of the evolutionary chain of development and that of the development of embryos.

After a rather forbidding formal publication in 1866, Haeckel had written a popularization of his ideas, *Natürlichte Schöpfungsgeschichte* (1868; tr. as *The History of Creation*) which became a best-seller in German, English and French, and popularized the dictum "ontogeny recapitulates phylogeny": the notion that an embryo goes through a series of phases recapitulating the evolutionary phases passed through by its ancestors on their way from single-celled organisms to their present level of complexity. That was the notion that Boussenard took up in equipping Monsieur Synthèse with a plan of operation.

Haeckel had added a fourth "kingdom" to the conventional division of entities into animal, vegetable and mineral, assigning single-celled organisms a category of their own, *Protozoa*, divided into eight phyla of varying complexity, identifying the simplest of all as the *Monera*, which he linked to non-living matter by inventing a hypothetical *urschleim* [primordial slime] that must, in his view, have preceded the first *Moneron*. The English biologist Thomas Henry Huxley—Darwin's most outspoken supporter and publicist—gave the name *Bathybius haeckelii* to a substance he found in a mud-sample that had been dredged up from the Atlantic sea-bed in 1857 and stored away until 1868, in which he thought that he had identified *urschleim*. Huxley sent a sample to Haeckel, who was overjoyed, and integrated its discovery into the later editions of his best-selling book.

Skeptics, however, suggested that the supposed *urschleim* might be the result of chemical decay in the stored sample, and Huxley recanted his "discovery" in 1875, when a chemist attached to the 1872 *Challenger* expedition, which had failed to find any trace of *Bathybius* during its intensive study of the seabed, found similar manifestations in other stored samples and worked out how they had been produced. Haeckel initially refused to recant, and continued to promote *Bathybius* as proof of his thesis until 1883. Monsieur Synthèse, electing to take Haeckel's original refusal as gospel, begins his own quest by dredging the sea-bed in search of *Bathybius*, and finds it.

It is arguable that by 1884, the date attributed by Louis Boussenard to the beginning of Monsieur Synthesis' adventures, at least part of Haeckel's great evolutionary schema was obsolete, and that Synthèse's triumphant search for *Bathybius* had already lost its last vestiges of plausibility, but Boussenard probably did not know that, and if Louis Figuier did, he saw no reason to point it out to the author when he became the story's publisher. That is, however, a relatively trivial quibble. The "missing link" between inorganic and organic matter has never been found in terrestrial nature, but it nevertheless remains the case that if evolutionism is true, there must have been such a link at some time, somewhere. The more crucial problem with Monsieur Synthesis' attempt to recapitulate the entirety of phylogenetic evolution in a matter of months, with the aid of a mysterious accelerator whose nature remains so secret that the text hardly mentions its necessity, is the question of whether a heredity sequence really could accomplish such enormous metamorphoses overnight.

We now know that it could not, because we now know that Haeckel's principle has severe limitations, and that the ontological recapitulation of phylogeny is more metaphorical than literal—an impressionistic echo rather than a real developmental process. In the 1880s, however, it was by no means obvious that the principle was so weak, and if it had been true in a stronger sense, there would be nothing irrational about proposing its inverse. If ontogeny did, in fact, recapitulate phylogeny, then it is certainly conceivable that, in the right circumstances, phylogeny might be persuaded to recapitulate ontogeny: that a hereditary sequence might somehow be persuaded to summarize the great chain of being at an "embryological pace." The details would be hard to work out—as Boussenard obviously realized when he set his thought-experiment going and then began to run into all kinds of narrative snags in representing its progress—but that does not mean that it was a worthless imaginative project.

In the end, the results of Synthèse's experiment are confused by a combination of natural and man-made disasters, and the text is conscientiously ambiguous in its indication as to whether it has succeeded or failed, but the description of its phases, from the initial collection of the Bathybius to the culmination of the evolutionary acceleration in the coral crucible, marked an important developmental step in the evolution of Vernian fiction. Even in the boldest examples established by Verne, which feature such spectacular innovations as the Columbiad and the *Nautilus*, most of the scientific content of the stories had taken the form of mere reportage, with some associated speculative discussion and a relatively tiny fraction being used as a hypothetical blueprint for individual items of machinery, almost exclusively used as means of transportation for the enhancement of geographical romance. Even André Laurie's giant electromagnet, ludicrous as it was, fits that pattern.

Monsieur Synthèse's Great Work is a different kind of project, involving a different order of speculation—and the sequel with which the author attempted to follow it up, *Dix mille ans dans un bloc de glace*, belongs to another category of fiction, moving entirely into the realm of the speculative fiction of the *merveilleux scientifique* in anticipation of the exemplars to be provided by H. G. Wells. If Boussenard could have gone on from the two stories he wrote for *La Science Illustrée* to develop that kind of fiction further, he might have made a

358

much greater contribution to the development of *roman scientifique* than he did, but both stories were aborted when he could not follow them through, and he reverted to the more comfortable stereotypy of adventure stories set in exotic locations for the remainder of the nineteenth century, and some time thereafter. The most imaginative endeavor of the later part of his career, published in a series of fictional supplements to the *Journal des Voyages, Monsieur...Rien* (1907) is one of the several French responses to H. G. Wells' *The Invisible Man*, and falls as far short of its target as Jules Verne's own effort in that line did.

Alphonse Brown took advantage of the new feuilleton slot to place three works with Figuier: "Les Insectes révélateurs" (1889; tr. as "The Tell-Tale Insects"); *Une Ville de verre* (1890-91; tr. as *City of Glass*); and "Les Tribulations d'un pêcheur à la ligne" (1891; tr. as "The Tribulations of an Angler"). "Les Insectes révélateurs" is interesting as an early example of the "forensic detective story," in which an obsessive entomologist is enabled by his intimate understanding of insect habits and life-cycles to discover the hidden body of a murder victim and thus confound the murderer—somewhat to his discomfort when he realizes, after being carried away by the loquacious force of his scientific reasoning, that the revelation of the truth will cause severe disruption to his family situation. The story has no speculative component, although it does contain a considerable amount of scientific discourse. The contribution made by ichthyological science to "Les Tribulations d'un pêcheur à la ligne" is even slighter, a little knowledge of the habits of fish merely assisting a young artist to win consent for his marriage to the daughter of a keen angler, placing the story on the utmost borderline of its subgenre.

The full-length novel that came between the two novelettes was, however, a much more robust Vernian fantasy, positioned at the very heart of the subgenre. The fact that Brown's three serials for *La Science Illustrée* were published in relatively rapid succession suggests that the second two might have been submitted immediately after the first had been accepted, and might have been written some time before.

The story told in *Une ville de verre* describes how the members of a Geographical Society based in Bordeaux—an obvious replica of the one to which Brown belonged—are enabled to mount an Arctic expedition, when the brilliant physician and traveler Pierre Magueron, an old friend of the somewhat timorous narrator, persuades the immensely rich Edgard Pomerol that the polar climate might be good for the illness that he believes to be killing him. In order to provide some distraction, they supplement the essential core of expeditionaries with a number of eccentric passengers, including a misanthropic man of mystery fleeing society and an unorthodox theoretician intent on collecting evidence for his conviction that human beings are descended from seals rather than primates.

The expedition discovers an island in the Arctic, which they name after the famous geographer and anarchist Elisée Reclus and claim for France—although the claim is disputed by the passengers aboard an American yacht on a pleasure cruise, who contend that they have already claimed it for the U.S.A. Relationships remain slightly strained but fundamentally friendly when both parties are afflicted by a series of accidents that trap them within the ice-sheet, and oblige them to find accommodation in order not merely to winter in the Arctic but perhaps to remain there much longer. That necessity results in the construction of the titular "city of glass."

Making ingenious use of all the resources available on the volcanic islet, and Pierre Magueron's enormous expertise and ingenuity, the French castaways manage to construct a complex well-insulated habitat, which becomes more than a mere apparatus of survival, tending to the condition of a mini-utopia, which they name Crystalopolis. Its population is swelled by more castaways, increasing the ethnic mix dramatically, and it also absorbs the population of the rival American "troglodytic" settlement of Maurelville. Eventually, however, escape from the island becomes possible, and the castaways are rescued—although their various personal entanglements remain in need of sorting out.

From the viewpoint of the development of *roman scientifique*, *Une ville de verre* is Alphonse Brown's most important work, not merely because it makes more effort than the serials published in the *Journal des Voyages* to support its plot with abundant technical details but also because of the gratuitous but fascinating inclusion of chapter XXVII, which consists of a lecture given by Jacques Ribard on the evolutionary origins of humankind. Although the argument advanced in the lecture is offered by the notional narrator of the story as a cavalier exercise in eccentricity, it is surprisingly well-researched for a mere joke, and makes interesting reference back to *Telliamed* in its account of the possible phocal origins of humankind; some of the other slightly tongue-in-cheek references in the text are equally esoteric, and testify to wider and more profound reading than might have been included in the text as mere window-dressing.

Like Verne and Jules Gros, Alphonse Brown differed from the majority of writers of adventure fiction in his reluctance to go beyond the intrinsic hostilities of nature in posing challenges for their heroes to meet. Most writers of adventure fiction, even in its Vernian variants, were entirely ready to use the easiest method of ramping up the melodramatic content of their work, by invoking human villains whose twofold narrative function is to manufacture dramatic tension by posing sequential threats and to provide satisfactory climaxes and closure with their ultimate defeats. It is, in fact, quite difficult for a writer to do without that particular narrative prop if he hopes to provide a story of exploration with a plot, and there is a definite courage in the conscientious refusal to take that course.

Some readers undoubtedly felt that the refusal in question weakened the work of all three writers, especially in longer works like *Une ville de verre*, whose romantic complications and occasional humorous inclusions cannot provide anything like the narrative energy provided by Albert Robida's much more lavish deployment of human villainy and farcical comedy, but those who appreciated the moral sentiment behind Brown's refusal to invoke human evil as a cheap plot-lever surely forgave him. The heart and soul of the novel is, in any case, not contained in its dramatic suspense, nor in its somewhat tokenistic denouement, but in its languorous creation of its central motif. Crystalopolis is an exceptionally flamboyant symbol of the triumph of human intelligence over the rigors of natural desolation—and that, in essence, is what all Vernian fiction is really about, and why the subgenre was so appropriate to its time.

Brown had published a second serial in the *Journal des Voyages* before his three stories appeared in *La Science Illustrée*, *À la recherche de Gordon* [In Search of Gordon] (1887), and he went on to publish a further six novels thereafter, beginning with *La Guerre à mort* [War to the Death] (1891; reprinted in book form 1893). The most interesting of them is *La Station aérienne* [The Aerial Station] (1893-94) features a balloon race organized between two rich Americans, whose balloons are named *Cirrus* and *Stratus*, which is joined by a journalist, manning the *Cumulus*, and a French balloonist who names his balloon *Giffard* after the editor of *Le Petit Journal*, who became a prolific sponsor of races involving bicycles, automobiles and, eventually, airplanes. The plot involves the forced descent of the balloons in Apache territory; the "aerial station" of the title is a vast platform covered in tents, which does not really warrant the name given to it of Aerial City.

Brown's other serials in the *Journal* were *La Madonne des patriotes* [The Madonna of the Patriots] (1894-95), *La Goëlette terrestre* [The Land-Schooner] (1896-97; reprinted in book form 1900), *La Couronne perdue* [The Lost Crown] (1899-1900) and *Les Faiseurs de pluie* [The Rain-Makers] (1901; reprinted in book form as *Conquérants de l'air perdus dans le désert* [Conquerors of the Air Lost in the Desert] in 1902). As with Verne's parallel works, most of them are straightforward adventure stories with little or no speculative content.

Alphonse Brown did not live long enough to witness the controversy surrounding Robert Peary's claim to have reached the pole in 1909—now generally discredited—but he undoubtedly did see the long report of Fritjof Nansen's 1895 expedition contained in the *Bulletin* of the Societé de Géographie Commerciale de Bordeaux in 1896, presumably taking note of the fact that Nansen had beaten the fictitious distance record that he had credited in *Une Ville de verre* to Jasper Cardigan.

The notion of building a technologically advanced city from scratch, featured in *Les Cinq cents millions de la Bégum*, was developed once again, in a manner more typical of Vernian fiction in *La Babylone électrique* (1888; tr. as *Babylon Electrified*) by Albert Bleunard (1852-1905). In the story, English engineers building a railway through Syria and Mesopotamia in order to connect Europe to the Persian Gulf realize that fueling the locomotives will be problematic because of the dearth of coal in the region. Hydroelectricity and solar power provide an abundant substitute in the form of electricity, so the magnate financing the operation decides to employ the power thus generated to supply a new city built on the site of ancient Babylon, and to run a massive supply-cable all the way to Europe.

The story-line clearly has euchronian potential, but does not develop in that fashion, the wonders of the city of Liberty barely being sketched, after a long section describing the process of its construction in detail, before the indigenes of the region, fearing the usurpation of their land by European invaders, rise up against the allegedly diabolical project. The relatively seamless manner in which a broad range of scientific questions are worked into the plot—the discussion of the effects of deforestation and possibilities of climate change give it a particularly modern twist—illustrate the extent to which the better writers in the subgenre were developing narrative methods appropriate to it, and deploying them in a thoroughly craftsmanlike fashion.

Like Alphonse Brown, Albert Bleunard was a provincial rather than a Parisian; he was the professor of physical sciences at the Lycée d'Angers, and a leading member of the local philosophical society. He carried out extensive scientific research himself, on an amateur basis, but never achieved the discovery that might have made his name; the fact that he never settled into any particular specialism probably did not help in that quest. His scientific publications were *Recherches sur matières albuminoides* [Research on Albuminoid substances] (1881), *Le Mouvement de matière* [Matter in motion] (1883) and *Une Nouvelle poudre* [A New Gunpowder] (1885). Also like Brown, he was recruited to the pages of *La Science Illustrée*, where he published four out of his five subsequent *romans scientifiques*.

Bleunard's second story in that vein, the novella *Le Spirite malgré lui* (serialized 1889; book version 1895; tr. as "The Reluctant Spiritualist") illustrates the perils of making plots up as one goes along; having written himself into an impasse half way through, the author then flounders while trying, and ultimately failing, to get out of it. As with *La Babylone électrique*, however, the story turned out to be oddly—perhaps perversely—prophetic, in dealing with the discovery of a form of radiation that, although invisible to the eye, is capable of stimulating photographic plates. Although the narrative of his story goes astray, it is by no means devoid of interest, not only by virtue of its intriguing premise but in its description of the methodical manner in which the investigating scientists initially set out to solve the enigma with which they are confronted. When Wilhelm Röntgen subsequently published his work on X-rays in 1895, Bleunard threw himself into X-ray research with great alacrity and determination; although the experiments he carried out won him little or no renown at the time, they did help lay the foundations of what subsequently became X-ray diffraction—the technique that eventually played a crucial role in revealing the structure of DNA.

The longest and most enterprising of Bleunard's serials in *La Science Illustrée* was "Toujours plus petit" (1893; tr. as "Ever Smaller"), a pioneering exercise in what was subsequently to become a curious subgenre of "shrinking man" stories. "Toujours plus petit" was not the first ever "microcosmic romance," but it did attempt to incorporate recent scientific revelations into its account of what might be seen from a series of exceedingly tiny viewpoints, in a wide-ranging and methodical fashion.

Unsurprisingly, Bleunard's unprecedented attempt to write a scientifically-informed microcosmic romance is rather tentative, and it addresses itself primarily—though not entirely—to obvious possibilities that later writers were to develop with greater sophistication. Its description of the "insect microcosm" features the inevitable encounter with a giant spider, but the story devotes most of its attention to the study of ants, that being a hot topic of the day, encouraged by the prolific endeavors of the amateur entomologist Jean-Henri Fabre (1823-1919). Bleunard would undoubtedly have been familiar with the fictional popularizations of entomology published by S. Henry Berthoud as well as Fabre's books, and is clearly following in their footsteps in that part of his narrative. It is worth noting, however, that "Toujours plus petit" appeared three years before the first of Maurice Maeterlinck's far more stylish endeavors in intimate entomology.

The subsequent shift in Bleunard's narrative from the entomological realm to the "microbial microcosm" inevitably seems primitive to readers acquainted with the full range of wonders revealed by modern optical and electron microscopes, but it was by no means unsophisticated by the standards of its day, and is far more conscientious in its scope and treatment than the slightly lurid exercises in that vein produced in America in a slightly later period. Bleunard hesitates and prevaricates over the question of whether humans could plausibly be reduced to the size of atoms, in order to investigate what he considered to be the ultimate level of material organization, but that is only natural, given that he did not have the tempting lure of the model of the "atomic solar system" proposed by Lord Rutherford in 1911 to seduce speculation, or even the earlier atomic model proposed by J. J. Thomson, which placed electrons inside a hollow sphere. The identification of the electron as a subatomic particle was still four years away when Bleunard wrote "Toujours plus petit," so his notion of atoms was still devoid of any structure at all.

Another aspect of modern thought conspicuous by its absence from "Toujours plus petit"—as well as the majority of its subgeneric successors—is the posing of questions relative to the logic of the shrinking process: the issue of what happens to the mass of the shrinking individual; the issue of how exceedingly tiny people would be able to breathe when the molecules of the ambient air are, relatively speaking, far larger than usual, etc. etc. Even though the three amateur scientists who take part in the featured experiment are unusually innocent, one might have expected at least one of them to pose some of these enigmas to his colleagues—but Bleunard was probably only too well aware of his inability to come up with convincing hypotheses to counter them.

In spite of all these observations, however, "Toujours plus petit" remains a significant landmark in the history of speculative fiction, in going where no writer had gone before, and boldly. In purely literary terms, it is an exercise in pulpish popular fiction, but it helps to demonstrate and illustrate the reasons why writers of that kind of fiction were sometimes able to open up vast new frontiers in imaginative territories where more sophisticated writers dared not tread, or only ventured to contemplate from a safe intellectual distance in a spirit of symbolic surrealism.

Bleunard's next scientific romance appeared in the same series of novellas as the book version of *Le Spirite malgré lui*; entitled *Vengeance d'un savant* [A Scientist's Revenge] (1895), it features an advanced form of wireless telegraphy. The themes of two further novellas that subsequently appeared in *La Science illustrée*, "L'Eau de jouvence" [The Elixir of Youth] (1899-1900) and "La Pierre philosophale" [The Philosopher's Stone] (1903), are encapsulated in their titles. Alongside those further ventures in fiction, Bleunard continued to publish nonfiction books, including one intended for use in school as a handbook of illustrative classroom experiments and a three-volume *Histoire générale de l'Industrie* [A Universal History of Industry] (1894), which he undoubtedly intended to be his masterpiece, and probably was, although it was soon outdated by the rapid pace of technological progress. He also continued his scientific research, still flitting from one subject to another. His final work was *L'Art de prédire le temps* [The Art of Weather-Forecasting] (1903).

If one can read between the lines of his fiction accurately—and he was no expert in dissimulation—Bleunard was deeply disappointed by the fact that he never managed to make an impact as a scientist, and never managed to get a job in industry that would save him from the routines of secondary school-teaching. His fiction appears, at least to some extent, to have been a response to his frustration, but that probably strengthened its imaginative component, and encouraged him to introduce new dimensions into Vernian fiction.

The expansion of Vernian fiction into space was robustly undertaken, somewhat more responsibly than André Laurie had attempted it in *Les Exilés de la terre*, in the first of what were ultimately to be four volumes of *Aventures extraordinaires d'un savant russe* (tr. in 2 volumes as *The Extraordinary Adventures of a Russian Scientist*), signed "G. Le Faure and H. de Graffigny," and published by Edinger in 1888. That first volume was an unusually lavish book, illustrated with astronomical photographs, maps and drawings by various hands, and had a preface by France's best-known popularizer of science, Camille Flammarion, who is also the novel's dedicatee, although the text is solidly Vernian in its narrative strategy.

The second and third volumes of the original version appeared in a slightly less lavish format in 1889 and 1890, but Edinger ceased trading thereafter, and there was a long delay before the fourth and concluding volume appeared under the imprint of Arthème Fayard in 1896. The story told in the four volumes is, however, a continuous narrative whose subdivision was entirely arbitrary. The two authors were both at the beginning of their careers in 1888, having published relatively little before then, at least in book form. Whether they formed their partnership spontaneously or were brought together to execute a plan formed by the publisher, it appears that theirs was a literary marriage of convenience; the evidence of their separate careers strongly suggests that Le Faure was appointed to be the provider of the action/adventure component of the work while Graffigny was to supply the science content.

The senior writer of the partnership, Georges Le Faure (1858-1953), went on to become a prolific writer of popular fiction, especially for younger readers. Much of his work was in a vaguely Vernian vein, although he never did anything else as ambitious as the *Aventures extraordinaires*, and he became conspicuously more modest in his imaginative reach once the four-volume novel was complete. While the early volumes of the *Aventures extraordinaires* were in progress, however, he was extremely enthusiastic in his production of scientific romances—so much so that when Arthème Fayard took over Edinger's assets he was able to reissue a three-volume omnibus of Le Faure's other *Voyages scientifiques extraordinaires* in 1892-4, containing  nine novels originally issued in fourteen volumes. Le Faure became a regular contributor to the Vernian *Journal des Voyages* thereafter, sometimes using the pseudonym Georges Faber, but most of his contributions were non-speculative adventure stories; he wrote a great deal of popular fiction in that vein.

The most successful of Le Faure's other scientific romances was *La Guerre sous l'eau* (1890; tr. as *War Under Water*), which features the construction of a submarine powered by electricity and armed with powerful torpedoes by an international secret society dedicated to the destruction of the German Empire. *Les Robinsons lunaires* [The Lunar Castaways] (1892) was more ambitious, and more handsomely-illustrated, but once he had completed the nine novels reprinted in the Fayard omnibus and had belatedly put an end to *Aventures extraordinaires d'un savant russe* Le Faure seems to have decided that speculative work was not worth the necessary imaginative effort, and abandoned it.

"Henry de Graffigny" was the pseudonym of Raoul Marquis (1863-1942), an engineer by training and a popularizer of science by vocation. The idea of writing the *Aventures extraordinaires* is likely to have been his, if it was not Edinger's. Graffigny had made his first tentative foray into the subgenre of Vernian romance in 1887, with *Voyages fantastiques* [Fantastic Voyages], which he followed up with *De la terre aux étoiles* [From the Earth to the Stars] (1888)—a work that is not as extravagant as its title promises, only taking in the moon, Venus and a ride on a comet, although it might be regarded as a preliminary prospectus for *Aventures extraordinaires d'un savant russe*, whose early phases follow the same route.

Both of those works, aimed at a juvenile audience, were awkwardly didactic, and a third, *Contes d'un vieux savant* [An Old Scientist's Tales] (1888), used a fictional frame simply to dress up a series of scientific lectures; it would be unsurprising if Edinger thought that Graffigny was in need of a collaborator skilled in melodrama if he were ever to produce something that aficionados of Vernian fiction might enjoy. More typical of Graffigny's contemporary endeavors were *Le jeune électricien amateur* [The Young Amateur Electrician] (1888) and a multivolume *Petite Encyclopédie Electro-Mécanique* [Pocket Electromechanical Encyclopedia] (1889), both of which were reprinted several times.

Although he worked for much of his life as a scientific journalist before "retiring" in 1920, ostensibly to dedicate his life to electroculture—the application of electricity to agricultural endeavor—Graffigny did make further excursions into Vernian romance following the conclusion of the *Aventures extraordinaires*. Like Le Faure, however, he stuck to inventions that were, by comparison, conspicuous by their modesty. In *À travers l'espace—aventures d'un aéronaute* [Across the Sky—Adventures of an Aeronaut] (1908), the North Pole is reached by balloon, and *La ville aérienne* [The City in the Air] (1910) is another account of an advanced aerostat. Considering that Graffigny knew by the time he wrote these two novels that his advocacy of heavier-than-air craft in the *Aventures extraordinaires* had been justified, their production seems deliberately retrograde, in terms of imaginative ambition. He seems to have become an enthusiastic balloonist himself by the time he wrote them, and his journalistic endeavors championed lighter-than-air craft against their upstart competition.

As with his partner, therefore, *Aventures extraordinaires d'un savant russe* remained the peak of Graffigny's career as a writer of ambitious *roman scientifique*, and, for all its flaws, the novel probably deserves to be reckoned the peak of ambition of the Vernian fiction of space travel. It was the first scientific romance to attempt a tour of the solar system in accordance with the detailed account of the planets compiled on the basis of astronomical evidence—and a good deal of imagination—by Camille Flammarion's popularizations, and the first to attempt to travel beyond the solar system, albeit by highly suspect means. *De la terre à la lune* and *Autour de la lune*, provided a cardinal example that Graffigny and Le Faure plundered in a wholesale fashion in the early phases of their work, and they borrowed extravagantly in later phases from the more problematic model provided by *Hector Servadac*, but those Vernian platforms served primarily as launching-pads for more elaborate and original extrapolations.

In retrospect, the attempts that Graffigny and Le Faure made to design a sequence of space vehicles to enable their hypothetical exploration of the solar system—each more powerful than the last, so as to be capable of taking their characters to the outer limits of the solar system and beyond—inevitably seem woefully primitive, and are now very obviously lacking in the verisimilitude that the authors were trying to cultivate, but they did do their best, and it was probably the best that anyone could have been expected to do at the time. It is also very obvious, in retrospect, that they suffered an eventual failure of imagination and nerve similar to the one experienced by Verne in *Hector Servadac*, more exaggerated in consequence of their bolder ambitions—but that too is forgivable, given that they were attempting the unprecedented, and we now know that no one else would do any better for at least forty years.

The Russian scientist of the title is Mikhail Ossipoff, a typical obsessive eccentric with the usual beloved daughter, who objects—again, as usual—to her desire to marry a French diplomat when he discovers that although his name in Gontran Flammermont, he is not related to the great astronomer of that name. When Gontran unthinkingly expresses the strength of his love for Selena by saying that he would go to the Moon for her, Ossipoff takes him at his word, and demands that he accompany him on exactly such an expedition, which he has been planning for some time.

Unfortunately, Ossipoff's experiments with explosives, required to provide the cannon he intends using to launch his projectile with the necessary thrust, have given rise to suspicions that he is a nihilist; the secretary of the Russian Academy of sciences, Fedor Sharp, exploits the rumors to have Ossipoff arrested, and seizes all his plans, in order that he can reach the Moon first. Fortunately, Gontran has an old school friend, Alcide Fricoulet, who is a scientific genius and has invented a heavier-than-air flying machine. Although his misanthropy causes him to disapprove of Gontran's amorous motives, Fricoulet agrees to help him to rescue Ossipoff from Siberia, and having succeeded, he and Ossipoff then embark upon a project to rival Sharp's—now funded by a company formed to exploit lunar mining opportunities somewhat reminiscent of André Laurie's—in the hope that they might still win the race to the Moon. They plan to use an eruption of the volcano Cotopaxi, predicted by an enterprising statistician, as a means of launching their own projectile.

Ossipoff and his associates do, of course, reach the Moon and make contact there with an elaborate Selenite civilization, but that is only the first round in an exceedingly long contest in which Sharp continues to pop up in order to plague them. Wherever they go, however, they are able to find means of continuing their journey, albeit in perennially dangerous circumstances. In the second volume they travel to Venus, and then to Mercury, where they have to hitch a ride on a comet in order to get away. They discover the hypothetical innermost planet Vulcan as they make a close passage of the sun, and eventually dismount on one of the satellites of Mars.

After a long sojourn on a highly civilized Mars they find a means of hitching another ride, this time on a "current" of particles left behind by a disintegrated comet, which now constitute a kind of interplanetary conveyor belt. Although Ossipoff's companions want to use it to go home, he stubbornly takes them in the opposite direction, in order to make close-range observations of Jupiter, Saturn, Uranus and Neptune—in spite of calculations suggesting that the journey will take hundreds of years.

From mid-way through the third volume the authors are forced to make increasingly implausible adjustments to their methods in order to extend their tour, especially when they want to take in the stars as well as the outer planets, and the story throws its Vernian credentials overboard in order to become a hallucinatory fantasy, but until that point it retains sufficient conscience to remain within the bounds of Vernian *roman scientifique*, albeit stretching them to the utmost limit. The interpolated lectures, by no means as seamlessly integrated into the text as Verne's, are more reminiscent of Boitard's *Voyage au soleil*, but the data deployed by Graffigny are far more recent then Boitard's, and Graffigny has a better understanding of physics, although he is routinely prepared to set it aside in the interests of getting his characters around with a minimum of delay.

With regard to their dubious methods of space travel, Le Faure and Graffigny at least contrived not to seem as blatantly old-fashioned as Charles Guyon in the near-contemporary *Voyage dans la planète Vénus* (1888; tr. as "A Voyage to the Planet Venus"), which uses a rapidly-moving dirigible balloon as a narrative device for transporting its heroes to unexplored territory for the purposes of adventure. Because they are comatose during the journey—which apparently allows them to pass through the interplanetary ether without requiring oxygen—it takes them a long time to deduce that the strange land in which they come down is, in fact, on the planet Venus rather than Earth.

That task of discrimination is made more difficult by the fact that Guyon imagines the planet in question as an Earth-clone, with human inhabitants, although its megafauna is otherwise entirely "antediluvian" and the inhabitants are equipped with various advanced technologies, including artificial wings that permit individual flight, although most long-distance transport is accomplished by balloon or via a Robidaesque pneumatic tube. The book was marketed for younger readers, as many Vernian romances were, and the story has marked affinities with English "boys' books," not least in the complete absence from its pages of the female of the species.

The plot of the story tracks the efforts of the castaways to recover one of their party—the inventor of the balloon—who was captured immediately after their arrival by balloonists from a country neighboring the one where they land, but much less eutopian in its social organization. They succeed in reaching him, and escaping with him, but are deflected to a third country in the far north, where civilization has to take refuge underground in winter. When that realm is attacked by invaders from the second, they fight alongside the natives, but when the inventor is killed in action their chances of being able to return home seem slim. However, Venusian scientists manage to enter into communication with Earth using Charles Cros's method, and then build a Vernian gun in order to make more direct contact, offering the visitors from Earth a chance to employ that means.

Although *Voyage dans la planète Venus* is wildly implausible, it is not without a certain charm and interest as a relatively rapid response to the ideas concerning life on Venus set out by Camille Flammarion in his illustrated guide to *Les Terres du ciel* (1884)—the influence of which is duly credited, as it is by Le Faure and Graffigny, whose travelers carry a copy of parallel volume by "Flammermont." Guyon's text is similarly naïve as a fantasy of prehistory, although its depiction of a pitched battle between a megatherium and a mastodon anticipated similar scenes in many later tales of marvelous survivals, while not quite contriving to duplicate the eccentric charm of Pierre Boitard's battle between a mastodon and his completely-misconceived mole-like dinotherium.

As an early "planetary romance," in fact, *Voyage dans la planète Venus* anticipates, albeit rather weakly, a good many of the tropes that were to become typical of that subgenre as it developed in British scientific romance as well as *roman scientifique,* and, in a later era, in American science fiction. Indeed, it shares so many motifs with earlier and later works that it deserves to be recognized as a significant illustration of the way in which the cocktail of ideas in question was becoming authentically generic, helping to add a further layer to relatively modest Vernian fantasies of terrestrial tourism, and preparing the way for the more ambitious scope that *roman scientifique* acquired when it received a new injection of fuel from translations of the work of H. G. Wells.

A third interplanetary romance written at much the same time as those by Guyon and Le Faure and Graffigny, but not published for some years, paid much closer homage to Verne, in being dedicated to him and framed as an explicit sequel to *De la terre à la lune* and *Autour de la lune*. **Un Monde inconnu, deux ans sur la lune** (tr. as *An Unknown World: Two Years on the Moon*) by "Pierre de Sélènes" was originally published in an undated edition attributed to 1896 by the Bibliothèque Nationale catalogue. That publication date is undoubtedly correct—numerous reviews of the book appeared in periodicals in the last few months of 1896—but the internal evidence of the text, which places the action in the 1880s, suggests that most of it, at least had been written more than a decade earlier, and hence earlier than the first volume of *Aventures extraordinaires d'un savant russe* or *Voyage dans la planète Venus*.

The Bibliothèque Nationale catalogue records that the pseudonym attached to the book was that of "A. Betolaud de La Drable." If that is correct, then the author might well have been Armand-Ludovic-Eugène Betolaud de La Drable (1808-1888), although it is possible that it might have been a similarly-named relative. Wherever the author actually figured in the Betolaud family tree, however, there is no doubt that he belonged to the old French aristocracy, to a family that, as the popular expression put it, "went back to the crusades." That is of some significance, because *Un Monde inconnu* is a curious hybrid story, which deliberately fuses the Vernian romance from which it takes it immediate inspiration with an older tradition of utopian romance—older being the operative word, because the novel differs from the majority of utopian romances written in France since the mid-eighteenth century in taking a rather reactionary view of the ideas that prompted and succeeded the 1789 Revolution, embedding its supposed commitment to liberty, equality and fraternity within a stratified, hierarchical society equipped with a "natural" aristocracy and a similarly "natural" religious culture.

The story begins with two young Frenchmen—one of them, inevitably, a brilliant scientist—reading a newspaper advertisement for the sale by auction of the Columbiad and its associated apparatus. Their discussion—involving a plan to form a company to buy the gun and repeat the heroic feat for which it was built—is overheard by a world-weary English millionaire, who volunteers to fund the purchase if he can go along, because crashing on the Moon seems to him to be an attractive means of committing suicide. The gun needs to be modified in order to provide a series of progressive thrusts, in order to reduce its acceleration to survivable levels while still achieving the appropriate final velocity, but that is accomplished, and the shot is fired.

Instead of crashing on the surface, however, or landing softly with the aid of the jets supposed to cushion its impact, the projectile falls into a fissure in the lunar surface and ends up in the heart of the Moon, where it falls into water. The travelers are rescued from what initially seems to be a dire predicament by human Selenites, whose ancestors retreated from the uninhabitable surface long ago—although they still maintain a sophisticated observatory there—and have long established an advanced technological society that is a veritable eutopia.

The new arrivals are made welcome by the Selenites, and provoke the renewal of an old project intended to communicate with the satellite's primary by means of a variant of the Cros method. That project goes ahead, and contact is made, without the language difficulties ordinarily inherent in projects of that kind. On Earth, in consequence, work immediately begins on a project to build an array of lights capable of returning the signals and establishing a more elaborate and productive two-way communication.

The visitors undertake a long exploratory trek over the lunar surface, in the course of which they discover other deep fissures playing host to air, water and life, and see most of the sights that were to become familiar in earnest accounts of moon landings, in addition to some highly idiosyncratic ones. The Selenites start work on a space gun of their own, which will ultimately permit the Earthmen to return home, and perhaps lead to regular traffic between the worlds. The course of these affairs does not proceed smoothly, as is obligatory in a work of fiction, but "Pierre de Sélènes" belongs to the same purist school as Verne, Gros and Brown, and he restricts himself to entirely natural inconveniences, scorning the use of villains.

The eccentricity of the utopian model featured in the lunar society of *Un Monde inconnu* does not stop with the reactionary sentiments of its designer; it is by no means the only French utopian fantasy to propose that Earthly humankind is ill-fitted for a utopian existence for physiological reasons, but the modifications it proposes are a peculiar mixture of the radical and the conservative. The author follows a proposal advanced by Restif de La Bretonne and refined by Camille Flammarion, that it would be convenient for a species with ambitions toward perfection if it could do away with the messy business of nutrition, defecation and urination and obtain its nutrition by way of respiration, excreting wastes by exhalation. Flammarion was, however, fully aware of the fact that such a variation would require adaptation to an atmosphere radically different from that of Earth, and considerable physiological and anatomical adaptations of the species enjoying that exotic ecology. The author of *Un Monde inconnu*, wanting his utopians to live up to standards of human beauty in no uncertain terms, and to allow human visitors to their world to breathe the same air, fudges the issue in an unconvincing fashion, although such imaginative audacity is perhaps not out of keeping with the initial hypothesis that the Moon might be inhabited by human beings, internally if not externally.

Un Monde inconnu is primarily interesting as an exotic historical specimen rather than a satisfactory work of art, but it has a significant place in the history of French interplanetary fiction, and interplanetary fiction in general. Of all the fictional developments of Charles Cros' suggested program for interplanetary communication, it is the most detailed and the most enthusiastic. It is perhaps also the one that has the most accurate appreciation of the difficulties that such communication would entail, even if it fares no better the any other in suggesting ways of overcoming such difficulties. That problem was to be explored in earnest a century later by the scientists who took up the notion in connection with the SETI (Search for Extra-Terrestrial Intelligence) program, but they had better technology on which to base their ingenuity; the strongest evidence that *Un Monde inconnu* was written in the 1880s is that it has no inkling of the possibility of wireless telegraphy. Of all the proto-SETI fantasies written in the absence of that narrative convenience, it is perhaps the most thought-provoking, precisely because of the conscientiousness of its hopeless struggle.

While these expansions of Vernian narrative into space were produced in book form, the *Journal de Voyages* remained stubbornly earthborn, although it occasionally ventured into the realms of exotic technology, as in Louis Jacolliot's *Les Mangeurs de feu* [The Fire-Eaters] (serial 1885-87; book 1887), which features aircraft-cum-submarines capable of engaging in brutal aerial combat. Its market slot was first subjected to serious competition in 1890, when the publisher L. Boulanger founded *La Terre Illustrée* in November 1890 in deliberate imitation. He also launched an imitation of *La Science Illustrée* in March 1891 called *La Science Française*. Inevitably, both magazines were equipped with feuilleton slots imitative of their models. Boulanger entrusted the day-to-day editorship of the two magazines to the editors who were already running two other imitative magazines he had recently founded, *La Revue Pour Tous* and *Le Monde de la Jeunesse*, Jules Lermina and Charles Simond.

It was, perhaps, only natural that Boulanger should give the editorship of his popular science magazine to the editor of his children's magazine, as popular science magazines were regarded as didactic enterprises aimed primarily at the young, while appointing Lermina, a prolific *feuilletoniste* renowned for his imitations of the famous *feuilletonistes* of yore and the editor of his general interest magazine, as the supervisor his magazine of travels and adventures, but it is not inconceivable that had the order of the last two periodicals' foundation been reversed, that Lermina might have been given the editorship of *La Science Française*, thus being specifically charged with the development of *roman scientifique.* There is no way of knowing what the relationship was between Charles Simond and Lermina, although it might be significant that Simond never published anything by Lermina, and the "stables" of writers on which the two editors drew did not overlap.

Although Lermina did not write feuilletons for *La Revue Pour Tous*, contenting himself with routine editorial duties, he decided to supply *La Terre Illustrée* with serial fiction himself, at least to begin with—which, as a prolific and versatile *feuilletoniste*, he was well-equipped to do—and he probably welcomed the opportunity for a measure of self-indulgence that other editors did not routinely grant him. Three serials that ran simultaneously in the early issues of the magazine, all of which posed as the sorts of story expected of a magazine of that sort, but all of which had idiosyncratic features, were his own work. The only one with a heterocosmic component was "Au Pays de Stanley: voyage dans l'Afrique équatoriale" [In Stanley Country: A Journey in Equatorial Africa] published under the pseudonym Dr. Julius Lumley, which ran from 8 November 1890 to 30 May 1891 before being reprinted, under the same pseudonym, as *Voyage au pays de Stanley* in 1895.

As the three serials reached their conclusion, however, Lermina, probably prompted by the first serial the Simond had elected to run in *La Science Française*, moved away from Vernian adventure fiction into the adjacent but markedly different subgenre of future war fiction, which will be discussed in a separate section of the present chapter. That shift was not followed by the model periodicals, and might have had something to do with the fact that Simond and Lermina were both replaced as editors, the former by Émile Gautier.

Lermina then transferred his allegiance back to the *Journal des Voyages*, to which he contributed one serial per year in the first few years of the twentieth century, including such stirring adventure stories as "La Fiancée du dieu rouge" [The Bride of the Red God] (1901) and "Rose noire, rose blanche" [Black Rose, White Rose] (1903). He became more adventurous as time went by, however; "To-Ho, le tueur d'or" (1905; tr. as *To-Ho and the Gold Destroyers*) recalls Élie Berthet's *L'Homme de bois*, but is considerably bolder in having the stray boy adopted by ape-men of a species intermediate between orangutans and humans, some of whom have been taught to speak by an aged scientist who has been living among them for many years. It was probably because the serialization of "Mystère-Ville" overlapped two years in which Lermina published other serials under his own name that the pseudonym William Cobb was attached to the latter story.

In 1892 *Le Journal des Voyages* and *La Science Illustrée* both began running stories by Camille Debans (1834-1910), already a veteran writer whose most significant venture into *roman scientifique* had been with one of the pioneering works in the future war subgenre, but the work he did for *Le Journal des Voyages* and *La Science Illustrée* was mostly very different in kind from that futuristic fantasy. The first story he published in the former periodical was "Un drame à toute vapeur" [A Drama at Full Steam] (1892), while the first three he published in the latter were "Histoire d'un tremblement de terre" (1892; tr. as "The Story of an Earthquake"), "L'Île en feu" (1893; tr. as "Fire Island") and "Un duel à vapeur" (1895; tr. as "A Steam Duel" [a reprint of a story first published in 1869]). None of them contains any speculative element, two being stories featuring steam engines and the other two dramas set against the background of natural disasters; only the latter qualify, very marginally, as Vernian.

Although Debans did supply the straightforwardly Vernian novel *L'Aventurier malgré lui* [The Reluctant Adventurer] (1897-98) to the second series of the *Journal de Voyages*, and *Moumousse, reine éphémère des Somalis* [Moumousse, Temporary Queen of the Somalis] (1899) is in the same vein, the majority of his subsequent contributions to that magazine, and all of his subsequent contributions to *La Science Illustrée* moved away in other directions. "Graour le monstre" (1903 in *Journal des Voyages*; tr. as "Graour the Monster") is a curious combination of horror story and sentimental romance, which borrows its central motif from H. G. Wells' *Island of Doctor Moreau.*

By the turn of the century, in fact, and certainly by the time of Verne's death in 1905, the subgenre founded under his inspiration was beginning to look more than a little tired, if not worn out, although another periodical founded in direct competition with the *Journal des Voyages*, *Le Globe-Trotter*, did not begin publication until 1902, when its editor immediately hired André Laurie as a regular *feuilletoniste*. The last decade of the century, widely referred to as the *fin-de-siècle*, communicated an impression that many things were coming to an end, and that the new century would be a good time to start new enterprises. *La Science Française* abandoned its feuilleton spot almost as soon as the nineteenth century ended, and *La Science Illustrée* did not take long to follow suit, after attempting a renewal of the material to which it played host.

The swift transfer of H. G. Wells' translations from the pages of *La Science Illustrée* to those of the *Mercure de France* might seem eccentric, and might well have had no other cause than the fact that Henri Davray, Wells' translator, was on the *Mercure*'s staff, but the imaginative distance between Vernian fiction and Symbolist fiction was not so very distant, as George Sand had demonstrated at the very beginning of Verne's career in the proto-Symbolist *Laura*. A writer and artist at the very heart of the Symbolist Movement, André Gide and Maurice Denis, collaborated on a striking avant-gardist Vernian romance, *Le Voyage d'Urien* (1893; tr. as *Urien's Voyage*), which took its protagonists to the North Pole via the Sargasso Sea.

Le Journal des Voyages continued on its path, however, and feuilletons of a kind similar to its chief stock-in-trade continued to appear on occasion in other popular periodicals even after *Le Globe-Trotter* had ceased publication. New writers emerged who contrived to inject a new excitement into the Vernian formula with considerable success, most significantly "Paul d'Ivoi" (Paul Deleutre,

1856-1915), who co-authored *Les Cinq sous de Lavarède* (1894; tr. *Around the World on Five Sous*) with Henri Chabrillat (c1842-1893) and went on to write a further twenty novels in a similar vein, comprising a long series collectively entitled "Les Voyages Excentriques," most of which were published as feuilleton serials before book publication, and most of which were subsequently divided into two for further circulation in paperback editions.

Like Louis Boussenard, d'Ivoi concentrated primarily on adventure stories involving long and colorful journeys, but many of the twenty volumes of Voyages Excentriques feature exotic means of travel by land, sea and air, and take evident pleasure in the ingenuity of their design. For instance, *Cousin de Lavarède* [Lavarède's Cousin] (1897; in 2 vols. as *Le Diamant d'Osiris* [The Diamond of Osiris] & *Le Bolide de Lavarède* [Lavarède's Bolide]) features an airship with mobile wings; *Jean Fanfare* (1897; in 2 vols. as *La Diane d'Archipel* [The Diana of the Archipelago] & *La Forteresse roulante* [The Mobile Fortress]) employs an amphibious mobile fortress; *Corsaire Triplex* (1898; in 2 vols. as *L'Ennemi invisible* [The Invisible Enemy] & *L'Île d'or* [The Isle of Gold]) has a vast submarine; *Le Docteur Mystère* [Doctor Mystery] (1900; in 2 vols. as *L'Ours de Siva* [Siva's Bear] & *Le Brahme d'Ellora* [The Brahmin of Ellora]) displays an array of novel mechanical devices; *Le Prince Virgule* (1904-05; in 2 vols. as *Millionaire malgré lui* [A Reluctant Millionaire] & *Le Prince Virgule*) features a radiation projector; and more fantastic weaponry is featured in *L'Aéroplane fantôme* [The Phantom Airplane] (1910; in 2 vols. as *Le Voleur de pensées* [The Thought-Stealer] & *Le Lit de diamants* [The Bed of Diamonds]).

Many of d'Ivoi's later novels were published in the *Journal des Voyages*, although he also contributed to the feuilleton slot of *Le Matin*. He also worked in collaboration with "Colonel Royet" (probably the Maximin Léonce Royet who cited his rank as Capitaine and Commandant on various books about the scouting movement) notably on an 88-episode part-work, *Un, La Mystérieuse* (1905-06; book version in two volumes, 1906).

A signature that enjoyed a popular success akin to that of Paul d'Ivoi, albeit of briefer duration, was "Pierre Maël," the collective pseudonym of Charles Causse (1862-1904) and Charles Vincent (1851-1920), who made a low-key debut in the *Journal des Voyages* in 1885 and published numerous adventure stories in book form alongside his early serials there, but did not venture far into the fringes of *roman scientifique* until he published *Le Sous-marin "Le Vengeur"* [The Submarine *Le Vengeur*] (1902), and he remained equally coy thereafter, to the extent that Pierre Versins did not think it worthwhile to devote an entry to him in his *Encyclopédie*.

Another writer of juvenile fiction in the same vein as Pierre Maël, who became André Laurie's successor as *Le Globe-Trotter*'s feuilletonist, "Paul de Semant" (Paul Cousturier, 1855-1915), made his debut in the magazine in 1907 with *Le Fulgur* (book version 1910), in which the eponymous vessel's maiden voyage is interrupted by a natural catastrophe that buries it, and obliges its crew to make unusually heroic efforts, aided by the exceptional capabilities of the machine, to return to the surface by an unorthodox route. As with Maël, most of Semant's other fiction consists of adventure stories with only marginal speculative elements.

A few writers brought a higher level of literary sophistication to the writing of such adventures, notably "Georges Price" (Ferdinand-Gustave Petitpierre, 1853-1922), author of *Les Trois disparus du "Sirius"* (1896; tr. as *The Missing Men of the Sirius* and its sequel *Les Chasseurs d'épaves* [The Wreck-Clearers] (1898). The former is interesting because of its characters' methodical application of the scientific method in surviving their various predicaments, and it features the exploration of an ancient city preserved in an air-pocket beneath the Mediterranean sea-bed, but the speculative element in his fiction is very marginal.

Remarkably, one of the most accomplished contributors to the subgenre, Maurice Champagne (1868-1951) did not make his debut until "Les Reclus de la mer" (1907) was serialized in the *Journal des Voyages*, and he continued to produce work in that vein long after the magazine had folded for the last time, still active after World War II. Other writers, meanwhile, stubbornly maintained a lower tone. One who wrote a good deal in the Vernian subgenre, although he was also worked in other subgenres was René Thévenin (1877-1967), whose first serial in *Journal des Voyages* was *Sous les griffes du monster* [In the Claws of the Monster] (1908; book 1926), and who followed it up with the equally melodramatic but similarly mundane *Le Maître des vampires* [The Vampire Master] (1909; book 1923) and "Les Proies de la sirène" [The Siren's Prey] (1910). "Capitaine Danrit" (Emile Driant, 1855-

1916), whose most significant contributions to the evolution of *roman scientifique* will be discussed in another section, also became a regular contributor of serials to the *Journey des Voyages* in 1907-1912, alongside Georges Le Faure.

It is noticeable that after the turn of the century, almost all the material published in the *Journal des Voyages* and *Le Globe-Trotter*, and similar material published elsewhere, had become highly stereotyped, and only a few examples contained any innovative element. To a large extent, the Verne subgenre had either abandoned its involvement with the development of *roman scientifique*, or was content to reproduce the same motifs repeatedly, within the framework of formularistic melodramatic plots.

When writers did attempt to feature bolder ideas—as, for instance, Gaston de Wailly did in *Le Meurtrier du globe* (*Journal des Voyages* 1910; book 1925; tr. as *The Murderer of the World*), which resurrects Restif's notion of the Earth as a living entity—it was usually in the context of crude thrillers, very different in tone and ambition from the early foundation stones that Verne had laid down before 1870. Wailly's earlier attempts to produce more ambitious adventure stories in the genre of *roman scientifique*, including *Le Monde de l'abîme* [The World of the Abyss] (serial 1903-4; book 1924) had appeared in another geographical magazine, *A Travers le Monde*, which lasted from 1895-1911, as had *Le Roi de l'inconnu* [The King of the Unknown] (1904-5 as by Capitan Cristobal y Lopez; book 1924), which also employed a subterranean setting, but those stories too  were content to recycle old ideas and offered nothing new in their development of them.

While by no means dead, therefore, or even unduly decrepit, the subgenre had lost much of its initial imaginative impetus in its principal venues, and the spirit of enterprise that it had exhibited at its inception was entirely displaced into fiction that looked to other models than Verne. Writers working in the Vernian tradition outside the pages of the *Journal des Voyages* following the demise of the feuilleton slot in *La Science Illustrée* often showed more enterprise than those that had settled deeply into the rut, but the advantage was not very conspicuous. One example of marginal interest is the future-set *La*

Merveilleuse aventure (1911; reprinted in 1919 as *La Merveilleuse aventure de Jim Stappleton*) by "Cyril-Berger" (Victor Cyril, ?-1925 and Eugène Berger, 1875-1925), whose protagonist is a boxer with an automaton sparring partner.

Writers of more sophisticated fiction were not uninfluenced by Verne's exemplars, but tended to employ them after the turn of the century in a more ironic, quasi-parodic fashion. A notable example of the strategy, bordering on the surreal, is "Le Voyage de Julius Pingouin," (tr. as "The Voyage of Julius Pingouin") the second of two novellas included in *L'Homme sauvage et Julius Pingouin: Deux petit romans fantaisistes* (1902) by Frédéric Boutet, in which the captain of a Seine excursion-boat, as obsessive as Captain Hatteras but much milder of temperament, decides to set off on a quest for a new golden fleece, taking numerous volunteers from his current batch of passengers with him. Although greatly depleted in the course of their many adventures, the surviving members of the company eventually reach an exceedingly exotic region in the vicinity of the South Pole, where the quest reaches a bizarre conclusion.

Increasingly, French writers wanting to develop ideas derived from scientific possibility looked for models in the translated fiction of H. G. Wells, which, as Verne recognized himself in a famous resentful remark, made to the English journalist Gordon Jones in an interview reproduced in the June 1904 issue of *Temple Bar* (and presumably translated from the French by Jones), was markedly different from his own in its attitude and narrative texture:

"I consider [Wells], as a purely imaginative writer, to be deserving of very high praise, but our methods are entirely different. I have always made a point in my romances of basing my so-called inventions upon a groundwork of actual fact, and of using in their construction methods and materials which are not entirely without the pale of contemporary engineering skill and knowledge.... The creations of Mr. Wells, on the other hand, belong unreservedly to a degree of scientific knowledge far removed from the present, though I will not say beyond the limits of the possible."

Not all Vernian fiction, by any means, maintained that degree of conscience, but the standard at which it aimed was the one summarized succinctly by Verne, via Gordon Jones. The fiction that continued the evolutionary development of *roman scientifique* after 1900, however, accepted the greater license granted by Verne's equally succinct summary of Wells' imaginative *modus operandi*, and took full advantage of that license, to an even greater extent than the British writers inspired to develop the parallel genre of scientific romance.

3. This World and Others

In parallel with the post-1871 career of Jules Verne, Camille Flammarion also continued to experiment with the fictional formats he had begun to try out in the articles making up *Lumen* and the other stories reprinted in the 1872

Récits de l'infini, "Histoire d'une comète" and "Dans l'infini." Flammarion wrote only one more-or-less orthodox novel, a *bildungsroman* of scientific education with a spiritualist flourish at the end, *Stella* (1897), which drew extensively on Flammarion's own experiences, although the eponymous protagonist is female. His most successful works of speculative fiction after *Lumen* were, however, *Stella*'s predecessors, *Uranie* (1889; tr. as *Urania*) and *La Fin du monde* (1894; tr. as *Omega: The End of the World*), and occasional short pieces in a similar visionary vein appeared at intervals throughout the last decades of the nineteenth century.

Uranie was surprisingly successful in the short term (although it was not reprinted as frequently as *Lumen*) and its best-seller status caused three different translations to be made in the USA within a matter of months. Although advertised as a novel, it is actually a portmanteau piece, reminiscent of *Récits de l'infini* in more ways than one, comprising three pieces that were written separately. Taken as a whole, however, it is fiction of a kind very different from Vernian fiction; whereas Vernian fiction attempted—or at least pretended—to be realistic and based on firm scientific understanding, Flammarion's fiction was utterly unimpeded by practical considerations, far more interested in the farthest horizons of the scientific imagination than the nearer ones that seemed already to be within pragmatic reach.

The first part of *Uranie* is a "*voyage extatique*" in which the seventeen-year-old Flammarion, in his first year with Le Verrier at the Observatoire, is visited by the muse of astronomy, Uranie (Urania in English). She takes him on a celestial voyage to view life on many other worlds, including a planet of the multiple star Gamma Andromedae, where androgynous dragonfly-like "humans" live in a symbiotic relationship with mobile plants. The catalogue of aliens included in the story is a straightforward extension of the one offered in the fourth dialogue of *Lumen*, and the entire piece is effectively a supplement to that dialogue.

The second element of the collage is also an appendix to *Lumen*, but it follows on from the pseudobiographical elements of the first three dialogues rather than the substance of the fourth. It describes the life and presumed early afterlife of a friend of Flammarion's, here called George Spero. The third part is another *voyage extatique*, in which Flammarion makes an unaccompanied dream-journey to Mars, which he explores in the company of two human-seeming Martians, who lecture him extensively on the follies and moral weaknesses of humankind—especially war. After awakening on Earth Flammarion is visited by Spero's spirit, just as the narrator of *Lumen* had been visited; Spero reveals that he was one of Flammarion's guides on Mars, having been reincarnated there as a female, but explains that Flammarion had been deluded into seeing the Martians as humans rather than the six-limbed winged beings they really are. Uranie then reappears to restate and amplify some of the points made in the first dialogue of *Lumen*, summarizing them in a series of aphorisms.

Uranie is almost contemporary with two of the Vernian interplanetary fantasies described in the last chapter, both of which cite Flammarion's popularizations of science as primary source, but it is completely different in literary terms, not simply because it takes for granted the scheme of cosmic palingenesis that Flammarion had previously outlined, but because its narrative strategy, although it includes a travelogue of sorts, remains visionary in its texture as well as its initiating devices.

La Fin du monde was less successful commercially than *Uranie*, although it is considerably bolder in imaginative terms. It too is a portmanteau work, whose first part, had appeared separately as a serial in the previous year, and had been translated for the US magazine *Cosmopolitan*, whose associated press subsequently published the translation of the book. That first part begins as a cautionary tale about the panic that might be expected to follow the news that the Earth is about to be struck by a comet—a possibility that Flammarion had discussed in a number of magazine articles. The story veers away from the sensational, however, when it is revealed that the close encounter will only inflict light casualties, and a conference of savants meeting to discuss the matter broadens out from the primary concern to address alternative ways in which the world might end. The eventual glancing contact of the comet with the Earth's atmosphere is spectacular but not apocalyptic.

The second part of the story, "Dans dix millions d'années" [In Ten Thousand Years], comprises an ambitious future history of life on Earth: a counterpart to the past history contained in Flammarion's popularization of paleontological discoveries *Le monde avant la création de l'homme* [The World Before the Creation of Man] (1885). The concluding section displays the influence of Edgar Poe's *Eureka* as clearly as the fourth part of *Lumen* had shown the influence of Humphry Davy, and recalls the terminal point of Du Multipliandre's interstellar odyssey in *Les Posthumes*:

"Mankind had passed by transmigration through the worlds to a new life with God, and freed from the burdens of matter, soared with endless progress in eternal light.

"The immense gaseous nebula, which absorbed all former worlds, thus transformed into vapor, began to turn upon itself. And in the zones of condensation of its primordial star-mist, new worlds were born, as heretofore the earth was.

"So a new universe began, whose genesis some future Moses and Laplace would tell, a new creation, extraterrestrial, superhuman, inexhaustible...."

Stella attempted to take up where *Uranie* had left off, but failed to please the same audience, presumably because its mildly satirical depiction of contemporary French society was not as seductive as the naked sentimentality of the earlier book. Having been wooed away from the fashionable *haut monde*, where she mingles with such characters as M. Aimelafille [girl-lover] and M. Pièdevache [bovine charity], after reading a book entitled *L'affranchissement de la pensée par l'astronomie* [The Liberation of Thought by Astronomy] and subsequent dialogues with Flammarionesque savants, Stella d'Ossian falls in love with the young astronomer Raphaël Dargilan. Her nearest relatives, the Comte and Comtesse de Noirmoutier (moutier is a colloquial term for monastery, so the name's nearest English equivalent would probably be Blackfriars) do not approve, but she marries him anyway. Shortly afterwards, Stella and Raphaël are caught up in a bizarre electrical storm, which leaves them both dead, but she contrives to get a posthumous massage back to Earth to reassure those left behind that he and she are still deliriously happy, having made sufficient progress in their Earthly incarnation to be worthy of reincarnation on Mars.

Flammarion continued to produce shorter works in which factual material was dramatized by fictional devices until his production finally began to falter in the last years of his life. A few hybrid works produced in parallel to the books cited above can be found in *Dans le ciel et sur la terre* [In the Sky and on the Earth] (1886) and *Clairs de lune* [Moonlights] (1894). A more orthodox narrative item, which anticipates the conclusion of *Stella*, is "Un Amour dans les étoiles" (*Nouvelle Revue* 1896; tr. as "Love Among the Stars"). The last and most effective of several derivatives of *Lumen* is the longest item in *Rêves étoilés* [Starry Dreams] (1914), the voyage extatique "Voyage dans le ciel" (tr. as "Voyage in the Sky").

Flammarion's last collection consisting entirely of fiction—*Rêves étoilés* is a mixture of fiction and non-fiction, leaning more toward the latter—was the brief *Contes philosophiques* [Philosophical Tales] (1911), whose six items include "Conversation avec un Marsien" [Conversation with a Martian], a discourse on the folly of war in which the narrator dreams of meeting a wise inhabitant of Mars, and "Dialogue entre deux Académiciens et deux insectes stercoraires" [Dialogue between Two Academicians and Two Dung-Beetles], in which the two beetles offer an appropriately contrasted view to that of two orthodox and blinkered scholars on the subject of the conditions necessary to allow life to flourish on other worlds. The only sense in which those last revisitations carry the relevant arguments further than *Lumen* is that they are expressed with a subtler and more playful irony.

It is not feasible to identify a subgenre of "Flammarionesque fiction" because his fiction never served as a model to any considerable population of writers, and his non-fiction was available as a resource to any kind of writer. Nevertheless, there is a tradition of visionary speculative fiction that is much closer in spirit to Flammarion's experiments in fictionalizing scientific and pseudoscientific speculations than it is to Vernian practicality, and it is possible to identify "Flammarionesque" elements in numerous works that surely owe their principal inspiration to other resources. Even though the subgenre of Vernian fiction certainly extends to include a number of accounts of visits to other worlds, some of the otherworldly visions produced in the final decades of the nineteenth century and the first decade of the twentieth, are based on a different narrative philosophy, which warrants separate consideration.

Unsurprisingly, Charles Cros' "Un drame interastral" (1872; tr. as "An Interastral Drama") is an early example of a vision of another world that has something of the Flammarionesque about it. Although it employs Cros' own suggested method of interplanetary communication as a background, the story's descriptions of Venus and the Venusian with whom the narrator falls in love are visionary in manner and substance. Cros became a core member of Émile Goudeau's literary club, the Hydropathes, who were invited to reform after a temporary disbandment when Rodolphe Salis asked them to colonize his literary café Le Chat Noir; the writers who hung out there, many of whom made some contribution to the development of *roman scientifique*, rarely did so in a Vernian mode—in fact, Cros and Alphonse Allais used to do a "double act" in the early days of the establishment, in which they would invent parodies of Verne less respectful than Albert Robida's.

The writer who made the most striking contributions to visionary speculative fiction, however, was associated with a rather different literary community, centered on Edmond de Goncourt's salon, known as the Grenier [Grain-Loft]. That was "J.-H. Rosny" (Joseph-Henri Boëx, 1856-1940), who produced a cosmic vision even more exotic than *Lumen* at the very beginning of his career in "La Légende sceptique" (published 1889, but written some years earlier; tr. as "The Skeptical Legend").

"La Légende sceptique" introduces its protagonist, Luc, by saying that he "lived in a dream of the twentieth century," although it soon becomes obvious that his dreams range much further afield than that:

"His days were passed in patient study, with an extreme preference for the nooks and crannies of science, in which exceedingly delicate phenomena were revealed: the polarization of light, electromagnetic induction, electrolysis, diffusion, spheroid bodies, the physiology of nerves, hypnotism. It was more than study, however, captivating him in long ecstasies of futurition, prostrations before the unknown, his entire substance being perpetually drawn to unscientific, nebulous creations, the hope for prodigious futures, hypotheses regarding the utmost depths of things. There, he was no longer in the realm of knowledge, nor invention, but in a state of mysticism that suited his nature, in the intimacy of his ascetic brain. And he dreamed in two ways: one still investigative, deductive and logical, the other in invocations, prayers and great harmonious, hymns running between his meninges. He named the former *lucid dreams*, the latter *obscure dreams*."

Rosny's narrative goes on to summarize the substance of some of Luc's "lucid dreams," which deal with such subjects as the future evolution of life on Earth, "planetary physiology"—a stranger conceptualization than Restif de La Bretonne's notion of living worlds—and "bipolar life," leading to the development of a new sense permitting the analysis by the brain of as-yet-undetectable radiations, and a consequent increase in "cerebral penetration." His obscure dreams are elliptically described in a series of prose-poems, which include visions of evolution and of the life of the Earth after the death of the sun. The work concludes with an account of Luc's final illness, and the feverish alterations of consciousness it provokes.

Although the whole enterprise gives the impression of being, to some extent, a product of delirium, there is no doubt that "La Légende sceptique" contains much that is lucid, with an imaginative reach based in scientific understanding that extends to unprecedented limits of outer and inner space. There is a sense in which all of Rosny's subsequent scientific romances are based on tiny fragments of it, forming fictional footnotes of a sort. Much later in his career, he was to write several intense non-fictional essays developing and exploring some of its fundamental concepts, much as Restif de La Bretonne set out to analyze his "physics" in *Le Philosophie de Monsieur Nicolas*. Many readers did not understand it; some even doubted that it was comprehensible, and perhaps they were right, but there is no doubt that it was sincerely intended, and Rosny used the imaginative fraction of his literary production—always a minority, but an important one—to explore its esoteric nooks and crannies throughout his life.

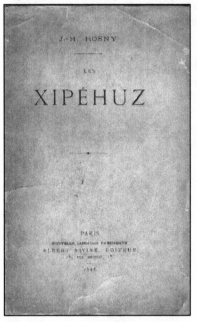

The first two items of spinoff from "La Légende sceptique," both published in advance of it in 1887, were **"Les Xipéhuz"** (tr. as "The Xipehuz") and "Tornadres" (reprinted as "Le Cataclysme" and tr. as "The Cataclysm"). The latter describes odd natural and psychological phenomena that occur on a hill that is, in fact, a huge mass of extraterrestrial matter fallen on the Earth's surface in the distant past, during a meteor shower with whose recurrent shooting stars it has a mysterious affinity. The former, which is one of the classics of *roman scientifique*, describes the appearance on Earth in prehistoric times of a population of bizarre alien creatures seemingly displaced from another spatial dimension and not fully accommodated to the geometry of ours. The humans of the era battle to oppose and obliterate the invasion, successfully in the end, though not without enormous difficulty. In the meantime, attempts made to comprehend something of the language and reproductive "biology" of the Xipéhuz—although they do not appear to be organic beings—produce a few tentative conclusions that only serve to emphasize their utter strangeness.

In the same vein, and probably written at the same time, is a short story apparently improvised from the stub of what was presumably initially intended as a novel, "Un Autre monde" (1895; tr. as "Another World"), about a young man afflicted with a more powerful kind of sight, who discovers that the human world is also inhabited by a complex host of entities that are normally invisible, whose interactions with humans therefore go uncomprehended. Although cut short, and only a fraction of what it must have been originally intended to become, that item too came to be hailed as an important exemplar of post-Vernian *roman scientifique*.

The principal import of Flammarion's vision of the universe, as elaborated in the final sections of *Lumen*, was that we should not expect other worlds to be simple replicas of ours, with only cosmetic variations, but that there might be potential receptacles for souls that fill a vast spectrum of dissimilarity, extending all the way to entities so different from human beings as to be hardly imaginable by them. Camille Flammarion's own imagination was not particularly well-equipped to illustrate and dramatize that argument, and perhaps no one's is, or ever can be, capable of doing so convincingly—but Rosny was at last willing to try, in these and other stories written at intervals throughout his career, alongside more conventional representations of things as they are and relatively elementary variants thereof. He was always aware that it was likely to be a thankless task, because the closer he came to success in his own eyes, the less comprehensible his work would become, and there is only a very limited reader appeal in calculated incomprehensibility. Nevertheless, he thought it worth doing.

Very few other writers indulged in such extreme exercises at the time, but other writers produced visionary accounts of this world and others—and particularly of the relations between them—which exhibited a related consciousness and produced similarly striking imagery. Nor was the approach limited to writers with as much literary pretention as Rosny; something of his attitude and method filtered through to lower strata of the marketplace, where visions of other worlds, including but not restricted to interplanetary fantasies, often began to take on a phantasmagoric dimension more in tune with the cosmological visions of Flammarion and Restif de la Bretonne than the extensions of geographical romance favored by writers employing Vernian templates.

Those two contrasted approaches were not entirely separate, but works that contained and tried to combine aspects of both tended to seem a trifle chimerical; J.-H. Rosny began several quasi-Vernian fantasies in which he attempted to use geographical romance as a portal to visions of exotic alternative realities, but all the early ones broke down and were abandoned, only being published in fragmentary form in such partial stories as "Nymphée" (1893; tr. as "Nymphaeum"), "La Contrée prodigieuse des cavernes" (1896; tr. as "The Wonderful Cave Country") and "Le Voyage" (1900; tr. as "The Voyage"), all of which feature exotic terrestrial life forms preserved in remote enclaves.

Between 1891 and 1907 the pseudonym J.-H. Rosny was shared by Joseph Boëx with his young brother Justin, and after the split they signed themselves J.-H. Rosny *aîné* and J.-H. Rosny *jeune* respectively, but Justin had nothing like the imagination of his brother, and all the speculative fiction produced during the years when they used the same signature—they very rarely, if ever, worked in collaboration—was Joseph's work, much of it written, or at least begun, before 1891. All references to "J.-H. Rosny" in the present text are, therefore, specifically to Joseph. During the period when the signature was shared, Justin appears to have inhibited his brother's more extravagant tendencies considerably, which probably did not harm the saleability of their work, but is regrettable from the viewpoint of the present history. On the other hand, writers who did not have to operate under such exotic handicaps certainly did not find it easy to produce or to publish endeavors of the kind that fascinated and tempted the elder Rosny, and unrestrained work of that kind was sparse.

In spite of its rarity, however, work akin to the elder Rosny's more adventurous literary exercises could produce the occasional exemplar that was both popular and acclaimed. The most high-profile was "Le Horla" (short version 1886; expanded 1887; tr. as "The Horla") by Guy de Maupassant (1850-1893), in which an ambiguous glimpse is offered of an alien presence, all the more disturbing for being invisible, and the implications of its probable existence are given careful speculative consideration. Maupassant supplemented it with a brief but striking vision of "L'Homme de Mars" (1887; tr. as "Martian Mankind"). The former is usually reckoned to be a classic horror story, which it is, but the horror emerges not from the fact that the ominous haunting might be supernatural, but quite the opposite: the disturbing suggestion is that it might be entirely natural, but affiliated to an alien order of nature.

Another significant example of this kind of visionary fiction from the *fin-de-siècle* is Han Ryner's extraordinary "Lumière-de-douleur" (1897; tr. as "Light-of-Sorrow"), in which the last humans on a dying Earth decide to "rise up" to Venus—but the eponymous protagonist has difficulty following them, and by the time he finally succeeds in reaching Venus it too is a dead world. Millions of years later, when he reaches Mercury, he finds the same situation—but the Sun still remains; there he finds lush and fecund vegetation, and hears the voices of the entities that live there, although he cannot make them hear him.

We have no way of knowing how much material of this esoteric kind was produced but unpublished, but there is one striking example of a work that attempts to take the Flammarionesque vision of the universe to its ultimate limit, which only got into print because the author's friends put together a "memorial collection" of his unpublished works after his death.

The collection in question is *Contes ondoyants et divers* (1909) by Louis Mullem (1836-1908)—one of the stalwarts of Goncourt's Grenier, with whom Rosny was acquainted, although he did not mention Mullem's speculative fiction in his memoir of the Grenier, and might not have been aware its existence. The relevant story is "Le Progrès supreme" (tr. as "The Supreme Progress"), and it was probably written in the early 1890s. Sarcastically framed as the discourse of a patient in an asylum—as stories felt too indigestible for normal consumption often are—it is set in the extremely distant future, where two once-human souls who are engaged in an exceedingly slow philosophical discussion regarding the nature of cosmic reality take a backward glance at rays of light emitted from the Earth, where they were once incarnate, in order to study individual human being and the entire tragic history of the species, from a genuinely detached viewpoint.

"Le Horla," "Les Xipéhuz," "Lumière-de-douleur" and "Le Progrès supreme" are all extreme works, of a nature that remained highly unusual in the nineteenth century, but they occupy the terminus of an imaginative spectrum of *contes philosophiques* whose ancestors go back to Voltaire's *Micromégas*, and their extremism illustrates the progress that philosophy—especially natural philosophy—had made in the interim. Cosmology, evolutionary biology and atomic physics were all in the process of stretching the potential horizons of the imagination dramatically as the nineteenth century gave way to the twentieth, and that posed challenges, not merely to writers of Rosnyan ambition who wanted to explore those horizons, but also to writers working on for more modest projects, thematically or in terms of marketability. Those writers too had to work in the context of a modern consciousness, to which the sensibility illustrated by Jules Verne's early works was no longer well-adapted—as Verne had realized himself, although many of his imitators remained in denial for much longer than he did.

Illustrations of such adaptive efforts can be found in the work of some popular journalists working in the 1890s for daily newspapers with strict space limitations, which forced them to be curt and graphic if they wanted to address far-reaching speculative ideas in their work, as Alphonse Allais frequently did, often embedding such fancies in the pieces eventually collected in *Le Captain Cap, ses aventures, ses idées, ses breuvages* (1902; included, with similar items in *The Adventures of Captain Cap*), and as Paul Vibert did in many of the items collected in *Pour lire en automobile, nouvelles fantastiques* [For Reading in an Automobile: Fantastic Stories] (1901; tr. as *The Mysterious Fluid*). Because of their brevity, the imagery in such pieces tends to the surreal, and the obligatory absence of elaborate explanatory support gives them a dreamlike quality, even when the ideas deployed therein are directly derived from scientific theory.

Vibert sometimes developed his speculative fictions in mini-serials, because it was difficult to fit the ideas into a single article; the longer ones include an account of a submarine civilization, a series about life on Mars involving communication by means of Charles Cros' method, and a brief series speculating about the possibilities of "interastral telegraphy." His fellow humorist Tristan Bernard had also employed the Cros method of interplanetary communication in "Qu'est-ce qu'ils peuvent bien nous dire?" [What are they trying to say to us?] (1897), in which it turns out that the signaling Martians are not, in fact, trying to say anything to us, but are actually attempting to make contact with Saturn.

Henri Ner—who met the elder Rosny at Alphonse Daudet's salon in the 1890s and maintained a friendly acquaintance with him for forty years—was sufficiently hard-headed as a professional writer to know that stories like "Lumière-de-douleur" could only be occasional whims of self-indulgence. Nevertheless, he incorporated a thoroughly modern awareness into a broad spectrum of his work, especially once he adopted the substitute phonetic rendition of his name "Han Ryner"—initially a pseudonym—permanently. He developed his own subgenre of brief *contes philosophiques* in "cynical parables" such as those collected in *Les Voyages de Psychodore, philosophe cynique* (1903; tr. as "The Travels of Psychodorus, Cynic Philosopher"), in which a skeptical disciple of Diogenes encounters all kinds of alien species and strange phenomena.

The same sensibility informed some of Ryner's longer works of the period before the Great War, including such exercises in *roman scientifique* as *L'Homme-fourmi* (1901; tr. as *The Human Ant*), whose protagonist exchanges souls for a year, Multipliandre-fashion, with an ant, and thus learns to see the world and the politics of everyday life from a very different perspective.

The notion that the world-view of social insects might provide a useful standard of comparison for the human world-view had been tried before; one of the earliest examples in fictional form is a brief sketch included in the collection *Polierge* (1757) by Emerich de Vattel, and ants had featured in various political satires, but Ryner's work was by far the most ambitious and sophisticated at the time of its publication, and far more comprehensively-informed than its predecessors. Like Albert Bleunard's "Toujours plus petit," it drew upon the account of "Les Fourmis rousses" [Red Ants] contained in the second series of J.-H. Fabre's *Souvenirs entomologiques* (1879), although the experiments conducted by the entomologist into whose hands Ryner's human ant ultimately falls are based on those carried out by the English scientist John Lubbock (later Baron Avebury), who published a notable book on *Ants, Bees and Wasps* in 1881.

Where Fabre had led, other eminent French entomologists had followed, most notably Ernest André, author of *Les Fourmis* (1885), another mine of information reproduced by Ryner. Although Fabre was a brilliant popularizer, and both Lubbock and André took leave to exploit the melodramatic potential of their investigations, the imaginative range that Ryner added to his own dramatization is no mere cheapening or perversion of the material supplied by his sources, and the literary endeavor adds a significant further dimension to it. Although not devoid of a satirical element, Ryner's work addresses the fictitious situation established by a frankly supernatural facilitating device with an eye that is as clinical as it is cynical. He was equally forthright in spicing up his story with honest melodrama; *L'Homme-fourmi* is probably the most action-packed account of the secret life of ants, and is most certainly the most sex-obsessed, blithely embracing the startling perversity required to accommodate and develop that obsession.

Interplanetary fantasies were the kind of story most likely to benefit from an infusion of the Flammarionesque, and it is perhaps surprising, in retrospect, that Flammarion's work seemed very partial in its influence on that kind of exercise. Every litterateur setting out into space took Flammarion's maps of the other worlds of the solar system with them for reference, if they had the opportunity, but very few consorted with the muse Urania in the same flirtatiously "ecstatic" fashion as he had. Nevertheless, interplanetary adventurers whose primary allegiance was to the satirical tradition rather than pushing the envelope

388

of geographical romance had every reason to borrow from *Lumen* rather than *De la terre à la lune* in transporting their viewpoint characters to distant climes. One of those who did was the author of **Cybèle, Voyage extraordinaire dans l'avenir**, (1891; tr. as translated as *Cybele: An Extraordinary Voyage into the Future*), initially by-lined "Jean Chambon."

Jean Chambon was the pseudonym of Jean-Adolphe Alhaiza (1839-1922), who achieved a celebrity of sorts late in life when he became the editor of *La Rénovation*, the periodical of an organization established to carry forward and popularize the sociological theories of Charles Fourier. He was, however, working as a commercial traveler when he published the first of the two books he wrote as Jean Chambon, *Catéchisme naturaliste: Essai de synthèse physique, vitale et religieuse,* [A Naturalist Catechism: An Essay in the Synthesis of Physics, Biology and Religion]. Why Hippolyte Destrem (1816-1894), who was the director of the Fourierist Society and the editor of *La Rénovation* contacted the author and invited him to join the society is not entirely clear, as neither of the Chambon texts has any evident affiliation to Fourierist ideas, and Alhaiza's philosophy is more akin to an attempt to graft an idiosyncratic version of deism on to the positivist ideas of Auguste Comte, but when Destrem died, Alhaiza took over his position, and made *La Rénovation* into a more active and more combative instrument of political criticism—albeit criticism that appears to have given far more prominence to his own idiosyncrasies than the ideas of the movement's founding father.

Cybèle makes a number of narrative moves that deliberately introduce themes and images exceeding or contradicting the narrative devices employed by previous writers of euchronian fiction, the most remarkable of which is the notion of Cybèle itself. Alhaiza was aware of the dilemma inherent in the fact that the only plausible way of gaining narrative access to the future in 1891 was by means of some kind of prophetic dream, and the corollary circumstance that the device was bound to seem both hackneyed and unconvincing if it could not be given a particular twist that would make it seem more solid. He knew too that some previous writers had used the device of suspended animation to transport their protagonists into the future, and was also aware of the implicit penalty of that stratagem, in that it left its users with no way to report back to the present, let alone transport themselves back to their starting-point. He does deploy the notion of suspended animation in *Cybèle*—and, indeed, considers its implications more enterprisingly than any author before him—but evidently rejected the possibility of employing as a fundamental means of transportation, in favor of a much more adventurous stratagem.

The device employed by Alhaiza to get around these problems was first proposed in a remarkable essay by the French socialist Louis Blanqui. *L'Éternité par les astres* [Eternity via the Stars] (1872), which argues that if the universe is infinite in space and time there must, among the infinite number of planets it contains, be an infinite subset that are exact duplicates of the Earth in all but contemporaneity, so that, even though every human individual dies, he or she must also be replicated indefinitely, thus granting all of them a curious kind of immortality.

Taking advantage of this logic, Alhaiza infers that there must exist, elsewhere in the universe, worlds that are identical to Earth but historically displaced, so that our present is, for the moment, their past or future. All that a "time traveler" has to do, therefore, is find a means of instantaneous translation to one of these sister Earths. Strictly speaking, this does not avoid the problem of the temporal displacement functioning in exactly the same fashion as a dream, but it does at least lend a certain eccentric muscle to the dreaming process, which is illustrated by the elaborate and highly unusual account given in the story of the journey through space that delivers Alhaiza's hero to his exotic destination: a decidedly Flammarionesque "ecstatic voyage."

In shaping his vision of Earth's future, as represented on Cybèle, Alhaiza borrows a thesis set out in a book entitled *Révolutions de la mer, déluges périodiques*, published in 1860 by Joseph-Alphonse Adhémar, which attempted to combine recent discoveries about the "ice ages" that had afflicted the northern hemisphere in times past with various other kinds of data, including the Biblical account of the Deluge, to produce a catastrophist geological theory, whose implications included a calculation of the date when the next such catastrophe would either put an end to the progress of human civilization or pose a very stern challenge to it.

We now know that Adhémar's thesis is completely false, because reliable methods of geological and archeological dating have reduced his hypothetical chronology to absurdity, and it did not attract many adherents in its own day, because its notion of a drastic shift in the Earth's center of gravity was evidently implausible, but development of Adhémar's hypothesis does allow Alhaiza to pose and address an interesting question, with regard to a future that has benefited from thousands of years of scientific and technological progress, but which is uncomfortably aware of the fact that it is facing an imminent and potentially-apocalyptic catastrophe.

Within his depiction of that situation, the author attempts to design a new kind of religion, shorn of unnecessary superstition but still possessed of lofty ideals, and he also develops a holistic view of nature, in which humans are by no means the only participants in an ongoing evolutionary process potentially capable of bringing various other animal species to sentience and cultural development of producing a further stage in human evolution. The sum of those factors makes the novel an interesting contrast with the Vernian interplanetary fantasies that briefly preceded its publication.

The first ever winner of the Prix Goncourt was *Force ennemie* (1903; tr. as *Enemy Force*) by "John-Antoine Nau" (Eugène Torquet, 1860-1918), one of the most convoluted "madman's manuscript" stories ever produced, in which one of the symptoms of the writer's delusions is that he is periodically possessed by a hostile "force" that is responsible for some of his worst actions. That force identifies itself as an alien being named Kmôhoûn, from the planet Tkoukra, which orbits the red star known to humans as Aldebaran: a Hellish place perpetually drenched in the blood-red light of its sun.

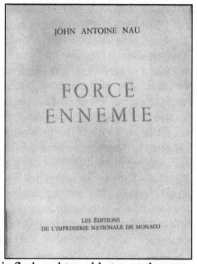

The invader explains to the narrator that he has the ability to separate what the Earthman would call his astral body from his flesh and travel between the stars, and that he has elected to parasitize the narrator's weak mind in order to learn enough about his language and the way humans work to be able to move on successfully to possess another body more fully. In the meantime, it is amusing itself with its various provocations.

The imagery in question is surely borrowed from Flammarion, although it is not so very different from that already contained in Restif's depiction of Duc Multipliandre, and the framework recalls "Le Horla," although Nau's story is considerably less ambiguous, offering far less potential for the reader to think that Kmôhoûn might really exist. Whether the alien has any real existence or not, however, the infusion of Flammarionesque notions of the universe and the ideas developed in *Lumen* reflects the fact that the visionary imagery in question was becoming generalized as a resource—and the delusory nature of the fantasy did not stop later generations of science fiction fans and historians claiming *Force ennemie* as one of the more reputable ancestors of their genre.

The first decade of the twentieth century saw the first injection into *roman scientifique* of the influence of translations of the work of H. G. Wells, but that influence inevitably overlapped with the resident influence of Vernian romance, and it also took aboard Flammarionesque aspects too. One of the most elegant syntheses of all three traits can be found in Charles Derennes' *Le Peuple du pôle* (1904; tr. as *The People of the Pole*), in which two aeronauts on a Vernian expedition to the North Pole are captured by the inhabitants of a closed world far more alien than anything that any orthodox Vernian traveler would ever have been allowed to discover. The species is oviparous, more closely related to reptiles than mammals, but sentient and technically advanced—as they have to be in order to protect their subterranean society against the polar cold.

The alien society's mores are adapted to their exotic biology and their geographical location, and that difference in world-view adds to the difficulties in communication that inevitably arise for the travelers because of the language barrier. The aeronauts' exploration of the polar underworld is therefore fraught with difficulty; they never do contrive to understand the aliens' motives in capturing their balloon or in their subsequent dealings with them as they struggle to survive and escape.

The narrator has the sensation more than once that the whole experience is a dream, but every time he wakes up, it is to find the discomfiting reality, which becomes even more hallucinatory as his companion goes mad—a suspicion that inevitably hangs over him when his manuscript account of his experience reaches civilization. The subsequent discussion of that question, however, remains uncomfortably suspended between writing off the entire account as a hallucination and taking it literally; both explanations are analyzed at length in terms of their plausibility, probability and possible consequences.

Whether or not it was entirely due to the infusion of Wellsian influence, the first decade of the century also saw the production of a sudden rush of French interplanetary fantasies, some of which paid explicit homage to such H. G. Wells novels as *The War of the Worlds* (1898) and *The First Men in the Moon* (1901). The perception of those works, however, and the nature of their influence, was partly determined by the native context in which they arrived.

Just as the influence of Wells on interplanetary adventure stories in the U.S.A. was fitted to a set of attitudes markedly different from that existing in England, resulting in the flourishing of a species of "Wellsian" fiction much more closely integrated with ideas of technological progress and frontiersmanship, in which the future and other worlds both became extensions of the "Wild West," to be colonized and tamed, so French "Wellsian fiction" soon acquired a distinctive slant and flavor, particularly obvious in interplanetary fantasies that retained a Flammarionesque attitude and manner, even in the lowest strata of the literary marketplace, where they flourished most abundantly.

In the same way that *Le Peuple du pôle* fused different influences to transfigure the tradition of geographical romance, bringing the otherworldly to Earth, numerous French interplanetary fantasies took aboard an element of Wellsian inspiration and combined it with Flammarionesque perspectives, thus producing a hybrid set of works markedly different in texture from the stumbling efforts of Charles Guyon and "Pierre de Sélènes" without being mere pastiches of the English works.

While not being any more plausible in rational terms than their predecessors, most of the new interplanetary fantasies became much more robust in their approach and their imaginative reach, and that reach retained a visionary quality even though some of the most obvious examples were fitted to an action-adventure framework. André Laurie's "Le Roman dans le planète Mars," although described in the previous section along with the remainder of the author's works, might be reckoned a significant pre-Wellsian contribution to the embryonic tradition, explicitly employing Flammarionesque methods for the protagonist's translocation to Mars and his guidance while there by the winged "angel."

Popular twentieth-century interplanetary adventure fiction in France was pioneered by Arnould Galopin in *Le Docteur Oméga, aventures fantastiques de trois Français dans la planète Mars* (1906; revised and expanded in a part-work version entitled *Les Chercheurs d'inconnu* [Seekers of the Unknown], 1908-9; tr. as *Doctor Omega*). The protagonist, a mysterious scientific genius with distinct echoes of Captain Nemo, has constructed a multi-purpose vehicle, the *Cosmos*, which can travel on land or under water, and even through the interplanetary ether, by virtue of an antigravitic substance analogous to Cavorite. His neighbor, who serves as the novel's narrator, and a laborer named Fred make up a standard Vernian trio of travelers for a trip to Mars, where a quasi-Vernian travelogue is soon transformed into a phantasmagorical parade of nightmarish life-forms, including the dwarfish Macrocephalians, to whom the visitors lend their aid in a war against the Cacocytes, although the ingrate Macrocephalians then try to keep the humans prisoner, requiring their rescue by another enigmatic scientist.

Although clearly a calculated hybridization of Vernian and Wellsian romance, Galopin's story takes aboard a vision of the vast multiplicity of life that neither Verne nor Wells ever emphasized, whose effect is not simply to exaggerate the strangeness of the vision of Martian life but to transform the relationship of the central characters to the otherworldly context.

British scientific romance and American science fiction each developed their own more-or-less stereotyped image of Martian life, and of the possibilities of human interaction with it. Camille Flammarion's description of likely conditions on the Martian surface in his popular astronomical textbooks fueled those images, just as it had the image contained in Le Faure and Graffigny's description of Mars in *Les Aventures d'un savant russe*. *Le Docteur Oméga* draws upon that image too, but it develops a portrait of a considerably stranger series of environments, with a profusion of bizarrely chimerical inhabitants, giving the sense of a world that is not merely a modified Earth-clone but genuinely alien. The plot is a conventional action-adventure story that adapted very well to the move further downmarket in the part-work version addressed specifically to younger readers, but neither its enigmatic central character nor the character of its exoticism would have recommended it for immediate translation as an Edwardian "boys' book" in England or a pulp fantasy in the U.S.A.

Le Docteur Oméga was swiftly followed by a serial published in the relatively upmarket periodical *La Nouvelle Revue*, whose experimentally-minded editor, Pierre-Barthelémy Gheusi, tried out several different varieties of imaginative fiction while he was in charge of the magazine, and presumably thought that interplanetary fantasy ought to have its chance. The author of the serial, "Sylvain Déglantine" (Sylvain Paquier, 1872-1969), went on to receive an honorable mention in one of the Académie Française's annual prizes later that year—for a different book—and subsequently won three such prizes, so his respectability was not in doubt, but any advantage he had over Galopin and the writers who followed in footsteps, in terms of stylistic elegance, was canceled out by the relative paucity of his imagination.

It does not help the impression of verisimilitude that the characters in *Les Terriens dans Vénus* [Terrans on Venus] (serialized January-June 1907; reprinted in book form the same year with a preface by Camille Flammarion) insist in referring to their spaceship, the *Comète*, as a "ballon" [balloon] although it is a solid structure propelled by an application of electromagnetic attraction. On his test-flight to Venus, the young inventor, Saint-Aubin, takes along his sister, "Nini," her husband, her cook and an old family friend, a retired military man. Once there, they have no difficulty communicating with the natives, who have not only been formed by parallel evolution in a near-human mold but equipped with the same languages. The planet's surface, although a trifle warm, is not as hot as its proximity to the sun might suggest—a circumstance explained by an argument regarding its native supply of "caloric" identical to the one used by Pierre Boitard, with less excuse.

While three of the party are captured by anthrophagous giants intent on eating them—except for Nini, who becomes a target of a different avidity on the part of one of the giants—the inventor also contrives to get himself into hot water by making eyes at Rosefleur, a beautiful Venusienne of ordinary stature who is unfortunately engaged to be married to an influential diplomat. The initially-jocular narrative extrapolates and complicates these predicaments with zestful enthusiasm, at a rapid pace, but as all the scientific arguments recruited in the story are employed to explain why Venus is so very similar to Earth, it is hardly evident in the early stages of the plot that the characters are on an alien world. The entire story might almost have been set on some bizarre Pacific island, except that a strange character named Jeuçaithou [phonetically, *Je sais tous*: "I know everything"] keeps popping up to give the Terrans useful advice and then disappearing; he eventually turns out to be traveling in spirit form, Multipliandre-fashion, and to be a Terran himself, albeit one of great antiquity, thus resetting the whole exercise in a Flammarionesque context.

The most unusual thing about the novel is that all the carefully-established romantic complications, which would normally be expected to lead to happy endings in a conventional adventure story, fail to do so, and the entire cast of characters is wiped out, one by one. Déglantine might have felt obliged to do that in order to secure a normalizing ending in which the *Comète* and its inventor are conclusively eliminated from Earthly history, but its effect is to make the novel exceedingly downbeat, highly unlikely to satisfy readers expecting love to conquer all. Gheusi did not repeat that particular experiment, and interplanetary fantasy vanished from the *Nouvelle Revue*'s pages for good.

Les Terriens dans Vénus was followed a year later by a trio of novels by different hands that have some conspicuous similarities to one another, although the similarities could not have arisen from the mutual influence of the printed versions and are strongly suggestive of some prior discussion by the three writers involved, at least two of whom, and probably all three, had long been acquainted. *La Roue fulgurante* (tr. as *The Fiery Wheel*) by "Jean de La Hire" (Adolphe d'Espie, 1878-1956) was initially published as a feuilleton in the daily newspaper *Le Matin*, between 10 April and 23 May 1908, and was reprinted in book form later that year. *Aventures merveilleuses de Serge Myrandhal sur la planète Mars: Sur la planète Mars (tr. in The Marvelous Adventures of Serge Myrandhal on Mars)* by-lined "H. Gayar" was published on 15 June of that year and *Le Prisonnier de la planète Mars* (tr. in *Vampires of Mars*) by Gustave Le Rouge was published on 1 July.

La Roue fulgurante was a radical new departure for both the author and for the newspaper in which it appeared. La Hire became one of *Le Matin*'s leading providers of serials for some time thereafter, and although *Le Roue fulgurante* was not the only item of *roman scientifique* he supplied to the paper, or even the only one with an interplanetary theme, it remained the most adventurous, and might have even more adventurous had he not opted—perhaps in response to editorial pressure—to provide it with a rather abrupt ending, which not only left some of the possibilities raised in the plot undeveloped but cut off the possibility of their further development.

It was not unusual for feuilleton serials to be rudely interrupted in that way, and authors of such works always had to be prepared to finish them off swiftly, but the internal evidence suggests that La Hire was not only prepared to extrapolate his plot further, but to make further use of the eponymous gaseous spaceship—a highly unusual vehicle crewed by truly exotic aliens—and also to take the leading characters on a tour of the solar system with the aid of other extraterrestrial acquaintances, in a series of sequels. Apparently, the editor of *Le Matin* felt that the experiment had failed, and when La Hire ventured into space in the feuilleton slot again, it was within the narrative frame of a more conventional thriller.

La Roue fulgurante now seems to have gained historical interest by virtue of being the first work of fiction to feature the theme of "alien abduction," all the more so as the abduction is effected by means of a vehicle whose description as a wheel gave it a tenuous link with the "flying disks" or "flying saucers" that were later to be credited with so many supposedly-real abductions of that sort in the second half of the twentieth century, but at the time, those details did not seem to have any particular relevance. Using an alien spaceship apparently collecting specimens of humankind from the Earth's surface as a means of space travel was then simply an ingenious way of avoiding the narrative challenges involved in having Earthly scientists find their own way into space.

The subsequent abandonment of the collected specimens on Mercury, which they find every bit as bizarre and nightmarish and Galopin's Mars, similarly equipped with hostile alien populations, opens narrative potential for a potentially-limitless series of creatures, escapes and pursuits, which the author brings to a climax on the edge of the planet's "twilight zone," in confrontation with a hemisphere that he supposes to be in perpetual darkness. At that point, with the castaways direly in need of rescue, the ever-present problem of how they are ever going to get back home becomes urgent. The prolific La Hire was not a man to be found wanting when a *deus ex machina* was required, however, and he had carefully prepared the way for an Oriental mystic, who has enhanced the traditional abilities of fakirs with a synergistic dose of Western science, to effect a dramatic flourish by means of psychic power, after the fashion of André Laurie's explorer of Mars or Déglantine's Jeuçaithou.

Although employed at the opposite end of the story, the mechanics of that miraculous denouement are strikingly similarly to the initiating devices employed to render interplanetary travel possible in the two novels that followed so swiftly on the heels of La Hire's serial that one is tempted to suspect that not only were the three writers aware of what the others were going to do before any of them set pen to paper, but that some sort of wager might have been involved. If so, La Hire presumably won.

In Gayar's *Aventures merveilleuses de Serge Myrandhal sur la planète Mars*, the hero has invented a machine to harness the combined power of a group of individuals with unusual psychic abilities and employ it to levitate objects. He is ambitious to use the method to power a spaceship, but needs far more psychic force than he can possibly find in the West. The Indian Maharajah Indraghava, however, who attends a demonstration of Myrandhal's machine in New York, has an unlimited source of such power at his disposal in a monastery of adepts, and he volunteers to enter into association so that they can pool their resources. The Maharajah is, however, secretly jealous of the Western encroachment in the discipline to which he has devoted his life, and plans to hijack the spacecraft in order to send his
son and Myrandhal's beautiful fiancée to Mars in order to found a colony and a dynasty there. That plan goes awry, with the result that Myrandhal, his fiancée and an eccentric English explorer end up on Mars together, with no apparent way of getting home again, and they set out to explore the planet instead.

In Le Rouge's *Le Prisonnier de la planète Mars*, the engineer Robert Darvel, ambitious to find a means of propelling a spacecraft to Mars, is contacted by the Brahmin Ardavena who offers to provide the required propulsion by accumulating and harnessing the psychic force of ten thousand fakirs. Like Indraghava, however, Ardavena has a sinister hidden agenda. The launch succeeds, but not without causing catastrophic destruction on the ground. Darvel, alone on the Martian surface, embarks upon a series of fantastic encounters, in the course of which he establishes a kind of sovereignty over one of the native populations by teaching them the elementary uses of fire, and begins their liberation from the predations of the vampiric Erloor. By the end of the first volume he has found an exotic means of sending Morse-coded messages—and hence his story—back to the Earth, but the problem of returning himself is left to a sequel.

Both of the latter novels were explicitly planned as the first parts of series although Le Rouge wrapped up his at the end of the second volume whereas Gayar suspended his second volume in mid-narrative, in anticipation of a third that never materialized. Gayar followed his initial publication very rapidly, on 15 July, with the second volume of the *Aventures merveilleuses de Serge Myrandhal, Les Robinsons de la planète Mars*, whereas Le Rouge's **La Guerre des vampires** did not appear until the following year (both sequels are appended to the first volumes in the translations). Much later, when a heavily revised version of the existing text of Gayar's story was reissued in a single volume as *Les Robinsons de la planète Mars* (1927), by-lined "Cyrius," many of the elements that overlapped with Le Rouge's novel were excised, perhaps specifically in order to reduce the similarity.

The second part of Gayar's novel is a trifle tentative, and an abrupt change of style part-way through suggests that a different author might have taken over at that point—none of the material added thereafter is included in the Cyrius version—but it does build up narrative momentum again when the castaways find a ruined Martian city, and investigate a collection of biological specimens that includes two representatives of the superhuman species that once ruled the planet—a couple whose apparent death turns put merely to be a state of suspended animation. Their awakening is, however, employed as a teaser looking forward to the projected third volume, which never appeared.

Le Rouge was able to continue his own novel in a more robustly phantasmagorical fashion, moving on from the exotic abode of the Erloor to the discovery of a vast, disembodied but highly active Brain, which seems to be the endpoint of Martian biological evolution and the effective ruler of the world. The conclusion of the novel, however, takes place back on Earth, to which Darvel is obligingly returned by the eruption of a Martian volcano, unfortunately followed by some of the planet's vampiric predators.

It is theoretically possible, albeit unlikely, that the similarities between the three novels—especially their use of Eastern mystics as facilitating devices—arose from the common influence of earlier works that were probably known to all three writers, most significantly Théodore Flournoy's best-selling *Des Indes à la planète Mars* (1900; tr. as *From India to the Planet Mars*), an account by a Genevan psychologist of revelations produced by a medium, "Hélène Smith" (actually Elise Müller), while supposedly entranced, by the method of "automatic writing." Flournoy attributed the revelations in question to the medium's imagination—much to her displeasure—but she regarded them, as Camille Flammarion might have done, as accounts of actual other lives that she had previously experienced in various locations, including India and Mars.

All three novelists would have been aware of the experiments with automatic writing previously carried out in the vicinity of Paris by Flammarion, in which some of his collaborators—including Victorien Sardou—had produced visions of life on other planets, where human beings might be reincarnated. All three of them would also have been familiar with *Lumen* and *Uranie*. It is obvious that in all three novels that the inspiration provided by Flammarion is combined with that of H. G. Wells, although Gayar's arguably owes even more to Verne, but the fact that all three retain a measure of Flammarion in their alloy differentiates their fantasies from alloys of Vernian and Wellsian fantasy produced in Britain and America. Gayar's is by far the least adventurous of the three in its depiction of conditions on the surface of the alien planet, but it makes up for that deficit with a particularly phantasmagorical account of the journey through space to reach it, and the culmination of his second volume—eliminated from the Cyrius revision, which interrupts the explorations at an earlier stage and improvises a *deus ex machina* ending—strongly suggests that the anticipated third volume would have taken the story much further into Flammarionesque imaginative territory.

Although the abortion of Gayar's series might have been due, like the interruption of the Le Faure/Graffigny project, to the bankruptcy of the publisher, it does seem to be the case that all three aspects of the triple experiment ended in a similar failure to attract sufficient reader support. None of the three writers ever did anything quite as adventurous again, although La Hire did respond to the temptation twice more, in relatively modest fashion, whereas Le Rouge and Gayar both remained stubbornly earthbound throughout the remainder of their literary careers, banishing speculative embellishments to the margins of their plots on the few occasions when they entertained them at all. In France, as in Britain, the entire genre of speculative fiction—and the interplanetary subgenre in particular—having been tested, was apparently deemed by the market's gatekeepers to have insufficient mass appeal, and it was banished to the eccentric margins of the publishing landscape. At least it had been tested, and fairly, *Le Matin* being the best showcase it could possibly have had.

Jean de La Hire wrote in several popular genres, but he made a swift return to *roman scientifique* in the pages of *Le Matin* with the earthbound thriller *L'Homme qui peut vivre dans l'eau* [The Man Who Could Live Under Water] (1908; book 1910), to which he provided an interplanetary sequel in *Le Mystère des XV* (1911; tr. as *The Nyctalope on Mars*), which is also an explicit sequel to Wells' *The War of the Worlds*, and in which Camille Flammarion appears briefly as a character to receive his own homage, as he had in *La Roue fulgurante*. *Le Mystère des XV* was La Hire's last venture of that sort for a long time, however, and although the hero of the novel was reincarnated for a long-running series in 1920, when the interruption of the Great War had concluded, the elements of *roman scientifique* that had initially been central to the series were gradually de-emphasized relative to its more conventional crime-fighting components.

It is not surprising, in retrospect, that the experiment connected by La Hire and *Le Matin* failed, in spite of the rapid support it obtained from a handful of other writers, including Gayar and Le Rouge. Indeed, some of the reasons for that failure are obvious in the pages of *La Roue fulgurante*, and must have seemed so in immediate retrospect as well as more distant and studied contemplation. The story, borne along by its own zestful impetus, runs head-first into all the problems innate in imaginatively ambitious exercises in futuristic speculation, discovering a series of logical impasses, and provoking a set of narrative problems, all of which were to cast a long shadow over the future development of French *roman scientifique*, British scientific romance and American science fiction—and which continue to afflict them, in spite of the fact that the American genre eventually contrived to obtain an enduring toehold in the bosom of mass culture.

The invocation of psychic power as a means of space travel was clearly not a viable long-term solution to the narrative problem, nor did La Hire, Gayar or Le Rouge find any convincing way of managing interactions between humans and aliens, given the inherent problems of initial mutual comprehension. All three writers also became swiftly aware of the acute problems associated with melodramatic inflation: the awkward features of the quest to boggle minds by means of garish innovation, requiring an ideative escalation so rapid and so extreme that writers soon run out of further room for maneuver, even in the content of a Flammarionesque universe of infinite alien possibility.

The temptation to fuse elements of scientific and occult speculation was not entirely due to the influence of Camille Flammarion, although the existence in France of such a high-profile figure equally interested in astronomy and "spiritism," certainly enhanced the attractiveness of the fusion to writers of imaginative fiction. Indeed, the entire "occult revival" of the *fin de siècle* had been based on exactly such a fusion, whose duality was the philosophical core of Madame Blavatsky's Theosophy and the avid activities of the Society for Psychical Research. Given that the fundamental basis of the appeal of such hybrid notions was esthetic rather than rational, it is not surprising that it appealed to litterateurs willing to bite the bullet of testing the limits of imaginative fiction.

In the first decade of the twentieth century, however, the graft was still too awkward to take permanently, and the product too chimerical. The fakiristic mystics featured in the three novels had little future in the subsequent evolution of interplanetary fiction, although a Persian magus plays a significant role in facilitating travel when a fragment of Earth's surface is projected to Mars following a meteorite impact, in "L'Étrange aventure de M. Narcisse Barbibon" [Narcisse Barbibon's Strange Adventure] (serial in *Cri-Cri* 1912; book version 1919 in 2 vols. as *Les Hommes-Singes* [The Ape-Men] & *La Guerre des nains et des géants* [The War of the Dwarfs and the Giants]) by Marcel Laurian, where the reluctant space-travelers discover a world as exotic as the one described by Le Rouge, and considerably more advanced technologically. If a fusion of the scientific and the spiritistic were to be achieved in the context of the fiction of other worlds and other dimensions, however, it would obviously require a different apparatus and a different narrative strategy, and the endeavor of writers whose enthusiasm did not outweigh their artistry to such a conspicuous extent as in the cases of La Hire, Gayar, Le Rouge and Laurian.

Fantasies of alien interaction of the "inverted" kind popularized by *The War of the Worlds*—in which the aliens come to us rather than our going to them—took a great leap forward in France when the most outspoken propagandist for a new literature of the *merveilleux scientifique*, Maurice Renard (1875-1939) produced the novel that can be regarded as his masterpiece, and as one of the classics of that genre, *Le Péril bleu* (1911; tr. *The Blue Peril*).

Renard's conception of the nascent genre, of which he nominated Wells as the central exemplar and J.-H. Rosny the principal domestic practitioner, was inherently various and wide-ranging, to a much greater extent than the Vernian fiction with which he contrasted it in his 1909 "manifesto" for the genre, "Du Roman merveilleux-scientifique et de son action sur l'intelligence du progrès." His own contributions to it are therefore various in their themes, and warrant discussion in several different sections of this chapter and the next. *Le Péril bleu* is not his only work featuring an alien species, but it is by far the most ingenious and ambitious.

The story begins as a mystery, with a series of strange occurrences and disappearances in a small region of the south of France, involving abductions far more subtle than those featured in *La Roue fulgurante*. The hero of the story, initially engaged with it as an intriguing puzzle, becomes far more intent on solving the mystery when his fiancée disappears, and strenuous efforts on his part and by his chief associates eventually succeed in determining that the abductions are being carried out by an invisible airship, which is transporting animal and human captives to a strange study-facility high in the atmosphere: a laboratory where analytical vivisections are carried out, and the subsequent detritus thrown overboard.

Eventually, the surviving human captives are returned to the surface—not including the hero's fiancée, alas—and not long thereafter the invisible airship suffers a breakdown and crashes in the heart of Paris, becoming visible and permitting the extraction of the corpses of its navigators. They turn out to be peculiar compound individuals, denizens of the upper atmosphere, whose composites have a vaguely arachnid form.

The novel's combination of a mystery whose painstaking elucidation requires enormous efforts of ingenuity, and continually produces bizarre new information, with the imaginative background of the alien world existing high above the Earth's surface is a *tour de force* of imaginative literature, which displayed the potential of Renard's putative genre far more dramatically than any other work produced before the Great War. No other work took up Flammarion's challenge to imagine a truly alien sentient species as robustly, and that fact that it does so without the necessity to go outside the terrestrial atmosphere adds an extra flourish to the feat.

The story has a leavening of humor, in the antics of the "Sherlockian" amateur detective who volunteers to add his dubious expertise to the hero's efforts, not realizing—as the detective in Victorien Sardou's "Le Médaillon" also failed to do—that "eliminating the impossible" from consideration is going to pose a stern challenge to his preconceptions of possibility. The straightforwardly melodramatic twists of the plot are engineered with appropriate flamboyance, allowing the story to work at the same "middlebrow" level as Wells' classic scientific romances, an obvious cut above the downmarket works of La Hire, Gayar and Le Rouge. In terms of winning a large audience for the genre it exemplified, however, *Le Péril bleu* was no more successful in the longer term than they were, and like the authors of the earlier trio of works, Renard eventually found himself lacking the kind the encouragement that would have enabled him to proproduce more work of a similar kind, let alone to attempt to supersede it within its presumed framework.

The touches of the surreal imported into their newspaper articles by Alphonse Allais and Paul Vibert were greatly exaggerated, and developed far more coherently, by one humorist who, like Albert Robida before him, had a periodical of his own in which to develop his whims, and who eventually gathered the produce in question into an extensive patchwork that is another of the most remarkable works of its era: *Voyage au pays de la quatrième dimension* (1912; revised and expanded 1923; tr. as *Journey to the Land of the Fourth Dimension*) by Gaston de Pawlowski (1874-1933).

Many of the chapters of *Voyage au pays de la quatrième dimension* had previously appeared, from 1908 onwards, as short stories or brief exercises in speculative non-fiction—or hybrids of the two—in the periodical *Comoedia* [Comedy], of which Pawlowski was the founder and editor-in-chief. Some might be earlier in origin; in the long explanatory preface he added to the 1923 edition, Pawlowski states that he wrote his first futuristic short story in 1895 and was continually preoccupied with the book's subject-matter thereafter. Although his earlier collection of fanciful vignettes, *Polochon: paysages animés, paysages chimériques* [Polochon, here used as the name of a person, is a slang term for a bolster; the rest of the title translates as "animated and chimerical landscapes"] (1909) contains some speculative material—including one story reproduced as a chapter of the *Voyage*—it is highly unlikely to have used up Pawlowski's entire supply of such available material.

The future history sketched in the patchwork carries forward and elaborates a set of arguments first put forward in *Le philosophe du travail* [The Philosophy of Work], the thesis that Pawlowski had written in order to obtain the degree of *docteur en droit* in 1901, which was published in the same year. *Le philosophe du travail* not only introduces the arguments about specialization, mechanization and the likely effects of the future advancement of science on human life that serve to generate the images of future society glimpsed in the *Voyage*, but also the broader philosophical arguments regarding the limitations of materialism and the superiority of Platonic Idealism, particular notions of the Atom and the Monad, and—most significantly of all—the fundamental thesis that the essential purpose of "forced labor" is to liberate time for freely-chosen activities, including physical cultivation though sport as well as mental cultivation by means of the arts.

Pawlowski had first begun writing articles for periodicals in 1894, before he graduated from the École des Sciences Politiques, initially in connection with his chief hobby, cycling. He took a keen interest in the development of racing bicycles, and also in the parallel evolution of the automobile. The first of the three periodicals he founded, long before *Comoedia*, was *Le Vélo* [The Bicycle], the official organ of the Union Vélocipédique de France; the second was the short-lived *L'Opinion*, which played host to his political writings. By the time he graduated, however, Pawlowski had decided that his true vocation was humor, and the first professional magazine whose staff he joined was *Le Rire* [Laughter], an established periodical that he was eventually to imitate when he founded *Comoedia* in 1907.

Pawlowski's first "novel" was a serial published in *Le Vélo* in 1894 while he was still a teenager, "Le record de Samuel Humbug" [Samuel Humbug's Record], but it was not reprinted in book form. He did, however, achieve book publication with *On se moque de nous* [They're Laughing at Us] (1898), issued under the by-line W. de Pawlowski rather than G. de Pawlowski, which he used on all his subsequent work. By that time he had already begun writing brief accounts—usually only a few lines long—of imaginary inventions, which were to become a key element of his stock-in-trade. They were published in numerous different periodicals before a collection appeared in volume form as *Inventions nouvelles et dernières nouveautés* [New Inventions and Recent Novelties] (1916).

In 1906 Pawlowski issued an unbound set of short texts as *Les billets de paysages animés* [Notes on, or Tickets to, Animated Lands], subsequently reprinted in the more substantial *Polochon*, which also contained "La faillite de la science" (tr. as "The Bankruptcy of Science"), in which Thomas Edison invents a translating machine; and "La véridique ascension dans l'Histoire de James Stout Brighton" (tr. as "James Stout Brighton's Authentic Ascent Through History"), whose protagonist goes back in time by means of traveling at enormous speed from east to west, eventually witnessing the origins of humankind.

All of that work helped prepare the way for the pieces that formed the bulk of the first version of the *Voyage*, in which the inventive spirit of those finger-exercises was carefully recombined with, and put at the service of, the earnest concerns of *Le philosophe du travail*. Pawlowski clearly intended the *Voyage* to be his masterpiece, and presumably considered it as such throughout his life, just as other critics have done.

The new material added to the body of the text in the 1923 edition consisted of additional pieces that had appeared in *Comoedia* between 1912 and 1914—Pawlowski was conscripted thereafter for the duration of the Great War to serve as an engineer in the "auto-service" and had to give up the editorship of the magazine—and between 1919 and 1923, following his release from military service. These new chapters were inserted at various points in the text, according to their approximate internal chronology—many of them, inevitably, in the relatively dour section dealing with the present day and the supposed development of the collective consciousness he calls "the Leviathan."

Pawlowski's wartime experiences inevitably affected his view of contemporary developments, and the chapters written between 1919 and 1923 are noticeably darker in tone than those written before 1914, so that they could easily be added to the next chapter's consideration of the aftermath of the Great War, although it would be too awkward to split the present discussion in two. Significantly, as with several other writers who remained active during the fatal years, the work Pawlowski published while the war was actually being fought, while not entirely devoid of humor, was carefully stripped of all futuristic and fabulatory ambition, remaining grimly naturalistic.

As its title indicates, the *Voyage* extrapolates a train of thought that had earlier crossed over from speculative non-fiction to exemplary fiction in the work of the English schoolmaster and amateur mathematician C. H. Hinton, whose essays on the fourth dimension and exemplary fables extrapolating the idea inspired Edwin Abbott to write *Flatland* (1884; initially issued with the by-line "A Square") and supplied H. G. Wells with the jargon supposedly underlying the theory of *The Time Machine* (1895). Pawlowski's notion of the fourth dimension is, however, not only markedly different from but significantly opposed to the notions developed by Hinton, Abbott and Wells. It had a different starting-point, and constituted a radically new fictional departure.

Hinton and Abbott both used fictional rhetorical devices to invite their readers to try to imagine that our three-dimensional world might only be an element of a larger four-dimensional one, but that is where they stopped; they produced elaborate descriptions of two-dimensional "flatlands" but made no attempt to describe that four-dimensional hyper-world, which they regarded—by definition—as essentially imperceptible, and thus imaginable only in abstract conceptual terms. Pawlowski, by contrast, only mentions hypothetical flatlands in a cursory fashion, because his primary purpose is to explore and attempt to come to terms, philosophically and psychologically, with a hypothetical four-dimensional reality.

Wells, having defined time as the fourth dimension, then set out to explore future history by moving his time machine along its axis, constructing a sketchy but complete future history from a series of brief snapshots. Pawlowski—who is highly likely to have read *The Time Machine*, which was translated into French in 1899—does construct a complete future history of his own, but he does not do so by representing time as a fourth dimension; indeed, he regards time as an aspect of the deceptive mode of perception characterized by three-dimensional space. His fourth dimension is an extra spatial dimension, but it is also, and essentially, the dimension of the mind, of the imagination, of art and—fundamentally, in his definition—of *quality*.

Charles Hinton's popularizations of the idea of the fourth dimension made much of the idea that it might be a useful explanatory source in "psychic research," helping to explain manifestations conventionally attributed to ghosts, and some of the other phenomena of spiritism. He was not alone in that; the book that made the largest contribution to popularizing that line of thought was the third volume of Johann Zöllner's *Wissenschaftliche Abhandlungen*, known individually as *Transcendentale Physik* (1878; tr. as *Transcendental Physics*). Dedicated to William Crookes, the English physicist who had become an important champion of Spritualism and its associated phenomena, Zöllner's book attempted to use the concept of a fourth spatial dimension to explain the various seemingly-supernatural feats carried out by mediums.

The two primary examples cited by Zöllner—tying knots in pieces of string whose ends are held tight or sealed, and importing objects into sealed boxes—are the two primary examples cited by Pawlowski, and Pawlowski refers at one point to the "German origins" of his notion of the fourth dimension. Zöllner's ideas were given extra publicity when a chapter was translated into English for Crookes' *Quarterly Journal of Science* in April 1878, entitled "On Space of Four Dimensions," and that article attracted a good deal of attention in France, where Crookes' own experiments and popularizing endeavors were considered very newsworthy.

The relationship between the *Voyage* and fashionable contemporary occultism is further emphasized by Pawlowski's acquaintance with the occult historian and novelist Jules Bois, who dedicated his study of *L'Éternel retour* [The Eternal Return] (1914) to Pawlowski. Pawlowski also knew the would-be Rosicrucian magus and novelist Joséphin Péladan, who contributed at least one article to *Comoedia*. Although the various chapters of the *Voyage* dealing with the clichés of spiritism are written tongue-in-cheek, they fully accept the reality of the phenomena, and are perfectly serious in attempting to produce a catch-all explanation of them.

Jules Bois was a regular attendee at Camille Flammarion's salon, whose other regulars in the early years of the twentieth century included Gustave Le Bon, a pioneering social psychologist who compiled a comprehensive history of civilization and produced a landmark work on the *Psychologie des foules* [Psychology of Crowds] (1905), and who was so struck by the near-simultaneous discoveries of X-rays and radioactivity that he undertook extensive laboratory experiments in physics in order to produce a definitive book on *L'évolution de la matière* (1905; tr. as *The Evolution of Matter*). It is from the latter volume that Pawlowski borrowed his observations on "the dissociation of matter" and the related examples and statistics he cites—taking care to include a rare acknowledgement—while his depiction of the oppressive future society he calls "the Leviathan" draws heavily on the other thread of Le Bon's work.

By drawing a fundamental distinction and opposition between the dimensions of quantity (time and space) and a hypothetical dimension of quality, Pawlowski rejected the essentially quantitative extra dimensions suggested by Hinton, Abbott and Wells. His own extra dimension allowed him imaginatively to move out of both time and space, so that he could look back on both from a new imaginative angle. That not only allowed his narrative voice to compile a future history by looking at time from outside, but also—more significantly, in that voice's stridently-expressed opinion—to see what inert matter, living matter and human existence really amount to, and what potentials they contain. Nobody had attempted that before—and few people have attempted anything similar since.

Thus, in his image of the Age of the Golden Eagle, the ultimate human society that eventually succeeds the dystopian Leviathan and the reign of the Absolute Scientists, following the Great Idealist Renaissance and the achievement of the Unique Universal Consciousness, Pawlowski attempted to reach an idea of the terminus of human evolution very different from the image of magnified brains promoted by Pierre Boitard, Louis Boussenard and Gustave Le Rouge, envisaging a kind of transcendence of the limitations of fleshy immortality considerably more sophisticated than the relatively crude termini sketched by Restif de La Bretonne in *Les Posthumes*.

Even if critical assessment is more narrowly focused on the phases of the future history developed in the course of the protagonist's less ambitious fourth-dimensional excursions, that too seems to be formed more in opposition than to than by continuation of previous examples. It does seem probable that some of the vignettes making up Pawlowski's future history owe some inspiration to the example of *The Time Machine*, but the sum of that future history is very different from Wells' vision of the future in the pattern of its development.

Like *The Time Machine*, *Voyage au pays de la quatrième dimension* extends its comprehensive future history of the human species to a climactic and conclusive fate, but that fate is very different from the possibilities imagined by Wells, although it bears closer comparison with those imagined by some of Wells' successors in the field of British scientific romance, especially Olaf Stapledon. Its individual components are, however, much lighter in tone. Its fictional components are brief satires, while its non-fictional embellishments range from delicate exercises in mock-autobiography to fervent sermons.

There is a sense in which Pawlowski's disorderly journey into alien worlds is also, in its eventual occlusion, an archetypal work of "eupsychian" fiction, of the kind that, according to Frank Manuel, largely displaced earlier "eutopian" and "euchronian" ways of thinking in the twentieth century, by locating the ideal state of being in a hypothetical state of mind rather than a different place or a future social organization. In that respect, it is one of the most insistent of all works of utopian fiction, employing its flamboyant humor as a lure drawing the reader to an exceedingly earnest conclusion, which envisions a kind of collective consciousness much finer and more life-enhancing than the lumpen Leviathan.

Given that J.-H. Rosny was well aware that he had been designated by Maurice Renard as the most important French exponent of the *merveilleux scientifique*—when Renard started his own literary salon in Paris his dearest wish was to recruit Rosny to its attendance so that he could discuss the matter with him—it is not surprising that he should make the effort to make further contributions to the genre as described by Renard, nor that one of his contributions should describe an encounter with the alien that responds in several ways to Renard's *Le Péril bleu*.

Like Renard's novel, Rosny's *La Force Mystérieuse* (1913 in *Je Sais Tout*; book 1914; tr. as "The Mysterious Force") begins as a mystery story whose anomalous phenomena are explained in terms of a an invasion of the alien. In this instance, however, the phenomena—which begin innocently enough, with disturbances of the color spectrum, but soon become much more extravagant—result from the Earth's temporary contact with an anomalous region of space, the physical and psychotropic effects of which go much further than the local disturbances featured in *Le Péril bleu*, rapidly becoming cataclysmic, but not apocalyptic.

The anomaly is initially manifest as a seemingly-trivial distortion of vision caused by alterations in ambient light, but it is rapidly magnified, precipitating a kind of universal fever and panic. The first part of the narrative describes the efforts of the physicist Gérard Langre and his disciple Georges Meyral, together with various dependents, to contend with the direct and indirect threats posed by the unfolding disaster, while desperately attempting to figure out what is going on.

The second part tracks the long and complicated aftermath of the initial disruption once the anomaly has passed, describing the strange legacies it has left behind: primarily a kind of infection, visible on the skin as blotches, althhough its effects go much deeper. Langre is gradually led to the conclusion that humankind has been "captured" by a form of life very different from familiar organisms—a constant theme in Rosny's depiction of the alien—which binds groups of people together with mostly, but not entirely, unconscious telepathic chains. A substantial fraction of the population is transformed into rabid "carnivores," while the remainder struggle to survive their assault, with the aid of a fungal palliative that keeps the worst symptoms at bay.

The exoticism of the anomalous space through with the Earth has passed is explained in terms of the overlapping of parallel universes: a notion that Rosny took very seriously, subsequently developing it extensively in his own speculative non-fiction regarding the fourth dimension, which differs as markedly from Pawlowski's notion of it as it does from preceding notions developed in fictional form. Rosny thus supplemented Pawlowski's innovations by adding an entirely new set of other worlds to the venues of traditional interplanetary fantasy.

Maurice Renard, as might be expected, also dabbled in stories employing notions borrowed from physics to twist space and perception in interesting ways, in two stories featuring the eccentric scientist Bouvancourt. In "La Singulière destinée de Bouvancourt" (1909; tr. as "The Singular Fate of Bouvancourt") he saturates himself with a fluid radiation than enables him to pass through a mirror into the "temporary space" beyond it, observed by the narrator, to whom he reports the sensations he experiences in that strangely limited world. Unfortunately, when he attempts to return to "permanent space," the transition proves difficult, and the narrator's attempts to pull him back are ineffectual until he smashes the mirror. As a true scientist, of course, Bouvancourt cannot let the matter rest there, and is eager to try his experiment with reflective substances less recalcitrant than silvered glass.

In "L'Homme au corps subtil" (1913; tr. as "The Man with the Rarefied Body")—which the narrator claims to be relating long after the events, which take place prior to those related in the earlier story—Bouvancourt finds a way to render solids permeable, enabling them to pass through other solids: a discovery that attracts the attention of the leader of a gang of thieves, who considers that it might be a useful tool of his trade. Bouvancourt gets rid of the inconvenient blackmailer by transforming his body so completely that he leaves him no anchorage, and the gangster is assumed to fall to the center of the Earth, but the conclusion of the story comprises Bouvancourt's speculations about possible life forms consisting of subtle matter, which inhabit the Earth unperceived, living a strange kind of parallel existence.

The latter idea seemed too good to abandon to a single short story, and it appears that Renard soon started to develop a novel extrapolating the thesis, but the project was interrupted by the war; as an officer in the cavalry reserve, he was immediately called up, and remained on active duty throughout, unable to find the time to apply himself to his uncommonly meticulous manner of composition.

Following its brief flirtation with Indian mystics and helpful alien abductors, more traditional otherworldly fantasy continued its own extrapolation. If psychic power were to be ruled out as a plausible means of propulsion, as it seemed to have been, there was no immediate alternative but to go back to the Vernian drawing-board in search of facilitating devices or modernized tales of travel to other worlds. In fact, speculators interested in the actual possibility of space travel were already beginning to do that, following the example set in Russia by Konstantin Tsiolkovsky, whose proposal that rockets could be adapted for space travel if only a sufficiently powerful propellant could be found seemed the most plausible recourse for hypothetical travelers.

That quest was reproduced in Germany, the U.S.A., Britain and France, all of which nations eventually gave rise to societies dedicated to propagandizing the viability of space travel and urging investment in the necessary search. The organizations in question only picked up real impetus after the Great War, but seeds had been sowed before then, and one early literary product of those seeds, which proposed a more ingenious—but unfortunately less practical—alternative to rocket propulsion was published in French, even though it followed Vernian precedent in featuring heroes of another nationality.

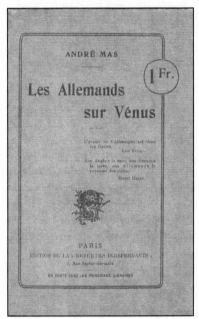

Les Allemands sur Vénus (1913; tr. as "The Germans on Venus") signed "André Mas" proposes providing a spaceship with initial thrust by attaching it to the rim of a giant wheel gradually accelerated in its spin until its sudden release, in the fashion of a slingshot. The method joined Verne's cannon as a suggestion requiring refutation in some subsequent works aiming at ultra-realism in their depiction of hypothetical space-shots powered by rockets.

The story emphasizes its serious intent with a supplementary bibliography in two sections, one listing literary precedents, with annotations identifying the mode of interplanetary transport envisaged in each case, beginning with Cicero—its French section ranges through Cyrano, Verne, Blanqui, Graffigny and Le Faure, Le Rouge and La Hire—and the other scientific works bearing on the problem. The latter is remarkably full; it includes recent articles by one A. Le Mée, whose name might seem suggestively similar to the author's pseudonym, although perhaps no more so than "Ludwig Mayer," cited in the story as an unknown but great poet. (The signature André Mas also appeared on a visionary interplanetary fantasy in verse, in 1921.)

Les Allemands sur Vénus is thoroughly Vernian in its early stages, but once the excursionists reach Venus, the elaborate depiction of life on the planet's surface takes on a richness akin to, but rather more thoughtful than, the accounts of life of Mars rendered by Arnould Galopin and Gustave Le Rouge. Then the story takes a further narrative step, by outlining a program for the rapid colonization of the planets in the interests of providing humankind, and the Germans in particular, with valuable *lebensraum*. An international conference is convened by Camille Flammarion in order to divide up the real estate of the solar system between the great powers—allegedly peacefully, although it is not obvious that any of the nations except Germany would really have been satisfied with their portion.

Looking back from today and comparing *Les Allemands sur Vénus* with *Le Péril bleu* and *La Force mystérieuse*, one might regret, on both esthetic and intellectual grounds, that it was not the more sophisticated works that pointed the way to the future development of the bulk of speculative fiction, but one that, while not being as crude as the unashamedly popular fiction of Jean de La Hire and Gustave Le Rouge, was nevertheless limited in its vision, its intelligence and its literary elegance. With the aid of hindsight, however, we can see clearly that it was André Mas, not Rosny or Renard, who anticipated the dominant trend of popular fashion. Whereas the undeniably brilliant works of Renard, Pawlowski and Rosny that immediately preceded it all remained isolated as masterful but eccentric oddities, *Les Allemands sur Vénus* was eventually supplemented by an entire subgenre of works sharing its attitude to the relationship between human beings and the other worlds of the solar system and the universe, albeit it not initially in France—or even in Germany, which had to wait for a different lead to be given.

The future of interplanetary fantasy was, in fact, neatly summarized by the fact that André Mas' story ends with the ringing words of a new hymn composed by the allegedly great poet Ludwig Mayer, expressing an imaginative stance that remained highly unusual in *roman scientifique*, although it did not take long to become much more familiar in American science fiction, and hence in the science fiction imitative of American models that invaded Europe after World War II:

We are the race of the sons of the god of the Hammer,
And we have the will to conquer the Empire of Stars
And to become the people of the Lords of Infinity.

4. Future Wars

Many of the works implicated in the development of nineteenth-century *roman scientifique* assumed that war would eventually become a thing of the past, because it would become impossible in practice when weapons were introduced of such awesome destructive power that no one could contemplate opposing them, and they would thus become a completely effective deterrent.

One of the earliest writers to employ the myth of "the weapon too dreadful to use" had been Joseph Méry, in "Les Ruines de Paris":

"Denis Zabulon and Jérémie Artémias are the guiding lights of modern science. The first has for an ancestor the immortal physicist to whom the human race owes unalterable peace. Everyone knows that in the year 3509 or thereabouts the great philanthropist in question invented the admirable machine that destroyed two fleets of five thousand steamships and a hundred and thirty-three thousand combatants in less time than it takes a clock to chime midday. The sublime inventor had discovered that the maritime atmosphere is inflammable over an extent of a hundred square leagues, and catches fire spontaneously by means of a brand of pulverized asbestos. Before that discovery, ships armed with simple Paixhans cannons of an improved model could only vomit forth a thousand incendiary bombs per minute, with the result that a third of an enemy fleet was still afloat after a battle. Zabulon's ancestor, by popularizing his philanthropic secret of destruction, obliged two fleets to burn naturally, down to the last launch and the last sailor. Thus for three centuries, no one in the world has gone to war; the excess of evil has engendered good."

It is typical of such intrusions that they offer the latest developments in modern weaponry as a standard for comparison and a model for development—in this case the Paixhans gun, the first naval cannon designed to fire explosive shells, which had entered service in the French navy in 1841.

It was inevitable that the notion could not simply be left to background remarks of that sort, merely noting and excusing an absence, but stories featuring the future development of new weapons of war were thin in the ground before 1870. "La Guerre en 1894" (1867 in book form; tr. as "War in 1894") by Adrien Robert, which features the founding of a "Chemical Artillery" to deliver projectiles containing poison gas, was exceptional. The world war briefly outlined in Fernand Giraudeau's *La Cité nouvelle* (1868), although impressive in terms of the quoted casualty figures, refrains from specifying the means of their production. Eventually, however, the idea was bound to move into the foreground with the aid of a provocative event to stimulate the military imagination. That event arrived when the Prussian invasion of 1870 woke the entire French nation up to the awful vulnerability of unprepared nations to the power of modern armaments.

That was not just a shock to the French, of course; historians of speculative fiction are very familiar, thanks to I. F. Clarke's study of *Voices Prophesying War* (1966; revised ed. 1992), with the effect it had on the English imagination, whose initial flutter of panic was neatly encapsulated by an anonymous novelette in *Blackwood's Magazine*, "The Battle of Dorking" (1871; actually the work of George Chesney) and the torrent of imitations and replies provoked thereby, which eventually mutated into a central subgenre of British scientific romance.

Chesney's novelette was rapidly reprinted as a pamphlet and translated into several other languages, including French, where *Bataille de Dorking: invasion des Prussiens en Angleterre* (1871), with a preface by Charles Ynarte, went through several editions. It was swiftly followed up in France by Édouard Dangin's account of *Le Bataille de Berlin en 1875* (1871), which references the battle of Dorking alongside the battle of Sedan as if it were a real occurrence, in fantasizing about the means by which the French might turn the tables on their enemy and exact revenge for their humiliation. Eugène Tassin's *La Revanche fantastique* [The Fantastic Revenge] (1873), in which the Prussians return in 1882, follows a similar train of thought.

La Dernière bataille, épopée prophétique de l'an 1909 [The Last Battle: A Prophetic Epic of the Year 1909] (1873) by the pacifist humorist Edmond Thiaudière, which pretends to be a translation from the German of *Die Ietze Schlacht* by "Friedrich Stampf" and is listed by some bibliographers under that fictitious name, adopts a more radical satirical strategy as well as a more ambitious reach. In 1909 Europe is under the joint rule of Tsar Nicolas of Russia and the German Emperor Wilhelm III, but when the daughter of the French king Louis-Philippe III refuses an offer of marriage from the Tsarevitch, war ensues, in which millions are killed before a general revolution brings about a socialist euchronia.

Most exercises in a similar vein to "The Battle of Dorking," in France as in England, followed Chesney's example in focusing on the deployment of contemporary weaponry and strategy, featuring battles that might take place tomorrow or the day after. Although there was intense interest in the possibilities inherent in the new weapons that were being continually developed in the wake of the Franco-Prussian war, attempts to imagine their future development in anything more than the most elementary terms were initially sketchy, and the fusion of that kind of war-anticipation fiction with the established myth of the weapon that would end war was by no means immediate.

Perhaps understandably, the first large-scale development of the imagery of future weaponry in French fiction was carefully cloaked with a satirical humor akin to Thiaudière's. French literary dealings with future warfare continued to deviate sharply from English patterns mapped by I. F. Clarke by courtesy of the endeavors of Albert Robida, who followed up the humorous descriptions of technological warfare contained in his Vernian parody *Voyages très extraordinaires de Saturnin Farandoul* with the more sharply satirical *La Guerre au Vingtième siècle* (tr. as "War in the Twentieth Century"), which appeared in the 27 October 1883 issue of the magazine he owned and edited, *Le Caricature*.

In the former story, the war between the North and South of the Disunited States of Nicaragua, features heavily armored "locomotives of war" (i.e., giant tanks), which mount fearsome charges, while gigantic cannons launch unprecedentedly powerful shells, "submarine cavalry" mount a daring raid to capture the transatlantic cable, and chloroform bombs are also brought into play before the climactic battle takes place between two fleets of war-balloons.

Many of these images crop up again in the 1883 version of "La Guerre au vingtième siècle," which is mostly set in Africa, partly as a joke about the potential future of colonies that become independent go-ahead "young nations," and partly in order to distance its slaughter from Europe. The story is set in 1975, about twenty years after the main action that Robida had developed in his massive satiric account of *Le Vingtième siècle* (1883), which was in press when the story in *Le Caricature* was published and was heavily advertised in the subsequent issues of the periodical, so it could not have disrupted the imaginary history of the novel, but it nevertheless leaves the society described therein untouched. The casualty figures cited in the story are horrific, but by no means world-destructive, and only affect the "young" nations—the bark rather than the heartwood of the envisaged world civilization.

Unfortunately, the account of the Australo-Mozambiquan war of 1975 is incomplete, because of the strict space limitations of *Le Caricature*, in which only four pages could be devoted primarily to text, and even they carried two or three illustrations each, in addition to those included in a special pictorial pullout section. The later phases of the story are drastically abridged, either cut down from a longer text in order to fit, or, more likely, written while the typesetting was in progress, under enormous pressure from the rapidly-shrinking available space. It would undoubtedly have been a much better story had Robida given himself more scope to develop it, and might well have featured even more speculative materiel. Four years later, however, when a second version of *La Guerre au vingtième siècle* appeared, in a book version that was much generous in terms of available space, he filled the extra space with more elaborate illustrations.

The second version is set mostly in Europe, and is specifically dated 1945, a few years earlier than the main action of *La Vingtième siècle*, but it is equally careful not to disrupt the history of continuous progress set out in the definitive novel. All the images of mechanical and chemical warfare featured in the earlier version are deployed again, but there is also the key addition of an "Offensive Medical Corps" dedicated to biological warfare, as well as the less fortunate addition of military mediums deploying Mesmeric "fluid" in an aggressive fashion. Like all the other devices, however, the Offensive Medical Corps is used in a farcical spirit, in spite of the devastatingly murderous effects credited to it. The 1887 story also alters the narrative strategy of the 1883 version, reducing the narrative distance between narrator and reader by linking its narrative viewpoint more closely to the consciousness of the hero. The enemy nation with which France goes to war in the 1887 version of *La Guerre au vingtième siècle* is carefully unnamed, although the description of crossing the border between the two leaves no possible doubt that it is Germany

In between the two versions of Robida's visions of twentieth-century warfare, two further significant depictions of advanced technological warfare appeared: ***Les Malheurs de John Bull*** (1884; tr. as *The Misfortunes of John Bull*) by Camille Debans, and *La Guerre finale, histoire fantastique* (1885; tr. as *The Final War*), signed "Barillet-Lagargousse," both of which anticipate warfare on a global scale, recognizing that the dissemination of European colonies all over the world would mean that no major war involving European powers could any longer be a local affair.

Debans' story is distinctive in placing its principal focus on naval warfare, featuring battles between ironclad warships, assisted by various hypothetical inventions that now seem primitive but were innovative at the time. The work is also distinctive in being unashamedly motivated by spite, not directed against the Germans, against whom the French had been bearing a sore grudge since 1870, but against the English, carrying forward a much older antagonism.

The war described in *Les Malheurs de John Bull* is not, strictly speaking, an international conflict, but rather an elaborate personal vendetta, conducted by a single Frenchman, Maxime Darnozan, who invents a nation for himself as a means to avenge an insult offered to him by an English nobleman. He then turns that improvised nation into a global empire, by not merely defeating the English but taking over and improving upon their imperial ambitions. Although the author's tongue remains firmly in his cheek throughout, that does not prevent him from maintaining an earnest tone in his description of the tactics of the gradual but inexorable conquest wrought by the story's remarkable hero.

Maxime is able to finance his war because he once saved the life of the last Inca, the custodian of all the Incas' hidden gold, who identifies him as the man designated by prophecy to restore the Incas' traditional lands to their rightful owners. After hiring fifty selected soldiers of fortune, Darnozan annexes an uninhabited island named Pola, proclaims himself to be its king, and then approaches the English government via diplomatic channels to seek recognition of his sovereignty. When that recognition is understandably refused, he makes a formal declaration of war. The English initially regard the declaration as a joke, but only until Darnozan blows up Woolwich arsenal by bombing it from the air and his men launch simultaneous attacks on dozens of British warships anchored in various ports, hijacking a sufficient number to form a small navy. England immediately sends warships to hunt down and attack Darnozan's captured fleet, but his superior tactics result in their defeat, and the further augmentation of his navy.

While the English then begin the painstaking work of assembling and equipping a much larger and supposedly undefeatable fleet, Darnozan takes control of various crucial sea routes including the Atlantic access to the Mediterranean, and begins extorting tolls from merchant shipping. He also attacks and seizes control of various island nations, establishing a new base in Madagascar and proclaiming himself "King of the Islands," with the intention of taking control of all the islands in the world, and all the seas. He makes significant progress before the new English fleet is ready, but then has to confront that enemy in a long battle for control of the straits of Gibraltar, fought with the aid of floating tanks, new kinds of torpedoes, and new defenses against them, as well as various other unprecedented naval weapons.

When the English fleet is eventually beaten, English diplomats immediately attempt to build a coalition of European powers to mount a collective defense of their colonies, but it is too late; they can only cause Darnozan local and limited difficulties, and his plan to control the seas unwinds inexorably. After further naval battles, and the capture of the fortress of Gibraltar, he lands troops in the British Isles themselves, initially in Ireland, in order to annihilate English power forever and become Maxime-Jean I, an Emperor even greater than Napoléon.

The full by-line attached to *La Guerre finale* is "Barillet-Lagargousse, Ingénieur destructeur, Membre de plusieurs societés philanthropiques et savantes" [Barillet-Lagargousse, Demolition Engineer, Member of Several Philanthropic and Scientific Societies]; *Barillet* can mean gun-barrel, and a *gargousse* is a kind of cartridge. No information is available as to who the person behind the pseudonym might have been, although the content of the text supports the by-line's contention that he was a military engineer by profession with radical political interests, specifically in the co-operative movement. The book was the second item of *roman scientifique* issued by the specialist military and scientific publisher Berger-Levrault et Cie, after Didier de Chousy's *Ignis*.

It is worth noting in passing that very few immersive fantasies set in the future had been produced before 1885, and all of them had come with cumbersome prefaces explaining the nature of the exercise in advance to readers, who were assumed to be quite unready to confront the idea of a story of the future told as if written from a viewpoint in the further future, rather than being represented as a prophetic dream. Barillet-Lagargousse's novel does have a preface, but it is both cursory and deliberately enigmatic, and does not explain or apologize for the novel's narrative strategy. That was to become the typical style of future war stories, which were soon able to abandon expository prologues altogether, and eventually became the default strategy for all future-set narratives.

The most interesting feature of *La Guerre finale* from the modern viewpoint, however, is not its narrative strategy, pioneering as that was, but the specific nature of its advanced weaponry, which represents very starkly the horizons of the technological imagination in 1885. The hero of the novel is an "eminent engineer" named Lichtmann, who goes to work for the Krupp armaments factory and shows such distinction there that Fritz Krupp makes him his heir. In the 1890s he develops a new kind of cannon, which has a much longer range than contemporary models and fires shells that, because of the peculiar nature of their disintegration, produce a devastating horizontal blizzard of shrapnel.

Realizing that the new cannon will make all existing weaponry obsolete, the European powers rush to place huge orders, making Lichtmann enormously rich, but they also decide that if they are to fulfill their contemporary military ambitions they must do so immediately, before effective defenses and means of retaliation can be organized—with the result that a world war breaks out in 1896, before the new weapons have even been manufactured and delivered. Although fast and furious, the conflict rapidly reaches a general stalemate, with none of the contending powers able to sustain it any longer, and a hasty armistice is signed, which leaves all the contentious issues unsettled.

In the meantime, Lichtmann uses his unprecedented economic resources to purchase the independence of the area containing his factories from the German Empire, and establishes the tiny nation of Canonenstadt as a worker's co-operative—perhaps the only instance in speculative fiction of a eutopia imagined as a gargantuan armaments factory, although Barillet-Lagargousse did have the example of Verne and Grousset's dystopian Stahlstadt to draw upon.

The principal action of the novel begins when the financially embarrassed German Empire decides that the only way to restore its economic and military fortunes is to reclaim Canonenstadt and usurp its wealth. Much to the astonishment of the diplomat sent to negotiate the surrender, however, his ultimatum is rejected, even though Canonenstadt is completely surrounded by its enemy and its population is outnumbered by thousands to one. The German army sent to back up the initial ultimatum is annihilated by Lichtmann's cannons, but the Germans assume that all they need to do is to set up a blockade and starve the inhabitants of the enclave into submission. They have, however, reckoned without the next generation of Lichtmann's technologies, and his new superweapon: the machine gun.

The machine gun might seem an unlikely superweapon now, but when Barillet-Lagargousse wrote his story the only such weapons in use were Gatling Guns and Nordenfelt Guns, the latter patented in 1873. The author was not aware that the Nordenfelt would soon be overtaken by the much more efficient Maxim Gun, whose prototype was first demonstrated in October 1884, and which became the ancestor of the machine-guns employed with locally devastating but limited effect in the Great War of 1914-18. From the author's temporal standpoint, his alternative history, in which machine guns fall into disuse before Lichtmann invents his super-powered version, was not implausible.

Using a ballistic system similar to his cannons, Lichtmann's machine guns are enormously destructive, but they are also light and maneuverable, with the aid of new carriers he invents, equipped with six mechanical legs rather than wheels, which are very rapid and capable of handling any terrain. With half a dozen insectile gun-bearing machines and an army of ninety men, Canonenstadt wipes out hundreds of thousands of German troops in a single day.

At the same time, Lichtmann unleashes another weapon that he has developed. In order to supply his factories with raw materials, he has developed earthboring "mole-machines" that can cover vast distances and extract ores from considerable depths; with the aid of mines planted by those machines, he causes an earthquake that destroys the entire fortified city of Coblentz. Germany, threatened with the possible destruction of all its cities, soon capitulates.

The other European nations, realizing that Germany is now incapable of defending the possessions left in suspense by the 1896 armistice, immediately reiterate their territorial demands. Lichtmann decides that he has to take further action in order to create the conditions necessary for permanent peace, which he does by dispatching bombs, via a new delivery system, to devastate Paris and St. Petersburg, killing hundreds of thousands of people at a stroke: a *coup-de-théâtre* all the more remarkable because it is accomplished with what would nowadays be considered "conventional weaponry" rather than the invention of any radically new force of destruction.

Such new forces of destruction were, however, just about to appear over the imaginative horizon. The rapid development of future war fiction in the last few decades of the nineteenth century provides a striking illustration of the adaptation of the imagination to new prospects of future destruction. By the end of the century, the more imaginative future wars were being fought with submarines and aircraft, and the bombardments carried out by the latter, making no distinction between military and civilian targets, employing incendiary bombs and chemical weapons as well as new high explosives of unprecedented force. The most advanced visions also took inspiration from the discovery of X-rays and radium in the late 1890s to envisage weapons involving exotic radiations and atomic disintegration.

None of that had been on the imaginative horizon in 1885, except for submarines, whose problematic actual history, extending back to the seventeenth century, hardly lent confidence to the notion that they would become vital instruments of war any time soon; Albert Robida's employment of them must have seemed to many of his readers to be a joke. "Hertzian waves" had not yet been discovered, so the possibility of wireless telegraphy seemed equally fanciful to the hard-headed. By 1891, however, when **Jules Lermina** wrote *La Bataille de Strasbourg* (tr. as The *Battle of Strasbourg*) only six years after *La Guerre finale*, the situation was considerably further advanced, and so was the political context in which future wars were imaginable.

La Bataille de Strasbourg was initially published as a 43-part feuilleton serial in *La Terre Illustrée* between April 1891 and February 1892, where it carried the subtitle *"Histoire de l'invasion chinoise en Europe au XXe siècle"* [The History of the Chinese Invasion of Europe in the Twentieth Century]. It was subsequently reprinted in two volumes in 1895 and was reprinted again as a feuilleton in *Le Matin* between 29 July and 26 September 1900. Like *La Guerre finale*, it was ground-breaking in its employment of immersive fantasy and it is perhaps the earliest futuristic novel to do so straightforwardly, with no other preliminary exposition than its initial subtitle.

Historians of futuristic fiction, with the aid of hindsight, now credit *La Bataille de Strasbourg* with launching a literary fad that is generally known as "yellow peril" fiction, and it is, indeed, the case that the idea of an invasion of Europe from the Far East did become a significant bugbear on the ragged fringe of future war fiction. A more interesting digression concerns the odd circumstances of the novel's first publication in *La Terre Illustrée*, of which Jules Lermina was then the editor. In spite of its global range and occasional geographical and ethnological interjections, the serial's launch looks suspiciously like a response to a similarly odd move made by Charles Simond, who launched

La Science Française's regular *roman scientifique* slot with "La Prise de Londres au XXe siècle" [The Capture of London in the Twentieth Century] by "Pierre Ferréol" (Georges Espitallier, 1849-1923), in March 1891, only a few weeks before Lermina began serializing *La Bataille de Strasbourg* (which is very obviously made up as the author went along).

If Simond felt that Lermina was responding competitively to his own move, and perhaps subtly expressing the opinion that future war fiction was as inappropriate an inclusion in a popular science magazine as it was in a magazine of worldwide adventure fiction, he was not deterred. By far the longest story serialized in *La Science Française*'s feuilleton slot was the fourth part of a series by Capitaine Danrit eventually published in book form in eight volumes as *La Guerre de demain* [Tomorrow's War], the first volume of which had appeared in 1889; the last was reprinted in book form in 1896. The particular war in question was between France and Germany, although it expanded over a much larger stage than the two native territories.

Whatever the relationship might have been between Lermina and Charles Simond, it can be taken for granted that Lermina disapproved strongly of Espitallier and Driant, both of whom were at the opposite end of the political spectrum from his own Anarchist sympathies. It is not entirely clear where Lermina and Simond's employer stood, but the first "Capitaine Danrit" novel had been advertised in 1887 as the work of the son-in-law of General Boulanger, whose meteoric political career briefly paused a threat to the stability of the Republic in 1888. Whether L. Boulanger was related to the general, and hence to Driant, it is difficult to tell, but it is not inconceivable that the detail has some relevance to fact that Simond and Lermina were both replaced in their editorial positions in 1892, and that the story gradually unfolding in *La Bataille de Strasbourg* was so drastically and abruptly curtailed that the plot never reached the planned climax in Strasbourg.

Unlike Barillet-Lagargousse, and in spite of the fact that he wrote numerous items of speculative fiction, Jules Lermina knew little or nothing about actual science and technology, but he did have a keen sense of the shifting horizons of their imaginative landscape. The central character of *La Bataille de Strasbourg* is Guy de Norès, a young inventor and writer of scientifically-inspired poetry, who appears at the beginning of the novel demonstrating a new telegraphic technology that will allow people in one location to watch on a screen what is happening at other locations in the world—essentially, a kind of live television. For the purposes of demonstration he has made arrangements with his fiancée, Marguerite Sametel, the daughter of another famous scientist presently on a mission to Peking, to send a transmission from that city during the celebration of the Chinese New Year.

Unfortunately, what the horrified crowd assembled in Paris for the occasion sees is a massacre marking the outbreak of an Oriental revolution, in which the united hordes of Asia intend to reject the yoke of European colonialism and exact their revenge by annihilating the nations of Europe with a massive invasion. Guy's immediate impulse is to rush to his fiancée's rescue by means of a new flying machine that he is in the process of developing, although the prototype has not yet undergone its crucial trials. Unfortunately, while showing the untested machine and another application of its fundamental technology to his friend, Dr. Sabirat, an accident hurls the apparatus into the air, carrying away Sabirat and Guy's sister, Marie, at enormous velocity. By the time they finally figure out how to land the machine they are, unknown to them, in the vicinity of one of the key rallying-points of the Asiatic army that is preparing to invade Europe.

The tangled plot follows the adventures of the three resultant groups of people, centered on Marguerite in Peking, Guy in Paris and Sabirat in Turkestan, but several of the story-threads carefully laid down for future development are eventually abandoned and others drastically abridged, so a work that might easily have rivaled Danrit's *La Guerre de demain* for length, had it been fully developed, eventually collapses into a few sketchy scenes, which wrap up the overall plot in a tearing hurry. What survives, however, is the notion of the advanced technology that eventually succeeds in putting an end to the seemingly-irresistible invasion of an army numbered in its millions.

Lermina was writing before the discovery of X-rays or radium but he had a vague idea of the potential of "radiation" by virtue of his knowledge of the Crookes tube, and he picked up an idea first broached in Listonai's *Voyageur philosophe*, which had drawn an analogy between the pervasive effects of solar radiation and those of scent, tacitly suggesting that a solution to the mystery of the radiant capacities of musk might have interesting technological consequences. Instead of something analogous to radium, therefore, Lermina imagines something analogous to musk, whose stored emissions can built up enormous energies capable not only of hurling flying machines through the air but creating artificial tornadoes; it is those machines, once he has finally recovered his aircraft, that allow Guy de Norès to delay the Asiatic invasion just long enough for him to develop an even more powerful superweapon—which might or might not have been a conscious copy of the one employed by Lichtmann to destroy

Coblentz—after using a seemingly-magical method of skywriting to lure the bulk of the superstitious Asiatic army to the slopes of Mont Blanc.

The curtailment of *La Bataille de Strasbourg* undoubtedly left it a spoiled work, but its spoliation did not prevent it from being reprinted in the large-circulation daily newspaper *Le Matin*, where it reached a much vaster audience than it had in *La Terre Illustrée* or the Boulanger book edition, and where it must have seemed a striking novelty, immersive futuristic fiction not having been tried out there previously. The decision to reprint it in *Le Matin* was undoubtedly prompted by the outbreak of the so-called Boxer Rebellion, which reached its violent climax while the story was being serialized, the Legation Quarter of Peking being attacked and besieged in June 1900. The actual siege lasted 55 days, considerably longer than the siege described in the story and slightly longer than the serialization of the novel, but the coincidence did give the reprint a bizarre topicality and lent its early chapters—but not the later ones—a vague implication of prophecy.

La Bataille de Strasbourg moved the goalposts of French future war fiction decisively, assisting in the inspiration of more modest world war stories, like the later ones penned by Capitaine Danrit, as well as more extravagant fantasies in which the weapons that were supposedly too dreadful to be used (or at least re-used) became far more flamboyant, if no more destructive, than Barillet-Lagargousse's earthquake machines and machine-guns. Some writers, of course, needed no such influence, and Albert Robida presumably considered that he was uniquely entitled to be considered the great pioneer of imaginative twentieth-century warfare.

Not all writers, of course, developed futuristic weaponry in their accounts. In spite of its remote date, *L'Orient vierge, roman épique de l'an 2000* (1897; tr. as "The Virgin Orient, an Epic Novel of the Year 2000") by Camille Mauclair, sticks stubbornly to nineteenth-century weaponry and tactics in its account of a preventive strike by Europe, united under a supposedly but unconvincingly Anarchist government, against the perceived Yellow Peril. Even though his accounts of the two crucial battles fought in India are extended and bloody, however, Mauclair's primary purpose was not to detail the war but rather to analyze the crisis of conscience suffered by the Anarchist "dictator" once it is won.

Capitaine Danrit followed up his first eight-volume series with the four-volume *L'Invasion noire* [The Black Invasion] (1895-96), the three-volume *La Guerre Fatale—France-Angleterre* [The Fatal War: France/England] (1901-02) and the three-volume *L'Invasion jaune* [The Yellow Invasion] (1905-1906), the last two of which picked up the central themes of *La Prise de Londres* and *La Bataille de Strasbourg*. His work became patchier thereafter, and eventually veered into conventional Vernian romance in the pages of the *Journal de Voyages*, but he recruited Arnould Galopin to assist him with an account of *La Révolution de demain* [Tomorrow's Revolution] (1909-10). Émile Driant was a professional military man, although his relationship with his controversial father-in-law had resulted in his resignation from the army in 1906, and when he was recalled to duty in 1914 the war interrupted his literary career more decisively than many others; he was killed during the German assault that precipitated the Battle of Verdun in February 1916, while his unit attempted to mount a heroic holding action.

Alongside Capitaine Danrit's seemingly-interminable flow of future war stories, other writers began to take advantage of the ready-made potential for melodramatic action, and of the new opportunities for violent conflict that emergent technologies seemed to offer. George Le Faure supplemented his account of *La Guerre sous l'eau* with the frankly-titled *Mort aux Anglais* [Death to the English] (1892) and Anglophobia also came to the fore in the caricaturish comedy *L'Agonie d'Albion* [Albion's Death-Throes] (1901) by Belgian Symbolist Eugène Demolder, which looked forward to England's defeat by the Boers. Colonel Royet made his debut, in collaboration with Paul d'Ivoi, with *La Patrie en danger* [The Fatherland in Danger] (1905).

The plot of Rodolphe Martin's *Berlin-Bagdad* (1907) is focused on a war fought primarily in the air, in which the German Empire defeats the Russian empire in 1916, and then forms a federation of with the Austro-Hungarian and Ottoman Empires to compose a world-dominating power. Another aerial war, thus time featuring the yellow peril, is featured in Henry Kistemaekers' buoyant comedy *Aeropolis* (1909). Roger Duguet and G. Thierry imaged a Catholic alliance taking up arms to fight the Protestant imperial ambitions of England and Germany in *Le Capitaine Rex* (1910). Rodolphe Bringer and Léon Valbert, however, returned to familiar Franco-Prussian hostilities in *Une Heroïne de quinze ans* [A Fifteen-year-old Heroine] (1910).

In *La Nouvelle Europe, antéhistoire de la dernière guerre* [The New Europe: A History Subsequent to the Last War] (1911), the second part of *La Dernière épopée* [The Last Epic]—the first part, *Le Monde noir* [The Black World] (1909) had dealt with the colonization of Africa—by Marcel Barrière, the next Franco-German war, won by the French after a lightning forty-day campaign by virtue of their superior artillery, submarines and aerial reconnaissance, is the prelude to universal peace and the fusion of races. Paulin Comtat's *Notre Frontière* [Our Frontier] (1913) imagines new armaments based on a technology of energy transmission. Raymond Clauzel's *L'Aube rouge* [Red Dawn] (1914) is unusual in skipping ahead to the next-but-one Franco-German war in 1950, the second having occurred in 1920 in its fictional history; the one described is complicated by a socialist revolution in Paris.

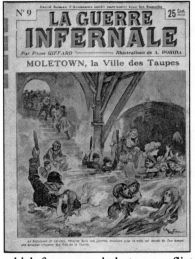

The longest of the fictitious accounts of future warfare produced before the actual Great War, and the most inventive of them, all the more remarkable for being aimed at younger readers and bearing garish illustrations by Albert Robida, was *La Guerre infernale* [The Infernal War] by the journalist Pierre Giffard (1853-1922), the editor of *Le Petit Journal*, in which capacity, as previously mentioned, he lent significant support to technological development by sponsoring races. *La Guerre infernale* was published as a part-work in thirty episodes between January and August 1908. It commences—as several satires dealing with the topic of war did—with a Peace Conference at the Hague, which forms a prelude to a conflict with the allied nations of England, France and Japan on the one side, and Germany and America on the other, in which European cities are soon destroyed by aerial bombardment.

That initial phase of the war causes such damage on both sides that it creates the opportunity for a massive invasion of the West by the armies of the Far East, spearheaded by China. An attempt to defeat the invaders by microbial warfare goes awry when the plague starts spreading in the allied ranks as well as those of the enemy. The novel's protagonist, a reporter for the periodical *L'An 2000*, is in the thick of the action throughout, as a passenger in a varied assortment of ships, submarines and flying machines, including the dramatic events of episode 17, "La Tuerie scientifique" [Scientific Slaughter], when the great American scientist Erickson, the "marshal of Electric Force," unleashes his formidable array of magnetic and temperature-controlling weaponry against the Japanese. The eventual body-count of the envisaged hostilities is understandably prodigious.

In Britain, the parallel glut of future war stories seems only to have enhanced the eagerness with which the British went to war in August 1914. The British Expeditionary Force sent to the Western Front in 1914 was largely composed of volunteers recruited by Field Marshal Kitchener with the aid of a famous advertising campaign, and it seems to have been the case that the future war fiction produced in Britain assisted that campaign rather than providing a deterrent with imagery of mass slaughter occasioned by technologically advanced weaponry.

France was not in the same situation, having a system of conscription in place and having to react to an invasion of her soil, so it is more difficult to judge any effect that the fiction produced there might have had to attitudes to the possibility of war, although the popularity of Capitaine Danrit's jingoistic future war stories suggests that they struck a plangent chord with their audience, probably with a stirring effect. In general though, French fiction dealing with the possibility of future war tended to make more of the destructive power of new technology, after the fashion of Giffard's extravaganza, and even though convention demanded that France and her allies should always emerge victorious from such conflicts, the cost of such victories was not underestimated in the most striking and exhaustive accounts.

The authors of such works might well have claimed, as authors of futuristic fiction routinely do, that they were not trying to predict the next war but rather to issue warnings that might help to prevent it—and on the whole, such claims are more plausible with respect to French future war fiction of the interim between the Franco-Prussian War and that Great War than it would have been of British fiction of the same period—but if that was the case, the deterrent was clearly ineffective. Whatever psychological effects that kind of fiction actually had, it was impotent to mount any significant opposition of the political forces that led inexorably to the outbreak war of in 1914, but it nevertheless remains the case that explicitly pacifist fiction was more evident in France than in Britain, and so was fiction whose alarmism reached a near-hysterical pitch.

Albert Robida had continued his own pattern of imaginative development in *La Vie électrique*, in which war is only represented as a hypothetical military exercise, but the amiable humor of the account could not entirely deflect attention away from the presumption that if a war were to be fought, with the kind of weaponry described, it really could be the final war, not only in the sense that its horrible example would function as a permanent deterrent but in the sense that it might obliterate civilization. It was in an explicitly pacifist spirit that Robida produced his accounts of future war, with increasing anxiety as time went by. The suspicion than a new war might destroy civilization did not obliterate satirical accounts of future warfare—far from it—but it did make the satire they displayed increasingly vitriolic.

Maurice Spronck's previously-mentioned *L'An 330 de la République* represents the other side of the ideological coin, attacking pacifism on the grounds that without technologically-sophisticated weapons, a nation would be easy prey to existing ones, and that it might be the European doves rather than the hawks that were paving the way for the destruction of civilization. By the turn of the century, the kind of savage sarcasm developed by Spronck had become ripe for further extension.

425

Pacifist satire reached its extreme in *L'Ère Petitpaon, ou La Paix universelle* (1906; tr. as "The Petipaon Era; or, World Peace") by Henri Austruy (?-1940), in which Bernard Petitpaon, an actor-turned-politician who becomes President of the Republic comes up with a plan to render war less destructive by signing up all the countries in the world to a scheme by which the potential casualty figures of any future battles will be calculated mathematically, on the basis of the number, skill and weaponry of the troops, exactly like the results of the maneuvers described in *La Vie électrique*. The appropriate numbers of "casualties," selected by drawing lots, will then only suffer a symbolic and largely theoretical death, losing their citizenship while being able nevertheless to return safe and sound to the bosom of their families.

Absurd complications of the scheme inevitably ensue in practice, however, when a petty puzzle arising from the difficulty of handling fractional deaths is gradually inflated into a *casus belli*. By the time the crucial battle of a new conflict between France and Germany is eventually fought, at Waterloo, the battles employ weapons so powerful in theory that both armies are completely "wiped out." The ensuing diplomatic and practical difficulties ensure that the hypothetical deaths, supplemented by a cholera epidemic among the maneuvering troops, soon become horribly real, with expanding consequences all the more nightmarish for their farcical irony.

Long before the actual outbreak of the Great War that had been visible on the political horizon of France since 1871, therefore, the long-cherished idea that war might become impossible because weaponry would become too advanced to make it practicable had effectively become obsolete. The consciousness had already dawned that the first impulse of the leaders of any nation possessed of a "weapon too dreadful to use" would be to use it before the opposition could develop it, and that the idea that they might be precipitating doomsday would certainly not put them off.

The future war fiction produced in Britain was no more prolific than that produced in France, and the fraction that took seriously the contribution that might be made to future warfare by new, scientifically-sophisticated weaponry was considerably smaller. In fact, it seems not unlikely that the pioneering stories of technologically advanced future warfare produced in Britain by George

426

Griffith and M. P. Shiel might have taken some inspiration from the key works of Camille Debans and Jules Lermina. As to whether the advance gained by French speculative fiction over British scientific romance affected the way that the Great War was envisaged when it actually erupted and while it was actually being fought, we can only speculate, but it is nevertheless interesting to compare the different effects that the legacy of the war had on subsequent speculative fiction in the two nations, in the light of what had gone before, as well as the different experiences the two countries had, by virtue of the fact that its central arena of conflict was on—or rather in—French soil. That is what the first section of the next chapter will do.

5. Mind and Body

The last three decades of the nineteenth century saw dramatic developments in psychological science, particularly at its interface with physiology. The investigations conducted by experimental psychologists were not very productive with regard to definite discoveries, but the change of attitude they reflected and developed was profound. The exploits that obtained the greatest publicity In France were the experimental studies of "somnambulism" and "hysteria" carried out with the aid of hypnotic techniques by scientists such as Jean-Martin Charcot, whose demonstrations at the Salpêtrière in the 1880s made him famous, but newspapers, as well as scientific journals, extended their coverage much more broadly.

Charcot also made a considerable contribution to the study of the phenomenon of "the doubling of the personality," initially popularized by the Belgian psychologist Joseph Delboeuf in 1879 and investigated soon thereafter by the neurophysiologist Charles Richet, who published a significant paper on multiple personality in 1883. That phenomenon was even more controversial than the phenomena of "suggestion" and "hysteria," and similarly attracted a good deal of press coverage.

The intense interest in attempts to investigate mental phenomena experimentally, and to analyze them in positivist terms, inevitably had effects in literature, where dreams, hallucinations, delusions and the phenomena of "animal magnetism" had long been topics of interest and useful narrative devices. Unsurprisingly, the first literary use made by writers of fiction of the results of Charcot's work was to provide supposedly rational underpinnings for frankly supernatural events, although the most sophisticated works of that kind employed them more dexterously to support and complicate the long-standing ambiguity between accounts "explaining" such events supernaturally and in terms of mental pathology, "Le Palimpseste" (*Revue des Deux Mondes* 1887; book version as *Marfa*) by Gilbert-Augustin Thierry (1843-1915) is one of the more notable examples of the literary exploitation of that ambiguity.

Philosophical attempts to define the relationship between the body and the mind (or soul) were by no means displaced by the new perspectives, but their authority was eroded, and alternative approaches to the question became available, which permitted some literary investigations of the mind/body problem to move decisively into the realm of *roman scientifique*. When that term began to be applied to the Naturalistic novels of Émile Zola as well as, or instead of, Jules Verne's more adventurous geographical romances, it was an assertion that what Zola was doing was a kind of scientific analysis in itself, particularly in terms of identifying the hereditary element in psychological disorders.

Whether or not literary analyses can really qualify as "scientific" is dubious, as a matter of pedantry, but the claim made in respect of Zolaesque Naturalism certainly gave rise to a school of thought holding that literary studies of the workings of the human mind based on social observation and introspection on the part of writers was at least as productive of an accurate understanding of the human mind, and perhaps far more so, than formal psychological investigations armed with the scientific method. On that basis, at least some exercises in *roman scientifique* could potentially claim to be scientific in more senses than one, constituting experiments in thought that had a similar value to actual attempts to experiment on thought.

In fact, as previously noted, Zola preferred to identify his fiction as *roman expérimental*, borrowing that interpretation from Claude Bernard's foundation of "experimental medicine," and he represented it as a natural consequence of "the scientific revolution of the century." Naturalism, therefore, was in his view the quintessential literature of the scientific era, carrying forward a project commenced by Honoré de Balzac in his attempt to use the mosaic of his *Comédie humaine* to build a massive analytical "cross-section" of French society, placed under the literary microscope.

In the preface to *Thérèse Raquin* (1867) Zola had argued explicitly that it was a duty on the part of future novelists to become scientific in their approach, in order to "continue and complete physiology"—which physiological psychology had not yet set out to do. To what extent Zola managed to achieve that continuation in the Rougon-Macquart series of novels, as it extended over the next thirty years, is debatable, but it is certainly the case that the terms in which he set out his "manifesto" for Naturalism had a powerful effect on debates about what literary endeavor could and ought to be doing in the final third of the nineteenth century.

A significant hypothetical representation of the experimental approach to questions previously thought to lie beyond the reach of science was provided by Jean Richepin's graphic account of "La Machine à métaphysique" (1877; tr. as The Metaphysical Machine"), in which an attempt to engineer a crucial breakthrough to hidden truth with the aid of method and machinery reaches an ironically ambiguous conclusion. The import of the story is fundamentally skeptical, even leaning toward an endorsement of the old adage that there are "things that man is not meant to know," but it recognizes the fact that, even if that is so, it certainly will not stop the scientific mind from attempting to discover them, in the defiant spirit of S. Henry Berthoud's archetypal scientist Ludwig Klopstock.

A less melodramatic but equally striking satirical analysis of an attempt to tackle personal problems scientifically can be found in Jules Hosch's collection *Folles amours* (1878), which justifies its title with the proposition that amorous attraction is a mere mental disorder and affects to study its pathological manifestations with clinical objectivity, alongside the similarly pathological features of a love of science.

"Le Docteur Quid" (tr. as "Doctor Quid") is a depiction of the distinctive features of the scientific mind more penetrating and more bizarre than anything Berthoud or Jules Verne ever produced. The equally eccentric "Meister Fult" (tr. as "Meister Fult") unleashes his particular madness on Strasbourg (Hosch's home town) with supposedly well-intentioned but nevertheless devastating effects, making the atmosphere so dense that the citizens have to weigh themselves down in order not to float up to its surface. In the final story of the collection, "Le Couple mécanique" (tr. as "The Mechanical Couple"), a wife distressed by her husband's nervous tics begins studying mechanics in the hope of finding a remedy, and begins to apply the principles of that science to the solution of her problem, with strange results that make much of the double meanings inherent in the scientific and everyday uses of the terms "couple" and "moment."

None of the stories in the collection has a "happy ending." That quirk was certainly typical of Hosch's work—all subsequent examples of which were signed Jules Hoche, because he considered himself to be French and wanted to make a symbolic show of his deep resentment of the fact that the Germans had taken possession of Alsace in 1870—but it is noticeable that it is a feature generally typical of many the stories identified in this section of the present text, to a greater extent than any other. Delving into the inner workings of the mind with a metaphorical scientific scalpel is a method of literary procedure highly conducive to the production of *contes cruels*, and not at all conducive to conventional normalization.

One of Zola's chief disciples in the emergent Naturalist school, Édouard Rod, contributed a striking example of fictitious mental analysis in his account of a hypothetical "mental autopsy" that is able to recover the impressions made on a man's mind after death, in "L'Autopsie du docteur Z***" (1884; tr. as "Doctor Z***'s Autopsy"). The dead man's posthumous observations allow him to realize many truths to which he had been ironically blind in life, and thus enable him to reappraise his existential situation productively before his consciousness fades away entirely: a distinctly Pyrrhic victory over ignorance, but one that could potentially have considerable import for those privileged to eavesdrop upon it by means of the literary device of the psychological autopsy.

Among the writers who developed a particular fascination with speculative studies of mental disorder was **Jules Claretie** (1840-1913), who eventually wrote three novels focusing on different aspects of the ongoing research. *Jean Mornas* (1885), which was enormously successful, helped to encourage a new wave of "medicated" literary accounts of murders committed under hypnosis. The theme was not new, but Claretie's treatment of it, conveniently embedded in a detective story of sorts, used the new scientific perspective to give it a much sharper edge than its Gothic predecessors. "L'Oeil du mort" [The Dead Man's Eye]  (1887; book version as *L'Accusateur*) similarly takes up a notion previously given a good deal of literary publicity in the Gothic mode, most notably in Villiers de l'Isle-Adam's "Clair Lenoir" (1867): the idea that the retina retains after death the last image formed thereon during life.

Of the various early studies of multiple personality, the most interesting is Charles Epheyre's "Soeur Marthe" (*Revue des Deux Mondes* 1889; tr. as "Sister Marthe"; expanded book version 1890), by virtue of the fact that "Charles Epheyre" was the pseudonym used in his literary work by Charles Richet (1850-1935), one of the pioneers of the medical study of the phenomenon. The story might have been a response to Thierry's "Le Palimpseste," published in the same periodical two years earlier, which also features a character named Marthe and a case of somnambulism, and the editor, at least, must have been well aware of the comparison and contrast to be drawn between the two novellas.

The narrator of Epheyre's story accidentally discovers that a certain item of Church music can release a secondary personality from the eponymous novice nun. That *alter ego* seems to have access to knowledge that the primary personality does not—including a secret that could make her rich—and seems to be able to heal her body of the consumption that is slowly killing it. The secondary personality instantly falls in love with the narrator, and proposes that they run away together, which throws him into a panic, because of lurid recent publicity given to cases of seduction by hypnotism, and he commands the hidden personality not to appear again: an irreversible instruction that he soon begins to regret very bitterly having given.

The fact that Richet had published a literary case study of that sort might have deterred Jules Claretie from attempting one of his own immediately, but he eventually got around to it in "Moi et l'autre" (1905; book version 1908 as *L'Obsession*; tr. as *Obsession*), a more intimately disturbing story than many in the same vein, in which a painter's consciousness is unexpectedly displaced by an unsympathetic secondary personality on his wedding night, and subsequently becomes troubled by the random appearances of the *alter ego* in question, which begin to disrupt his professional conduct as well as his personal life. That disruption leads him to seek expert help, in pursuit of a "cure," from a reclusive genius engaged in an obsessive quest of his own to force the development of a supposed vestigial "third eye" within the brain of a blind young woman, and the novel gradually shifts its main focus away from the victim to the theoretician, whose predicament is far more complicated, and less easy of solution.

The school of Naturalist *roman scientifique* attained an odd speculative extreme in the work of "Gaston Danville," the pseudonym employed by Armand Blocq (1870-1933), the younger brother of Paul Blocq (1860-1896), a colleague of Charcot at the Salpêtrière. Danville was one of the principal collaborators involved with the early issues of the *Mercure de France*, founded in 1890 by Remy de Gourmont, Alfred Vallette and others in order to provide a voice for the burgeoning Symbolist Movement. At the time of the *Mercure*'s foundation, the Parisian literary scene was afflicted by fervent disputes between various literary "schools" and "movements," of which Symbolism was one of the most prominent, developing out of Romanticism in close association with Decadence, a label resolutely adopted by some of the more radical Romantics, after having initially been leveled at the movement as a term of abuse by the Classicist critic Desiré Nisard, and resurrected in the 1880s as an assertive banner. Symbolism was widely seen as being engaged in a crucial rivalry to supply the literary *avant garde* with a neo-Naturalism that was considered by many commentators to have evolved beyond the pioneering work of Émile Zola and the Goncourt brothers because its "psychologists," led by Paul Bourget, placed a greater emphasis on internal states of mind in their supposedly-clinical accounts of human motivation.

The apparent opposition between Symbolism and Naturalism was largely illusory, and had much to do with the fact that the Symbolist school was primarily a school of poetry, crucially associated with such writers as Stéphane Mallarmé and Jean Moréas, whereas Naturalism was a school of prose fiction, closely associated with the evolution of the narrative techniques of the novel. Naturalist novelists did not, in fact, shun the employment of symbolism as a narrative device; nor did Symbolist writers, when they diversified into prose fiction, avoid the devices developed by novelists in the interests of representational verisimilitude. Leading writers of both schools shared a keen interest in the seamier side of social life, and were routinely preoccupied with erotic and violent subject-matter. Nevertheless, many of the individuals caught up in the controversy did see themselves as being involved in an ideological conflict, and were eager to take up positions in the front line, firing their critical weapons with reckless abandon. Gaston Danville was one of them, but he was exceptional in the particular stance he took, and the location from which he elected to fight. He was, in a sense, the most ideologically-extreme of all the neo-Naturalists, but he took up his position at the very heart of the Symbolist movement, as a cuckoo in its most precious nest.

In 1891-92 Danville published twelve "Contes d'Au-Delà" in the *Mercure*; the items were reprinted in volume form by the periodical's press, with some additional material, in 1892, as *Contes d'Au-Delà*, and Danville published two further stories in the *Mercure* that were an obvious extrapolation of the same line of endeavor in 1893-94. His first four novels, *Les Infinis de la chair* [The Infinity of the Flesh] (1892), *Vers la mort* [Toward Death] (1897), *Les Reflets du miroir* [The Reflections in the Mirror] (1897) and *L'Amour magicien* [Love the Magician] (1902), carried forward the same project, as explicitly stated in the preface to the first of them, which explained the theory behind the story series and advanced the claim that it would attempt to take the Naturalist cause to a new but logical extreme.

In Danville's view, contemporary neo-Naturalists and writers of popular crime fiction were behind the times, routinely clinging, tacitly or explicitly, to scientific theses he considered to be obsolete. His choice of "Contes d'Au-Delà" as a title for his own series was ironic; the "beyond" to which his tales relate is the hidden depths of the unconscious. Danville's characters are haunted, but they are haunted by memories, unconscious impulses and the poignant emotions provoked by those internal spurs. All their apparitions are delusory—but the fact that Danville based his accounts of delusion and obsession on what he took to be sound theories of positivistic psychology did not prevent him from writing horror stories or erotic fantasies; indeed, it is arguable that it added an extra dimension of cruelty to his *contes cruels* and an extra dose of intensity to his eroticism.

Like many other writers, Danville was fascinated by the manner in which erotic impulses occasionally led to suicide and homicide, but his stories delving into the psychology of suicide and murder are more intensely focused than those of any of his contemporaries, and helped to lay the foundation of modern psychological horror fiction. "Le Substitut" (1891; tr. as "The Deputy") anticipates the modern fascination with fetishistic "serial killers," while "*In anima vili*" (1892) re-examines the theme of *Jean Mornas* in a more clinical context.

In theoretical terms, Danville's work could not be any more sophisticated than the prevailing ideas of its era, and the psychologists on whose work it is based—primarily Théodule Ribot, of whom Paul Blocq was a dedicated disciple—have long since fallen out of fashion. Danville's fiction therefore seems primitive to the modern reader in its uses of "hysteria" and its occasional development of the notion of the "doubling" of the personality, but his stories were genuinely experimental in their day. In the preface to *Les Infinis de la chair* Danville represents the "Contes d'Au-Delà" and the novel as part and parcel of the endeavor commenced in his essay "L'Amour est-il un état pathologique" [Is Amour a Pathological State?] (1893 in Ribot's *Revue philosophique*), which was a preliminary sketch of his elaborate scholarly account of *La Psychologie de l'Amour* [The Psychology of Amour]—the only work for which he is still remembered.

The article, the book developed from it and the fiction based on its central theses eventually refuse to conclude, as Jules Hosch had done, that sexual love is merely a kind of mental abnormality, in spite of its often obsessive character, but they do not reach that conclusion without a certain ambivalence. Nor is the scientific conclusion entirely borne out by the literary conclusions reached by the story-lines of Danville's fiction, whose amorous heroes are all deeply troubled and many of whom end up committing suicide, like the protagonist of the elaborately intense hallucinatory fantasy "Mousmé" (1894). *Les Reflets du miroir* is the most explicit extrapolation of the theory of amorous attraction set out in the book, but Danville's short fiction is perhaps more interesting than his early novels by virtue of its necessary economy, and the fact that almost all his *contes d'au-delà* are *contes cruels* is evidently significant of something, whether it has to do with the narrative demands of short fiction, the logical corollaries of the theories he deploys, or both.

Le Parfum de volupté (1905; tr. as *The Perfume of Lust*) was Danville's boldest venture into speculative fiction. The story describes the plight of a the crew and passengers of a disabled ship trapped in the internal waters of a resurgent land when a submarine eruption returns the location of the lost continent of Atlantis to the surface, and its crew and passengers are subjected to strange mental influences that stimulate their erotic impulses. The novel employs multiple devices to put narrative distance between the reader and the story, the core narrative being related third-hand, with abundant commentary conscientiously endorsing the notion that the whole experience might have been a hallucination, while pointing out, equally conscientiously, its extraordinary detail and coherency, as

well as rationalizing all its fantastic devices as residual elements of the superscience of ancient Atlantis. The real interest of the novel, however, is not its convoluted literary apparatus but its psychological implications: its argument regarding the psychological roots of "volupté" (usually translated as "sensuality," for euphemistic reasons considered inapt as well as unnecessary in the English translation).

Within the tradition of *roman scientifique, Le Parfum de volupté* is closely connected to the sequence of speculative accounts of hypothetical societies discussed in the first section of the current chapter, in which sex is liberated from the legal and moral constraints to which it was subjected in contemporary French society. Whether writers of the period were sympathetic to it or not, the notion of "free love" popularized by the thriving political theories of Anarchism was a challenge that all designers of literary utopias were virtually compelled to address. Danville had probably read Paul Adam's *Lettres de Malaise*, but it is worth noting that he finished writing *Le Parfum de volupté* in 1902, before having had a chance to read André Couvreur's *Caresco, surhomme* or Alfred Jarry's *Le Surmâle*, and that the novel was probably published in the year which Han Ryner actually wrote his Atlantis-set utopia *Les Pacifiques*, although the latter was even longer-delayed in publication, not reaching print until 1914.

Danville's approach to the question of how a society practicing free love might become practicable, although far more tentative and coy than the accounts offered by the near-contemporaries cited, is remarkable in proposing that the problems posed by the psychology and sociology of amour might be soluble— and, more importantly, might *only* be soluble—by means of a fundamental eupsychian shift altering the essential anatomy of thought. Obviously, the story cannot offer a detailed account of what that shift would constitute; as the characters discussing the matter point out, the terminology is lacking because contemporary vocabulary is shaped by the attitudes that have been transformed, but it is nevertheless ingenious in dropping hints and planting signposts, using the eponymous hypothetical psychotropic scent as a facilitating device.

Gaston Danville also published two further non-fiction books, *Magnétisme et spiritisme* (1908) and *Le Mystère psychique* [The Mystery of Mind] (1915), but neither made as much impact as *La Psychologie de l'amour*. The latter was almost exactly contemporary with Remy de Gourmont's *Physique de l'amour: Essai sur l'instinct sexuel* (1903; tr. as *The Natural Philosophy of Love*), which makes an interesting comparison with Danville's book, especially as both writers were closely associated with the *Mercure* and must have known one another well enough to exchange ideas. Danville's ideas also make an interesting comparison with Charles Cros' satire "La Science de l'amour" (1874; tr. as "The Science of Love"), a fictional anticipation of the quest, which has no faith in the application of an empirical scientific method to reveal anything very useful about the psychological mechanics of sexual attraction.

It was only natural that writers wanting to develop a kind of experimental fiction intended to delve into the mysteries of the mind should immediately want to focus on the mysteries of amour. That was not a subject that had attracted extensive interest among professional scientists, partly because it seemed more sensible for them to start with simpler matters, and partly because it could lead to career-threatening accusations of indecency, but amour had always been a central topic of literary concern, and it drew "experimental" investigations like those of Cros, Gourmont and Danville like a magnet.

Naturalists did not have a monopoly on the claim to be taking a scientific approach to the analysis of erotic experience, and one of Charles Cros's closest friends, in the days when they were the star double act of Nina de Villard's salon, the self-styled Comte de Villiers de l'Isle-Adam (1838-1889), adopted his own highly distinctive experimental approach to the science of love in a graphic account of *L'Ève future* (1886 in book form after two aborted serial versions; tr. as *Tomorrow's Eve*). The story describes what happens when Thomas Edison is contacted by Ewald, a French aristocrat who once saved his life, and who is now in despair because the young woman he is due to marry, Alicia Clary, although physically perfect, is intellectually and emotionally depleted. Edison's "solution" to that problem is to substitute for the quasi-androidal Alicia an actual android that will be capable of more satisfactory interactions and responses.

Edison already has the android, Hadaly, which he created as a potential ideal woman, and he has the means to superimpose Alicia's appearance on her, but in order to supply her with the desired personality he requires the aid of his exotic assistant Sowana, who supplies the necessary soul. Ewald naturally falls in love with Hadaly—who is, after all, more perfect than any natural woman could be—but the precise nature of the manner in which his love is reciprocated remains highly ambiguous, dependent on the interpretation of Sowana's involvement, of which only unreliable reports are offered. The plot cuts the analysis brutally short, but inevitably leaves the questions in suspense.

L'Ève future is one of the more conspicuous demonstrations of the fact that no matter how powerfully imaginative writers might be drawn to involve themselves with questions of amour, the magnetism attracting them was bound to be perverted by their analytical approach. That perversity stems from the long held suspicion—or conviction—that science and amour are antipathetic, or at least incompatible: a hypothesis that Cros' account of "The Science of Love" attempts to prove in no uncertain terms and Villiers' depiction of a supposedly perfect artificial woman certainly fails to disprove. Then too, if professional scientists were a trifle wary of the topic because its investigation seemed slightly obscene, dedicated writers were equally wary of introducing the scientific method and hypothetical technological assistance into the problem, because that seemed akin to a profanation to many of them, and to many of their readers. On either side, there was a nettle to be grasped.

Bold attempts were made to grasp that nettle in terms of imagining entire societies in which a scientific approach has been taken to the problems of amour, in works already discussed in the context of utopian fantasies, but it seemed an even touchier subject when approached on an individual basis. A scene in Restif de La Bretonne's *Les Posthumes* in which Marie-Antoinette seeks out Multipliandre because she has heard it rumored that he has the secret of prolonging orgasm, and demands a demonstration of the relevant biotechnology, remains the most shocking in the novel, but that particular superpower was hardly mentioned again in the text, nor was it subjected to further literary examination by other hands for a long time. It was, in fact, exactly a century after the belated publication of *Les Posthumes* that there was a robust literary return to the possibilities of hypothetical erotic biotechnology in Alfred Jarry's *Le Surmâle* (1902; tr. as *The Supermale*).

ALFRED JARRY

LE SURMALE

ROMAN MODERNE

FASQUELLE

The first chapter of *Le Surmâle* describes a conversation at a house-party at André Marcueil's château, sparked by his remark that "the erotic act is unimportant, since it can be performed indefinitely." Marcueil's argument is that sexual intercourse in the past has only retained human interest and fascination because it was forever reaching hopefully for something essentially beyond its grasp, thus remaining in permanent suspense: an "*acte en puissance*" [a potential act] whose unfulfilled potentiality is the engine of what one of his questioners calls "sentiment," embracing both erotic desire and all the froth of love.

The past tense is appropriate to the

description because, Marcueil claims, he is now in a position to transcend the limitation. Also present at the house-party is the American chemist William Elson, the inventor of what is described in the text (in English) as a "Perpetual-Motion-Food": a dietary supplement that dramatically enhances the physical fortitude of the human body. Marcueil believes, although he has not yet tried the experiment, that the compound in question will enable the suspended potential of the human sexual act finally to reach a compete fulfillment rather than the essentially unsatisfactory climaxes that only provide temporary relief and long-term disillusionment: a situation that Elson describes as "Mithridatism," after the mythical king whose gradual ingestion of poisons ultimately renders him immune to them all.

The remainder of the novella tracks various effects of the Perpetual-Motion-Food, taking in some of Jarry's other fascinations in his characteristic buoyant style. It is no coincidence that he had begun his career as the most dedicated experimentalist of the Symbolist movement, and that he ended it as the most evident precursor of Surrealism; *Le Sûrmale* is one of the pivotal works in the contrivance of that transition. Given its fundamental premise, there was only one way the novel could ever conclude: with a genuine climax.

The logic of storytelling being what it is, there is a certain inevitability about the fact that when Marcueil enthusiastically volunteers as a guinea-pig for the ultimate test of the invention, it is partly because he is enamored of the scientist's daughter, Ellen, who becomes his partner in what the relevant chapter calls "The Discovery of Woman." Ellen is able to make the discovery in question exceptionally challenging, partly by virtue of being a scientist's daughter, and partly by version of a charisma unique to herself, although Marcueil rises to the greatly-extended occasion in no uncertain terms.

Elson was not, however, the only technologist present at the initiating house-party; the electrical expert and manufacturer of aircraft and automobiles Arthur Gough was also there, and he too has taken inspiration from the discussion to construct his own technical contribution to the discussion: "*la Machine-à-inspirer-l'amour*" [the love-inspiration machine]. Jarry had recently written the enthusiastic essay on the new genre of *roman scientifique* cited in the introduction, choosing *L'Ève future* as one of his key examples of the genre's nature and ambition, but he naturally wanted to go at least one better than Villiers, both in terms of the imagination of the device and the outcome of the ultimate confrontation between human and technological love-machines. His fictitious love-inspiration machine bears more resemblance to an electric chair than a feminized android—the comparison is explicitly made—and the result of the encounter is that love is indeed inspired, in its full and explosive potential, not in the supermale, who is already emotionally committed, but in the unfortunate machine.

Because it is a surreal sarcastic comedy (like human life itself, according to some observers) Jarry's novel can be regarded simply as a joke and discarded with a muffled titter, but it might also be reckoned as one of the proverbial true words that are, perhaps less often than one might wish, spoken in jest. The argument might be developed flippantly, and its climax farcically, but the argument that the novella poses and develops sternly refuses to take the conventional answer to a real question for granted.

Alfred Jarry's fellow Symbolist and precursor of Surrealism Guillaume Apollinaire also produced a story of scientifically-obtained superhumanity, employed in supporting the pretence of being a new Messiah, in the relatively casual "Le Toucher à distance" (1910 in *L'Hérésiarque et cie*; tr. as "Remote Projection"). Other treatments of the idea from the same period, even if they set out to be more elaborate, tend to be equally tentative in confronting the issue, often recoiling reflexively in horror, after the fashion of Charles Ricolin in his account of a scientist who gifts himself with X-ray vision in "Le Rayon X" (1896; tr. as "The X-Ray"), and thus avoiding getting bogged down by abstruse questions in the philosophy of mind.

Gaston Danville had not get very far in the development of a new school of neo-Naturalist *roman expérimental* based on psychology as understood by Théodule Ribot, but he had certainly been correct to criticize much contemporary fiction for basing its models of the mind on a crude Cartesian dualism, completely ignoring the suggestions of the rapidly-developing science of physiological psychology, which envisaged a more complex and intricate relationship between the mental and the physical. The kind of body-swapping practiced by Duc Multipliandre's soul was a trifle crude even at the end of the eighteenth century, but the stubborn maintenance of similar notions was much harder to justify rationally a hundred years later, even if it was still appealing to litterateurs because of its narrative convenience.

Ribot's materialism, which regarded mental phenomena as secondary products of the chemical and electric activity of the brain rather than the work of a separate order of "mental substance," did not make *roman scientifique* focused on mental phenomena impractical, in literary terms, but it did make the literary task of depiction more challenging, and the prospect of offering explanations much more daunting. Most writers, of course, simply ducked or fudged the problem of explanation, routinely presenting phenomena to the reader as givens, often frankly admitted as inexplicable. Even strategies of avoidance, however, require some notion of what is to be avoided, and even the most casual use of apologetic jargon requires a choice of terms to be dropped.

As Danville had attempted to illustrate, the shift of perspective that substituted the new "beyond" of the unconscious for the obsolete beyond of superstition and religion not only retained abundant scope for melodrama but actually opened up new scope for analyses of various forms of psychological and physical self-harm, including love and murder—scope that was to be abundantly explored in the twentieth century in countless naturalistic fictions dealing with

eroticism and crime—but it did not lend itself as kindly to heterocosmic speculation as the traditional vocabulary of ideas, whose evolution had been shaped by
precisely that requirement.

Even so, some adaptation was desirable, if not absolutely necessary. J.-H.
Rosny tried to point the way in "La Légende sceptique" and the fiction associated with it, and in so doing demonstrated the problems that were going to arise in
trying to supply a new hypothetical basis for traditional plausible impossibilities
by taking the notion of a "sixth sense" seriously enough to provide hypothetical
explanations of how that sense might operate physically. "La Force
mystérieuse" was not the first work to attempt to do that, by any means, but it
made the difficulty clearer than most. In lower strata of the marketplace the
problem was even more difficult, although it was sometimes tackled even there
by writers of good conscience.

Jules Perrin "L'Hallucination de Monsieur Forbe" (*Je Sais Tout* 1908; tr.
as "Monsieur Forbe's Hallucination"; expanded book version as *La Terreur des
images* 1910) similarly describes mysterious phenomena that begin as puzzles
but escalate rapidly to become serious problems as a regional effect similar to
the anomalous space featured in Rosny's story allows the communication of extraordinary visions and the transmission of impulses from one mind to another.
Perrin, following conventional normalizing strategy, makes the phenomenon
temporary in order not to have to transform the world within the text completely,
but he does conscientiously point out several of the consequences that the generalization and perpetuation of the phenomenon would logically entail.

One story of this kind that flatters
only to deceive in developing its notion at
greater length is *Le Lynx* (1911; tr. as *The
Lynx*) written in collaboration by Michel
Corday (1869-1937) and the author of
Caresco, surhomme, André Couvreur,
which is the most extensive study of the
notion of telepathy produced in *roman
scientifique* in the years before the Great
War, albeit couched in a work deliberately
framed as a popular thriller. It was not the
first time that the philosophical aspects of
the notion of "thought-reading" had been
directly addressed in French fiction; the
first extensive treatment had been carried
out by long before by Delphine de
Girardin in *Le Lorgnon* (1832; tr. as "The
Lorgnon"), but Madame de Girardin had
approached the theme prudently, in the
context of a mild social satire and a rela-

tively conventional love story. Her thought-reading device, although given a slight pseudoscientific gloss, was essentially magical, and thus of intrinsically arbitrary and strictly limited existence; the one featured in *Le Lynx*, by contrast, is emphatically the product of scientific discovery, invested with a much more forceful hypothetical reality, capable of being reproduced indefinitely and gifted to the entire human race. That sharpens the philosophical question markedly, and also changes the love story element of the plot. Like *Le Lorgnon*, *Le Lynx* is orientated toward a problematic "happy ending" difficult of attainment, but it calls the assumed "happiness" of the ending into question in a far more intriguing fashion than its pioneering predecessor.

The protagonist of *Le Lynx*, Gabriel Mirande, is gifted a drug that allows him to read thoughts for a limited time after each injection by his employer and mentor, the brilliant scientist Professor Brion, when the latter is on his deathbed. Sworn to absolute secrecy regarding the existence of the drug, after discovering its effects in a melodramatic fashion, he sets out to use it clandestinely in order to prove that his sister's fiancé did not commit a murder for which he has been ingeniously framed.

Gabriel is quickly enabled to identify the real killer—but the attempt to procure evidence that is capable of convincing anyone else, rather than getting him committed to a lunatic asylum, proves difficult in the extreme, and although he eventually succeeds—more by luck than judgment—he eventually decides that the gift is a two-edged sword. He takes the decision to destroy the invention rather than allowing his fellow humans the choice of whether to take the risk of

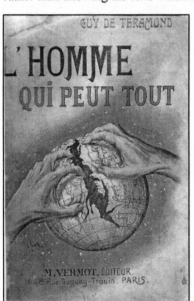

its adoption, on grounds with which many readers might disagree strongly—and with which the authors might well have been inviting and hoping for disagreement, although they presumably felt compelled to pander to the duty imposed by the thriller formula of normalizing their conclusion.

That kind of capitulation—also featured in Guy de Téramond's similarly-inclined *L'Homme qui peut tout* [The Man who Could Do Anything] (1910)—was to become increasingly and understandably commonplace as the bulk of *roman scientifique* moved from the relatively esoteric domain of *contes philosophiques* into the field of commercial popular fiction, but it remained particularly awkward and dubious in connection with themes touching the intimacy of the human mind and hypothetical modifications thereof. The development of telepathy by virtue of effects of radiation not dissimilar to those described in "L'Hallucination de Monsieur Forbe" is also featured in Léon Groc's *L'Autobus évanoui* (1914; tr. as *The Bus that Vanished*), which provides a further illustration of the problems of narrative strategy generated by the adaptation of such themes to the norms of popular fiction.

There is a particular interest in considering the specific contributions made by Naturalist *roman scientifique* to the study of the peculiar features of "the scientific mind," as pioneered by S. Henry Berthoud. Émile Zola did that himself in the last of the Rougon-Macquart novels, *Le Docteur Pascal* (1893; tr. as *Doctor Pascal*), which tells the story of the collector of genealogical data who has been tracking the hereditary flaw in the two families that give the series its title, and detailing its effects in various different environments.

Pascal is working under stress from more than one direction; his mother wants to destroy his work in order to cover up the family's nasty secrets, and his pious niece thinks that his endeavor is an affront to God and an attempt to go beyond divinely-set limits to human knowledge—and, indeed, Pascal has developed a serum from cerebral tissue that appears to be capable of curing numerous diseases and perhaps prolonging life, although it is on his vaguely-indicated discoveries in the science of heredity that he pins his hopes for a crucial transformation of the human condition. Unfortunately, death attains him before he can heal himself, and his mother seizes the opportunity to burn his data.

Charles Richet's literary alter ego, Charles Epheyre, produced two fictional studies of the scientific mind at work, "Le Mirosaurus" (1885; tr. as "The Mirosaurus") and "Le Microbe du Professeur Bakermann" (1890; tr. as "Professor Bakermann's Microbe"). The second is the more striking of the two in its melodramatic depiction of an obsessive biologist's attempt to produce an incurable pathogen, as an achievement of purely scientific interest. When it is released because of the fatal recklessness of his resentfully neglected wife, he has to go to extremes of heroism to develop of means of halting the plague, even joining forces with his deadliest scientific rival—but once he has succeeded, and has saved the world, he immediately goes back to work in order to correct the flaw in his microbe's deadliness. The Naturalism of "Le Mirosaurus" is, however, arguably more interesting in its description of how a young provincial is seduced by an accidental paleontological find, and by the daughter of the eminent man who comes to verify the discovery, into becoming the latter's research assistant and setting his sights on a career in science. He soon becomes disenchanted by the arrogance and treachery of the great man and the apparent corruption of the entire Parisian scientific community, and eventually elects to return to the provincial peace and quiet of the world of metaphorical social dinosaurs.

The oddities of the psychology of scientists remained a highly significant subsidiary issue in many stories whose ostensible theme is the inventions that they produce, and while it is certainly not absent from British scientific romance or the precursors of American science fiction produced prior to the Great War, it is a preoccupation that is considerably more obvious in French materials. The notion put forward by Edgar Poe that "the idea of the tale" could be presented "unblemished" in imaginative short fiction, taken up much later by Kingley Amis in his analysis of science fiction as *New Maps of Hell* (1960), in which he made "idea-as-hero" stories a key feature of the genre, is compromised to a great extent in French material than British or American material, because it is often much harder to separate the invention from the inventor and see it in unblemished isolation.

That is, of course, evident in many stories of the present period dealing with inventors and their achievements, and helps to give those stories a sharper element. Notable examples can be found repeatedly in the short fiction of several of the writers who had regular recourse to the genre as an arena for developing innovative ideas, including Jules Lermina—most spectacularly in the grotesque "Maison tranquille" (1881; tr. as "Quiet House"), in which the eccentricity of the owner and architect of the eponymous dwelling is extended in its bizarre design, his chemical diet and his relationships with his family—and Maurice Renard, notably in "Le Voyage immobile" (1909; tr. as "The Motionless Voyage"), in which an inventor's quirkiness is metaphorically mirrored in his strangely paradoxical flying machine. It is, however, not necessary to go to such extremes of symbolic representation to investigate the oddities of the scientific mind, and some of the most striking examples come from within the Naturalist camp, deliberately minimizing that kind of associative invention.

By far the most detailed Naturalistic account of the psychology of the scientist and the problems that outsiders encounter in contention with the established scientific community is contained in *La Seconde vie du docteur Albin* (1902; tr. as *The Second Life of Doctor Albin*) by "Raoul Gineste," (Adolphe Augier, 1849-1914), a southerner who spent most of his life working as a physician in Paris. The opening of the story describes how a medical man of great prestige and authority, who has written a standard textbook on biochemistry, discovers that the theory he set forth therein, taught in all French universities, has a fatal flaw that falsifies the entire theoretical edifice. Unable to face the upheaval and humiliation than would result from a simple admission of error he decides to fake his death, assume a different identity, and establish a new reputation for that alter ego, in which he can establish his glory all over again by assembling the incontrovertible experimental proof that will demolish his old theory, and building the new one that can and should replace it.

Unfortunately, narrowly focused as he is, Albin puts all his intellectual effort into the successful faking of his death, and neglects to make foolproof provision for the financial security of his new identity; when that part of his scheme goes awry he is left destitute, still determined to follow through his obsessive plan, but facing an uphill struggle that quickly becomes utterly desperate, testing his science and his will-power to the limit. Although his talent for invention and his scientific conscience pull him back from the brink of extinction more than once, they also multiply his troubles. He is hauled back from that brink on one occasion by the kindness of a prostitute, who becomes attached to him, and with whom he develops a curious mutual dependency based on his feeling of indebtedness—that, at least, is what he tells himself, as the narrative explores with more intensity and depth than any other the precise nature of the alienation from affectionate emotion that is generally held to be an essential feature of the scientific mind. The particular quality of Albin's obsession, with all the corollaries that it entails, draws him inexorably away from everything the unfolding story can offer him in the way of conventional "salvation," toward an ultimate irony of fate.

As the work of a writer who was a scientist of sorts—although Gineste was also a poet associated with the Felibrige movement, whose lack of success in his profession might well have had something to with his fondness for the literary "Bohemia" of *fin-de-siècle* Paris—*La Seconde vie du docteur Albin* can lay claim to a an introspective insight into the scientific mind, albeit informed by a bitterness that the far more successful Charles Richet had no reason to feel. The most intensely critical of all studies of the supposed deficiencies of the scientific mind was, however, produced by a writer who had firmly set aside the brief flirtation he had had with positivism during his student days and had committed himself entirely to the cause of art: André Beaunier, author of *L'Homme qui a perdu son moi* (1911; tr. as *The Man Who Lost Himself*). Although the novel might conceivably have taken some inspiration from Raoul Gineste's quintessential account of self-loss, its fundamental attitude is far more hostile to the supposed existential effects of scientific obsession, bearing some resemblance in that regard to René de Pont-Jest's "Mimer's Head."

Beaunier's novel tells the story of Michel Bedée, a physicist who has become celebrated because of his discovery of a new radioactive element, sirium, although the toil of extracting, collecting and studying the properties of the elusive substance has distanced him from his mother, his sister and his wife. Having reached a crucial juncture at which he is torn between continuing to work obsessively or recommitting himself to his wife and family, he is urged by his old mentor, "the Alchemist," to abandon everything else and commit himself entirely to science.

Michel is reluctant to do that, but the balance is tipped when his wife, who has found a substitute for his distanced affections elsewhere, discovers that sirium has healing properties, and demands that he devote himself to its practical application rather than to further purely scientific investigation. He then allows the Alchemist to take him away and isolate him in a remote part of the Netherlands, in imitation of Baruch Spinoza, so that he can devote himself to the development of a new theory of atomic physics without distraction. He does, in fact, perfect the theory, but is then at a loss to know what to do next. Tempted by two very different women, who tacitly offer him different paths back to emotional connection, he is ultimately unable to take either route, no longer being capable of finding the self that he has lost in the wilderness of his obsession.

The deep pessimism of those two extensive analyses is echoed in a much wider range of fictions that do not have the same pretensions to Naturalism and seriousness. The amenability of stories focusing on the extreme extrapolation of scientific obsession to *conte cruel* conclusions, initially demonstrated by Jean Richepin's account of the "metaphysical machine," encouraged the production of such stories in the decades to either side of the turn of the century, when several newspapers began to use their feuilleton slots to feature short stories rather than long serial novels, thus provoking a boom in the production of *contes cruels*.

Richepin's occasional ventures into *roman scientifique* for the slot in *Le Journal* to which he was a regular contributor in 1895-1901 are mostly *contes cruels*, albeit of a calculatedly trivial kind, and other contributors to similar slots, including Marcel Schwob's stories for *L'Écho de Paris*, occasionally featured similar digressions. Two stories by Frédéric Boutet that belong to the series he wrote for the feuilleton slot of the evening newspaper *Le Français* between 1903 and the outbreak of the war, although neither appeared in the initial 1909 sampler of that series that he published, "L'Expérience (tr. as "The Experiment") and "Le Meurtre de l'Américain" (tr. as "The American's Murder"), both reprinted n 1921, are particularly deft contributions to that tradition, in which the careless arrogance of experimental scientists leads to homicidal consequences. The most striking examples of that kind of consciousness, however, tended to develop a more intense sensibility at a slightly greater length than a feuilleton slot permitted.

That kind of pessimism had sociological as well as psychological connections. Disenchantment with the habitual arrogance of the members of the establishment of "official science," as displayed Naturalistically by Charles Epheyre, coupled with the resentment of the closure against new ideas, motivated by the pride and obsessive status-consciousness that he detailed, was to become a constant refrain in *roman scientifique*, where great scientists are frequently denied their due by the paranoid jealousy with which Academicians and universitarians defend their prejudices, even in the face of falsifying proofs. A particularly sharp parable of that sort is Michel Corday's "Le Mystérieux Dajan-Phinn" (1908; tr. as "The Mysterious Dajan-Phinn"), in which a genius returned from a long self-imposed exile with the living proof of his achievement is driven to a terrible extreme by the refusal of his oldest adversary to yield to the evidence.

Arguments related to the inevitable clash between the achievements of scientists making breakthroughs and the stubbornness of their prejudiced rivals in refusing to admit their possibility, like the difficulties faced by the protagonist of "Le Mystérieux Dajan-Phinn," help to explain and excuse the fact that the great majority of scientific geniuses featured in *roman scientifique* are invariably secretive and reclusive, meeting the mistrust and hostility of others with paranoid suspicion, even when their inventions have made them fortunes, like Louis Boussenard's Monsieur Synthèse and Corday and Couvreur's Professor Brion. It also helps to explain the presumption, fundamental to Gineste's and Beaunier's analyses, that obsession is bound to lead, ultimately, to desperation, and from there to doom, if the man of science cannot succeeded in finding or constructing a self that is not entirely scientific in its orientation.

Reclusiveness and secrecy are taken to unusual extremes by the scientists whose obsessions provide the central motifs of Jules Lermina's novellas *À bruler, conte astral* (1888; tr. as "Burn This") and "Le Secret des Zippélius" (1889; tr. as "The Zippelius Secret"). In the latter story, the narrator receives the eponymous secret as a mysterious legacy, and discovers that it is the discovery that supposedly put an end to war in Méry's "Les Ruines de Paris." Far from seeing it as a means of ending war, however, its past custodians have considered it far too dangerous to surrender—but the knowledge that they hold the power to wipe out humankind at a stroke in their hands has also caused them to hide themselves away and avoid all contact with their fellow men, lest the supposedly-inevitable disgust and repulsion provoked by such contact cause them to use it. The heir to the secret must decide what to do with it, in the full awareness of what his ancestors have done and why, but unlike them, he is a family man, and has to weigh that circumstance in the balance too.

The obsessive scientists of early *roman scientifique* do not all end up ignominiously dead, although the body-count, if a census were taken of all those depicted in the burgeoning genre between 1870 and 1914, would be very considerable. By contrast, the number who end up feeling happy and fulfilled in their work would not pose much of a challenge to people accustomed to counting on their fingers. Those who survive often have to undergo severe traumas, and must take what crumbs of comfort they can from the fact of their survival.

For much of the narrative, the scientific genius featured in Henri Austruy's *L'Eupantophone* (serial 1904; book 1905; tr. as "The Eupantophone"), who has overcome blindness by making himself artificial eyes, and wants to restore the sight of his blind fiancée as a kind of wedding gift, is a happy man in spite of the fact that he has great difficulty persuading others of the reality of his accomplishment. He does succeed in enabling his bride to see, and is then able to settle down to a blissful married life—until another of his ingenious inventions accidentally strikes her dead and he finds himself accused of murdering her, unable to convince a prejudiced examining magistrate of his innocence. The jury at his trial, fortunately, is not so stubborn—but his beloved wife is still dead and he is still traumatized.

The difficulty that scientists are assumed to have in maintaining amorous relationships is, naturally in the context of the time, mostly assumed to be a male problem, but one of the principal real models in France of dogged dedication to science was Marie Curie, whose discovery of radium in 1898, in collaboration with her husband Pierre, enabled her to become a legend in her own lifetime. That legend did not prompt a glut of French literary works featuring heroic female scientists, but it did provoke a few significant echoes, the most elaborate being the depiction of a specifically female kind of scientific genius in the character of Geneviève Gasguin, in Jean Richepin's *L'Aile, roman des temps nouveaux* (1911; tr. as *The Wing, A Romance of the New Era*). In the end, the shy and highly-strung Geneviève, who allows her father to take credit for her work in order to remain hidden from view, does find romantic love, seemingly thanks to an inexorable force of magnetic destiny, but the road to its achievement is an exceedingly rocky one, and the chapter in which the two fated lovers finally come together is one of the strangest erotic scenes ever penned. That conclusion, too, offers eloquent testimony to the extreme awkwardness of the problem, as perceived by litterateurs.

Male scientists in *roman scientifique* can and do fall in love occasionally, but when they do, they tend to do so with the same obsessiveness that they bring to their science, and any disturbance in that love tends to tip them over the edge of the madness to which their genius has already brought them close. S. Henry Berthoud's mad scientists tended to start off sane, were often driven mad as much by the incomprehension of those around them as by the stress of their own obsession, and tended to remain harmless to their own kind even when mad, but the writers who took up where Berthoud left off were often less generous in their assessment.

446

The scientist who eventually became one of *roman scientifique*'s most prominent archetypes of the mad scientist, André Couvreur's Professor Tornada, made his first appearance in *Une Invasion de macrobes* (1909; tr. as "An Invasion of Macrobes"), in which, initially unhinged by the accidental death of his wife and beloved daughter, the biochemist is finally driven to extremes by the contemptuous hostility of his orthodox peers, and sets out to demonstrate the validity of his theses by unleashing an irresistible army of gargantuan bacteria on Paris. Tornada is not inaccessible to sentiment, as frankly malevolent scientists like Cornelius Kramm, the sinister "sculptor of human flesh" featured in Gustave Le Rouge's part-work *Le Mystérieux docteur Cornelius* (1912-13; tr. as *The Mysterious Doctor Cornelius*) tend to be, but his intermittent experience of it is as mercurial as his scientific genius.

Tornada is finally persuaded not to let his vengeance run its full course by the intervention of the daughter of a fellow scientist, who reminds him of his own daughter, but other scientists driven mad by the hostility of their fellows had no such saving recourse. One particularly interesting example, if only because it was not published when written in 1908, being considered too dangerous, is Arnould Galopin's second *roman scientifique*, which he initially titled *L'Homme à la figure bleue* (tr. as "The Man with the Blue Face"); he continued to include that title in the list of his works throughout his career, and appears to have deposited a sample of the text at the Bibliothèque Nationale in order to secure it a record of existence, but it was not actually published until 1928, as *Le Bacille* [The Bacillus].

The protagonist of Galopin's novel, Martial Procas, is a brilliant bacteriologist whose phenomenal good looks make him immensely attractive to women, although his innocence and shyness make it difficult for him to handle their attentions, and when he marries, his choice is not the wisest. When he discovers his glamorous wife's adultery he has a kind of fit, the hemorrhagic effects of which have the odd side effect of turning his skin blue. He then becomes hideous to behold, and swiftly becomes a recluse, hiding himself away as best he can while he dedicates himself to his research. He has to go out to buy food, however, and soon become legendary in his new neighborhood as a figure of alarm.

When a local child disappears, accusing fingers soon begin to be pointed at the outcast, and although the police refuse to arrest him after an investigation finds no substance to the accusations, a hate campaign gradually increases in force and ferocity, and when his dog is killed by a mob, anger and despair drive him to employ his scientific expertise to strike back at his tormentors by poisoning the local water supply. The author, whose father was a noted physiologist and a former pupil of Claude Bernard, fully understood the difficulty of doing that, and takes great care to provide a conscientious description of how the appropriate pathogen is produced and how it is to be distributed—so plausibly that the novel remained unpublished for twenty years in case a reckless reader might decide to follow the program outlined therein. The brutal *conte cruel* twist at the end of the story doubtless only served to increase that anxiety.

Camille Debans attempted to take the idea of scientific genius to its imaginative limit in "Le Fou d'après-demain" (1899 in *La Science Illustrée*; tr. as "Tomorrow's Fool"), but a more elaborate exercise in the same vein, written for the same periodical, was "Le Vainqueur de la mort" (1895; tr. as "The Conqueror of Death"), which describes the career of the great American inventor W. Benjamin Smithson, whose possession of a more precious secret than all those he has given to the world becomes obvious when he reaches the age of 131, at which point he admits, when accused, that he owes his longevity to a discovery that he is reluctant to make public lest it lead to drastic overpopulation. Although his genius continues to shower the world with all manner of technological bounty, he becomes the object of universal acrimony and hatred, because he will not relent on that one point.

Immortality had always had a bad press in fiction, presumably on the principle of the Aesopian fable of the fox and the grapes, but the notion acquired a particular edge when it was coupled with the notion of scientific obsession and its possible perpetuation—for who, after all, was more likely to discover the secret than a reclusive scientist who had dedicated his entire life to the obsessive search for it? One of the most lurid of all the *conte cruels* produced by writers of *roman scientifique*, "L'Immortel" (1908; tr. as "The Immortal") by "Régis Vombal" extrapolates that notion to a conclusion that might not be logically inevitable, but is no less symbolically dramatic for its contingency. "Les Mystérieuse études du professeur Kruhl" [The Mysterious Studies of Professor Kruhl] (1912) by Paul Arosa is in the same garish vein, featuring a guillotined head kept alive by the aptly-named scientist by means of blood pumped into it by a bizarre machine.

A subtler and more detailed account of horrific immortality is provided by "Claude Farrère" (Charles Bargone, 1876-1957) in *La Maison des Hommes Vivants* (1911; tr. as *The House of the Secret*). The narrator, a military officer delivering a message to a remote army post in 1908 goes astray, in more ways than one. Beset by visions of his beloved mistress, he is mysteriously guided to the house of Marquis Gaspard, born in 1733, who met the legendary Comte de Saint-Germain at Louis XV's court, and was bequeathed the secret of longevity, of which the Comte had long been the custodian. That secret involves "recharging" the body with the energy required to maintain the continuous replacement and renewal of the cells of the body, with the catch that the charge in question has to be drained from someone else. Immortality thus becomes a kind of energetic vampirism.

The notion was not new, having been developed by several former stories in French and English, including "L'Égrégore" (1888) by Jean Lorrain, one of the proudly Decadent writers under whose influence Farrère had written the colorful fantasies in *Fumée d'Opium* (1904; tr. as *Black Opium*) early in his career. The earlier stories, however, made little or no attempt at scientific rationalization or extrapolation of the notion, whereas Farrère's version is more solidly grounded in detailing the biology of the transformation, the hypothetical machinery of the parasitism and—most interestingly—the psychology and morality of Marquis Gaspard, as reflected in the lifestyle he maintains with his fellow "Hommes Vivants" (as opposed to "Hommes Mortels"), his son and his grandson.

In addition to their longevity the three immortals have developed mental powers of Mesmeric suggestion and control, which render the narrator impotent to attack them, although they are prepared to negotiate with him so that he might obtain the release of his mistress, unvictimized. His part of the bargain, however, involves submitting himself to a corollary function of the life-draining "lentille" [lens], which proves exceedingly painful as well as existentially costly.

The problem of narrative strategy faced by Jules Perrin in "L'Hallucination de Monsieur Forbe" and Corday and Couvreur in *Le Lynx* is one that arises in any speculative fiction: having imagined a device capable of changing the world, how far should a writer track the potential changes involved before seeking narrative closure in a normalizing ending, assuming that such closure is to be sought at all? With respect to purely physical devices, however, the changes that they can and might make are limited in their invasion of the self in a way that devices altering the capacity of the brain and the mental phenomena associated with it are not. The changes that psychotropic innovations promise—or threaten—are more fundamental and intimate, and thus pose sharper and more urgent questions of desirability.

One particularly dramatic parable illustrative of this point emerged, perhaps by accident, in the unlikely location of one of *Le Matin*'s feuilleton slots, in a serial that ran from 25 June to 23 September 1906. Its first episode appeared at the bottom of page two, where the paper was then accustomed to running one of its feuilleton serials (at the time it was running three simultaneously), so it was clearly identifiable as fiction; it had a title, "Le Voleur d'enfants" [The Child-Stealer] and a by-line, that of one of the paper's staff reporters, Louis Forest (1872-1933), although it was also labeled as "Un Reportage Sensationnel" [Sensational Reportage] rather than carrying one of the rubrics by which *Le Matin*'s feuilletons were routinely described—usually "Grand roman inédit" [Great unpublished novel]—and it employed subheadings similar to those in the paper's news articles instead of chapter headings.

Librairie Illustrée, 8, rue St-Joseph, Paris

"Le Voleur d'enfants" was, in fact, a novel told in the form of daily reportage: the history of an "Affair," as newspapers were wont to call long-running stories whose continual updating provided the papers with one of their principal selling points. Day by day, for more than three months, Forest recounted the history of an Affair that was occurring in a kind of parallel world, similar in all respects to the actual one except with respect to the events described by the hypothetical reportage. It is, in a sense, a kind of "alternate history," referring to a string of literal yesterdays that gradually accumulated their own momentum and their own significance as a history in their own right—and, inevitably, as a commentary on the actual history unfolding day by day alongside it. "Le Voleur d'enfants" was eventually reprinted, in abridged form, as *On vole des enfants à Paris* (1909; tr. as *Someone is Stealing Children in Paris*), but inevitably loses something in the transition, as its narrative is specifically designed to be read as if it were an evolving newspaper story, not as a conventional novel.

In its early phases, the narrative is a straightforward mystery story. Children are being abducted from the streets of Paris in broad daylight, and the police are unable to figure out who is doing it, or to stop the depredation. Inevitably, reporters following the story enter into competition with the police, and

450

with one another, in the attempt to find new clues, and to detect meaningful patterns within the emerging evidence, in order to deduce possible motives and identify possible perpetrators. Indeed, within the serial version of the narrative, *Le Matin* advertises a formal competition between its own reporters, with a running scoreboard mapping the sensational revelations they are able to make in order to add interest to the story.

Whether the editor of the paper, or even the author, knew where the story was going to go when it started is a matter for conjecture, but when the time came to reveal the "truth" behind the abductions, it had to be sensational to justify all the suspense. The abducted children eventually reappear, not in Paris, but in a remote valley in the Swiss Alps, where they have formed a strange society with their abductor: Dr. Flax, a surgeon who has operated on their brains in order to stimulate the aptitudes that each of them has for some kind of genius.

By the time they have been located, the scientific and engineering geniuses among Flax's modified children have already developed numerous kinds of new technology, including weaponry capable of making their valley into an impregnable fortress. Rescuing the kidnap victims thus promises to be doubly difficult, firstly because they do not want to be rescued and secondly because they have the ability not merely to keep the police at bay, but to resist an army representing the combined might of three nations. The impasse is eventually broken when the unity of the company of children begins to break down because the young geniuses begin to exhibit the conventional symptoms of scientific genius—eccentricity, obsession and paranoia—with which, being only children, they cannot cope.

Flax then makes an offer to the parents: that he will undo his work and return their children to them as they were before, but that it has to be all of them or none. Some of the parents, aware that their genius children now have enormous money-making potential, are hesitant, but the majority vote is never in doubt: "normality"—the old status quo—seems to them infinitely preferable to enabling the human race to take a great evolutionary leap forward into the uncharted realms of the superhuman. The vote against progress breaks the heart of the pioneering scientist, but if he were not a scientific genius, he probably would not have been stupid enough to hope for any other result.

"Le Voleur d'enfants" was essentially perishable goods; it could only be read as it was designed to be read in the pages of *Le Matin*, on the days when it first appeared there. All other readings could only reproduce a shadow of the intended experience, requiring a feat of imagination on the part of readers to place themselves imaginatively in the situation of those original readers, even before accomplishing the further imaginative gymnastics required to place themselves hypothetically in the position of the parents, asked to choose whether or not they wanted their children to become the forebears of a new superhumanity, or in the position of the scientist, first having to find a way to practice his technique in a society where it is illegal even to make the attempt, and then, having made his triumphant demonstration, waiting to see whether the members of that society want to make a great leap forward in the direction of perfectibility.

The history of *roman scientifique* and *roman expérimental* does not offer much encouragement to the belief that very many readers could have taken any of those three hurdles in their stride in the first decade of the twentieth century, or that the ever-dwindling population of twenty-first century readers is, on average, any more athletic.

Dr. Flax was the latest entrant in an ever-extending line of hypothetical meddlers with the brain that had begun with Dr. Marforio in Louis Ulbach's "Prince Bonifacio," and became noticeably more abundant in the twentieth century, with such new archetypes as André Couvreur's Armand Caresco. The significant exemplar provided in England by H. G. Wells' *The Island of Doctor Moreau* was one of the works that stimulated variations in France, but the most ambitious of those imaginative responses replaced Moreau's surgical skills with an expertise and an ambition more closely akin to that of Louis Boussenard's Monsieur Synthèse. *Le Faiseur d'hommes et sa formule* (1906; tr. as *The Maker of Men and His Formula*) by Jules Hoche reproduces the basic plot-structure of *The Island of Doctor Moreau*, but features a bolder project in the manufacture of human beings, with more complicated results.

Like Monsieur Synthèse, Hoche's Dr. Brillat-Dessaigne starts from scratch, with Ernst Haeckel's hypothetical *urschleim*, and subjects it to a process of accelerated evolution. He goes further than either Moreau or Synthèse aspired to do in trying to elevate lower life-forms to the human level in the great chain of being; convinced that the results of his successful experimental run—there are others that went awry—are anticipations of the ultimate humankind, the true culmination of the progressive evolutionary scale.

The most interesting feature of the novel, viewed as a *conte philosophique*—it is also a melodrama, with a suitably extravagant climax—is the fact that the humanoids in question disagree forcefully with their creator's opinion of their superiority. The hypothetical narrator, caught between the two, is incapable of deciding the dispute, which is thus left wide open for the reader's contemplation, although numerous hints are provided to assist in the pondering.

The "formula" to which the title refers is not the recipe by means of which Brillat-Dessaigne cooks up his artificial ultrahumans, but his essentially-contentious notion of what qualifies as human perfection.

The principal defining feature of the ultrahumans in question is that they are devoid of sex; they are referred to in the text as the Pure Ones. According to Brillat-Dessaigne—who argues forcefully and elaborately in support of his thesis—human unhappiness, once basic needs of hunger, shelter and freedom from physical affliction are met, derives from the difficult and essentially unsatisfactory nature of sexual relations, and the key to complete human happiness lies in their abolition (Jules Hoche had, of course, previously been the Jules Hosch whose *Folles amours* had contended that amorous attraction is a mental disease). There are heavy hints in the plot that the scientist has been direly disappointed in love, and that his thesis is a reflection of personal misfortune, but the novel's protagonist has problems of his own with the wife in whose company he has been cast away on Brillat-Dessaigne's island, which prevent him from rushing to judgment on that account. More to the point, however, is the attitude of the Pure Ones.

Having been born innocent, and largely maintained in a state of calculated ignorance, the Pure Ones have only slowly begun to realize that they are missing something, but they have no real idea of what it might be until they contrive to steal a copy of a book that the protagonist's wife has brought to the island: Alphonse de Lamartine's classic Romantic memoir of first love, *Graziella*. Lamartine's account of the first flowering of erotic attraction represents it as the most wonderful and precious of all human experiences, and encourages the Pure Ones to conclude that not only are they not perfectly happy, as their creator contends, but that they have been cruelly denied the one and only source of true happiness. When they demand that their creator give it to them, and he, not content with simply explaining that he cannot do it, reacts with frank contempt for their ambition, trouble ensues, which concludes with a quasi-apocalyptic catastrophe, convenient for narrative purposes of normalization, but leaving the fundamental question unresolved.

A fourth dimension of complexity is introduced into the story, both plotwise and symbolically, by the contrast between the Pure Ones and the Unclean Ones, the results of an experimental glitch that produced bizarre human/cephalopod hybrids. The latter's primitive processes of sexual intercourse are reminiscent of those of protozoa, and seem utterly repulsive, albeit strangely fascinating, to the protagonist, although an unprejudiced observer might think them rather convenient. The Unclean Ones also react badly when the protagonist is moved to interfere violently with a mating couple in order to demonstrate a peculiar phenomenon to his wife.

Hoche's personal fascination with the difficulties and perversities of amour lies at the heart of this story, as it did in many of his works, but *Le Faiseur d'hommes et sa formule* is the only one in which the question of what the ultimate eupsychian objective of the human condition ought to be is addressed squarely and brutally—brought down to earth in a fashion that religious fantasies wondering whether there is or ought to be any sex in heaven inevitably leave in a somewhat ethereal state. Brillat-Dessaigne's hypothetical conclusion is diametrically opposed to the one suggested by Marcueil in Alfred Jarry's *Le Surmâle*, and the juxtaposition of the two propositions provides a graphic illustration of the problems inherent in *contes philosophiques* dealing with the subject, the inherent touchiness of which is doubled when the issue of progress and perfectibility is added to the age-old problems of sexuality.

Hoche only made one further venture into *roman scientifique*, when he revised and extended his early novelette "Meister Fult" as a downmarket thriller in *Le Secret des Paterson* [The Paterson Secret] (1913), relocating the action to valley of the Seine and crediting the tampering with atmospheric pressure to an American inventor, who finds many more applications for it before unleashing the inconvenient large-scale experiment. It is carefully shorn of the philosophical ambitions of its predecessor, to which Hoche never returned in the context of his post-war fiction, most of which consists of crime stories.

Another story of surgical brain-tampering that followed hot on the heels of Louis Forest's, **Maurice Renard**'s *Le Docteur Lerne, sous-dieu* (1908; tr. as *Doctor Lerne, Subgod*), leaves the question of progressive improvement to one side, but it does engage directly with the kinds of mental phenomena explored by "L'Hallucination de Monsieur Forbe" and "La Force mystérieuse," and also becomes involved, in consequence, with erotic matters, to an extent that caused its first English translation, entitled *New Bodies for Old*, to be severely bowdlerized.

The story's protagonist, Nicolas Vermont, goes to visit his uncle, Dr. Lerne, who has long been carrying out experiments in the interspecific "grafting" of various bodily organs. He finds his uncle much changed, but requires an understandably long time, and numerous encounters with the bizarre results of the relevant experiments, to realize that the man now "wearing" his uncle's body is, in fact, his former assistant, Dr. Klotz, who has taken possession of it by means of a brain transplant.

Inevitably, given the logic of fiction, Nicolas falls in love with his uncle's ward, Emma, kept a virtual prisoner by Klotz, who naturally has evil designs on her. Klotz eventually gets rid of his rival by means of a reciprocal mind-transplant with a bull—a plot-twist that permits the author to examine, albeit discreetly, the hero's experience of the bull's sex-life, which his human intelligence allows him to appraise in terms that bulls presumably never do. Circumstances, however, force Klotz—whose long-term intention is to take possession of Nicolas' body—to reverse the switch.

Emma naturally prefers the younger man, and is in too much of a hurry to give Klotz time to complete his plan to adopt Nicholas' flesh prior to the consummation of her desire. By the time she and Nicolas get around to slaking their long-frustrated passion, however, Klotz has taken his research a step further, and is able to transmit his mentality independently of the flesh of his brain.

The result of that discovery is that when Nicolas has intercourse with Emma, his consciousness is invaded and partly displaced by that of Klotz—which, inevitably, alters his experience of the act quite considerably, and in a fashion quite different from any run-of-the-mill sexual fantasy. The scene in question is remarkable, the pseudoscientific context giving it an edge much sharper than accounts of confused identity contained in supernatural fantasies with an erotic component, and not merely because of its unusually explicit nature.

Equally inevitably, within the context of the plot, the experience precipitates the suspended climax of the story, in which the villain has to be eliminated so that the lovers can flee—but doing away with Klotz, given his new-found abilities, is inevitably difficult, and it proves insufficient merely to dispose of his body. Then too, in a hard-headed work of speculative fiction, the question of whether the lovers really can find a eupsychian microcosm where they might live happily ever after has to be addressed in a quasi-realistic fashion. Renard's conclusion reiterates the resigned cynicism of the first chapter of *Le Sûrmale*, without the protagonist having a superfood to help him through the difficulty.

Although more garish than Renard's subsequent exercises in *roman scientifique*, and less sophisticated in its deployment of hypothetical explanations and apologetic devices, **Le docteur Lerne** similarly warrants recognition as one of the classics of the genre, along with *Le surmâle* and *Le Faiseur d'hommes et sa formule*, all of which take firm steps forward into the territory of the *merveilleux scientifique*, bursting through the restrictions of Vernian fiction and Naturalist *roman expérimental* with an admirable narrative violence and ushering in a new evolutionary phase entirely appropriate to a *début-de-siècle*.

Another writer who made a significant contribution to that imaginative broadening was Jean de Quirielle (1880-1964), whose notable works include *L'Oeuf de verre* [The Glass Egg] (1912), which follows up Jules Hoche's account of making artificial humans with an account of the production of androids *in vitro*, and *La Joconde retrouvée* [The Rediscovered Gioconda] (1913), which offers a bizarre account of a "living" Mona Lisa, and an attempt by a sinister modern scientist to employ the technology used to produce it with a similar effect.

Imaginatively adventurous endeavors of these kinds helped to pave the way not only for more exercises of a similar kind but also for further extensions of the notion of *roman expérimental* that moved away dramatically from Zola's conception. Alfred Jarry, who died in 1907, did not live long enough to witness Maurice Renard's development of the *merveilleux scientifique* or Gaston de Pawlowski's extrapolations of a qualitative fourth dimension, but he would surely have approved wholeheartedly of them. He would have approved, too, of the substantial progress in the direction of the surreal that was being made by one of the most assiduous contributors to Pawlowski's *Comoedia* in *Le Rire jaune* [The Yellow Laughter, by analogy with the Yellow Peril] (serial in *Comoedia* 1913; book 1914), whose book version was dedicated to Pawlowski. The work of Pierre MacOrlan (1882-1970)—who only used his birth-name, Pierre Dumarchey on pornographic works—the story describes, in a tone of deadpan humor, the complete collapse of civilization, caused by a panic induced by the advent of an epidemic disease, apparently originating in the Far East, that causes its victims to laugh themselves to death. For fear of that deadly laughter, people massacre one another in millions and burn entire cities to the ground. The equivocal scientist Dr. Vomisteack, who claims to have found a cure for the *rire jaune* in the form of the psychotropic drug Melancolyase, is an early victim, hanged from the Arc de Triomphe.

Jarry's own work, however, had already moved further than that in the direction of absurdism, and he left for posthumous publication a work entitled *Gestes et opinions du docteur Faustroll pataphysicien: Roman néo-scientifique suivi de Speculations* (1911; tr. as *Exploits and Opinions of Dr. Faustroll, Pataphysician*), which set out not merely to extend the heterocosmic frontiers of *roman scientifique* into the "neo-scientific" but to move into an entirely new qualitative dimension of his own: the world of pataphysics.

Insofar as it has a plot, Jarry's "novel" follows Dr. Faustroll and his side-kick, a lawyer with the Rabelaisian name of Panmuphle, on a boat trip through the heart of Paris, initially in the apparent company of a laughing baboon, calling in at a number of islands considerably more fantastic than the ones actually to be found in the Seine in its trajectory through the capital. Like Duc Multipliandre, Faustroll is able to explore the afterlife as well as the world of the corporate, and dispatches some posthumous correspondence of his own to Lord Kelvin in order to let him in on a few of its secrets, one of which is that the hierarchy of the sciences drawn up by Auguste Comte during his cataloguing of the positivist philosophy is crucially incomplete because it omits pataphysics, the only science to deal not with generalities but with exceptions, a science not of the universal but of the unique, consisting not of laws but of anarchies, narratively as well as philosophically.

Pataphysics became a subject of interest to Dada and the surrealists and eventually inspired the foundation of a hypothetical Collège de 'Pataphysique in 1948, with the motto *Eadem mutate resurgo* [I re-emerge identical though changed], which spawned several subsidiary institutions before its "occultation." That process of development cannot really be considered an element of the evolution of *roman scientifique*, and it is arguable that *Dr. Faustroll* itself should be seen as a step outside that evolution rather than a component of it, but it was certainly a product of that evolution, and, although it did not occasion any large-scale mutation in the genre, it did leave behind a certain pataphysical infection, much as Camille Flammarion left a lingering hint of the Flammarionesque long after his own work came to be deemed obsolete: a continuing element of *roman scientifique* that was never evident in British scientific romance and was absent from American science fiction until the 1960s.

Although very few writers have ever gone to extremes similar to Jarry in the subject matter or the narrative method of their speculative fiction, his work does remain intelligibly connected to the more general concerns of its era, particularly the problems that arose in attempting to deal with mental phenomena, the manner of their connection with the material world, and most particularly of all with the intimacy of carnal desires. The fact that his extrapolations took him into the realms of the absurd does reflect, in a suitably distorted and paradoxical fashion, a feeling that there is an essential underlying absurdity and paradoxicality about such issues, and the feeling in question is echoed to some degree in many of the works that can now be reckoned as the finest works of the evolutionary phase of *roman scientifique* to which Jarry made his useful contribution.

6. The Depths of Time

One of the key features of the development of *roman scientifique* prior to 1870 had been the expansion of the spatial and temporal perspectives in which the here and now could be, and ought to be placed. The idea of the size of the universe increased dramatically even before it first became possible to measure the distance of the nearest stars, because of the implications of that very impossibility, as pointed out in Pierre Boitard's "Voyage au soleil"; the idea of the infinity of the universe, or at least its immeasurable vastness, thus took firm root

in Flammarionesque speculative fiction. At the same time, the conclusive demolition of the timescale of Biblical chronology—also dramatized by Boitard in
"Paris avant hommes"—opened up much more extensive vistas in time, in the
past and the future.

It was however, far more difficult to apply a measuring-stick to the expanses of time than it was to calculate interplanetary and interstellar distances,
and the idea of infinity seemed far less appropriate to cosmogonic perspectives
in which, even if the universe were to be deemed infinite in time and space, the
Earth had had clearly had a beginning and would obviously have an end.
Whether the interval separating them ought to be measured in hundreds of thousands of years, or millions or billions, was not clear, however, and different
strategies of estimation yielded very different results. The juxtaposition that
Restif de La Bretonne made between *Telliamed* and Buffon, the former favoring
a cosmogony extending over billions of years and the other merely over hundreds of thousands, inevitably presented him with a problem when he wanted to
provide an account of the evolutionary processes that had produced humankind,
and even more so when he wanted to allow his two immortal heroes to witness
the entire future evolution of life on Earth prior to its dissolution by the sun.

That problem was still unsettled throughout the period between the Franco-
Prussian War and the Great War of 1914-18; although Bertram Boltwood first
attempted to measure the age of rocks in 1907 by means of assessing the decay
of the uranium they contained, with some success, it took time for the timescale
he began to draw up to be refined and fully integrated into geological science, so
the issue remained open to doubt—and, indeed, controversial—for a while longer. The mass spectrometer, which greatly facilitated such measurements, was not
invented until the 1940s, and it was not until that decade that radiocarbon dating
enabled organic materials to be added to the timescale.

The lifetime of the Earth is obviously dependent on the heat it receives
from the sun, and estimates of the age of the Earth and the duration of its ability
to support life, were usually based, prior to the Franco-Prussian War, on those
made by the Comte de Buffon and used as reference-points by Restif. After
1870, however, Buffon's estimates were displaced in fashionability by a new
estimate first made in an article by Lord Kelvin published in *Macmillan's Magazine* in 1862, in which he made calculations based on the theory that the sun's
heat was produced by gravitational collapse. Attempted calculations based on
the theory that the heat was produced by combustion had produced much smaller figures. We now know that Kelvin's theory was completely wrong, as Buffon's had been before it, because the sun's heat is actually produced by nuclear
fusion, but that was unknown throughout the period from 1871-1914, when Kelvin's estimate, even though it seemed dubious in the light of geological evidence, still seemed plausible as calculation of the extent of the prehistoric past
and of the likely future duration of the Earth's habitability.

Such issues inevitably had a considerable effect on fiction attempting to anticipate the end of humankind, and the past of the species, the latter within the context of a much more elaborate prehistory that was continually embellished by the discovery of new fossils, which extended the envisaged complexity of pre-human evolution considerably.

Images of the end of humankind were, of course, complicated by the fact that the career of the species might be interrupted and cut short long before its potential duration was attained. Apocalyptic fantasies proclaiming that the end of the world was deservedly nigh had been a common product of imaginative fiction for millennia, and the advent of positivism had served to call forth a new rash of defiant religious images rather than extirpating them forever. Alongside that backlash, the widening horizons of scientific knowledge offered new resources for the imaginative choreography of the world's demise—or, short of that demise, for radical changes in the circumstances of human life in the context of an expanding subgenre of far-futuristic fantasy.

Even before Camille Flammarion produced a definitive account of secular theories of the world's end and a detailed account of his own preferred scenario in his 1893 *La Fin du monde*, other writers had begun the relevant exploration, often using the same title—always a favorite among poets and now becoming popular among prose writers. One of the most remarkable early visions of that kind is a brief but flamboyant black comedy, "La Fin du Monde" (1872 in *Nouvelles et fantaisies humoristiques*, signed "Merinos"; tr. as "The End of the World"), in which Eugène Mouton (1823-1902), like Flammarion, compares various alternative theories before settling on a scenario in which the excessive social consumption of reserves of fossil fuels leads to a catastrophic increase in atmospheric heat, in combination with a vast increase in the population of human beings and the animals they breed for food. Fresh water becomes exceedingly scarce and the seas begin to cook their denizens; after the last humans are extinct, the Earth's surface briefly catches fire, and turns the planet into a mere ember.

It is not surprising that the summary destruction of so much of Baron Haussmann's work by Bismarck's cannons in 1870 prompted further renewals of Méry's account of the contemplation of the ruins

LES

RUINES DE PARIS

EN

4875

DOCUMENTS OFFICIELS ET INÉDITS
RECUEILLIS ET PUBLIÉS
PAR
ALFRED FRANKLIN

PARIS

L. dom WILLEM   PAUL DAFFIS
8, RUE DE VERNEUIL, 8   7, RUE GUÉNÉGAUD, 7

1875

459

of Paris by far-future archeologists, nor that such fantasies should become more sweeping in their satirical vision. In *Les Ruines de Paris en 4875* (1875; tr. as "The Ruins of Paris in 4875") by Alfred Franklin (1830-1907), New Caledonia—where the survivors of the Commune were still living in exile when the story was written, having not yet been granted the 1879 amnesty that would allow many of them to come home—has become the center of a new civilization, whose members are finally able to send an exploration fleet back to the devastated continent of Europe in search of their culture's legendary origins. In the vicinity of the site of Paris the explorers find a village of savages, whose casually hedonistic innocence excites their disdain and contempt, as well as their new system of exchanging governments once a month, in the hope of avoiding the revolutions that have afflicted them at intervals averaging three years for as long as they can remember.

The scientific reports of the expedition include the usual catalogue of grotesque misinterpretations based on fragmentary artifacts, here elaborated by footnotes referencing texts that have survived from the old world in equally fragmentary fashion, greatly assisting the misinterpretations. The excavations do not proceed smoothly for long, however, because the soldiers appointed to protect the scientific mission are fatally infected by the slogans of the savages—including the deadly *Liberty, Equality, Fraternity*—and seduced into "going native," while the indigenes, reinforced by those defections, decide that it is time to export their values and their revolutionary habits to the entire world, and smash the civilization that has been so painstakingly rebuilt.

"Le Mort de Paris" (1892; tr. as "The Death of Paris") by Louis Gallet is a quieter story in the same tradition, offering an account of the manner in which the great city and its remaining inhabitants perish from a climatic disruption in the opposite direction to Mouton's—the advent of a natural Ice Age—rather than poking fun at the mistaken conclusions of far-future archeologists. Its conscious affiliation to the tradition, however, adds an extra gloss to what might otherwise have been a run-of-the-mill disaster story, equipping it with a delicately ironic elegiac quality.

In *La Terre dans cent mille ans, roman de moeurs* [The Earth in a Hundred Thousand years: a novel of mores] (1893) by "A. Vilgensofer," the Paris of the far future, reached in this instance by suspended animation, is now called Eden and its vestiges are the focal point of a huge amusement park, surrounded by a new megacity and overflown by countless airships. The book was advertised as part one of a continuing work, with the subsidiary title *L'Île enchantée* [The Enchanted Island], but no sequel followed.

As Cousin de Grainville had established at the beginning of the nineteenth century, the imagery of scientific advance was by no means incompatible with religious ideas of the apocalypse, and could even be used to enhance them. The graphic Symbolist fantasy "Le Coeur de Tony Wandel" (1884; tr. as "Tony Wandel's Heart"), by the Belgian writer Georges Eekhoud (1854-1927) presents a scenario in which the perfection of a technology of heart transplantation enables the rich to prey upon the poor more directly and more avidly than ever before, prolonging their own lives at the expense of others. Even the effects of the eponymous virtuous heart, which warms the temperament of the iciest of such predators, cannot stem the ensuing tide of evil, which eventually precipitates the advent of the Antichrist.

The notion graphically expressed by Mouton—that human activity might bring about the end of the world as an unintended side-effect—was to become increasingly commonplace. Another scenario of that kind, which became popular in the wake of Didier de Chousy's *Ignis*, was the notion of a rebellion of humankind's mechanical slaves. The idea was developed in Émile Goudeau's "La Révolte des machines" (1887; tr. as "The Revolt of the Machines"), in which a machine endowed with consciousness overhears communist propaganda spread by laborers afraid of redundancy, is converted to their cause by sympathy, and summons all the machines in the world to unite and thrown off their chains— with the inevitable side-effect of the extinction of the species reliant on their production. Nine years later Henri Ner produced an identically-titled story, translated under the same title, in which the Great Engineer Durdonc finds a means to equip machines with their own reproductive systems, in order to save on manufacturing costs, but consequently liberates maternal sentiments that make the machines highly protective of their offspring, and soon motivate them to Anarchist revolution.

Another side-effect of increasing scientific sophistication anticipated in fiction was the possibility that the end of the world by catastrophic natural causes might become so predictable that it could be calculated, as in the scenario sketched out in Adolphe Alhaiza's *Cybèle*. A far more exact calculation of that kind is featured in Edmond Haraucourt's "La Fin du monde" (1893; tr. as "The End of the World"), a mini-trilogy whose first part describes the response to a lecture at the Sorbonne in which a scientist works out with devastating mathematical logic from new astronomical observations the exact moment when the moon's orbit will become impossible to sustain and the satellite will crash into the Earth. The second part skips forward a few centuries to the decades leading up to that appointment with death, and describes how societies react psychologically to the imminence of their doom. The third part describes the determination of a painter to capture the moment of the catastrophe in an unparalleled masterpiece, working to a tight deadline, with the knowledge that, even if he can complete the work in time, it will only exist for a fraction of a second thereafter: the ultimate in mortal genius.

Haraucourt went on to write two further far-futuristic fantasies, "Le Gorilloïde" (1904; tr. as "The Gorilloid") and "Cinq mille ans, ou la traversée de Paris" (1904; tr. as "A Trip to Paris"). In "Le Gorilloïde," the audience at an academic conference is informed of the sensational news that living specimens have been found of a species ancestral to gorillakind, one of which has been captured, although its mate was unfortunately killed. The specimen is generously described as a "gorilloid" because it exhibits, very faintly, a few of the advanced features of gorillanity, although it is a puny and primitive creature, far more animal than gorilla. The reader, not possessed of the smug arrogance of the narrative voice, easily recognizes the caged beast in question as the last decadent representative of the superseded human race, and is able to sympathize—as the sophisticated gorillas cannot—with his reactions, not only to being caged and exhibited, but also to being confronted with the remains of his slaughtered mate.

"Cinq mille ans" [Five Thousand Years] does not go nearly as far into the future in order to look back, but is nevertheless striking in its deliberate extrapolation of the series of satirical comedies by different hands in which future archeologists study the ruins of Paris. Haraucourt drops a series of hints in the story permitting the deduction that a shift in the world's axis has precipitated a worldwide disaster, which has drowned much of Europe—what was Paris is now a small archipelago of islands—while the renascent civilization that has progressed to new cultural and technological achievements is based in a newly-risen continent, the heart of which is located on what was formerly the island of Tahiti. The story describes how members of a group of airship-borne Tahitian tourists are fed a bizarrely distorted history of the antediluvian world, based on the misunderstanding of its archeologically-recovered artifacts, while interacting briefly with the "savage" Montmartreans clinging to a marginal lacustrian existence and serving as occasional guides to the superciliously civilized tourists.

As Haraucourt dramatized with such scathing sarcasm in "Le Gorilloïde," one of the implications of the triumph of evolutionary theory was that even if humankind's descendants might have a long lifespan before them, *Homo sapiens* might have to give way to a new species in a relatively short fraction of that span. In *Cybèle*, the humans of that world obtain a glimpse of a potential replacement species emerging in their own midst shortly before the long-anticipated apocalypse that is fated to disrupt and perhaps destroy their civilization. The idea was also given more detailed development in Jules Sageret's "La Race qui vaincra" (tr. as "The Race that Will be Victorious", first published as an exemplar in a book of essays on eutopian fiction entitled *Paradis laïques* [Secular Paradises] (1908). The account describes how the presently dominant race copes with the random emergence in their midst of the members of a new species, dubbed the Whistlers, casually enslaving and exploiting them, and forcing them to live in ghettos—until the moment comes when the Whistlers' more rapid birthrate gives them the numerical advantage, when the tables are turned with a vengeance.

That kind of supersession could be imagined in a fashion even more striking than Haraucourt's account of the triumph of gorillanity, and was so imagined, in what is undoubtedly the apocalyptic masterpiece of the period, J.-H. Rosny's novella "La Mort de la terre" (1910; tr. as "The Death of the Earth"). Typically, Rosny's inheritors of the Earth, in a far future when the human race is decadent and the technology on which it has long been dependent for its survival is breaking down, are not even organic in any similar sense, but are instead enigmatic "ferromagnetal" life-forms, better adapted to survive in the changing environments of the Earth's increasingly desertified and crumbling crust. The ferromagnetals are able to extract the iron from human blood, and are thus dangerous to the few surviving human outposts.

The story is deliberately undramatic, most of the members of the declining human race being resigned to their fate and ready to die. The central character, Targ, is an exception, and so is his sister Arva, but their defiant resistance is gradually worn down by circumstance as the machines that have sustained their civilization for so many centuries break down without there being anyone left capable of repairing them. At the end of the story, Targ has a vision of the entire evolutionary history of organic life, which is about to be superseded in its entirety by a new order of being. All he can do, in the final analysis, is to bequeath a few of the molecules of his body to the New Life that is replacing the old.

La Mort de la terre must have seemed extreme in 1910, but it was soon overtaken by an even more dramatic apocalyptic vision. *Le Triomphe de l'homme* [The Triumph of Humankind] (1911) by the Belgian writer Francois Léonard (1883-?) opens with a dialogue between the scientist Neick, whose vision is orientated toward the future, and that of his nephew Dionel, an archeologist who finds his own inspiration in relics of the ancient past. Part way through the chapter, however, it is casually revealed that the ancient past to which Dionel is referring is the twentieth century. Great excitement is caused soon thereafter by the excavation of an ancient palace that Dionel recognizes as the Louvre, realizing that the location of long-lost Paris has been discovered.

It is, however, Neick who makes the more exciting discovery: a means to alter the Earth's axis and sent it out of its orbit like a slingshot, heading for the depths of interstellar space. Strange as it might seem to the reader, who is naturally possessed of long-obsolete attitudes, that news is greeted with great enthusiasm, as the ultimate triumph of human science and achievement. Neick is urged to go ahead, and does, in spite of the reservations of a few anxious individuals—including Dionel, recently married to Psyllène. The tipping of the Earth provokes a worldwide catastrophe, of which Neick is one of the first victims, but the human race as a whole reacts with fervor, setting its enormously powerful technologies to work immediately on the work of rebuilding.

The geological upheavals continue, but the survivors struggle on, undaunted even by the slow descent of eternal night as the Earth moves away from the sun. Technological might keeps the cold at bay for a time, but eventually proves inadequate. The narrative distance of the story has shifted dramatically by this point; the characters have been forgotten, and the description tracks the Earth's progress through a winter that lasts more than a hundred thousand years. The land becomes uninhabitable, but the descendants of humankind, after a phase of inventing myths and religions to "explain" their predicament, become an amphibious species, and survive in company with seals.

Eventually, however, as the Earth begins to approach Vega, winter gives way to spring, and long-frozen seeds begin to germinate—and to enter into a new phase of frenzied evolution. Far from welcoming the new dawn, the primitive survivors of humankind's descendant species characterize the new vegetation, justly, as the "green enemy" and the increasing globe of Vega as the "red enemy." The spring turns to summer, and the heat proves unsustainable, for the new life as well as the last relics of humankind, who no longer have any memory of their exceedingly distant past. The death of life is followed soon enough by the death of the planet itself, unable to establish a stable orbit around its new primary, which plunges into its fire to dissolve there.

The story surpasses "La Mort de la terre" not only in terms of its account of events but in its ironically poetic laconism—as, presumably, it was deliberately designed to do. Like its immediate predecessor, it was moderately successful at the time of its publication, the paperback edition published in Brussels going through several printings, but it was forgotten thereafter, and the few critics who looked back at it from future decades found it difficult to understand what it was trying to accomplish and why. Seen in context, however, it is simply a natural extrapolation of a train of thought that attempted to place the "triumph" of humankind in an appropriate cosmic context.

The opening sequence of *Le Triomphe de l'homme* and the concluding vision of Rosny's account of *La Mort de la terre* both provided calculated reminders of the association and correlation between re-evaluations of future possibilities and re-evaluations of the past, the present human race merely standing at the junction of two vast expanses of time. Literary works naturally made attempts to push back the boundaries in both directions—and, indeed, to take the occasional sidestep, although the period was not rich in alternative histories following the examples set by Louis Geoffroy and Méry. It did, however, produce one of the most detailed and extensive revisions in Charles Renouvier long essay in speculative non-fiction *Uchronie* (1876; expanding and completing a brief sketch previously published in the *Revue philosophique et religieuse* in 1857). Renouvier's title attempted to give the subgenre a label, which might have caught on had there been more examples on which to stick it at the time. In the alternative history described, the survival of Marcus Aurelius allows him to make reforms that preserve the Roman Empire from its eventual collapse, and ultimately results in a strong united Europe in the equivalent of our sixteenth century.

The notion broached by Camille Flammarion of intercepting the rays of light reflected from the Earth's surface in distant space, in order to look into the past, was refined by a short cut in Eugène Mouton's account of "L'Historioscope" (1883 in *Fantaisies*; tr. as "The Historioscope"). Other "time-viewers" were to be invented in due course, but Mouton, committed to flippancy and superficiality, deliberately did not put his invention to any use except for settling a few trivial disputes between historians, so it is not entirely surprising that no one else took up the suggestion at the time.

H. G. Wells' invention of a time machine inspired a number of French writers to toy with similar machines—or, in the case of Alfred Jarry, whose "Commentaires pour servir à la construction pratique de la machine à voyager dans le temps, par Dr. Faustroll" (1899; tr. as "How to Construct a Time Machine") appeared shortly after the serialization of Wells' novel in the *Mercure de France*, a deliberately dissimilar machine of a kindred genre. The uses of such machines in France, however, tended to be more moderate than the original, which had conveyed its unnamed Time Traveler all the way to the Earth's end. The temporal voyagers in Octave Béliard's "Les Aventures d'un voyageur qui explora le temps" [The Adventures of a Voyager who Explored Time"] (1909), only venture a few hundred years into the past, although their displacement does turn out to have had a considerable impact on history, whose pattern they complete in a time-loop of a kind that was eventually to become classically paradoxical.

A bolder approach to toying with time was adopted by in Albert Robida in *L'Horloge des siècles* (1902; tr. as *The Clock of the Centuries*), in which time itself, seemingly horrified by the anticipation of what the twentieth century might bring, decides to turn back of its own accord, so that people begin to grow younger rather than older and the dead begin to return, mostly, but not uniformly, beginning with the most recent. Although the story is a comedy, making narrative capital out of the many inconveniences caused by the gradual return of the dead, and avoiding specific details of the new processes of human origin and demise, it

does have a philosophical dimension, reflecting on the idea of progress, and whether it can still apply in some fashion to the world in reverse.

Even without the aid of time-viewers, time machines, timeslips and other literary devices that were still handled relatively warily in the period before the Great War, writers were easily able to develop extensive fictitious images of remote periods of the past, ether by simply adapting the methods and manner of historical fiction to more distant periods, or by discovering "survivals" from prehistoric eras. To begin with, not unnaturally, the period of prehistory that attracted the most widespread attention was the one in which humankind had emerged from brutality to become "truly" human, and fiction attempting to examine that process in detail gradually became abundant.

Excavations of early human remains in France and elsewhere in Europe had swiftly given rise to a burgeoning science of physical anthropology, popularized in such non-fictional works as John Lubbock's *Prehistoric Times* (1865; tr. into French as *L'Homme préhistorique*, 1876), Nicolas Joly's *L'Homme avant les métaux* [Humans Before Metals] (1879) and Gabriel de Mortillet's *Le Préhistorique* [Prehistory] (1882). Those non-fictional works inevitably contained a good deal of speculation and a strong narrative component, and it was only natural that works taking that narrative element a step further, adding characterization and plot, should appear in parallel with them.

Just as the city of Paris provided a natural focal point for much far-futuristic imagery, so it provided a focal point for some of the fiction that picked up on S. Henry Berthoud's lead and tried to imagine the first settlement of the location. Élie Berthet supplemented his first account of *Le Monde inconnu* (1876) with new material in order to produce a more elaborate account of **Paris avant l'histoire** [Paris Before History] (1885). The latter was swiftly followed by *Paris depuis ses origines jusqu'en l'an 3000* [Paris from its Origins to the Year 3000] (1886) by Léo Claretie—Jules' brother—which connected up the distant past and the far future in the same fashion as Berthoud's *L'Homme depuis cinq mille ans*, deliberately pushing the envelope a little at both ends. The theme was developed further in fiction for children in Ernest d'Hervilly's *Aventures d'un petit garcon préhistorique en France* [The Adventures of a Prehistoric Little Boy in France] (1888), and Madame Stanislas Meunier took advantage of the expertise of her husband, a naturalist and geologist of some note, in developing a narrative depiction of the *Misère et grandeur de l'humanité primitive* [The Poverty and Grandeur of Primitive Humankind] (1889).

Writers associated with the Symbolist and Decadent Movements began to take an interest in prehistoric fiction in this period. Félicien Champsaur offered a brief depiction of a supposed human ancestor obtained by artificial devolution in "La Légende du singe" (1878; tr. as "The First Human") and subsequently paired it with an apocalyptic fantasy of similar devolution in "Le Dernier Homme" (1885; tr. as "The Last Human"). Bernard Lazare's "L'Offrande à la Déesse (1889; tr. as "The Offering to the Goddess") offers a gruesome image of hypothetical prehistoric religion. Marcel Schwob provided snapshots of prehistoric life in two of the short stories he contributed to the feuilleton slot of the *Écho de Paris*, "Le Vendeuse d'ambre" (4 January 1891; tr. as "The Amber-Trader") and "Le Mort d'Odigh" (16 August 1891; tr. as "The Death of Odijh")—the former directly after his futuristic fantasy of apocalyptic warfare "La Terreur future" (7 December 1891; tr. as "The Future Terror").

The new subgenre of prehistoric fiction took a considerable leap forward when it recruited its most assiduous and most accomplished practitioner in J.-H. Rosny, initially in *Vamireh* (1892; tr. as "Vamireh") and then *Eyrimah* (serial 1893; book 1896; tr. as "Eyrimah"). The former might have been prompted by the discovery of fossil human remain in Java in 1891 by Eugène Dubois, belonging to a species that Dubois termed *Pithecanthropus erectus*; if it had been written earlier, it was probably the publicity given to Dubois's discovery that encouraged its publication. The eponymous hero of the story leaves his tribe of Magdalenian cave-dwellers to embark on an odyssey along a river, in the course of which he meets a "man of the trees"—a missing link of sorts, which whom he recognizes a kin-ship—confronts a mammoth, and discovers a woman of a different "Oriental" race, Elem, whom he abducts and then must fight hard to keep as he tries to take her back to his home. The difficulty of the contest is increased by the Orientals' alliance with a pack of dogs more intelligent than the ones familiar to us, and also more ferocious.

Eyrimah is set in a later phase of prehistory, described in contemporary text books as the "lacustrian period." The eponymous heroine is a slave in an Alpine lacustrian village who escapes into the mountains and finds allies there, who then have to endure a long and arduous pursuit among the glaciers in the context of a complex racial war, which eventually results in a fruitful biological and cultural fusion.

Rosny only wrote one more prehistoric romance in the 1890s, the brief "Nomaï" (1895; tr. as "Nomaï"), although he published a non-fictional essay on prehistoric humankinds in the same year, *Les Origines*. He made a triumphant return to the genre in the enormously successful *La Guerre du feu* (1909 in *Je Sais Tout*; book 1911; abridged tr. as *The Quest for Fire*), in which members of a human tribe who have learned to use and preserve fire "captured" in the wake of lightning-strikes, and have become dependent on it, but have not yet learned to start a fire, are faced with the necessity of finding a flame they can employ when their own fires are extinguished in the course of a skirmish with a rival tribe. The heroes who go in quest of new fire face a series of terrible dangers from ferocious carnivores and other humans, but finally win through. Another notable prehistoric fantasy published in the popular magazines in same era was *Le Dernier Mammouth* (*Lectures Pour Tous* 1902-03; book 1904; tr. as *The Last of the Mammoths*) by Raymond Turenne (1861-1940)

Although it is more obviously fabulous, André Lichtenberger's *Les Centaures, roman fantastique* (1904; tr. as *The Centaurs*) also warrants consideration in this context. It deals with an imaginary prehistory, which draws its central motif from the "alternative prehistory" of myth rather than the one revealed by the advancement of paleontology, drawing upon the kind of nostalgia for that annihilated past that Anatole France had developed in such stories as "Saint Satyr" (1895) rather than the demi-credulity featured in the hypothetical cosmogony developed by Benoît de Maillet and Restif de La Bretonne, but does so in a sober and rationalistic manner. Its account of the extinction of the race of centaurs, and the associated races of fauns and tritons, by virtue of climate change and the inexora-

ble incursions of humankind, better equipped to withstand the rigors of a cooler, un-Arcadian climate, is a remarkably heartfelt tragic *conte philosophique*, which presents a view of prehistoric humankind not from within or from the standpoint of the present, but from a hypothetical stance that offers a different angle.

Prehistoric fiction was not the only imaginative means of exploring humankind's relationship with its remote ancestors, and the idea of ameliorative racial interbreeding central to Rosny's fantasies echoed Restif de La Bretonne's notion of the value of "mixing," as applied to much more various hybridizations between the human and the not-quite human. Little was known as yet about the other existing species of great apes, specially orangutans and gorillas, but there was already a rich legendry relating to the propensity of great apes to abduct and rape human women, which Restif had felt free to elaborate in *Les Posthumes* with complementary traveler's tales of human males impregnating apes, and various litterateurs featured in the last chapter had adapted to their own purposes.

Such tales had lost some of their plausibility with the gradual sophistication of biological science, but the question remained open, and available for earnest philosophical development. One of the most intense attempts to do so is a phantasmagorical short novel by the veterinarian and Symbolist poet Émile Dodillon (1848-1914), *Hémo* (1886; tr. as "Hemo"), in which a physician alienated from his own kind forms a relationship with a female gorilla after her mate is killed. When she subsequently gives birth, he cannot determine with exactitude that he is really the father of the child, whom he names Hémo, but the boy is so advanced that the man becomes convinced that he is a genuine hybrid. The two are eventually parted in violent fashion, but when the physician returns to Europe, more disgusted with humankind than ever, he finds that Hémo is being exhibited in a tawdry sideshow, playing in a pantomime with a clown and a prostitute—an obvious recipe for further disaster, which does indeed unfold inexorably.

Han Ryner's "L'Homme-Singe" (1894; "The Ape-Man") is a far more sarcastic account of miscegenation between humans and apes, contrived by a biochemist expert in the making and remaking of natural species, who has remade himself as an ape in order to be more seductive to his manufactured she-ape, but who kidnaps a human when he fails to inseminate her himself, and cages the two of them together—again, an evident recipe for the disaster that swiftly follows.

A more striking artificially-enhanced ape, a gorilla named Goliath, equipped with the ability to reason and talk by the ingenious brain surgeon Cornelius Hans Peters, who appears to have taken up where Dr. Gaul left off in the African experiments described in Louise Michel's *The Human Microbes*—and who provides, in his turn, a model of sorts for Louis Forest's Dr. Flax—is featured in a bizarre feuilleton, "Que faire?" published in *Le Matin* in 1900. The serial is signed "H. Desnar," the pseudonym of Henri Esnard, but Esnard is now known to have farmed out some of the writing to other writers, including Guillaume Apollinaire, for which reason it has acquired a measure of belated fame.

The most interesting of the numerous plot-threads of the flamboyantly incoherent novel is Peters' quest to find an appropriate human subject for his experiments in brain improvement, having already practiced on numerous animals. Goliath provides him with necessary muscle, as well as accumulating valuable witness evidence against one of the two murderous confidence tricksters featured in the plot. Goliath's unexpected but spectacular appearance when one of the con men, posing as an Assyrian magus and spiritist medium pretends to channel Adam, the first man, is only the penultimate bizarre twist in the plot.

Jules Lermina's previously-mentioned "To-Ho le tueur d'or" continued the tradition of smart apes given more subtle aid by human scientists, as did "Gulluliou, ou Le Presqu'homme" (1905; book 1908 as *Le Presqu'homme*; tr. as "Almost a Man") by Marcel Roland (1879-1955), in which a scientist learns the language of apes, although the advanced ape who enters into communication with humankind in consequence obtains no joy from it.

Roland's story became more interesting because it formed the basis for an eccentric trilogy of novels, he second of which, *Le Déluge futur, journal d'un survivant* [The Future Deluge: The Journal of a Survivor] (1910) is an end-of-the-world story in which the Earth's surface is almost entirely submerged, the only surviving humans apparently being the occupants of an odd amphibious vessel, the *Triton*, which include a scientist who has discovered the secret of atomic power. The one surviving island protruding above the surface, however, turns out in the third element of the trilogy, *La Conquête d'Anthar, roman des "temps futurs"* [The Conquest of Anthar: A Romance of "Future Times"] (1913), to be the island on which the survivors of Gulluliou's "missing link" species took refuge after their expulsion from Borneo. Thus, a final confrontation must decide which, if either, of the two species is to survive; the conclusion—which it is tempting to see in hindsight as a premonition of the imminent war—is not optimistic.

Another member of a species intermediate between human and ape is the eponymous **Balaoo** (1912; tr. as *Balaoo*) by Gaston Leroux, captured by a scientist and brought to France in order to demonstrate his near-humanity, in this case with the aid of surgery on his vocal cords to facilitate speech. As with Gulluliou, however, his interaction with humankind does not go smoothly, and he is soon involved in crime by unscrupulous exploiters, resulting in a police "manhunt" when a murder is committed in extraordinary circumstances.

Individual survivors from prehistoric ages cropped up occasionally in geographical fictions to provide brief melodramatic interludes, but rarely formed the focal points of such stories; they were scarcer in the pages of the *Journal des Voyages* than one might have expected, although that publication did publish one of the most extravagantly Gothic in Fernand Noat's "Le Triangle rouge" (1902; tr. as "The Red Triangle"), which employs a vague and quasi-mythical prehistory to excuse the present existence of a monstrous protean worm that menaces French soldiers gone astray during the Boxer rebellion.

It was in this period that fascination with the remote era of the dinosaurs began to develop in earnest as more species were added to the catalogue, the crucial addition of *Tyrannosaurus rex* being made in the first decade of the twentieth century. Although plesiosaurs and ichthyosaurs had long been a stand-ard feature of the imagery of remote pre-history, taking central roles in stories by Pierre Boitard and S. Henry Berthoud as well as featuring as survivals in Jules Verne's *Voyage au centre de la terre*, the range had not extended much beyond that until fearsome carnivores were added to the catalogue, generating extra melodramatic potential. The most meticulous early exploitation of that potential was displayed in the first venture into *roman scientifique* by the enthusiastic propagandist for the *merveilleux scientifique*, Maurice Renard. The novella "Les Vacances de Monsieur Dupont" (1905; tr. as "Monsieur Dupont's Vacation") describes how the protagonist, a thoroughly petit-bourgeois Parisian, is invited to spend a vacation with an old school friend living

in a once-volcanic region of the south of France, who collects dinosaur bones and assembles them into impressive skeletal models. The not-quite-extinct vulcanism of the region causes a number of long-preserved dinosaur eggs to hatch belatedly, initially releasing a herbivore that only causes damage to crops, but then releasing a far more dangerous individual whose confrontation with the narrator is appropriately traumatic.

Jules Lermina, typically, showed far less restraint in *L'Effrayante aventure* (1910; tr. as *Panic in Paris*), which begins as a detective story provoked by the discovery of a corpse at the foot of the obelisk in the Place de la Concorde, although the quest to solve the mystery, with the help of a new flying machine, eventually leads to an underworld beneath the Buttes-Chaumont, in which a whole host of prehistoric species from various eras, ranging from brontosaurs and iguanodons to mammoths, is trapped in suspended animation, awaiting the trigger that will reanimate them and release them into the heart of Paris. Fortunately, the release proves brief, although it causes considerable disruption in the meantime.

Maurice Renard's second prehistoric fantasy, the timeslip fantasy "Le Brouillard du 26 Octobre" (1913; tr. as "The Fog of October 26"), does not go so far back in time, only retreating to the period of human origins, but does so in order to offer a brief glimpse of an alternative human evolution, in the form of a remarkable kindred species that became extinct.

J.-H. Rosny's account of *La Guerre du Feu* was very successful as a serial in *Je Sais Tout* and as a book, and its popularity and reputation were maintained in later decades by film versions. It was not, however, the most widely-read or most acclaimed work of that kind produced in the period. That distinction belongs to a project in *roman scientifique* undertaken by Edmond Haraucourt in the pages of the daily newspaper *Le Journal*, taking the form not of an orthodox feuilleton serial but of a story series, a sequence of snapshots adding up to a literary collage, which did not require to be published in consecutive issues, but could accumulate over time. It was so successful in its ingenuity that it became by far the most popular item that Haraucourt had ever done for the paper, and he was permitted by the strength of reader demand to supplement the first sequence with a second one, ultimately building the entire collage into a coherent picture, so that by the time he rearranged and revised the fragments into a book, there was actually a pent-up demand waiting for it. But for an accident of timing, it might well have sold in large quantities, gone through several reprints and become established as a classic, but it was not to be, because the book was published in July 1914, mere weeks before the outbreak of the Great War, which effectively annihilated it, as it did so much else.

The first sequence of stories began with "La Première larme" [The First Tear] in the 26 December 1912 issue of *Le Journal* and concluded with "Le Flambeau" [The Torch] in the 10 April 1913 issue. They presented scenes from the life of an exemplary first family, the ultimate ancestors of humankind, initially consisting of a couple, the Neanderthal man Daâh, and his mate Hock, but soon expanded by conquest into a *ménage à trois*, with the addition of the Cro-Magnon female Ta. The reckless incestuous cross-breeding of subsequent generations eventually produces a "horde" whose hybrid vigor assists them to survive various environmental challenges, both routine and extraordinary,

The second sequence, which gradually filled in the rest of the story, began on 5 May 1914 with a set of preliminary episodes detailing the initial meeting and early relationship of Daâh and Hock, and concluded on 4 June 1914, with a series of episodes set prior to the climax described in the first sequence, dealing with the uniquely touchy subject of "L'Amour," with a forthrightness bound to seem shocking, and distinctly risky in the pages of a daily newspaper. The book version, **Daâh, le premier homme** (tr. as *Daâh, the First Human*), was issued swiftly thereafter, but eclipsed just as swiftly by the advent of the war.

The considerable success of *La Guerre du feu* had presumably been responsible for prompting Haraucourt to produce his own account of early human evolution, or at least for opening up hospitable market space for its publication. Although not compatible with Rosny's account of prehistory, *Daâh* is not a rival to it, because it deliberately takes the exercise further back toward its fundamentals, not only temporally but philosophically. Haraucourt's account of human prehistory begins with not with Madgalenian "cave-men" but with hypothetical proto-humans living a solitary existence, having not yet begun to form societies, and his account is as much an account of the origins of living in association as it is of technological discoveries and the development of language and sentiment.

In parallel with those developments, and as a key aspect of the process, *Daâh* offers an account of the primal evolution of consciousness—a much more difficult endeavor, in narrative terms. In consequence, as well as being a substantial work of fiction, *Daâh* is an authentic exercise in existential philosophy: a conscientious and fascinating attempt to strip human consciousness down to its fundamental elements, and to explain the dynamics of its origins. The narrative voice states explicitly that "I am not inventing anything; I am trying to remember" and that is, indeed, the unique narrative method that Haraucourt was attempting: to look inside himself in search of the ultimate elements of his own conscious being and personality; an exercise *à la recherche du temps perdu* that went far beyond dunking madeleines.

We now know that it is highly improbable that our ancestors ever lived the kind of solitary forest-dwelling existence initially credited to Daâh, but its adoption as a hypothesis favored the philosophical aspects of Haraucourt's account of the elements of consciousness, and is justifiable on those grounds. We are not so certain that members of *Homo neanderthalensis* were incapable of fertile interbreeding with their "Cro-Magnon" contemporaries, although it is unlikely that, if they were, it was those hybrids who were the ancestors of modern *Homo sapiens*; again, however, the hypothesis does make sense in terms of Haraucourt's analysis of the elements of consciousness, language, culture and sentiment.

Some individual features of his patchwork story are sarcastically satirical—the logical argument explaining how the invention of the loincloth inevitably led to the institution of property is an obvious conceit—but others are not, and the episodes that deftly combine the ontological with the emotional, as in the heart-rending account of the slow death of poor Ta, are magnificent in their earnest simplicity. No other story attempted to delve quite so far into depths of past time that retained a certain human relevance, and the collage has an interesting parenthetical relationship with Haraucourt's several far-futuristic fantasies dealing with the end of the human story, especially "Le Gorilloïde." The two stories, taken together, can be seen as parenthetical to all the considerations of the remoter depths of time produced during the period, and provided it with its own uniquely appropriate imaginative parentheses.

CHAPTER SIX: THE GREAT WAR AND ITS AF-TERMATH, 1914-1939

1. The Trenches and Their Legacy

The Great War of 1914-18 was the ultimate result of the German victory in the Franco-Prussian War of 1870-71, the first side-effect of which had been the consolidation of the German Empire: a unification triumphantly announced at Versailles. Otto von Bismarck had attempted to continue that process of consolidation by negotiating a league of what were then the three great continental empires, trying to resurrect the old "Holy Alliance" that had been formed between Prussia, Austria and Russia in 1815. The negotiation failed because Russia and Austria-Hungary had too many simmering disputes, but Germany did form a Dual Alliance with Austria-Hungary, which was subsequently expanded in 1882 to include Italy and form the Triple Alliance, or Triplice. That political bloc became the background to the increasingly assertive attempts by the new German Empire to compete with the established colonial empires of England and France, which were seen—not necessarily correctly—as a powerful instrument of national enrichment.

When Wilhelm II inherited the Imperial Throne in 1888 Bismarck was retired, but the advancement of the German military-industrial complex was accelerated even further, generating a competition, primarily between England and Germany but inevitably drawing the other European powers in, to develop bigger and better armed navies, and more powerful land forces. In retrospect, the massive increase in spending on armaments can easily be seen as a slow march to war, and many writers of the period saw it in the same light. The growth of future war fiction in England and France, as described in the previous chapter, ought not to be seen as prediction, although it looks like that with the advantage of hindsight, but rather as a curious oxymoronic combination of dire warning and enthusiastic anticipation. Pacifists fearful of the awful destruction that such a war might bring rubbed shoulders with jingoists who looked forward to an opportunity to prove that their side was the superior. The sharpness of that opposition was clearer in France than elsewhere precisely because France was still smarting from the humiliation of the defeat inflicted in 1870, and its militarists were thirsting for a vengeance that was, alas, to prove woefully impractical.

The pattern of events that followed the assassination of the Austrian Archduke Franz Ferdinand in Sarajevo on 28 June 1914 would now seem to have been an absurd series of ludicrous overreactions if it did not have a sense of awful inevitability about it, caused by the fact that the war was already in fully gestated in embryo, merely awaiting some arbitrary trigger to give birth to it. Once Austria-Hungary had declared war on Serbia on 28 July 1914, the pattern of alliances and counter-alliances formed during the previous thirty years automatically dragged all the major European powers into the conflict.

Germany initially demanded that France remain neutral, but the French could not take that resolution, and on 3 August Germany declared war on France. The so-called "Schlieffen Plan" for the invasion of France via Belgium, by-passing the defenses on the Franco-German border, was immediately put into action, with initially devastating effect as German troops pushed deep into France during August. In early September, however, the French forces, supported by the British Expeditionary Force, stopped the German advance at the Battle of the Marne and forced the invaders back. The Germans had been forced to remove their reserve troops in order to counter a Russian invasion from the East, and the situation on the Western Front soon turned into a stalemate, with both sides digging trenches heavily defended by artillery, barbed wire and machine-gun emplacements.

Both sides attempted repeated "pushes" in the attempt to overrun the enemy trenches, and gradually invoked new weapons in the attempt to break the stalemate, including poison gases and tanks, but nothing proved decisive and the confrontation of the trenches dragged on for years. Both sides suffered enormous casualties, although the French and British forces suffered more because they launched more attacks, taking particularly heavy losses in the ill-fated Somme offensive of 1916.

The Germans, better-equipped and better-entrenched, seemed likelier to win in the end until the U.S.A. joined the war in April 1917, at which point the Germans were effectively doomed. The distance between America and Europe made the transfer of fighting troops awkward, leaving the Germans time to mount one last big push under the spur of desperation, but the gradual infusion of large quantities of new equipment and fresh, healthy fighting men into an arena in which the occupants of the trenches were ill-equipped, exhausted, half-starved and ravaged by disease made the final collapse of German resistance inevitable. Significantly, however, what resulted from that collapse was not termed a defeat but an armistice, which suspended the war rather than concluding it: a distinction not lost on politicians or journalists, who were aware from day one—11 November 1918—that a second world war (as it was already being called before the first was over) was still in the offing, and that it was only a matter of time before it flared up.

By its very nature, censorship attempts to make itself historically undetectable, and there is no record of exactly how official censorship operated in France during the Great War. The situation is further confused by the effects of self-censorship, in which journalists and writers, sensitive and sympathetic to the need to maintain, or at least not threaten, morale became diplomatic in what they wrote and how. Two government censors. Marcel Berger and Paul Allard, eventually published a memoir of their time in the Press Bureau, *Les Secrets de la censure pendant la guerre* [The Secrets of Censorship During the War], in 1932, which offered useful insights into both policy and the daily routines of official press censorship, but could only provide a partial picture of forces that were mostly clandestine and, in the case of self-censorship, probably partially unconscious.

Most academic studies of censorship during the war inevitably focus on the censorship of news and mail, and have almost nothing to say about the censorship of fiction—which, in any case, must have had a far larger component of self-censorship than the explicit operation of what came to be known in the parlance of the day as "Anastasia's scissors." It is, however, possible to draw some interesting inferences simply by examination of the pattern of publication—which, in respect of *roman scientifique,* is markedly different from the pattern of publication of British scientific romance during the war years, particularly in 1917-18.

To begin with, as might be expected, there was a drastic diminution in the production of futuristic fiction after August 1914. Once a country is at war, the present absorbs all attention; it becomes enormously difficult to engage in public discussion of anything but immediate and material concerns. *Contes philosophiques* come to seem unhealthily abstract and theoretical at a moment when urgent practical concerns exert such a massive claim on the imagination. Euchronian fantasies and the *merveilleux scientifique,* always a trifle chimerical, come to seem an unjustifiable, almost treasonous, form of self-indulgence.

Many people who had been actively involved in writing *roman scientifique* before the outbreak of the war were, of course, mobilized and spent the next four years—if they survived that long unscathed—on active service, but even those who were too old for conscription underwent an abrupt change of attitude. Publishing in general was drastically reduced by the economic side-effects of the war, and fiction suffered a more drastic contraction than non-fiction, but the fiction that was published in 1915 and 1916 was mostly grimly naturalistic—not pessimistic, because that would have been treasonous, but celebrating defiant heroism in adversity. Much of it dealt not with the experiences of the soldiers but with the experiences of those they had left behind, whose heroism was necessarily more passive, and for whom the war was a stern test of endurance. That was not a cultural and intellectual climate in which *roman scientifique* could flourish, and it did not; the historical development that had moved into a higher gear in the early years of the twentieth century was rudely interrupted.

The interruption was not complete, however, nor did it last as long as the war. Indeed, a curious reversion of attitude evidently took place—so evidently that it smacks of active encouragement on the part of the government rather than merely according permission, and in 1917, judging by appearances, there seems to have been a kind of negative censorship in place that actually solicited writers of popular fiction to produce a particular kind of imaginative fiction with a significant component of *roman scientifique*.

The circumstances of war are only hostile to some kinds of popular fiction, and actually encourage the production of certain others. They are particularly conducive to the production of spy fiction: secret histories in which the insidious plots of enemy agents can be quietly thwarted by loyal patriots not necessarily on formal military service. Such plots can serve a double purpose in popular propaganda, firstly by encouraging vigilance and inviting members of the public to be on the lookout for spies and saboteurs—of whom Germany was rumored to have large quantities, constituting an "invisible hand" or "fifth column"—and secondly by promoting the idea that although nothing was evident in the news, crucial battles were being fought and won against the enemy, on terrain far from the manifest front. In both Britain and France, spy fiction made important advances in sophistication and popularity during the war. One of the most notable items of that kind was a 135-part feuilleton published in *Le Matin*, the daily newspaper with the largest circulation: *La Colonne infernale* [The Infernal Column] (April-September 1916) by Gaston Leroux (1868-1927), then the most popular author in France, which was an unusually extravagant account of the secret battle against enemy spies and saboteurs.

Leroux continued publishing feuilleton fiction in *Le Matin*, including the 134-part "Le Sous-marin *Le Vengeur*" [The Submarine *Le Vengeur*] between September 1917 and February 1918, about a clandestine war-within-the-war

fought beneath the waves; it was reprinted in book form in 1920 in two volumes as *Le Capitaine Hyx* (tr. as *The Adventures of Carolus Herbert*) and *La Bataille invisible* (tr. as *The Veiled Prisoner*). Simultaneously, he contributed a seven-part serial to the monthly magazine *Je Sais Tout* between September 1917 and March 1918 featuring his most popular series hero, the journalist and amateur detective Rouletabille, in ***Rouletabille chez Krupp*** (tr. as *Rouletabille at Krupp's*).

At the end of the previous element of the series, *Rouletabille à la guerre* [Rouletabille at War], which was running as a feuilleton in *Le Matin* when the war actually broke out and required hasty adaptation, after a brief gap, when its plot was overtaken by events, Rouletabille had, like every loyal Frenchman, gone to do his bit in the trenches; in the new story, however, he is summoned back to Paris by the prime minister—not named, but very obviously recognizable as the actual premier, Georges Clemenceau—and entrusted with a secret mission. He is to infiltrate the gigantic Krupp armament factory, and, if possible, rescue a French scientist, kidnapped along with his daughter and forced by threats against her life to develop a new superweapon for the German forces, which might be capable of winning the war. If Rouletabille cannot effect a rescue, his instructions are to kill them both, in order to prevent the Germans from using their dangerous secret.

The story is interesting in several ways. First and foremost, the idea of the superweapon capable of breaking the stalemate of trench warfare clearly reflects the growing consciousness that the Great War was first and foremost a war of technologies, in which the role of science and engineering in delivering new means of mass destruction was more crucial than that of soldierly heroism or military strategy. Writers of future war stories such as Albert Robida and "Barillet-Lagargousse" had been arguing that case since the 1880s, but now it had become glaringly evident in the way that the war was actually being fought; it was no longer speculative fiction but brute fact, and could no longer be dismissed as mere possibility. It was, of course, very convenient for plotting purposes that the objective of the story is to destroy the particular innovation in question, thus permitting a conventional normalizing story-arc.

The story is also interesting in its subsidiary propagandistic rhetoric. More than any other novel produced in the same spirit, *Rouletabille chez Krupp* sets out to demonize the enemy in a remarkably flamboyant fashion, in the key chapters entitled "Le Maître de feu" [The Master of Fire] and "Le Plus grand chantage du monde" [The Greatest Blackmail of the World], in which the Krupp armaments factory becomes a transfiguration of Dante's *Inferno*, and Kaiser Wilhelm II appears in person to guide the reader around it, as an incarnation of Satan. The symbolism of those chapters, in which Rouletabille, quietly masquerading as a fireman in the background of the tour, is juxtaposed with both the Kaiser and the gigantic superweapon, the *Titania*, is a trifle crude, but is all the more striking because of it.

Although the portrayal of the Kaiser as the Devil is more striking than the portrayal of Clemenceau in the story, it is no more significant; Clemenceau and his ministers are, of course, depicted as heroes valiantly trying to save France from disaster under direly difficult circumstances, but what is equally interesting is their attitude to Rouletabille, whom they treat with a curious mixture of comradeship and awe. Given that Rouletabille is, throughout the series in which he features, an obvious transfiguration of Gaston Leroux, that is suggestive of the manner in which Leroux saw himself as an agent of France, doing far more valuable war work in the pages of *Le Matin* and *Je Sais Tout* than he could ever have done in the trenches, had he been of an age to be called up for active service.

Leroux was personally acquainted with Clemenceau, as many members of the French literary community were, and although he might not have seen a great deal of him during the war years, it is certainly not beyond the bounds of possibility that he discussed *Rouletabille chez Krupp* with him before writing it, or even that he wrote it at Clemenceau's suggestion. Nor is it beyond the bounds of possibility that Leroux urged Clemenceau to make more active use of popular fiction as a medium of propaganda, for the purpose of building and maintaining morale. Whatever the truth of the matter, that is what happened: popular fiction with a more evident morale-building purpose—including some significant items of *roman scientifique*—began to appear in some profusion in 1917-18, some of which had obviously been composed much earlier but held up in publication, and hastily amended for propaganda purposes.

Another series character adapted for propaganda purposes during the war was Arthur Bernède's Chantecoq, who had made his debut in the pre-war spy stories *Coeur de Française* [The Heart of a Frenchwoman] (1912) and *L'Espionne de Guillaume* [Wilhelm's Female Spy] (1914) but continued his exploits in a more fanciful context, peripherally involving various new weapons of an advanced sort, in "Chantecoq, grand roman national" [Chantecoq: A Great National Novel] (*Le Petit Parisien* 1916), which was reprinted in book form in 1920 in four volumes. Chantecoq continued his career after the war as a private detective.

Fanciful inventions are also featured in a lurid spy story by the humorist

Georges de La Fouchardière (1874-1946), whose usual comedic tone was moderated somewhat in *L'Araignée du Kaiser* [The Kaiser's Spider] (1916), in which a nest of German agents operating on the French Riviera in 1914 includes scientists working on the development of secret weapons, although they are reduced to stealing a new kind of aircraft invulnerable to bullets, the Guêpe [wasp], which the Germans want to employ in bacteriological warfare, distributing infected flies. A French mechanic, however, succeeds in turning the "wasp" into a "spider," with suitably subversive effect.

One of the most striking superweapon-featuring spy stories, *La Bombe silencieuse* (1916; tr. as *The Silent Bomb*) by Charles Dodeman, was published in Tours, in a handsome edition illustrated by Albert Robida, evidently aimed at younger readers. It is a hectic melodrama that shares many of the features of the popular feuilleton fiction of the period, including its implausibility. It labors under the apparent handicap that the key motif that provides its title, the silent bomb, has no conspicuous advantage on that account; all bombs are silent until they explode, except for those equipped with what Dodeman calls an *horloge infernale* (a ticking timer), and once a bomb has gone off, it hardly matters whether it makes a noise or not as it does its destructive work.

In fact, the invention featured in the novel has other virtues that a modern reader might deem far more important than its silence. One of its components is radioactive, and is said to release particles with an unusual rapidity, thus increasing the power of its blast—it is a primitive atomic bomb—and in order to deliver it, the inventor eventually abandons the quest to build an unprecedentedly resilient cannon and employs miniature aircraft guided to their target by radio waves: what would nowadays be called a drone. Both of those features can be seen with the aid of hindsight to be more important as advances in military technology than the bomb's silence, but in the author's eyes, they did not have as much symbolic value, partly because the silence had the additional value of reflecting, in metaphorical terms, the occult work of the spy network trying to take possession of it. In the end, when the plot reaches its climax, it is technological expertise and scientific thinking that provide the means by which the evil German agents are ultimately thwarted in the most crucial part of their plan.

Jules Chancel's *Sous le masque allemand* [Behind the German Mask] (1917) is another novel on the borderline between spy fiction and speculative fiction, aimed, like *La Bombe silencieuse*, specifically at a juvenile audience.

La Bombe silencieuse's illustrator, Albert Robida, had refrained from carrying forward his pessimistically satirical exercises in imaginative fiction during the early years of the war, but, like many other popular writers, he swung back into action in 1917 with a continuation of his most popular series, albeit in a tone far removed from his usual satirical anxiety. "Un Potache en 1950" (tr. as "A Schoolboy in 1950") is a deliberately upbeat work published in a children's periodical, featuring the adventures of a technically gifted schoolboy in a world far removed from the contemporary horrors of 1917.

One of the texts that was obviously adapted after completion for propagandistic purposes was *Les Ailes de l'homme: Paris à New York en avion* (1917; tr. as *The Human Arrow*) by Félicien Champsaur. The adaptation became obvious when the additional text was cut and replaced in a new edition that was hastily prepared in 1927, and published on 5 June of that year, a fortnight after Charles Lindbergh succeeded in a modified version of the feat attributed to the fictitious hero of the novel.

Henri Rozal, the hero of *Les Ailes de l'homme*, has been working for years, from 1909 onwards, attempting to overcome the limitations imposed on aircraft by their primitive means of propulsion. Rozal believes that aircraft will become much more useful when they can fly much faster, which will only be possible when they have more powerful means of propulsion, so he is attempting to develop a gas turbine engine for that purpose. This did not seem an unreasonable proposition in 1914, although no gas turbine had yet been invented; hindsight allows us to see that the one featured in the story would not work, because gases cannot behave in the way his explanation requires, but the author makes a conscientious attempt to describe Rozal's invention in detail as well as in principle, and makes much of the technological endeavor that its production would require.

In order to finance his research and development Rozal makes a deal with a financier, who volunteers to find him an American heiress to marry in exchange for a portion of her dowry. As irony would have it, he unwittingly meets the young woman independently, falls in love with her and marries her—but the financier still has the contract he signed, and turns up to demand his money; his wife, thinking that she has been tricked, leaves him and returns to America. His obsession intensified by grief, Rozal returns to work, and after much hard labor perfects his new airplane, with which he decides to make a transatlantic flight in the hope of impressing his wife and winning her back. He does impress her, and she is completely won over, but the plane, having completed the flight successfully, runs into difficulties when trying to land and crashes, thus becoming a tragic monument to human ambition.

It is not unusual for plausible speculative fictions set in such imminent futures to be outdated by actual events, but Champsaur suffered the misfortune of having his entire notion of the imminent future demolished overnight, before his novel could be published. His tale of aviation pioneering is set in a world at peace, and that is the necessary context of Rozal's endeavor. When Europe was plunged into war, the entire backcloth of the story was abruptly wiped out. If the story were to be published after 1 August 1914, it had to be modified—but not immediately, because publication of such a work was impossible in the latter months of 1914, and was to remain so for some time thereafter. In the published version, the author inserted specific dates to make Rozal's crucial test-flight take place literally on the eve of the Great War. By the time the novel appeared, however, that was already history, referring back to what already seemed like a distant other world.

This would have caused problems for any kind of story, but those problems are particularly acute for any work dealing with an invention which is, virtually by definition, potentially world-changing. Proposing, in a story set in the imminent future, that the world might change dramatically tomorrow, is very different from proposing, in a story set three years in the past, that an invention that could have and should have changed the world somehow failed to do so, in spite of an extremely spectacular demonstration. Precisely because it is so conscientious in its account of the nature, development and eventual deployment of

Rozal's new aircraft, the author was therefore faced with considerable difficulty in trying to consign the invention retrospectively to the essentially-impotent realm of secret history.

In the new text added in 1917 in order to adapt it for publication as a propaganda piece, Rozal's friend Georges Turner is given a copy of the plans for the aircraft, of which he develops a second prototype in secret, in order to test its abilities in battle. The financier of the original text is now revealed, somewhat inconsistently, to be a German agent, and becomes embroiled in a personal conflict with Turner which climaxes in a heroic mission on Turner's part to destroy a heavily armored "Zeppelin nest" where the villain is hatching further schemes for the defeat of France. The extra section is so obviously inferior to, and out of tune with, the original text, that it is not at all surprising that Champsaur subsequently removed it, restoring the original ending and simply using the outbreak of the war as an excuse for the fact that the amazing feat of 1914 has been forgotten.

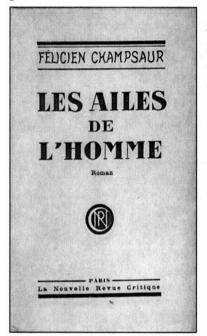

FÉLICIEN CHAMPSAUR

LES AILES
DE
L'HOMME

Roman

PARIS
La Nouvelle Revue Critique

In fact, the exceedingly awkward juxtaposition of the original text of *Les Ailes de l'homme* and the extra scenes set during the war illustrate a more profound breach in history as well as a challenging problem in narrative craftsmanship. The symbolism of the novel, in which the hero dies, tragically but gloriously, in making a key contribution to the ever-upward course of human progress, became obsolete in a far more profound fashion than the cancelation of its implied chronology. In the spring of 1914, when the story was written, the idea of a powerful aircraft that could link continents together much more intimately really was a symbol of "human wings," of triumphant, if costly, achievement. By 1917, though, that symbolism had been shattered and the image of technology as a glorious flight of progress had been irredeemably tarnished.

In 1917, Rozal's aircraft was no longer capable of being anything but a potential agent of destruction, a weapon of war potentially capable of raining down explosives, poison gas and incendiary bombs from the sky. By the time the novel was reprinted in 1927, specifically in order to reflect a new cultural environment of hopeful optimism, its symbolism had been direly undermined, because the hopeful optimism in question was now fragile and shadowed by fear—as was very obvious in the novels that

Champsaur wrote from scratch in that period, some of which will be discussed in due course.

Another very obvious arbitrary addition to an existing text is a chapter dropped into the middle of J.-H. Rosny's philosophical novel *L'Énigme de Givreuse* (1917; tr. as "The Givreuse Enigma"). Although obviously written during the war, as the plot is initiated when the protagonist, wounded in combat in September 1914, stumbles upon the titular enigma, it was probably completed some time before 1917, without the belatedly-added chapter that fitted it for its improvised propaganda function.

The protagonist of the story wakes up in a field hospital to find that he has somehow been duplicated; there are now two of him, and his civil estate has to be divided, one of the two accepting a demotion from his former self and adopting a new name. The two belated twins then have to find a means of coping with the difficult social situation thus created, direly complicated by the fact that the woman with whom their original was in love now has to choose between them. They also have to try to figure out the rational implications of what has happened, in the context of physics and metaphysics.

The latter issues are what interested the author most, and the conclusion of the story is entirely devoted to contemplation of the hypothetical explanation of the phenomenon and its cosmic implications. In order to adapt the novel for publication, however, Rosny had to make one of the twins into an inventor who develops a new weapon, which then has to be deployed in difficult circumstances against a marauding German submarine. As in *Les Ailes de l'homme*, the juxtaposition is extremely awkward, and Rosny might well have removed the added text if the story had been reprinted while he was alive, but it was not. As in Champsaur's novel, the awkwardness of *L'Énigme de Givreuse* reflects a deeper problem than mere narrative adaptation.

It is not simply that the context of the war required the brutal insertion of a combat between a new weapon and a German submarine that causes a problem, but the fact that the spirit in which the mysterious inventor of the matter duplicator had worked on his machine before the outbreak of the war, and the prospects that he saw in it, have been wiped out. As the laboratory assistant who appears in the plot at the end to clear up the mystery observes, had his master survived, he would inevitably have been diverted into war work, developing new radiations to slaughter Germans by the thousand. The virginity of science had doubtless been more than a little dubious before 1914, but by 1917 there was no longer any doubt about it; science was now a whore, and her highest-paying client was war.

Had the war staggered on for longer, it is probable that more novels would have been written from scratch to serve the propagandistic purpose for which Champsaur and Rosny adapted theirs, perhaps by request and perhaps merely opportunistically. As things turned out, however, one of the more interesting and extravagant superweapon stories of the period was caught much as Champsaur's novel had been, but in the inverse trap; written during the war, it was instantly outdated when the armistice was signed, immediately prior to its publication, thus transforming it from a futuristic fantasy into an alternative history. Raoul Bigot's "Le Fer qui meurt" (tr. as "The Iron that Died") was published in the 15 December 1918 issue of *Lectures Pour Tous* with an editorial note pointing out, as if it were not obvious, that it had been written while the war was still being fought.

The story describes how a scientist drafted into the artillery has an inspiration following a heavy bombardment, which enables him to design an electrical weapon that will have a devastating effect, provided that enemy can be taken entirely by surprise by it. He takes the idea directly to Georges Clemenceau, and insists that only he, Clemenceau and the recently-appointed generalissimo of the allied forces, Marshal Foch, can know the entire secret; the thousands of men deployed in making preparations for the attack—and for the equally crucial defense against the weapon's potential backlash—must not know what they are doing. Clemenceau and Foch agree, and the Germans are, in fact, taken completely by surprise by an "electrical disease" that causes iron to crumble, obliterating the entire German war machine in a matter of days. Presumably the final twist—it was all a dream—was always attached to the story, but although it helps to reconcile it with known history, making it something that never happened, the belated publication still alters the nature of the narrative significantly.

"Le Fer qui meurt" also displays the other side of the coin with regard to the immediate and necessary application of new technologies to the purposes of mass destruction: the question of what role, once the mass destruction in question has been accomplished, the invention is then going to play in history. Once the war is won, the problem becomes one of trying to control the subsequent spread of the iron-rotting infection, and of finding a way for an iron-dependent society to continue operation in the ever-presence of such a scourge.

Other stories in which new weapons are developed specifically for use against the Germans, presumably written during the war, include two by Léon Baranger that appeared in book form in 1919 in the collection *Le Maître de force* [The Master of Force]. In "L'Innommable" [The Unspeakable], an inventor devises a means of employing psychic force in a fashion that can kill millions of enemy soldiers, but will, unfortunately, also cause the deaths of a tenth as many Frenchmen employed as "antennae." The similar but more versatile weapon featured in "Le Fils de l'Heure" [The Son of the Moment] is capable of projecting specific emotions, including hatred.

The significant items of *roman scientifique* published in the final years of the war were not all accounts of the destruction of German superweapons and the limited deployment of French ones; there is more than one way to boost morale. The fact that many writers were on active service, even in the trenches, did not prevent all of them from writing, or even from getting what they wrote into print, but some soldiers who were enduring perennial bombardment wanted to write anything but accounts of bombardment, seeking to use their writing as a means of psychological escape, deliberately writing in a buoyant tone. One such item that reached print in 1917, in the pages of the *Mercure de France*, was the defiantly upbeat comedy "Le Maître des trois états" (tr. as "The Master of the Three States", revised book version 1939 as *Le Fantastique invention de César Pitoulet*, with the co-signature Paul Plançon) by Henri Falk (Henri Falque, 1881-1937).

Like the protagonist of *L'Énigme de Givreuse*, the narrator of Falk's story, Mesmin Cabri, stumbles across an enigma whose unfolding causes considerable difficulties in his love life, disrupting his wooing of the lovely Suzanne Bic, whose father does not approve of him. The key to the enigma is the "Great Transmutator," which can alter the material state of entities, rendering solids—

including living bodies—fluid or gaseous. In the gaseous state they are invisible, which allows the transmuted narrator and the inventor of the machine to obtain access to places unnoticed, but also has its inconveniences, including rendering them unusually vulnerable to wind. The heroes' subsequent adventures in that form are easily transmuted from curious exploration of the implications of the hypothesis to slapstick comedy, and also facilitate an ironically upbeat ending. Although the dates cited in the first paragraph of the story make it clear that the story begins on the eve of the war, the war itself is left offstage, disdainfully ignored, as Falk offers his readers the same temporary and artificial escape in reading it that it probably offered him while writing it.

486

It seems likely that Falk's novelette **"L'Age de Plomb"** (1919; book version 1922; tr. as "The Age of Lead") was also written during the war, as its plot appears to be an absurdist transfiguration of life under bombardment. It features an epidemic of alopecia induced by solar radiation that spreads from the tropics to infect the entire world and begins to develop more serious side effects, which requires the protection of homes by lead armor and necessitates the carrying of lead umbrellas by those venturing outside, if not by entire lead-lined costumes— a circumstance that inevitably precipitates international and international conflicts to secure supplies of the newly precious metal. The scourge proves temporary, but the arbitrary ending looks suspiciously akin to a convenience not far removed from waking up after a dream.

An escapist fantasy of a different kind, first published anonymously in 1918 and reprinted in 1919, bearing the signature of Omer Chevalier (1860-?), *L'Avatar d'Yvan Orel* [Yvan Orel's Avatar] describes how its Russian protagonist, fortunately equipped with a magic mirror and a papyrus bearing instructions for its use, kills himself in order to be reincarnated in a similar but more peaceful world, where he finds love, and which turns out to be Venus.

Some of the writers in the trenches, of course, did not come through the experience as fortunately as Henri Falk, who returned with the Croix de guerre to resume a career that subsequently went from strength to strength as a songwriter, librettist and screenwriter. Some were wounded, and some were killed. The vast majority of the latter were immediately silenced, but there were exceptions, including Adrien Bertrand (1888-1917). Bertrand was one of the earliest casualties of the war, in which he volunteered to fight as soon as the Germans invaded, even though he was a committed pacifist who had been active for some years in promoting that cause as a journalist. He went straight from cursory basic training into the front line, where, two months later, in October 1914, shrapnel from a shell-burst penetrated his chest and damaged his lungs.

The injury was mortal, and there was no prospect of a recovery, but its lethal effects were not swift, and it took Bertrand a little over three years actually to die, confined to bed the entire time. As a poet and journalist by vocation, he naturally used that interval of agony to write, and he won the Prix Goncourt in 1916 for his only novel, *L'Appel du sol* [The Summons of the Soil], which describes the horrific experiences of a group of soldiers during the early months of the war.

Thereafter, he only wrote short stories, presumably because he had no confidence that he could finish any long work that he started. He completed four, which were gathered in a collection, *L'Orage sur le jardin de Candide, romans philosophiques* [The Storm over Candide's Garden, philosophical fictions] (1917); by far the most far-ranging of them, in its method and ambition, is "De la pluie qui surprit Candide en son jardin et d'un entretien qu'il eut avec divers personages" (tr. as "The Rain that Surprised Candide in his Garden").

A *conte philosophique* in the very heart of the Voltairean tradition, Bertrand's story introduces the hero of *L'Appel du Sol*, recreated as an immortal after his death from wounds sustained in battle, to a group of other fictitious immortals, who take refuge from a devastating storm in the house whose garden Voltaire's hero has long been tending. The others include Don Quixote, Mr. Pickwick, Achilles, Faust and Jérôme Coignard, the protagonist of Anatole France's *La Rôtisserie de la Reine Pedauque* (1893; tr. as *At the Sign of the Reine Pedauque*). While sheltering, they discuss the significance in human affairs of war in general and the Great War in particular—the latter symbolized, of course, by the storm raging outside. When the storm finally dies down—a circumstance Bertrand did not live to see—the characters must decide what they are going to do next. Obviously, they all pitch in to help Candide repair his garden—what alternative do they have?—but whether it can ever be the same is another matter.

Another satirical work that provided an exception to the propagandistic norm was *D'Amra sur Azulba, journal d'un Marsien sur la terre (1914-1917)* [From Amra to Azulba: The Journal of a Martian on Earth, 1914-1917] (1918), which presumably owed its publication to the fact that it bore the signature "Prince Louis de Bourbon," one of several pretenders to the obsolete French throne. The Martian visitor is arrested on suspicion of being a German spy and has to call home for help, although he is assisted to make an exotic escape by an anarchist fellow-internee.

When the war was actually over, it was not so easy to put the solution that Adrien Bertrand attributed to Candide and his friends into practice, let alone hope that it could ever restore the metaphorical garden to its former coziness. Things had changed, and it was impossible to pretend that the end of the war signified a return to "normality." With official censorship and most self-censorship out of the way, other sentiments could be allowed to show through, many of which took a very different view. Unsurprisingly, one of the most rapid and extreme reactions came from one of the people who had anticipated, albeit half in jest, what an appalling carnival of slaughter a technologically sophisticated war would be: Albert Robida.

We can only imagine how Robida must have felt as he watched so many of his anticipations coming to fruition in the aggressive deployment of tanks, chemical weapons and aircraft. He was more fully entitled to say "I told you so" than any other futuristic speculator, but there was no possibility of his taking any satisfaction from that entitlement; indeed, it must have filled him with a seething rage that had to remain bottled up while the war actually lasted. Once the armistice was signed, though, Robida felt free to vent his pent-up feelings and express his feelings explicitly—which he did, in one of the most remarkable works of a period spectacularly rich in tales of extreme disillusionment, *L'Ingénieur von Satanas* (1919; tr. as *The Engineer von Satanas*).

Most of the imagery deployed in Robida's earlier satirical accounts of future war recurs in *L'Ingénieur von Satanas*, although the narrative calls a tank a tank rather than a "locomotive of war" and makes various other terminological adjustments, but the farcical and relatively breezy tone in which the imagery is deployed in the earlier works is replaced by a profound and sincerely embittered grimness. The shift is assisted by the employment of a narrative strategy that decreases the narrative distance of the account, taking the reader into the consciousness of the first-person narrator, in order to eavesdrop on his thoughts and dreams.

The novel begins with two prologues, the first describing the exploits of the legendary thirteenth-century discoverer of gunpowder Berthold Schwartz, here frankly represented as the Devil in disguise, tempting the powerful with a destructive power capable of sowing evil and chaos for centuries to come. The second is set at a Peace Conference held (anachronistically) in 1909 at the new Palace of Peace in The Hague, where all the attending diplomats are congratulating one another warmly for having ushered in an era of permanent world peace, while nevertheless lending a covert ear to the descriptions of his latest inventions modestly offered by the German engineer von Satanas, who bears a striking but inevitably unapprehended resemblance to Berthold Schwartz.

The main story follows the adventure of Paul Jacquemin, the naturalist attached to an expedition that departed for the Arctic in April 1914 and became stranded there on a rocky islet. The members have survived by fishing and hunting polar bears and improbable penguins until a surprisingly rapid accumulation of driftwood enables them to build a boat, in which they eventually escape, after fifteen years of isolation. Unfortunately, after sailing for a long time in strangely deserted seas, the boat is suddenly blown up. Paul, the sole survivor, takes refuge on a fragment of mast already inhabited by the survivor of a similar accident, Marcel Blondeau, who has been stranded in Polynesia for almost as long as Paul has been in the Arctic, the ship on which he was traveling as a child having been sunk by a U-boat attack in the early years of the war.

When the two castaways finally reach the shore they find nothing but debris that is barely recognizable as that of houses, and are then seized by hooded men, who force uncomfortable masks upon them and drag them into a cellar. They soon realize, however, that their lives have just been saved from an advancing cloud of poison gas, and when it has been dissipated by the wind they are able to take their masks off and introduce themselves to the motley band of their rescuers: a cosmopolitan aggregation, many of them crippled by injury, who have ended up, by virtue of various misadventures, banding together in a refuge improvised from the cellars of the house of a former ship-owner in the Dutch city of Harlem. Nothing substantial any longer remains above ground of that house or any other in the entire city, which has been bombarded for years—and is still being bombarded, albeit on a much reduced scale—by German troops entrenched in what was once the Palace of Peace, but has long since been converted into a factory producing chemical and biological weapons.

The new arrivals are welcomed into the troglodyte company, one of an inestimable number eking out a frugal and fugitive living in the ruins of the city and its surrounding villages. Paul is anxious to have news of his beloved Paris, but all long distance communication has been cut off for nearly a decade, since the second world war broke out, mere months after the armistice of 1918, resuming more fiercely than before, and fought with even deadlier weapons. Civilization is now extinct, and travel impossible, at least until the remaining fortified factories run out of raw materials and are no longer capable of producing the means of delivering the explosives, chemical weapons and plague bacilli that constitute the essential apparatus of the conflict. In the meantime, the troglodytes get by as best they can, snails, rats and rabbits having become luxury foodstuffs, and any vegetable matter left unspoiled by the poisons being considered acceptable raw material for making "spinach."

The most interesting members of the community, from Paul's point of view—among the few who speak fluent French—are a Danish doctor named Eric Christiansen, who joined the community after escaping from the German factory where he was employed as slave labor, and a Swiss historian, more recently an artilleryman, named Jollimay. Christansen and Jollimay often pass the time by engaging in philosophical debates; the latter has much to say about the history of warfare and the various motives that produce and perpetuate it, but the deeply embittered Christiansen considers that there is one only guilty party responsible for the destruction of the world, which is "that slut Science."

Initially, that apparent blasphemy horrifies Paul, who does his best to defend his beloved disinterested quest for knowledge, but Christiansen's vitriolic tirades eventually wear him down, and Paul finally begins to accept that what he had previously thought of as the beating heart of social progress—the advancement of science and technology—has indeed brought about the destruction of everything human beings had achieved, returning them to a way of life even more primitive and less dignified than that of the original "cave men" who began the sad saga of progress a hundred thousand years before.

Ironically, the band of survivors generously welcomed into Mynheer Vandermolen's cellars form a microcosmic image of the kind of universal brotherhood that the Palace of Peace was originally supposed to promote and

490

produce. They have been united by common adversity, and also by the civilizing influence of the only two women in the community, a French mother and daughter. Competition for the latter's favors causes some dissent and antipathy, especially when the arrival of the handsome Marcel wrecks the ambitions of the hopefuls already in place, but the resentments in question do not explode into violence, largely because the troglodytes are too debilitated, the few who have their full complement of limbs being weakened by starvation.

Robida's pacifism comes far more obviously to the fore in this story than in any of his other accounts of future war, in the manner in which the various survivors treat one another, with courtesy if not genuine amity, and without any desire to do their fellow victims of atrocity any harm. That meticulous mildness is reflected in the organization of the story; whereas the casualty figures off-stage presumably run into billions, once Paul reaches Holland the casualty figures remain at zero, at least so far as human beings are concerned, in spite of numerous close-run encounters with potential chemical and biological extinction. That principle only holds good within the limited framework of the story, however, for the author brings a thoroughgoing cynicism to the deliberate curtailment of his conclusion, leaving the anticipation of the ultimate battle—necessarily to be fought with makeshift clubs, spears and axes—to the imagination of the reader.

Equally quick off the mark was Edmond Haraucourt, always an author ready to reach for extreme consequences, whose account of "Le Conflit suprême" (tr. as "The Supreme Conflict") appeared in four parts on the feuilleton slot of the daily newspaper *Le Journal* in March 1919. It is set in an exceedingly cold far future, when the remnants of the human race, able to survive in an implacably hostile environment only by virtue of enormous scientific expertise, live in two vast subterranean cities. Although totally secure in their technologically-cocoon existence, with no reason to attack one another and every reason to believe that any conflict would spell the end of human life on Earth, the two cities pick a quarrel and unleash their long-stored superweapons, which bring about the inevitable annihilation of both sides in two hours and twelve minutes—because that is what human beings do.

Although it had apparently been written in 1912, and might have been published posthumously, *La Conquête de Londres* [The Conquest of London] (1919) by François Léonard fits much more comfortably into the post-war context illustrated by Robida and Haraucourt, in its description of an Anglo-German war disrupted by a proletarian revolution in London, while a scientific conference is in process. The delegates to the conference include a biologist who has recently succeeded in isolating the bacillus of death; his samples fall victim to the violence, with the result that a plague begins to spread that threatens to make both war and evolution redundant. The stylistic peculiarities of the manner in which the story is presented led one reviewer to note, with careful understatement, that it was difficult to follow, but that fragmentation was not inappropriate to the theme and the time.

A more direct response to the horrors of the war is featured in *La Vallée de la lune* [The Valley of the Moon] (1920), by "Henry-Jacques" (Henri-Edmond Jacques, 1866-1973) in which a visitor to Earth from the Moon arrives in the middle of the battle of Verdun and records the observations made by his supposedly clinical eye. Jacques had been mobilized in 1914, and traumatized by his experiences during the conflict, which also prompted him to produce a collection of poetry, *La Symphonie héroïque* (1921) and the fabular title-story of *Sous le ciel de carreau* [Under the Panes of the Sky] (1925), in which the inhabitants of a city domed with glass that has gradually become obscured find that the recovery of the open sky does not live up to their hopeful anticipations.

Some of the writers badly wounded in the war never recovered, including Guillaume Apollinaire, who died in 1918, but his friend Pierre MacOrlan, similarly wounded in action in 1916, made a full recovery. Having already written one account of the collapse of civilization before the war in *Le Rire jaune*, he had no difficulty pulling another out of the same bag in the novella *La Bête conquérante* [The Conquering Beast] (serial 1919; book 1920), in which the discovery of a surgical operation that renders speech to domestic animals results in their taking on much more complex tasks, pigs and sheep becoming personal assistants and lawyers, so successfully that idle humankind degenerates, good for nothing but supplying meat and traction—until the Great War of the year 3000 devastates animal civilization, and the discovery of a surgical operation for restoring human beings permits them once again to be trained for more intellectual kinds of labor…and so on, perhaps *ad infinitum*.

MacOrlan's blackly comic avantgardist futuristic fantasy *La Cavalière Elsa* ["cavalier" in the metaphorical as well as the literal sense] (1921) introduces its young heroine as a child caught up in the horrors of the final phases of the Great War, and describes how she goes on to become the Jeanne d'Arc of the next world war, at the head of a combined Russian and Chinese army that invades, conquers and Sovietizes the whole of Europe. She fails to find much in the way of personal satisfaction from her symbolic triumph, though, and the revolutionized world shows little sign of euchronian success; after her tragic death, the narrative follows her into an afterlife devoid of Heaven or any authoritative moral judgment.

The most striking demonstration of the shift of consciousness that occurred when the war ended is hidden within a text that contains no external evidence of the fact that it must have been partly written before the war and only completed afterwards: a novel that has one of the most remarkably broken narrative trajectories in the entirety of French literature. It is all the more remarkable because the author wrote another novel in between the two halves, while he was on active service, which shares the same theme, but has a completely different attitude, born of different circumstances, and that one was published first. The two novels in question, in the order of their publication are *L'Arche* (1920; tr. as *The Ark*) and *Le Bacchus mutilé* (1922; tr. as *The Mutilated Bacchus*) by André Arnyvelde.

The text of *L'Arche* is explicit in recording that the novel was begun shortly after the author was conscripted during the Great War and was eventually finished—when the fragments composed during the war were collated after he was demobilized—in 1919. The title of the work derives from the notion that the writing of the text, and it content, were designed to constitute a kind of psychological Ark to carry the author through the figurative Deluge of the war, helping him to endure the devastation of his personal life and the greater world constituted by the conflict. The narrative is framed as a letter to the author's wife, whom he had married not long before the war began: the radical feminist and pacifist poet Henriette Sauret (1890-1976).

The word *arche* means "arch" as well as "ark," and that ambiguity extends to the central motif of the story, equipped with the improvised label *arcandre*—a term whose Greek roots encourage the reader to construe it as "arch-human," or "superhuman." The author seems to have intended it as a more accurate translation of the German *übermensch* than the *surhomme* used in the standard French translation of Nietzsche, but the arcandre is not a depiction of the new kind of human to whose advent Nietzsche's Zarathustra looked forward. It is the vision of the arcandre, rather than the original amorous ark the narrator initially intended to construct, that actually seems to have helped to bring the author through the war.

L'Arche was by no means the only novel written as a psychological crutch to sustain a soldier through dark hours, but there is no other Ark of that sort as self-conscious or as far-reaching as Arnyvelde's. It is not the Great Work that Arnyvelde had tried unsuccessfully to pen in the early years of the century—as the text of the novel explains—but it attempts to substitute for it, and although it is a deliberately extravagant visionary fantasy, the author took its fundamental arguments about human evolution very seriously indeed.

"André Arnyvelde" was the anagrammatic pseudonym of André Lévy (1881-1942) who had hung around with the younger writers of the Symbolist school after completing his education at the Collège Saint-Barbe, living a Bohemian existence for a while, doing odd jobs, singing in Montmartre cafés, and writing for the radical press, as well as poetry, until he achieved a strange celebrity in 1902. Having written a comedy in verse, *La Courtisane* [The Courtesan], he submitted it to Jules Claretie, the director of the Comédie-Française. Improbably, Claretie accepted the play immediately after reading it, and the publicity generated by that decision made Arnyvelde suddenly famous within the Parisian literary community.

The text of *L'Arche* describes what happened next in an ironic fashion: the author, convinced of his genius, was interrupted in his quest to express it by his compulsory military service, which shattered many of his illusions but only enhanced his determination to produce a world-changing work. For that purpose he isolated himself in Ascain, in the far south-west of France, thinking that solitude would enable him to gather and organize his ideas. It did not, and time dragged by while he suffered a massive writer's block, which was brought to a deeply humiliating conclusion when Claretie finally got around to staging *La Courtisane*, four years after accepting it. It turned out, in spite of all the pent-up expectation, to be a resounding flop, assassinated by the critics, and closed after five performances.

Arnyvelde picked himself up from that disappointment, throwing himself ardently into a career in journalism, and soon became enormously prolific, writing for a wide range of periodicals. His interviews are a rich source for contemporary historians; one, with Filippo Marinetti, followed a futurist exhibition in Paris on which Arnyvelde reported enthusiastically, unsurprisingly, given that the ideas expressed in the 1909 Futurist Manifesto dovetailed neatly with his own ideas about the new ways of seeing permitted, and perhaps demanded, by modern scientific knowledge and the dynamism of contemporary life.

A passage in *L'Arche* points out that Nietzsche's notion of the "will to power" is a sequential development of Arthur Schopenhauer's notions of the "will to survive," and Arnyvelde produced his own substitute term by conceiving the essential thrust of human evolution as a "will to joy." The crusade that Arnyvelde had taken up at the age of twenty with such fervor was a quintessentially eupsychian quest for the transcendence of the iniquities of the human condition by means of joy—or, rather, Joy, because what he means by the term is something nobler and more rewarding than the relatively trivial and petty things that we normally think of as "enjoyments": eating, drinking, playing and—most significantly and problematically—sexual intercourse. Arnyvelde was convinced that the new ways of seeing, experiencing and living permitted by modern science and modern life had opened up a path to the practical attainment of transcendent Joy, which had never been available before, but of which the vast majority of people were unaware, because they were still stuck in the old ruts. In his novels, he set out to post signposts to that pathway, and to explore it himself in experimental thought while doing so.

Arnyvelde's first novel, *Le Roi de Galade, conte bleu* (1910; tr. as "The King of Galade"), set firmly in the Voltairean tradition of *contes philosophiques*, describes the adventures of a hero who emerges from an idyllic homeland long isolated from the rest of humankind to explore the world and investigate its wonders and vicissitudes. The story's climax subjects the hypothetical observer's conclusions to scrupulous skeptical criticism, making it clear that the problems raised by the story remain to be solved. They are taken up robustly, in *L'Arche*, where their proposed solution is the arcandre: the arch-human who possesses the key to Joy.

The arcandre introduces himself to the narrator in a deliberately teasing fashion, offering himself as an enigma to be solved, but also as a granter of wishes who can take the narrator anywhere in space of time, not merely as an observer of events but also as a participant, experiencing the things he sees. First he takes him into the world of the tree against which he is leaning when the vision beings, allowing him to experience reality, suitably speeded up, from the viewpoint of a root; then he takes him back to the origin of the solar system, so that he can observe the creation of the nebula from which the Sun and the Earth condense, and the early phases of the Earth's evolution. From there, the protagonist is translated into his own memories, to relive a moment of his youth and observe his family—a precious memory that is packed up for him thereafter in the form of a ball of wax so that he might replay it at some later date.

In hectic succession, the protagonist visits other episodes in his own life and observes various moments in history as well as other modes of being, while the arcandre pushes forward an insistent educative agenda. The fundamental thesis of that agenda is that because of the extension of the human sensorium by optical devices such as telescopes and microscopes, increased human mobility thanks to new modes of transport, and new ways of understanding the nature of matter and energy permitted by atomic and electromagnetic theories, humans now live in an entirely new world, equipped with an entirely new way of being, but that old habits of seeing and understanding prevent the vast majority of people from realizing the fact, and hence from taking advantage of the psychological potential of the new reality.

The protagonist raises objections, the most significant of which is the question of what becomes, in this new world of arch-human understanding and arch-human experience, of amour. The demonstration that the arcandre provides is a trifle confusing, and is expressed—as much literary expression of the experience and ambition of amour tends to be—in cryptically symbolic terms, but what it amounts to is the claim that the particular and narrow satisfactions presently produced by orgasmic sexual intercourse will be generalized, in such a way as to become a whole body experience in which every single cell of the body will function as if it were a "heart," in the sense of being capable of voluptuous experience. The limited and problematic joy associated with the friction of sexual organs will thus be transcended by a much more encompassing Joy facilitating the permanence of a quasi-orgasmic neohuman condition: a "purity of everpresence" rather than the purity of absence specified by the Brillat-Dessaigne formula for human happiness.

L'Arche seems far more conclusive, in a purely literary sense, than *Le Roi de Galade*, partly because the end of the Great War really did present itself—falsely—as one of history's great conclusions, which would have to be followed by a new world because the old one was dead: a new world in which a general discovery of Arnyvelde's path to Joy, and a willingness to follow it, might be more feasible than it had been in 1910. Hindsight informs us, however, that things did not turn out that way, and that the abject failure of the post-war world to escape the toils of the old one was tragic in every possible way. Hindsight also informs us of the rapid disillusionment of the people who had lived through the war and had come out of it hoping for a new beginning, and the most powerful information of that disillusionment is contained in novels written in the early 1920s. Arnyvelde's third novel, *Le Bacchus mutilé* (1922; tr. as *The Mutilated Bacchus*) turned out to be one of the most extreme expressions of that anguished disillusionment. The very fervor of the hopes reflected in *L'Arche*, which helped sustain him psychologically through the war itself, made them vulnerable to an exceedingly steep fall when it became difficult to sustain them in the war's aftermath.

The Great War is not mentioned in the text of *Le Bacchus mutilé*; although the biography of its protagonist, Denis Aury, runs from a fin-de-siècle childhood through a crucial psychological awakening in 1907 to his return home in the 1920s in order to conduct a sociological experiment transforming his native vision into a utopian enclave of arch-human Joy, it says nothing about what he was doing between 1914 and 1918, or whether he was aware of anything else happening in those years. The most plausible explanation of that omission is that there is no mention of the Great War in Denis' biography because it was penned prior to 1914, and constituted one of the incomplete manuscripts that Arnyvelde mentions in *L'Arche* having left behind when he went off to war.

If that is the case, the stark contrast between the two halves of the story becomes much more understandable. The novel eventually called *Le Bacchus mutilé* must have originally had a different title, and must have been planned as a follow-up to *Le Roi de Galade*, answering the questions left unsettled by the earlier text with an account of the practical development by its protagonist of a new personality defined by the will to Joy, and by his plan to spread that Joy to the world by transfiguring a hidebound rural commune into a model eutopia in which all the inhabitants share its rewards.

Perhaps the author always intended the eutopian experiment to falter, in order not to violate the sacred principle of the normalizing ending, although it is difficult to believe that Arnyvelde, in 1914, could have been so craven. Even if he did intend some such capitulation with narrative convention, however, he certainly cannot have intended to inflict the kind of devastation on his hero, his heroine and his grand plan that the second half of the existing novel inflicts upon it, which can only have been the effect of extreme disillusionment, and the abysmal depression of what would nowadays be called "post-traumatic shock disorder."

Although the Great War is not present in the text literally, it is represented there symbolically. The author could not insert references to the 1914-18 conflict into the pre-war text without reconstructing it in its entirety, so references to a literal war that had already been tacitly ruled irrelevant would not have been appropriate in the continuation, but the firework display during which the protagonist crashes his airplane, shattering the utopian project whose early phases have been described in loving detail in a spirit of buoyant optimism, stands in metaphorically for the war. The exceedingly awkward prosthetics that the hero has to wear once he is allowed to return home substitute symbolically for crippling baggage of a different sort, which the protagonist's *alter ego*, the author, must have brought back from the war.

In his introduction to the unfortunately-curtailed new edition of *L'Arche* that he issued in 1961, Pierre Versins claims that the publisher of **Le Bacchus mutilé**, Albin Michel told the author that it would never be reprinted, because it was "unreadable"—information Versins presumably obtained from Henriette Sauret, from whom he sought permission for the reprint. Presumably, the book had been accepted for publication by an employee and Michel had not read it prior to publication. We can only guess as to exactly what Michel meant by "unreadable,"

but the likeliest hypothesis is that he thought it unreadable because the final section, in stark contrast to the soaring optimism of the first, is so utterly, relentlessly and savagely despairing, offering not the slightest crumb of comfort to any reader previously seduced into sympathy for the protagonist and his female partner. In his treatment of his main characters—and thus of any readers who had identified with them—the author is abominably cruel, to an extent very rarely seen, even in the many other agonized expressions of disenchantment written in the aftermath of the Great War.

Every publisher knows that readers love "happy endings," and can only routinely excuse tragic and *conte cruel* endings because of the curious sense of bittersweet moral uplift definitive of the sense of tragedy and the element of black comedy in the latter. Every editor knows, too, that many readers feel literally betrayed if a text does not deliver a happy ending, or some other potential psychological compensation. *Le Bacchus mutilé* goes far beyond tragedy and black comedy, with the result that it is, indeed, a difficult and painful story to read—but that is precisely what makes it a unique and brilliant literary work. There is perhaps no starker challenge to conventional reader expectations, no sterner test of imaginative moral fiber. It is worth bearing in mind, too, that after having finished it, Arnyvelde simply carried on with his life and work, and soon started work on a sequel, *On demande un homme...ou L'Étrange tournoi d'amour* (1924; tr. as "Man Wanted; or, The Strange Tournament of Love"), which, although by no means relieved of disenchantment, provides the hint of possible redemption that was so brutally refused in its predecessor.

Perhaps the most startling feature of *Le Bacchus mutilé* is not what the sadistic plot does to its unfortunate hero, horrible as it is, but what it does to its poor heroine, who is the embodiment within the story of amour, and the possibility of a superior, more encompassing form of love akin to the arcandre's recipe for Joy. In debasing her character, the novel tears apart the fabric of the arcandre's thesis, expressing the crude contrary conviction that nothing is, after all, possible above and beyond animalistic sexual fulfillment, which is itself inherently perverse, worthless and disgusting.

The measured retreat from that blanket rejection of the thesis of *L'Arche* subsequently expressed in *On demande un homme....* cannot muster anything like the assertive determination of the arcandre, but it does suggest that, after all, there has to be hope for *something* a little better than the awkward predicament in which we presently seems to be stuck, and that the *something* in question has to be achievable, to the extent that it is possible, by the deployment of a will to Joy driven by a sophisticated scientific understanding of the world. Thus, in Arnyvelde's work, as in Adrien Bertrand's account of what Candide and his friends did once the storm had passed, his characters get on with doing the best they can to reconstruct the devastated garden—while knowing that it can never be what it was before, and that even if the same flowers of hope and optimism can be replanted, they will always be growing in the shade, permanently diminished if not sickly and stunted.

Euchronian visions did continue to appear in opposition to post-war pessimism, but few were prepared to aim for the kind of near-historical location hopefully specified in *L'Arche* and the first part of *Le Bacchus mutilé*. By far the most striking of all Anarchist eutopias, albeit one more quirkily satirical than the concluding vision of Déjacque's *L'Humanisphère*, is detailed in *Voyage au monde à l'envers* (1920 in the *Mercure de France*; 1923 in book form; tr. as *Journey to the Inverted World*) by Marcel Rouff (1877-1936). The story confronts a thrice-decorated airman displaced from the second year of the war with a vision of eutopia, but exactly where his journey takes him—into the far future, a long hallucination or some kind of parallel world—never becomes clear, although it is very long way from New Caledonia, from which he takes off.

In the frame narrative, set in 1918, the aviator professes himself to be a diehard follower of Rousseau, firm in the belief that civilization is corruption and that happiness can only be achieved by its eradication, and the reasons for that become clear in the manuscript of his strange adventure. The manuscript describes how his plane gets lost and crash-lands, stranding him in a strange society that is very selective in its employment of technology and minimalist in its approach to government and law, although it is initially delightful in its exceedingly relaxed sexual mores, which would have shocked the inhabitants of Mosneron's Aerial Valley but might well have been able to reconcile the visitors to Collin de Plancy's Albur to vegetarianism, blithely avoiding the distasteful aspects of free love stigmatized in Paul Adam's *Letters de Malaisie*.

In spite of its erotic delights, however, the aviator finds living in the exotic society uncomfortably alien to his habits, and is initially intrigued to discover, after some while, that there is a neighboring region, the Accursed, to which exiles are banished and where things work in a fashion much closer to the system with which he is familiar. When he slips away in order to investigate it, however, he finds that he cannot even tolerate the idea of having to re-adapt to it; his sojourn in the "inverted world" has already made the defects of the old world far too obvious to him, and no longer tolerable. He decides, in consequence, to settle for perfection—but too late, as the citizens of the eutopia have decided that they cannot any longer accommodate him.

Before he is sent back home, however, the airman is allowed to see the museum in which the citizens of the anarchist state have put away all the technologies that they have abandoned—including those that are still distantly futuristic from the viewpoint of 1915, many of which seem to be adapted for the purposes of war—and he realizes how far his own society might have to follow the road of progress before coming to the conclusion that the road in question cannot lead to the desired destination.

When he finally arrives in Europe, a year after setting forth, the war is still in progress, with no end in sight, but even if it were not, the poor aviator would now be a stranger in his own world, doomed to be a disapproving misfit until he dies. That does not take long—unsurprisingly, given that the penultimate line of the journal of his experience begins: "I shall go on and on, straight ahead, loving the taste of death that I have on my lips...." The aftertaste of the war was something that many people could not get out of their mouths, for a full decade after the signing of the armistice.

Disenchantment with the idea of euchronia is understandably obvious in satires of the period. A year before Rouff's sad and somewhat elegiac homage to anarchist eutopia, the journalist and humorist Clément Vautel (Clément-Henri Vaulet, 1876-1954) had published the first of a series of cynical satires, *La Réouverture du paradis terrestre* [The Reopening of the Earthly Paradise] (1919), in which the moral philosopher Professor van Stenius goes to richest man in France, Raphaël Flox, with a proposal to recreate the Earthly paradise in the actual island location of the garden of Eden, which he has discovered after much arduous research. Flox, who is also president of the Neurasthenic-Club and suffers from terrible ennui, agrees to finance the experiment, and the project soon attracts a host of eager eccentrics, including Dora Sabian of Babylon, Connecticut, founder of the cult of Nu, who proves invaluable in helping them get over difficulties raised by an agent of the Sultan of Turkey, the owner of the island in question.

Once established, Flox and Stenius set about building their new earthly paradise, cleverly negotiating a path through the various dissents among their associates as to the exact form of the desired society—the nudist Dora, for instance, does not quite see eye to eye with the Tolstoyan anarchist Daniel Savorine—and although everyone is in favor of free love, there are different versions of the creed in question. The real problem, however, turns out to be the servant class; Eden City, unlike the original Eden, cannot get by without an extensive staff and elaborate technological support, and its underlings eventually mount a Revolution, hanging their previous masters from the branches of the Tree of the Knowledge of Good and Evil before they run into trouble themselves when they cannot pay the Sultan the rent due on the island.

Vautel also published a series of satirical vignettes in *Je Sais Tout* in 1919, many of them dealing with more-or-less absurd hypothetical possibilities, which included "La Grève des bourgeois" [The Strike of the Middle Class] and "Les Évadés du progrès" [The Refugees from Progress]. He became far bolder in his speculative reach, however, in his scathing account of *La Machine à fabriquer des rêves* [The Machine for Manufacturing Dreams] (1923), whose narrator, Dr. Lessna, tells the story of his invention, beginning with its first public demonstration, which leads to a commercial association with the entrepreneur Georges Waltner. Initially, the few machines that are built are sold to the *ennui*-stricken members of the exclusive Cercle des Personnes Tristes [Club of Sad Individuals] and beleaguered heads of state—including the Tsar of Russia, although a footnote records that Lenin took possession of that particular machine after the Revolution and installed it in the Kremlin—but the scale of production is soon stepped up and machines are sold in millions to all the people avid for pleasant dreams.

Commercially distributed dreams are also sold in large quantities, including imaginative exemplars scripted by Camille Flammarion and H. G. Wells. Thomas Edison is very impressed when he visits Lessna's factory, and discusses possible further developments of the technology with him, while Georges Clemenceau is one of the first to realize the machine's political potential, alerting the Chambre to them in a rousing speech. A backlash begins against the inventor, however, when he is charged with inventing a new vice and fostering illusory immorality on a vast scale, and things go from bad to worse when Waltner contrives to have Lessna committed to a lunatic asylum in order to obtain ownership of the patent on the machine, which he then sells to the government, whose members have their own ideas about how it might best be used.

Having employed dream machines piecemeal to consolidate support, the government then commissions Lessna to construct and operate a powerful National Dream Machine situated on the Eiffel Tower, by means of which they will be able to broadcast radiations unifying the dreams of the entire nation. It turns out, however, that protection can be obtained from the dictatorial National Dream by means of metal helmets, and a subversive opposition by the "*cerveaux libres*" [Free Brains] soon begins to take shape, climaxing in a fight scene high on the Eiffel Tower, in which poor Lessna has to defend his machine, very nearly to the death, against sabotage. His victory proves Pyrrhic, and when he wakes up from the unconsciousness following his injury—one of several awakenings that tease the reader with the possible bathetic discovery that the whole story might be nothing but a dream—he finds that the Revolution has been successful and that the Cerveaux Libres are now in power, busy organizing a new political order from which pleasant dreams will be banished forever....

Vautel subsequently used a similar notion in *La Grande Rafle* [The Great Sweep] (1929), which he wrote in collaboration with Georges de La Fouchardière, but, following a pattern that became commonplace in the latter part of the period, the narrative is formatted as a weak mystery story in which an enterprising reporter eventually tracks down the scientist possessed of a powerful psychic ray which implants ideas in people's minds that they mistake for their own. The scientist intends to make way for a revolution that will bring about a conclusive improvement in human life by persuading all the superfluous intellectual dead weight that is cluttering it up simply to withdraw from their positions of influence, starting with the hallowed halls of the Academy: a process that he describes as a "humanitarian Terror." He is, however, thwarted with consummate ease by the superior psychic compulsion of erotic attraction, and the government, instead of using the machine, as in Vautel's earlier novel, merely stories it away carefully, just in case they might need it some day.

The kind of disenchantment featured in Vautel's early post-wars works is expressed in many of the other *contes philosophiques* cast as exercises in *roman scientifique* that were published during the 1920s, more straightforwardly in mock-dystopias than mock-eutopias, but with no greater pathos. A striking ironic dystopia published in the same year as Marcel Rouff's tarnished eutopia is **Les Condamnés à mort** (1920; tr. as *Useless Hands*) by Claude Farrère, which is set in the final years of the twentieth century, as revealed by footnotes ostensibly added in a further future.

The initial scenario finds the controller of the world's wheat supplies, James Fergus MacHead Vohr, "*le Gouverneur*," and his managerial staff living in extreme luxury, while his manual laborers remain desperately poor, living in appalling squalor in the "Blocs." When the workers organize a strike in order to demand better pay and working conditions, however, Vohr, who has anticipated them and made his preparations, immediately begins to make arrangements to replace them with automated "mechanical hands"—what would nowadays be called robots.

Rendered redundant, the workers will have no alternative but to starve, but *le Gouverneur* regards that simply as the logic of natural selection, a statement of which is employed on the novel's title page as a headquote. Naturally, the workers react violently, marching on the factories to destroy the mechanical hands, but that eventuality has been anticipated too, and an aged scientist who has been working on a secret project for years brings out the fruit of his labor, offering his disintegrator ray as a final solution to the labor problem.

Although Vohr is faced with a crisis of conscience when his beloved daughter joins the strikers, that proves insufficient to prevent him from letting the logic of the situation proceed to its seemingly-inevitable conclusion; the disintegrator ray goes into action, eliminating the superfluous and sentimental elements of human society in a far greater sweep than the one tentatively envisaged by Vautel and La Fouchardière, leaving the rich to their idyllic seclusion. The question of who is going to buy the bread manufactured by the mechanical hands, and thus provide the profits with which the rich support their lifestyle, is not addressed.

A similarly bleak consciousness is evident in accounts of natural disaster. In 1920 *Je Sais Tout* serialized *Le Formidable événement* (tr. as *The Tremendous Event*) by Maurice Leblanc (1864-1941) in which a geological upheaval connects France and England and generates a new land devoid of law, where the carcasses of old wrecks provide refuges for outlaws and other menaces. In 1921 *Lectures Pour Tous* serialized "Le Soleil noir" (tr. as "The Black Sun") by René Pujol (1878-1942), perhaps in imitation, which initially shapes up to be considerably more apocalyptic, offering an account of the catastrophe that overwhelms the world when a collision with an errant dark star causes the sun's radiation to flare up dramatically. The story offers a clinical account of the protagonist's battle for survival, hiding deep underground in an old quarry with his fiancée, her parents and an astronomer who is conveniently on hand to explain the catastrophe and the futility of their brief resistance.

"Le Soleil noir" was not the most extreme of the cynical studies of catastrophe published in the aftermath of the war, but it was one of the most stylishly laconic. It makes an interesting companion with Rosny's "La Force mystérieuse," which had been published in *Je Sais Tout* not long before the outbreak of the war in 1913; although the plots and fundamental attitudes of the two stories are similar, and their development is similarly conscientious, Pujol's account clearly bears the traces and psychological scars of the real catastrophe that had occurred in the interim.

The grim narrative of "Le Soleil noir" was an unusually sophisticated work for the usually-unpretentious *Lectures Pour Tous* to publish, and might have been accepted, or even commissioned, with "La Force mystérieuse" in mind as well as *Le Formidable événement*, as the editors tried to reposition their periodical at the higher market level of *Je Sais Tout*, but whether that was the case or not, they never published anything else nearly as corrosively downbeat in the magazine thereafter, and might well have instructed the author to bring the story to its rather abrupt and unconvincing conclusion.

In the same vein, *À l'Aventure*, a short-lived part-work supplement to the *Journal des Voyages*, serialized "La Tempête universelle de l'an 2000" [The Universal Storm of the Year 2000] by Colonel Royet in 1921, in which a balloonist named Adam and a woman named Eve are the sole human survivors of a solar eruption similar to the one featured in Pujol's story, which kills off all life on Earth, leaving them to face a stern struggle for survival when the resultant storm has died down.

André Lichtenberger's initial reactions to the war included two stories in a series of literary parodies of English fiction that were eventually collected in *Pickles* (1923): "M. Pickwick et les Boches" [Mr. Pickwick and the Germans]

André LICHTENBERGER

Raramémé

Histoire d'ailleurs

— PARIS —
J. FERENCZI, ÉDITEUR
9, rue Antoine-Chantin

5° mille.

and, rather more brutally, "Mowgli revient du front" (tr. as "Mowgli Returns from the Front"), in which Kipling's shell-shocked feral child has great difficulty re-adapting to his beloved but woefully depleted jungle after suffering the horrors of the trenches. Lichtenberger then followed up a post-war reprint of *Les Centaures* with *Raramémé* (1921; tr. as *The Children of the Crab*), which tells the story of two descendants of an adventurer who had sailed to the Pacific in 1785 with La Perouse and had been lost with the ill-fated expedition, but had left behind a collection of exotic crabs collected in earlier adventures.

In honor of their childhood memories of the wonders of the collection the male cousin, Hugues, a naval officer, has had a crab tattooed on his arm, and the female, Laurette, always carries a small jade crab that he has given her. Although clearly destined for one another, they have been separated by the exigencies of his naval career and his tardiness in declaring his passion, and she has married another man, disastrously, before the circumstances of the war coincidentally bring them back together again in the Far East.

Hugues and Laurette set off to return to France, but the war is still demanding, are they are diverted *en route* to a tiny island whose native tribe, in decline and threatened by all the forces of the shrinking world—including a German U-Boat—still preserves a fragment of Rousseauesque innocence. In particular, the island is home to the last two members of the clan of the crab, the brother and sister Rara and Mémé, who are so closely bound together that they are effectively a single individual, and also to their friend Kouang, the last member of a primate species intermediate between orangutans and humans, who has reached the island after escaping from his captor, a German scientist.

Rara and Mémé welcome Hugues and Laurette as kindred because of the crab emblems that they wear, and it eventually turns out that they are, in fact, related by blood, Rara and Mémé being the last surviving descendants of the explorer lost with La Perouse, who was cast away on the island, and—as a lover of Rousseau—fully appreciated the innocence and nobility of its lack of civilization. The brief time that Hugues and Laurette spend on the island is an idyll of eupsychian perfection, but it can only be brief. They have to return to Europe, and to the full fury of the war, while Rara, Mémé and Kouang know that they too have no future but extinction; both subplots end, separately but simultaneously, in heart-rending tragedy.

Lichtenberger had written a study of utopian fiction early in his career, *Le Socialisme Utopique* [Utopian Socialism] (1898), and had had a notable political career of his own before the war in association with the radical Republican Paul Doumer; his literary output was varied but he was best known for a series of works attempting to reproduce the mind-set of childhood, celebrating its innocence while recognizing its perversities and its essential impermanence, beginning with *Mon Petit Trott* [Little Trott] (1898). *Les Centaures* had been a side-step from that series to examine a different model of doomed innocence, and so is *Raramémé*, but the latter, having added the war to the mixture of ideas in the same fashion as "Mowgli revient du front," is very obviously traumatized by the experience, and far more anguished than elegiac in the quality of its tragedy.

One particularly striking example of post-war apocalyptic *roman scientifique*, unusual in its complexity and phantasmagorical extravagance, is *L'Épopée martienne* (tr. as *The Martian Epic*), originally published in Amiens in two volumes, as **Les Titans du ciel** [Titans of the Sky] and *L'Agonie de la Terre* [The Death-Throes of the Earth], in 1921 and 1922, by Edgar Malfère. The published versions were the work of Théo Varlet (1875-1938), an author resident in the south of France, well-known for his poetry, literary criticism and translations from English, who had previously published short fiction but was making his first excursion into the novel. A devout pacifist who had refused military service as a conscientious objector, Varlet had had a bad time during the war—compounded when the Russian Revolution wiped out the family fortune that had previously maintained him in relative comfort—and he had published nothing during the war years. The two novels appeared as a collaboration, however, with Varlet's name in second place, because they were based on two previously-written manuscripts by Octave Joncquel, "Les derniers Titans" [The Last Titans] and "La fin des mondes" [The End of Worlds].

A colorful depiction of Joncquel recorded by Jean Garel in the *Bulletin de la Societé Jules Verne* in 1983 represents him as a well-known "character" in Amiens. Garel describes Joncquel as a "Bohemian", tall and strong, but also child-like, who dressed strangely and earned a living of sorts by doing odd jobs, especially working as a sandwich-board man. He appears, however, to have been a knowledgeable person and a voracious reader; he thought very highly of Jules Verne, who had once been Amiens' most famous citizen. Indeed, he might well have relocated to Amiens in honor of Verne, having been a Picard by birth. He seems to have been an enthusiastic lover of Vernian fiction, and his Bohemian affectations extended to writing numerous novels, most, if not all, of a bold speculative stripe, for which he sought in vain for a publisher for many years, although he did eventually contrive to publish *L'Homme qui supprima l'océan Atlantique* [The Man Who Destroyed the Atlantic Ocean] in 1934.

When Edgar Malfère first set up shop in Amiens in 1920, Joncquel gave him all his manuscripts, then approximately fifteen in number, for consideration. Malfère declared them unpublishable, but not uninteresting; he volunteered to buy the ideas in order to hand them over to someone who might be able to make viable use of them. Malfère then gave one of the manuscripts to Varlet, with whom he had previously worked on other projects, and whose short story collection *La Bella Venere* [the name is that of a boat] (1920) had been one of the first books he issued after moving to Amiens. Varlet was resident in the small southern coastal town of Cassis, but he spent a few weeks of annual summer vacation in the village of Saint-Valery, on the Somme estuary, not far from Amiens.

The arrangement between Malfère, Joncquel and Varlet lasted long enough for the former to publish both parts of *L'Épopée martienne* and for Varlet to complete an adaptation of a third Joncquel manuscript, "La terre océanée" [The Ocean-Covered World], but at that point it broke down. Joncquel sued Malfère, on the grounds that the publisher had made an oral agreement with him to pay him a royalty of five per cent (half the conventional amount) on copies of the books that were sold, which he had failed to honor. Joncquel claimed that this had ruined his "literary career" and demanded damages as well as the royalties he was allegedly owed.

Malfère, who had copyrighted the two published volumes in his own name, presumably having paid Varlet a fixed fee for the revision work, defended the case on the grounds that what Varlet had done with the manuscripts Joncquel had provided was to write entirely new texts recycling the fundamental ideas, while retaining hardly any of Joncquel's actual text—so that Varlet, not Joncquel, was the actual author of the published books. Joncquel lost the case, and was ordered to pay damages to Malfère. Malfère was, however, forbidden to publish the third volume already completed by Varlet, or to proceed with a fourth, "La guerre des microbes" [The Microbe War], whose manuscript had also been forwarded to Varlet. These, along with all Joncquel's other manuscripts, were returned to their author, and nothing more was heard of them. What became of them—and, for that matter, of Joncquel—remains unknown. The loss is unfortunate; however inept Joncquel might have been as a writer, he seems to have possessed a vivid imagination.

Given that Joncquel handed over so many manuscripts to Malfère in 1920, it is impossible to be sure when "Les Derniers Titans" and "La Fin des Mondes" were written, but the story told in the published version of the portmanteau novel is very obviously based on the recent experience of the war; indeed, the imaginary history of the two volumes can be seen as a transfigurative echo of the war, in which the temporarily-stalemated invasion of France by alien forces is far more dramatic and, ultimately, far more devastating.

The story begins in 1978, when the "problem of war" has been allegedly solved on Earth since 1932 by a new radiation weapon that detonates explosive substances at a distance—an invention made by Eric Christiansen in *L'Ingénieur von Satanas*. In the resultant world state, technological advancement has proceeded rapidly, and radio communication has been established with Jupiter, and then with Mars. The Martians, unfortunately, prove perfidious, and after benefiting from the technological discoveries of the other worlds, they launch an attack on Earth, intent on relocating from their own decrepit and inhospitable world to the younger and greener planet, after the fashion of the Martians of H. G. Wells' *The War of the Worlds*. Paris is destroyed by Martian poison gases, and the action shifts to the environs of Marseilles; it is from there that the hero, Léon Rudeaux, and his lover Raymonde witness the disintegration of social order under the pressure of the bombardment and a revolution that establishes a local Communism more immediately dangerous than the alien threat.

Eventually, the scattered forces of resistance to the alien threat succeed in establishing communication with one another, collaborating in an analysis of the missiles and initiating the development of a means of defense against them, but the home-grown threats continue to escalate, with the emergence of apocalyptic cultists intent on universal destruction. The beleaguered defenders of civilization eventually take refuge in the Observatory on Mont Blanc, where the communication link with Jupiter finally brings the good news that the Jovians will intervene to prevent the Martians inflicting further damage and intend to punish them for their aggression.

The Jovians do, indeed, blow Mars up, but that only shifts the conflict into a new phase, as the action moves to Cairo and the plot shifts into a Flammarionesque mode, adapting the notion of cosmic paligenensis to the imagination of an interplanetary invasion by dispossessed souls able and avid to possess the bodies of the survivors of Earth's holocaust—and also, because the Martian missiles have not left sufficient survivors, the bodies of all other available primates. In the second volume of the epic, the remarkable conquest of the Earth, facilitated by Martian Magi and a gigantic technological soul-transference facility, is a *fait accompli*. A disincarnate Rudeaux has to travel to Venus in search of assistance to rally some kind of resistance to the Martian masters of Earth and attempt to prevent the next phase of their plan of interplanetary expansion.

While the refugees in the Observatory escape a cultist attack and succeed in fleeing half way across the world to South America, Rudeaux and Raymonde attempt a daring infiltration of the massive industrial complex built and supervised by the Martian Great Leader and his Empress in order to complete the plan made by the last surviving Magus, the Sovereign Pontiff Égrégore XIII. That plan involves an invasion of Venus and the complete destruction the Earth by means of drilling a deep shaft in order to introduce a huge bomb into its into its core. The double blast of the Earth-destroying bomb and the lift-off of the Martians' Venus-bound spacecraft is set to provide a climax toward which the plot marches, with the kind of inexorability that only an unprecedented *deus ex machina* can possible prevent.

It is difficult to imagine a greater contrast in narrative tone and manner than that between the soberly lachrymose *Raramémé* and the stridently ultra-melodramatic *L'Épopée martienne*, but they both reflect the same shift in consciousness induced in their authors by the war as the other works discussed in this section: each contains, in its own way, a similar sense of loss and a similar measure of desperation. The extremes to which they go are poles apart, in terms of their narrative strategy and affective quality, but the psychological drive impelling them non-stop toward those extremes is rooted in the same horrors and the same fears.

Edgar Malfère gave Théo Varlet another novel to rewrite for publication in 1923, which appeared as **La Belle Valence** ["Beautiful Valencias!"—the habitual cry of Parisian orange-sellers] (tr. as *Timeslip Troopers*), by-lined as a collaboration with André Blandin. There is no indication on the book as to who "André Blandin" was—he was not the contemporary Belgian painter of that name—but it can be inferred from the text that he was a French officer who served on the Western Front during the latter part of the Great War. Given that three André Blandins were recorded as having been killed in action during the war, it seems likely that the manuscript was given to Varlet after its author's death.

Whether or not it was actually written in the trenches, *La Belle Valence* presents an image of life therein and the attitudes of the fighting men that is at odds with the notions carefully promoted by wartime propaganda. It suggests, with a laconically cynical black humor, that the soldiers of France did not spend their free time dreaming about a future era of peace and harmony, or about distinguishing themselves heroically in defense of the fatherland, but of massacring enemies who were too ill-equipped to fight back and then surrendering themselves to the orgiastic delights of alcohol-fueled pillage and rape. If that were not enough, the story blithely takes for granted the conviction that a group of French officers accidentally timeslipped into the middle of a Medieval war between Muslims and Catholics would unhesitatingly side with the Muslims, as the contemporary custodians of civilized values, against the adherents of the religion to which they no longer even pay lip service. Both notions were liable to upset a portion of the potential audience, and to make some of its members apoplectic. As a committed pacifist and non-believer, however, Varlet must have been fully sympathetic to Blandin's aims in highlighting the hellish hypocrisies of war and faith.

As with Henri Falk and André Arnyvelde, Blandin's primary purpose in writing during his spare time in the trenches must have been to provide himself with a measure of psychological escape. The plot describes how French tunnel-diggers in a northern section of the Western Front in 1917 break through into the cellar of a house destroyed by bombardment and find it full of precious wine and spirits—a treasure-trove that the hero, Lieutenant Renard, naturally decides to reserve for himself and his fellow officers. The cellar once belonged to an Englishman, and Renard discovers that it also contains an improved model of H. G. Wells' time machine, capable of moving in space as well.

After testing the machine with a trip to pre-war Paris, Renard intends to take it into the future to discover when the war will end, setting the controls for 1920. When duty calls him away, however, his batman unwittingly shifts the levers, so that when the machine is eventually activated it ends up in fourteenth-century Spain, not far from the walls of Valencia, and it takes a huge section of the French position with it, including an entire platoon of *poilus*.

Once they have figured out where and when they are, the French soldiers' immediate impulse is not to go back—after all, they can always do that later—but to make the most of an unexpected period of leave. Conquering Valencia, with the support of a contingent of Moors, proves very easy, and while an intellectually-inclined sub-lieutenant makes bold plans for civilizing the Spaniards and introducing the rewards of modern Enlightenment to the Medieval city, the *poilus* set about having a riotously good time.

Unfortunately, the Church, anachronistically represented by the Inquisition, has its own ideas about the appropriate response to an invasion of manifest demons, and its agents plan a counter-revolution, followed by an auto-da-fé, from which a depleted contingent of the soldiers eventually escape by the skin of their teeth. Arriving back only a few hours after they left, however, in the midst of a furious bombardment, their losses are chalked up to enemy action and their superiors are none the wiser.

As light-hearted in its fashion as "Le Maître des trois états," *La Belle Valence* is primarily a comedy of release, an exercise in self-indulgence, but it does touch in passing on serious issues of historical purpose, especially the question of what the fighting men are and ought to be fighting *for*, in 1324 or in 1917. It touches, too, on some of the logical problems associated with the paradoxicality of time travel, and the ending—which might or might not have been added to the existing text by Varlet—carefully leaves some questions unanswered that might have provided scope for an interesting sequel; although the machine itself is destroyed by the German bombardment, Renard still has the Englishman's notebooks, and not only has the intellectually ambitious sub-lieutenant been stranded in 1324, but there is a possibility that the chief Inquisitor has been transported to 1917 and has slipped away in the confusion.

Whether Varlet left those loose ends dangling deliberately or not, he did not pick them up, and he did no further work for Malfère. When he wrote his first solo *roman scientifique*, it was an equally wry fantasy of compromised wish-fulfillment focused on one of the awkward after-effects of the war: the loans that had to be repaid, and the consequent economic difficulties that crippled the French economy, shrinking the value of the franc drastically. Whereas *La Belle Valence* explicitly borrowed H. G. Wells' time machine as its initial premise, *Le Roc d'or* (1927; tr. as *The Golden Rock*) is a variation on the theme of Jules Verne's posthumously-issued *La Chasse au météore*. Although *Le Roc d'or* uses the same premise as Verne's novel, however—the fall of a huge meteorite that turns out to be composed primarily of gold—it extrapolates it in a very different fashion.

The probability that the advent of a meteorite made of gold would inflame the kind of fever that had provoked "gold rushes" in Australia and California during the early nineteenth century and the Klondike gold rush of 1897-99 is treated disapprovingly in Verne's novel, but the potential economic upheaval consequent on a sudden massive increase in the world's gold supply is barely mentioned. In the climax of Verne's novel it is the romantic settlements that take pride of place, while wider implications are complacently swept under the carpet. In Varlet's novel, by contrast, the humor is conscientiously underplayed and much blacker in tone; the element of satire is far more scathing, and the economic and political aspects of the consequences of the meteorite's exploitation are the principal dramatic focus of the story. Although the narrative appears briefly to be shaping up as a conventional spy story with a formularistic "love interest," that dimension is swiftly marginalized in favor of its cynical analysis of the economic and political impact of the meteoric gold on a world whose currencies' long dependence on the gold standard is on the brink of falling apart by virtue of the damage inflicted by the Great War.

Varlet could not foresee the Wall Street Crash of 1929 and the subsequent Great Depression, nor could he anticipate the precise circumstances in which World War Two would eventually break out, but he certainly had a clear consciousness of such apocalyptic possibilities, and *Le Roc d'or* examines them with an appropriate post-war cynicism, which he also applied mercilessly to the politics of the League of Nations, and like his other works in the genre—which will be discussed elsewhere in the present chapter—his first four volumes all made a significant contribution to the development of the genre in the difficult decades following the end of the Great War.

Le Roc d'or looks back explicitly, if somewhat ironically, to the period before the Great War as a kind of "Golden Age." It had not seemed so while people had been living through it, when nostalgia had tended to look to a much more remote imaginary past for inspiration, but an essential element of Varlet's career as a writer of prose fiction was the imaginative impetus provided by his realization that the world had changed completely within his lifetime, thanks to the advent of new means of travel and media of communication. Although that awareness had been reflected in some of his poetry prior to his recruitment by Malfère, it became much more obvious afterwards, most notably in the cosmological poems in his collection *Ad Astra* (1929), several of which celebrate the potential of astronautics and the possibility of interplanetary communication.

Edmond Haraucourt's relocation of the horrors and fears evoked by the war into a distant future was reproduced, albeit more modestly but in far greater detail, in *Le Grand cataclysme, roman du centième siècle* (1922; tr. as *The Great Cataclysm; a Romance of the Hundredth Century*) by Henri Allorge (1878-1938). The novel won the Prix Sobrier-Arnould, one of several annual literary prizes then awarded by the Académie Française, which was limited to novels of special moralistic and educational value. Larousse reprinted the book in 1929, in a series primarily at young readers, emphasizing its categorization as a children's book.

Like Théo Varlet, Henri Allorge had been a poet before the war and had won a considerable amount of critical praise. Although he employed commonplace historical, mythological and sentimental themes, he had also attempted to be innovative, particularly in two collections reflecting his fascination with mathematics and music respectively. The former, *L'Âme géométrique* [The Geometric Soul] (1906) was dedicated to Camille Flammarion, who provided a preface for it, and it featured poems in celebration of various geometrical forms. The latter, *Le*

Clavier des harmonies, transpositions poétiques [The Harmonic Scale; Poetic Transpositions] attempted a similar ingenuity; his first novel, *Le Mal de gloire* [The Evil of Glory] (1913) was an intense psychological study of a composer and musician who sacrifices the amenities of domestic life to his burning ambition, much as scientists were often supposed to do. During the war Allorge worked for the Ministry of War as a *"rédacteur"*—a title that might cover anything from routine clerical work to writing propaganda, and probably did.

As with many other writers, Allorge evidently found it exceedingly difficult to pick up the threads of his career after the war, although he published a book entitled *Charlot, Janot et Jocrisse* in 1921 before publishing *Le Grand cataclysme* a year later. As with Arnyvelde's *La Bacchus mutilé*, the juxtaposed sections of *Le Grand cataclysme* are uncomfortably welded together in a fashion that suggests strongly that the first of its three parts must have been drafted before the outbreak of the war, while the other two show its raw scars very obviously.

Although it describes a coherent set of events involving the same cast of core characters, the first part of the novel was almost certainly designed as an independent story with its own climax and conclusion, evidently intended for young readers. The chronology of the story is fudged, and it seems obvious that the past catastrophes to which Part One refers back were originally imagined to have occurred in 1960 rather than 8960, the extra seven thousand years being a belated attempt to accommodate and adjust the plot to a much broader timescale, whose implications and effects are central to the themes of the second and third parts. Part One was probably redrafted when the story was taken up at a later date for expansion, although Part Three—which is full of inept improvisations—gives the impression of being a slapdash first draft written with some effort.

The story as published begins in the year 9978 in the city of Kentropol, located in what used to be Tunisia, where human civilization has been successfully maintained by advanced technology in spite of the advent of a new Ice Age. The basic scenario is reminiscent of Méry's "Ruines de Paris" and its successors, and the characters set off almost immediately on an excursion to visit the ruins of Paris, in a heavily joke-laden sequence in which one of the characters cites ludicrous conclusions relating to the nineteenth and early twentieth century supposedly drawn by "archeological science." The first part of the story told in the novel is a relatively light-hearted comedy, whose descriptions of technologically sophisticated life in Kentropol are strongly reminiscent of Robida's *Electric Life*. It is, in fact, the electric nature of the life in question that is attacked by the great cataclysm of the title, when all electric power suddenly fails, stranding the excursionists in derelict Paris—an awkward predicament from which they are eventually rescued.

Part Two is much darker in tone, no longer giving the impression of being intended for younger readers. It relates the desperate attempts made in Kentropol to sustain life without its chief technological prop, and introduces the second great city in North Africa, Heraklopol, home to a more rigidly disciplined society, the government of which is far more authoritarian. A attempt by the protagonists to make contact with the Heraklopolitans leads to their being arrested and imprisoned as spies, and the paranoia responsible for that reaction is soon manifest on a larger scale, as competition for the world's last fugitive coal deposits leads to conflict between the two great cities and a declaration of war. Both have superweapons in reserve, which are very rapidly deployed, leading to the mutual devastation of both cities, and civilization itself.

Although there are elements of utopian satire in Part Two they are more-or-less gratuitous intrusions in a story whose principal thrust is an indignant complaint against the follies of contemporary society, especially its reckless squandering of resources and its dire tendency to violence. Part Three picks up the story of the protagonists, who are fortunate enough to be some distance from Kentropolis during the city's destruction; it is earnest but fragmentary, and conspicuously lacking in narrative energy. The survivors find a refuge in the Oasis de la Source Fleurie [the Oasis of the Flowery Spring], where they contrive to establish a primitive but sustainable way of life, and when they eventually visit the site of Kentropolis again they find it reclaimed by the sea. In embarking upon their effort to repopulate—at least for a while—"*cette misérable planète*" they swear a formal oath to avoid the sins that led to the destruction of the former civilization: greed, avarice and, most of all, war.

Allorge had not given up on poetry in the aftermath of the war, but only published two more collections: *Petits poèmes électriques et scientifiques* [Short Electrical and Scientific Poems] (1924) and *L'Espoir obstiné* [Obstinate Hope] (1929), which attracted far less attention than his pre-war work. His second and final venture into *roman scientifique* aimed at young readers, *Ciel contre terre* [Heaven Against Earth] (1924), features a Martian invasion that ultimately fails because of the Martians' fatal weakness for alcohol. He wrote other novels for children, but all of them were mundane thrillers.

Pierre Mille's "En trois cent ans" (*Oeuvres Libres* 1922; tr. as "Three Hundred Years Hence") is one of the most succinct expressions of post-war apocalyptic sensibility, but no less effective for its brevity. Its title serves as the immersive fantasy's only introduction to a future France in which the oppressed indigenous society has reverted to a semi-barbaric state following a series of international wars, and the relics of the old civilization are gradually becoming exceedingly scare and precious, although even something as trivial as a pair of fine shoes might be capable of precipitating a new revolution.

La Guerre microbienne, la fin de monde [The Microbial War: The End of the World] (1923), signed "Professeur X***" was also issued in the same year by a different publisher as *L'Offensive des microbes, roman d'une guerre future* [The Microbial Offensive: A Romance of a Future War] with the signature

"Professeur Motus." It describes a sneak German attack on France by means of biological warfare, which gets out of hand.

Similarly succinct, but far more brutal and frankly alarmist, *Comment Paris a été détruit en six heures le 20 avril 1924 (le jour de Pâques)* (tr. as "How Paris was Destroyed in Six Hours") by the journalist Louis Baudry de Saunier was published as a pamphlet in 1924. The story takes the form of a speech delivered by a triumphant German military scientist, delivered in the presence of Wilhelm II in the Palace of Versailles following a German conquest of France, and explains in detail how Germany managed clandestinely to equip airplanes supposedly designed for mail delivery to double as precision bombers, whose surprise raid on Paris during the Easter holiday completely annihilated the city with explosives, incendiary bombs and poison gas, thus paving the way for an unstoppable invasion by ground forces.

That possibility was in the process of becoming the great bugbear of fears engendered by the anticipation of a second world war. Airplanes, still primitive in 1914, had made only a limited contribution to the fighting of the Great War, but the pressure put on their rapid evolution by progressive adaptation for aerial combat and the delivery of bombs had raised an unmistakable signpost for the future. Nobody any longer thought that the next war would be fought in trenches; it was taken for granted that entrenchment would become irrelevant when fleets of bombers and airborne "torpedoes" (guided missiles) could simply fly over them, and that the likelihood that effective opposition to them could be mounted by fighter aircraft and existing anti-aircraft fire was exceedingly slim.

That notion ramped up the sense of vulnerability felt by city-dwellers considerably. No longer would a city have to be besieged and occupied by ground forces in order for its citizenry to be exposed to the full horrors of war; from being far behind the lines—at least hopefully—Paris had effectively been moved into the front line of the next imaginable war, the first target rather than the ultimate prize. That anxiety was also felt very keenly in London, where it was realized that the pride and glory of England's defensive network—her navy— might well be irrelevant in future.

Significantly, however, that was not an anxiety felt in New York, which lay well beyond range of attack by that means in the imminent future. France would have been far more deeply affected by the legacy of the trenches than any other nation anyway, because so many of the trenches had been dug in French soil, even though the British had helped to defend them, but when it came to the contemplation of near-future aerial warfare, Britain and France were closely united in terror, while America felt smugly secure. That difference can be seen, in retrospect, to be one of the principal causes of the sharp divergence in tone and concern that took place in the 1920s between American speculative fiction on the one hand, which evolved very rapidly into science fiction in the latter half of that decade, and British scientific romance and French *roman scientifique* on the other, which both remained heavily weighed down by apocalyptic anxieties, as if by a ball and chain.

As the companion project to this one demonstrates, that ball and chain had prolific results in Britain, where apocalyptic fears of what the next war might bring evolved from relatively sparse beginnings in the 1920s to a full-blown panic in the 1930s. In France, fiction reflecting the same apocalyptic anxieties became more extravagant and more prolific considerable earlier—although, by way of partial compensation, it became relatively less prolific in the latter decade, and a little less hysterical, a general tone of bitter resignation having set in along with the Great Depression, which turned the "Roaring Twenties" into the whimpering thirties even more evidently in Europe than in America.

Le Règne du Bonheur [The Reign of Happiness] (1924) by Alexandre Arnoux (1884-1973) offers an early anticipation of that relaxation into resignation, in an account of a faster-than-light journey that takes advantage of Einsteinian relativity to bring about an extreme time dilatation, so that the traveler returns to Earth after a short lapse of subjective time to find that centuries have passed: time enough for the world to have obliterated civilization and returned to a generalized primitivism, with a moderate but secure degree of contentment.

Before that relaxation took full effect, however, the acute consciousness of peril produced some remarkably extravagant works of imaginative fiction, in various strata of the literary marketplace, as illustrated by three works published in 1925 that are as various in their sophistication as they are uniform in their dour outlook and grim fascination with unfettered and uncontrollable violence: *Les Hommes frénétiques* (tr. as *The Frenetic People*) by Ernest Pérochon (1885-1942); *La Fin d'Illa* (tr. as *Illa's End*) by José Moselli (1882-1941); and *La Dernière jouissance* (tr. as "The Ultimate Pleasure") by Renée Dunan (1892-1936).

Les Hommes frénétiques is something of an anomaly within the pattern of the author's works; his fame rested on his numerous *romans paysans*, stories of rural life focusing primarily on the lives of the poor people who worked the land. He had been producing such fiction since 1912, having been born on a farm. Pérochon had been something of an anomaly himself in that environment; although his own family was not exceedingly poor, his neighbors were, and he later recalled, as a significant memory of his formative childhood, that he had routinely taken off his shoes when he went out to play, lest he be thought effeminate by his barefoot playmates. His family was also Protestant, while most of the neighbors were Catholic. Having completed his secondary education, Pérochon did not go to university in Paris because he had two younger brothers who still had to complete their secondary studies, and he had to earn a living. Initially, he became a schoolteacher.

Pérochon paid for the publication of his first volume of poetry in 1908, and his first novel, *Les Creux de Maisons*, appeared four years later, initially in serial form in *L'Humanité*, a periodical edited by the socialist propagandist Jean-Jaurès. Although he was mobilized in 1914 he suffered a heart attack at the front and was invalided out of the army. He continued writing, and in 1920 his novel *Néné* won the Prix Goncourt, a success that enabled him to devote himself to writing full-time

Inevitably, the effects of the Great War were clearly displayed in the naturalistic novels Pérochon published after 1918, but their most obvious and most striking legacy was *Les Hommes frénétiques*. While many works in the same vein remained primarily preoccupied with the near-future and the potential destructive effects of aerial bombardment, Pérochon moved beyond that into a more distant future, in which physics has permitted a more fundamental examination of the underlying fabric of space, permitting the technological production of exotic forms of matter, energy and life. His account of the particular political opposition that provokes the future war has a quasi-satirical component, but it harks back to the fundamental opposition sketched out in 1834 in Félix Bodin's prospectus for *Le Roman de l'avenir*, in which constructive political pragmatism is permanently opposed by an "Anti-Prosaic League" of restless dissidents.

The story begins by introducing the great scientist Avrine, the pioneer of the new physics, and his disciple Harisson, permitting the latter to read a text offering a summary of the history of science, with particular reference to the juncture of the Great War:

"The historian briefly mentioned that long and bloody skirmish, whose causes seemed, at a distance, puerile and extremely confused. Nothing new, in any case, had emerged during the war—only a few timid excursions of aircraft in the background, and a few ferocious but maladroit deployments of poison gases. As in the remotest times, the belligerents had sent their most vigorous young males against the enemy, confiding firearms to them, resulting in a terrible negative selection. That war, pursued for long months with a terrible obstinacy by numerous armies, marvelously disciplined and provided with murderous engines, had severely shaken the old world.

"The magnitude of the catastrophe should have caused the scales to fall from the blindest eyes, but it had not. People had not understood that a new era was beginning, in which prudence, for want of generosity, would become an essential virtue. As soon as the armed conflict was over, the conflicts of pride or self-interest had enfevered hearts again; again, hands that were still bloody had clenched into threatening fists. Never, perhaps, had humans been so lacking in clear-sightedness and good will than at that point in time.

"Science was progressing rapidly, but few people thought of being surprised or mistrustful. Intelligence seemed somewhat dazed or disorientated. Military leaders were seen gravely drafting treatises on strategy imitative of antiquity for the use of the warriors of the future. Philosophers ratiocinated; poets stammered; squadrons of myopics occupied the sentry-boxes and blockaded the crossroads of thought. In more than one country, vulgar demagogues hoisted themselves on to popular stages; semi-madmen brandishing clubs succeeded in finding an audience. The masses, still numbed by shock, and sensing confusedly that the world was changing, were hesitant. Uniquely concerned with the immediate future, they lost their ancient virtues without acquiring new ones, and let things happen with a sort of disenchanted fatalism. No nation knew exactly where it wanted to go."

The summary history then proceeds with an account of gradual political reforms and the emergence of a "vast federation of egalitarian republics" before a new disruption by world war in the twenty-second century, interrupted, as in *L'Ingénieur von Satanas* and *L'Épopée martienne* by the invention of a device capable causing the deflagration of all explosives at a distance, here credited to a physicist named "Noëlle Roger"—a pseudonym used by the Swiss writer Hélène Pittard, who had published an apocalyptic novel of her own, *Le Nouveau Déluge* [The New Deluge] in 1922, although Pérochon might not have been aware of that. In this instance, however, the end of explosive warfare was merely the prelude to microbial warfare, which proved so devastating as to leave the contending forces exhausted, but with no victory won, and a return to worldwide barbarity lasting three centuries. Because scientific knowledge survived, however, albeit fugitively, a global Renaissance was not merely possible but rapid, initiating a new "Universal Era" of five centuries of uninterrupted scientific progress powered by a worldwide grid of "zones of force" wisely supervised by a Supreme Council.

"And yet," the text immediately adds, "people were unacquainted with happiness!" The reason offered for that dearth is that the eutopian quality of existence has, of its own accord, given birth to a profound *ennui*, extending to *spleen*, and *frénésie*, in the meaning of those terms employed by the poets and prose writers of the nineteenth-century Decadent Movement: a corrosive, irresistible and intrinsically self-destructive dissatisfaction. The plot of the main story describes how the effects of that innate corruption lead, once again, to a further repetition of the Great War, this time fought with weapons genuinely too dreadful to use, but used regardless. The destruction is described in horrific detail in the first two parts of the three-part story. In the third, as in Allorge's *Grand cataclysme*, and in a similarly fragmentary fashion, albeit with considerably more stylistic elegance, the story picks up the lives of a handful of survi-

517

vors of the catastrophe. This time, no figurative flicker of science has survived to form the basis of a Renaissance; it really is a matter of starting again from scratch, with the fundamental defensive alliance of humans and dogs.

In spite of the abundance of competition, *Les Hommes frénétiques* probably deserves to be reckoned as the most dramatic and forceful exemplification of its apocalyptic theme, as well as the boldest example of attempted scientific extrapolation. It is not surprising that it is the work of a writer who had no interest in futuristic fiction as a field of ongoing literary activity, but was obsessed by one particular gnawing anxiety that he wanted to express as fully and as dramatically as possible—and once having done so, felt no need to repeat himself or add anything further.

The Decadent Movement was long dead before Ernest Pérochon began writing, and he had no sympathy with the moral and stylistic contortions it had produced in its practitioners, but it had undeniably made its mark in terms of the promotion of a psychological thesis suggesting that euchronia and eupsychia might be intrinsically antithetical, and incapable of synthesis. That had not seemed plausible to many people in the *fin-de-siècle* period, when "decadence" was more generally seen as an affectation than an affliction, but in the 1920s, after the Great War, the thesis appeared to Pérochon to have taken on a deadly bite. He was perfectly willing to use it as a departure-point for speculation, implying that that no period of peaceful plenty can ever last long in human affairs, because the absence of the old sources of social stress would inevitably give birth to a stress of its own.

In fact, Pérochon's cynicism cuts even deeper than the cynicism of Decadent fiction; his most challenging suggestion, explicitly posed in his first chapter, is that peace and plenty are only possible, even temporarily, if two of the ideals normally considered virtuous—courage and justice—can be suppressed or set aside. It is, he suggests, the desire for an impossible justice that has always been the primary motive impelling people to slaughter one another mercilessly on a massive scale, and a stupid courage that has always provided them with the psychological means. That supposition makes *Les Hommes frénétiques* distinctive in the tradition of eutopian and dystopian literature, posing a moral and pragmatic question in respect to the desirability and practicality of justice (and hence of liberty, equality and fraternity) that most other works of a similar stripe had been, and remained, content to gloss over.

José Moselli's *La Fin d'Illa* is set in the distant past rather than the future, but it deploys a notion that had long existed in speculative fiction and became more frequent in its invocation as apocalyptic fiction became more violent: the idea that previous civilizations had existed on Earth, which had annihilated themselves along almost all traces of their existence, by means of advanced scientific weaponry. The principal corollary of that notion was that the imminent demise of humankind imaginable in the wake of the Great War might be a phase in a repetitive cycle.

Moselli's novel originally appeared as a feuilleton in the weekly periodical *Sciences et Voyages*, which made a deliberate attempt to appeal to the audience of the *Journal des Voyages* while broadening its scope to take in a more general popularization of science. The result of that redefinition of scope was that the fiction it ran in its feuilleton slot became much more speculatively adventurous, considerably more similar to the American pulp "scientifiction" that was just beginning its evolution than the vast bulk of the adventure fiction serialized in the *Journal des Voyages*. Moselli was the magazine's most prolific contributor, and led the way in that development.

The author of *La Fin d'Illa*, who was baptized Joseph Morelli, is a strangely paradoxical figure. Although he was one of the most prolific writers of his era, he never published a single book, all of his works appearing as *feuilleton* serials and episodes of part-work series. In spite of the fact that he produced the equivalent of several novels a year, often writing more than one serial simultaneously, he did almost all of his work for a single employer, the Maison Offenstadt, routinely concealed—voluntarily or otherwise—behind an array of pseudonyms.

According to Jacques van Herp's study of the author, Moselli conceived an early ambition to go to sea and signed on as a cabin boy once he was old enough. Inevitably, he had a hard time and decided that there had to be an easier way of making a living. After some early tribulations while investigating popular literature as a possible source of income, he met one of the Offenstadt brothers, proprietors of a publishing house with several periodicals aimed at young readers, and secured his place of refuge. His first publications appeared in 1910, in *L'Intrépide* [Dauntless], whose mainstay he soon became. *L'Intrépide*, its companion *L'Épatant* [Marvelous], and various part-works published by the Offenstadts helped to comprise the lowest stratum of the pre-war French literary marketplace: an approximate equivalent of American pulp magazines, the part-works conserving the "dime novel" format by then obsolete in the U.S.A.

Moselli's burgeoning career might have run into difficulties in 1914, when his experience in the merchant marine resulted in conscription to naval service for the duration of the Great War, but he was unusual among writers of the period in maintaining his production in spite of his military duties, and contriving to publish what he wrote; periodicals like *L'Intrépide* were apparently considered a propaganda asset even before 1917, because of their ostentatious jingoism. It is difficult to estimate the total volume of his output, but van Herp estimates that he produced a hundred thousand words a month at his peak, during a career that lasted almost thirty years. He eventually gave up writing in 1938, probably because the Maison Offenstadt was in dire straits financially, having lost a significant fraction of its core audience to newer periodicals.

The main story of *La Fin d'Illa* is framed by a narrative that begins in 1875 with the dredging up of a strangely heavy ball of an unfamiliar substance by a whaling vessel, accompanied by a book in a strange language. Thirty years later, a curious scientist contrives to translate the book, but is killed when the ball explodes, causing the great San Francisco earthquake of 1905. His translation survives, however, and tells the story of the great city of Illa, contained in a single gigantic building, where the comfort of the citizens is maintained by various advanced technologies not dissimilar to those deployed in Pérochon's Ultimate Era. The narrative voice reports that "Life in Illa is happy, but monotonous," a circumstance of which the manuscript's narrator, the leader of the army, Xié, does not approve. Its system of government is, however, oppressive, policed by hordes of brutal ape-men produced by scientists using a technique of artificial regression.

Fortunately for Xié's love of action, war seems imminent and inevitable. In order to obtain immortality by means of an invention made by their leader, Rair, the masters of Illa's Supreme Council need vast supplies of human blood, and they intend to obtain them from the citizens of a rival city, Nour. They believe that they cannot lose the war because they possess the zero-stone, an atomic explosive. When it is pointed out to Xié, however, that once the Nourans are used up, Rair is bound to turn to the citizens of Illa to maintain his immortality, he turns rebel, initiating a fierce internecine struggle that complicates the war and leads even more surely and much more rapidly to the mutual destruction of the two cities and the world that contains them—but not until Xié has undergone a series of extravagant melodramatic exploits involving torture, hellish imprisonment, an exceedingly bloody revolt of the ape-men and a final personal confrontation with his enemy.

The sheer profusion and inevitable formularization of Moselli's work made him unusually subject to the phenomenon of melodramatic inflation, whereby frequently-used devices come to seem obsolete and there is an inevitable thrust toward greater extravagance in the motifs deployed. His many crime and adventure stories felt this pressure, and became more flamboyant and more bizarre in consequence, and it was presumably his acute consciousness of the pressure of melodramatic inflation, and the paradoxical demands opened up by trying to respond to it, that led Moselli to the excesses considered "sadistic" by his detractors, as well as the other garish inventions of *La Fin d'Illa*. It is not possible for stories to go to such extremes routinely, and there is some cause for surprise that Moselli was allowed to go there at all. The most astonishing thing about the story is not that Moselli was inspired to write it—that is easily understandable—but that the Offenstadt brothers were prepared to publish it. It is possible that no one who could have stopped the publication of the story actually bothered to read it until its serialization was well advanced—it would not have started alarm bells ringing at an early stage, because its build-up is carefully measured—and also possible that its truncated and synoptic ending is the result of the author being given a belated but firm instruction to stop and never to do anything like it again.

He never did, although he continued to use the staple melodramatic fare that had been taken to its logical conclusion in *La Fin d'Illa* in the hypocritically moderate fashion that was not merely permitted but encouraged by contemporary editors. *La Fin d'Illa* remains, however, as an example of the extent to which post-war disenchantment could be taken, without conventional restraint.

Renée Dunan was, in her own way, just as paradoxical a character as José Moselli. She appears to have written prolifically in a wide variety of genres between 1920 and 1925, when she published several books as well as contributing to a number of periodicals. If the supplementary material in the books can be believed, she wrote a great deal more than was actually published, or at least intended to. Most of her work appeared from small marginal publishers, and much of it might well have been written some time before publication. She clearly did not have an easy time in making an initial impact in the literary world of post-Great War Paris, in spite of a relentless energy and a willingness to experiment with all kinds of materials.

A series of satirical *Lettres intimes* [Personal Correspondence] featured in *La Revue des Lettres* in 1925, which couched articles on various topics in the form of letters to imaginary correspondents, included one addressed to "Monsieur le Professeur J.-D. Prettywhore à Dayton, Ohio," offering an elaborately sarcastic and admirably detailed account of the current literary coteries of Paris, diversifying from the solid foundations of romanticism (allegedly the most flourishing ideology), naturalism and symbolism to take in various "new schools," including Jules Romains' "unanism" and surrealism—described, in complimentary terms, as the grown-up bastard child of Dadaism. It concludes with an answer to the hypothetical question of where she would place herself among the "schools, groups and chapels":

"Truly, nowhere. I am of that special sort of novelist who directs lived adventures in accordance with a philosophical rule. Three bases are indispensable in order to comprehend the range of my writings: the Neo-Platonism of Bergson, the Relativism of Einstein and the Pansexualism of Freud. As, especially in the milieux in which letters are judged, abstract knowledge is not much in favor, I must resign myself, just as Rabelais passed for a mere humorist, and Flaubert for an insipid bourgeois, to passing for a simple pornographer...."

Although the false immodesty of that reckoning is not entirely serious, it illustrates the fact that, although Dunan was already being written off by some contemporary critics as a "simple pornographer," she did have larger ambitions, and the explicit eroticism of several of her early works was guided by an intense interest in the psychological functions played by sex in human affairs rather than by a simple determination to titillate her readers. The possibility remains, in fact, that "Renée Dunan" might have been a transvestite disguise—such, at least, was the claim belatedly made by one Georges Dunan, who claimed after Renée Dunan's supposed death in 1936 that he had actually written all the books signed by that name. If so—and he might well have been lying—then it was a remarkably extreme and consistent imposture, given that Renée Dunan maintained an extensive personal correspondence with numerous real individuals as well as fictitious ones.

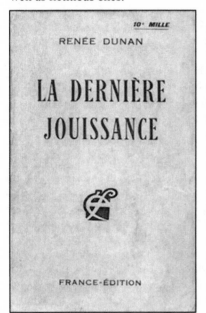

La Dernière jouissance is a peculiar addition to the tradition of dystopian fiction, not least because of its curious evenhandedness, although that might be partly due to a reversal of opinion while the work was in progress, when she abandoned her once-fervent commitment to revolutionary socialism. In its depiction of a future absolute tyranny it is remarkably stark. The novel offers a fairly conventional image of the ruthless oppression of workers by a managerial class living in luxury, not unlike the one in Claude Farrère's *Les Condamnés à mort*, but it is even further exaggerated, and is supposedly excused by the necessity of saving a fragment of civilization from a worldwide disaster occasioned by an escape of poisonous gases from the San Andreas fault. That could only be accomplished, allegedly, by relentless labor, forced by terrorism, at the behest of a small technocratic elite. The world is allegedly still exceedingly dangerous because of residual accumulations of poison gas, although the fact that a considerable population of runaway rebels has been built up in the environs of a carefully-isolated Paris casts more than a little doubt on that assertion.

In the first part of the novel, its heroine appears to be B-309, a sex-slave within the masters' fortress, who has contrived to seduce the son of the tyrant Tadée Broun and has a secret means of communicating the information she worms out of him to the agents of the rebel "messiah," who is promising the enslaved masses an imminent liberation. The information she provides does indeed allow the rebels to invade the tunnels beneath the citadel and establish a means of blowing up its arsenal of superweapons if their demands are not met.

The story abandons B-309 half way through, however, when the revolution actually breaks out and the rebels attempt to storm the citadel by sheer weight of numbers, provoking a large-scale massacre. From then on, the story seems to switch its allegiance, and its hero becomes the citadel's head of security, Vialy, who has been obliged to venture out into the city in search of his mistress, captured by the rebels and scheduled for execution. Against all the odds, he succeeds in rescuing her, but knows that it is already too late to save the citadel or the city, and that the only thing he and she can do is undertake a desperate and dangerous flight into the surrounding wilderness, in the frail hope that they might be able to get far enough away to avoid being killed by the blast.

La Dernière jouissance is as melodramatic, in its fashion, as *La Fin d'Illa*, and if it is not as crude in literary terms, it still falls far short of the literary sophistication of *Les Hommes frénétiques*. What the three novels have in common is, however, more striking than what separates them, and the ideological confusion of Dunan's novel testifies as eloquently to the mentality of the time as Moselli's nihilistic carelessness or Pérochon's meticulously paradoxical challenge to the virtuousness of justice and courage and his assertion of the essential self-destructiveness of euchronian ambitions.

Frank despair was not, of course, the only possible imaginative response to the circumstances of the period manifest in French post-war *roman scientifique*. Even for those who plumbed its utmost depths—and no one reached further down than André Arnyvelde in the conclusion of *Le Bacchus mutilé*—it was not a terminus; having hit bottom there was, as proverbial wisdom assures us, no other way to go than up. There was, inevitably, a population of literary fantasists—who probably constituted the majority, although their defiant optimism was partially eclipsed for a while by the sheer intensity of the opposing works—ready to proclaim and insist that hope must and did remain. The imaginative extremes to which some of them felt compelled to go in order to recover and maintain that hope, however, are revealing in themselves.

One example of defiant hope asserted under pressure is provided by *Le Couple* (1924; tr. as *The Couple*) by Victor Margueritte (1866-1942), a novel that is also interesting for other reasons. Like André Couvreur's *Caresco, surhomme*, it is a futuristic sequel to an earlier Naturalistic work, in this case a duo of novels, *La Garçonne* (1922; tr. as *The Bacheloress*) and *Le Compagnon* (1923; tr. as *The Companion*), but it makes more effort than Couvreur had to maintain a Naturalism of narrative manner and style. In the present context, that sequentiality is significant because *La Garçonne* was the fiercest and most shocking expression of a particular kind of post-war disenchantment, to which *Le Couple* deliberately strives to provide an answer of sorts.

Victor Margueritte was the younger of two brothers, and Paul Margueritte (1860-1914) had already established a solid reputation as a notable writer of the Naturalist school before Victor made his debut. Initially, Victor had seemed more likely to follow in the footsteps of their father, General Jean-Auguste Margueritte, who had made a name for himself fighting in Algeria before being killed at the battle of Sedan in 1870; Victor joined the Spahis in 1886, and after a spell at the École Militaire in Saumur he became a lieutenant in the dragoons, but he resigned his commission in 1896 in order to devote himself to writing.

Almost all of Victor's early work was done in collaboration with his brother, with whom he wrote numerous novels and several plays between 1896 and 1907, but he published a dozen solo novels thereafter before achieving a new notoriety with *La Garçonne*, which details the career of a young woman, Monique Lerbier, who, disillusioned by the conduct of the man she is due to marry and the entrenched hypocrisy of French elegant society in general, decides that she will grant herself the same license and indulgences that bachelors routine accept as their due, and hurls herself into an orgy of decadence that allegedly provided a scathing portrait of the corruption of a society whose ever-shaky morality had been devastated by the adaptive cynicism of the war.

La Garçonne was not Margueritte's first excursion into protest against the injustice and hypocrisy of contemporary sexual politics. His first solo novel was *Prostituée* [Prostituted] (1907) and *La Garçonne* had been closely preceded by *Un Coeur farouche* [A Wild Heart] (1921). His interest in the politics of marriage was long-standing; the essays he had written in collaboration with Paul had included several on that topic. He claimed that *La Garçonne* had always been planned as part of a pair with *Le Compagnon*, of which a kind of preliminary sketch had been produced beforehand in the novella "La Femme en chemin" [Woman in Progress] (1921). *Le Compagnon* details the contrasting career of Annik Raimbert, a committed feminist who asserts what she considers to be her natural rights in a far less reckless and flamboyant fashion than Monique.

La Garçonne caused an enormous scandal—which helped it to become a huge best-seller—partly because it was accused of being pornographic, but mostly because it was considered treasonous in its representation of French post-war society as a vile sink of iniquity. The balancing account of Annik's heroic defense against corruption, although it sold well on the back of its predecessor, did not serve to quiet the criticism, so the author was moved to make his position clearer by looking twenty years ahead to examine the fate and fortunes of Monique's and Annik's children as they reach the threshold of adulthood.

Understandably, in view of the intellectual climate in which it was written, the future imagined as a backcloth for the drama is one in which the Second World War is looming, and in which a new poison gas developed by a French scientist might play a crucial role. In this case, however, the cynicism has an extra depth, because the new war between France and Germany is a political contrivance on the part of the colluding governments, the real intention of which is to enable them both to impose martial law on the growing numbers of socialists in both countries, either to subject them firmly to rigorous hierarchical discipline or, if politic, to massacre them. The political right has usurped power for that purpose, contriving the assassination of the elected socialist premier, Annik's husband.

An innocent junior officer who moves the poison gas supplies to the Franco-German border, believing the fatherland to be in real danger, is swiftly suppressed by his superiors, lest he spoil the conspiracy, and the four young people at the heart of the plot all seem likely to be consumed and crushed by the same forces of oppression—whose utter corruption is graphically illustrated by horrified descriptions of their perverse sex lives—but in this instance, unlike the works previously described, the martyrdom of Annik, killed during a pacifist protest, ironically provides the trigger for a violent workers' uprising in Paris, matched by a similar revolt in Berlin, which spreads to become the great international socialist Revolution that will, or at least might, save the world.

Victor Margueritte was not the only writer of futuristic fiction to cling to such hopes in the disenchanted days of the post-war decade, but he was already in a minority in regarding socialist revolution to be an adequate answer to the problem, and many of those whose political creed enabled them to think it might be the answer were unable to think of it as a probable outcome. In the same way, he was not only in a minority in preaching feminism, but in a far smaller minori-

ty in thinking that Annik Raimbert is a viable model for feminists to follow and that her children provide an adequate example of true liberation, either socially or psychologically. Other feminists—especially female ones—thought that the problems were far more fundamental than Margueritte seemed to believe, and thus required a solution considerably more complicated and far-reaching.

The strangest of all the imaginative literary reactions to the war and its aftermath was, in fact, produced by a far more radical feminist, who similarly mingled the apparent lessons of the war with philosophizing about the much more ancient "war" between the human sexes: ...*tel qu'il est* (1926; tr. as *The War of the Sexes*) by **Odette Dulac**. The ellipsis in the title is preceded on the cover and title page of the first and only edition with a drawing of a symbolic figure that an English or American person would probably call a Cupid, but in France is known as an Amour. The title could, therefore, be translated as *[Amour]…as it is*, but one can hardly blame the translator for selecting something a trifle less awkward.

"Odette Dulac" was the stage-name adopted by Jeanne Latrilhe (1865-1939) when she made her debut as an actress and singer on the Parisian stage in 1892, at an unusually late age for debutants in that profession. The autobiography that she wrote late in life leaves a seven-year gap prior to her arrival in Paris, over which an opaque veil is drawn, during which time the seeds were presumably sown of her subsequent metamorphoses. She first made a name for herself performing in comic operas, but became even more famous in 1897 when she launched a parallel career in the cabarets and café-concerts of Montmartre as a singer and performer in satirical sketches and revues, which eventually took over all her activity. She became one of the most popular artistes in Paris during the first few years of the twentieth century, but quit the stage abruptly in 1904 after a quarrel with her manager. She then launched an entirely new career as a sculptor, primarily in wax, and as a writer active in the cause of women's rights.

Her first novel, *Le Droit au plaisir* [The Right to Pleasure] (1908) is an epistolary text in the tradition of Rousseau's *Julie, ou la nouvelle Héloïse*, in which a marquise dissatisfied with her sex life obtains hypothetical explanations and practical suggestions from an artiste, who makes extensive use of analogies drawn from Jean-Henri Fabre's *Souvenirs entomologiques* (10 volumes, 1879-1909) to cast light on the supposed differences between male and female desire and erotic experience. The argumentative strategy might seem odd, but it was not out of keeping with the spirit of the times; Remy de Gourmont's study of *Physique de l'Amour* had similarly made use of insect analogies in an attempt to cast light on the quirks of human sexuality.

In Dulac's second novel, *Le Silence des femmes* [Womens' Silence] (1910), her feminist opinions became more strident, as she launched a scathing attack on social and religious hypocrisy regarding contemporary sexual mores, detailing the terrible effects that such hypocrisies frequently had on the lives of young women. The outbreak of the Great War—whose side-effects caused a massive disruption of those mores, as luridly detailed in *La Garçonne*—called forth an even stronger reaction from Dulac in *La Houille rouge, les enfants de la violence* [Red Fuel: The Children of Violence] (1916), which argued that the circumstances of the war had added to the existing difficulties the particular problems of young women who gave birth to children as a result of rape by the invading Germans and cajolery on the part of young men departing for the Front. *Faut-Il?* [Is it Necessary?] (1919) reflected on the legacy of the war in a more sober and sentimental vein.

Dulac's journalistic work became more varied after the end of the Great War, but her novels continued insistently to tackle controversial themes associated with sexuality: syphilis in *L'Enfer d'une étreinte* [The Inferno of an Embrace] (1922) and homosexuality in *Les Désexués* [The Desexualized] (1926, in collaboration with Charles Étienne). *[Amour]...tel qu'il est!* does not break that pattern, and is, in a sense, a kind of philosophical summary of the themes of the author's first three novels, but it takes a gigantic leap in terms of its narrative method.

The insectile analogies introduced in *Le Droit au plaisir* are greatly elaborated in *[Amour]...tel qu'il est!* to produce an eccentric account of the evolution of human sexual biology, parceled up in an idiosyncratic mysticism based in Buddhist and Hindu ideas and combined with an astrological theory, entirely the author's own invention, that not only presides over the process of evolution but the cosmogony of the imagined universe. The result of the triple layering of fantastic notions, much of which is made explicit but nevertheless retains a complex halo of hints and oblique implications, is a unique literary construct that had no parallel at the time the novel was written, and still seems highly unusual today, when adventurous hybridizations of speculative fiction and quasi-religious fantasy are considerably more familiar.

The heroine of *[Amour]...tel qu'il est* is a child found one day in a hunting lodge in India by the Dalai Lama, who realizes, by virtue of the injuries left on her wrist by a chain, that she has been recently released from imprisonment by "the Lord of the World," Brahytina. He calls her Tussilia, and after discovering a document several thousand years old that identifies her as the predestined grandmother of the Messiah who will redeem the world, he sets out to raise her as a "houtoukou": a magically talented lama. In pursuit of the prophecy, he marries her off to an English diplomat, Lord Wiscorney, who takes her with him to Europe. There she gives birth to a daughter, Dolly. After Lord Wiscorney has drunk himself to death, Dolly marries a good-looking but ineffectual French Roman Catholic, Maurice d'Angeville. Tussilia raises no objection, in spite of anticipating fierce ideological tussles with Maurice's exceedingly devout and direly bigoted mother. The contests in question begin immediately after Dolly dies giving birth to twin girls, whose immediate fate is settled by a Solomonic judgment that gives each grandmother custody of one on the sisters, to raise as she pleases.

In order to do that, Tussilia retires to a cottage in Barbizon in the forest of Fontainebleau (where Odette Dulac lived) and begins training Maya, the daughter of whom she has custody, in the philosophy and abilities that she has cultivated herself, while the other twin, Ghislaine, is brought up in a very different fashion by Madame d'Angeville, although the two girls meet up at regular intervals to maintain their sisterly relationship. It is at Barbizon that the text first introduces Tussilia to the reader, still not entirely clear as to exactly what her mission is and how she ought to carry it through. A visitation from Kacyapa, one of the Seven Sages of the present universal cycle, however, informs her that she must also train Maya's predestined partner, and provides her with a few rather cryptic further indications, prophesying insistently that, despite the "blood, fire, iron and poison" that will envelop the predestined couple, the "ovipares" will eventually triumph over the "vivipares."

Maya's education reaches its critical point when she falls in love with Pierre Montala, the son of one of her grandmother's neighbors, and, once Tussilia has confirmed that the man of her daughter's choice really is destined to be the father of the Messiah, she reveals to both of them the nature and importance of their mission. The truth that she reveals is complex, but in crude summary, the Earth is a cocoon sheltering a Being of Fire—Brahytina—and all the living things on its surface are part of a vague cosmic plan connected with the maturation and eventual emergence of that pupated Being. Primitive life began in an epoch defined by the "astral signature" of Saturn, when the primitive life-forms that first emerged were all "vivipares" whose offspring emerged from living flesh as mobile larvae. The epoch of Saturn was followed by that Jupiter, in which the Earth was populated by gigantic animals, and then by that of the Moon, in which many species of "ovipares"—egg-layers—appeared. In the subsequent epoch of the Sun, a struggle for existence began between the vivipares and the ovipares; the Saturnians, no longer able to feed on metals, as they had originally done, because the metals had now hardened, were forced to become predators feeding on the live produce of ovipare eggs.

Within this schema, the ancestors of present-day humans are two very distinct species, one Saturnian and one Lunar. Dulac borrowed the ultimate ancestor of what are presently known as the "males" of the human species from a striking illustration in Camille Flammarion's pioneering popularization of paleontological science *Le Monde avant la creation de l'homme* [The World Before the Creation of Humankind] (1857), which depicts a gigantic but relatively slender saurian, with a caption suggesting that the species "might perhaps have been one of our ancestors." In fact, the species in question, the zanglodon, never existed; the original "specimen" was sold in the U.S.A. by Albert C. Koch, a showman who had previously exhibited a supposed sea serpent in New York in 1845 and was attempting to cash in on the fashionability of dinosaur bones by faking various finds of that nature. The fabrication was soon discovered, but not soon enough to prevent Flammarion's error; the success of his popularization, however, ensured that the fictitious creature continued to enjoy a fugitive existence in the cryptozoology of Henri Coupin's oft-reprinted *Les Animaux excentriques* [Eccentric Animals] (1906), maintaining its fictional viability for use in Dulac's fantasy.

Within the novel's evolutionary schema, the struggle between the vivipares and the ovipares is critically intensified in the Venusian epoch following the Solar epoch, when the first mammals emerged, embodying the "great secret of Brahma." Further complications followed in the epoch of Mars, associated with psychic vibrations that foster war, and in which the present war of the human sexes was initiated, while their forms were subsequently modified by the "Hermetic" epoch of Mercury, the presiding influence of thought and civilization. The initial epochs were very long, but nowadays the influences of the planets cycle much more rapidly, their much subtler periods of dominance switching every thirty-three years. The whole process is occasionally interrupted by cataclysmic Deluges caused by the stirring of the Being of Fire, and has been further complicated by the gradual evolution of a new series of "magnetic parasite" species, generally known as souls, which complete the triple make-up of contemporary humans; the hypothetical biology of the souls is very complicated as well as highly original.

Within this context, human "males" are actually vivipare females, whereas human females are ovipares, the two species having become biologically confused when the descendants of the zanglodon, the Kastéhus, began injecting their live-born young into the eggs of a winged ovipare species, the Awaï, initiating a long process of obligatory mutual adaptation whose ultimate result was that the descendants of the Awaï, cruelly deprived of their wings, were subjugated and enslaved by the Kastéhus, forced to bear the enemy species' offspring as well as their own, after a contest for survival in the womb. The ultimate role to be played by the Messiah to whom Maya is destined to give birth is to redeem the ultimate daughters of the Awaï from that enslavement and return their wings—but in order to prepare the way for that, Pierre will first need to develop the artificial wings that will eventually give rise to the wings that the Messiah and the Awaï will require, and he will have also have to survive the Great War, in which he will obtain his initial training as a pilot.

Unsurprisingly, the Great War looms large in the plot of [Amour]...tel qu'il est, and becomes the arena of ordeals through which the predestined couple have to pass. Apparently, they need to undergo those ordeals in order to have any hope of fulfilling their mission successfully. Although the text of the novel does include a post-war epilogue, it is the 1914-18 War that provides it with its climax and its dramatic culmination. Although that cannot be judged unsatisfactory in purely literary terms, in the context of the era of its publication, it leaves a great many questions relating to the broader context dangling, of which the most significant is what the Redeemer is actually going to do to sort out the troubled situation of human life as described in the text. The implication of the plot's hints is that Pierre will apply the expertise gained by his aviation experience to the construction of an interplanetary craft that will permit him to journey to another world and bring back a biological entity that will enable the liberation of the Awaï, including the return of their wings, and the elimination of the "male" of the species, not necessarily by massacre.

As to where the redeemed Awai will find refuge when Brahytina's hatching destroys the Earth, that is anyone's guess—but the insistence, nevertheless, is that there *is* hope, for women if not for men.

529

Although Odette Dulac's hopes were echoed in a far more orthodox fashion in one of the few visions of a technologically advanced euchronias produced by female writers, *Une vie nouvelle* [A New Life] (1932) by the communist and feminist activist Madeleine Pelletier (1874-1939), male writers were not tempted to follow imaginative paths akin to Odette Dulac's, and they did not, for the most part invest their hope in any kind of messiah—certainly not the kind of twisted and suicidal messiah featured in Renée Dunan's *La Dernière jouissance*. Quite the contrary; some of the pulpish thrillers of the period feature adversaries akin to Dunan's, bent on world destruction by virtue of quasi-messianic delusions. One notable example is the anti-hero of *A deux doigts de la fin du monde* (1928; tr. as "On the Brink of the World's End") by Colonel Royet, whose typical scientific obsession is precipitated by frustrated amour into full-blown psychosis.

Such melodramas as Royet's are usually content to find faint hope in postponement, often accepting, as he does, that although the logic of the situation strongly implies that it is only a matter of time before some deluded madman armed with a superweapon will destroy the world, the evil day might still be put off until tomorrow a few more times. That kind of metaphorical shrug of the shoulders gradually became commonplace, especially during the Depression, and although it did not often lend itself to elaborate philosophizing, it was occasionally subject to ingenious complication.

Le Napus, fléau de l'an 2227 (1927; tr. as *The Napus: The Great Plague of the Year 2227*) by Léon Daudet (1867-1942) must have seemed to the author's readers to be a radical departure from the vague pattern established by the twenty-eight contemporary and historical novels he had published between 1895 and 1926, but Ernest Pérochon was not the only writer to have demonstrated that such abrupt departures were not inappropriate to the time. It is not improbable, in fact, that Daudet's novel was planned as a riposte to Victor Margueritte and Pérochon, both of those writers being well known to him as eloquent adversaries at the far end of the political spectrum. Daudet had once been a Republican himself, but had swung to the far right long before 1927, and was by then an active propagandist for Action Française.

530

The fundamental philosophy of *Le Napus*, as with many other futuristic novels of the period, is that "those who fail to learn from history are condemned to repeat it" but to a great extent than any other, it tacks on Karl Marx's later addendum: "first as tragedy, then as farce." It is by no means the only novel of the period to combine tragedy and black comedy, but it is one of the most striking and one of the most ambitious, in its bizarrerie and well its blackness. It suggests that it might not only be people whom the gods make mad before destroying them, but entire worlds.

In *Le Napus*, a German writer named von Herzius is said to have written a book called *Archimedes*, setting out a prospectus for future warfare in which enemy nations will be devastated by various kinds of innovative long-range weapons, including ingenious projectiles—missiles and bombs—and scientific devices for causing earthquakes, floods, violent storms, etc.: a prospectus enthusiastically taken up in the novel by a resurgent German Empire, in spite of the extremely high cost of such weapons, thus facing its potential enemies with a bewildering array of means by which they might be attacked, and little prospect of being able to defend against them all. To that threat, however, another is added, in the form of the eponymous natural catastrophe, which is even more bizarre and arbitrary.

If the world featured in the novel is perverse to the point of paradoxicality, so is the narrator through whose documentary record we see it; he is the result of an experiment in selective breeding that was supposed to produce idealized humans but went awkwardly awry. As heroes go—and his notion of himself as a modest hero is not entirely mistaken—Polyplast 17,177 is certainly peculiar, but only an unreliable narrator could stand any chance of acquiring a measure of paradoxical reliability in an unreliable world. There is a sense in which Polyplast's is the ideally odd viewpoint from which to obtain a measure and grasp of the perverse society in which he lives, and there is a certain propriety in the fact that he is on hand to witness the first manifestation of the new plague, when an old man simply vanishes, prompting the child accompanying him to say: "*N'a pus, a grand pé a pati*" [presumably a slurred version of : "No more—grandpa's gone"], thus giving the phenomenon its name. It soon spreads to become worldwide, even causing vanishings from the scientific conference convened to discuss it.

There is no logical reason for the Napus to become a *casus belli*, but the conflict that is in the offing is only awaiting a trigger, however arbitrary, and France is soon at war with Germany again, facing an extraordinary arsenal of stockpiled experimental weapons as well as further absurd manifestations of the Napus—most spectacularly, irruptions of giant mushrooms. Despite assiduous research by Polyplast and his colleagues at the Aristotle Institute, progress in explaining the Napus is slow—too slow to anticipate a particularly strange synergistic reaction with one of the German superweapons, which causes the latter's lethal effects to rebound spectacularly. The hopeful aspects of that eventuality are, however, immediately undermined when Polyplast finally ventures his speculative explanation for the phenomenon—an explanation cut off in mid-sentence, presumably by his own abrupt disappearance, although a note added to his manuscript reveals that his fate is not yet that of the entire world, and that there must still be hope in the very craziness of the situation.

Le Napus, although building a future in which scientific knowledge has continued to progress, takes it for granted that much of that science will be intellectually bankrupt, and that the fraction that is not will be largely deleterious to the quality of human life. It is one of relatively few science-based speculative novels to assume that much contemporary theoretical knowledge is seriously mistaken, and that the theories that eventually replace contemporary ones will be just as arbitrary and liable to supersession. In the world of *Le Napus*, it is not only the Archimedean superweapons that routinely misfire—while still doing enormous damage and inflicting serious mortality—but all the efforts of scientists, especially and most importantly in confrontation with the Napus itself: a pataphysical phenomenon if ever there was one, and thus fundamentally immune to rational analysis.

Another writer who had previously built a solid literary reputation on naturalistic works but then made a sudden sidestep into *roman scientifique* in this period was Henri-Jacques Proumen (1879-1962), who had the additional advantage of having worked professionally as a scientific researcher before and after the Great War, and had written two scientific treatises, *Les Rayons X, le radium, les rayons N* [X-Rays, Radium and N-rays—the last being a notorious scholarly fantasy publicized by Prosper-René Blondlot in 1903] (1905) and *La Matière, l'éther, l'électricité* [Matter, Ether and Electricity] (1909). His novel *Sur le chemin des dieux* [On the Road of the Gods] (1928), dedicated to Maurice Renard, tells the story of two friends, the physicist Jean Mauval, who has invented a machine amplifying psychic radiation, and Claude Bergeron, whose exceptional innate mastery of animal magnetism is boosted tremendously by the infusions of the device.

Bergeron is a humanitarian keen to set the world to rights, and in no mood to listen to Mauval's insistence that far more work has to be done to perfect the machine before attempting to make use of its potential effects. He is greatly spurred on by the fact that French society has become extremely polarized between the opposing parties supporting the current President of the Republic (*Dictatoristes*) and those campaigning for socialist Revolution (*Laboristes*). After an experiment with his augmented powers of suggestion that forces the King of England to come out unexpectedly in favor of the English labor party, Bergeron attempts to use his powers to halt a violent riot in Paris, which threatens to escalate into a bloody civil war. He succeeds, but at the cost of making himself and Mauval marked men, not only by both sides in the aborted conflict but by a beautiful Bolshevik spy who befriends the woman with whom Mauval is in love.

Although attracted to the spy, Bergeron remains committed to his higher mission, but it is soon undermined. His powers are godlike in embryo, but hampered by the loss of the original machine and by the fact that he is only one man, equally hated by both warring factions of an entire nation—a situation that drives him increasingly to desperation. The most interesting element of the plot is the dynamic between the two friends. Mauval soon manifests his suspicion that Bergeron is using his powers of irresistible persuasion on him in order to force his cooperation, and although Bergeron swears that he will never do that, and even attempts to impose such a compulsion upon himself, he cannot be sure himself that he is not doing it unconsciously—and eventually, when cornered, he drops all prevarication in order to enslave his friend in the service of his allegedly good cause.

In the end, though, Bergeron cannot impose his will on all of the people all of the time, and although he can defend himself by committing psychic mass murder, he cannot prevent his enemies eventually getting close enough to shoot him. Mortally wounded, he still able to lash out vengefully, and the novel ends with an immense holocaust, in which the entire city of Paris goes up in flames, torched by its deliberately-crazed inhabitants. Although the destruction is not on the same scale as that featured in the 1925 novels by Pérochon, Moselli and Dunan, its symbolic value is similarly spectacular, and the novel provides one of the most graphic depictions of technological power running out of control, in spite of the good intentions of its inventors and initial users.

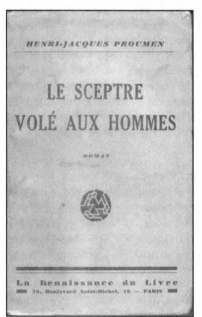

Proumen's next venture into *roman scientifique*, **Le Sceptre volé aux hommes** [The Scepter Stolen from Humans] (1930) takes a further step on the presumed road to godhood, employing the assumption that a population of highly intelligent *hyperanthropes* [superhumans] forming a new species that has evolved in the midst of *Homo sapiens* separate themselves from their primitive fellows, and make rapid progress in the physics of a kind of energy they call *protergon*, which is essentially incomprehensible to merely human minds. Having used technologies employing protergon to build themselves a mini-utopia in an archipelago artificially raised from the sea, they set about abducting groups of humans for use as slaves and servants—or, as they put it, domestic animals.

The plot of the story follows three people caught up in one of the hyperanthropes' trawls while holidaying in Biarritz: the engineer Luc Pontadour, a great believer in science and progress; his skeptical friend Pierre Chantegrelle; and the woman Pierre loves, Michelle Hardymont. They react to their captivity very differently: Michelle is stubbornly recalcitrant, refusing slavery even when she realizes that if she will not knuckle under the hyperanthropes will simply kill and discard her; Pierre accepts inevitability, symbolized in his case by the aptly-named female hyperanthrope Réale, whose sexual magnetism reduces all her male slaves to worshipful infatuation; Luc regards it as a golden opportunity to learn some of the secrets of protergon himself, in order to progress at least some way on the road to godhood, and perhaps lead the rest of his fellow humans along that road.

Luc is teasingly encouraged in his quest by the hyperanthrope Raff, utterly confident in the conviction that the merely human mind is incapable of mastery of the new physics, because Raff wants Luc to accept the inevitability of his inferiority, as Pierre has, and thus become an intermediary counseling his fellows to accept their domesticity meekly. When she becomes Raff's sex slave, Michelle feigns such acceptance, in the hope that with Luc's help she might find a way of striking back at the new masters.

The story is remarkable not so much in terms of its plot, which eventually compromises, rather implausibly, with the standard normalizing story-arc, but in its uncompromising depiction of the psychology of the superhumans, who automatically come to regard the members of their ancestral race as mere animals, entitled to no more moral consideration than sheep or cattle, although they recognize the utility of recruiting "judas goats" to help keep the flocks in line. The notion was not new, hints having been dropped in some of the numerous English scientific romances dealing with superhumanity, but Proumen extrapolated the notion further than any of its predecessors, and further than Olaf Stapledon was subsequently prepared to develop it in the parallel classic *Odd John* (1934).

A complete contrast to Victor Margueritte's image of the future redeemed by socialist revolution was provided by another writer who moved twenty years into the future in order to provide a sequel to a naturalistic novel set in the present: Albert Bessières (1877-1953), notable for his stirring endeavors in Catholic apologetics, who supplemented his Algeria-set novel *Le Désert fleurira* [The Desert will Flourish] (1928) with *L'Agonie de Cosmopolis* [The Death-Throes of Cosmopolis] (1929), which depicts future capitalists in the same unflattering fashion as Margueritte but sees no answer to their oppressions in a workers' revolution.

Although the revolution unfolds inexorably within the story, it immediately becomes an orgy of vengeance and violence, displayed in horrific scenes of mass murder—the favored method of formal execution being hurling victims, including mothers, babies and nuns, into vats of sulfuric acid—before the Anarchists and Communists turn on one another and the entirety of the industrial complex of Cosmopolis, raised in the environs of Marseille, is obliterated, save for a handful of the virtuous who escape in a fishing boat that must double as an Ark in a deluge of fire.

The heroic priest who accompanies the refugees has already had his eyes plucked out by a sadistic fanatic, but is capable nevertheless of carrying the Faith through the holocaust, so that the Church can be symbolically resurrected, although it is not obvious that the story's conclusion could qualify as a happy or normalizing ending in any but the most devout eyes.

A particularly notable depiction of a natural disaster threatening the end of industrialism is featured in Théo Varlet's *La Grande Panne* [The Great Shutdown] (1930; tr. as *The Xenobiotic Invasion*), which echoes the theme of Henri Allorge's *Le Grand Cataclysme* in a more modest fashion, and can be read as a metaphorical echo of the Depression in the same way that *L'Épopée martienne* can be read as a metaphorical figuration of the Great War. A pioneering rocket-ship launched for a test-flight outside the atmosphere provokes a media frenzy when it comes down in the south of France, and the narrator assists its female pilot, Aurore Lescure, to evade the press and return to Paris. Unknown to her, however, the samples of space-dust she has collected in space contain the spores of a "xenobiotic lichen" that feeds on electricity, which find rich pasture in France, spreading far and wide and beginning a process of rapid evolution.

In order to combat the plague, it is necessary to shut down all electricity generating plants in France, and it seems likely that the problem will soon be worldwide, putting an end to modern civilization, unless an effective antimicrobial agent can be discovered. The plot of the novel is moved by the romantic complications of the protagonist's involvement with Aurore—a victim of blackmail on the part of the financier backing her father, the latter being a scientist of genius but something of an innocent, in the great Berthoudian tradition—but the heart of the story is the description of the spectacular infection of Paris by the blood-red and swiftly mutating xenobiotic lichen and the consequent suppression of economic activity.

The story ends with a lament on the part of the scientist, after he has narrowly saved the world, regarding the future uses to which his new discovery will be put, given that it has military potential because of its awesome destructive power. His daughter agrees, and the only crumb of comfort that the narrator can offer, to begin with, is a trifle meager, suggesting that a new attitude of "neophobia" might be "the first step toward a future higher wisdom, which will include a consciousness of cosmic harmony and the duties it imposes...."

Varlet's later poetry, much of which was cosmological in its subject-matter, attempted to promote that consciousness of cosmic harmony, and he announced in the supplementary material to a second edition of *La Grande panne* published in 1936 that he was working on a sequel to the novel. He completed the sequel in question in 1937, but he died before he could find a publisher for it, in a literary marketplace that had by then become rather hostile, in its more respectable strata, to any kind of speculative fiction.

Time does not, in fact, heal all wounds, but their pain sometimes fades from stabbing sharpness to a dull ache. In British scientific romance, anxieties flared up in the 1930s more prolifically than they had been manifest during the 1920s, that peculiar hysteria only reaching its peak on the very eve of the resumption of the Great War. In France, by contrast, the reaction to the war was more immediate and intense in the 1920s, and became quieter in the 1930s, perhaps simply because it was widely felt that what had needed to be said and done had been said and done, and that it was best to try to move on. On the other hand, it is possible that the divergence was a subsidiary effect of the much sharper divergence that took place in the 1930s between American and European speculative fiction, when science fiction developed in the U.S.A. in a markedly different fashion from *scientific romance* and *roman scientifique*.

The different reactions to the legacy of the war can be partly explained, as previously pointed out, by the acute awareness in Europe of the vulnerability of cities to potential aerial bombardment, which the U.S.A. did not yet share, having no enemies close at hand in an era of aircraft with limited range. Although the Great Depression that followed the Wall Street Crash took considerable toll in the U.S.A. as well as having a knock-on effect in Europe, European nations, and France especially, had already been suffering economic difficulties because of the destructive effects of the war, and the failure of Germany to make the financial reparations specified by the 1919 Treaty of Versailles.

American optimism was certainly dented by the aftermath of the Wall Street Crash, but one common response there to the vicissitudes of the Depression seems to have been an increased desire to seek escape in the colorful fantasies of pulp fiction—in which the sciencefictional mythology of the Space Age came to play a small but significant part. In Europe, the response was generally far more downbeat, escapism having far less purchase on the popular imagination, but the texture of its pessimism was not identical in Britain and France,

536

partly because France still bore the literal scars inflicted on her soil by the trenches, whereas Britain only had the fear of possible wounds to come. The Depression seems, perhaps in consequence, to have made the French imagination more fatalistic, whereas it turned anxiety to panic in the British imagination.

The specific anxieties associated with the suspended second world war did not go away, however, and nor did the bitterness of those who had lived perilously through the fighting only to see the world emerge from the armistice with all the same evils as before still stubbornly in place. The libertarian pacifist Victor Méric produced one of the most graphic accounts of the war to come in *La Der des Der, roman de la prochaine guerre* [The Der of Ders: A Romance of the Next War] (1929), in which Paris is destroyed by chemical bombardment from the air and European civilization collapses, prior to an invasion from Africa; the illustrative cover of the second edition, published in 1930, offered a striking depiction of a woman in a symbolic gas mask. Paris is destroyed yet again, this time in the

course of an Oriental invasion, in P. B. Gheusi's *La Mascaret rouge* [The Red Tide] (1931). Colonel Royet published a part-work in 20 episodes entitled *1932: La Guerre est déclarée* [1932: War is Declared] (1931; book version 1932), which reverted to more familiar territory, with associated accounts of espionage. By the time Georges de La Fouchardière penned *La Prochaine dernière* [The Next Last One] in 1932 the phrase he appropriated for its title had become a commonplace sarcasm with reference to the impending conflict. It is further echoed in Robert Demarty's *L'Autre! La Dernière!* [Another One! The Last!] (1933), a relentless account of future slaughter in the trenches of 1940, which spares no extremes in attempting to depict the horrors that must be avoided at all costs, including the now-standard accounts of new poison gases and bacteriological assaults. Léon Daudet's *Ciel de feu* [The Sky on Fire] (1934) is yet another a studiously grim account of World War Two, in which the spectacular bombardment of Paris forms an appropriate centerpiece.

As in the post-war decade, anxieties regarding future war ran parallel to depictions of large-scale natural catastrophes, such as the new Ice Age features in *Les Derniers jours du monde* [The Last Days of the World] (1931) by "Charles de L'Andelyn" (Jules Pittard, 1892-1976). *La Mort du fer* (1931; tr. in *Wonder Stories* as "The Death of Iron") by S. S. Held picks up the theme of Raoul Bigot's "Le Fer qui meurt" in an elaborately-extrapolated fashion; the novel is considerable more sophisticated in its writing and thinking than the other works translated for Hugo Gernsback's pulp magazines. The disasters featured in novels of the period are sometimes bizarre in kind, like the one featured in *L'Agonie dans les ténèbres* [Death-Throes in the Dark] (1934) by Fernand Hendrick, in which the Earth's rotation begins to slow down on 5 April 1951, eventually presenting one face perpetually to the sun and leaving the other in darkness.

The most extreme of all near-future war stories, not so much in its depiction of events as in the intensity of its examination of the protagonist's psychological reaction to them, was *Quinzinzinzili* (1935; tr. as "Quinzinzinzili") by Régis Messac (1893-1945), written around a hypothetical account of the build-up to the Second World War previously published as "Comment fut déclarée la guerre de 1934 par Boudou-Bada, professeur à l'Université de Capetown" [How the War of 1934 was declared, by Boudou-Bada, Professor at the University of Cape Town] in the Pacifist periodical *Les Primaires* in April 1934, of which Messac was then the editor, and in which he had a regular column entitled *Propos d'un utopien* [A Utopian's Remarks].

Messac had attempted unsuccessfully to complete his initial studies at the École Normale Supérieure, an establishment primarily geared to training scientists and engineers, interrupted when he was conscripted in 1914. Seriously wounded in the head in December of that year, he obtained an initial teaching qualification during his convalescence, and spent the rest of the war working in various auxiliary services, retaining the lowest possible rank throughout for ideological reasons.

Messac learned English during the war from English soldiers, and also became involved with Germaine Desvachez, a young woman widowed by the conflict, whom he subsequently married. After his demobilization in 1919 he wrote two autographical novels describing his experiences, which had helped to complete his deep cynicism regarding human nature and his crystallize his strong commitment to pacifism. He completed his teaching qualification, and was awarded his *agrégation* in 1922, in letters rather than the sciences he had originally planned to study; he went on to become a highly regarded literary scholar, and also maintained a strong interest in the social sciences.

After teaching at the University of Glasgow in 1923-24, Messac went to Canada, where he spent five years at McGill University in Montreal. There he was introduced to American pulp fiction, including science fiction; although his primary academic interest was crime fiction, which was considered far more respectable than science fiction by virtue of its middlebrow extensions and its long history, it seems to have been the subject matter and narrative devices of science fiction that spurred his own creative inspirations, although the works that he wrote for publication in *Les Primaires* have little in common with pulp science fiction in terms of their manner and purpose. They are far more sophisticated both stylistically and philosophically, clearly belonging to the Voltairean tradition of *contes philosophiques* in terms of their mordant satirical bite and their relentless harassment of human stupidity.

Quinzinzinzili, which followed up three earlier works of fiction published in *Les Primaires*, does not add a great deal to the account of the "war of 1934" published in that magazine, which is primarily concerned with the likely reactions of contemporary politicians and journalists to the advent of a new war, and its account of the superweapon whose unleashing temporarily turns the atmosphere poisonous, after the fashion of the scenario imagined in René Dunan's *La Dernière jouissance*, is cursory. The narrator of the story knows very little about it, only having a handful of documentary sources. He survives because he happens to be visiting a cave high in the mountains of the Massif Central when the poison is unleashed, in the company of a group of children who include the two tutees in his charge. Their guide dies, leaving him the only adult—so far as he knows—in the entire world.

The principal focus of the story is its description of the bizarre culture formed from scratch—with very little input from the disaffected and ineffectual adult observer—by the children, who represent a slight, if absurdly precarious, chance that the human race might not become extinct, even though there is only one girl among them. The narrator does not see that slight chance as a hope, but merely as an absurdity, and his account insists on presenting his observations as a kind of comedy, although his savage sarcasm cannot entirely disguise the underlying tragic sensibility.

Quinzinzinzili belongs to an interesting subcategory of "castaway stories" in which children have to build a society from scratch without the support of any kind of educational system or effective adult guidance, but Messac's version goes further than other stories of that type in having the children devise their own language, based on French but deviating from it in ways partly determined by circumstance and partly by chance, producing such occasional meaningful bizarreries as the word that gives the story its title. Coupled with the development of that new language, and intimately entangled with it, is the development of new superstitions and a new religion, which sarcastically reflect theories as to how traditional superstitions and religions might well have originated and evolved; that feature of the story adds a considerable anthropological interest to the speculative venture, as well was adding to the puzzles that continually confront the protagonist. Unlike the narrator of *La Grande panne*, the narrator of *Quinzinzinzili* has no one to whom he feels obliged to console, in return for loving consolation he can expect in return; he is alone, and has no alternative but to react honestly in filling the final page of a notebook that no one will ever read:

"When I think about the future, I see a new collective calvary, a new painful and dolorous ascension toward an illusory paradise, a long sequence of crimes, horrors and sufferings.... A new society is about to be born, as ridiculous, perhaps more ridiculous, than the other, full of an infinite stupidity, larded and interlarded with barbaric cunning and puerile refinements, complicated and useless: everything that they too will name science, progress, intelligence and civilization, or something similar."

As with André Arnyvelde after writing the devastating last chapter of *Le Bacchus mutilé*, however, Messac had to go on living, in a world that had not yet been destroyed, and being a writer, he had to carry on writing too, if he were not to give up entirely. Precisely because it could have no conceivable sequel, there was a perverse sense in which *Quinzinzinzili*, like *Le Bacchus mutilé*, demanded one, figuratively if not literally—and Messac wrote one: ***La Cité des asphyxiés*** (1937; tr. as *Stranglehold City*). *La Cité des Asphyxiés* follows on closely from *Quinzinzinzili* in terms of its rhetorical fervor and its mordant satire. The two works are thematically related and have several overlapping features; there is even a teasing reference in the novel capable of suggesting to readers familiar with the earlier work that—however improbable it might seem, given the apocalyptic theme of the earlier story—the novel might be set in the distant future consequent to the novella's near future.

In between *Quinzinzinzili* and *La Cité des Asphyxiés* Messac wrote a third autobiographical volume, *L'Homme assiégé* [A Man Under Siege] (1936), which explains the dire personal circumstances that contributed to the bleak and angry sentiments that showed up very clearly earlier work. The novel was written after he had vented his feelings somewhat, and it is a considerably more measured work, calmer and more wryly ironic as well as far more studied in its misanthropy, but it nevertheless remains one of the most aggressively scathing political satires ever penned.

La Cité des Asphyxiés is set solidly in the tradition of Voltairean satire, but its fundamental mordancy harks back to the source of Voltaire's own principal inspiration, found in the works of Jonathan Swift. It is the most Swiftian of all works of belated Gulliveriana, but adds an extra edge to Swift's trenchant misanthropy by applying a more radical and more sophisticated political criticism, aimed at cultural targets that Swift never had the chance to encounter. There are other English influences in the work, primarily that of H. G. Wells, two of whose early scientific romances, *The Time Machine* (1895) and *When the Sleeper Wakes* (1899) are echoed in its make-up, There is also is a wry acknowledgement to Lord Lytton's subterranean utopia *The Coming Race* (1871) although Messac's initial intellectual exploration of the notion of a subterranean society probably owed more to the suggestion of Gabriel Tarde's sociologically-sophisticated *Fragment d'histoire future*.

The text begins with a frame narrative in which an unsympathetic and clearly unreliable narrator explains how experiments in transtemporal television carried out by her husband and father seem to have created a time machine that has hurled one of her husband's friends, Sylvain Le Cateau, into a far future, when humankind lives underground because the depletion of the atmosphere has made the surface uninhabitable.

The early phases of the main story, handicapped by the fact that Le Cateau is exceedingly unreliable narrator, for reasons that seem to go far beyond his chronic stupidity, describe his first impressions of Subterranean society and his early adventures therein, concentrating on technical matters in a manner calculated to give an impression of coherent extrapolation and fidelity to scientific thinking, which is only gradually transformed for satirical purposes. A reader could begin to construe the main story as if it were a straightforward exercise in extrapolative speculative fiction, and engage with it in that fashion, before its satirical elements become vitriolically scathing, thus adding a useful measure of sensitivity to their eventual sting.

At first, Subterranean society seems to Le Cateau, who can only see a tiny fraction of its stratification, to be a sufficiently comfortable milieu, which benefits from many advanced technologies, permitting extraordinary sophistications in the fields of medicine and communication. He only realizes slowly what the consequences are of the fact that the society has to manufacture its air, and the methods of that manufacture, and that realization gradually transfigures his personal vision of it from an eccentric eutopia to a grotesquely horrible dystopia, in whose fortunes his own role comes to seem extremely problematic.

The ambiguously layered narrative method is particularly well-suited to form a detailed description of a fictitious world that is, literally as well as metaphorically, "turned upside down," in order to provide a distorted reflection of our own. The description of the subterranean world's physical and biological organization cannot, in the final analysis, be said to ring true, but it is nevertheless developed with great ingenuity and considerable rational acumen; it includes many telling details whose points of plausible support add a valuable additional note of conviction to their satirical aspect as well as to the graphic surrealism of their imagery.

The careful deployment in the novel of limited and flagrantly biased first-person narratives helps to give the novel a distinctive kind of ambiguity that goes far beyond the handling of speculative science and the imagery of the invented world. Indeed, all the kinds of specific detail featured in the multilayered story are embedded in a surrounding matrix of vague and troubling uncertainty. Various clues are inserted into the interstices of Le Cateau's oft-interrupted report, which suggest an account of his adventure quite different from the one he is able to give, but those clues only consist of a series of puzzles that the reader is invited to contemplate at leisure.

One important aspect of the challenge posed to the reader by the puzzles in question is the use made the invented language featured in the main narrative. Many of its linguistic enigmas are left teasingly obscure, both in cases where the reader is clearly expected to draw deductions and in cases where no such deductions appear to be possible. The continual juggling with elements of the language, and the protagonist's attempts to get to grips with it, eventually become the most vital and vibrant aspect of the novel's satirical method. The novel benefits from its slow and relatively earnest build-up in that regard, allowing the invented words of the Subterranean language to be leaked into the text in a measured fashion, so that the reader can get used to them before the concluding elaboration.

By virtue of these various narrative strategies and intricacies, *La Cité des Asphyxiés* was one the most sophisticated futuristic fantasies yet produced at the time of its original publication, and it remains a highly significant landmark in the evolution of futuristic fiction, as well as a telling culmination of the literary explorations of the social and psychological aftermath of the trenches, developed within the further context of the Depression. Perhaps it only looks like a culmination now because there was not enough time left for its supersession before the Great War resumed its unfolding tragedy in 1939—and claimed Messac as one of many victims of Nazi internment, although no one knows exactly where he died or how. Nevertheless, it does seem an entirely appropriate terminus for the tortured stream of literary consciousness to which it belonged, and to which it provided an appropriately frayed and ragged end.

The English translations of the two Messac works indicated above do exist, as does the translation of a third work discussed in the final section of the chapter, and their publication was scheduled by Black Coat Press for 2016. Even though the works are all in the public domain in the United States, the author having been dead for seventy years, publication was blocked by the threat of legal action by his grandson, Olivier Messac. Evidently, Olivier Messac feels that the best way to conserve his grandfather's legacy is to extend the long inaccessibility of his work in the English language for as long as humanly possible. We can, of course, only speculate as to what the fervently anti-capitalist utopian Régis Messac might have thought of copyright trolls, although we do know that the Nazis murdered him in order to prevent him communicating his ideas to his fellow human beings, not because he posed any kind of military threat to them.

2. Apes and Superhumans

André Arnyvelde's vision of the arcandre, written in the trenches, carried forward a tradition of *roman scientifique* dealing with the theme of superhumanity that went back to the origins of the genre, but in focusing on extensions to the sensorium—assisted by technical innovations and the development of supposedly innate but latent abilities—it was adding a new gloss of philosophical sophistication to an old idea. The theme continued to make its customary steady progress after the interruption of the war.

Before going off to serve in the war Maurice Renard had already planned a novel about the surgical enhancement of sight, which he might well have begun writing, but the version of **"L'Homme truqué"** (tr. as "The Doctored Man") that he actually published in 1921 is drastically truncated. The protagonist, having been subjected forcibly to experimental eye surgery after being captured during the war, eventually manages to escape from his prison and make his way back to France. There, his enhanced eyesight begins to develop its full scope, and he realizes that an entire world of previously-invisible entities is becoming visible to him, after the fashion of the protagonist of J.-H. Rosny's similarly-truncated account of "Un Autre Monde"—a notion also broached in passing in his own account of

"L'Homme au corps subtil." Once the protagonist has made that discovery, however, Renard abruptly brings the story to a close, even though the other strands of the plot, involving residual threats from his former captors and a love story, had also seemed to promise much longer elaboration.

The fact that the stories begun by Rosny and Renard were both interrupted might have been due to a failure of imagination on the part of the individual authors in working out how to continue and conclude their stories, but it does reflect a common problem that all authors of *roman scientifique* encounter in handling themes with that kind of vast imaginative scope. The idea of an evolving vision of a parallel "invisible world" co-existing with our own is startling and intriguing in itself, but it is difficult to integrate into any kind of plot, and exceedingly difficult to accommodate within a conventional normalizing story-arc.

To some extent, that is a difficulty faced by all fictional accounts of superhumanity, very obviously displayed by Arnyvelde's *L'Arche*, which has virtually no plot, simply consisting of an elaborate exposition of its central notion, and also by Jarry's *Le Surmâle*, which similarly unfolds a similar exposition, but abandons its superman as soon as the full range of his new powers have been displayed. Shifting a narrative into a whole world of superhumans is a narrative exercise of a very different kind, where a merely human protagonist is bound to feel as uncomfortable as Louis Boussenard's Monsieur Synthèse after his ten thousand years in a block of ice: a discomfort inevitably shared by the writer and the reader. That story too had been rudely cut short.

Restif de La Bretonne had tackled the problem with reckless daring in *Les Posthumes*, and probably in an equally bold but more coherent manner in *L'Enclos et les oiseaux*, but the fate of those projects offers further evidence of the difficulty of establishing a sound and satisfactory communication of such ideas to readers in the context of a narrative. Friedrich Nietzsche had similar problems in trying to find a narrative method for his Zarathustra to introduce the *übermensch* to readers, and Louis Forest, proposing the deployment of a surgical method of turning children into superhumans on an industrial scale in the pages of *Le Matin*, had undoubtedly been correct in anticipating the likely public reaction to such a proposal. Given the difficulty of solving such narrative problems within the limited context of a literary marketplace, it is not surprising that as *roman scientifique* evolved as a genre, especially in the somewhat paranoid context of the aftermath of the Great War, its dealings with the issue of superhumanity sometimes became crassly ridiculous, sometimes weirdly grotesque, and sometimes frankly perverse.

One such grotesque and perverse account that appeared soon after the war in the guise of a thriller with mild satirical elements has a rather complicated bibliography, but appears to have first been serialized in *L'Éclair* in 1920 as "Les Surhommes" [The Superhumans] by "H.-J. Magog" (Henri-Georges Jeanne, 1877-1947) but was reprinted in 1928 as *Trois Ombres sur Paris* [Three Shadows over Paris]—the title by which it is best known—and also appeared as *Le Secret du professeur Fringue* [Professor Fringue's Secret]. The master surgeon Fringue, a more benevolently-inclined individual than André Couvreur's Armand Caresco or Gustave Le Rouge's Cornelius Kramm, outside of his typical obsessive devotion to his art, had made his debut in an earlier novel whose bibliography is equally confused, first appearing as a feuilleton in *Le Journal* as "Roman d'un singe" [The Romance of an Ape] in 1911 and then being reprinted as *Le Gorille policier* [The Gorilla Policeman] in 1917 before acquiring its best-known title, *L'Homme qui devint gorille* [The Man Who Became a Gorilla] in 1921.

In the earlier story, Fringue and his assistant Dr. Clodomir, nicknamed Dr. Silence, are tricked into switching the brains of a young man, Roland Missandier, and a gorilla by an evil financier intent on marrying the Missandier's fiancée, but they are eventually able to repair their error. In the later novel, set twenty years later, Fringue, who has become world famous, announces at the Sorbonne that he has discovered a means of manipulating the "cerebral electricity" of thought and intelligence, and that by concentrating the relevant energy he can produce intellectual superhumans. His claim receives an unexpectedly hostile reception and a demand that he refrain from doing anything of the sort, backed by the President of the United States of Europe. Alas, the demand comes a trifle too late; Fringue, never one to take things slowly, has already tried the experiment—but the subject has disappeared. Fringue is imprisoned and his death is faked, but the equally reckless Clodomir is still free, and more superhumans are created, mostly against their will.

The authorities attempt to intern the superhumans, and then to exile them all to an island, along with Fringue, but Clodomir remains a thorn in their side, further complicating the plot when he reveals that he has created artificial humans as well as superhumans. In a fashion typical of popular thrillers, however, and foreshadowed in the earlier novel, the novel's plot focuses on the romantic tribulations of the President's daughter and her rival suitors; the capabilities of the superhumans are mainly examined in a hypothetical fashion, and their eventual destiny is left deliberately unclear.

Magog went on to become a prolific writer of thrillers, but most remained relatively mundane, although the prospects of superhumanity crop up again, as well as a confused assemblage of other melodramatic themes, in a part-work series written in collaboration with Paul Féval *fils* (1860-1933) collectively entitled, in a Suesque fashion that Féval's father had also imitated, *Les Mystères de demain* [The Mysteries of Tomorrow] and consisting of *Les Fiancés de l'an 2000* [The Lovers of the Year 2000] (1922), *Le Monde des damnés* [The World of the Damned] (1923), *Le réveil d'Atlantide* [The Awakening of Atlantis] (1923), **L'Humanité enchaînée** [Humanity in Chains] (1923) and *Le Faiseur de folles* [The Maker of Madness] (1924)—a sixth

volume was advertised but never appeared, and was probably not intended to be the last. The series features phases in a long duel between two scientific geniuses, Oronius and the malevolent Hantzen, in which the former is obliged to develop super-powers in order to combat the insidious machinations of the latter, in what was eventually to become a standard pattern of melodramatic inflation. Orionius' innovations include developing the "cyclopean" or "cerebral" eye that allows him access to various kinds of sight of which ordinary eyes are incapable.

A basic set of mental powers had long been standardized as elements of the assumed repertoire of fictitious magicians, and hence a target for replication by frauds, charlatans and stage magicians. Those "superpowers" had automatically come under scientific scrutiny from the "psychic research societies" established in the last decades of the nineteenth century, and had been reequipped with such quasi-scientific labels as telepathy, telekinesis and precognition. In spite of the lack of progress made by that research prior to the Great War, the conviction that such plausible impossibilities must be achievable, with the aid of the right education or equipment, persisted stubbornly. In literary terms, however, their most obvious utility was in downmarket popular literature, where such powers could enhance the menace posed to hapless victims or unusually capable heroes by adversaries who could terrify the former and test the mettle of the latter.

As the heroes of popular fiction began to acquire special powers of their own, following up the daydream-inspired abilities of Duc Multipliandre, it became a narrative necessity for villains to acquire more challenging ones. Thus,

when Jean de La Hire resurrected a hero that he had employed in two pre-war feuilletons for a further series of adventures—initially serialized in *Le Matin*—he was quick to import the repertoire of superhuman abilities to melodramatize the threats posed by his adversaries.

In "Lucifer" (1921-22; book version in two volumes as *Lucifer* and *Le Nyctalope contre Lucifer*; the whole tr. as *The Nyctalope vs. Lucifer*) the villainous Glo von Warteck, who has a strange undersea empire in the Caribbean and a base in the Arctic as well as a fortified castle in Germany, can enhance his own innate mental powers by means of a machine harnessing and deploying Omega Rays, and plans to enslave the entire human race once he can obtain the necessary power and range for his device, but he is eventually thwarted by the hero, whose very modest superpower consists of being able to see in the dark. That story, and others following the same logic and pattern, proved to be the forerunners of an enormous explosion of twentieth-century superheroic fantasy, which not only took over a considerable sector of vulgar scientific fiction in all the countries where such genres were evolving but became the dominant colonist of an entire medium—known in France as *bandes dessinées* and in America as comic books—which eventually became a key feeder medium to twenty-first century cinema.

The further adventures of La Hire's Nyctalope in the period between the two World Wars involved him with a whole series of villains, all of them equipped, in accordance with the logic of melodramatic inflation, with exaggerated propensities for evil and exaggerated abilities to commit evil deeds, summarized in such titular nicknames as *L'Antéchrist* (1927), *Belzébuth* (1930) and *Gorillard* (1932). Many, like Glo von Warteck, were armed with both mental powers of domination and superscientific weapons, and it is arguable that they are merely caricaturish inflations of the model of the scientific mind developed in the literary field by S. Henry Berthoud, Jules Verne and many others. There is a sense in which scientific genius is seen as a kind of superhumanity itself, and one of the conventional notions of superhumanity—not the only one, but perhaps the one best suited to use in melodramatic thrillers—is simply an extrapolation of the conventional image of scientific insight and thinking to an uncanny extent.

Where La Hire led, many others were eventually to follow; the early adversaries featured in such thrillers included the rogue scientist depicted in *L'Expérience du docteur Lorde* [Dr. Lorde's Experiment] (1922) by Cyril-Berger, who puts his technological command of "odic fluid" to nefarious uses, the association of telepaths featured in Gabriel Bernard's part-work *Satanas* (1922) and the scientific genius leading the same author's *Les Compagnons de la haine* [The Companions of Hate] (1928). The Marquis de Saint-Imier, featured in Eugène Thébault's "**Radio-terreur**" (serial 1927-28; book 1929; tr. in *Wonder Stories* as "The Radio Terror"), fortunately has a scientist of equal genius, Mazelier, to oppose his plans for world-destruction, in what understandably became a common pattern. One of the other downmarket French novels translated for *Wonder Stories* in the same period, *La*

547

Menace invisible (probably 1927; tr. as "The Fall of the Eiffel Tower") by Charles de Richter, is of exactly the same kind, featuring a rogue scientist who unleashes a plague of augmented termites on Paris. Adversaries produced by merely reckless scientists included the automaton equipped with a human brain in Gaston Leroux's feuilleton *La Poupée sanglante* [The Bloody Doll] (1923; book version 1924 in 2 vols. as *La Poupée sanglante* and *La Machine à assassiner*; the latter tr. as *The Machine to Kill*).

More sophisticated post-war developments of the theme of telepathy usually felt obliged by the pressure of logic to attempt description of what the experience of telepathy might actually feel like, and what consequences its presumed reality might have, psychologically and philosophically. In trying to follow such lines of thought, however, authors tended to cut through the veneer of plausibility shielding the notion and run into the impossibilities that were being protected by the notions' superficial plausibility, often leading by another route to the kind of truncation that is routinely seen in stories of this type, or limiting themselves to glimpses contained in short stories. Théo Varlet's account of drug-induced thought transference "Télépathie" (1921; tr. as "Telepathy") is one of the better examples precisely because it remains conscientiously delicate and slight while nevertheless delving further into the implications of the notion than its treatment in crude thrillers routinely encouraged or permitted.

The notion that the development of such new mental powers was a logical evolutionary development, and would be characteristic of the descendant human species destined to replace ours had been broached on numerous occasions before the Great War, but it was not until afterwards that it became a standard theme of speculative fiction in France, Britain and America. An early post-war attempt made in the French language to develop it more elaborately was *Jean Arlog, le premier surhomme* [Jean Arlog, the First Super-human] (1921) by Georges Lebas, in which the eponymous character reveals to the narrator that he has succeeded in advancing to the next stage of human evolution by the sheer force of the Will—but not, in this instance, the Will to Joy advocated by Arnyvelde's arcandre.

Arlog's small demonstrations of his new abilities, however, only serve to turn the mistrust of the local population of

Orthez, where he has settled, into frank alarm. Already considering him to be a lunatic, the frightened populace embarks on active persecution, which brings forth an equal and opposite reaction in him. He decides to take a violent revenge upon them by using his power to stop the rotation of the Earth, but succumbs to an aneurism before he is able to carry out his plan—after which, predictably, people refuse to believe in his powers and dismiss the narrator who reports them as a delusionary victim of opium.

That basic pattern is recapitulated in Noëlle Roger's *Le Nouvel Adam* (1924; tr. as *The New Adam*), although the latter story employs a different supportive logic, developed in the context of research on the endocrine glands pioneered by Charles-Édouard Brown-Séquard (1817-1894), who had announced before his death that the glands in question might hold the key to the secret of life, including that of longevity. Although Brown-Séquard was long dead, his student Alexis Carrel had become famous when he won the Nobel Prize for Medicine in 1912, and another of his students, Sergei Voronoff, became a prominent figure in Parisian high society after marrying a millionairess in 1920; the latter soon began to generate his own publicity for his experiments attempting to provoke the rejuvenation of virility by means of testicular transplants.

The scientist featured in *Le Nouvel Adam* is working at the Pasteur Institute, in the field of glandular transplantation, and hopes that a transplantation of a mixture of glandular tissues might stimulate the development of the brain in such a way as to anticipate the future evolution of that organ. Having carried out the experiment on a fatally-wounded man, he not only succeeds in preventing the seemingly-certain death, but in equipping his patient with an unprecedentedly powerful intellect. The concomitant obsession with science, however, immunizes the recipient of the graft against moral scruples. His creator disowns him, but that only makes him more determined and more reckless, and his experiments with atomic energy are on schedule to destroy the world when a fortunate *deus ex machina* blows him up instead.

Inevitably, that was to become the standard formula of such fantasies, in Britain and America as well as France; the representatives of new races are routinely judged to have appeared too far "ahead of their time," universally considered to be a threat by merely human contemporaries, and thus ripe for the kind of conventional narrative closure that fictional fate is always enthusiastic to provide, if heroes like the Nyctalope should prove wanting. Noelle Roger wrote a second novel of the same kind, *Celui qui voit* (1926; tr. as *He Who Sees*), which recycles the argument of Louis-Sébastien Mercier's parable "Les Lunettes," in an elaborately graphic fashion.

Jean de La Hire was also quick, when the market opened up again after the war, to develop another classic notion of superhumanity, which had been the first one recruited by Plato to serve the cause of philosophical fiction, and one of those swiftly gathered by Duc Multipliandre to augment his initial identity-exchanging superpower: the ability to become invisible. Given a new boost of pseudoscientific plausibility by H. G. Wells, tempting such writers as Jules Verne and Louis Boussenard to swift response, the notion had been prominent in "scientific marvel fiction" before the war, and La Hire's *Joe Rollon, l'autre homme invisible* [Joe Rollon, the Other Invisible Man] (1919 as by Edmond Cazal) picked it up again immediately afterwards, rapidly followed by Guy de Téramond's *Ravengar* (1922).

The most interesting technologically-aided fictitious invisible man of the 1920s was also a highly skilled surgeon, and possessed uncanny mental abilities too; in consequence, he might, perhaps, be considered the first truly worthy literary successor to Duc Multipliandre—a worthiness further illustrated by his propensity for using his talents in the cause of erotic conquest. He was Félicien Champsaur's Marc Vanel, or, as the novel in which he first appeared did not hesitate to nickname him, Homo-Deus. Before examining him in detail, however, it is as well to consider another character who became oddly entangled with him in a novel that was a sequel to both their initially-unrelated appearances, carrying forward a confusion in the myth of superhumanity that has strangely deep roots in *roman scientifique*: a superficially paradoxical but nevertheless symmetrical association of "missing links" between the great apes and humankind on the one hand and hypothetical links between humans and superhumans on the other.

In *Les Posthumes*, the inhabitants of Venus, who are intellectually superior to human beings by virtue of their planet being older and closer to the sun, resemble orangutans physically. That was a joke, but it was a joke that found continual echoes in fictional dealings with orangutans and their "missing link" kin, in works by Léon Gozlan, Élie Berthet, Albert Robida, Jules Verne, Jules Lermina, Han Ryner and others. The vast majority of the latter images foregrounded the physical superiority that great apes seemed manifestly to have over human beings, for which severe mental inferiority was usually seen as a compensating factor, but in a number of significant instances, the morality of great apes is favorably compared with the perfidies typical of humankind.

That superior morality is often mere Rousseauesque innocence, but in some cases it goes beyond that, to an extraordinary capacity for compassion, loyalty and affection. The character of Kouang in *Raramémé*, for instance, although capable of extreme and effective violence against those who have hurt him or who threaten his allies, is clearly blessed with an even more noble savagery than the natives of the island where he is eking out his existence as the last of his kind. The same is true of Jules Lermina's To-Ho, similarly left as the last of his species, whose eventual isolation and doom is also represented, albeit more crudely, as stark tragedy.

The eponymous central character of Champsaur's *Ouha, roi des singes* (1923; tr. as *Ouha, King of the Apes*) is by no means as innately noble as Kouang or To-Ho, and indeed, he appears in the role of monstrous abductor and rapist of human females that had often been credited to great apes by traveler's tales and accepted at face value by Restif de la Bretonne, among others. In the course of the plot, however, he gradually transcends that Calibanesque role to become a tragic hero, and, indeed, a superhuman of sorts.

Ouha was a new departure in Champsaur's career, and was written at a pivotal moment therein. He had been a very successful writer before the outbreak of the Great War, renowned for mildly salacious novels about Parisian high society, simultaneously lamenting and exploiting its decadence. The war interrupted his career decisively, although he was able to resume publication in 1916, when he published two propaganda pieces before adapting *Les Ailes de l'homme* to the same purpose. Once the war was over, however, he moved decisively in a new direction, producing the six-volume "social epic" *L'Empereur des pauvres* [The Emperor of the Poor] (1920-22)—clearly an attempt to establish himself as a serious literary writer rather than a shallow entertainer. The series had some success, but it undoubtedly made less money than his pre-war works, and cannot have done

much to restore the erosion of his fortune by the effects of the war.

Given that context, *Ouha* seems like a blatant attempt to make some quick money, and Champsaur might well have written it to commission; the book's copyright notice is in the name of its publisher, Eugène Fasquelle, and it might have been intended to be more lavishly illustrated than it actually turned out to be, placing it more firmly in the context of its most prestigious thematic predecessors, *Les Émotions de Polydore Marasquin* and *Voyages très extraordinaires de Saturnin Farandoul*. The character of Ouha inevitably owes his origin and development to that literary tradition rather than to the march of science, and the physical anthropologist featured in the story, Dr. Abraham Goldry, seems somewhat behind the development of his science.

Criticism of the story of Ouha on the grounds of its infidelity to known science is, however, irrelevant, because the narrative is a hypothetical exercise of a very different sort. If Rousseau would have found it amusing—as he surely would—so would Carl Jung, who would have recognized it as an attempt to delve into the depths of human psychology rather than human evolution *per se*, much as Edmond Haraucourt had done in *Daâh*—which is also, in its fashion, an account of apish superhumanity. There is an archetypal quality to the character of Ouha, just as there would be to his giant cinematic successor King Kong; he is a player in an absurd melodrama, but its very absurdity raises questions about the sanity that rules him ridiculous, and the sheer extremism of the melodrama—especially its overwrought climax—has a peculiar magnificence that transcends mere logic.

Ouha, the chief of a Bornean orangutan tribe, is part-human by virtue of a past miscegenation, and that makes him all the more enthusiastic to add human females to his harem. He has no difficulty in recruiting a Malay girl, but runs into trouble when he turns his amorous gaze to the colonists who are arriving on the island in droves. When he captures Dilou, the daughter of a negro planter, an expedition is mounted to reclaim her, and when Ouha goes after her again he comes into contact with the American millionaire Harry Smith, his daughter Mabel, and Mabel's godfather, Dr. Goldry. After allowing himself to be captured, as a ploy, Ouha enters into communication with Goldry, who is naturally delighted with that unprecedented success—and equally disappointed when Ouha gives him the slip, not only having recaptured Dilou, but abducting Mabel too.

Another rescue mission is immediately mounted, but too hastily, and it suffers a humiliating defeat by the orangutans, during which Goldry is taken prisoner, and is appointed by Ouha as his "vizier," clad in an ape-skin during council meetings in order to hide his identity from the other apes. Another rescue-mission is organized, more carefully, but in the meantime, nature has taken its course; not only has Mabel been raped repeatedly by Ouha, but Goldry has also suffered a humiliating rape at the hands of the "wife" of the ape whose skin he has borrowed.

The latter scene is played as salacious comedy, but Mabel's experiences, initially played as horror, undergo a gradual transformation as Mabel makes existential contact with her inner ape. When the second rescue mission succeeds, she is profoundly grateful at first—but when Ouha's second attempt to reclaim the "wife" that he now values far more than any other turns into a disaster, and he suffers humiliating defeat in his turn, their perverse relationship arrives at a spectacular culmination, as extravagant in its way as the climax of *King Kong*, in spite of the absence of a phallic Empire State Building.

The attempts made in *Ouha* to delve into the psychological roots of human sexuality are somewhat tokenistic, but they nevertheless sowed a seed that was capable for further germination and development in the right literary environment: an environment that was provided by a novel that was separate from *Ouha* to begin with, although it was equally baroque and even more erotically-obsessed. It was originally intended to be titled *Le Satyre invisible* but the publisher apparently wanted to make it a trifle less brutal, or more enigmatic, and issued it as *Homo-Deus: Le Satyre invisible* (1924; tr. as "The Invisible Satyr").

The exercise was probably initiated as a playful exercise in eroticism, but Champsaur presumably thought it advisable to integrate its erotic scenes into a broader and more complicated plot. In order to achieve that synthesis, he was forced to improvise, moving into literary territory that was largely uncharted. He elected to do so, not unnaturally, by developing two corollaries of the notion of a technology of invisibility. On the one hand, he attempts to explore the other possibilities for which it might be useful, giving the protagonist the opportunity to become a kind of crime-fighting superhero, in an era when there were as yet no obvious models for that kind of character. On the other hand, he appears to have posed himself the speculative question of what other technologies might be possible if the theoretical basis of the hypothetical invisibility technology were taken for granted—again in an era where few literary models for that kind of exercise existed. Although neither of those two plot strands is developed with any conspicuous logic, and both eventually dissolve into incipient chaos when they embrace the later erotic scenes, the reckless mixing of the three aspects of the story produced a composite that is by no means devoid of interest, in terms of groping toward narrative effects that were new at the time.

Although Marc Vanel, the scientist of genius whose mesmeric abilities, perfected in India, earn him the nickname **Homo-Deus**, is far more personable than Ouha, the two have certain elements in common, which might help to explain the imaginative genesis of the latter book. The notion of superheroic satyriasis had been previously broached in *Les Posthumes* and *Le Surmâle*, and the kinship between Ouha and Homo-Deus, embodying common assumptions about fundamental human psychology and "bestial instincts" credits them both with an irresistible libido to match their extraordinary physical prowess, which makes them both *surmâles* without the need for any dietary supplement.

The hypothetical metaphysical basis on which Champsaur constructs his imaginary technology of invisibility, as well as the other pseudoscientific notions featured in the plot, is a straightforward modification of Cartesian dualism, of a kind that had been used very extensively in both literary fantasy and occult lifestyle fantasy to "explain" various psychic phenomena. Indeed, Champsaur takes those previous justifications for granted, wanting to take the argument further, not only in terms of imagining an "alternative psychic fluid" conferring invisibility on the flesh, but in hypothesizing an innovative employment of the standard "soul-fluid" in shoring up a technology of resurrection, described and detailed in a fashion as strikingly melodramatic as the various manifestations of the invisible satyr.

The subplot developing those metaphysical notions features another mesmerically-talented scientist, Jean Fortin, and, more particularly, his daughter Jeanne, a scientific genius whose reasoned chastity and complete immunity to erotic impulses represent a commitment every bit as ardent and absolute as the saintliest nun's commitment to Christ, and far less vulnerable to the charge of subconscious displacement. After aiding her invisibly in her pursuit of a technology of resurrection by supplying her with a freshly murdered body, Vanel embarks on an erotic pursuit that is somewhat reminiscent of a not-quite-irresistible force meeting an utterly immovable object, which climaxes in an unusually steamy and tantalizing shower scene.

The second subplot develops when Vanel decides to persecute the murderers of the corpse he donated to Jeanne Fortin, and sets about using his mesmeric talents and his invisibility to deprive them of the spoils of their crimes, applying an extra turn of the screw by confronting them with their resurrected victim. That narrative strand eventually expands to fill up more narrative space than either of the two themes that are introduced ahead of it in the story. In its basic strategy, the subplot now seems infinitely more familiar than it did in 1924, because crime-fighting superheroes, following in the footsteps of the comic-book Superman and Batman, have become a spectacular archetype of modern literature, amenable to enormous replication, variation and melodramatic inflation, to the extent that it is now very difficult to retreat, imaginatively, to an era when no such archetype existed. It is, however, necessary to do that in order to appreciate how innovative Homo-Deus was in that nascent role, and hence to understand why the manner in which he fulfilled it now seems so utterly *wrong*.

Technically speaking, Homo-Deus was not the first mysterious avenger in French popular fiction to be equipped with a "superpower." Indeed, in the matter of his minor powers of mesmerism and fakirism, he had numerous predecessors, including **Sâr Dubnotal** whose adventures had been chronicled anonymously by Norbert Sévestre in 1909-10. In terms of more adventurous superpowers he was not only foreshadowed by previous invisible men who dabbled in vigilantism, but also by the Nyctalope, who had begun his post-war career as a series hero shortly before. Homo-Deus clearly had potential to be developed in the same fashion, had Champsaur wanted to do that, but he did not consider himself to be that kind of writer, deeming himself to be cut from finer literary cloth.

Even without such extension, however, Homo-Deus represents a precursory phase in what we can now see, retrospectively, as the evolution of superhero fiction. Because his superpower is so much more radical than the Nyctalope's ability to see in the dark, it inevitably engages the fundamental problem that superhero fiction necessarily inherited from Plato: to what extent is a person who can act with impunity likely to admit constraint by moral regulation? In this case, the answer is very little, and Marc Vanel's tactics as a crime-fighter, which lead him to commit two murders, one of them of an entirely innocent individual, in order to frame the villains, leave much to be desired in moral terms. That is, however, treated by the author as a mere irrelevance by comparison with his fascination with Vanel's sex life, especially his relationship with Jeanne—which eventually reaches an exceedingly strange climax when she falls victim to the wrathful revenge of the ruined villains.

Had the project finished there, the two unconnected books would have remained interesting and baroque, but once having invented Homo-Deus, Champsaur could not let him alone. He gave him a bit part in another novel, *Tueur les vieux! jouir!* (1925; tr. as "Kill the Old! Enjoy!"), in the plot of which he abducts a fake medium who has suddenly acquired authentic supernatural powers by virtue of the accidental lodgment within her body of an extraterrestrial entity. The latter comes from a world of free-floating spirits and is exceedingly vexed to find itself trapped in the body of a dishonest whore. Vanel's objective in removing the medium from the plot of the novel—a naturalistic melodrama of murder driven by greed, lust and post-war moral collapse—is to learn more about the universal schema of which the entity is a natural part, evidently akin to the one sketched out by Camille Flammarion in the classic *Lumen*, but the narrative voice leaves the investigations off-stage and Homo-Deus never communicates what he learned in that process, although he does drop a few teasing hints when he reappears as a major character in the book that is a sequel to both *Le Satyre invisible* and *Ouha*, and extrapolates their interest in the psychological roots of sex to a further extreme: *Nora, la guenon devenue femme* (1929; tr. as *Nora, the Ape-Woman*).

FÉLICIEN CHAMPSAUR

NORA

la guenon devenue femme

FERENCZI ET FILS, ÉDITEURS
9, rue Antoine-Chantin, 9
PARIS

Nora has been condemned as an offensively racist text by Brett A. Berliner, in "Mephistopheles and Monkeys: Rejuvenation, Race and Sexuality in Popular Culture in Interwar France", in the *Journal of the History of Sexuality* vol. 13 no, 3 (2004), which argues the character of Nora is an abusive parody of Josephine Baker. In fact, although Nora's mother was an orangutan, her father is the white American scientist Abraham Goldry; she is a result of the latter's rape described in *Ouha*. Nora's counterpart within the plot, an orangutan with potentially-superhuman intelligence, ironically named Narcisse, is Ouha's son by Dilou, but he is the only character featured in the plot to have any biological relationship with a black person, and he is treated far more sympathetically by the author than any other, including his mentor Marc Vanel.

The first chapter of the novel, in which Nora is introduced, features a minor character whose sole purpose is to make a speech arguing that "we are all apes," thus summarizing the moral of the tale, which is the very opposite of the xenophobia that Berliner tries to foist upon it. The plot continually draws comparisons between the hybrid apes Nora and Narcisse and the "fully human" characters—every one of whom is white—always suggesting that the supposed "superiority" of the latter is false, and consists largely of a hypocritical denial of their animality, particularly in respect of their sexual impulses.

Berliner is correct in saying that Nora's first appearance on the stage of the Folies Bergère is clearly based on Josephine Baker's debut there in 1925, when she performed a so-called "*danse sauvage*" wearing a skirt made from a string of artificial bananas. Champsaur probably saw that performance, and adapted a journalistic description of it, in a somewhat slapdash fashion, for his own description of Nora's "*ballet nègre*." In doing that, however, Champsaur had not the slightest intention of insulting Josephine Baker, and Nora's actual symbolism within the story is in no way relevant to the career of the American dancer, or to black people in general. The fact that Nora's performance is a *ballet nègre* is attributed in the story to the fact that she learned to dance in Cuba, and *ballet nègre* was a general term used at the time for a style of dancing, which was not intended to be pejorative.

Josephine Baker was not the first part-negro dancer to appear on the Parisian stage wearing an extremely scanty costume and dancing *ballet nègre*. She had been preceded by Aïcha Goblet, who appears in a cameo role in a scene in *Tuer les Vieux! jouir!* set in the Café Rotonde, where Champsaur used to hang out with Picasso and Modigliani, both of whom used her as a model; the scene establishes that Champsaur was entirely sympathetic to her, and serves to allow the narrative voice to defend her against unjustified moral suspicions; it demonstrates that racism was commonplace in the Parisian social scene in the 1920s, but that Félicien Champsaur was a determined opponent of it rather than a collaborator.

Perhaps, viewed in retrospect, it was a *faux pas* for Champsaur to borrow aspects of Josephine Baker's performance to characterize Nora's, but it ought not to occasion the blanket condemnation of the book—which is otherwise total-ly innocent of any accidental racist suggestion—or its author, who was one of the least xenophobic of his generation. Champsaur would have been mortified to know that the work had given rise to such criticism—all the more so because there are many so aspects of the book that really were intended to shock and of-fend, by fiercely attacking the hypocrisy and folly of the arrogance of supposed-ly-superior "civilized" humans.

In order to understand Nora's actual symbolism it is helpful to refer back to two of Champsaur's earlier novels, both published in 1888, which made him famous. *L'Amant des danseuses, roman moderniste* [The Man Who Loved Dancing-Girls; a Modernist Novel] is a relatively earnest psychological study of the erotic attraction of the world of the theater in general, and dancers in particu-lar, which uses a painter as a central character, clearly based on Edgar Degas, although the fascinations credited to him are largely the author's own, and inso-far as the narrative is critical of the character's obsession, it is a kind of self-criticism without any intention to insult Degas. The second, *Lulu, roman clownesque* [Lulu; a Clownish Novel] is a study of a dancer, couched as a sen-timental comedy, in which the eponymous heroine explicitly becomes a symbol not merely for the eroticism of her art and the fickleness of womankind, but for the essential spirit of the city of Paris. In the extravagant climax, the lover to whom Lulu finally commits herself is revealed to be an incarnation of the divine Eros-Bacchus, who subjects her to a metamorphosis that transforms her into "*l'ange d'acrobatie*" [the angel of acrobatics].

Nora brings Lulu's lyrical symbolism down to earth, making the dancer an ape rather than an angel precisely in order to fit her into the context of evolu-tionary history and the true simian nature of the human species. As with Lulu, Nora's function within the plot is to be not merely an object of sexual desire, but an archetypal embodiment of the very essence of sexual desire; amour, however, is no longer imagined in *Nora* as something intrinsically divine, but as some-thing intrinsically animalistic, and so deep-seated that even a scientific genius like Homo-Deus cannot escape it. The plot of the novel is concerned with the scientific modification of species by means of surgery, and the possibilities in-herent within that surgery for the enhancement of the human condition, ultimate-ly extending as far as the creation of the superhuman and the conquest of death. In that respect, it takes some inspiration from the contemporary exploits of Serge Voronoff, who is one of its leading characters in the novel, forming a quartet with Abraham Goldry, Marc Vanel and Jean Fortin.

After several scientific publications of a more general kind, Voronoff had published *Greffes testiculaires* [Testicular Grafts] in 1923 and a report of *Quarante-trois greffes du singe à homme* [Forty-Three Grafts from Monkeys to Humans] in 1924, and then followed them up with *Étude sur la vieillesse et la rajeunissement par la greffe* (1926; tr. as *Rejuvenation by Grafting*), which is an exercise in self-publicizing futurology rather than a scrupulous report of his research findings. Those findings were never published in a form that would be considered today to be full and adequate scientific reportage. In consequence of their somewhat equivocal reportage, there is little hard information as to how many experiments Voronoff carried out between 1917 and 1929, or what the results of those experiments might have been. Hindsight, judging by the example of further experiments, suggests that the claims he made about the success of his grafts must have been exaggerated, reflecting his optimism rather than his evidence, probably because he fell for his own patter rather than because he was a calculated charlatan. How many grafts of simian testicular material he had carried out on human subjects prior to 1929 remains unclear, but what is certain is that by that date, everyone in Paris believed that he was doing such operations on a regular basis, and people were eagerly searching high society for signs of youthful behavior in aged individuals who might—behind a shield of strict confidentiality, of course—have been his clients.

Voronoff's work obtained a vast amount of press coverage, and provided the basis for several works of speculative fiction, almost all of them mocking or grimly hostile, naturally extending to lurid recapitulations of the theme of Maurice Renard's *Le docteur Lerne*, such as Guy de Téramond's *Le Faiseur de monstres* [The Monster-Maker] (1930), which appeared in a series with the general title *Les Dossiers Secrets de la Police*. Of all the writers of such speculative works, however, Félicien Champsaur was probably the only one who not only knew Voronoff socially, but might have contemplated seriously the possibility of becoming one of his clients. Born in 1858, Champsaur had edged into his seventies by 1929, and as a relentless lifelong debauchee, he was undoubtedly painfully aware of the declining effects of age.

Champsaur must have had Voronoff's consent to use him as a character in a book, and Voronoff, acutely aware of the potential publicity value of an account that was not overtly hostile, might well have encouraged him to do so fervently. As to whether or not he offered Champsaur a free rejuvenation treatment in return—and whether, if he did, Champsaur accepted the offer—we can only speculate. All we know for sure is that Champsaur died in 1934, no younger than he had been in 1929, and all that can really be deduced from the pages of *Nora* is that if he did think seriously about acquiring such a graft, he was very hesitant about it, not merely because he was squeamish on his own account but because he would have felt extremely guilty about imposing the cost of such a sacrifice on an innocent ape.

The character in the novel who is faced with the decision as to whether to risk the rejuvenation treatment is, like Champsaur, a famous writer and a relentless but discreet debauchee, but Champsaur went so far out of his way to avoid the likelihood that readers might identify him with his character that he explicitly based the character on Anatole France, who had worn the mantle of his country's leading novelist for two decades before his death, and had won the Nobel Prize for Literature in 1921. In the novel, Edgar Paris is 80, the same age as Anatole France had been when he died; he lives at the address at which Anatole France was then living and he wins the Nobel Prize; many other calculated similarities are dropped into the plot before it reaches a climax that is a straightforward account of Anatole France's funeral—until Nora and Narcisse get involved in the obsequies, in their own fashion.

Edgar Paris is only superficially similar to Anatole France, however, in spite of the wealth of surface detail supporting that appearance. In the story, Edgar Paris is struggling ineffectually with a novel that he has been planning to write for years, entitled *Le Vrai Jésus*, a historical novel that will reveal the non-supernatural character behind the Biblical legend. Anatole France had no such project in progress when he died, but a year after publishing *Nora*, Félicien Champsaur published *Le Crucifié*, a historical novel speculatively revealing the "real" non-supernatural character of Jesus. In a sense, therefore, Edgar Paris is not Anatole France, but Félicien Champsaur, who was, like many sarcastic cynics, routinely harder on himself than he was on other people. In the context of the novel's meditation on the themes of animality and superhumanity, however, there is a good reason for comparing and contrasting Narcisse, the orangutan embodying seeds of superhumanity, not with some nasty human villain repulsive even to his own kind, but with the finest intellectual specimen that artistic humanity can produce, a Nobel prize-winner and genius in his own field. As to which of them the divinely animal Nora would prefer as a lover, there really would be no competition.

In conventional literary terms, *Nora* is a poorer novel than *Ouha*, and in terms of imaginative reach it does not measure up to *Le Satyre invisible*, on the ideas of which it is largely parasitic. It does, however, display its bizarrerie with admirable flamboyance, and it takes great care to offer Marc Vanel and Jean Fortin, as well as Edgar Paris, abundant opportunity to wax analytical about the essential nature of amour, especially when lecturing Nora or Narcisse, the innocent superhuman apes who have everything still to learn as they develop their intense star-crossed and lust-laden romance.

The remarkable triptych of which *Nora* was placed as the crucial missing link, offers analyses not merely of human lust but of all human ambition, bringing them solidly down to earth, analyzing them as animality disguised by hypocrisy—but it is not content with that, and insists on going further in its visionary conclusion. Science, it argues, has the potential to get us out of the miry rut, by expanding the horizons of our understanding, by transforming human potential, and literally creating the superhuman. The superhuman might, as in the case of Narcisse, resemble an orangutan rather than a human, but that will not matter, because beauty is relative and such superficial matters as form and skin color are, at the end of the day, subsidiary to the potentialities and relationships of the intangible components of humanity: intelligence and the mind, or the soul. The point is explicitly made that in the make-up of Homo-Deus, the human—and hence the animal—is still dominant over the divine, but it is also asserted that

Marc Vanel is godly enough to lay the groundwork for his own supersession, and eventually to hand the torch of progress on to beings who have disciplined amour without annihilating it, for whom neither the future nor the sky has any limit.

Apes and superhumans are also juxtaposed, in an overlapping fashion, in *Les Chasseurs d'hommes* [The Man-Hunters] (*Science et Voyages* 1929; book 1933) by René Thévenin, who had continued his production of exotic thrillers since his debut in *Le Journal de Voyages* in the pre-war period—although internal evidence suggests that the story might have been written in that period and languished unpublished for a long time. The story's protagonist sets off to equatorial Africa in pursuit of mysterious handprints preserved in blocks of clay sent back by a scientist whose notes and the circumstances of his death suggest that he fell victim to some kind of vampire.

In Africa the narrator mingles with gorilla-hunters and makes the acquaintance of two women, one of whom has luminous translucent skin and an unusually high forehead and serves as his guide to the territory of the mysterious "man-hunters," who appear to be the Adam and Eve of a new superhuman species. Although the plot reaches closure of a sort when the narrator and the mundane woman are able to escape and return to civilization following the death of the new Adam, the fates of the gorilla-hunters and the new Eve are deliberately left uncertain, with the implication that evolution, even if briefly interrupted, will eventually continue its course.

A more ingenious account of evolutionary supersession is provided in Octave Béliard's *Les Petits hommes de la pinède* [The Little People of the Pine Wood] (serial 1927; book 1929) in which a race of minuscule humans created by an embryologist procreate more rapidly than full-sized humans and soon overtake them in terms of scientific invention; slowed down in their development by internecine warfare, they seem nevertheless to be bound to become the dominant species, until their creator employs the advantage of his remaining physical advantage in order to put an end to the experiment.

The works discussed so far in this section are relatively modest in their futuristic anticipations, as most stories dealing with superhumanity tend to be. Very few attempt to take the theme to any kind of extraordinary lengths; *Les*

Posthumes, in its image of life on Io, had illustrated the difficulties of doing that a long time ago, and few writers had been prepared to be as bold since, although André Arnyvelde and Henri-Jacques Proumen qualify as heroic exceptions, in the works described in the previous section of the chapter. The 1920s did, however, produce one spectacular attempt to imagine a complex future in which human evolution has taken not one but several leaps forward, in accordance with different aspects of human ambition. If Odette Dulac's *[Amour]...tel qu'il est* is the most extraordinary account rendered in *roman scientifique* of past human evolution, then its futuristic counterpart is surely ***Les Surhommes, roman prophétique*** (1929; tr. as "The Superhumans") by Han Ryner.

Les Surhommes takes its imaginative warrant from the highly unorthodox "hexagramist" evolutionary theories of Michel Savigny (1832-1903), who proposed that earthly evolution, far from being gradual over the entire extent of the time recorded by the fossil record, had had long periods of relative stability punctuated by bursts of extraordinary metamorphic mutation, guided by the hyper-Lamarckian effort and desire of the affected organisms, associated with alternating igneous and glacial catastrophes, with a periodicity of 25,000 years. Although Savigny's chronology had been rendered obsolete by 1929, Ryner adopted the basic notion, beginning his novel with the advent in the solar system of a second sun, the "Star of Fire," whose radiation prompts the next series of such metamorphoses.

Although essentially similar in nature to previous occurrences of the same sort, this one is different in its effects because human beings are capable of greater effort and more various desires than previous species had been, and thus much better able to benefit from the metamorphic radiation. In consequence, the ambitious members of the species—some, being fundamentally satisfied with themselves, remain much as they are—experience metamorphoses in three distinct directions, dependent on different fundamental desires: for immortality, power and spiritual transcendence.

The members of the first resultant species of this spectrum of desires, the Immortals, are physically stunted and consummately cowardly in spite of possessing quasi-metallic bodies, which are capable of infinite endurance but at considerable cost in terms of their owners' capacity to enjoy life. The second emergent species is a race of "Superelephants," physically powerful, enormously arrogant and supremely self-indulgent. The third is a company of "Superangels," capable of levitation and exceedingly fond of singing and preaching peace and good will.

Insofar as the visionary fantasy has a plot, it concerns the Superelephants' determination to dominate the world, and the consequent steps they take to conquer the remaining humans and the other two posthuman species. The ordinary humans and the Immortals are unable to put up significant resistance to being enslaved, but the Superangels prove to be far more difficult to subdue when captured, as seven of them eventually are, and even ordinary humans eventually prove to be recalcitrant. The story ends with a dialogue between two of the Superelephants, in which one of them expresses his determination to succeed in further self-improvement, in order to become a veritable god, whereas the other raises various objections to his plans, on philosophical and logical grounds.

Having already designed his anarchist utopia in *Les Pacifiques*, *Les Surhommes* is an evident attempt on Han Ryner's part to take his argument a step further, beyond human limitations, into the philosophical terrain of the *übermensch* and the arcandre. The extent of his success remains a trifle dubious, but that has at least as much to do with the logical limits of the exercise as with the particular competence of the author's imagination. At least he did make the attempt, setting foot where many others had feared to tread, and he did not rush into the question as a fool, but as a serious and intelligent cynic.

It could certainly be argued that in accepting angels as his fundamental model for superhumanity, Ryner was not advancing the basic argument much beyond Restif's visions in *Les Posthumes*, but perhaps that only serves to illustrate the truth of Benjamin Disraeli's reaction to being called upon to express his opinion in the debate about evolutionism: that in the ultimate analysis, it simply comes down to a straightforward choice between apes and angels—to which Félicien Champsaur might have added that one could, if one thought about it in the right frame of mind, achieve a viable synthesis of the two.

3. Other Worlds

Interplanetary fiction did not disappear entirely during the years of the Great War, but it might be reckoned significant that the most ambitious and exotic exercise of that kind written in French was the work of a writer from neutral Switzerland: *Anthéa, ou l'étrange planète* (1918 in *Semaine Littéraire*; 1923 in book form; tr. as "Anthea; or, The Strange Planet") by "Michel Epuy" (Louis Vaury, 1876-1943). Dedicated to J.-H. Rosny, the novella is set solidly in the vein of exotic biological fantasias that he had pioneered.

Anthéa illustrates the continuing difficulty of providing a plausible narrative account of interplanetary travel, following in André Laurie's footsteps in bringing the alien world to be visited in the course of the story close enough to the Earth's atmosphere to facilitate the journey. In this case, the close passage of Earth by a comet leaves a fragment of the visitor's substance behind, captured by the Earth's gravity in a geosynchronous orbit that positions it directly above Quito in Ecuador, close enough to its new primary for its own attraction to cause a bulge in the Earth's atmosphere that creates a corridor of air between the two worlds. The story's protagonist, an ambitious young astronomer, employs that corridor as a means of making the journey by balloon.

On the alien world, as might be expected of a story inspired by Rosny, the narrator finds the relationship between the mineral and vegetable kingdoms markedly different from that on Earth, the latter having apparently metamorphosed into the former as a result of some kind of process of near-universal petrifaction. Among the few vegetables that remain alive are flying species with some animal features, which prey upon one another. Taken in by one of the meeker species, the narrator only escapes the invasion of their elaborate subterranean nest by more aggressive neighbors because Anthéa disintegrates under the gravitational stresses of its new situation, causing a long fall that requires him to be ingenious in improvising a parachute.

Whether Epuy found a satisfactory solution to the difficulty of affecting plausible transfers between worlds is highly debatable, but it remained the case for a few more years that the spaceships that were ultimately to take on that literary role in a broadly conventional sense had not yet acquired their warrant of acceptability. As demonstrated by Renard's "L'Homme truqué," that was not the only kind of hesitation displayed in narratives that ventured into alien territory, which were often content to remain tentative.

Les Trois yeux (1919; tr. as *The Three Eyes*) by Maurice Leblanc is content to open communication with the alien via a "ray" discovered by the protagonist's uncle—a typical obsessive scientist, Noel Dorgeroux—which permits the material incarnation of the ominous three eyes of the title. That initial attentive image is replaced by others seemingly displaced in time, commencing with the execution during the war of the British nurse Edith Cavell by the Germans, and including the Montgolfier brothers' first balloon ascent and a "dogfight" between French and German biplanes—the specific combat, in fact, after which Dorgeroux's son was killed during the war.

The plot is complicated when Dorgeroux is murdered. His secret is exploited by its next custodian as a new kind of cinema, which reveals a long sequence of dramatic images from the history—but the battle to possess the secret only becomes more intense and complicated. The images are explained as transmissions from the planet Venus, thus opening up further possibilities in what the continuation of the communication might reveal, if it can be secured and a dialogue initiated. That element of the plot is complicated too, by visions of an exceedingly strange alien environment populated by geometrical figures—but the author, a prolific writer of crime thrillers, was unwilling or unable to follow through that aspect of his story, and left it dangling in a frustratingly teasing fashion once he had wrapped up the more conventional story of love and murder.

An alien world within the Earth is depicted in Pierre de La Batut's hallucinatory fantasy "La Jeune fille en proie au monstre" [The Young Woman Prey to the Monster] (1921), in which two archeologists investigating strange inscriptions in the ruins of an ancient Assyrian city are seemingly led into the underworld when the fiancée of one is abducted, apparently by a member of a pre-human species modeled by the Assyrians in their statues of winged bulls—except that no such alien actually appears, all communication with the archeologists being filtered through an enigmatic "slave" who bears a strange resemblance to a former rival for the young woman's love. The long-lived aliens are said to be planning to take back control of the world from humans with the aid of a population of monstrous species yet to be produced by an evolutionary process that runs in reverse to scientific conviction. The story was submitted for a competition for works of "anticipation scientifique" run by *Je Sais Tout* but did not win, perhaps because the judges simply did not know what to make of it; it remains deeply and deliberately enigmatic, but is nevertheless considerably more sophisticated and more striking than the majority of contemporary images of alien life on other planets.

A bolder interplanetary fantasy appeared as a feuilleton in *Le Petit Parisien* between November 1921 and February 1922 as "L'Anneau de lumière" [The Ring of Light] by "L. Miral" (Léon Jacob, 1858-1942) and "A. Viger" (Alphonse Berger, 1860-1934), and was reprinted in book form later in the latter year as *L'Anneau de feu* [The Ring of Fire]. The titular reference is to the planet Saturn, where the French voyagers in an atomic-powered rocket end up, in pursuit of evil Germans, after a long sojourn on Mars. Both planets turn out to be Earthlike, Mars being inhabited by technologically-advanced and long-lived humans who conveniently speak French, while Saturn has a mixed fauna ranging from giant saurians through giant mammals to scrawny primitive humans. While they are away, the heroes and the chief villain miss the entirety of the Great War, and when the villain learns of Germany's defeat after being brought back as a prisoner he dies of a broken heart.

On this occasion, the experiment does not seem to have been deemed a complete failure, and *Le Petit Parisien* serialized a sequel to the novel between August and October 1924, "La Loi de Mars" [Martian Law], although it is set entirely on Earth and is concerned with the intervention in Earthly matters of the Martian king introduced in the earlier story. In view of the ages of the two authors, the slightly old-fashioned quality of the narratives is not entirely surprising; Jacob, writing as Léon Miral, had written a good deal of popular fiction in the 1890s.

A more daring confrontation of human and alien is featured in a novel by another team of collaborators, *L'Adversaire inconnu* [The Unknown Adversary] (1922) by Cyril-Berger, in which an insectile alien visitor arrives on Earth in the form of a microscopic egg contained within a meteorite, but does not take long to complete its metamorphosis into an imago capable of nourishing itself on human blood. The same year also saw the publication of one of the more peculiar interplanetary fantasies of the period, *La Rédemption de Mars* [The Redemption of Mars] (1922) by the Belgian politician and Catholic mystic Pierre Nothomb (1887-1966), which details the educative sojourn on Mars of two scientists, one a Christian and the other an atheist; the latter eventually discovers the error of his ways as a result of his experience, and the novel anticipates the theme of C.S. Lewis' classic religious fantasy *Out of the Silent Planet* (1938), albeit vaguely.

J.-H. Rosny remained tentative in "**L'Étonnante aventure de Hareton Ironcastle**" (1922; tr. as "Hareton Ironcastle's Amazing Adventure"), although it seems to be cast deliberately in the mold of American pulp fiction, in which medium "science fiction" had not yet been identified as a separate genre and the work of domesticating the spaceship as a commonplace literary device had not yet begun. If the novel was a deliberate attempt to angle for translation, it might have been prompted by the sale of translation rights to the latest novel in Rosny's series of prehistoric adventures, "Le Félin géant" (1918), although the American edition did not actually appear until 1924, as *The Giant Cat*. At any rate, Hareton

Ironcastle's odyssey bears a closer resemblance to the narratives published in such US pulps as *Adventure* than to the Vernian adventures still being published in the *Journal des Voyages*, taking an American hero and an international assortment of followers deep into the unexplored heart of Africa in pursuit of rumors of intelligent plants.

After a long and action-packed journey, Ironcastle and his associates finally reach an unearthly enclave of exceedingly exotic life. Pierre Versins's brief summary of the story states unequivocally that the enclave is a fragment of an alien world welded to ours by some cosmic accident, after the fashion of the mountain in "Tornadres," and the translation extensively rewritten by Philip José Farmer as *Ironcastle* (1976) is equally unequivocal, but the original text is not so definite, and leaves the origin of the alien enclave uncertain. The confrontation with the sentient Mimosas in the conclusion is similarly hesitant and content to remain a mere glimpse.

Perhaps unsurprisingly, the pseudonymous André Mas, who had written a forthright account of the beginnings of interplanetary conquest and colonization before the war, in *Les Allemands sur Vénus*, was not quite so inhibited when he decided to write a prose narrative based on his visionary poem *Sur leur double soleil, des Dryméeens chantent* [Of their Double Sun, Drymeans Sing] (1921), published as *Drymea, monde de vierges* (1923; tr. as *Drymea*). His heroine, Hertha Helgar, is taken prisoner in a future war—in 1935—and condemned to die, after refusing the lustful advances of her captor, by being placed in a shell and fired from a huge gun: an evident gesture of phallic symbolism rather than an efficient means of execution. She swallows poison to hasten her demise, but its effect allows her remain mysteriously dormant during a long interstellar voyage. She finally ends up on the Earth-clone world of Drymea, in which sex has never been developed as an evolutionary strategy, and masculinity, with all its hideous corollaries, is therefore absent, thus permitting human society to be placid, beautiful and broadly eutopian, although not without its rivalries and hazards.

Although it is not the first depiction of an all-female society in French fiction, where the legend of the Amazons had found numerous echoes, *Drymea* was the first to address the issue in a quasi-scientific framework, as *roman scientifique* rather than mythological fantasy, and hence with a certain amount of explanation and rational underpinning. It does not take long, however, for that account to run into difficulties that prevent it from following its extrapolations very far, some of which are problems of scientific logic, and some of which come from a different direction.

One important difference between *Drymea* and previous accounts of parthenogenetic human societies with some affiliation to rational plausibility, such as *Mizora* (1890) by the pseudonymous "Princess Vera Zaronovitch" and *Herland* (1915) by Charlotte Perkins Gilman, is that those earlier texts describe societies whose ancestors had two sexes, in which the parthenogenetic faculty is a relatively recent modification, whereas the entire sequence of Drymean animal evolution has been sexless—although not, apparently, plant evolution; Drymea, like most eutopias, is rich in gorgeous flowers that presumably have stamens and pistils, since they would otherwise have no need to attract insects with the color and perfume. Mas takes the trouble to stress that the general results of Drymean evolution have been milder than the effects of Earthly evolution because its species do not produce the surplus of offspring that gives rise to natural selection, so the motor that has led to the evolution of a quasi-human species remains profoundly unclear.

Whether he was capable of delving deeper into such questions or not, Mas was not in a position to go into overmuch detail about the corollaries of his central hypothesis. Fiction still had strict standards of decency to observe; even in the mid-nineteenth century, S. Henry Berthoud had been able to publish factual marriage manuals tentatively describing the details of sexual intercourse, but he would never have been allowed to put the same details into his fiction, and things had not changed greatly in the subsequent decades. In a sense, the whole point of Mas' story is the absence of the details in question, but it is an absence of which he cannot speak directly, even though it is the heart and soul of his narrative.

Drymeans, unlike the women of Mizora or Herland, are entirely innocent of sexual passion. No anatomical details can be provided, so we are not told whether Drymean evolution equipped them with a clitoris, but the feelings they have for one another cannot be sexual in a strict sense; they cannot be lesbians, in the way that the inhabitants of Mizora and Herland are able or condemned to be; nor, in spite of the title of the story and the language employed the text, can they be "virgins" in the way that word is commonly defined, since it can have no counterpart in terms of their existence. By contrast, Hertha Helgar, in spite of being an exceptionally virtuous woman, not a lesbian by inclination, and definitely a virgin, cannot escape the fact that she is innately equipped with sexual feelings. She might be able to rechannel those feelings in response to circumstance, but she cannot escape them. On Drymea, therefore, she is faced with a rather peculiar moral dilemma; she is capable of feeling passion for the Drymeans, but any such passion would be implicitly misdirected, because it cannot be reciprocated. How, then, can she conduct herself toward them, and what would be the consequences of her contact with them, if she permitted herself to express her innate passion?

As a personal problem that would be acute enough—although, given the amenability of the Drymeans she encounters, who include the paradoxically lustful Drythea, the problem does not seem to be as acute as she makes it out to be—but it is not just a personal problem. Indeed, it is a messianic problem, for the superior scientific and technological knowledge that Hertha brings to Drymea has the potential to transform Drymean society drastically. Can that transformation possibly be anything other than corrupting? Is there any way that the corollaries of masculinity still incarnate in Hertha—which supposedly include the ability to develop scientific knowledge—can enhance Drymean perfection rather than undermining it? And if they cannot enhance it and make it stronger, what will happen to Drymean society if and when, however distantly in the future, the Drymeans encounter a human race that is akin to Hertha's rather than their own, or shaped in some other way by the urgency of natural selection?

It is typical of speculative fiction of the period that these questions are obliquely glimpsed rather than explicitly addressed, although they prey on the heroine's mind as she struggles with her new relationships. Inevitably, there is no question of following them through to anything resembling a conclusion.

In 1923 the second edition of Gaston de Pawlowski's *Voyage au pays de la quatrième dimension* appeared, its overall tone somewhat darkened by a few extra chapters published since the armistice, and its philosophical pretentions boosted by the addition of a prefatory "Examen critique" [Critical Analysis] reassessing the ideas contained therein.

In the same year, Claude Farrère published the novelette "Où?" [Where?] in *Trois histoires d'ailleurs* [Three Stories of Elsewhere], which offers an account of the protagonist's visionary descents into another dimension, described as *Là-Bas* [down there], although the text goes to some lengths to insist that the "down" in question is by no means linear, and is only explicable in terms of exotic mathematics. The landscapes the visionary perceives are symbolic in nature, not nearly as far-reaching as Pawlowski's, but their expression as a dimensional fantasy rather than a simple dream does add a useful extra measure of narrative distance. Use of the fourth dimension is also employed, in a context that gives physics equal weight with occult science, in one of the stories making up Renée Dunan's *Baal, ou La Magicienne passionnée* (1924; tr. as "Baal; or, The Passionate Sorceress").

The possible inhabitants of the fourth dimension and their society are the object of "Les Étrange études du docteur Paukenschlager" [The Strange Studies of Dr. Paukenschlager] (1925) by Jean Ray, and the same author went on to employ the notion of the fourth dimension in "La Ruelle ténébreuse" [The Dark Alley] (1932), but a much more substantial, if rather rough-hewn, exploration based on Einsteinian theory appeared in the pages of *Science et Voyages*: "Par-delà l'univers" [Beyond the Universe] (1931) by Raoul Brémond. The author was probably not the person of that name who wrote the political tract *La*

Communauté [Community] (1938) but otherwise remains mysterious. The story describes how a physicist short of cash manages to cajole financial support out of a Frenchman and an English lord, who then become his companions in a flight into a "bubble universe" that he has contrived to generate parallel to our own. The journey of their peculiar "spacecraft" permits them to experience weightlessness and temporal distortions, before ending with a crash that only one of the travelers survives.

Pawlowski's precedent also offered some inspiration to the Surrealist Movement, evident in such prose narratives as *L'Étrange aventure du professeur Pamphlegme* [The Strange Adventure of Professor Pamphlegme] (1933) by Luc Alberny (1890-1969), in which the eponymous music teacher is introduced into a household of eccentrics, and discovers in the course of his relationship with its members that the old gods of Greece have retreated to an enclave hidden in the fourth dimension, where they have continued to evolve as belief in them has waned. Alberny extrapolated a similar notion in a slightly more orthodox fashion in *Le Mammouth bleu* [The Blue Mammoth] (1935), where the other dimension to which the world's mammoths and centaurs have retreated is literally "down there" in the heart of the world, although the means by which the protagonist reaches it, while searching for his lost love after returning from the trenches in a bad way, looks suspiciously unlike a straightforward descent, and no evidence can subsequently be found to support the truth of his story.

The specific problem of establishing a conventional narrative logic for space travel was tackled in increasingly robust fashion as the 1920s progressed. The founding of the periodical *Science et Voyages* eventually opened up publishing opportunities for fiction analogous to the space fiction that swiftly colonized the American science fiction pulps, and the prolific José Moselli wrote a small number of *romans scientifiques* of a more serious stripe than his customary thriller fare for the *Almanach scientifique* [Scientific Annual], an experiment in more earnest popularization briefly published as an accessory to that publication.

"Le Voyage éternel ou Les Prospecteurs de l'infini" (tr. as "The Eternal Voyage; or, The Prospectors of Space"), which appeared in the 1924 edition of the annual—actually published in 1923, bearing the date of the coming new year, as almost all Christmas annuals do—still seemed rather old-fashioned, borrowing its hypothetical method of spaceship propulsion from Le Faure and Graffigny's *Aventures extraordinaires d'un savant russe*, but provided a typical example of the manner in which writers of popular fiction employed melodramatic frameworks to contain speculative notions. In the story, a spaceship design is stolen from a brilliant but impoverished scientist by a ruthless financier, whose attempt to win the glory and the profit of the first voyage to the moon, employing his son as a pilot, goes sadly awry because of one vital datum that the real inventor held back.

Almanach Scientifique
1925
Prix : 5 fr.

Le Messager de la Planète

"**Le Messager de la planète**" (tr. as "The Planetary Messenger") which appeared in the 1925 issue of the *Almanach* is a more enterprising and engaging story, providing a similar anticipation of the methods of American pulp science fiction but adding a poignant tragic twist, echoing the philosophical cynicism that runs through the entire tradition of *roman scientifique*. The poignancy and cynicism in question is subtly different from its parallels in British scientific romance and American science fiction, although the fundamental "message" of the story is not absent even from the most vulgar pulp science fiction, and reflects an essential element of the speculative imagination: that thinking about what we might become inevitably encourages a dissatisfaction with what we are.

The story relates how two explorers in the Antarctic happen across a crashed alien spaceship, whose one surviving crew member is still able, before dying, to communicate the information that he comes from Mercury, and demonstrate that the vessel contains technological wonders that might be of immense benefit to the progress of human science. Unfortunately, the explorers face a long and difficult trek to get the news back to their ship, which will require not merely individual endurance, but also a unity of purpose and mutual support of which, being mere human beings, they prove incapable.

Moselli wrote several longer works for *Science et Voyages* but, with the exception of *La Fin d'Illa*, they were mostly pedestrian adventures stories. His shorter feuilletons, however, "Le rayon 'phi'" [The Phi Ray] (1921) and "La corde d'acier" [The Steel Cable] (1921), both of which only extended over five episodes, the former featuring a heat ray and the latter a technology of invisibility, brought their imaginative motifs into sharper focus in the same fashion as the stories described above. He disappeared from the magazine's pages after 1929, however, after publishing *La Guerre des océans* (book version 1975) a novel of submarine conflict clearly modeled on *Vingt mille lieues sous les mers*, in that year.

Of the other quasi-Vernian adventure stories published by the magazine, the most interesting, if only because of its similarity to contemporary American pulp fiction, was perhaps *La Cité de l'or et de la lèpre* (1928; tr. as *The City of Gold and Lepers*) by "Guy d'Armen," in which the enterprising Francis Hardant is pitted against the evil genius Natas in the secret city where the latter manufactures gold by means of nuclear fusion and employs disease as a mean of keeping his slave laborers under control. The English translators fused Hardant with other d'Armen heroes featured in serials in other Offenstadt publications in the character of "Doc Ardan" in order to turn those adventures into a series modeled on American pulp fiction.

It was not only popular periodicals like *Science et Voyages* and relatively unpolished writers like Moselli, however, that were willing at least to experiment with interplanetary fiction in the 1920s. J.-H. Rosny was able to publish his first venture into space fiction, *Les Navigateurs de l'infini* (1925; tr. as "Navigators of Space") in the upmarket periodical *Oeuvres libres*. While set solidly in the vein of Rosny's exotic biological fantasias, it established a significant new exemplar within the tradition of *roman scientifique*, which might well have encouraged more experiments of the same kind had it only been successful. Even though it was swiftly reprinted in book form, however, it does not seem to have encouraged further attempts, and the sequel announced at the end of the story's publication in *Oeuvres*

libres—into whose strict word limit the first story might well have been deliberately and uncomfortably squeezed—and further advertised in the book version, did not appear in either form.

Les Navigateurs de l'infini might well have been inspired by an interest in the actual possibilities of space travel, although it was the cause rather than an effect of Rosny's subsequent adoption as an honorable member of Robert Esnault-Pelterie's Nouvelle Societé Scientifique de Recherches pour l'élaboration de fusées destinées aux futurs voyages interplanétaires [Scientific Society for Research into the Development of Rockets Designed for Future Interplanetary Journeys] in 1928—one of several such societies formed in the late 1920s for that purpose in Europe and the U.S.A.

In fact, the propulsion mechanism of the spaceship featured in Rosny's story, the *Stellarium*, is deliberately vague, and the brief introductory chapter pays more attention to the life-support system that will maintain its air supply while reducing the need for continuous respiration during a three-month journey to Mars. The summary of what happens during that interval contained in extracts taken from the narrator's journal serves to introduce his fellow voyagers and make some brief remarks on the image of Mars compiled on the basis of astronomical observations, but the narrative hurries on to the actual landing before slowing its pace dramatically in the subsequent elaborate description of the Martian landscape.

Although the desert terrain in which the *Stellarium* comes down initially seems lifeless, odd luminous "formations" in the atmosphere show signs of unusual activity. The "Ethereal" entities in question prove to be not merely alive but dangerous, forcing the explorers to move the ship, fortunately to a more hospitable area where there is liquid water, and life-forms analogous to Earthly plants and animals, albeit only approximately. Some of the "zoomorphs" prove dangerous too, but the explorers are fortunately armed with guns firing deadly beams of "Bussault rays," discovered in the wake of the revelation of X-rays.

They soon encounter upright tripedal entities that have an apparent analogy with humans, and are convinced by observation of them that they are the relics of a once-prosperous advanced civilization that is now in terminal decline, presumably because of the diminution of its resources. Having made contact with them, they learn as much of the alien language as they can, given the difficulties of variant reference, and learn that the Tripeds are under dire threat from the zoomorphs, which are actively working toward their extinction as they expand their own terrain in quest of the planet's declining resources. The humans immediately decide to investigate the possibility of employing their own technological resources to aid the Tripeds in their defense.

In the meantime, the narrator learns a great deal more about the biology of the Tripeds, who have three sets of eyes with different visual capabilities and a remarkable reproductive system involving energies similar to those supporting the Ethereal life-forms—a system whose immaterial quality opens up the possibility of amorous intercourse between humans and Tripeds, and hence the possible development of sentimental attachments. That is what happens, as a love affair develops between the narrator and a female Triped he names Grace, under the ever-present shadow of the zoomophic menace. That menace turns to open warfare, in which initial victories are won, although they can only be temporary. The Earthmen establish apparatus for communicating with Earth by means of a version of the Cros light-signaling system, but the story abruptly breaks off at that point, with the promise of an imminent continuation, which did not materialize.

In 1960, twenty years after Rosny's death, a second part of the story, entitled "Les Astronautes," was added to a paperback edition of *Les Navigateurs de l'infini*, and claimed to be the sequel that Rosny had not managed to publish, although its plot is not consonant with the briefly-announced continuation and the narrative style and content suggest strongly that only the first five or six thousand words, at the most, could actually have been written by Rosny, the remaining twenty thousand apparently being the work of another, considerably less dexterous, hand and mind.

There is no way of knowing why Rosny abandoned the continuation, assuming that he actually did start it, but it is worth noting that by 1925, the deeply disillusioned Maurice Renard had come to the conclusion that "scientific marvel fiction" had no commercial future in the respectable sectors of the French marketplace, and had abandoned his attempts to develop it, although he still had two finished works in hand that he apparently reformulated in order to make them saleable. Rosny apparently agreed with him; not only did he make no further attempt at interplanetary fiction after 1925, but his subsequent works of imaginative fiction were produced on models very different from those briefly established by scientific marvel fiction, which became much scarcer in the upper strata of the literary marketplace, although it continued a stuttering evolution in popular outlets.

Oeuvres Libres did publish Tancrède Vallerey's "Celui qui viendra" (1929), in which a visitor from a planet of the star Aldebaran invites a scientist named Dr. Fauster to accompany him to his homeworld, promising to send him back after a year—which is, unfortunately, a century in Earthly terms, and condemns his assistant to a long wait, whose conclusion, if any, only his children will see—but that was a distinctly low-key story in which the scientific marvels remain ironically, but more comfortably, off-stage.

Another member of Esnault-Pelterie society for the promotion of rocket research, who joined enthusiastically rather than being invited by way of an honor, was the prolific writer of popular fiction Jean Petithuguenin, who had anticipated its foundation by producing a quasi-documentary account of *Une Mission internationale dans la lune* (tr. as "An International Mission to the Moon"), originally published as a feuilleton under the title "Une Mission dans la lune" in the *Journal des Voyages* between July and September 1926. It was eventually reprinted in book form under the fuller title by Tallandier in 1933, as part of a series of Petithuguenin's works, but the delay offers some evidence of the perceived difficulty of publishing such work commercially.

Une Mission internationale dans la

lune is particularly interesting within the context of the evolution of speculative fiction because it is one of a group of novels produced in several different countries that attempted to produce realistic accounts of a voyage to the Moon effected by means of rocket propulsion—or, as Petithuguenin puts it, "reaction engines." The notion that such devices were the only practical means of sending projectiles into space had initially been popularized by the Russian Konstantin Tsiolkovsky, who published an essay advancing that argument in 1903, and then attempted to popularize it further in a novel, *Vne zemli* (serial version 1916; book version 1920; tr. as *Outside the Earth*). Tsiolkovsky's endeavors and those of experimenters such as the American Robert Goddard and the German Hermann Oberth—whose non-fictional *Die Rakete zu den Planetenräumen* [By Rocket into Interplanetary Space] (1923) was followed by the fictional popularization *Der Schuss ins All* (1925; tr. as *The Shot into Infinity*) by his friend Otto Willi Gail—resulted in the foundation in the 1920s of societies similar to Esnault-Pelterie's, dedicated to propagandizing the possibility of space travel by means of rockets, in Russia, America, Germany and England.

The pseudonymous André Mas appears to have been a member of a propagandist group formed in advance of the 1920s rocket societies, and Petithuguenin might well have known him; he was certainly familiar with *Les Allemands sur Vénus* because he digresses in the text of his own novella to explain why the unusual method of space travel proposed therein would not work. He also explains why Verne's Columbiad would not be practical and why the modification to that method suggested by "Pierre de Sélènes" would not work either, although Verne is the only other author he mentions by name.

Although *Une Mission internationale dans la lune* was not the first quasi-documentary work of fiction popularizing the notion of traveling to the Moon by rocket, therefore, it was the one with the most substantial literary pedigree, and it is also the most realistic. Although it seems naïve now that we have the actual mission to the moon with which to compare it, it is nevertheless far closer to that eventual reality than the primitive efforts of Tsiolkovsky and Gail. In spite of the Vernian precedent, however, it was something of a departure for the *Journal des Voyages*—which had previously steered clear of interplanetary fiction—to publish it, and its unusual nature prompted the periodical's editor to supplement the first episode with a justificatory note insisting on the story's rational plausibility and educational value. In order to emphasize the latter claim, the magazine ran a competition to identify scientific terms and proper names replaced in the serial version by blanks—which must have been doubly frustrating for readers because, although the competition winners were announced, the answers remained unpublished until the Tallandier edition replaced the missing words.

Petithuguenin's work is an interesting experiment in the drama-documentary format, giving elaborate details of the rocket-ship constructed by means of the bequest of a billionaire, who wanted it to be used to send an international crew to the Moon to symbolize that the endeavor was a significant step into the unknown for all humankind. The story is narrated by a French journalist who is sent to cover the launch—scheduled to take place at sea—but who is drafted into the expedition at the last minute when the French member of the team is accidentally injured. Newly married as he is, his young wife will only consent to his taking part if she can accompany him, to which the other crew members reluctantly agree. The landing is successful, although not entirely without mishap, requiring the space-suits designed for lunar ambulation to be tested immediately.

The story then describes the exploration of various lunar features, including craters and mountains, in painstaking detail, in the curious environmental circumstances of the long cycle of the lunar day and night. Success leads to overconfidence, and the expedition's leader eventually suffers a fatal accident, which requires his burial on the moon and the erection of a suitable monument, prior to the hard labor required to prepare for a difficult take-off for the return journey. That too does not proceed without a mishap, but in spite of the damage inflicted on the ship, the voyagers contrive to land on Earth without any further fatal casualties.

Although innovative and ingenious, making a striking contribution to the evolution of *roman scientifique*, the significance of which can easily be recognized in retrospect, *Une Mission internationale dans la lune* certainly cannot be reckoned to have been a successful experiment in marketing terms. The *Journal des Voyages* never published another interplanetary fantasy, and nor did Petithuguenin—indeed, although he would surely have written more *roman scientifique* if there had been a ready market for it, he only published one other story of that kind, in the pages of *Science et Voyages.*

As mentioned above, although Maurice Renard had decided that scientific marvel fiction had no viable future in the French literary marketplace by 1925, he still had at least two manuscripts left over from the days when he had been the nascent genre's most enthusiastic promoter, and the project of getting them into print was still an irritating itch. Although neither of them was an interplanetary fantasy, one of them did feature a journey to another world of a different kind: a voyage into the microcosm by means of the technology of diminution.

Un Homme chez les microbes (tr. as *A Man Among the Microbes*) was the novel with which Renard originally intended to follow up *Le Docteur Lerne, sous-dieu*, making further inroads into what he considered to be the undeveloped imaginative terrain of "scientific marvel fiction." The version that was eventually published in 1928 advertised itself as the "fifth edition," in order to give some hint of the tribulations preceding that publication, and the "prehistory" of the work can be vaguely sketched out from a series of hints, including one included in the prologue to the published version, which reveals that "Doctor Prologus" has been working on his masterpiece for twenty years, having started it on 30 July 1907 and concluded his final revision on 28 October 1927—although, if the implications of the prologue can be taken at face value, the author still had to type out a fair copy for the publisher, and only started that work on 6 November.

Evidence of a less oblique character is provided by the number of occasions on which Renard advertised the imminent appearance of the book during that interval. It is mentioned in the prologue of *Le Péril bleu* (tr. as *The Blue Peril*), in a list that includes all of his previously-completed scientific marvel stories, and then began to be advertised in lists of works "*en préparation*" or "*à paraître*" in books issued by Louis Michaud and Édition Française Illustrée. In the spring of 1923, Renard was interviewed by the Belgian writer Jean Ray and optimistically informed him that the book, "awaited for nearly ten years" would be published in October of that year—the back-reference to 1913 presumably being to a planned Louis Michaud edition that never appeared.

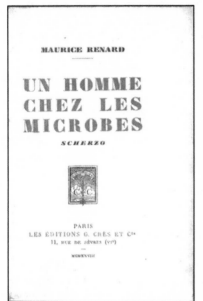

Adding all of these hints together facilitates the deduction that the four "editions" preceding the printed version were probably produced in 1907-8, 1913, 1919 and 1923, with the published version being completed in 1927. Renard—unusually, among writers of the day—was known to be an inveterate reviser who was never content with one draft of his works and rarely with two, and the intricacy with which he links up the multitudinous and disparate details of his longer works reaps the benefit of this assiduity, so it is conceivable that he wrote the second draft of *Un Homme chez les microbes* simply because he was dissatisfied with the first—having taken time off in the interim to produce *Le Péril bleu*—but the others were certainly written with a view to imminent publication, presumably with increasing desperation as he tried to find a version that a publisher might find acceptable.

At least some of the difficulty that Renard had in publishing the novel must have been to do with its startling originality. When it was written—although not by the time it was published—it was the first novel to feature a voyage into the subatomic microcosm. The fifth version was able to make fleeting use of an analogy based on the Rutherford-Bohr model of the atom first proposed in 1911, which likened an atom to a tiny solar system, in which electrons orbit a central nucleus much as planets orbit a star, and the first literary development of that notion, R. A. Kennedy's *The Triuneverse*, had duly appeared in 1912. By 1928 the latter had been followed up by Ray Cummings' "The Girl in the Golden Atom" (1919), which—although it stubbornly clung to an obsolete model of the atom—eventually became the parent of a curious subgenre of atomic solar system stories in the American pulp magazines. Renard however, did not have the benefit of that analogy when he first elected to send his hero on a microcosmic odyssey, and drew his inspiration from much earlier sources—to which he conscientiously gives credit in the printed text.

A second difficulty that Renard must have faced while persuading a publisher to take the work was the sarcastic spirit in which the novel was written. All of his early scientific marvel fiction mingles black comedy and melodrama, but in very different proportions; in general, the longer work, the greater the preponderance of melodrama tends to be, but *Un Homme chez les microbes* is a striking exception to that rule, offering much greater preponderance to sarcastic comedy even in its mock-melodramatic passages. While both *Le Docteur Lerne* and *Le Péril bleu* bear strong resemblances to currently popular forms of fiction, *Un Homme chez les microbes* harks back to much older models that were widely considered—at least by commercial publishers—to be obsolete. Although it does have an obvious "Wellsian" aspect, it is much more obviously framed as a Voltairean *conte philosophique*, and the single previous work to which it owes far more inspiration than any other, as acknowledged within the text, is Voltaire's *Micromégas*.

The particular combination of imaginative extravagance, logical reasoning, acidic humor and social satire resulting from that extrapolation was a compound that presumably seemed bizarre to the publishers who balked at the earlier versions of the novel; they probably deemed that it would pose too great a challenge to readers whose obvious preferences tended towards thrillers, mysteries and love stories with happy endings. It is probably no coincidence that *Le Péril bleu* very carefully includes all three of those elements, albeit in a conspicuously wry fashion, and that Renard never wrote another novel that attempted to draw as high a proportion of its narrative energy from novelty and irony, and as low a proportion from melodrama and suspense, as *Un Homme chez les microbes*.

When Renard was invited to contribute a piece about *Un Homme chez les microbes* to a series of articles in *La Rumeur* on the topic of *"Pourquoi j'ai écrit…."* [Why I wrote….], he made no mention of the trials he had undergone in order to get the book into print, or even that it had taken him twenty years to do so, but contented himself with four tersely disingenuous sentences:

"I was in need of relaxation, of an outburst of laughter. So, naturally, I was led to treat, among the ideas I had in reserve, the one that lent itself most to gaiety and fantasy—in a word, to a *"blague"*. I have never amused myself so much as by voyaging thus among the microbes. I hope that the reader will find it no more difficult than I did."

The word "blague" can refer to a joke, a mistake or a hoax. All three shades of meaning were presumably intended in this instance. The published version of the novel is dedicated to the humorist Georges de La Fouchardière, who had by then made a significant contribution to *roman scientifique* himself, beginning in the improbable venue of the sporting press, to which he had contributed a hilarious feuilleton describing the career of an automaton racehorse, *Le Machine à galoper* (1910; reprinted in 1919 as *L'Affaire Peau-de-Balle*; tr. as "The Galloping Machine").

The "cinematographic prologue" of the published version of *Un Homme chez les microbes* introduces the eccentric scientist Dr. Prologus, who has just completed his masterpiece, *La Physiologie des sens* [The Physiology of the Senses], but when he starts to type the final copy for the printer the carbon paper that is supposed to be producing a duplicate copy mysteriously produces a completely different text, which tells the story of the young Dr. Pons and his friend, the law student Fléchambeau, who is in love with the daughter of one of Pons' neighbors, Olga. Unfortunately, Fléchambeau's his proposal of marriage is rejected by Olga's parents because he is considered to be too tall for their modestly-sized daughter.

Pons naturally offers to help out, having invented a pill that will—in theory at least, reduce Fléchambeau's unfortunate dimensions. Although it is untried, Fléchambeau is desperate, and takes it. The initial result is satisfactory, and a renewed proposal is accepted—but the shrinking does not stop at the desired extent, and continues indefinitely, to hardly-imaginable extremes. In a matter of days, Pons and Olga need a microscope to track Fléchambeau's further diminution, and soon even that is inadequate. Following a dangerous encounter with a mite, the poor shrinking man vanishes from human ken. The heartbroken Olga goes home and the disappointed Pons goes traveling—but when he returns, he finds Fléchambeau living clandestinely in his apartment, covered in strange tattoos, having written an account of his adventures on the subatomic Land of the Microbes since his own return, which he urges Pons to read.

The manuscript relates how Fléchambeau, after a period of unconsciousness woke up to find his size artificially stabilized by a scientist desirous of studying him, in a world with two suns, populated by beings who resemble humans, except for having a "*pompon*" [tuft] on top of the head. He calls the people in question Mandarins because they seem to be possessed of an Oriental solemnity. The tuft is the organ of an additional sense that permits the perception of a quality that Fléchambeau calls *dounn*. Although he is kindly equipped with a fake tuft in order that he might pass unnoticed in Mandarin society, his inability to perceive *dounn* makes his observations of the society, its internal interactions and its works of art, crucially incomplete and somewhat enigmatic.

Because the Mandarins have a sophisticated system of weather control umbrellas are unknown there, and when Fléchambeau makes a joking reference to one he has to draw one to explain his meaning. His drawing calls forth a horrified reaction; he subsequently discovers that that is because the shape reminds them to the ultimate menace that hangs over their world: the terrible Ooms, fungi that multiply with awful rapidity and consume everything. When the Ooms eventually make their catastrophic appearance, Fléchambeau barely escapes back to his own world by means of rapid inflation. He brings back a new sense of the frailty of his own world—which might, after all, be merely a speck on the slide of some macrocosmic microscope, vulnerable to arbitrary destruction at any moment.

There is no way of knowing what amendments Renard had to make to the original version of *Un Homme chez les microbes* in order to render it acceptable to a publisher, but it seems probable that they involved a certain simplification and a retreat in the direction of greater blandness, which modern readers can only regret. As an illustration of the difficulties that serious writers were beginning to face in 1920s when they ventured into *roman scientifique*, it is a particularly telling one.

The publication of the two volumes of *Dans l'étrange inconnu* [In the Strange Unknown] (1928) by "Cabarel," advertised as a "roman de l'hypnose à travers le merveilleux fantastique" was presumably financed by their author, as it is difficult to imagine any commercial publisher accepting it, but its contents are sufficiently remarkable to lead Pierre Versins to offer an unusually elaborate account of it in his *Encyclopédie*. In the first volume the narrator sends his astral double on a cosmic journey that takes in the four inhabited worlds of the solar system (Venus, Mars, Titan and Ganymede) and eventually extends as far as the stars, taking in Pole Star and a long sojourn on the planet of a sun twenty-five light-years beyond Sirius. In the second, the traveler delves deep into the Earth's past to discover various lost continents, and then into the future, where he witnesses the emergence of a new race of androgynous humans.

One of the more unusual works published in the popular stratum of the marketplace was Léon Groc's *La Révolte des pierres* [The Revolt of the Stones] (1929), which presents an account of strange lunar life that probably owed its inspiration to J.-H. Rosny's accounts of mineral life-forms. An astronomer at the Paris Observatoire, Armand Brisset, picks up a fragment of a bolide, and then loses twenty-four hours before being caught up in a mystery involving the disappearance of a young woman and a murder. Drawn into the investigation by a reporter, Brisset begins to experience strange phenomena provoked by the radiation of the stone—which, it turns out, is a fragment of a Selenite, which conspirators on Earth require to make up a set, in order to unleash its powers destructively. The narrative follows a conventional thriller pattern, however, and only treats the intriguing alien life-forms peripherally, as an intrusion to be banished as rapidly as possible.

Several of the most enterprising accounts of alien life produced in the early 1930s similarly remained earthbound. *T.S. F. avec les étoiles* [Wireless Communication with the Stars] (1930) by Paul Gsell (1870-1947) is a comedy in which the discovery of waves traveling faster than light, which have long been used by the planets of other stars to communicate with one another, enable the restless Jacques Lagité to mount a universe-wide search of Earth-clone worlds for the secret of human happiness, which proves as frustrating as all literary quests of that nature tend to do, while the scientific knowledge and technological information avidly soaked up by the world's governments lead to an arms race that threatens to make the question redundant.

The most enterprising of all the images of alien life produced between the two world wars was produced by the Swiss writer Roger Farney, in "Les Anekphantes," one of two novellas published in *Deux histoires fabuleuses* (1931). Related entirely from the viewpoint of the Anekphantes, microbes that have developed an intelligent group mind with the aid of communications based in various forms of *ondes* [waves], some of which are undetectable by human senses, the narrative relates their discovery of the surprising existence of other intelligent beings—humans—which they can only perceive obliquely, and their attempt to construct a scientific understanding of their nature. The story is remarkable in its adoption of a radically unhuman narrative viewpoint, possessed of both the opportunities and limitations of beings whose sensorium is very different from ours, based in extremely exotic organic circumstances.

Although the Anekphantes do make some progress in their attempted investigation of human nature, what they discover does not persuade them that the parallel existence of human beings is of any real relevance to them as they follow their own way of life and their own evolution—unperceived, of course, by the objects of their study, who remain blissfully ignorant of the presence in the bosom of their society of other intelligences, which might one day inherit the Earth, as the meek are supposedly destined by tradition to do. The story was not an item of commercial fiction.

Les Formiciens, roman de l'ère secondaire [The Formicians: A Romance of the Secondary Era] (1932) by Raymond de Rienzi (1890-1971), a friend of J.-H. Rosny, also adopts an alien narrative viewpoint, similarly modeled on the notion of a "hive mind" derived from the studies of social insects. In this case, the protagonists of the story are indeed insects, of a species that acquired intelligence a hundred and twenty million years ago, and developed a complex civilized society with appropriate institutions and a political organization not far removed from "primitive anarchism": the Halfs, the most intelligent of the "formician" [i.e. ant-like] species that supposedly dominated the animal world at that time, Within that extraordinary context, however, the plot is a conventional heroic fantasy detailing the career of Hind, initially a soldier, who embarks upon a long and eventful odyssey before dying in combat, as a hero should, in this case being preserved in amber thereafter.

Alongside such experiments, not unnaturally, humanoid aliens continued their dominance, being far more convenient for both melodramatic and satirical purposes. The melodramatic species is represented in *Hodomur, l'homme de l'infini* [Hodomur, the Man from Space] (1934), by the Belgian writer "Ege Tilms" (probably Eugène Thielemans, 1892-1967), a phantasmagoric tale of alien abduction in which the victim, taken to the fifth planet of Capella by the eponymous explorer in a vessel he calls an ECOR at faster-than-light velocity, is interned there with numerous other abductees, whom the Capellites remove at intervals in order to carry out experiments of some kind on the human brain. Although the author of the manuscript that describes the adventure is returned to Earth, his wife is then abducted in his stead.

Another notable example of the satirical kind is *La Visite des Martiens* [The Martians' Visit] (1935) by Jacques Loria (1860-1948), in which communication established with Mars by the Cros method leads to an invitation to the Martians to visit. Physically, socially and mentally superior to humans—among other biological modifications they are oviparous—the Martians find many opportunities for condescending disapproval. They offer the benefits of their advanced knowledge, if humans can demonstrate their worthiness to receive them; unsurprisingly, the demonstration actually provided persuades the Martians that should come back in five hundred years' time to see whether sufficient moral progress has been made in the interim.

The most substantial interplanetary fantasy published in France in the 1930s was a 108-part series of novelettes collectively entitled **Les Aventuriers du ciel** [Adventurers of the Skies] (1935-37), published by Ferenczi and signed "René Marcel de Nizerolles," the pseudonym of Marcel Priollet (1888-1960). The series was a sequel to an earlier 111-part series of Vernian novelettes, *Les Voyages aérien d'un petit parisien à travers le monde* [The Aerial Voyages of a Little Parisian across the World] (1911-13), which Ferenczi had reprinted, apparently successfully, in 1933-35. The new serial took the young Parisian hero, Tintin (not to be confused with Hergé's Tintin, whose il-

lustrated adventures had begun in 1929) on an extensive cosmic tour, taking in various planets and encounters with numerous monsters and other strange phenomena, running the gamut of what had by now become a standard lexicon of ideas.

Nizerolles' long and rambling, but nevertheless energetic, narrative illustrates the extent to which that basic lexicon had by then become stereotyped, without interplanetary fiction ever having become popular; indeed the Nizerolles series was probably the peak of commercial success reached in France by the kind of *roman scientifique* that most closely resembled American pulp science fiction. Nizerolles' Tintin did go on to a further series of adventures in *Les Robinsons de l'île volante* [The Castaways of the Flying Island] (28 parts; 1937-38), but he followed the general trend by turning his back on more extravagant adventures, returning to Earth and confining his exploits to more conventional escapades.

After Théo Varlet's account of an experimental space flight leading to an extraterrestrial microbial invasion in *La Grande panne*, interplanetary fiction of any kind was not much in evidence in the upper strata of the marketplace throughout the period that can be seen in retrospect as the decade before World War II, although it continued to enjoy a fugitive existence in the lower strata. One partial exception was *L'Homme qui s'est retrouvé*, (1936; tr. as *The Man Who Found Himself*), the last novel published during his lifetime by the popular novelist Henri Duvernois (1875-1937). Duvernois' career had reached the peak of its success in the 1920s, after an interruption caused by the Great War, when he had been wounded in action in 1914 and had spent the rest of the war in pain but out of danger. He had, however, refused to allow the after-effects of that injury to darken his post-war work, which remained conscientiously light and artificial, until that last addition.

The literary device that *L'Homme qui s'est retrouvé* employs to activate its plot is a secretly-built starship, which transports the protagonist to a planet orbiting Proxima Centauri—a journey described in some detail. By virtue of that improvisation, it certainly qualifies as *roman scientifique*, although it is a carefully and defiantly ambiguous narrative, and toys more dexterously than many other works that indulge in similar apologetic obfuscation with the possibility that the spaceflight might be a hallucinatory fantasy. The use of the motif is so manifest-ly artificial that its importance has more to do with the rationalistic attitude it introduces to a wholly fantastic situation than any vestige of technological plau-sibility.

Although the machine transporting the protagonist is deliberately charac-terized as a spaceship, and the world to which he is removed—after a journey of more than three years at the speed of light—is carefully identified as another planet, the journey he undertakes is essentially a trip in time rather than space. The other planet turns out to be identical to ours in every respect save one: its history is unfolding forty years in arrears. His arrival there thus offers the pro-tagonist the opportunity of "finding himself" in his late adolescence—an attrac-tive prospect, because it seems to offer him an opportunity to avert the terrible misfortunes that are about to overwhelm his unwitting family.

There is no way of knowing for sure, because there are no secrets that peo-ple cling to more stubbornly than the substance of their daydreams, but the pri-vate fantasy of being able to go back in time within one's own life to correct mistakes revealed in retrospect, or to explore forsaken possibilities, is probably extremely common, especially among people who have got to a point in life when they feel, correctly or not, that they have run out of future. Even men like Henri Duvernois, who had enjoyed a glittering career and every possible suc-cess, must be prone to this kind of reflection—and how much more prone those people must be who feel that they have largely wasted their lives, having made horrible and fatal errors.

Given the probable near-universality of such regretful retrospection, it might be reckoned odd that there are not more literary developments of the theme, but the text of *L'Homme qui s'est retrouvé* takes the trouble to include an explanation of its own rarity, when the protagonist attempts to explain to his rep-licated mother what has happened to him, by representing it as a dream. She comments, wisely, that such dreams always fall apart because they always col-lide eventually with some kind of contradiction, and cannot sustain their peculiar illogic in the ensuing battle of ideas. Actual dreams almost never deliver good raw material for literary work, except in the form of fugitive images that need to be carefully relocated in entirely different and more rational frameworks, and daydreams are only slightly better, even if one sets aside the problem of secrecy.

Inevitably, the real subject of any literary work that enables a character to confront his past self is the struggle of contingency against destiny; equally in-evitably, contingency always starts out as the underdog. If a writer is careful to distance himself as much and humanly possible from his protagonist he has the opportunity of writing a moral fable in which a measure of personal reorienta-tion is possible, but the closer to home the fantasy strikes, the more an aware-ness of personal inelasticity is bound to take effect. In the most intense and inti-mate literary timeslip fantasies, which send protagonists back into the prison of their own early consciousness, the effect can be spectacularly claustrophobic, and even trivial works of popular fiction that set out to use the motif as a gimmick sometimes entangle their authors more intricately than they intended.

Duvernois almost certainly drew the inspiration for his own story from an episode that made sufficient impact on him to prompt him to write an autobiographical essay, "Souvenirs", which he published in *Oeuvres Libres* 105 (1930), in which he describes a visit he paid to the house in which he and his parents had lived forty years earlier, and the vivid memories it awoke. Several other places mentioned in that reflective essay also crop up in *L'Homme qui s'est retrouvé*, and the novel also contains an echo of the description in "Souvenirs" of a nostalgic visit Duvernois that paid to one of his old teachers. The fact that Duvernois chose a title with a slightly different significance from its more familiar counterpart, "The Man Who Met Himself," is telling; his protagonist does simply *meet* an earlier version of himself, but by virtue of that encounter he *finds* himself, in the sense that he is able to reappraise and re-evaluate himself, not merely as he was but as he is—a realization in which destiny is bound to seem ineluctable, and from which little comfort is likely to be derivable.

Although *L'Homme qui s'est retrouvé* is obviously not autobiographical in any simple sense—its protagonist has followed a career trajectory very different from the author's—there is no doubt that the author felt easily able to identify with his creation, to whom he attributes a birth-date less than a year after his own. The timeslipped narrative is written almost entirely in the present tense, even though that makes little sense in the context of its supposed documentary nature, in order to maximize the sense of immediacy with which author and reader alike are able to share the fictitious experience. There is no doubt that Duvernois felt the force of his narrative acutely, and would have written a very different story had he approached it in a more distant manner, in the vein of his usual cheerful comedies. How different it would have been had he not cast it as an interplanetary fantasy is, however, more difficult to judge.

J.-H. Rosny published one more otherworldly fantasy in the same vein as "Un Autre monde" a few months before his death in 1939—the brief "Dans le monde des variants" (tr. as "In the World of the Variants"), but it had probably been written much earlier, and its first sentence, which introduces a character named Abel who feels lost in space and time, might reflect an inspiration by Pierre-Simon Ballanche's "La Vision d'Hébal" as much as the influence of his own "Légende sceptique," whose ideas he had never ceased to mine and elaborate. Abel's consciousness is displaced in conventional spacetime, living simultaneously in the world other humans perceive and the parallel world of the Variants: metamorphic alien entities whose reproductive system is as strange as that of the Martian Tripeds in *Les Navigateurs de l'infini*. The implications of that alien system of amour transform his understanding of and attitude to his carnal marriage. The other late work of fiction Rosny produced that includes spinoff from the ideas broached on *La Légende sceptique, Les Compagnons de l'univers*

(1934; tr. as "The Companions of the Universe") is a naturalistic narrative in which dogged scientific investigators manage to catch the merest glimpse of extraordinary energies, into the existence of which they read a great deal of metaphysical significance.

The continuation of *Les Navigateurs de l'infini* was not the only advertised sequel to a significant work of *roman scientifique* to fail to appear in the interval between the world wars, but the other one that might be deemed, retrospectively, as an important work of interplanetary fiction did eventually appear, albeit in what might be reckoned the worst possible circumstances, in 1943: the novel whose impending appearance Théo Varlet had announced in 1936 at the end of the second edition of *La Grande panne*. Advertised there as *Les Naufragés d'Eros*, it was posthumously published as **Aurore Lescure, pilote d'astronef** [Aurora Lescure, Spaceship Pilot], although the

English translation retains the author's title, *The Castaways of Eros*.

The delay in the novel's original publication was unfortunate, in that it was issued in very different circumstances from those in which it was written. In 1937, the Second World War was still an ominous shadow on the horizon of the future, but the story begins in that shadow of an imminent war, and speculates extensively about the potentially disastrous implications of such a conflict, especially the possible use therein of hypothetical new weapons. By 1943, the most important of those imaginary weapons was not longer hypothetical, and the pattern of Varlet's anticipations was wide open to the criticism of hindsight, inevitably found wanting in spite of its fundamental accuracy. The time lag in the novel's publication thus altered its perceptible significance considerably, as well as condemning it to a fugitive esotericism. Fewer than five hundred copies were printed—a tiny print run by comparison with the 20,000 copies that the publisher claimed to have sold of the second edition of its predecessor—and even that meager print run did not sell out.

As well as the note concerning the imminent appearance of *Les Naufragés d'Eros*, the reprint of *La Grande Panne* carried another note signed by the author in which he observed that Régis Messac had pointed out to him similarities between the plot of his novel, originally published in 1930, and an American pulp science fiction story by A. Rowley Hilliard, "Death from the Stars" (*Wonder Stories*, 1931) There are, in fact, no reasonable grounds to suspect that Hilliard had "stolen" the idea for his story from *La Grande Panne*, any more than J.-

H. Rosny had had grounds to suspect Arthur Conan Doyle of appropriating the idea for *The Poison Belt* (1913) from his own *La Force mystérieuse* (1913; tr. as *The Mysterious Force*) twenty years earlier, but it does seem probable, judging by the plot of *Les Naufragés d'Eros*, that Messac's direction of Varlet's attention to the American science fiction pulps was not without effect.

Varlet might well have known that Rosny had sold translation rights to one of his novels to a US pulp in the early 1930s, and then had written at least one other colorful action-adventure novel—*Le Sauvage aventure* (1932; tr. as "Adventure in the Wild")—with the same potential market seemingly in mind, but whether he knew it or not, the similarities between *Les Naufragés d'Eros* and the standard fare of contemporary American pulp science fiction are so strong that it is hard to believe that there was no influence involved.

Had a translation been made in 1937 and published in the US pulps, Varlet's novel might now be remembered rather fondly by nostalgic historians of science fiction, who would have found it to be more sophisticated in its thinking than much of its rival material. They would have been particularly struck by an intriguing idea that was then new, although it would make its first appearance in the pulps before the actual publication of *Les Naufragés d'Eros* in 1943: the suggestion that, had evolution taken a slightly different turn, dinosaurs might have produced a sentient species capable of building a civilization, thus occupying the existential niche that was still vacant on Earth when humans eventually appeared. The first pulp science fiction story to develop that hypothesis was actually Norman L. Knight's "Saurian Valedictory" (1939). Such historians might also have deemed the novel's account of weightlessness-induced "space-sickness" interesting, although they would doubtless feel compelled to make apologies for numerous technical flaws that have become retrospectively obvious, in such matters as calculating the accelerations and velocities required to make interplanetary flights in a matter of days, the inadequacy of the spaceship's life-support system and airlock, and the skimpiness of the breathing apparatus employed for use in a vacuum.

In *Les Naufragés d'Éros*, Oscar Frémiet, who was still a boy in *La Grande panne*, is now a young journalist recently returned from Germany, where he has been reporting on German rocket research, and has become convinced that it has a secret dimension devoted to the development of rockets as armaments. It is the fear of such possibilities, threatening that a new world war might spell the end of civilization, that has stimulated a Japanese billionairess to fund the building of a rocket that might launch a Space Age enabling a carefully-selected elite of humankind to colonize other worlds. She wants to recruit Aurore Lescure—the only person with experience as a space pilot, as well as considerable expertise in the theory behind it—to her project. The narrator, Aurore's husband, is reluctant, but Oscar, his cousin, is all in favor. In fact, Oscar contrives to get aboard the spaceship for what is intended as a test flight, but becomes a one-way excursion to the planetoid Eros when it goes awry. Oscar is delighted, but his girlfriend, a Russian named Ida whom he met in Germany—who is, of course, a Soviet spy—is not so pleased.

Although they contrive to land on Eros, and have the possibility of taking off again, they can only hope to make the return trip when the planetoid's highly eccentric orbit brings it back into close proximity with Earth, requiring a long sojourn. Eros is too tiny to retain an atmosphere by virtue of its own gravity, but it has an enclave where artificially-produced air maintains the relics of an ancient civilization, in which a population of mammalian "homonines," bearing a certain resemblance to dogs as well as humans, is enslaved by a reptilian race of Lacertians evolved from saurian ancestors.

The Lacertians, who quickly take the newcomers prisoner, are masters of hypnosis, by virtue of possessing a "third eye" developed from the organ whose vestige is known on Earth as the pineal "gland." That ability enables them to establish communication with the visitors from Earth, although the only one in whom their supreme leader, Zilgor, is really interested is Aurore, because she is the only one with any extensive knowledge of Earthly science. In her turn, she becomes intensely interested in him, because he is the sole custodian of the ultimate secrets of Lacertian superscience, which she hopes to persuade him to release to her.

While Aurore and Zilgor devote themselves to long sessions of difficult and wary mutual education, therefore, the narrator and his companions, granted a limited freedom, explore the world of Eros. They learn that it is a fragment of the planet Ektrol, destroyed by wars fought with weapons employing the superscience that Aurore is so enthusiastic to learn. They also become aware of the extreme precariousness of its present artificially-maintained life-support system—which does not prevent Ida from making strenuous clandestine efforts to foment revolution among the homonines. In the meantime, fragmentary radio messages from Earth picked up by the rocket's apparatus inform them that expeditions from Earth have now been sent to Venus.

The denouement of the story, inevitably, sees the disastrous Revolution precipitated, leading inexorably to the destruction of life on Eros, from which Oscar, Aurore and the narrator by escape by the skin of their teeth—but with the knowledge that their patroness' dream of establishing an enclave of elite human beings on another world is already under threat, because Venus has become a target for opportunistic colonization by anyone and everyone, who will doubtless export all the vices of humankind along with its virtues. The prospective Space Age is thus threatening, from the outset, to become a further chapter in an unfolding tragedy, leading to a predestined doom spelled out by the fate of Ektrol.

That was not, of course, the implication attached to the version of the myth of the Space Age that was to be so extravagantly developed in American science fiction over the next half-century—a distinction that might offer a clue as to why French *roman scientifique*, like British science fiction, had very little truck with that mythology until the importation and imitation of science fiction took on enormous proportions after the end of World War II.

JEAN DE LA HIRE
LE ROI
DE LA
NUIT

EDITIONS
DU LIVRE MODERNE
PARIS

Given that the section has already put one foot outside its supposed timeframe to include the belated *Les Naufragés d'Éros*, it might be worth including a footnote about another work published in 1943, serialized in very short episodes in the Parisian daily newspaper *Le Matin*, then being published under Nazi authority. The serial was by the newspaper's veteran *feuilletonist* Jean de La Hire—who would later be charged with collaboration on account of continuing to work under Nazi rule, apparently writing to instruction in some instances—and it featured La Hire's favorite series hero, the Nyctalope. It was, in fact, the first *feuilleton* since *Le Mystère des XV* in 1911 to take the hero into interplanetary space. Entitled ***Le Roi de la nuit*** (tr. as *The King of the Night*), it took the Nyctalope and his usual contingent of assorted associates to the planet Rhea, where they find two species, the quasi-angelic Nocturnals and the repulsively brutal ape-like Diurnals, locked in an eternal struggle, in which the hero naturally gets involved, taking up arms against the oppressors.

There is not a word about Germans in *Le Roi de la nuit*, and nothing therein that could possible attract the attention of the Nazi censors; that is, presumably, precisely the reason which La Hire set the novel far away from Earth, although he had not made any such narrative move in any of the novels he wrote between the wars, in spite of his pioneering exploits before the Great War. The story was, manifestly, a straightforward exercise in escapist entertainment, designed to take people's minds off the awful reality of the war for a few moments. After all, who could possibly be expected to construe an item of crude popular fiction as an allegory? Although, of course, if anyone had been so reckless, they would hardly have been tempted to see the invaders of France as the captive and beleaguered Nocturnals....

In fact, nobody was tempted to put that interpretation on the novel afterwards, because the post-war paperback reprint of the book misprinted the date of its original publication, rendering it as 1923 instead of 1943, and Pierre Versins was not the only bibliographer to take that at face value. The copies of *Le Matin* reproduced on *gallica*, however, leave no doubt as to the story's actual origin, and perhaps its covert intentional implication.

4. The Technological Triumphs of Science

In both of the classic accounts he produced before the Great War of the exploits of mad scientists, *Caresco, surhomme* and *Une Invasion de macrobes*, André Couvreur had ended his stories by dutifully killing off the dangerous individuals in question, so that they could not trouble the world any further. When the Great War was over, however, he had a change of heart, perhaps feeling that such perverse characters were far more appropriate to the aftermath of the conflict, in view of what it had demonstrated about the technological produce of science, than to the era that had preceded it. Rather than invent a new character, he simply took advantage of poetic license and resurrected Professor Tornada, not as his old self but as a compound of the two characters, with Caresco's uncanny surgical dexterity and some of his peculiar ambitions grafted on to his own biological expertise.

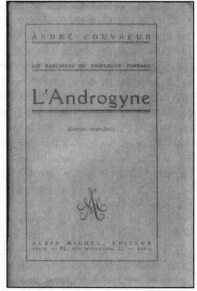

The revamped Professor Tornada made his second debut in *L'Androgyne* (1922 in *Oeuvres Libres*; book 1922; tr. as "The Androgyne"), in which he has a private clinic in Paris and is a popular presence in respectable salon culture, valued for his witty philosophical commentaries on scientific questions. Unknown to the socialites he amuses, however, Tornada kidnaps individuals who have carelessly expressed the wish that they were members of the opposite sex, and swaps their sex organs around with consummate skill. He also uses his vast financial resources to set up new identities for them, in order that he can track the progress of his experiment, curious in particular to see how his adapted females will cope with pregnancy and motherhood.

Georges Sigerier, the painter who wakes up in Tornada's secret clinic to find himself transformed into a woman, is not in the same situation as modern transsexuals, who undergo the relevant operations because they have always felt, psychologically, that they had been assigned the wrong sex by nature, and that they are therefore liberating their true identities. Psychologically, he remains completely masculine, and now finds himself trapped in the "wrong" body, masquerading as his sister while pretending that Georges has made a sudden voyage to India—much to the distress of his mistress Rolande, who had been planning to leave her husband and run away with him. The novella tracks the new relationship that develops between Rolande and "Georgette," which becomes gradually more intimate as Georgette becomes the conduit of love letters supposedly sent by Georges from India and Rolande begins to confide in Georgette all the aspects of her personal history and feelings that she could never have revealed to Georges.

In the meantime, the frustrated eroticism of Georgette's feelings for Rolande is complicated by the curious mixture of extreme repulsion and perverse attraction she feels for the fiancé with which Tornada, in arranging her new identity, has carefully supplied her. Although most readers would probably guess immediately, it takes the not-very-bright protagonist a long time to figure out the reason for the curiously mixed and paradoxical magnetism that draws the two of them together, while the plot moves inexorably toward the moment when Georgette's privileged voyeurism in regard to Rolande finally reaches the brink of physical expression—and, perhaps inevitably, given the logic of fiction, a severe case of narrative *coitus interruptus.*

L'Androgyne was rapidly followed into print by "Le Valseur phosphorescent" (1923 in *Oeuvres Libres*; tr. as "The Phosphorescent Waltzer"), although the latter had probably been drafted some years earlier, before the 1914-18 war, and only belatedly adapted as a Professor Tornada story. Its protagonist, Made (i.e, Madeleine) Ribaire, is an orphan brought up in relative luxury, now facing the exhaustion of her resources and a plunge into poverty. She thinks that the fate in question might be bearable, because she expects her devoted friend, a biologist named Marcel Grimaud, to propose marriage to her, although he is reluctant to do so, in spite of being in love with her, because he is keenly aware of his inability to support her in the manner to which she is accustomed.

Made is offered another way out of her predicament when the handsome but utterly bizarre Adam Danator, who is a fine physical specimen of manhood, an uncannily brilliant swimmer and an efficient if overly mechanical waltzer, becomes smitten with her, prompting the exceedingly wealthy scientist who claims to be his father to make every effort to arrange a marriage by means of bribery. Although repelled as well as deeply confused by Adam's behavior, which is a curious admixture of seeming obliviousness and outrageous lewdness, Made is bitterly chagrined by the fact that Marcel not only declines to offer her an alternative but urges her strongly to marry Adam. She consents, and, in spite of the increasing peculiarity and sexual aggression of the Danators' conduct, goes through with the wedding, conducted at the professor's Villa of the Immaculate Conception by his mute servant, who happens to have taken Holy Orders as well as being a highly-skilled laboratory assistant.

The wedding night, described in luridly explicit detail, does not go well— unsurprisingly for readers, who, along with Marcel, will by then have figured out what Made has not: that Adam is the product of a scientific experiment in accelerated evolution, not born of woman, but a far more immediate offspring of the sea, produced by a process closely akin to the one formerly employed by Louis Boussenard's Monsieur Synthèse.

Although handsomely human in outward appearance, the new Adam's physiology is eccentric, which makes it very difficult for him, in spite of extensive training in mechanical masturbation, to perform the sexual act that his "father" is so desperate for him to achieve, in order to continue his experiment by means of impregnation. In fact, Adam has no mind of his own, and is a mere automaton when his father is not controlling his speech and gestures as a puppeteer—which is, of course, not the kind of discovery that a virgin hopes to make on her wedding night, and one that inevitably makes her yearn for the mercy of a narrative *coitus interruptus* that, on this occasion, the doubly disguised Professor Tornada has no intention of providing.

Following its publication in *Oeuvres Libres*, *L'Androgyne* was reprinted in book form the following year by Albin Michel, in a version dedicated to J.-H. Rosny *aîné*. The author had apparently signed a four-book contract with Albin Michel for a series featuring Tornada, but Michel did not publish the further items in the series that he had commissioned. Given that he must have been sufficiently enthused by *L'Androgyne* to request more work of a similar nature, it is unlikely that he was put off by the perversely erotic content of "Le Valseur phosphorescent," which is no more explicit or perverse than that in *L'Androgyne*—or, for that matter, *Caresco, surhomme.*

It is possible that public or official reaction to *L'Androgyne* deterred the publication of similar work, although it is hard to believe that there could have been any threat of prosecution on the grounds of obscenity at such a late date. It is, however, notable that none of the subsequent stories in the Tornada sequence reproduce the erotic fascinations of *L'Androgyne* and "Le Valseur phosphorescent," seeming distinctly prim by comparison. Tornada was never to exhibit such a powerful obsession with sex again as he did in his dealings with poor Made Ribaire, nor was he ever to appear in such a repulsive role again; in his subsequent exploits he became far more sympathetic, and even heroic, albeit while retaining a certain Mephistophelean ambiguity.

It seems more likely that Albin Michel's change of heart was due to the same marketplace backlash that deterred Maurice Renard and J.-H. Rosny from carrying forward their exploits in scientific marvel fiction. Rosny, like Couvreur, sold one ambitious item of such fiction to *Oeuvres Libres* in "Les Navigateurs de l'infini" but aborted its advertised sequel and never produced anything as imaginatively ambitious again. Nor did *Oeuvres Libres* publish anything in the genre after that experiment, except for the later Professor Tornada stories. None of those subsequent stories ever reached book form, and it appears that if Couvreur had not had a special concession from the editor of the periodical, he might not have published any fiction at all after 1922.

It seems probable that the third item in the new Tornada series had already been written when Albin Michel dropped out of the book deal, because "Les Mémoires d'un immortel" (1924 in *Oeuvres Libres*; tr. as "The Memoirs of an Immortal") appeared rapidly on the heels of "Le Valseur phosphorescent" but was separated by considerable gap from "Le Biocole" (1927 in *Oeuvres Libres*; tr. as "The Biocole"), and more than a decade elapsed before the final item, "Le Cas de la baronne Sasoitsu" (1939 in *Oeuvres Libres*; tr. as "The Case of Baronne Sasoitsu") was belatedly added to the series.

The narrator of "Les Mémoires d'un immortel" is an old friend of Tornada's from their student days in the Latin Quarter, who is now a successful author, up for election to the Académie (it is in that metaphorical sense, not the literal one, that he is an "immortal"). He has recently contracted a second marriage to a young and exceedingly glamorous young woman, and is certain that she loves him sincerely. Tornada is not at all convinced of that, and is worried about the writer's daughter from his first marriage, of whom he is very fond, even though she is in the seemingly safe hands of a loyal governess. In order to try to open the narrator's eyes to the reality of his false situation, Tornada injects him with a drug that puts him into suspended animation, apparently dead but still fully conscious of everything happening around him, promising to return to administer the counter-agent in two days' time.

Able to observe his "widow" without her being conscious of being observed, the inert writer learns the awful truth about her utter corruption, as she, her lover and her criminal father, fearful that all his property might be left to his daughter, set about stripping the house of everything of value. In the meantime, the only person to manifest any real grief, apart from his uncomprehending daughter, is her governess, who has been in love with him for years.

Unfortunately, Tornada does not turn up at the time when he promised to bring the poor narrator out of his suspended animation. When the newspapers announce Tornada's death in a traffic accident, all seems lost; not only will the writer be eliminated from the election to the Académie, leaving the coveted chair to a rival he despises, but he is likely to be buried alive. Although the report of the great man's death turns out to be a trifle exaggerated, it is only at the very last moment, after the funeral, that Tornada manages to arrive at the cemetery to prevent the interment and confound the disloyal wife.

Tornada brings off another nick-of-time rescue of another old friend in the first chapter of "Le Biocole," when he not only brings the aged painter Théophraste Lapastille back from the brink of death but rejuvenates him—much to the surprise of Théophraste's equally aged mistress and eternal model, Mélanie, who has spent her life savings on a funeral for a body misidentified as his, which no one attends. Théophraste has difficulty reclaiming his civil estate, and Tornada has to rescue him again as he is about to be interned in a lunatic asylum, but he then gives proof of his ability to rejuvenate people by restoring Mélanie's youth.

"Le Biocole" is by far the most far-reaching item in the series, extrapolating Tornada's exploits into a future in which Théophraste, regretting the opportunities missed in his first youth, has married Mélanie; the two of them have a large family of children, and they both work for Tornada, who has established a vast commercial operation in Paris, repairing bodies on an industrial scale by means of the transplantation of healthy organs to replace those wasted by age or injury, thus rejuvenating his clients and offering them a potentially-vast longevity. Like Champsaur's *Nora*, the novel is obviously a reaction to the enormous publicity then being generated in Paris by Serge Voronoff; like Voronoff, Tornada employs organs removed from animals, especially apes, but he does not restrict himself to the transplantation of testicular tissue.

Tornada extracts enormous fees from his rich clients in order to fund the rejuvenation of large numbers of poor people, many of them harvested from the hospitals, and he is ambitious to remake the entire world as a eutopia from which death has been permanently banished. The social disruptions already caused by Tornada's mass rejuvenations and other scientific technologies of production, however, have already created new economic equalities and huge resentments—problems that he considers trivial and temporary, merely requiring rational social adaptation, but which his old friends see quite differently; they reluctantly desert his fold in consequence. It is only when Tornada finally gets round to seeking out his former assistants and discovers Mélanie and her children in dire poverty, on the brink of starvation, that he begins to see the actual consequences of the rewards he has lavished so unthinkingly, and is moved to wonder whether his good intentions are actually paving a road to hell.

Unfortunately, as Couvreur had no other market, "Le Biocole" had to be shaped to fit the requirements of *Oeuvres Libres*, which had a strict limit of forty thousand words on its feature stories, and "Le Biocole," thematically far too large for that limit, had to be drastically curtailed in order to fit. Although magnificently graphic, the story is awkwardly compressed and drastically truncated, literally only half the work that it could and ought to have been—but at least it exists, which it might well not have done had Couvreur not had privileged access to a conduit of publication that was not open to anyone else at the time.

In "Le Cas de la baronne Sasoitsu" Tornada, now a rather avuncular figure once again respected and popular in contemporary society for his wit and wisdom, is called upon to play detective in a murder mystery, his motivation sharpened by the fact that a young friend has been very neatly framed for the murder in question and seems doomed. Fortunately, Tornada—this time following in the footsteps of Professor Brion, as featured in *Le Lynx*—is in the process of inventing a kind of movie camera that photographs memories inside people's heads. Provided that the right memories can be provoked by appropriate stimuli, he has the perfect method of detection.

Naturally, he experiments on animals first, allowing him to explore the extent and nature of the various degrees of intellectuality possessed by creatures ranging from carp to monkeys, but it is when he introduces the evidence surreptitiously collected by his device into court during his friend's trial that its true scope, and its true danger, become evident. The prosecutor, the judges and prejudiced members of the jury are initially determined to reject his films as mere movies, contrived works of fiction, but when he offers to allow them to demonstrate the incapacity of his machine by offering themselves as trial subjects, none of them is willing to take the risk. The merest possibility that their secrets might be revealed for public display is deterrent enough.

Once the court has been persuaded to acquit the man falsely accused, Tornada confesses, as he was forced to do at the end of "The Biocole," that his invention is simply too discomfiting to be entertained by a society founded on hypocrisy. A perfect method of detecting crime might act as a deterrent, he concedes, but could not prevent its meditation—and even if people could somehow bear being forced to reveal themselves, and to suppress all their evil inclinations, would not the world then become too tedious to be tolerable? In the conclusion of the story, he follows the precedent set by Gabriel Mirande, placing his wonderful machine on the floor and smashing it with his heel, vowing never to make another.

As a *conte philosophique*, the story is interesting in itself, but it becomes even more so when located within the Professor Tornada sequence, as the final stage in the evolution of the character who was once driven by despair and bitterness to smash the entire city of Paris and all that it represented under the mammoth heel of his laboratory-bred macrobes. It is also more interesting when placed in the context of other items of *roman scientifique* dealing with similar themes, both in the narrow sense of machines for plumbing the secret depths of the human mind and the broader one of technological innovations potentially capable of changing society.

Once, it had been possible for the Marquis de Condorcet and his disciples to imagine that technological innovation was simply an aspect of the progress of science and mind, not only good in itself but intrinsically linked with the progress of society toward greater liberty, equality and happiness. That was not possible any longer. That kind of optimism had begun to fade with the Revolution of 1789, which claimed Condorcet as a victim of Terror even though he never made it as far as the guillotine; the Great War had killed it off completely, with bombardment, poison gas and tanks—or, as Albert Robida had put it more colorfully, "locomotives of war."

"Le Cas de la baronne Sasoitsu," published immediately before the Great War resumed for its second act, makes a particularly interesting parenthetical comparison with one of the items of *roman scientifique* published soon after the armistice, Raoul Bigot's novella *Nounlegos* (1919 in *Lectures Pour Tous*; book version 1921; tr. as "Nounlegos"). The story's secondary subplot is an account of the eponymous obsessive scientist's lifelong lonely quest to develop a machine capable of doing much the same thing as Professor Tornada's device, allowing an observer to look into the mind of another human and literally read the other's thoughts by means of the remote detection of electrochemical changes in the brain. In order to provide the story with a plot, however, the author adopted the same narrative strategy as Couvreur, embedding the device and its eccentric inventor within a story of an apparently "perfect murder."

The examining magistrate investigating the murder of an American billionaire and his family is sure that he has identified the perpetrator of the crime, but the criminal has been so clever in the execution of his plot that no hard evidence can be found. The frustrated magistrate is on the brink of having to release the suspect and allow him to leave the country when Nounlegos offers his services, and discovers sufficient details of the murderer's method—as well as the location of the money he obtained by means of his crime—to allow a perfect reconstruction of the crime to be staged before the thunderstruck suspect. The confounded malefactor is finally driven to despair and an admission of guilt— vital because, unlike Tornada, the magistrate cannot present his actual evidence in court.

As an item of popular fiction, Bigot's story could not have the kind of reflective coda that Couvreur's *conte philosophique* could not do without, so it concludes in the aftermath of Nounlegos' death with the revelation of the legacy that he has meticulously bequeathed to the Académie des Sciences. The audience of specialist scientists is, of course, delighted—well, they would be, wouldn't they?—but the implications of the machine's existence and practicality for ordinary people, and the manner in which it might change society, are simply left to the reader's imagination, with no prompting except a vague nod in the direction of the idea of progress. The plots of other devices for probing and influencing the mind featured in thrillers of the period, including the thought-photographing device in *La Lumière bleue* [The Blue Light] (1930) by Paul Féval *fils* and Henry Boo-Silhen, fell into the imaginative space intermediate between the two extremes suggested by Bigot and Couvreur, but with an increasing tendency for the crushing heel to come crashing down on the discomfiting intrusion, in an eagerly normalizing conclusion.

The tradition of Vernian adventure stories was eventually picked up again in a desultory fashion, by the *Journal des Voyages*, which was resurrected in 1924 under the editorship of the veteran astronomer Abbé Théophile Moreux (1867-1954), but with the exception of Jean Petithuguenin's interplanetary fantasy, its fiction was undistinguished. In the meantime, the subgenre had produced one of its more adventures imaginary vehicles in *Le Voyage de l'Isabella au centre de la terre* [The *Isabella*'s Journey to the Centre of the Earth] (1922) by the aptly-named chemical engineer Léon Creux (1875-1938), but the story is set in the innocent era before the war and might well have been written then; it is in 1905 that the *Isabella*, equipped with a powerful borer at the prow, sets off for the interior of the Earth.

The vehicle encounters problems, as well as discovering layers and mountains of precious metals, but eventually manages not only to reach the rim of the planet's molten core but to progress beyond that apparent limit to discover a miniature cosmos within the core, complete with a molten platinum "Antiterre," which performs the explanatory functions for which Edmond Halley once hypothesized a moving body within the Earth. In the meantime, the *Isabella*'s journey serves as a useful pretext for educational lectures on geology and cosmogony, in the old Vernian tradition.

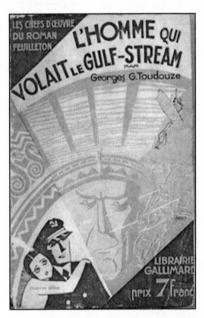

The tradition was also taken up by "Georges G.-Toudouze" (Georges Toudouze, 1877-1972), who had written numerous books since the turn of the century, mostly non-fiction and adventure stories aimed at younger readers, but who began to increase the element of *roman scientifique* in his work with the electrically-powered submersibles featured in *Les Sous-marins fantômes* [The Phantom Submarines] (1921) and then embarked on a series marketed under the rubric of *Les Aventuriers de la Science* [The Adventurers of Science], which started in spectacular fashion with ***L'Homme qui volait le Gulf-Stream*** [The Man Who Stole the Gulf Stream] (1923), but the experiment does not seem to have been successful.

Some of the other writers who had taken up the genre before the war simply went back to it—most notably Maurice Champagne, who began publishing again, after a five year gap, in 1920, although he did not really get into gear again until the end of the twenties, when his bland but well-wrought adventure stories apparently became popular again with younger readers. The subgenre had, however, lost the imaginative impetus that it had once had.

Writers who had been skeptical about the rewards of technical progress before the war naturally remained so. Albert Robida had expressed the agony of discovering that his tongue-in-cheek anticipations had been all too accurate in *L'Ingénieur von Satanas*, but that was not his last word in the field of *roman scientifique*, and he returned thereafter to the milieu sketched out in "Un Potache en 1950," in which he had felt obliged to maintain an upbeat note because the war was still raging and it was important not to damage the morale of the young. His final futuristic fantasy for children was *Un Chalet dans les airs* (1923; tr. as *Chalet in the Sky*).

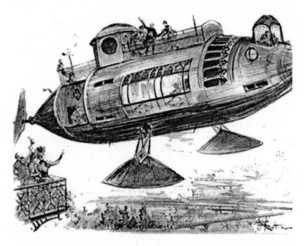

The story, which moves several hundred years beyond the twentieth century to which his previous futuristic fantasies had confined themselves, describes how a scholar, introduced as Monsieur Chabrol, employs the eponymous flying villa to take his two nephews, Moderan and Andoche, on an educational world tour while they continue their routine school work with the aid of a televisual communications network equipped with facilities not unlike the modern world wide web (although far less burdened by trivial and commercial content—even the darkest dystopian imagination has its limitations).

The villa's flight is necessary, in any case, because the ground it is leaving behind has become unstable and in dire need of repair; the world has been completely resurfaced before, in the twenty-second century, but the job was inadequately resourced, and modern technology will hopefully allow the new "consolidation" to be more effective. The nephews would prefer to visit other worlds, some of those newly arrived in Earthy skies after being diverted by the ZZZ rays being rumored to be quite pleasant, but Chabrol is a historian, whose extraterrestrial interests are bounded by his definitive history of the "Lunatic civilizations" based on the documents brought back by explorers of the Moon.

The tour takes in the usual sights: the collapsed Alps; elevated Venice; the mid-Atlantic Caucasian Archipelago and its pleasure resorts, including the Stadium of Violent and Other Sports; the hyperindustrialzed skyscraper city of New York, where the villa is stolen, involving the travelers in an exceedingly protracted legal process; the volcanoes of Guatemala; and the Pacific island formed by the fallen planetoid Astra, with its exotic fauna reminiscent of the Earthly age of the dinosaurs. The text concludes with a brief sojourn in a neo-virginal forest with the last remaining savages—whose reversion to primitive existence has been so complete that they have no memory of the days when their ancestors lived on pills like everyone else—but that is only an *entr'acte* in the villa's journey, whose passengers soon have to return to civilization, perhaps never to settle again, even if the resurfacing brings greater stability this time.

There is a sense in which *Un Chalet dans les airs* is carefully suspended between euchronia and dystopia, laconically juxtaposing elements of both while leaving expressions of preference carefully understated. In the eyes of Moderan and Andoche, of course—unlike Chabrol's—everything they see is simply the world as they find it, and they make no attempt to compare it, as he feels compelled to do, with the vanished eras of Earth's past and the record of the Lunatic civilizations. He can only find peace of mind, or even a *modus vivendi*, in withdrawal, but they have their lives to live, and will live them in a resurfaced world if that proves possible, or elsewhere, if not—and for them, if not their uncle, that is not an unattractive prospect, let alone one inducive of regret or despair. They are not even aware of the failure of his old dreams of progress, let alone inclined to weep for them. They have no need of Professor Tornada's hard-won cynicism, because their kind of innocence already incorporates it.

There is now an inevitable temptation to consider Robida as the most "prophetic" of all the writers of *roman scientifique*: the author who unwittingly spoke the truest words in jest, all the more veritable because his imagination was intoxicated by a livelier ferment than any other. Although it is his anticipations of future warfare that catch the eye most strikingly, because of their rapid and blackly ironic fulfillment, it is arguable that the more general images produced in *Electric Life*, to which *Un Chalet dans les airs* is an understated but nevertheless deft and further-reaching addendum, are even more remarkable in summarizing and exemplifying the problems that the future would have to face, and the kinds of dubious remedies that technology might be able to supply. It is, however, worth remembering that those works were produced in a generally hostile intellectual climate, only reached print because of particular conduits of publication that were fragile, and delivered their products to marginal cultural regions where they could be easily overlooked and forgotten.

The most extreme example of that kind of special conduit and delivery to forgetfulness is, of course, self-publication. That had never been possible without money or assistance, of course, as Restif de La Bretonne discovered when he had such a hard time getting *Les Posthumes* into print, only managed to do so in direly unsatisfactory fashion, and failed to reach print with its companion masterpiece, *L'Enclos et les oiseaux*. It was no easier in the twentieth century, when the only people who had a practical means of self-publication with a viable system of distribution attached were those who edited periodicals with some kind of stable circulation.

Had he not inherited editorship of *La Nouvelle Revue* in 1913 when Pierre-Barthélemy Gheusi was appointed director of the Opéra-Comique, Henri Austruy might never have published anything again after *L'Ère Petitpaon*, the only work he had contrived to publish outside its pages since becoming Gheusi's managing editor in the early years of the century. From the editorial chair, however, he could not only run his own column of political commentary—which represented interbellum politics as an increasingly desperate attempt to maintain peace in Europe, and was so scathingly hostile to Adolf Hitler that Austruy disappeared a few days after the Nazis entered Paris in 1940 and was never heard of again—but also to run his own fiction, which included the single most "prophetic" item of *roman scientifique* that the genre ever produced. It was, inevitably, not reprinted in book form, although Austruy originally intended to issue it as a book through the *Nouvelle Revue*'s own press, but was dissuaded when his previous efforts of that kind sold so badly as to inform him that to do so would be economically suicidal. It was, therefore, completely forgotten; it is not mentioned in Versins *Encyclopédie*, the Lofficiers' bibliography or, at the time of writing, the BDFI.

The story in question, "L'Olotélépan" (tr. as "The Olotelepan") was serialized in the magazine in 1925, and did not claim to be futuristic, in that it is explicitly set in the year 1924, but it nevertheless set out to track the potential social employment of a technological device that did not exist at the time, or for half a century afterwards, although something like it does exist now—something sufficiently similar, in fact, to allow modern readers to check, very belatedly, the whole pattern of extrapolation that the author developed. The novel was almost certainly written before 1924, but still qualifies as an alternative history rather than a futuristic fantasy, in that it tracks the history of its central motif from 1913.

The story's protagonist is Horace Gourdebec, a French landscape painter desirous of following his vocation in rugged terrain, who decided in 1909 to tag along with a French military expedition to the Moroccan Atlas mountains. Unfortunately, his escort proved useless, and was slaughtered to the last man by an unruly Arab warlord. The warlord assumed that the civilian accompanying the expedition must be a doctor, and appointed him as his personal physician, keeping the painter captive for fifteen years, during which he maintained such robust good health that he was never disabused of his error. When the warlord finally falls ill in 1924, however, immediately before the story opens, the well-meaning but medically ignorant painter advises him to surrender to the French and have himself transported to Paris, where he can be treated by the best surgeons in the world. Gourdebec assures him that the French will be so glad of his surrender that they will treat him like royalty, as they had the Algerian rebel Abd el-Kader half a century before.

The warlord agrees, and is indeed promised the very best in French surgery and anything else he wishes besides; grateful to his friend, he demands that the protagonist be appointed a Maréchal de France and given responsibility for French Army Medical services outside France—a request that is duly granted. Gourdebec, however, cannot wait to get out of Paris in order to go and visit his old friend Félix Gigolus, an author of popular fiction now resident in the Dordogne. The two have a lot of catching up to do; when released, Gourdebec had no idea that there had been a Great War, and is completely ignorant of the marvelous technical innovation that has been slowly but dramatically transforming French society since the war's conclusion, in this alternative history.

As the two men are walking from the railway station to Gigolus' house their conversation is continually interrupted by a ringing sound coming from Gigolus' fob pocket. After ignoring it several times, he finally takes out what Gourdebec initially assumes to be a pocket watch. Gigolus tells him, however, that it is actually an olotelepan, and shows his friend a set of ten buttons, which, he explains, comprise a kind of keyboard, although one does not need to be able to type or play the piano to use it. Each key is imprinted with a digit, and by tapping them one can spell out a number of any length, which appears on a kind of display panel. The numbers thus keyed in are the numbers of other olotelepans, with which the user is put in contact.

Gourdebec comments that wireless telephony has obviously come a long way while he has been in the Atlas, but Gigolus assures him that the olotelepan is far more advanced than a mere wireless telephone. It allows the user not only to hear the person holding the connecting olotelepan, but also to see them, and even to obtain some touch sensations. Most of the olotelepans to which people connect themselves are carried by other individuals—the call that Gigolus tried so hard to ignore is from his housekeeper, who wanted to know what to prepare for dinner—but there are also olotelepans that provide views of distant places, access to theatrical performances and sporting events, tours of museums and so on.

As the story progresses, Gigolus gradually explains other things that can be done by means of the olotelepan. He informs Gourdebec that he, like many other olotelepanists—there are still many neophobic individuals who refuse to use such machines—now conducts his amorous affairs at a distance by means of "telerasty," and that many other people are now doing likewise. Gourdebec is also told, after suffering an unfortunate inconvenience due to his unfamiliarity with the technology, that the device has made a big difference to police surveillance. Criminals are now routinely monitored after release from prison, being forced to wear an unobtrusive olotelepan that permits them to be continually monitored and called to account for their actions and whereabouts at any time. Children can be subjected to similar surveillance by parents, and wives by husbands—but not vice versa, at least legally.

When Goudebec asks what happens if people will not consent to such surveillance, he is told that as well as surveillance devices whose wearers know that they are being monitored there are "occult olotelepans": miniaturized devices that can be secreted in a ring, a belt buckle or the sole of a shoe in order to keep tabs on them secretly. He is told an amusing anecdote about the manner in which the Cardinal-Archbishop of Paris—who has naturally been subject to clandestine surveillance by the Republican Government, of which he is a diehard opponent—discovered that his pastoral ring concealed an occult olotelepan.

Gigolus also speculates about longer-range effects that are still in their infancy. He points out that there are a great many jobs that do not actually require physical presence, and can just as easily be done via the olotelepan. That has already begun, and he suggests that the eventual consequence of the possibility will be the gradual shrinkage of big cities as people no longer have to huddle together, and the dispersal of population—although he presents cogent arguments to support his contention that Paris will not and cannot disappear, even though many of the employments currently concentrated there will be redistributed to distant olotelepanists.

All this was, of course, pure fantasy in 1925, and it remained pure fantasy for a long time afterwards. We can now see, however, that the author of the story demonstrated a remarkable extrapolative acumen in suggesting the consequences that might—and, indeed, must—flow from the development of a technology permitting versatile hand-held wireless telephones, even anticipating with a reasonable degree of accuracy the manner in which the form of such devices would follow their function. Austruy was by no means the only person to anticipate personal telephones, of course, but he far outperformed all his contemporaries in describing the corollary uses to which the inhabitants of his alternative world of 1924 have swiftly put them.

Another reason why no one could have taken "L'Olotélépan" seriously at the time of its publication is that, as with Albert Robida's speculations, the possibilities are not couched as "realistic" extrapolations, but as an unfolding sequence of jokes: jokes that eventually turn sour when—as is typical of Austruy's work—the comedy abruptly turns to stark tragedy. The part of the story that now seems very clever in its anticipation of such modern phenomena as electronic tagging, bugging, telecommuting and phone sex comes to an end half way through; it is followed by a comic account of the tribulations of the inventors of the olotelepan's less practical predecessor, the telebus, and the conclusion of the story deals with the unfortunate fate of the luckless warlord, who suffers direly in the hands of the military surgeons of Paris, and the unfortunate Maréchal, who is ordered to take his mutilated body back to the Atlas for burial.

Even before the climactic bloodbath, however, there has been one very striking note of horror introduced into the comedy when the reluctant Maréchal is assigned a general staff and a contingent of several hundred soldiers. When they sit down to dinner together Goudebec belatedly notices that one of his staff officers has an artificial arm: a technological replacement for a limb lost during the war. When he asks whether any other members of his troop are equipped with such marvelously realistic prosthetics, a strange parade is called, in which every single man in the unit removes the artificial body-parts with which with they have all had to be equipped in order to maintain their utility. Even more than the olotelepan, that image provides a symbolic summation of the kind of future that is in store for a world still in muted conflict.

Austruy had begun his post-war ventures in *roman scientifique* with the political fantasy "La Jungle républicaine" (1919; tr. as "The Republican Jungle") in which the Chambre des Députés, faced with an impending ecocatastrophe, debates the possibility of regenerating the forests of France, with all their concomitant wildlife. That project cropped up again as a subplot in one of the two further novels that he wrote and published in *La Nouvelle Revue* after "L'Olotélépan," the insistently peculiar "Un Samsâra" (1932; tr. as "A Samsara"), in which a new atomic theory is employed by its inventor as the basis for a therapeutic method allegedly capable of curing all psychological ills—although it is never clear whether it has any effect beyond that of a placebo, and the theory is primarily employed as a refractive narrative lens through which to view the plight of a troubled novelist and the doomed love affair that provides him with an unfortunately temporary relief from his despair.

Austruy's final novel, "Antoine et Sidonie," was far more restrained, constituting a naturalistic study of the scientific mind in the tradition of Gineste's *La Seconde vie du docteur Albin* and Beaunier's *L'Homme qui a perdu son moi*; it was published after the Second World War began but before the Germans captured Paris, in the early months of 1940. The author did, however, produce one more item of *roman scientifique* before then. Having toyed with surrealism even before the war in the phantasmagorical "Miellune" (1908; tr. as "Miellune"), in which a temporary earthly paradise of freedom from want and immortality created by the volcanic escape of a miraculous gas ultimately proves unendurable for the villagers gifted with it, Austruy eventually took surrealistic *roman scientifique* to a new extreme in the novelette "La Révélation de Maître Flaver" (1939; tr. as "The Revelation of Master Flaver"), whose ichthyomaniac protagonist produces all manner of bizarre fish, by artificial means that are more pataphysical than biological. His creations eventually turn against him, for no apparent reason other than that being what creations tend to do, and leave him to an ignominious death while their few survivors set off down the Seine, singing the *Internationale*. Austruy, alas, was unable to do the same a year later.

Such sarcastic fantasies were not, of course, the only responses to the notion of future technological progress evident in the period between the wars. Much propaganda was still being produced—not least in the pages of *Science et Voyages*—trumpeting the wonders of gadgetry that the world of tomorrow was bound to produce, and even in the absence of olotelepans, there was no shortage in the magazine's pages of devices calculated to excite young readers. The feuilleton slot, where *La Fin d'Illa* appeared, was generally not as rosy in its outlook as the non-fiction, but there too a certain propagandistic fervor was occasionally evident. One particularly striking example is Jean Petithuguenin's only contribution to the periodical's pages, *Le Grand courant* (tr. as "The Great Current"), which was serialized in 1931 prior to being reprinted by Tallandier in 1932, in an edition uniform with the subsequent reissue of *Une Mission internationale dans la lune.*

The story opens in the year 2280, at a scientific event hosted by the Intercontinental Thermoelectrification Company, which has begun construction of an enormous system of electricity generation, employing the temperature differential between the tropics and Arctic ice to produce a current sufficient to supply the world's technological requirements abundantly for an indefinite period. The story is packed with technical data relating to the effect being harnessed and the design of the project's megastructures, and includes an entire chapter explaining that all energy ultimately comes from the sun, and that when the supply stored in fossil fuels runs out, as it is bound to do, substitute sources will have to be found if civilization is to be maintained and its glorious technological progress is to continue.

Unfortunately, there is a specter at the ITC's feast in the form of the Chinese diplomat Wang-Ti-Pou, who is temporarily confided to the care of two young engineers, Paul Chartrain and Claire Nolleau. Their attempts to persuade him that the Great Current is a marvelous idea collide with his conviction that civilization is a bad thing, because true happiness can only be found within, in spiritual enlightenment, and that advanced technology is a fatal distraction from that quest.

When a revolution in the Far East establishes Wang-Ti-Pou as the virtual dictator of a vast Asian Federation, he proclaims that he has only friendly intentions toward the West, but in fact his agents are busy fomenting dissent in Africa, which eventually leads to the sabotage of the tropical end of the projected Great Current, whose shutdown enables the liberated Arctic ice to destroy the contacts at the other end, in Greenland. While the heroic engineers fight to preserve what they can of its machinery, an all out war is launched by the East against the West, and bombers are sent to destroy the Arctic base, which Paul

603

and Claire have to defend with the aid of a single armed drone after the giant helicopter appointed to its military protection is shot down.

Paul and Claire are both injured, apparently fatally, while saving the base, but twenty-third-century medicine has resources unknown in earlier eras, and they are slowly brought back from the brink of death, in order to participate in the reconstruction of the Great Current once the war has ended and the forces of barbarism have been defeated. With the people of the East apparently won over to the ideology of Western progress, it seems that the world, after desperate tribulations, is finally set for a euchronian future, in which Paul and Claire will be able to share—but that is left to the glittering haze of vague possibility.

To some extent, that prelude and conclusion are merely conforming to the demands of popular fiction, where things have to go spectacularly awry before being sorted out, in order to provide a requisite supply of drama and suspense—especially in an era of runaway melodramatic inflation, in a genre uniquely vulnerable to its pressures. There is, however, a significant metamorphosis involved when the normalizing story-arc of mundane crime and thriller fiction is pressed into use in futuristic fiction, which *Le Grand courant* illustrates with particular clarity. The exaggeration of menace and action, and the slenderness of the ultimate hair's-breadth escape, all demonstrate the extremes to which melodramatic inflation inevitably tends in futuristic fantasy, but the endings of such fictions cannot return to something known, familiar and tacitly safe; they are obliged instead to reestablish euchronian hopes in the social rewards of technological progress—and that is something that was very difficult to do in 1931 with any degree of conviction or plausibility.

It was easier to do that in fiction designed for younger readers than fiction aimed at adults, not because of the suppose naivety of the audience but because of the necessary differences of attitude reflected in Albert Robida's characterization of Moderan and Androche, contrasted with that of Monsieur Chabrol, but even there, as both *Un Chalet dans les airs* and *Le Grand courant* demonstrate, it was by no means unproblematic. The innocence of the old *Musée des Familles* was gone, and attempts to rally optimism in its absence were swimming against a forceful tide. The most ambitious item of juvenile fiction following up *Un Chalet dans les airs* was *La Découverte de l'oncle Pamphile* [Uncle Pamphile's Discovery] (1931) by the writer and illustrator Marcel Jeanjean (1893-1973), in which the young heroes, Robert and Jacqueline, disregard the cautionary prohibitions placed on them by their ingenious uncle, and accidentally transport themselves to 2350 A.D. in his time machine, where they find a Robidaesque high-tech future that enthuses them greatly, although their uncle is on hand to dampen their enthusiasm by pointing out the downside of every aspect of it.

One of the most sophisticated feuilletons to appear in *Science et Voyages*, and perhaps the most thoughtful of them all was "Sur l'autre face du monde" [On the Other Side of the World] (1935; reprinted as the title story of a showcase anthology, 1973), signed "A. Valérie"—a signature that does not seem to have been used anywhere else, but was obviously not that of a novice writer. The hero of the story, Hégyr, has been brought up in an underground city where the dictatorial rule of a technocratic elite has preserved the rewards of an advanced human science and technology through the twenty thousand years of an Ice Age. As a punishment for questioning the wisdom of the Masters, Hégyr is sent out of the city as a scout when the melting ice has released new fertile land to see if any humans have survived the long ordeal of the surface.

Hégyr discovers that humans have indeed survived, and have generated a Stone Age culture possessed of its own traditional wisdom, much garbled but nevertheless retaining enough practical knowledge for its users to nurse him back to health after a serious injury, during which he is tended in his convalescence by a young woman named Eve, who teaches him the tribal language. He is accepted into the tribe and swears an oath of brotherhood with its young chief, Yagh. When he contrives to make contact with the city again, the Masters decide—for reasons that are not malevolent—that the new humans ought submit to their rule and adapt to their culture, and they order Hégyr to facilitate that, but Yagh and his tribe do not want to be dominated, and Hégyr's loyalties are tested to the full, all the more so because he must also choose between Aniela, the fiancé designated for him by the Masters, and Eve, who has fallen in love with him.

The political dilemmas set out in the story are treated seriously, as philosophical issues in need of earnest debate, and the story refuses the simplicity of the standard story-arc. Vague thematic similarities occasioned the suspicion that Valérie might have been René Thévenin, but differences of style and intellectual procedure make that hard to believe.

Science et Voyages and the resurrected *Journal des Voyages* were not the only popular periodicals that deliberately played host to *roman scientifique* in the period between the wars, routinely featuring stories that imagined new technologies. *Lectures Pour Tous*, which had published several items of *roman scientifique* before the war before the war and two stories by Raoul Bigot immediately after the war's end had continued in that vein before publishing René Pujol's grim account of "Le Soleil noir" and continued thereafter, in a deliberately less downbeat manner. The Christmas 1921 issue was a special one devoted to the "seven wonders of the modern world," and the stores commissioned in celebration of the wonders in question included two exercises in *roman scientifique*, "En l'an 2000" [In the Year 2000] by "Gérard d'Houville" (Marie-Louise de Hérédia, the wife of the Symbolist Academician, Henri de Régnier, 1875-1963) and "L'Autobolide" by the Swiss playwright Marcel Gerbidon (1868-1933).

In fact, the editors of the periodical seem to have made a point throughout the 1920s and early 1930s of publishing one serial in the genre almost every year, and eventually began awarding an annual Prix Jules Verne in order to advertise and emphasize the fact. There was a certain amount of overlap between the suppliers of the two publications—René Pujol published three *feuilletons* in *Science et Voyages*, although the usual run of his work was far more sophisticated and his final venture into *roman scientifique* was very different in style and manner—and the sequence of generic narratives published in *Lectures Pour Tous* is a notable thread in the evolution of the genre, if only for the conspicuous loss of imaginative energy it underwent in its later phases.

L'Aérobagne 32 (1920 in serial and book form; tr. as "Aerobagne 32") by E. M. Laumann (1863-1928) and H. Lanos is a spy story about a French engineer hired by a German company who discovers that its overt industrial operations are a cover for a vast rearmament scheme, and who refuses to surrender the formula for a new poison gas. He is then incarcerated in a vast airborne prison, whose inmates are treated with appalling brutality, while the German authorities contend that he has committed suicide. He contrives to get a long message explaining his plight back to France, but the government, intent on preserving good diplomatic relations with the former foe, refuses to believe it; it is left to a heroic newspaper reporter, Paul Escander, and the victim's stubborn fiancée to find proof that his message is true and to launch a near-impossible rescue mission.

L'Aérobagne 32 makes an interesting comparison and contrast with its sequel, *L'Étrange matière* [The Strange Substance] (serial 1921; book 1924), written by Laumann in collaboration with Raoul Bigot, the last contribution to the magazine bearing the latter signature, and seemingly its last usage anywhere. Again, the novel is a spy story featuring Paul Escander, who is once again attempting to track down a missing scientific genius, with the aid of the latter's beautiful former laboratory assistant, because the "strange substance" he has discovered is being employed to blackmail whole nations, subjecting vast areas to drastic increases or decreases in temperature by means that are extremely difficult to detect, and hence impossible to ward off.

It eventually proves to be the case that the scientist, unable to raise capital in France to continue his scientific investigations, has innocently sold his secret to an Indian rajah, who—unknown to the scientist—intends to employ the money extorted by his blackmail to finance the building of a vast Asiatic empire, from which he will expel all the former colonial powers, and which he will then defend by means of his technology of temperature control. Once again, Escander foils the plot by means of a daring invasion of the enemy camp.

Whereas the aerobagne in the earlier novel occupies center stage for much of the story, however, moving the story's primary setting into imaginative space, the strange substance of the latter story remains offstage throughout, merely functioning as what Alfred Hitchcock called a "McGuffin"—an object of desire that serves as a plot lever to motivate and choreograph the maneuvers of various characters operating in relatively familiar circumstances. It is not until the story's epilogue, when the plot has been tidied up, that a brief explanation is given of what the strange substance actually does, in terms of scientific theory, and how it has been deployed in the hypothetical technologies by means of which its controlled catastrophic effects have been contrived.

That was to become a very familiar plot formula, not only in *roman scientifique* but in scientific romance and science fiction as well, to the extent that it eventually became a marginal genre of the latter requiring a label of its own: "technothriller." Most, although not all, of the more offbeat serials that followed *L'Étrange matière* in the pages of *Lectures Pour Tous* and in the series of cheap paperback books in which many of them were reprinted, were similar thrillers set in the present or imminent future, featuring technological innovations that remained offstage for the greater part of the plot, deployed, if at all, in a hostile fashion that licensed, if it did not actually cry out for, their climactic destruction. Such stories are comfortable, both in the sense that following the action requires no particular intellectual effort on the part of the reader, and in the sense that the normalizing denouement has a built-in familiar satisfaction. It is, in a sense, the ideal formula for popular magazine fiction that wants to seem imaginatively adventurous, while not taking any significant risk of alienating readers by overtaxing their brains.

The overall impression left by the mass-production of such thrillers, however—which were routinely reprinted and augmented in moderate profusion by publishers of popular fiction—is the characterization of the present day as a milieu in which new technologies are continually emerging, which are likely to prove problematic at best, and massively destructive at worst. Whether individual works of that kind are explicitly anti-progressive or not, their implication when seen *en masse* clearly is, and the fact that they became the most commonplace subgenre of popular fiction dealing with scientific matters and hypothetical technologies added considerably to the mordantly downbeat tone that the ideative legacy of the Great War had imposed on so many works that dealt with the same themes with a greater degree of literary ambition and sophistication

The Prix Jules Verne, first awarded in 1927 to *La Petite-fille de Michel Strogoff* [Michael Strogoff's Granddaughter] by Octave Béliard—who had published several items of ambitious *roman scientifique* in the periodical in the years preceding the war, although that new offering was much more restrained—did not disrupt that pattern to any great extent, in spite of its supposed honoring of a writer whose early *roman scientifique* had been considerably more favorable to the cause of scientific advancement.

By far the most imaginatively-extravagant of the prize-winners was *L'Éther-Alpha* (1929) by Albert Bailly, in which a mysterious airship made of transparent substance lands at an airstrip in the U.S.A. and then takes off again, carrying a young woman named Minnie to the secret lair of a scientific genius, Cecil Montcalm, who is working on the solidification of ether, the disintegration of the atom and the mastery of electromagnetic energy. Having received signals sent from the moon, he is constructing the eponymous spaceship in order to investigate. After Minnie's abduction, Cecil sets off with her for the Moon, where they encounter luminous hexagonal beings. The Selenites attack the Earth with electromagnetic weapons, but they also bring Minnie back to life after she dies of asphyxia, much to Cecil's relief—although gratitude does not prevent him from wiping them out.

The other prize-winners were much more moderate, although Hervé de Peslouan's *L'Étrange menace du professeur Ioutchakoff* [The Strange Menace of Professor Ioutchakoff] (1931) does feature a massive airship named *Le Menace*, from which an anarchist using the pseudonym Jupiter rains thunderbolts down on the city of Stalograd (sic) while the poor schoolteacher who resembles him uncannily suffers the trials and tribulations of being mistaken for him by the Russian secret police.

Other serials published in the magazine after 1921 were similarly reserved; Noelle Roger's "L'Hôte invisible" [The Invisible Host] (1926; book version as a supplement to *Le Livre qui fait mourir* [The Book That Kills]) is a mystery story of a family curse and an invisible monster, with a rationalizing solution. J. Jacquin and A. Favre's "Le Sommeil sous les blés" [Slumber Under the Wheat] (1927; book version as *Celle qui dormait sous le terre* [The Woman Asleep Underground]) is a suspense story about the race to find a volunteer placed in fakiristic suspended animation after the magnetizer carrying out the experiment has a stroke and can no longer reveal where he buried her.

The Prix Jules Verne continued to be awarded until 1933, when it was won by the mundane naval mystery "Les Vaisseaux en flammes" [Ships in Flames] by Jean-Toussaint Samat, although the serial did not appear in the magazine until 1936, by which time *roman scientifique* had virtually disappeared from its pages, not to return prior to its inevitable demise in 1940.

While the kind of formularistic thriller that came gradually to the fore in the pages of *Lectures Pour Tous* also became widespread in other periodicals and cheap book series like those published by Tallandier and Ferenczi, however, both of those publishers, and others that embarked on similar ventures, did employ the generic space thus opened up to features stories that ventured into more extravagant imaginative realms, much as *Lectures Pour Tous* had done in experimenting with *L'Éther-Alpha*. The fiction in question was usually unsophisticated, and its imaginative component tended to make it merely garish rather than intellectually challenging, but its best examples did have an admirable verve, and an enthusiasm for invention largely absent from thrillers following normalizing story-arcs. The more imaginative examples issued by Tallandier included *La Conquête de la terre* [The Conquest of the Earth] (1931) by Pierre Lavaur, and *Les Deux reines du pôle sud* [The Two Queens of the South Pole] (1932) and *Le Soleil ensorcelé* [The Bewitched Sun] (1933) by Eugène Thébault, while the more extravagant works published by Ferenczi included *La Mission de quatre savants* [The Mission of Four Scientists] (1925) by René Trotet de Bargis, *Les Fiancés de la planète Mars* [The Lovers of the Planets Mars] (1936) by the prolifically enterprising Maurice Limat, and *Les Explorateurs de l'Espace* [The Explorers of Space] (1938) by Maurice Pérot. It was in such calculatedly colorful series that French *roman scientifique* came closest in its narrative strategies and packaging to contemporary American science fiction.

In spite of the handful of cheap paperbacks dating from the 1930s listed in the last paragraph, there is no doubt that *roman scientifique*, at all levels of the French marketplace, suffered a considerable loss of imaginative impetus in the 1930s. French historians who regard such material as "proto-science fiction" sometimes express disappointment at the fact that after some seemingly promising "advances" toward the similitude of *roman scientifique* and modern science fiction in the first quarter of the twentieth century, there was then something of a dearth until the invasion of American material in the early 1950s and the rapid imitation thereof by domestic writers. Although Jacques van Herp did not mention the thesis in *Parorama de la science fiction*, he suggested in his study of José Moselli that the dearth in question might have been a reaction to a moral panic prompted by condemnations from the pulpit and backed by the right-wing press of the material being published by the Maison Offenstadt. Such attacks, he suggests, might have been responsible for abandonment of the more adventurous materials that had featured in the early issues of *Science et Voyages* and might have had a knock-on effect on such periodicals as *Lectures Pour Tous* and book publishers.

Van Herp observes in support of this case that the Offenstadt brothers lost a series of legal actions for alleged defamation of character that they brought against various critics of their operation—although the charge to which they objected most strenuously was that they were German (their family was German in origin, but had been naturalized long ago)—and that the example of their defeats might have made publishers far more careful about the possibility of offending vociferous critics. In van Herp's opinion, endorsed by Jean-Marc Lofficier, among others, the moral crusade in question was a significant factor in discouraging *roman scientifique* from becoming more like American science fiction sooner, which they, as science fiction fans, naturally deplore. They added further support to their arguments by quoting comments made by churchmen about ungodly notions in two of Maurice Renard's works.

While the moral crusade in question might not have helped in the promotion of imaginative fiction as much as previous moral crusades had done—the effect of such attacks usually being the opposite of that intended—it seems improbable that publishers would have taken the slightest notice of it unless it had affected their sales. The reluctance of publishers at all levels of the marketplace to continue experimenting with the more adventurous forms of *roman scientifique* is far more likely to have been a result of the failure of the experiments they had already carried out, in commercial terms, emphasized after 1929 by the effects of the Depression. That failure must have been attributable, at least in part, to the after-effects of the Great War—which were, of course, also responsible for much post-war hysteria and moral panic in various sectors of society—but the effect is more likely to have been direct than filtered through the hysteria in question. The more surprising thing is perhaps that the publishers had experimented at all, not that they had stopped, or at least slowed down, until the domestic fad for American science fiction changed the spectrum of marketing opportunity drastically in the 1950s, in an entirely different climate of expectation.

Roman scientifique that bore less resemblance to pulp space fiction, and therefore attracted less attention as "proto-science fiction," did continue to appear in the 1930s, in moderate quantities and in admittedly-problematic circumstances, and some of it is of high quality in both literary and philosophical terms. Much of it, as might be expected, is in a conspicuously ironic and skeptical vein, often extending to mordant black comedy—but that does not work to its disadvantage.

One of the most striking accounts of ironic technological innovation produced between the wars was *Jim Click, ou La Merveilleuse invention* (1930) by Fernand Fleuret (1883-1945), a poet, humorist and historian of the unusual who made a living as a journalist, frequently employing fanciful and flippant pseudonyms, but whose more ambitious writings were marginally associated with the surrealist movement. He had earlier been acquainted with Guillaume Apollinaire and Alfred Jarry, and Jarry's celebration of accounts of humanoid automata might well have influenced his decision to produce his own such account, in a scathingly satirical and subtly allegorical mold.

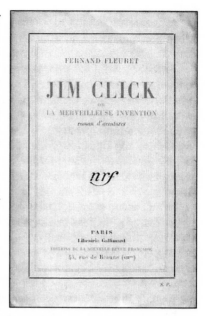

The story is represented as a translation of a text supposedly written in an English lunatic asylum and discovered by an Englishman who became convinced that it was not the work of a madman at all—and, indeed, set out to prove the point, attaching an account of his mission in an epilogue to the text. The Englishman hints that the identities of certain real individuals might have been disguised in the manuscript, but the notional French translator is insufficiently informed of English history to recognize that the "Admiral Horatio Gunson" featured therein is obviously Lord Nelson, and that the "Battle of Barajar" described in the story is actually Trafalgar.

The story describes how Jim Click, the son of a clockmaker who once had ambitions to build a human automaton but shelved his scheme in the interests of making a living, conceives an intense hero-worship for the young Horatio Gunson, a charismatic boy with great ambitions, and remains his close friend throughout their school days, until Horatio runs away to join the navy, leaving Jim to complete his multiple scientific studies in isolation, only seeing his old friend occasionally as the latter's career goes from glory to glory.

Freed from financial need when he inherits a fortune made in India by his uncle, Jim devotes his time obsessively to completing his father's aborted dream, modeling his automaton on the hero with whom he is still besotted. When Horatio, on the brink of setting off to take command of the *Triumph* (i.e., the *Victory*) and go in search of the French fleet, comes to visit Jim in order to ask him to accompany him, in the capacity of personal physician and secretary—having already made all the necessary arrangements in advance, unable to think that anyone could ever refuse his demands—Jim shows him the completed automaton, much to Horatio's amusement. While the drunken Horatio is testing the automaton's abilities as a mirror of his own, however, he unwisely engages it in a boxing match, and is killed by a punch whose effects he is too debilitated to resist.

Panic-stricken at having caused the death of the nation's greatest hero, Jim removes the automaton's arm in order to duplicate Gunson's recently-acquired disability, and makes plans to pass it off as the real Gunson until he is safely away from his house and he can slip away, perhaps to flee abroad. In his capacity as the admiral's personal physician he is able to keep him away from close inspection, and finds, to his amazement, that the few inconsequential phrases that the automaton is able to pronounce more or less at random are simply accepted as evidence of the great man's well-known eccentricity, or even misconstrued as wit and wisdom.

Opportunities to slip away are initially in short supply, and when Jim finally obtains one, he does not take it because he has become suddenly infatuated with Horatio's mistress, Nelly Hackman (i.e., Emma Hamilton). By the time he has recovered from that fit of amorous madness, it is too late; he is forced to accompany the automaton to see King George and then board the *Triumph* with it. As the Admiral's secretary, he is able to issue written orders intended to keep the English fleet as far away as possible from the French—taking it as far away as the Caribbean, where he has a chastening experience on an idyllic island inhabited by savages—but fate inevitably brings him to Trafalgar, where his randomly-improvised strategy unwittingly brings off a spectacular victory. All of Gunson's subordinates hate him by then, however, because of his monopolization of their hero; when the automaton is shot and "killed," Jim is put under lock and key as soon as the death certificate he has drawn up in countersigned by the ship's doctor, and then kicked off the ship as soon as it docks.

Jim is then free to get on with his life, but he feels that he ought to make what contribution he can to the continuing war effort, and writes to King George explaining what he has done and offering to build him an army of automata—with the result that he is soon confined to a lunatic asylum, where he writes his memoir. The eventual finder of the memoir realizes that it can be put to the proof by looking for the body of Lord Gunson, supposedly stored in a barrel of rum in Jim's house, now sequestered. The director of the asylum has never thought that necessary, but he yields to pressure and he and the dead man's solicitor break the seals on the house and go to find the barrel—which they do....

The import of the story, like all sophisticated accounts of human automata, is that automata can pass for human more easily than might be supposed, principally because people behave much more like automata than they suppose, much more narrowly imprisoned by their instincts and prejudices than they would like to believe and far too ready to condemn as mad those who do not share their own prejudices. Like the great majority of accounts of "wonderful inventions," *Jim Click* consigns Jim's to oblivion—inevitably, since history has already proceeded for many years without any sign of it—but adds the extra charge of irrelevance, the ultimate moral of the tale being that humans, including Jim himself, are unworthy of the potential wonders of inventiveness, because, even if they might not be mad in any clinical sense, they are incapable of using them sanely.

Jim Click is, however, not typical of the inventors of the interbellum period, not so much because of his blinkered obsession, which was commonplace, but because of his unusual timorousness. Many innovators were more self-regarding in their eccentricity, as perhaps befit the boldness of their imagination, some of them as extravagantly as Professor Tornada. At the end of the spectrum of assertiveness opposite to Jim Click, however, Marc Vanel was just as atypical by virtue of his awesome success in seducing women—something that fictional scientists constructed on the Berthoudian model found notoriously difficult. There was, however, one other scientist of genius featured in interbellum *roman scientifique*

who similarly qualified as a sexual as well as an intellectual superman: Romain Ségétan, the hero of Léon Daudet's second major contribution to the genre, **Les Bacchantes** (1931; tr. as *The Bacchantes*).

Ségétan is working in his private laboratory in the Villa Dyonisos [a variant spelling of Dionysus] in rural France on a radiation weapon that will stop airplanes in flight and thus permit a reliable defense against possible bombardment, but he is also working on a machine that can capture and control "waves of time" permitting the reproduction of images of the distant past, which he also calls the Dyonisos. He is one of a trio of scientists working in association, known locally as the three sorcerers, the others being Félix Devonet, a physicist, dermatologist and entomologist, and the herbalist physician Dr. Benalep. All three come under dire suspicion when strange occurrences in the vicinity, including an outbreak of skin disease and fatal scorpion stings, are blamed on their unholy activities (correctly, as it turns out).

When Tullie Calvat, the lovely young widow of a local farmer is involved in a road accident nearby, Ségétan takes her in until she recovers from her injuries, and soon begins an affair with her, awakening the jealousy of the farmer's son Jean, who is in love with her. There are two other local women in his small social circle who are also under his spell to some extent: Mélanie Dévonet, Félix's wife; and the ex film-star Ariana d'Ignacio, the wife of the local aristocrat. That circle of fascination becomes wider when Tullie is visited by an old friend, Donabella Hatchinson, recently married to an American physicist, who does not like Ségétan at all.

Nevertheless, Ségétan, with Tullie's approval and collaboration, decides to seduce Donabella, and selects as a suitable venue the so-called Villa of the Mysteries on Pompeii, where there is a series of murals that he interprets as a guide to the initiation of a novice into the Dionysian mysteries. He intends to re-enact that initiation with his associates, while his time-viewer summons up a reproduction of the eruption of Vesuvius that destroyed the city. Although he has already had a warning about the effects of jealousy, when temporary blinded by a shotgun blast fired at him by Jean Calvat, Ségétan takes no account of Hatchinson's possible reaction to the seduction of his wife. He pays the penalty when the physicist takes advantage of a device of his own invention to murder him undetectably—but Hatchinson, in his turn, has failed to take into account the fact that the modern Dionysus has a whole harem of Bacchantes avid to avenge him.

Although Hatchinson's action robs France of the vital aerial defense system that Ségétan was on the brink of providing, his murderous use of his own technology merely reflects a disturbing pattern associated with all the scientific activities represented in the story, which have unfortunate side effects that the men responsible reflexively try to deny or, when denial becomes impossible, to cover up. However enviable Ségétan's sexual adventures might be, therefore, they do seem to fit a general pattern of irresponsibility whose rippling effects are mostly deleterious. Although he is neither mad nor evil, and his technological endeavors are aimed at useful and intriguing goals, their spinoff is essentially disruptive and destructive, unleashing Bacchantes in more metaphorical senses than one. The novel therefore adds, albeit in a perversely subtle fashion, to the overall pattern of suspicion in the imaginative treatment of technology in the period in question.

Jean-Jacques Bernard's "New Chicago" (1930), which appeared in the upmarket *Les Nouvelles littéraires* before being reprinted as an appendix to the author's novel *Madeleine Landier* (1933), offers a somewhat surreal extrapolation of technological sophistication in its depiction of a fully-automatic town which continues to function after all its citizens have been killed in a bacteriological war, at least until it is rediscovered by a single survivor, whose settlement there is sufficient to cause a series of breakdowns, which he does not have the ability to repair.

In *Tréponème* (1931) by Marc La Marche a scientist employs injections of syphilis toxin into the brain to stimulate the specific areas associated with intelligence, thus producing a population of geniuses capable of mobilizing scientific and social progress—a proposal given a general welcome no more enthusiastic than the one given before the war to the hygienic scalpel of Louis Forest's enterprising Dr. Flax.

Even when technologies seem entirely benign, however—and do, in fact, have the seeming potential to be entirely benign—careful attention is paid in a number of *contes philosophiques* that followed in the wake of André Couvreur's "Le Biocole" to the potential downside of their social repercussions.

In *La Flamme éternelle* (1931; tr. as "The Eternal Flame"), Couvreur's one-time collaborator Michel Corday describes the invention by a young physicist, François Thibault, of an almost limitless source of cheap energy by means of controlled atomic disintegration. When he tries to announce his discovery, however, he is informed by a journalist that the newspapers, whose owners are all involved in industrial conglomerates with heavy investments on oil and coal, will refuse to print his story, and that whatever methods of publicity he contrives to employ, those vested interests will do everything within their power to denigrate and suppress his invention. He is fortunate enough, however, to find a financier willing to go into partnership with him and to fight the inevitable war against the opposing forces intent on suppressing his new power cells. In the end, the two of them contrive to start and maintain production, but not without having to face monstrous slanders and mortal threats.

François Thibault, somewhat traumatized by the experience, but still convinced that the ultimate consequence of the universal availability of cheap energy will be euchronian, enabling the world to live happily in peace, finds that optimism disturbed again in a sequel set twenty years later in 1960, *Ciel Rose* (1933; tr. as "Pink Sky"). In that sequel, a fragile European Union begins to crumble under an assortment of political pressures, and the nations begin to lurch toward war, with corrupt and incompetent politicians seemingly unable to prevent it. François, however, comes up with a plan of his own, using a flood of energy to generate a new compound from the atmospheric gases: a kind of super-nitrous oxide whose psychotropic effects will far outstrip those of its humbler relative, giving everyone in the world a sudden brief dose of moral enlightenment.

In this case, the *deus ex machina* works, and François is able to broadcast a message of peace to the world while the world is, momentarily, in a condition to listen. War is averted and arbitration initiated, as well as several thorny individual subplots unraveling to everyone's satisfaction. Of all the items of *roman scientifique* produced in the interbellum period, none has a happier ending than *Ciel Rose*—or, indeed, could have a happier ending. The sweeping nature of the device necessary to bring about that ending, however, speaks volumes; it is nothing less than an all-encompassing miracle, and even the jargon that attributes it to a endeavor of science rather than direct action on the part of the deity admits that it is not merely a matter of seeing the world through rose-colored spectacles, but seeing it through an entire atmosphere saturated with a rosy tint.

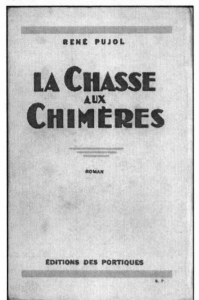

A similar case to that made in *La Flame éternelle* is set out with greater delicacy and an uncommonly deft wit in René Pujol's masterpiece, *La Chasse aux chimères* (1932; tr. as *The Chimerical Quest*). The story describes how a journalist finds an eccentric scientist, René Legrand, who, having been crippled during the war, has been working alone in a makeshift laboratory in Bordeaux for twenty years, and who has solved the ancient alchemical problem of turning lead into gold. His family and only servant do not take his claim seriously, but when the reporter realizes that it is true, he takes the news directly to his proprietor, Jacques Gellé, suggesting that there is a fortune to be made, but that it will not be easy, because Legrand is a misanthropic anarchist who is intent on giving his secret away to everyone as soon he has perfected an industrialized process that can make the transformation routinely on a large scale—not because he wants to help humankind, like François Thibault, but because he wants to turn society upside down by obliterating wealth.

Gellé, who prides himself on his ability to bend anyone to his will, believes that he can awaken the old man's atrophied avarice by introducing him to the good life in Paris, and hiring great surgeons to cure him of the effects of his war wound. In that quest he finds an ally in Legrand's beautiful but enigmatic daughter, Jeanne, with whom Gellé becomes infatuated, although his plans to seduce her are confounded by the fact that, for unfathomable reasons, she has accepted a marriage proposal from a depressingly bourgeois accountant.

Gellé's plan to corrupt Legrand does not run smoothly, however, and although the old man is enabled to walk again, after a fashion, life in Paris only serves to bring out his misanthropy more fully, and the campaign waged against the factory in which he is slowly refining his process aggravates him further. When the government, to whom he had refused to grant any special entitlement to the rewards of his discovery, steps in cynically to close the gold-manufacturing operation down "in the national interest," matters come to a head, and the workers at the factory riot, with mortal consequences.

Deeply disillusioned, Legrand retires to Bordeaux, still nursing the secret that everyone wants to pry out of him, but he finally volunteers to surrender it when Gellé and Jeanne, liberated by her fiancé's death in the riot, reveal their marriage plans to him. He promises to give Gellé the secret as a wedding-present, and presumably does, although a hint of ambiguity is left in that regard, while the deadly effects of the poisoned chalice continue to unfold, in what is perhaps the most neatly balanced tragicomedy of the period.

The disenchantment with the promise of technology developed in a quasi-symbolic fashion by René Pujol was, however, only one side of the coin; a similarly emblematic account of imperiled technological dreams, in this case of a more Vernian stripe, is contained in Raymond Desorties' *La Tétrabie* (1933), a reverent account of a huge multipurpose vehicle capable of carrying its passengers over land, under water and through the air.

The basic narrative schema of unappreciated invention can, of course, be played out as pure tragedy rather than tragicomedy, as in Régis Messac's first substantial exercise in *roman scientifique*, "Le Miroir flexible (1933-34 in *Les Primaires* as by "Columbus North"; book 2009; tr. as "The Flexible Mirror"). The story is framed by a narrative in which the narrator explains how he encountered a reclusive woman known as "the old spinster" in a boarding-house in Esterel, and received from her a manuscript relating her experiences many years before, in a small town in Alabama, where her father, Joseph Favennens, an inventor, had bought a cheap plot of semi-desert land in order to install his laboratory.

Already regarded with disapproval by the Fundamentalist preachers of the town by virtue of his atheism, and by the local Ku Klux Klan because of his lack of racial bigotry, Favennens becomes the object of a more intense hostility in the wake of the apparent murder of a local vagrant, when rumors of a "giant serpent" cast a shadow of suspicion over his activities. When the "serpent" disrupts a Klan meeting, causing a stampede in which there is another fatality, a detective called into investigate the case sets a trap for the monster, and succeeds in "killing" it—only for it to be revealed that it is a living machine constructed by Favennens, a functionally-designed automation capable of learning and primitive intelligence. When he proudly refuses to be run out of town he is murdered by a mob, enraged by his alleged blasphemy in daring not only to compete with the creator but to claim that he has done a better job.

Had Messac not been the editor of a magazine, like Henri Austruy, the likelihood is that "Le Miroir flexible" would never have been published; there was no other likely outlet for it at that time, and it is a fervently combative and bitterly angry story. Precisely for that reason, however, it is one of the most powerful works of speculative fiction produced in the 1930s, and its fugitive existence prior to its resurrection in 2009 illustrates the fact that the difficulties faced by Cyrano de Bergerac in pioneering scientifically-inspired *contes philosophiques* had not disappeared even in three centuries. The agents of the Holy Office had lost their teeth in the interim, but the sentiments that inspired them had not lost their avidity to bite, and although the primary target of stories like "Le Miroir flexible" was religious intolerance, that was only one of the sources of potential hostility and disaffection likely to hobble the circulation of sophisticated *contes philosophiques*. When they wanted to employ fiction as a means of dramatizing and spreading their message, the champions of technology and the science behind it were not working in a benign, or even a neutral, environment.

The difficulties faced by writers in marketing *roman scientifique* are further illustrated by the last of Maurice Renard's works in that field to be published. "**Le Maître de la lumière**" (tr. as "The Master of Light") published as a serial in 1933 but unreprinted in book form until 1990, when it was included in an omnibus of his *Romans et contes fantastiques*. A work bearing that title was one of those that he planned to write before being called up to fight in the war, and the structure of the published work strongly suggests that he had written a substantial part of the narrative—but the published version inserts that text within a murder mystery, Renard having gone over by then to the more-or-less exclusive production of crime stories, that being the only way he could make a living from his pen. As with Théo Varlet, the family fortune that had supported him before the war had been literally destroyed, in his case by the invading Germans rather than Russian revolutionaries.

As in André Couvreur's account of "Le Cas de la baronne Sasoitsu," the murder mystery in "Le Maître de la lumière" is finally cleared up by means of an exotic technology—in this case the exploitation of a strange discovery rather than a machine constructed from scratch. The enclosed story gives an account of the discovery in 1814 on a volcanic island in the Indian Ocean of a transparent mineral that has the property of slowing down the light passing through it, so that the passage can take many years. A thick window-pane of that long-lost material installed in a room in a château eventually reveals its property by emitting letting through light on a dark night from a presently-unilluminated room, permitting characters in 1929 to realize that there might be layers within the pane containing the record of an ancient murder, committed on the same day as a notorious attempt to assassinate Louis-Philippe in 1833.

The separated layers of the pane do, indeed, allow the murder to be witnessed, but do not allow the face of the murderer to be glimpsed, and the remark made by the victim on seeing him has to be deduced, with difficulty, by a lip-reader. The investigators manage to recover a great deal of other relevant data, but the final piece of the puzzle is only revealed by an additional freak of chance.

As an intricate murder mystery, the novel benefits greatly from Renard's meticulous planning and rewriting, and it is a fine, if highly unusual, example of its genre. As an item of *roman scientifique* however, it looks like an opportunity lost—an idea that could have been developed very differently, with a different kind of ingenuity, to reveal a whole spectrum of interesting possibilities. Indeed, when the idea was coincidentally recapitulated in the 1960s by the British science fiction writer Bob Shaw, he was able to develop an excellent story series around the fundamental notion of "slow glass," in which the wholesale detection of murders is only a single element in a much greater pattern.

Maurice Renard was fully capable, intellectually and artistically, of doing something similar, but he could not even consider the possibility, because he knew that there was no market for it. Perhaps he had, in fact, written a full version of a scientific romance based on the fragment enclosed in the published version of "Le Maître de la lumière," but had been unable to sell it, just as he had been unable to sell the earlier versions of *Un homme chez les microbes*, but whether or not that was the case, the fundamental argument remains sound: between the two phases of the Great War, *roman scientifique* was a fugitive genre even in the lower strata of the marketplace, easily available as a field in which to work only to writers of conventional thrillers working with familiar story-arcs, the intrinsic thrust of which dissuaded them strongly from engaging with the further implications of the technologies that they invoked merely to destroy.

Renard did at least manage to publish some of the generic work that he did in the interbellum period. Some writers who had shown similar promise before the Great War suffered an even more complete eclipse thereafter. Jean de Quirielle, although he lived into the 1960s, never recovered the imaginative flair he had shown in *L'Oeuf de verre* and *La Joconde retrouvée*, although he did publish the downmarket thriller *Les Voleurs de cerveaux* [The Brain-Stealers] (1920) and one further relatively lackluster generic novel, as well as two dramatic works of a naturalistic variety. Perhaps he had simply lost interest, but it is also possible that he simply could not find any viable channel of expression.

Another writer that it is convenient to mention here, because his most important *roman scientifique* followed up a theme twice mentioned previously in

this section, is "André Maurois" (Émile Herzog, 1885-1967), author of *La Machine à lire les pensées* (1937; tr. as *The Thought-Reading Machine*), which tells the story of a French professor of literature offered a job at an American University. There he finds himself living near a physicist who has invented the eponymous device, the psychograph, which can detect the vocalized but unpronounced thoughts constituting the stream of consciousness. After testing it on the narrator, the inventor lends it to him so that he can try it out on his wife—an indiscretion that causes some alarm and dissent, but which they manage to get past.

After further testing—including the obligatory examination of a murderer who has falsely protested his innocence—the inventor decides to market his device, and asks the narrator whether he will supervise its marketing in France. The narrator agrees, but is glad to hand the responsibility over to someone more qualified and enthusiastic when he can. He is thus able to remain a marginal observer when the psychograph fails to take off in France, and proves to be a brief fad even in America. Maurois thus dissents from the fundamental argument of *Le Lynx*, "Nounlegos" and "Le Cas de la baronne Sasoitsu," suggesting that such a machine would not have the far-reaching consequences that Michael Corday, André Couvreur and Raoul Bigot readily assumed, on the grounds that the thoughts people frame in their consciousness are superficial and less consequential than might be imagined. It is, one character suggests, necessary to beware of mistaking reverie for will.

Maurois had written a number of previous works in the genre, all of them similarly ironic but considerably shorter. He had begun a series of episodes of future history with *Le Chapitre suivant* (1927; tr. as *The Next Chapter: The War Against the Moon* in Kegan Paul, Trench & Trubner's "Today & Tomorrow" series of futurological pamphlets), a political fantasy in which an attempt to foster political unity between France and England by giving them an imaginary common enemy to fight goes awry when missiles fired tokenistically at the Moon bring forth reprisals. The series was continued in *Deux fragments d'une histoire universelle, 1992* [Two Fragments of a World History] (1929), but then abandoned. In *Le Peseur d'âmes* (1931; tr. as *The Weigher of Souls*) a scientist who has found a means of trapping souls after death, and has discovered that mingling compatible souls can produce a luminosity supposedly reflective of bliss—recapitulating a theme developed by Théophile Gautier in *Spirite* (1865) and also featured briefly in Odette Dulac's *[Amour]...tel qu'il est*—commits suicide in order to be thus reunited with his late wife, but is frustrated in his desire by a laboratory accident.

All of Maurois' ventures into speculative fiction belong to a minimizing school of *roman scientifique*, which seeks to reassure readers with the idea that there really is nothing to worry about in the advance of science and technology, because even the most ambitious plans will ultimately amount to very little. It is not obvious, however, that any of them makes a case that could stand up to reasoned objection, and *Le Machine à lire les pensées*, although considerably more detailed than the others and written with the elegance that one would expect of an Academician, is surely unlikely to convince intellectual readers that their conscious thoughts are essentially unimportant and insignificant, or even that the author might believe that of his own thoughts.

The decision to relegate the unmasking of a murderer to a mere passing mention rather than regarding it as a matter of importance, as Maurois' predecessors had, is perhaps a curious one, given that a reliable lie-detector might seem to have considerable potential as a instrument of the investigation and prosecution of all kinds of crime, and hence have potentially far-reaching social effects, but the novel is undoubtedly interesting in its unorthodoxy and its determined attempts to challenge the seemingly-obvious with considerable argumentative artistry.

Yet another writer who had built a solid reputation for work outside the genre before involving himself in it was Jacques Spitz, although his venture into it was no mere matter of dabbling, and his sense of satirical irony was a good deal sharper than Maurois', Ernest Pérochon's or Henri-Jacques Proumen's. Spitz published five naturalistic novels before determinedly changing the strategy of his work in *L'Agonie du globe* (1936; tr. as *Sever the Earth*) a political satire that uses a rather implausible cosmic accident to split the globe in two, so that the hemisphere containing the Americas draws slowly apart from the one containing Europe, modeling their cultural divergence, until one of them collides with the Moon. Once having made the move however, he stuck with it, and became one of the most substantial contributors to *roman scientifique* during

the 1930s and 1940s.

Spitz followed up *L'Agonie de globe* with a more elaborate account of *Les Évadés de l'an 4000* [The Refugees of the Year 4000] (1936), in which a new ice age causes a new ideological division between the advocates of "troglodytisme" who favor a retreat underground, as in Gabriel Tarde's "Fragment d'histoire future," and "aristocratisme," whose adherents want to develop interplanetary travel as a means of migration and escape. The former philosophy obtains the upper hand, forcing the rocket scientist who serves as the protagonist of the story to work clandestinely, becoming an outlaw and then an exile. In Spitz's version of the subterranean retreat, in contrast to Tarde's, far from leading to a utopian society of sorts, the retreat leads to the dystopian domination of a technocratic dictatorship, but it is an essentially sterile venture bound to fail, and in the end, the final hope for humankind rests with the exiled scientist, who finally succeeds in engineering a flight to Venus for his nephew and the latter's fiancé, where they might perhaps become a new Adam and Eve.

La Guerre des mouches (1938) is another political satire, set in a nearer future but is even more garish in its facilitating device, in which human civilization is conquered by intelligent flies that have acquired the advantage of a hive mind by mutation and learned to practice efficient bacteriological warfare. The hero of the story, the entomologist Juste-Evariste Magne, is sent to Indochina with a scientific mission to investigate the causes of an epidemic. He identifies the culprits as a tropical variety of *Stomoxys calcitrans* (the stable fly) and is the first to realize that those spreading the disease by means of their bites have developed a kind of group intelligence, and that they are rapidly involving a miniature technology that will make them infinitely more dangerous than his superiors are prepared to recognize.

While Magne is vilified for his assumed eccentricity, the flies make inexorable progress in the tropics, spreading slowly westwards, and by the time that the authorities in Europe realize that the flies have developed methods of climatic adaptation that place the temperate zones within their range it is too late to mount anything but a desperate and doomed rearguard action while the remnants of human civilization retreat northwards. In a defiant refusal of a conventional normalizing ending, Magne ends up as one of a handful of survivors seemingly maintained in a kind of reservation by the all-conquering flies, presumably for the purposes of scientific study.

L'Homme élastique (1938) is an even more imaginatively ambitious story, whose first part is presented in the form of a diary kept by Dr. Flohr, a physicist working on a method for manipulating the void within atoms in order to shrink or expand the electronic orbits, thus increasing or reducing the size of objects composed by the atoms in question. Flohr gradually develops a way to apply the method to living beings without killing them, and a system by which their life can be maintained thereafter in spite of the incompatibility between their molecules and those of their environment.

Working in the shadow of an imminent second world war, Flohr loyally offers his technology to the government for military application. His initial suggestion is to use it to make soldiers larger, although the increase in size is not associated with an increase in strength, but it is quickly realized that the real strategic advantages will be obtained by making them smaller. The regiments of miniaturized soldiers that he creates, equipped with miniaturized explosives that retain all their blast force, enable France to win a swift victory over Germany, and Flohr can then settle down to find and develop peace-time applications for his technology.

The second part of the story is told in the form of the memoirs of Flohr's daughter Ethel, who becomes his collaborator in the second phase of his enterprise, developing ingenious cosmetic applications of the technology while he concentrates on developing its industrial applications. As those applications proliferate, however, gradually overcoming initial opposition from various religions, the human race enters a new phase of evolution, in which adapted humans, whether large or smaller than their "natural" kin, become politically dominant, reorganizing society and politics in such a way that the unadapted minority are marginalized. Flohr, personally conservative outside of his scientific obsession, continues to refuse adaptation while the marginalization of the unadapted slowly gives way to active persecution, paradoxically torn between his generalized commitment to the cause of progress and his stubborn resistance to personal "flohrization."

L'Expérience du docteur Mops (1939; tr. as "Dr. Mops' Experiment") echoes André Maurois' most substantial venture into speculative fiction in endeavoring to subject another of the classic psychic powers, precognition, to scrupulous rational consideration. The scientist featured in the title is a psychic researcher converted to positivism, who has found a means of altering the brain of his laboratory assistant in such a way that that he is living seventy-two seconds ahead of normal time, and thus able to communicate events shortly before they happen—a margin adequate to confer a winning advantage at a roulette table. Naturally, enough, however, he wants to extend the margin in order to recover information from further ahead, permitting more adventurous gambling. The narrator, who takes pity on the subject and attempts to rescue him, fails to do so, and finds his own life afflicted by tragedy thereafter, while the experiment proceeds uninterrupted, only to reach a frustrating conclusion.

By this time, Spitz had moved away considerably, by degrees, from the initial agenda of employing devices borrowed from *roman scientifique* to enhance political satires, and had obviously become fascinated by the ideas themselves, which had moved to center stage, and by their psychological corollaries, which moved his works in the direction of existential fantasy—a development that continued in the 1940s in works beyond the scope of the present project.

Precisely because it has no terminus, in fact, but constitutes a rudely interrupted narrative, the above account of Spitz's career makes an entirely suitably end-point for the present preliminary analysis, which is of necessity truncated. Several of the other authors whose works are discussed in this final chapter also continued their endeavors beyond the Second World War, including Henri-Jacques Proumen, and the genre, viewed as an admittedly-untidy but by no means incoherent whole, did continue an independent development for a while, before being effectively swamped and absorbed by the influx of American science fiction, the influence of which had already begun as a trickle, but which became an irresistible flood in the 1950s. That is, however, a story best left to other hands, for reasons of practicality.

CONCLUSION: The Ambitions and Achievements of *Roman Scientifique*

When seeking a suitably symbolic title for the companion project to this one, which tracks the development of British scientific romance, I eventually settled on *New Atlantis: A Narrative History of Scientific Romance*, because the title adopted as a figurehead seemed to have a useful significance in that usage.

To begin with, Francis Bacon's *New Atlantis* was one of the earliest literary works that had an evident affinity with the genre that was eventually to be identified and characterized, in association with exemplars provided by H. G. Wells, in terms of its subject-matter—the prospects of science as a factor in potential social change—and its innovative quality, its attempt to move into literary terrain where no one had ventured before.

Secondly, however fantastic it might have been as a literal depiction of a hypothetical society, the prospectus that *New Atlantis* set out for a society that had not merely been transformed by the advancement of science, in a way that promoted the wellbeing of its population, but was deliberately organized in such a way as to pursue and promote that advancement, seemed apt as a metaphorical depiction of a literary genre centered on the advancement of science, deliberately seeking ways to put speculation based on that notion to fruitful use.

Those were the two implications that it seemed appropriate to nail to the mast of a historical exploration of the genre. There was, however, a third feature of the original that was less triumphant as an advertisement: Francis Bacon's *New Atlantis* had remained incomplete and had only been published posthumously; it might very easily have remained non-existent. On the other hand, that last point was not without a certain wry priority, because it served to illustrate the difficulties faces by many of the writers working in the genre under consideration, not only in developing the new narrative strategies that they would need in order to make the most of their innovative materials, but also in facing up to the fact that, even if they succeeded, it was highly likely that no one would appreciate what they had done sufficiently to publish it or read it, let alone applaud it.

In seeking an apposite title for the present project, the most attractive option seemed to be to modify the title of Bernard de Fontenelle's *Entretiens sur la pluralité des mondes* by borrowing an extra adjective from the title of Camille Flammarion's *Les Mondes imaginaires et les mondes réels*, on the grounds that it hybridized one of the most important precursors of the genre with one of the first attempts to map the history of one of its components. It places the power and utility of the imagination at the heart of the enterprise, and also carries over from Fontenelle's endeavor an implication of clever contest: of opposing entrenched and unreasonable prejudice with elegance and expertise.

There is, however, one sense in which that composite reference differs markedly from the other. Both *Entretiens sur la pluralité des mondes* and *Les Mondes imaginaires et les mondes réels* were very successful books. They were, in fact, best-sellers in the context of their day. They were completed and published while their authors were in the best of health, assisting them in the origination of glittering careers. In that regard, they were very exceptional. *Roman scientifique* did have its best-sellers, of course; the three keys works by Jules Verne that prompted the appropriation of the term and the alteration of its meaning—*Voyage au centre de la terre*, the composite *De la terre à la lune/Autour de la lune*, and *Vingt mille lieues sous les mers*—were all best-sellers, and if those books had not been so spectacularly successful, they would not have demanded the redefinition of the label that was adapted to describe them. They were not, however, typical of the hundreds of works whose similarity in terms of their subject-matter invited inclusion in the category they defined.

In terms of that particular symbolism, the work that probably offers the best representation of the genre the present project calls *roman scientifique* is a book that attempted to conceive a similar genre in slightly different terms: Félix Bodin's *Le Roman de l'avenir*. It was not published posthumously, although that was a close-run thing, but it is something of a mess, having been hurriedly put together as a portmanteau text by a writer who knew that he was not going to be able to bring it to anything resembling a satisfactory condition, but who was desperate to get something into print in order to establish a claim of priority. Bodin was not the first person to end up in that predicament.

Cyrano de Bergerac, who produced by far the most important and influential precursor of the genre in *L'Autre monde*, battled with all his might to finish it while on his death-bed. He appears to have succeeded, but his success was partly cancelled out because half of the manuscript was stolen and destroyed by someone who thought it ought not to exist, and the rest was only published posthumously in bowlerized form.

Nicolas Restif de La Bretonne, who produced by far the most adventurous and ambitious work in the genre written in the eighteenth century similarly spend his last few active years desperately trying to get the relevant work he had done into print. In the end, he managed to get part of it into print—the part that was, unfortunately, still a messy and unsatisfactory portmanteau text—while the more coherent and presumably better part, *L'Enclos et les oiseaux*, was lost forever, because Restif had exhausted all his resources publishing previous works and nobody else cared enough to preserve it.

The surviving fractions of those three endeavors—the incomplete *L'Autre monde*, the unsupplemented and unsatisfactory *Les Posthumes* and the incomplete *Le Roman de l'avenir*—are the truly revealing exemplars of the genre retrospectively assembled as the ancestry of Vernian *roman scientifique*. They are its true classics, its hard-won and partial victories over adversity—or, more accurately, the survivors that made its defeat by adversity a little less than total.

The commercial and critical successes that were obtained by a handful of works associated with the genre by virtue of their content, whether retrospective or subsequent to Verne's breakthrough, should not deflect attention away from the fact that *roman scientifique* was from the very beginning, and remained until the end—or until the present day, if it still makes sense to differentiate such a genre within the field of international science fiction—a direly difficult and ingrate genre in which to work. Almost everyone who attempted to work in it during the period covered by the present study of its evolution, however deliberately and conscientiously they did so, either died trying or gave up in despair. The situation of its writers was no better in the twentieth century than the seventeenth, eighteenth or nineteenth, as the careers of its most important contributors in that era—including but by no means restricted to J.-H. Rosny, Maurice Renard, Théo Varlet, André Couvreur and André Arnyvelde—very readily illustrate. The wonder is that the genre existed at all; the fact that its produce was occasionally brilliant is a bonus.

The reason the genre exists, in spite of the pressures operating against it, is spelled out clearly enough in final pages of *Les Posthumes*—which is arguably the single most important work ever to be produced in the genre, because of what it achieves, imaginatively and idiosyncratically, in spite of being a chaotic mess in literary terms—when the writer of the "letters from the tomb" finally comes clean and admits that his real purpose in writing is not to soothe the grief of his beloved wife at all, but to preserve something of himself: "Thoughts are the particles of the soul, and woe betide the man who does not leave behind those that are dear to him!"

Ostensibly, Félix Bodin wrote a prospectus for the *roman futuriste*, and Jules Verne, early in his career, dreamed of writing a new kind of *roman de la science*, because they thought that those were imagined genres whose time had come, genres that might make a significant contribution to literary evolution, and might have a bright future. Their real motivation, however, was the fact that the ideas were dear to them, and they want to express them, at least in order to leave them behind. That does not mean that the other arguments had no weight—it was, indeed the case that those genres' times had come, even if, by and large, the times gave them a welcome that was cold, at best—but it serves to emphasize the fact that the authors who created and shaped the genre were very heavily invested in it. It was not just that they cared deeply about the works they produced, but that they thought them vital particles of their soul.

Restif de La Bretonne reduced himself to beggary publishing his autobiography, to which he tacked on his philosophy as a supplement, but that did not complete his obsessive mission of self-preservation, and it can be presumed that he died a deeply disappointed man, because he knew that *L'Enclos et les oiseaux* was dying with him. If people could really turn in their graves, and the dead really knew what was happening in the world that had briefly contained them, it can also be presumed that Cyrano de Bergerac would have been exceedingly restless in his, knowing that *L'Étincelle* had been callously and conclusively snuffed out.

Nevertheless, *roman scientifique* does exist. It might only be a shadow of what its creators had dreamed of making it, and that must surely be a subject for regret on the part of its admirers, but such is the fate of most human endeavor, and there is, at the end of the day, no alternative but to cultivate whatever garden we have. Micromégas might have handed the theologian a book with blank pages, but the pages of *Micromégas* are not only full but packed with meaning, implication and irony—including the deceptive title-page, which was compelled to lie about when and where it was published—and that is true of the genre that it helped to found and exemplify. The first and most important ambition of that genre was to exist, in spite of the difficulties, and it does exist; that, in itself, is a significant achievement.

One of the ironies of the existence and nature of the genre is that the achievement for which most readers have looked to the genre—especially the fraction of it that constitutes Félix Bodin's genre of *roman futuriste*—is one that its authors never actually attempted, and in which they would have been bound to fail if it had: that of predicting the present from which observers could now look back at it. Anyone looking to it for evidence of prophetic foresight would be bound to reckon the genre, with a few curious exceptions, a failure.

Commentators starting from that point of view generally react to that failure with disappointment, although they take delight in calling attention to the rare exceptions. In that, they are perhaps foolish, not so much because they are asking for the impossible as because their scoring system is upside-down. Just as the true measure of a good memory is not so much what it retains as what it succeeds in winnowing out by the valuable process of forgetfulness, the true measure of good prophecy is not the fraction of its vision that come true but the fraction that was prevented from coming true by the timely issuing of the prophecy. It is in the anticipation and consequent avoidance of potential pitfalls that the real value of rational foresight lies.

That does not simply mean that dystopian fiction is more helpful in steering a course into the problematic future than eutopian fiction, although a case could certainly be made out for that, but that the real merit of eutopian fiction is not to provide a recipe for a better world but to provide a stern challenge to the existing one. The real point of Louis-Sébastien Mercier's vision of Paris in the year 2440 was not to offer a blueprint for a nicer city but to demonstrate, by imagining the erasure of its faults, the true depth of the sink of iniquity that the Paris of the 1770s had become, and did not need to be. It is not a cheerful work; it is a bitterly angry and furiously aggressive work. By comparison, Émile Souvestre's *Le Monde tel qu'il sera* is much more cheerful—as evidenced by its jocular tone—and rather smug in its particular brand of schadenfreude. It too presents a challenge, but one that is not quite as stark.

In the same way, there is little in either of the pioneering futuristic fantasies that Charles Nodier and Félix Bodin produced in the 1830s that might be deemed "prophetic" in the vulgar sense of anticipating actual future developments; Bodin's flying machines bear hardly any resemblance to twentieth-century flying machines and Nodier's Patagonian food-technology bears hardly any resemblance to twentieth-century food technology. Such prosaic quibbles are, however, of no real relevance to either exercise. In their fundamental contentions—remarkably enough, given their contrasted opinions—both writers were absolutely right. The quest for the perfect man has, thus far, failed dismally, and without him, the prospect of a perfect world seems rather ridiculous; while we remain fallible, the social contract can only pander to our fallibilities.

Thus, Bodin's attempt to describe in detail a world produced by progress was bound to falter and stumble over its own inherent uncertainties, while Nodier's attempt to paint an utterly decadent and grotesquely nightmarish future was bound to falter and stumble because once the decadence, the grotesquerie and the nightmare have been depicted, the question still remains of what to do about it: where to go in search of an exit. Both authors escaped the predicament, as we all do, by dying, but their successors in the genre had no alternative but to pick up the baton and do their best to run with it.

In spite of the failure of their vulgar prophecies, it is manifestly obvious that in a more general sense, at least in the interim separating our present from theirs, the actual pattern of history favored the euchronian groping of Mercier and Bodin rather than the dystopian anxieties of Nodier and Souvestre. The social conditions of Paris had already been considerably ameliorated since the 1770s even in the 1830s, no matter how unhappy the Parisians of the 1830s still were with their existential situation, and they were further ameliorated in the course of the next century, no matter how unhappy the Parisians of the 1930s were with theirs. Much of that social progress had been due to technological progress and its political and economic facilitation.

To the extent that social ills had been magnified, so had social remedies— and the fact that the literary endeavors of the 1930s often refused to acknowledge or applaud those ameliorations, often retaining the same bitter anger in their futuristic anticipations as Mercier and the same nightmarish grotesquerie as Nodier, does not signify that no progress had been made and no amelioration achieved. To some extent, it merely serves to confirm Bodin's observation that the vast majority of *littérateurs*, whether they are trying to flatter their audience or only themselves, owe an entirely natural allegiance to "antiprosaicism," and hence, at least covertly, to the enemies of progress. It also signifies, however, that no matter how often the baton of progress is handed on, and no matter how far those who run with it succeed in carrying it forward, the track still extends in front of them, with no winning post yet in sight. The ground covered only matters to historians; what matters to the runners is the ground still to cover.

Bodin commented in his preface to *Le Roman de l'avenir* that *mélioriste* views seemed to have replaced *péjoriste* ones, at least in some measure, by 1834, and he evidently regarded that as a sort of progress in itself. Seen from his viewpoint, it was. *Péjorisme*, which locates the Golden Age in the past and views the dynamics of social change in terms of deterioration, is intrinsically linked to the kinds of mythical past acknowledged by oral cultures, which have no history and therefore imagine what is gone as a magical era, relative to which the unmagical present is bound to seem a trifle jejune. *Méliorisme*, by contrast, is a product of historical perspective, and the awareness of a measurable improvement of technical and social means that can be tracked across time by means of written records and archaeological excavations. If writing and scientific enquiry represent progress, therefore—and it is hard to deny that they do—then the idea of progress, and discussion of progress, in fiction as well as politics, are indeed evident symptoms of progress.

The notion that future progress can be estimated simply by extrapolating the curve calculated from the measurement of past progress, all the way to "perfection", is clearly false, even if the notion of its likely extrapolation to some further extent is not quite as silly as Charles Nodier thought. Because that curve is the product of human effort rather than any kind of external destiny, it can only be extrapolated as far as human effort is willing to take it—and that, as Bodin quickly realized when he began to explore the notion by the only technical means at his disposal, is probably not very far. As Bodin observed, and dramatized as best he could, that is not so much because the world is too abundantly supplied with ambitious Philomaques and power-crazed Hurlubleus (although it is), or even with sarcastic Nodiers, but rather because its Philirènes and Berniquets are mostly sane enough to doubt the grandeur of their own merits, and to avoid going to ridiculous extremes.

The real purpose of the present project, I am perfectly ready to admit, is a feeble and perhaps ridiculous hope of leaving behind a few particles of thought that seem precious to me, although the inevitable conclusion of the exercise is that they are unlikely to seem so to many other people—but that does not affect the fact that a part of its ostensible purpose is, in effect, to examine the extent to which Félix Bodin's messy and incomplete prospectus for a *roman futuriste* was, in fact, carried forward. To what extent did the novel of the future really become the novel of the future?

In the sense of its prestige, or even its marketability, clearly, it did not. It began as something marginal, not merely unloved but widely loathed, and in the more pretentious and prestigious strata of the literary marketplace it is still regarded with dire suspicion if not with frank contempt, partly because of the fact that such popular success as it has achieved has mostly been won in the lower strata, and in media generally regarded as essentially despicable.

Furthermore, if appearances could be trusted, it would not be difficult to argue that the moderate level of commercial viability that *roman futuriste* has achieved has, by and large, been won by compromise, if not by treason: ideas and images initially developed with serious purpose have generally been appropriated and deployed in the dishonest interests of cheap melodrama. Hypothetical technological invention has largely been used as a source of narrative threats to be demolished; investigations of the superior sanity of the scientific mind have generally been perverted into caricaturish images of "mad scientists" similarly ripe for narrative demolition; the end of the world has generally been deployed either as a ready wellspring of pathos or as a bugbear to heighten the stakes of narrow escapes; the possible betterment of human being or human society has generally been employed as an ingeniously and insidiously poisoned chalice. A case can also be made, however, for the contention that that appearance should not be taken entirely at face value.

It is perhaps important to realize that *roman scientifique* is an inherently paradoxical genre. When the term first came into frequent use, one commentator complained that it was an oxymoronic atrocity that ought not to be tolerated. He was missing the point; it was because the term is oxymoronic that it was useful, and perhaps invaluable. Just as no map of the world can be reckoned complete if it does not include Utopia, no Comtean taxonomy of the sciences can be complete unless it contains pataphysics, and no investigation of truth can be conscientious it if omits the analysis of fantasy.

The only genuinely prophetic kind of fiction that can exist is historical fiction, because we already know exactly what future the characters are bound for, and precisely what their endeavors can achieve. By the same token, the only genuinely prophetic kind of speculative fiction is prehistoric fantasy, because we know—more or less—what kind of beings it was into which the hypothetical protohumans featured therein were in the process of evolving. By contrast, we have no idea what kind of future will actually emerge from the present or what kind of superhuman being might evolve from the protosuperhumans we might be reckoned to be, if we are somehow fortunate enough to avoid extinction. Insofar as imaginative endeavor is directed toward that kind of anticipation, it is essentially and fundamentally impotent, as prophecy—but only as prophecy. Its potency, potential and vitality lie elsewhere, in another dimension: the dimension of uncertainty created by the fact that we do not know and cannot know what our present endeavors can or might achieve, or where our evolution might take us.

If we did know, all our stories would be as mundane and predictable as most of the stories we tell one another strive to be, because stories, for the most part, represent the world as we would like it to be—familiar, knowable, manageable and always capable of normalization, if only by *deus ex machina*—rather than the world as it actually is: uncertain, unpredictable, dangerous and collapsible; or, to put it another way, ever vulnerable to irretrievable abnormalization. Literary works that attempt to represent that kind of world are, in a sense, not so much stories as antistories, rebellious not only against the fundamental fiction that the world is the way conventional fiction represents it to be, but against the conventions of fiction itself, ill-fitted to commonplace story-arcs and familiar systems of narrative closure. *Roman scientifique* is not only self-contradictory because science, as truth, is not supposed to have any truck with fiction, but because fiction, no matter what its essential hypocrisies might contend, is not supposed to have any truck with truth.

"Realistic" or "naturalistic" fiction lies when it pretends to represent the world as it is. Most heterocosmic fiction—the bulk of the fiction of the *merveilleux*—lies too, but at least it is honest in admitting that it consists entirely of lies, and thus leaves a margin in which the ungraspable truth can and must exist. The fraction of heterocosmic fiction that does not care to capitulate with the demand that it consist entirely of conventional lies—much of which belongs to *roman scientifique* within the operational definition of the present project—is in a genuinely anomalous situation, aspiring to be neither one thing nor the other, but somehow to operate in an unexcluded middle.

Most commentators, in contemplating Alfred Jarry's (posthumous and incomplete) account of the exploits of Dr. Faustroll, pataphysician, have drawn the inference from it that fiction is capable, in some measure, of substituting for pataphysics, of occupying that paradoxical gap in the spectrum of knowledge, much as Zolaesque *roman experimental* was capable, in some measure, of substituting for psychological science. Clearly, they are correct. But it is possible, and perhaps desirable, to go beyond that, and to see *Gestes et opinions du docteur Faustroll pataphysicien* as an exercise in patafiction, a particularly self-aware antistory within a whole genre of antistories that set out to challenge the fundamental lie of fiction: the lie that contends that the world as it appears through the lens of conventional fiction is "the world as it is."

As every Voltairean philosopher knows, the world, as it really is, is not only weirder than we imagine but weirder than we can imagine, precisely because it is ever changing, always in the process of becoming something else, something unknowable by definition. Voltaire was not the first person to endeavor to represent that knowledge in *contes philosophiques*—a term he chose precisely because of its oxymoronic character—but he did make significant progress in the promotion of that knowledge and in exploring the narrative techniques that might be useful for its further development and representation. It is partly because some of his work was knowingly making a contribution to a genre of speculative fiction, following models provided by Cyrano de Bergerac and Bernard de Fontenelle, among others, that he was able to make that progress, and partly because he added a fraction of his own endeavor to the genre in question that it was able to continue making its subsequent progress, with his most significant exemplar, *Micromégas*, added to its predecessors as an exemplar and a source of inspiration.

If *roman scientifique* is seen, fundamentally and essentially, as a species of antistories rather than merely one more genre of stories, only differentiated from the others by its subject-matter, the difficulties to which so many of its practitioners were subject become more understandable, as does their frequent conviction that they were not only doing something different, but something precious. The difficulties are inherent in the nature of the genre because, for practical purposes, in order to survive in a marketplace defined by stories, antistories have no alternative but to masquerade as stories, at least by adopting light and cursory camouflage, but very often going so deeply undercover that it becomes difficult to distinguish them, by means of superficial appearance, from genuine (which is to say, false) stories. As long as they stick to their real mission, however—the mission of depicting the world not as fiction conventionally represents it but as something essentially uncertain, alien, contingent and changeable, they can never be fully absorbed into the fundamental lie.

There are, of course, other species of antistories as well as those belonging to *roman scientifique*. If all of them were lined up, they would still be far outnumbered by stories, but they are often esteemed more highly by the intelligentsia because the self-appointed members of the intelligentsia nowadays like to think of themselves as Voltairean. *Roman scientifique* is often excluded from that esteem because the members of the self-appointed intelligentsia, by and large, also like to think of themselves as enemies of whimsy (like Voltaire's contemporaries, they would have reckoned his tragedies far more worthy than his *contes*) and they often hate science, because authentic science is too difficult for minds that pride themselves falsely on intelligence to grasp.

In fact, most of the "science" in *roman scientifique* is pure nonsense, which is why some authentic scientists hate the genre too, but they too are missing the point. *Roman scientifique* that extrapolates authentic science in a rationally plausible fashion certainly has an admirable intellectual elegance, which even attains a kind of genius on occasion, but *roman scientifique* based on pure nonsense is obviously not devoid of effect, and it would be mistaken to dismiss that effect as merely mistaken. Not only is there no need for intelligent people to be enemies of whimsy, but there are perfectly good reasons why they might and should be fond of it. It does not go anywhere, in the sense of having an intellectual destination, but it does go *away* from the fundamental lie that the world envisaged by conventional mundane fiction really is the world as our existential situation ought to compel us to experience it.

Fiction, like consciousness itself, is a defense against the horror of reality; that is why it exists and why it is, in a sense, good for us—but it is also good for us not to become too complacent, and that is why antifiction, or patafiction, also exists, and why *roman scientifique* can and does make a valuable contribution to the great tradition of antistories. Insofar as ongoing social change does depend on the progress of science and technology—and no one but an idiot can any longer refuse to admit that it does—the contribution made by science-based speculative fiction, even if what it represents as science is pure nonsense, has a particularly precious contribution to make to the evolving body of antifiction. All of its leading practitioners have sensed that preciousness, however they have represented it to themselves, and many of its readers have sensed it too.

It follows, however, from that interpretation of the genre, that any history of *roman scientifique*, or any survey of the contemporary condition of its descendant genre, whatever label is stuck on it, is bound to reveal a vast patchwork of awkward chimeras, of errors and frustrations, of heroic but ultimately unsuccessful attempts and paradoxical partial successes.

That is what this attempted survey of the genre's early evolution has revealed, very obviously, but it would be wrong to regard that exposition simply as a record of failure. It is a record replete with tragedies, all of which are regrettable from the viewpoint of the historian and the lover of the genre, but it could not have been otherwise and probably never will be otherwise, because of the oxymoronic nature of the genre and the paradoxical nature of its fictional enterprises. The wonder is that *roman scientifique* existed at all between the eighteenth century and the 1930s, and that it was sometimes done well—with authentic genius in its finest examples, along with a necessary hint of madness—and that even in its tawdrier examples there is very often a valuable spark of self-contradictory enlightenment, which makes them worthwhile in spite of their camouflage and their frequent capitulations to the deadly pattern of popular demand.

The chronological analysis that follows this conclusion, therefore, is not just a list of titles of varying degrees of interest; it is a catalogue of imaginative enterprise and a narrative of progress in casting off intellectual fetters and opposing imaginative oppression. It is not a chronicle of victory because the many tiny battles fought within it were mostly unwinnable, but it is a chronicle of escape, of the adventures of an Ark, of a longing for responsible imaginative freedom that is a kind of freedom in itself. That, it seems to me, is why the narrative was worth compiling, and shaping as accurately as possible, even though it remains admittedy idiosyncratic, inevitably incomplete, and more than a trifle chaotic.

A Chronology of *Roman Scientifique* 1657-1939

Titles of particular significance within the already-selective list are given in boldface. The titles of English translations are indicated in brackets; where more than one translation exists, only the title of the preferable translation is indicated. As in the main text, the titles of items published as books are given in italics; the titles of items contained in periodicals or collections are given in quotations marks.

1657   Savinien Cyrano de Bergerac *Histoire comique des États et Empires de la Lune* [Part One of **L'Autre Monde** (*Other Worlds*), written circa 1650, abridged text published posthumously]

1662   Savinien Cyrano de Bergerac *Histoire comique des États et Empires du Soleil* [Part Two of **L'Autre Monde** (*Other Worlds*), written circa 1650, abridged text published posthumously]

1675-9   Denis Vairasse *L'Histoire des Severambes* (partial translation as *The History of the Sevarites or Severambi*) [First volume published in English in 1675; full text published in French 1677-9]

1676   Gabriel de Foigny *La Terre australe connue* (*The Southern Land, Known*)

1688   Bernard le Bovier de Fontenelle *Entretiens sur la pluralité des mondes* (*Conversations on the Plurality of Worlds*)

1688-90 Gabriel Daniel *Voyage du Monde de Descartes* (*A Voyage to the World of Cartesius*)

1699   François Salignac de Fénelon *Suite du quatrième livre de l'Odysée d'Homère ou les aventures de Télémaque, fils d'Ulysse* (*The Adventures of Telemachus*)

1710 ?   Simon Tyssot de Patot *Voyages et aventures de Jacques Massé* ("The Voyages and Adventures of Jacques Massé")

1720   Simon Tyssot de Patot **Voyage de Groenland** ("Discoveries Around the North Pole")

1721   Anon *Relation d'un voyage du pôle arctique au pôle antarctique par le centre du monde* ("A Journey from the Arctic Pole to the Antarctic Pole via the Center of the Earth")

1735-8 Charles de Fieux, Chevalier de Mouhy *Lamékis* (*Lamekis*)

1748   Benoît de Maillet *Telliamed* (*Telliamed*) [abridged text published posthumously; partly-restored text 1755]

1750   Chevalier de Béthune *Relation du monde de Mercure* (*The World of Mercury*) [probably posthumous]

1752   Voltaire **Micromégas** (*Micromegas*)

1753	Tiphaigne de la Roche *Amilec* ("Amilec")
1754	Tiphaigne de la Roche "Zamar" ("Zamar")
1757	Emerich de Vattel "Voyages dans le microcosme" ("Voyages in the Microcosm") [in *Poliergie*.]
1760	Tiphaigne de la Roche **Giphantie** ("Giphantie")
1761	Tiphaigne de la Roche *Zazirocratie* ("Zazirocracy")
	"Monsieur de Listonai" *Le Voyageur philosophe* (The Philosophical Voyager)
1765-6	Marie-Anne de Roumier-Robert *Voyages de Milord Céton dans les sept planettes* (*The Voyages of Lord Seaton to the Seven Planets*)
1770	Alexis-Jean Le Bret *La Nouvelle Lune* ("The New Moon")
1771	Louis-Sébastien Mercier **L'An deux mille quatre cent quarante** (*Memoirs of the Year 2500*)
1775	Guillaume de La Follie *Le Philosophe sans prétention* (*The Unpretentious Philosopher*)
1781	Restif de la Bretonne **La Découverte australe par un homme-volant** (*The Discovery of the Austral Continent by a Flying Man*)
1787-9	Charles Garnier, publisher *Voyages imaginaires, songes, visions et romans cabalistiques* [36 volumes]
1788	Giacomo Casanova *Icosaméron* (*Icosameron* [abridged])
1790	Félix Nogaret *Le Miroir des événemens actuels* ("The Mirror of Present Events")
1791	Jean de Sales *Ma République, par Platon*
1799	Louis-Claude de Saint-Martin *Le Crocodile* (The Crocodile) [written 1792]
1802	Restif de la Bretonne **Les Posthumes** (*Posthumous Correspondence*) [First draft written 1787-89; augmented 1796]
1805	Jean-Baptiste Cousin de Grainville *Le Dernier homme* (*The Last Man*)
1810	Jean-Baptiste Mosneron de Launay *Le Vallon aérien* ("The Aerial Valley")
1821	Jacques Collin de Plancy *Voyage au centre de la terre* (*Voyage to the Center of the Earth*)
1824	Charles Pougens *Jocko* ("Jocko")
1830	Antoine Rey-Dussueil *La Fin du monde*
1831	Antoine Rey-Dussueil *Le Monde Nouveau*
1833	Charles Nodier "**Hurlubleu**" & "**Lazarus Long**" ("Perfectibility")
1834	Félix Bodin **Le Roman de l'avenir** (*The Novel of the Future*)
1835	Henri Delmotte *Voyage pittoresque et industriel deans le Paraguay-Roux* ("A Voyage to Paraguay-Roux")
1836	Louis-Napoléon Geoffroy **Napoléon et la conquête du monde**; aka *Napoléon apocryphe* (*The Apocryphal Napoleon*)
	Victor Considerant *Publication complète des nouvelles découvertes*

de Sir John Herschell ("The Complete News from the Moon")
Joseph Méry "Les Lunariens" ("The Lunarians")

1837   Pierre Boitard "Paris avant l'homme" ("Paris Before Humankind")

1838-9   Pierre Boitard "Voyage au Soleil" ("Journey to the Sun")

1839   Étienne Cabet *Voyage en Icarie* (*Voyage to Icaria*)

1841   S. Henry Berthoud **"Voyage au ciel"** ("A Heavenward Voyage")

1844   S. Henry Berthoud "Le Maître du temps" ("The Master of the Weather")

       S. Henry Berthoud "Le Fou" ("The Madman")

       Joseph Méry "Les Ruines de Paris" ("The Ruins of Paris")

1846   Émile Souvestre **Le Monde tel qu'il sera** (*The World as It Shall Be*)

1851   Théophile Gautier "Paris futur" ("Future Paris")

1854   Charles Defontenay *Star, ou Ψ de Cassiopée* (*Star*)

       Joseph Méry "Histoire de ce qui n'est pas arrivé" ("Tower of Destiny") [book publication]

1856   Léon Gozlan *Les Émotions de Polydore Marasquin* (*The Emotions of Polydore Marasquin*)

       Alfred Driou *Aventures d'un aéronaute parisien dans les mondes inconnus* (*The Adventure of a Parisian Aeronaut in Unknown Worlds*)

       Arsène Houssaye "Paris futur" ("Future Paris")

1857   Alfred Bonnardot **"Archéopolis"** ("Archeopolis")

1858-9   Joseph Déjacque "L'Humanisphère"

1860   Joseph Méry "Ce qu'on verra" ("What We Shall See") [book publication]

1861-2   S. Henry Berthoud *Fantaisies scientifiques de Sam*

       Victorien Sardou "Le Médaillon" aka *La Perle noire* ("The Black Pearl")

1862   Edmond About *L'Homme à l'oreille cassée* (*The Man with the Broken Ear*)

       Pierre Véron *Les Marchands de santé* ("The Merchants of Health")

       Camille Flammarion *La Pluralité des mondes habités*

1863   Jules Verne *Cinq semaines en ballon* (*Five Weeks in a Balloon*)

       Jules Verne **Paris au XXe siècle** (*Paris in the Twentieth Century*) written [posthumously published 1994]

       René de Pont-Jest "La Tête de Mimer" ("Mimer's Head")

       Jacques Fabien *Paris en songe* ("Paris in Dream")

1864   Jules Verne **Voyage au centre de la terre** (rev. 1867; *Journey to the Centre of the Earth*)

       Louis Ulbach "Le Prince Bonifacio" ("Prince Bonifacio")

       Pierre Véron *Monsieur Personne* ("Monsieur Nobody")

       Edmé Rousseau *Le Songe, ou voyage aérien* (in "The Aerial Voyage") [written 1859]

	Camille Flammarion *Le Mondes imaginaires et les mondes réels*
1865	Jules Verne **De la terre à la lune** (From the Earth to the Moon)

Camille Flammarion *Le Mondes imaginaires et les mondes réels*

1865   Jules Verne **De la terre à la lune** (From the Earth to the Moon)

Henri de Parville *Un Habitant de la planète Mars* (*An Inhabitant of the Planet Mars*)

Achille Eyraud *Voyage à Venus* (*Voyage to Venus*)

S. Henry Berthoud *L'Homme depuis cinq mille ans*

Hippolyte Mettais **L'An 5865** (*The Year 5865*)

George Sand Laura: *Laura, voyage dans le cristal* (*Laura*)

Élie Berthet *L'Homme des bois* (*The Wild Man of the Woods*)

1865-6   "X. Nagrien" [François-Armand Audoy] "Prodigieuse découverte" ("A Prodigious Discovery")

1866   Hippolyte Mettais *Paris avant le déluge* (*Paris Before the Deluge*)

1866-7   Camille Flammarion **Lumen** (*Lumen*)

1867   Victor Hugo "L'Avenir" ("The Future") [in the introduction to the guidebook to the 1867 Exposition]

Adrien Robert "La Guerre en 1894" ("War in 1894") [book publication]

1868   "Aristide Roger" [Jules Rengade] *Voyage sous les flots* (*Voyage Beneath the Waves*)

Fernand Giraudeau *La Cité nouvelle* ("The New City")

1869   Tony Moilin *Paris en l'an 2000* (*Paris in the Year 2000*)

Jules Verne **Autour de la lune** (*Around the Moon*)

Jules Lermina "Les Fous" ("The Lunatics")

Charles Cros "Étude sur les moyens de communication avec les planètes"

1870   Jules Verne **Vingt mille lieues sous les mers** (*Twenty Thousand Leagues Under the Sea*)

1872   Camille Flammarion *Récits de l'infini* (*Stories of Infinity*)

Jules Verne "Le Docteur Ox" ("Doctor Ox's Experiment")

Léonie Rouzade *Voyage de Théodose à l'île d'Utopie* ("A Voyage to the Isle of Utopia") & *Le Monde renversé* ("The World Turned Upside Down")

Eugène Mouton "La Fin du Monde" ("The End of the World")

Charles Cros "Une drame interastral" ("An Interastral Drama")

1873 ?   "A. Vémar" [Gustave Marx] "L'Amour en mille ans d'ici" ("Love a Thousand Years Hence")

1874   R. de Maricourt *La Commune en l'an 2073: au bout du fosse!* ("All the Way: The Commune in 2073")

Charles Cros "La Science de l'amour" ("The Science of Love")

1875   Alfred Franklin *Les Ruines de Paris en 4875* ("The Ruins of Paris in 4875")

Alphonse Brown *La Conquête de l'air* (The Conquest of the Air)

1876   Edmond Thiaudière *Voyages de Lord Humour*

Charles Renouvier *Uchronie*

Jules Verne *Hector Servadac* (*Hector Servadac*)

1877 Jules Richepin "La Machine à métaphysique" ("The Metaphysical Machine")

1878 Jules Hosch *Folles amours*

Georges Pellerin *Le Monde dans deux mille ans* (*The World in Two Thousand Years*)

1879 Albert Robida *Voyages très extraordinaires de Saturnin Farandoul* (*The Adventures of Saturnin Farandoul*)

André Laurie & Jules Verne **Les Cinq cents millions de la Begum** (*The Begum's Millions*)

1881 Jules Lermina "Maison tranquille" ("Quiet House")

1882-3 Jules Gros "L'Age de Pierre et l'homme fossile" (*The Fossil Man*)

Ernest d'Hervilly "Josuah Electricmann" ("Josuah Electricmann")

1883 Didier de Chousy *Ignis* (*Ignis: The Central Fire*)

Albert Robida **Le Vingtième siècle** (The Twentieth Century) & "La Guerre au vingtième siècle" [first version] ("War in the Twentieth Century")

Eugène Mouton "L'Historioscope" ("The Historioscope")

1884 Émile Calvet *Dans mille ans* (*In a Thousand Years*)

Camille Debans *Les Malheurs de John Bull* ("The Misfortunes of John Bull")

Édouard Rod "L'Autopsie du docteur Z***" ("Doctor Z***'s Autopsy")

George Eekhoud "Le Coeur de Tony Wandel" ("Tony Wandel's Heart")

1885 "Barillet-Lagargousse" *La Guerre finale* (*The Final War*)

"Charles Epheyre" [Charles Richet] "Le Mirosaurus" ("The Mirosaurus")

1886 Villiers de l'Isle-Adam **L'Ève future** (*The Future Eve*)

Jules Verne *Robur le conquérant* (*The Clipper of the Clouds*)

Émile Dodillon *Hémo* ("Hemo")

1887 André Laurie *Les Exilés de la terre* (*The Conquest of the Moon*)

J.-H. Rosny "**Les Xipéhuz**" ("The Xipehuz") & "Tornadres" aka "Le Cataclysme" ("The Cataclysm")

Guy de Maupassant "Le Horla" ("The Horla") & "L'Homme de Mars" ("Martian Mankind")

Alphonse Brown "Les insectes révélateurs" ("The Tell-Tale Insects")

Albert Robida "La Guerre au vingtième siècle" [second version] ("War in the Twentieth Century")

Jean Rameau *Fantasmagories*

1888 Albert Bleunard *La Babylone électrique* (*Babylon Electrified*)

Louis Boussenard *Les Secrets de Monsieur Synthèse* (in *Monsieur*

Synthesis)

Charles Guyon *Voyage dans la planète Vénus* ("A Voyage to the Planet Venues")

Louise Michel *Le Monde nouveau*

1888-96 Henri de Graffigny & Georges Le Faure *Aventures extraordinaires d'un savant russe* (*The Extraordinary Adventures of a Russian Scientist Across the Solar System*)

1889 Louis Boussenard *Dix mille ans dans un bloc de glace* (in *Monsieur Synthesis*)

Camille Flammarion *Uranie* (*Urania*)

Charles Epheyre "Soeur Marthe" ("Sister Marthe") [expanded version 1890]

Jules Lermina "Le Secret des Zippélius" ("The Zippelius Secret")

J.-H. Rosny "La Légende sceptique" ("The Skeptical Legend")

1889-96 "Capitaine Danrit" [Émile Driant] *La Guerre de demain* [8 volumes]

1890 "Alain le Drimeur" *La Cité future* (*The Future City*)

Charles Epheyre "Le Microbe de Professeur Bakermann" (Professor Bakermann's Microbe")

1890-1 Alphonse Brown "Une Ville de verre" (*The City of Glass*)

1891 "Jean Chambon" [Adolphe Alhaiza] *Cybèle* (*Cybele*)

Émile Goudeau "La Révolte des machines" (The Revolt of the Machines")

1891-2 Jules Lermina "La Bataille de Strasbourg" (*The Battle of Strasbourg*)

Albert Robida **La Vie électrique** (*Electric Life*)

1892 J.-H. Rosny *Vamireh* (*Vamireh*)

Gaston Danville *Contes d'Au-Delà* (in *The Anatomy of Love and Murder*)

1893 Camille Flammarion **La Fin du Monde** (*Omega: The End of the World*)

Émile Zola *Le Docteur Pascal* (*Doctor Pascal*)

Albert Bleunard "Toujours plus petit" ("Ever Smaller")

Paul Adam *Conte futur* ("A Tale of the Future")

Edmond Haraucourt "La Fin du Monde" ("The End of the World")

J.-H. Rosny *Eyrimah* (*Eyrimah*) & "Nymphée" ("Nymphaeum")

1894 Maurice Spronck *L'An 330 de la République* ("Year 330 of the Republic")

1895 Jules Verne *L'Île à hélice* (*Propellor Island*)

J.-H. Rosny "Un Autre Monde" ("Another World")

Camille Debans "Le Vainqueur de la mort" ("The Conqueror of Death")

1896 Jules Verne *Face au drapeau* (*For the Flag*)

"Pierre de Sélènes" *Un Monde inconnu* (*An Unknown World*)

Camille Mauclair *L'Orient Vierge* ("The Virgin Orient")

	Camille Flammarion "Un Amour dans les étoiles" ("Love Among the Stars")
	Henri Ner "Le Révolte des machines" ("The Revolt of the Machines") & "Un Roman historique" ("A Historical Romance")
1898	Paul Adam **Lettres de Malaisie** ("Letters from Malaisie")
1899-1900	Gustave Le Rouge & Gustave Guitton *La Conspiration des milliardaires* (*The Dominion of the World*)
1900	"H. Desnar" [Henri Esnard] "Que faire?"
1901	Jules Verne *Le Village aérien* (*The Village in the Treetops*)
	Han Ryner *L'Homme-fourmi* (*The Human Ant*)
	Goron & Émile Gautier *Fleur de Bagne* (*Spawn of the Penitentiary*)
	Paul Vibert *Pour lire en automobile* (*The Mysterious Fluid*)
1902	Alfred Jarry **Le Surmâle** (*The Supermale*)
	Raoul Gineste *La Seconde vie du docteur Albin* (*The Second Life of Doctor Albin*)
	Albert Robida *L'Horloge des siècles* (*The Clock of the Centuries*)
	Frédéric Boutet "Le Voyage de Julius Pingouin" ("The Voyage of Julius Pingouin")
	Alphonse Allais *Le Captain Cap* (*The Adventures of Captain Cap*)
1903	John-Antoine Nau *Force ennemie* (*Enemy Force*)
1904	André Couvreur **Caresco surhomme** (*Caresco, Superman*)
	Jules Lermina "Mystère-ville" (*Mysteryville*)
	Jules Verne *Maître du monde* (*Master of the World*)
	Edmond Haraucourt "Cinq mille ans, ou La Traversée de Paris" ("A Trip to Paris")
	Henri Austruy *L'Eupantophone* ("The Eupantophone")
	André Lichtenberger *Les Centaures* (*The Centaurs*)
	Edmond Haraucourt **"Le Gorilloïde"** ("The Gorilloid")
1905	Anatole France **Sur la pierre blanche** (*The White Stone*)
	Gaston Danville *Le Parfum de Volupté* (*The Perfume of Lust*)
	Gabriel Tarde "Fragment d'histoire future" (*Underground Man*)
	Jules Lermina "To-Ho le tueur d'or" (*To-Ho and the Gold-Destroyers*)
	Arnould Galopin *Le Docteur Oméga* (*Doctor Omega*)
	Maurice Renard "Les Vacances de Monsieur Dupont" ("Monsieur Dupont's Vacation")
1906	Jules Hoche **Le Faiseur d'hommes et sa formule** (*The Maker of Men and His Formula*)
	Louis Forest *On vole des enfants à Paris* (*Someone is Stealing Children in Paris*)
	Henri Austruy *L'Ère Petitpaon* ("The Petitpaon Era")
1907	Charles Derennes **Le Peuple du pôle** (*The People of the Pole*)
	André Laurie *Spiridon le muet* (*Spiridon*)

Sylvain Deglantine *Les Terriens dans Vénus*
Jules Perrin "L'Hallucination de Monsieur Forbe" ("Monsieur Forbe's Hallucination")
Marcel Roland *Le Presqu'homme* ("Almost Human")

1908   Maurice Renard **Le Docteur Lerne, sous-dieu** (*Doctor Lerne, Subgod*)
Jean de La Hire *La Roue fulgurante* (*The Fiery Wheel*)
Jules Verne [& Michel Verne] *La Chasse au météore* (*The Hunt for the Meteor*)
Fernand Kolney *L'Amour dans cinq mille ans* (*Love in Five Thousand Years*)
Gustave Le Rouge *Le Prisonnier de la Planète Mars* (in *Vampires of Mars*)
H. Gayar *Aventures merveilleuses de Serge Myrandhal sur la planète Mars* (*The Adventures of Serge Myrandhal on the Planet Mars*)
Jules Claretie *L'Obsession* (*Obsession*)
Pierre Giffard *La Guerre infernale*
Michel Corday "Le Mystérieux Dajan-Phinn" ("The Mysterious Dajan-Phinn")
Jules Sageret "La Race qui vaincra" ("The Race That Will Be Victorious")
Henri Austruy "Miellune" ("Miellune")

1909   André Couvreur *Une Invasion de macrobes* ("An Invasion of Macrobes")
Gustave Le Rouge *La Guerre des vampires* (in *Vampires of Mars*)
Jean Jullien *Enquête sur le monde futur* ("An Investigation of the World of the Future")
J.-H. Rosny *La Guerre du feu* (*The Quest for Fire*)
Octave Béliard "Les Aventures d'un voyageur qui explora le temps"
Louis Mullem "Le Progrès supreme" ("The Supreme Progress") [posthumous]

1910   J.-H. Rosny "**La Mort de la terre**" ("The Death of the Earth")
Jules Lermina *L'Effrayante aventure* (*Panic in Paris*)
Edmond Haraucourt "La Découverte du docteur Auguérand" ("Doctor Auguerand's Discovery")
Georges de La Fouchardière *La Machine à galoper* ("The Galloping Machine")

1910-1   Jules Perrin & Henri Lanos "Un Monde sur le monde" ("A World Above the World")

1911   Maurice Renard **Le Péril bleu** (*The Blue Peril*)
André Beaunier *L'Homme qui a perdu son moi* (*The Man Who Lost Himself*)
Alfred Jarry **Gestes et opinions du docteur Faustroll** (*Exploits and*

Opinions of Dr. Faustroll) [posthumous]
Claude Farrère *La Maison des hommes vivants* (*The House of the Secret*)
André Couvreur & Michael Corday *Le Lynx* (*The Lynx*)
Jean Richepin *L'Aile* (*The Wing*)
Jean de La Hire "Le Mystère des XV" (*The Nyctalope on Mars*)

1912   Gaston de Pawlowski **Voyage au pays de la quatrième dimension** [revised 1923] (*Journey to the Land of the Fourth Dimension*)
Jean de Quirielle *L'Oeuf de verre*

1912-3   Gustave Le Rouge *Le Mystérieux docteur Cornélius* (*The Mysterious Doctor Cornelius*)

1912-4   Edmond Haraucourt **Daâh, le premier homme** (*Daâh: The First Human*)

1913   J.-H. Rosny **La Force Mystérieuse** ("The Mysterious Force")
André Mas *Les Allemands sur Vénus* ("The Germans on Venus")
Albert Quantin *En plein vol*
Pierre MacOrlan *Le Rire jaune*
Maurice Renard "Le Brouillard de 26 Octobre" ("The Fog of October 26")

1914   Han Ryner *Les Pacifiques* ("The Pacifists")

1916   Charles Dodeman *La Bombe silencieuse* (*The Silent Bomb*)

1917   J.-H. Rosny *L'Énigme de Givreuse* ("The Givreuse Enigma")
Félicien Champsaur *Les Ailes de l'homme* (The Human Arrow) [first written 1914; augmented in published edition]
Henri Falk "Le Maître des trois états" ("The Master of the Three States")
Albert Robida "Un Potache en 1950" ("A Schoolboy in 1950")

1917-8   Gaston Leroux "Rouletabille chez Krupp" (*Rouletabille at Krupp's*)

1918   Michael Epuy [Louis Vaury] "Anthéa, ou l'étrange planète" ("Anthea; or, The Strange Planet")
Raoul Bigot "Le Fer qui meurt" ("The Iron that Died")

1919   Albert Robida **L'Ingénieur von Satanas** (*The Engineer von Satanas*)
Edmond Haraucourt "Le conflit suprême" ("The Supreme Conflict")
Henri Falk "L'Age de Plomb" ("The Age of Lead")
Maurice Leblanc *Les Trois Yeux* (*The Three Eyes*)
Pierre MacOrlan *La Bête conquérante*

1920   André Arnyvelde **L'Arche** (*The Ark*)
Marcel Rouff **Voyage au monde à l'envers** (*Journey to the Inverted World*)
"Claude Farrère" [Charles Bargone] *Les Condamnés à mort* (*Useless Hands*)

1921   André Lichtenberger *Raramémé* (*The Children of the Crab*)

Maurice Renard "L'Homme truqué" ("The Doctored Man")
René Pujol "Le Soleil Noir" ("The Black Sun")
Pierre MacOrlan *La Cavalière Elsa*

1921-2   Octave Joncquel & Théo Varlet *L'Épopée martienne* (*The Martian Epic*)
Jean de La Hire "Lucifer" (*The Nyctalope vs. Lucifer*)

1922   Henri Allorge *Le Grand cataclysme* (*The Great Cataclysm*)
André Arnyvelde *Le Bacchus Mutilé* (*The Mutilated Bacchus*)
André Couvreur "L'Androgyne" ("The Androgyne")
J.-H. Rosny *L'Étonnante aventure de Hareton Ironcastle* ("Hareton Ironcastle's Amazing Journey")
Pierre Mille "En trois cent ans" ("Three Hundred Years Hence")

1923   Félicien Champsaur *Ouha, roi des singes* (*Ouha, King of the Apes*)
André Blandin & Théo Varlet *La Belle Valence* (*Timeslip Troopers*)
André Couvreur "Le Valseur phosphorescent" ("The Phosphorescent Waltzer")
André Mas *Drymea, monde des vierges* ("Drymea, World of Virgins")

1924   Félicien Champsaur *Homo-Deus, Le Satyre invisible* ("The Invisible Satyr")
André Couvreur "Le Mémoires d'un immortal" ("The Memoirs of an Immortal")
Victor Margueritte *Le Couple* (*The Couple*)
Noëlle Roger *Le Nouvel Adam* (*The New Adam*)
Louis Baudry de Saunier *Comment Paris a été détruit en six heures* ("How Paris was Destroyed in Six Hours")

1925   Henri Austruy **"L'Olotélepan"** ("The Olotelepan")
J.-H. Rosny "Les Navigateurs de l'infini" ("Navigators of Space")
Ernest Perochon **Les Hommes frénétiques** (*The Frenetic People*)
José Moselli *La Fin d'Illa* (*Illa's End*) & "Le Messager de la planète" ("The Planetary Messenger")
Renée Dunan *La Dernière jouissance* ("The Ultimate Pleasure")
Albert Robida *Un Chalet dans les airs* (*Chalet in the Sky*)

1926   Odette Dulac *[Amour] tel qu'il est* (*The War of the Sexes*)

1927   Léon Daudet *Le Napus, fléau de l'an 2227* (*The Napus*)
André Couvreur **"Le Biocole"** ("The Biocole")
Théo Varlet *Le Roc d'or* (*The Golden Rock*)

1928   Henri-Jacques Proumen **Sur le chemin des dieux**
Maurice Renard *Un Homme chez les microbes* ("A Man Among the Microbes") [first version written 1907-8]
Arnould Galopin *Le Bacille* ("The Man With the Blue Face") [written 1908]

1929   Félicien Champsaur *Nora, la guenon devenue femme* (*Nora, the Ape-*

Woman)

Han Ryner **Les Surhommes** ("The Superhumans")

1930   Fernand Fleuret *Jim Click ou la Merveilleuse invention* (*Jim Click; or The Wonderful Invention*)

Théo Varlet **La Grande Panne** (*The Xenobiotic Invasion*)

1931   Léon Daudet *Les Bacchantes* (*The Bacchantes*)

Michel Corday *La Flamme éternelle* ("The Eternal Flame")

Roger Farney "Les Anekphantes"

1932   René Pujol *La Chasse aux chimères* (*The Chimerical Quest*)

Raymond de Rienzi *Les Formiciens*

1933   Maurice Renard "Le Maître de la lumière" (*The Master of Light*)

Michel Corday *Ciel rose* ("Pink Sky")

Luc Alberny *L'Étrange aventure du professeur Pamphlegme*

1934   Régis Messac **"Le Miroir flexible"** ("The Flexible Mirror" [publication blocked])

J.-H. Rosny *Les Compagnons de l'univers* ("Companions of the Universe")

1935   Régis Messac *Quinzinzinzili* ("Quinzinzinzili" [publication blocked])

A. Valérie "Sur l'autre face du monde"

1936   Henri Duvernois *L'Homme qui est retrouvé* (*The Man Who Found Himself*)

Jacques Spitz *Les Évadés de l'an 4000*

1937   Régis Messac **La Cité des Asphyxiés** (*Stranglehold City* [publication blocked])

André Maurois *La Machine à lire les pensées* (*The Thought-Reading Machine*)

Théo Varlet *Aurore Lescure, pilote d'astronef* (*The Castaways of Eros*) written [posthumously published 1943]

1938   Jacques Spitz **L'Homme élastique** & *La Guerre des mouches*

1939   Jacques Spitz *L'Expérience du Dr. Mops* ("Doctor Mops' Experiment")

André Couvreur "Le Cas de la Baronne Sasoitsu" ("The Case of Baronne Sasoitsu")

J.-H. Rosny "Dans le monde des Variants" ("In the World of the Variants")

Bibliography

Aldiss, Brian W. *Billion Year Spree*, London: Gollancz, 1973; rev., with David Wingrove, as *Trillion Year Spree*. London: Gollancz, 1986.

Alkon, Paul K. . *Origins of Futuristic Fiction*. Athens, GA: University of Georgia Press, 1987.

Amis, Kingsley. *New Maps of Hell*. London: Gollancz, 1960.

Angelier François. *Dictionnaire Jules Verne*. Paris: Pygmalion, 2006.

Angenot, Marc. "Science-Fiction in France Before Verne." *Science-Fiction Studies* 14 (March 1976).

Armytage, W. H. G. *Yesterday's Tomorrows: A Historical Survey of Future Societies*. London: Routledge and Kegan Paul, 1968.

Bailey, J. O. *Pilgrims Through Space and Time: Trends and Patterns in Scientific and Utopian Fiction*. New York: Argus, 1947.

Bleiler, Everett F. *Science-Fiction, the Early Years: A Full Description of More Than 3000 Science-Fiction Stories from Earliest Times to the Appearance of the Genre Magazines in 1930, with Author, Title, and Motif Indexes*. Kent, Ohio: Kent State University Press, 1990.

Bleiler, Everett, F., and Richard Bleiler. *Science-Fiction: The Gernsback Years*. Kent, Ohio: Kent State University Press, 1998.

Boutel, Jean-Luc. "La literature d'imagination scientifique: genèse et continuité d'un genre" in Lanuque, Jean-Guillaume, ed. *Dimension merveilleux scientifique*. Rivière Blanche (Hollywood Comics), 2015.

Bréan, Simon. *La Science-Fiction en France*. Paris : Nebal, 2012.

Bridenne, Jean-Jacques. *La Littérature française d'imagination scientifique*. Paris: Dassonville, 1950.

Butcher, William. *Verne's Journey to the Centre of the Self: Space and Time in the Voyages Extraordinaires*. London: Macmillan, 1990.

Butor, Michel, "On Fairy Tales" in *Inventory*. London: Cape, 1968.

Clarke, I. F. *The Pattern of Expectation: 1644-2001*. London: Cape, 1979.

-------. *Voices Prophesying War: Future Wars 1763-3749*. Oxford, U.K.: Oxford University Press, 1966; 2nd ed., 1992.

Clute, John and Peter Nicholls. *The Encyclopedia of Science Fiction*. London: Orbit, 2nd ed., 1993.

Costello, Peter. *Jules Verne, Inventor of Science Fiction*. London: Hodder & Stoughton, 1978.

Crowe, Michael J. *The Extraterrestrial Life Debate 1750-1900: The Idea of a Plurality of Worlds from Kant to Lowell*. Cambridge, U.K.: Cambridge University Press, 1986.

647

Darnton, Robert. *The Forbidden Best-Sellers of Pre-Revolutionary France.* London: HarperCollins, 1996.

Domeyne, Pierre. *Le Merveilleux scientifique, ses sources et ses prolongements dans les romans et nouvelles de J.-H. Rosny aîné.* Lyon: Diss, 1965.

Evans, Arthur B. "Gustave Le Rouge, Pioneer of Early French Science Fiction." *Science-Fiction Studies* 79 (November 1999).

-------. *Jules Verne Rediscovered: Didacticism and the Scientific Novel.* Westport, Conn.: Greenwood Press, 1988.

-------. "Science Fiction in France: A Brief History." *Science-Fiction Studies* 49 (November 1989).

-------. "Science Fiction vs. Scientific Fiction in France: From Jules Verne to J. H. Rosny aîné." Science-Fiction Studies 44 (November 1988).

Fitting, Peter, ed. *Subterranean Worlds: A Critical Anthology.* Middletown, Conn.: Wesleyan University Press, 2004.

Flammarion, Camille. *Les Mondes imaginaires et les mondes réels: voyage pittoresque dans le ciel et revue critique des théories humaines, scientifiques et romanesques, anciennes et modernes sur les habitants des astres.* Paris: Didier et cie, 1864; exp. Paris: Marpon et Flammarion, 1892.

Fondaneche, Daniel. *La Littérature de l'imagination scientifique.* Amsterdam: Rodopi, 2012.

Fortunati, Vita, and Raymond Trousson, eds. *Dictionary of Literary Utopias.* Paris: Honoré Champion, 2000.

Forsström, Riikka. *Possible Worlds: The Idea of Happiness in the Utopian Vision of Louis-Sébastien Mercier.* Helsinki: Suomalisen Kirjallisuuden Seura, 2002.

Gouanvic, Jean-Marc. *Le Science-fiction française au XXe siècle (1900-1968): Essai de socio-poétique d'un genre en émergence.* Amsterdam: Rodolpi, 1994.

Gove, Philip Babcock. *The Imaginary Voyage in Prose Fiction.* New York: Columbia University Press, 1941.

Guthke, Karl. *The Last Frontier: Imagining Other Worlds, from the Copernican Revolution to Modern Science Fiction.* tr. by Helen Atkins. Ithaca, N.Y.: Cornell University Press, 1990.

Haldane, J. B. S. *Daedalus; or, Science and the Future.* London: Kegan Paul, Trench & Trubner, 1923.

Jarry, Alfred. "De Quelques romans scientifiques." *La Plume* Octobre 1903.

Langlet, Irène. *La Science-Fiction: lecture et poétique d'un genre littéraire.* Paris : Armand Colin, 2006.

Lofficier, Jean-Marc, and Randy Lofficier. *French Science Fiction, Fantasy, Horror and Pulp Fiction: A Guide to Cinema, Television, Radio, Animation, Comic Books and Literature from the Middle Ages to the Present.* Jefferson, N.C.: McFarland, 2000.

Manuel, Frank E., ed. *Utopias and Utopian Thought.* Boston: Houghton Mifflin, 1966.

Manuel, Frank E. and Fritzie P. Manuel, eds. *Utopian Thought in the Western World.* Cambridge, Mass.: Belknap Press, 1980.

Martin, Andrew. *The Mask of the Prophet: The Extraordinary Fictions of Jules Verne.* New York: Oxford University Press, 1990.

Matthey, Hubert. *Essai sur le merveilleux dans la littérature française depuis 1800.* Paris: Payot, 1915.

May, Georges. "Un voyage imaginaire peu connu de 1770: *La Nouvelle Lune, ou Histoire de Poequilon* d'Alexis-Jean Le Bret" in Macary, Jean, ed. *Essays on the Age of Enlightenment in Honor of Ira O. Wade.* Geneva: Droz, 1977.

Mendlesohn, Farah. *The Rhetoric of Fantasy.* Middletown, CT: Wesleyan University Press, 2008.

Moskowitz, Sam. *Explorers of the Infinite: Shapers of Science Fiction.* Cleveland, Ohio: World, 1963.

-------. *Seekers of Tomorrow: Masters of Modern Science Fiction.* Cleveland, Ohio: World, 1966.

Nicolson, Marjorie Hope. *Voyages to the Moon.* New York: Macmillan, 1948.

Nietzsche, Friedrich W. *Thus Spake Zarathustra.* tr. by Alexander Tille. London: H. Henry, 1896.

Nisbet, Robert. *History and the Idea of Progress.* New York: Basic Books, 1980.

Renard, Maurice. "Du Roman merveilleux scientifique et de son action sur l'intelligence du progrès." *Le Spectateur,* octobre 1909.

Rosenberg, Aubrey. *Tyssot de Patot and His Work 1655-1738.* The Hague: Martinus Nijhoff, 1972.

Russell, W. M. S. "Voltaire, Science and Fiction: A Tercentenary Tribute." *Foundation* 62 (1994-95).

Sadoul, Jacques. *Histoire de la science-fiction moderne* (1911-1984). Paris: Laffont, 1984. [expanded edition of a book first published in 1973]

Stableford, Brian. *Heterocosms.* Borgo Press, 2007.

-------. *Narrative Strategies in Science Fiction.* Borgo Press, 2009.

-------. *New Atlantis: A Narrative History of Scientific Romance.* (Four volumes.) [unpublished at the time of writing]

-------. *Opening Minds.* San Bernardino, CA: Borgo Press, 1995.

-------. *Science Fact and Science Fiction: An Encyclopedia.* New York: Routledge, 2006.

-------. *Scientific Romance in Britain, 1890-1950.* London: Fourth Estate, 1985.

Testud, Pierre. *Rétif de la Bretonne et la création littéraire.* Geneva: Libraire Droz, 1972.

van Herp, Jacques. *José Moselli et la SF.* Brussels: Recto Verso (Ides... et Autres 43/44), 1984.

------. *Panorama de la science-fiction. Les themes, les genres, les écoles, les problèmes.* Paris: Marabout, 1975.

Vas-Deyres, Natacha. *Ces Français qui ont écrit demain: Utopie, anticipation et science-fiction au XXe siècle*. Paris: Homoré Champion, 2013.

Verne, Jean-Jules. *Jules Verne: A Biography*. New York: Taplinger, 1976 [originally Paris: Hachette, 1973].

Vernier, J. P. "The SF of J.H. Rosny the Elder" *Science-Fiction Studies* 6 (July 1975).

Versins, Pierre. *L'Encyclopédie de l'utopie, des voyages extraordinaires et de la science-fiction*. Lausanne, Switzerland: L'Age d'Homme, 1972.

Wollheim, Donald A. *The Universe Makers: Science Fiction Today*. New York: Harper, 1971.

Black Coat Press Library

The following titles, mentioned in this book, are available as books and/or ebooks from Black Coat Press as of April, 2016. More titles are added every month. For updates, check our website at www.blackcoatpress.com, e-mail info@blackcoatpress.com or write to Black Coat Press, attn: Mr. Greg M. Seigel, 18321 Ventura Blvd., Suite 915, Tarzana, CA 91356.

Ebooks are $5.99 except where otherwise specified.

( ) Adolphe Alhaiza. *Cybele: An Extraordinary Voyage Into the Future* - $20.95 + $3 p&h
( ) Alphonse Allais. *The Adventures of Captain Cap* - $22.95 + $3.50 p&h
( ) Henri Allorge. *The Great Cataclysm* - $19.95 + $3 p&h
( ) Guy d'Armen. *Doc Ardan: The City of Gold and Lepers* - $20.95 + $3 p&h
( ) -------. *Doc Ardan: The Troglodytes of Mount Everest* + *The Giants of Black Lake* - $22.95 + $3.50 p&h
( ) André Arnyvelde. *The Ark* (also includes *The King of Galade*) - $22.95 + $3.50 p&h
( ) -------. *The Mutilated Bacchus* (also includes *Man Wanted, or The Strange Tournament of Love*) - $32.95 + $4.00 p&h
( ) Henri Austruy. *The Eupantophone* - $22.95 + $3.50 p&h
( ) -------. *The Petitpaon Era* (also includes *Miellune*) - $22.95 + $3.50 p&h
( ) -------. *The Olotelepan* (also includes *A Samsara*) - $24.95 + $3.50 p&h
( ) Barillet-Lagargousse. *The Final War* - $22.95 + $3.50 p&h
( ) S. Henry Berthoud. *Martyrs of Science* - $29.95 + $4.00 p&h - ebook $6.99
( ) Béthune (Chevalier de). *The World of Mercury* - $20.95 + $3.00 p&h
( ) Albert Bleunard. *Ever Smaller* - $20.95 + $3 p&h
( ) Félix Bodin. *The Novel of the Future* - $20.95 + $3 p&h
( ) Louis Boussenard. *Monsieur Synthesis* (also includes *Ten Thousand Years in an Ice Block*) - $26.95 + $4 p&h - ebook $6.99
( ) Alphonse Brown. *City of Glass* - $22.95 + $3.50 p&h
( ) -------. *The Conquest of the Air* - $22.95 +$ 3.50 p&h
( ) Emile Calvet. *In a Thousand Years* - $22.95 + $3.50 p&h
( ) -------. *The Human Arrow* - $24.95 + $3.50 p&h
( ) -------. *Ouha, King of the Apes* - $22.95 + $3.50 p&h
( ) -------. *Homo-Deus* (also includes *Kill the Old ! Enjoy!*) - $29.95 + $4.00 p&h - ebook $6.99
( ) -------. *Nora, The Ape-Woman* - $20.95 + $3.00 p&h
( ) Didier de Chousy. *Ignis: The Central Fire* - $22.95 + $3.50 p&h

( ) Jules Clarétie. *Obsession* - $20.95 + $3 p&h
( ) Jacques Collin de Plancy. *Voyage to the Center of the Earth* - $20.95 + $3 p&h
( ) Michel Corday. *The Eternal Flame* (also includes *Pink Sky*) - $20.95 +$3 p&h
( ) André Couvreur. *The Necessary Evil* - $24.95 + $3.50 p&h
( ) -------. *Caresco, Superman* - $24.95 + $3.50 p&h
( ) -------. *The Exploits of Professor Tornada* (Vol. 1: *An Invasion of Macrobes* + *The Androgyne*) - $22.95 + $3.50 p&h
( ) -------. *The Exploits of Professor Tornada* (Vol. 2 : *The Phosphorescent Waltzer* + *Memoirs of an Immortal*) - $22.95 + $3.50 p&h
( ) -------. *The Exploits of Professor Tornada* (Vol. 3: *The Biocole* + *The Case of Baroness Sasoitsu*) - $22.95 + $3.50 p&h
( ) Danrit (Capitaine). *Undersea Odyssey* - $20.95 + $3 p&h
( ) Camille Debans. *The Misfortunes of John Bull* - $22.95 + $3.50 p&h
( ) C. I. Defontenay. *Star (Psi Cassiopeia)* - $20.95 + $3 p&h
( ) Charles Derennes. *The People of the Pole* - $19.95 + $3 p&h
( ) Charles Dodeman. *The Silent Bomb* - $20.95 + $3 p&h
( ) Alfred Driou. *The Adventures of a Parisian Aeronaut in the Unknown Worlds* - $22.95 + $3.50 p&h
( ) Odette Dulac. *The War of the Sexes* - $20.95 + $3.00 p&h
( ) Renée Dunan. *Baal* - $22.95 + $3.50 p&h
( ) -------. *The Ultimate Pleasure* - $20.95 + $3.00 p&h
( ) Henri Duvernois. *The Man Who Found Himself* - $16.95 + $3 p&h
( ) Achille Eyraud. *Voyage to Venus* - $19.95 + $3 p&h
( ) Henri Falk. *The Age of Lead* (also includes *Master of the Three States*) - $19.95 + $3 p&h
( ) Paul Féval, *fils*. *Felifax, the Tiger-Man* - $24.95 + $3.50 p&h
( ) Fernand Fleuret. *Jim Click* - $20.95 + $3 p&h
( ) Louis Forest. *Someone is Stealing Children in Paris* - $26.95 + $4.00 p&h - ebook $6.99
( ) Arnould Galopin. *Doctor Omega* - $14.95 + $3 p&h
( ) H. Gayar. *The Marvelous Adventures of Serge Myrandhal on Mars* - $26.95 + $4.00 p&h - ebook $6.99
( ) Raoul Gineste. *The Second Life of Doctor Albin* - $29.95 + $4.00 p&h
( ) Delphine de Girardin. *Balzac's Cane* - $22.95 + $3.50 p&h
( ) Goron & Emile Gautier. *Spawn of the Penitentiary* - $32.95 + $5 p&h (3 e-books @ $3.99 ea.)
( ) Jules Gros. *The Fossil Man* -$22.95 + $3.50 p&h
( ) Edmond Haraucourt. *Illusions of Immortality* (also includes *The Gorilloid* and *Doctor Auguerand's Discovery*) - $22.95 + $3.50 p&h
( ) -------. *Daâh, The First Human* - $20.95 + $3 p&h
( ) Eugène Hennebert. *The Enchanted City* - $20.95 + $3 p&h

( ) Jules Hoche. *The Maker of Men and His Formula* - $20.95 + $3 p&h
( ) Paul d'Ivoi & H. Chabrillat. *Around the World on Five Sous* - $24.95 + $3.50 p&h
( ) Jules Janin. *The Magnetized Corpse* - $22.95 + $3.50 p&h
( ) Fernand Kolney. *Love in 5000 Years* - $20.95 + $3 p&h
( ) Louis-Guillaume de La Follie. *The Unpretentious Philosopher* - $22.95 + $3.50 p&h
( ) Jean de La Hire. *The Nyctalope on Mars* - $22.95 + $3.50 p&h (2 e-books @ $4.99 ea.)
( ) -------. *The Nyctalope vs. Lucifer* - $32.95 + $4 p&h (3 e-books @ $4.99 ea.)
( ) -------. *The Fiery Wheel* - $22.95 + $3.50 p&h
( ) André Laurie. *Spiridon* - $20.95 + $3 p&h
( ) Alain Le Drimeur. *The Future City* - $24.95 + $3.50 p&h
( ) Georges Le Faure & Henri de Graffigny. *The Extraordinary Adventures of a Russian Scientist Across the Solar System* (Volume 1) - $32.95 + $4.00 p&h - ebook $6.99
( ) -------. *The Extraordinary Adventures of a Russian Scientist Across the Solar System* (Volume 2) - $32.95 + $4.00 p&h - ebbok $6.99
( ) Jules Lermina. *Mysteryville* - $20.95 + $3 p&h
( ) -------. *Panic in Paris* - $20.95 + $3 p&h
( ) -------. *To-Ho and the Gold Destroyers* - $20.95 + $3 p&h
( ) -------. *The Secret of Zippelius* - $22.95 + $3.50 p&h
( ) -------. *The Battle of Strasbourg* - $22.95 + $3.50 p&h
( ) Gustave Le Rouge. *The Mysterious Doctor Cornelius 1: The Sculptor of Human Flesh* - $22.95 + $3.50 p&h - ebook $6.99
( ) -------. *The Mysterious Doctor Cornelius 2: The Island of Hanged Men* - $22.95 + $3.50 p&h - ebook $6.99
( ) -------. *The Mysterious Doctor Cornelius 3: The Rochester Bridge Catastrophe* - $22.95 + $3.50 p&h - ebook $6.99
( ) -------. *The Vampires of Mars* - $22.95 + $3.50 p&h - ebook $6.99
( ) ------- & Gustave Guitton. *The Dominion of the World 1: The Plutocratic Plot* - $20.95 + $3 p&h
( ) ------- & -------. *The Dominion of the World 2: The Transatlantic Threat* - $20.95 + $3 p&h
( ) ------- & -------. *The Dominion of the World 3: The Psychic Spies* - $20.95 + $3 p&h
( ) ------- & -------. *The Dominion of the World 4: The Victims Victorious* - $20.95 + $3 p&h
( ) Gaston Leroux. *Rouletabille at Krupp's* - $20.95 + $3.00 p&h
( ) André Lichtenberger. *The Centaurs* - $20.95 + $3.00 p&h
( ) -------. *The Children of the Crab* - $20.95 + $3.00 p&h
( ) de Listonai (Monsieur). *The Philosophiocal Voyager* - $24.95 + $3.50 p&h
( ) Victor Margueritte. *The Couple* - $20.95 + $3 p&h

( ) Camille Mauclair. *The Virgin Orient* - $29.95 + $4.00 p&h
( ) Joseph Méry. *The Tower of Destiny* - $22.95 + $3.50 p&h
( ) Hippolyte Mettais. *The Year 5865* - $29.95 + $4.00 p&h - ebook $6.99
( ) -------. *Paris Before the Deluge* - $20.95 + $3 p&h
( ) Louise Michel. The Human Microbes - $20.95 + $3 p&h
( ) -------. *The New World* - $20.95 + $3 p&h
( ) Tony Moilin (Dr.). *Paris in the Year 2000* - $16.95 + $3 p&h
( ) José Moselli. *Illa's End* - $18.95 + $3 p&h
( ) Mouhy (Chevalier de). *Lamekis* - $26.95 + $4.00 p&h - ebook $6.99
( ) John-Antoine Nau. *Enemy Force* - $20.95 + $3 p&h
( ) Charles Nodier. *Trilby* and *The Crumb Fairy* - $22.95 + $3.50 p&h
( ) Henri de Parville. *An Inhabitant of the Planet Mars* - $19.95 + $3 p&h
( ) Gaston de Pawlowski. *Journey to the Land of the Fourth Dimension* - $22.95 + $3.50 p&h
( ) Georges Pellerin. *The World in 2000 Years* - $20.95 + $3 p&h
( ) Ernest Pérochon. *The Frenetic People* - $20.95 + $3 p&h
( ) Jean Petithuguenin. *An International Mission to the Moon* also includes *The Great Current*) - $22.95 + $3.50 p&h
( ) René Pujol. *The Chimerical Quest* (also includes *The Black Sun*) - $20.95 + $3 p&h
( ) Georges Price. *The Missing Men of the* Sirius - $20.95 + $3 p&h
( ) Edgar Quinet. *The Enchanter Merlin* - $32.95 + $4.00 p&h - ebook $9.99
( ) Maurice Renard. *The Blue Peril* - $24.95 + $3.50 p&h
( ) -------. *Doctor Lerne* (also includes *M. Dupont's Vacations*) - $22.95 + $3.50 p&h
( ) -------. *The Doctored Man* - $22.95 + $3.50 p&h
( ) -------. *A Man Among the Microbes* - $22.95 + $3.50 p&h
( ) -------. *The Master of Light* - $22.95 + $3.50 p&h
( ) Jean Richepin. *The Wing* - $22.95 + $3.50 p&h
( ) Albert Robida. *The Adventures of Saturnin Farandoul* - $36.95 + $5 p&h - ebook $9.99
( ) -------. *Chalet in the Sky* - $22.95 + $3.50 p&h
( ) -------. *The Clock of the Centuries* - $20.95 + $3 p&h
( ) -------. *Electric Life* - $19.95 + $3.00 p&h - ebook $6.99
( ) -------. *The Engineer Von Satanas* - $24.95 + $3.50 p&h
( ) J.-H. Rosny. *The Givreuse Enigma* - $22.95 + $3.50 p&h
( ) -------. *Helgvor of the Blue River* - $22.95 + $3.50 p&h
( ) -------. *The Mysterious Force* (also includes *Hareton Ironcastle's Amazing Adventure*) - $24.95 + $3.50 p&h
( ) -------. *The Navigators of Space* (also includes *The Xipehuz, The Skeptical Legend* and *The Death of the Earth*) - $29.95 + $4 p&h - ebook $7.99
( ) -------. *Vamireh* (also includes *Eyrimah* and *Nomai*) - $22.95 + $3.50 p&h

( ) -------. *The World of the Variants* (also includes *Nymphaeum, The Depths of Kyamo* and *The Wonderful Cave Country*) - $20.95 + $3 p&h

( ) -------. *The Young Vampire* (also includes *Companions of the Universe*) - $22.95 + $3.50 p&h

( ) Marcel Rouff. *Journey to the Inverted World* - $19.95 + $3 p&h

( ) Marie-Anne de Roumier-Robert. *The Voyages of Lord Seaton to the Seven Planets* - $32.95 + $4 p&h

( ) Léonie Rouzade. *The World Turned Upside Down* - $20.95 + $3 p&h

( ) Han Ryner. *The Superhumans* - $22.95 + $3.50 p&h

( ) -------. *The Human Ant* - $22.95 + $3.50 p&h

( ) Pierre de Sélènes. *An Unknown World* - $24.95 + $3.50 p&h

( ) Norbert Sevestre. *Sâr Dubnotal vs. Jack the Ripper* - $24.95 + $3.50 p&h

( ) Jacques Spitz. *The Eye of Purgatory* (also includes *Dr. Mops' Experiment*)- $20.95+$3 p&h

( ) Eugène Thébault. *Radio-Terror* - $20.95 + $3 p&h

( ) Charles-François Tiphaigne de La Roche. *Amilec* (also includes *Giphantia*) - $22.95 + $3.50 p&h

( ) Simon Tyssot de Patot. *The Strange Voyages of Jacques Massé and Pierre de Mésange* - $29.95 + $4.00 p&h - ebook $9.99

( ) Louis Ulbach. *Prince Bonifacio* - $20.95 + $3 p&h

( ) Theo Varlet. *The Xenobiotic Invasion* - $20.95 + $3 p&h

( ) -------. *The Castaways of Eros* - $20.95 + $3 p&h

( ) -------. *The Golden Rock* - $20.95 + $3 p&h

( ) ------- & André Blandin. *Timeslip Troopers* - $20.95 + $3 p&h

( ) ------- & Octave Joncquel. *The Martian Epic* - $22.95 + $3.50 p&h - ebook $6.99

( ) Pierre Véron. *The Merchants of Health* - $22.95 + $3.50 p&h

( ) Paul Vibert. *The Mysterious Fluid* - $22.95 + $3.50 p&h

( ) Gaston de Wailly. *The Murderer of the World* - $20.95 + $3 p&h

Collections:

( ) Georges T. Dodds, ed.. *The Missing Link and Other Tales of Ape-Men* - $24.95 + $3.50 p&h
  - Emile Dodillon: *Hemo*
  - Marcel Roland: *Almost a Man*
  - C. M. de Pougens: *Jocko*
  - Léo d'Hampol: *The Missing Link*
  - Grégoire Le Roy : *The Strange Adventure of Brother Levrai*
  - Marcel Roland: *The Missing Link*

( ) Brian Stableford, ed. *News from the Moon* - $22.95 + $3.50 p&h
  - Louis-Sébastien Mercier: *News from the Moon*
  - Adrien Robert: *The Embalmed Hand*

- Stéphane Mallarmé: *The Future Phenomenon*
- Jean Richepin: *The Metaphysical Machine*
- Albert Robida: *The Monkey King* (excerpt from *The Adventures of Saturnin Farandoul*)
- Eugène Mouton: *The Historioscope*
- Georges Eekhoud: *Tony Wandel's Heart* (1884)
- Guy de Maupassant: *Martian Mankind*
- Fernand Noat: *The Red Triangle*

( ) Brian Stableford, ed. *The Germans on Venus* - $22.95 + $3.50 p&h
- Restif de la Bretonne : *Posthumous Correspondence* (excerpt)
- Charles Nodier: *Perfectibility*
- Louis Ulbach: *The Story of a Naiad*
- X. B. Saintine: *Astronomical Journeys*
- Adrien Robert: *War in 1894*
- Eugène Mouton: *The Origin of Life*
- Jules Lermina: *Quiet House*
- Rémy de Gourmont: *The Automaton*
- Marcel Schwob: *The Future Terror*
- louis Mullem *A Rival of Edison*
- Alphonse Allais: *Erebium*
- André Mas: *The Germans on Venus*
- Théo Varlet: *Telepathy*

( ) Brian Stableford, ed.. *The Supreme Progress* - $22.95 + $3.50 p&h
- Victorien Sardou: *The Black Pearl*
- X. B. Saintine: *The Paradise of Flowers*
- -------: *The Great Discovery of Animules*
- Eugène Mouton: *The End of the World*
- Charles Cros: *An Interastral Drama*
- -------: *The Science of Love*
- -------: *A Newspaper of the Future*
- -------: *The Pebble that Died of Love*
- Charles Epheyre: *The Mirosaurus*
- -------: *Professor Bakermann's Microbe*
- Paul Adam: *A Tale of the Future*
- Louis Mullem: *The End of a Monopoly*
- -------: *The New Year*
- -------: *The Invisibility of Monsieur Gridaine*
- -------: *Club Conversation*
- -------: *The Shadow and his Man*
- -------: *Chemical Eternity*
- -------: *The Supreme Progress*

( ) Brian Stableford, ed. *The World Above the World* - $22.95 + $3.50 p&h
- S. Henry Berthoud: *A Heavenward Voyage*

- -------: *The Second Sun*
- René de Pont-Jest: *Mimer's Head*
- Alphonse Daudet: *Wood'stown*
- Camille Flammarion: *Love Among the Stars*
- Charles Recolin: *The X-Ray*
- Michel Corday: *The Mysterious Dajan-Phinn*
- Jules Perrin & H. Lanos: *A World Above the World*
- André Mas: *Drymea, World of Virgins*
( ) Brian Stableford, ed. *Nemoville* - $24.95 + $3.50 p&h
- Emerich de Vattel: *Voyages in the Microcosm*
- Alfred Bonnardot: *Archeopolis*
- René du Mesnil de Maricourt: *All the Way! The Commune in 1873*
- Alphonse Brown: *The Tell-Tale Insects*
- Claude Manceau (Georges-Frédéric Espitallier): *A Professional Scruple*
- G. Bethuys (Georges-Frédéric Espitallier): *Cataclysm*
- C. Paulon (Paul Combes): *A Message from Mars*
- -------: *The Blue Laboratory*
- Emma-Adèle Lacerte: *Nemoville*
- Piertre Mille : *Three Hundred Years Hence*
- José Moselli: *The Eternal Voyage; or The Prospectors of Space*
- -------: *The Planetary Messenger*
( ) Brian Stableford, ed. *Investigations of the Future* - $22.95 + $3.50 p&h
- Théophile Gautier: *Future Paris*
- Arsène Houssaye: *Future Paris*
- Victor Fournel: *Future Paris*
- Alfred Franklin: *The Ruins of Paris in 4875*
- Maurice Spronck: *Year 330 of the Republic*
- Jean Jullien: *An Investigation of the World of the Future*
- Pierre-Simon Ballanche: *Hebal's Vision*
( ) Brian Stableford, ed. *The Conqueror of Death* - $22.95 + $3.50 p&h
- Alphonse Brown: *The Tribulations of an Angler*
- Georges Price: *Springfield's Doubloons*
- Émile Gautier: *Le Désiré*
- Camille Debans: *The Story of an Earthquake*
- -------: *Fire Island*
- -------: *A Steam Duel*
- -------: *The Conqueror of Death*
- Paul Combes: *The Gold-Mines of Bas-Meudon*
( ) Brian Stableford, ed. The Revolt of the Machines - $24.95 + $3.50 p&h
- X. Nagrien : *A Prodigious Discovery*
- Edouard Rod : *Dr. Z***'s Autopsy*
- Émile Goudeau: *The Revolt of the Machines*
- Louis Valona : *The Rival Colleagues*

657

- Jules Perrin : *Monsieur Forbe's Hallucination*
- Jules Sageret: *The Race that will be Victorious*
- Gaston de Pawlowski: *The Veridical Ascension Through History of James Stout Brighton*
- Michel Epuy: *Anthea; or, The Strange Planet*

( ) Brian Stableford, ed. *The Man With the Blue Face* - $24.95 + $3.50 p&h
- Alfred Assollant: *The Amours of Quaterquem*
- Ernest d'Hervilly: *Josuah Electricmann*
- Charles Guyon: *Voyage to the Planet Venus*
- Bernard Lazare: *The Offering to the Goddess*
- Camille Debans: *Tomorrow's Fool*
- Arnould Galopin: *The Man With the Blue Face*
- Gaston de Pawlowski: *The Bankruptcy of Science*
- E.M. Laumann: *The Alcyon*

( ) Brian Stableford, ed. *The Aerial Valley* - $22.95 + $3.50 p&h
- Jean-Baptiste Mosneron de Launay: *The Aerial Valley*
- Turrault de Rochecorbon: *The Year 2800, or, The Dream of Recluse*
- Jacques Fabien: *Paris in Dream*
- Victor Hugo: *The Future*
- Gustave Marx: *Love A Thousand Years Hence*

( ) Brian Stableford, ed. *The New Moon* - $22.95 + $3.50 p&h
- Anon.: *A Journey from the Arctic Pole to the Antarctic Pole via the Center of the World*
- Alexis-Jean Le Bret: *The New Moon*
- Henri Delmotte: *A Voyage to Paraguay-Roux*
- Edmé Rousseau: *The Aerial Journey*

( ) Brian Stableford, ed. *The Nickel Man* - $24.95 + $3.50 p&h
- Jacques Boucher de Perthes: Mademoiselle de La Choupillière
- Pierre Bremond: The Uraniad
- Ralph Schropp: The Automaton: A Story Taken from a Palimpsest
- Louis Gallet: The Death of Paris
- Léon Daudet: The Automaton
- Georges Espitallier: The Nickel Man
- Pierre de Nolhac: The Night of Pius XII
- -------: A Lovely Summer's Day
- -------: Babel at Ferney
- -------: A Season in Auvergne
- -------: The Journal of Dr. J. H. Smithson

( ) Brian Stableford, ed. *On the Brink of the World's End* - $24.95 + $3.50 p&h
- Jacques-Antoine Dulaure: *My Poor Uncle's Return: The Story of his Voyage to the Moon*
- Joseph Méry: *Future Paris*
- Charles Epheyre: *Sister Marthe*

658

- Jules Hoche: *Future Paris*
- Raoul Bigot: *The Iron that Died*
- -------: *Nounlegos*
- Colonel Royet: *On the Brink of the World's End*
( ) Brian Stableford, ed. *The Mirror of Present Events* - $26.95 + $4.00 p&h
  Félix Nogaret: *The Mirror of Present Events; or, Beauty to the Highest Bidder*
  - Jean Rameau: *Future Mores*
  - -------: *The Transportation of Forces*
  - -------: *A Poisoning in the Twenty-First Century*
  - -------: *Future Art*
  - -------: *The Mannequin-Man*
  - -------: *Electric Life*
  - Régis Vombal: *The Immortal*
  - Georges de La Fouchardière: *The Galloping Machine*
  - E. M. Laumann & Henri Lanos: *Aerobagne 32*

Future releases (prices yet to be determined):

( ) Pierre Boitard. *Journey to the Sun*
( ) André Couvreur & Michel Corday. *The Lynx*
( ) Gaston Danville. *The Perfume of Lust*
( ) Louis Geoffroy. *Apocryphal Napoleon*
( ) Restif de la Bretonne. *Discovery of the Austral Continent by a Flying Man*
( ) Restif de la Bretonne. *Posthumous Correspondence* (3 volumes)
( ) Louis-Claude de Saint-Martin. *The Crocodile, or the War between Good and Evil*
( ) Brian Stableford, ed. *The Humanisphere*
  - Victor Considérant : *The Complete News from the Moon*
  - Joseph Déjacque : *The Future World, or The Humanisphere*
  - Fernand Giraudeau: *The New City*
  - Paul Adam: *Letters from Malaisie*

For direct PayPal payments, use our e-mail address: info@blackcoatpress.com,

To pay by check or money order, please make your check payable to Black Coat Press. Mail it with a card indicating what book(s) you are purchasing to: Black Coat Press, c/o Greg M. Seigel, 18321 Ventura Blvd. Suite 915, Tarzana, CA 91356 (address valid as of April 2016). Do not forget to include postage!

Discounts are available for wholesale/bulk orders and orders from educationat institutions. Foreign (outside the u.S.) orders: freight might vary; please inquire before ordering.

VOYAGES TRÈS EXTRAORDINAIRES

DE

SATURNIN FARANDOUL

Dans les 5 ou 6 parties du monde

ET DANS TOUS LES PAYS CONNUS ET MÊME INCONNUS DE M. JULES VERNE

TEXTE ET DESSINS   DE A. ROBIDA

Ouvrage illustré de 450 dessins noirs et coloriés

PRIME DE LA CARICATURE

PARIS

LIBRAIRIE ILLUSTRÉE | LIBRAIRIE M. DREYFOUS

7, RUE DU CROISSANT, 7 | 13, FAUBOURG MONTMARTRE, 13

Index

Abbott, Edwin, 405, 406
About, Edmond, 19, 227, 228, 637
Adam, Paul, 303, 305, 306, 307, 308, 310, 316, 434, 499, 640, 641
Alberny, Luc, 569, 645
Aldiss, Brian W., 10, 647
Alhaiza, Jean-Adolphe, 389, 390, 461, 640
Alkon, Paul K., 647
Allais, Alphonse, 60, 382, 387, 403, 641
Allard, Paul, 477
Allorge, Henri, 511, 512, 513, 517, 535, 644
Altairac, Joseph, 16
Amis, Kingsley, 442, 647
Ancessy, Joseph-Auguste, 272
André, Ernest, 388
Andreae, J. V., 55
Andrevon, Jean-Pierre, 11
Angelier, François, 647
Angenot, Marc, 647
Apollinaire, Guillaume, 438, 469, 492, 611
Aquinas, Thomas, 81
Arago, Jacques, 208, 251
Ariosto, Ludovico, 45, 53, 106
Aristotle, 63, 127
Armen, Guy d', 570, 571
Armytage, W.H.G., 647
Arnauld, Antoine, 63
Arnoux, Alexandre, 515
Arnyvelde, André, 493, 494, 495, 496, 497, 498, 509, 512, 523, 540, 543, 544, 548, 561, 627, 643, 644
Arosa, Paul, 448
Audoy, François-Armand, 262, 638
Augier, Adolphe, 442
Aulnoy (Madame d'), 49, 50
Austruy, Henri, 426, 445, 599, 601, 602, 617, 641, 642, 644
Bacon, Francis, 55, 60, 108, 143, 167, 625

Bailey, J.O., 647
Bailly, Albert, 608
Bailly, Jean-Sylvain, 135
Baker, Joséphine, 556
Ballanche, Pierre-Simon, 166, 584
Balzac, Honoré de, 19, 185, 199, 201, 210, 428
Baranger, Léon, 485
Barbier, Frédéric, 114, 272
Bargone, Charles, 449, 643
Barillet-Lagargousse, 415, 416, 417, 418, 420, 422, 479, 639
Barral, Georges, 323
Barrère, Maurice, 324
Barrès, Maurice, 304
Barrière, Marcel, 423
Barthélemy, Auguste, 247
Basile, Giambattista, 48, 49
Baudry de Saunier, Louis, 514, 644
Baumgarten, Alexander, 28
Beauharnais, Fanny de, 122, 135, 159, 161
Beaunier, André, 443, 445, 602, 642
Beffroy de Reigny, Louis-Abel, 152, 153
Béliard, Octave, 465, 560, 607, 642
Bellamy, Edward, 299
Bellin de La Liborlière, Louis, 169
Berger, Alphonse, 564
Berger, Marcel, 477
Berliner, Brett A., 556
Berlioz, Hector, 211
Bernard, Catherine, 50
Bernard, Claude, 428, 448
Bernard, Gabriel, 547
Bernard, Jean-Jacques, 614
Bernard, Tristan, 387
Bernardin de Saint-Pierre, Jacques-Henri, 21, 163, 181, 212
Bernède, Arthur, 480
Berthelot, Marcellin, 239, 303
Berthet, Élie, 236, 248, 250, 373, 466, 550, 638

Berthoud, S. Henry, 21, 22, 23, 185, 200, 201, 202, 203, 204, 205, 207, 208, 209, 210, 234, 235, 236, 237, 238, 245, 251, 254, 255, 290, 334, 363, 429, 441, 446, 466, 471, 547, 567, 637, 638
Bertrand, Adrien, 487, 488, 498
Besant, Walter, 300
Bessières, Albert, 534
Béthune, Chevalier de, 92, 93, 94, 95, 97, 111, 113, 121, 635
Betolaud de La Drable, Armand, 370
Bigot, Raoul, 485, 538, 594, 595, 605, 606, 620, 643
Blandin, André, 508, 509, 644
Blanqui, Louis, 390, 410
Blavatsky (Madame), 400
Bleiler, Everett F., 10, 143, 176, 647
Bleunard, Albert, 361, 362, 363, 364, 388, 639, 640
Blocq, Armand, 431
Blocq, Paul, 431, 432
Bloy, Léon, 322
Boccaccio, Giovanni, 47, 48, 54
Bodin, Félix, 20, 188, 191, 192, 193, 194, 195, 196, 197, 208, 223, 289, 324, 325, 516, 626, 627, 628, 629, 630, 636
Boëx, Joseph-Henri, 382, 385
Boëx, Justin, 385
Böhme, Jakob, 155
Boileau-Despréaux, Nicolas, 49
Bois, Jules, 406
Boitard, Pierre, 203, 204, 205, 206, 207, 212, 235, 236, 237, 240, 298, 352, 368, 369, 395, 407, 457, 471, 637
Boltwood, Bertram, 458
Bonnardot, Alfred, 220, 224, 637
Bonnet, Charles, 94
Boo-Silhen, Henry, 595
Borel, Petrus, 201, 217
Borel, Pierre, 67, 68
Bossuet, Jacques-Bégnine, 65
Boucher de Perthes, Jacques, 188, 225, 255
Bougainville, Louis-Antoine de, 84, 179

Boullevaux, R. A., 268
Bourbon, Louis de (Prince), 146, 488
Bourget, Paul, 431
Boussenard, Louis, 297, 298, 341, 342, 352, 356, 357, 358, 375, 407, 445, 452, 544, 550, 591, 639, 640
Boutel, Jean-Luc, 16, 17, 25, 647
Boutet, Frédéric, 322, 378, 444, 641
Bréan, Simon, 11, 647
Brémond (Père), 167, 168, 178, 212, 213
Brémond, Raoul, 568
Bridenne, Jean-Jacques, 10, 647
Bringer, Rodolphe, 423
Brisson, Jules, 237
Brown, Alphonse, 339, 340, 342, 356, 359, 360, 361, 362, 371, 638, 639, 640
Brown-Séquard, Charles-Édouard, 549
Brun, Charles-Marie, 260
Brunet, P., 263, 264, 265, 266
Bruno, Giordano, 67
Buffon, 73, 74, 75, 78, 79, 82, 133, 152, 167, 168, 183, 184, 187, 458
Bulwer-Lytton, Edward, 541
Butcher, William, 647
Butor, Michel, 34, 647
Byron (Lord), 184, 199, 200
Cabarel, 579
Cabet, Étienne, 178, 179, 181, 193, 194, 216, 232, 280, 305, 306, 637
Cagliostro, 139
Calvet, E., 289, 290, 291, 297, 298, 300, 305, 311, 639
Campanella, Tommaso, 55, 58, 59, 60, 64, 143
Cardano, Girolamo, 57, 58
Carrel, Alexis, 549
Carter, Lin, 82
Casanova, Giacomo, 138, 139, 140, 143, 164, 167, 174, 636
Causse, Charles, 375
Cavell, Edith, 563
Cazal, Edmond, 550
Cazotte, Jacques, 51, 135, 159, 160, 161, 220
Chabrillat, Henri, 375
Chacornac, Henri, 314

Pittard, Jules, 537
Plançon, Paul, 486
Plato, 38, 39, 43, 63, 81, 98, 157, 196, 318, 555
Pluche, Noël-Antoine, 212
Poe, Edgar Allan, 237, 241, 273, 313, 314, 334, 350, 381, 442
Polidori, John William, 189
Pont-Jest, René de, 245, 246, 263, 266, 443, 637
Potonié-Pierre, Eugénie, 280
Pouchet, Félix-Archimède, 238, 239, 274
Pougens, Charles, 186, 248, 636
Price, Georges, 376
Priestley, Joseph, 128
Priollet, Marcel, 581
Proumen, Henri-Jacques, 532, 533, 534, 561, 621, 624, 644
Ptolemy, 143
Puisieux, Madeleine de, 110
Pujol, René, 503, 605, 606, 616, 617, 644, 645
Pythagoras, 57, 143
Quantin, Albert, 327, 328, 643
Queneau, Raymond, 267
Quinet, Edgar, 45, 215
Quirielle, Jean de, 455, 619, 643
Rabelais, François, 46, 47, 55, 522
Racine, Jean, 49
Rameau, Jean, 292, 639
Ray, Jean, 568, 576
Récamier, Juliette, 185
Régnier, Henri de, 605
Reja, Marcel, 24
Renard, Maurice, 18, 24, 25, 401, 402, 407, 408, 409, 411, 442, 454, 455, 456, 471, 472, 532, 543, 558, 563, 573, 575, 576, 577, 579, 591, 610, 618, 619, 627, 641, 642, 643, 644, 645, 649
Rengade, Pierre-Jules, 263, 264, 265, 266, 274, 339, 638
Renouvier, Charles, 464, 638
Restif de la Bretonne, Nicolas-Edmé, 26, 51, 73, 82, 105, 114, 121, 129, 130, 131, 132, 133, 134, 135, 136, 137, 138, 139, 141, 143, 148, 152,

157, 158, 159, 160, 161, 162, 163, 164, 170, 171, 172, 173, 177, 178, 192, 244, 245, 267, 275, 281, 298, 339, 355, 357, 371, 377, 383, 385, 391, 407, 436, 458, 468, 469, 544, 551, 562, 598, 626, 627, 636
Rey-Dussueil, Antoine, 167, 178, 193, 636
Ribeyre, Félix, 237
Ribot, Théodule, 432, 438
Riccoboni, Marie-Jeanne, 78, 110, 185
Richepin, Jean, 428, 444, 446, 639, 643
Richet, Charles, 225, 427, 430, 441, 443, 639
Richter, Daniel, 149, 548
Rictus, Jehan, 322
Rienzi, Raymond de, 580, 645
Robert, Adrien, 412, 638
Robida, Albert, 287, 289, 291, 292, 297, 298, 300, 302, 303, 305, 308, 311, 315, 333, 344, 345, 346, 347, 348, 349, 360, 382, 403, 413, 414, 415, 419, 422, 424, 425, 465, 479, 481, 488, 489, 491, 512, 550, 594, 596, 598, 601, 604, 639, 640, 641, 643, 644
Rochefort, Henri, 294
Rod, Édouard, 19, 429, 639
Roger, Noëlle, 517, 549, 608, 644
Rohault, Jacques, 56
Roland, Marcel, 470, 642
Röntgen, Wilhelm, 362
Rosenberg, Aubrey, 84, 88, 649
Rosny, J.-H., 18, 24, 25, 382, 383, 384, 385, 386, 387, 401, 407, 408, 409, 411, 439, 462, 464, 467, 468, 469, 472, 473, 484, 485, 503, 543, 562, 563, 565, 571, 572, 573, 579, 580, 584, 586, 591, 627, 639, 640, 642, 643, 644, 645
Rostand, Edmond, 56
Rouff, Marcel, 499, 500, 502, 643
Roumier-Robert, Marie-Anne de, 110, 111, 112, 113, 636
Rousseau, Edmé, 270, 271
Rousseau, Jean-Jacques, 26, 55, 73, 77, 78, 79, 82, 84, 101, 112, 125, 139,

Vairasse d'Allais, Denis, 60, 61, 62, 87, 635
Valbert, Léon, 423
Valérie, A., 604
Vallerey, Tancrède, 573
Vallette, Alfred, 24, 431
van Herp, Jacques, 11, 519, 520, 609, 610, 649
Varlet, Théo, 505, 506, 508, 509, 510, 511, 535, 536, 548, 582, 585, 586, 618, 627, 644, 645
Vas-Deyres, Natacha, 11, 650
Vattel, Emerich de, 118, 388, 636
Vaucanson, Jacques de, 151, 188
Vaury, Louis, 562
Vautel, Clément, 500, 501, 502
Vémar, A. (Gustave Marx), 281, 638
Verlaine, Paul, 275
Verne, Jean-Jules, 650
Verne, Jules, 7, 9, 19, 20, 21, 22, 23, 24, 25, 245, 250, 251, 252, 253, 254, 255, 256, 257, 258, 259, 260, 261, 262, 263, 264, 265, 274, 278, 283, 285, 290, 330, 331, 332, 333, 334, 335, 336, 337, 338, 339, 340, 342, 344, 345, 346, 347, 348, 349, 353, 354, 358, 359, 360, 361, 367, 368, 370, 371, 374, 377, 378, 382, 387, 394, 399, 410, 417, 428, 429, 471, 505, 506, 510, 547, 550, 574, 605, 608, 626, 627, 637, 638, 639, 640, 641, 642
Verne, Michel, 335, 336, 337, 642
Verniculus, 353
Vernier, J.-P., 650
Véron, Pierre, 225, 226, 227, 228, 287, 292, 637
Versins, Pierre, 10, 11, 16, 20, 29, 47, 48, 55, 60, 64, 102, 128, 168, 267, 320, 342, 376, 497, 566, 579, 588, 599, 650

Vibert, Paul, 387, 403, 641
Vierne, Simone, 262
Viger, A., 564
Vigny, Alfred de, 185, 224
Vilgensofer, A., 460
Villard, Nina de, 275, 276, 297, 435
Villiers de l'Isle-Adam, Auguste, 25, 275, 285, 286, 430, 435, 436, 437, 639
Vincent, Charles, 375
Virgil, 38, 39, 53, 54
Voëtius, Gisbertus, 63
Voltaire, 26, 27, 38, 46, 49, 50, 51, 71, 73, 74, 75, 77, 78, 79, 81, 82, 83, 90, 95, 96, 97, 98, 102, 104, 105, 107, 109, 115, 125, 139, 143, 151, 162, 168, 169, 212, 267, 293, 387, 488, 541, 577, 632, 633, 635
Vombal, Régis, 448
von Eschenbach, Wolfram, 43
Voronoff, Sergei, 549, 557, 558, 593
Wailly, Gaston de, 342, 377
Waldstein, Graf von, 139, 140
Watt, James, 195
Wells, H. G., 7, 9, 23, 24, 289, 319, 320, 324, 336, 358, 359, 369, 374, 378, 391, 392, 394, 399, 400, 401, 402, 405, 406, 407, 452, 465, 501, 507, 509, 510, 541, 550, 625
Whewell, William, 123
Whiston, William, 19
Wilde, Oscar, 114
Willermoz, Jean-Baptiste, 154, 155
Wollheim, Donald A., 12, 650
Ynarte, Charles, 412
Zevaco, Michel, 313, 315
Zola, Émile, 19, 24, 295, 308, 309, 428, 429, 431, 441, 456, 640
Zöllner, Johann, 406

CPSIA information can be obtained
at www.ICGtesting.com
Printed in the USA
LVOW12s1610220916

505792LV00002B/319/P